# NORMAN THOMAS
## THE LAST IDEALIST

BOOKS BY W. A. SWANBERG

*Norman Thomas: The Last Idealist*
*Luce and His Empire*
*The Rector and the Rogue*
*Pulitzer*
*Dreiser*
*Citizen Hearst*
*Jim Fisk: The Career of an Improbable Rascal*
*First Blood: The Story of Fort Sumter*
*Sickles the Incredible*

# NORMAN THOMAS

## THE LAST IDEALIST

*W. A. Swanberg*

CHARLES SCRIBNER'S SONS / *NEW YORK*

FOR THE FOUR GENERATIONS

# REX
# DOROTHY
# JACK, SARA & MICHAEL
### A N D
# JESSICA & ZACHARY

Copyright © 1976 W. A. Swanberg

Library of Congress Cataloging in Publication Data

Swanberg, W. A.
  Norman Thomas, The Last Idealist.

  Includes index.
  1. Thomas, Norman Mattoon, 1884–1968. I. Title.
HX84.T47S9      329'81'00924 [B]      76–15591
ISBN 0–684–14768–8

1 3 5 7 9 11 13 15 17 19   H/C   20 18 16 14 12 10 8 6 4 2

PRINTED IN THE UNITED STATES OF AMERICA

Grateful acknowledgment is made to those publishers and individuals who have permitted the use of extracts from the following materials in copyright.

"To Some Bloodthirsty Writers" by Irwin Edman. Reprinted by permission; copyright
© 1943, 1971 The New Yorker Magazine, Inc.
  Latest Will, by Lenore Marshall, copyright © 1969, by permission of W. W. Norton &
Co., Inc. and James Marshall.
  Norman Thomas, A Biography: 1884–1968, by Harry Fleischman, copyright © 1964,
1967, by permission of W. W. Norton & Co., Inc.

# CONTENTS

# Contents

# Contents

# ILLUSTRATIONS

ix

# Illustrations

# Illustrations

# NORMAN THOMAS
## THE LAST IDEALIST

# I

## 1. Mama's Boy

Norman Mattoon Thomas, who would become a magnificent fighter, came very near losing the preliminary battle that made possible all the others—the fight for his own life. Evidently premature, he weighed only four pounds when he was born on November 20, 1884. The family doctor shook his head. For several struggling years, neighbors kept saying pityingly that he was not long for this world. Norman fooled them all by growing to prodigious strength and achieving an international fame that only one other fellow townsman of Marion, Ohio, would match, though in a very different way. The other was Warren Gamaliel Harding, nineteen years older, who like Thomas developed the affable personality that seemed the very distillation of the easygoing, neighborly atmosphere of a fresh-water county-seat town near the turn of the century. Both also would become men of great charm and handsomeness. The similarity ended there. What was said perhaps unfairly of Harding—that he was all personality and no character—could never be said of Thomas. These two would brush together in Marion, their paths would cross again and indeed Thomas would be a frequent visitor at the White House he could not win for himself, bringing admonition to Harding and to succeeding occupants for more than a generation after Harding was dead.

To follow these two Ohio men into the world, to compare their dreams and their friends and their acts, to see what politics did to them and what they did to politics, would be an American study with overtones ranging from the slapstick to the exalted and the tragic.

Marion was on the Erie and the Big Four, forty-five miles north of Columbus, seventy-five miles south of Toledo, a farm market town of

1

some 7,000 people, best known for its manufacture of threshing machines and steam-powered shovels. Its active Grand Army of the Republic post waved the bloody shirt and helped keep the Republicans in power. Both of Norman's parents were preoccupied with the good of Marion without forgetting more distant horizons. His father, the Reverend Welling Evan Thomas, was pastor of the Presbyterian church, good-looking, neat of dress, wearing a mustache that warranted the use of a hand-painted mustache cup. An independent Republican who would cheer Mr. McKinley's war against the Spaniards, he was yet nonconformist enough to make a hero of Gladstone and to urge Irish home rule, an issue unimportant to the Marion non-Irish. He was so reserved—at times even distant—that he had no intimates, though he had good friends, and he was an intellectual who unfortunately read interesting sermons in a dull monotone. Lacking push, he came to resent the failure of his elders to increase his $1,200 salary, something he would never suggest himself. His church was the prosperous and "aristocratic" one in town, having among its members Marion's richest man, sour old Amos Kling, who would become Harding's unwilling father-in-law, and many of the manufacturing executives. "A frock coat was a sort of uniform," Norman later recalled. "He lived for his family and his profession. He was a diligent pastor and preacher, a sincerely orthodox Presbyterian who frowned on playing cards, marbles for keeps, dancing and theater-going. He was sure that all drinking was immoral, and that smoking wasn't too much better."

Norman's mother, almost as tall as his father's five foot ten, was a dark-haired woman of great charm, vigor and principle, capable of making Marion stare a little. She had a college degree—something unusual among women at that time, as was her background. She had grown up, of all places, in Siam. But she was a pleasant and intelligent leader in church groups, a facile conversationalist, in contrast to her husband's reserve, a good hymn-singer and so generally kind and helpful that all suspicions were allayed. The Thomases lived in a two-story red brick house on Prospect Street regarded as substantial and even luxurious, for all its lack of inside plumbing. The modern bathroom was found only in the newer and more pretentious houses, among them the mansion of Kling. The Thomases were accustomed to touches of refinement not found in ordinary homes—that frock coat, for example, some fine pieces of furniture, a well-stocked library, a tea set from Bangkok, an intermittent "hired girl" and several fireplaces to complement the coal-burning stove. They were looked up to without being considered uppity. The ministerial salary, plus free rent, honorariums and Mrs. Thomas's modest income from an inheritance, permitted them more than average comfort. They tithed conscientiously. A half-century later, Norman Thomas would write a "secret autobiography" meant only for his children in which he commented on his boyhood and his family with insights that revealed both boy and man. "Both were the kind of people," he wrote of his parents, "who left a deep impression on the communities where they lived. But Mother, certainly in the home, was the more outstanding personality, and Father was content to have it so."

All the more because the first Thomas child, a daughter, had died at two of diphtheria, the spindly, blue-eyed Norman had special care. His mother sang hymns to put him to sleep: "Jesus, Lover of My Soul" and "Swing Low, Sweet Chariot" were among those he remembered. Too frail for public school, he was entrusted first to the tutoring of Evelyn Gailey, a member of his father's church who conducted a small class in her home. Being left-handed, he was forced to write and throw a ball right-handed as all normal people were expected to do. Later in his life, when medical theory pronounced this the cause of psychic disorders, he doubted wryly that it was responsible for his Socialism, but "I do suppose it added to my lack of manual skill." He was indeed terribly awkward—clumsy was the word for it. He even had trouble lighting a match. After two years with Miss Gailey he leaped easily into the fourth grade at public school, although still subject to colds and fearful attacks of croup that came near to suffocating him. His fragility, athletic ineptitude and bookishness were qualities that robust boys universally ridicule as sissy. The fact that he was spared such treatment suggests that already he had the charm, the smile and the true liking for people that would become magnetism in his manhood. He was nevertheless shy and remembered that he was inclined to talk too much among adults in trying to hide his diffidence. He was his father's son, after all, and his whole life would be an odd battleground between the outgoing public man and the man of reserve and privacy.

## 2. Spreading the Word

Among Norman Thomas's forebears were strains of religious faith mingled with powerful currents of initiative, independence and downright daring that might converge in him to send him in startling directions. If his parents were outstanding, he could hardly have picked more dashing and determined grandparents. His paternal grandfather, Thomas Thomas, had been taken in 1824 at age twelve from the family farm in Carmarthenshire, Wales, to cross the Atlantic by steerage and settle in the Welsh community of Neath in Bradford County, northern Pennsylvania. The early death of *his* father and the necessity of supporting a family still numbering seven made the going hard, but Thomas Thomas was not one easily discouraged. He was twenty-five before he was able to act on his yearning to become a preacher. In 1837 he walked almost a hundred miles to Easton, entered the preparatory department of Lafayette College and sustained himself with construction work and other labor that kept him out of school at intervals. When he graduated in 1843, he was thirty-one, the oldest man in his class. After two more years at Princeton Theological Seminary, he returned to Bradford County, married the Welsh-born Mary Evans, who had waited during these long efforts, and began the life of a circuit rider, preaching at four small Presbyterian churches. He was noted in that sylvan country for his firm religiosity, his physical stamina and his enormous annual vegetable garden—an essential in view of his small salary and five children. His son Welling, Norman's father, also went to Lafayette—the Thomases had a wide streak of loyalty—working much of his way. Then he studied briefly at Union Theological Seminary in New York City, a place he found "too advanced" in its theology. He soon transferred to Princeton, was ordained in 1878 and given a church in Ashley, Ohio.

Norman's mother's American ancestors on both sides went back to Revolutionary times. Her father, Stephen Mattoon, of Huguenot descent, came from the frigid St. Lawrence River country of Jefferson County, New York, studied at Union College and then went on in 1843 to Princeton Theological Seminary, where he was in the same class as Thomas Thomas. Hence Norman's two grandfathers must have met and known each other at the university that would in time become Norman's own; yet later family records seem to make nothing of this Princeton convergence of the two men who did not dream that they would share a grandson. Stephen Mattoon married Mary Lowrie at Cambridge, New York, near her farm birthplace, and they went in 1848 as pioneer Presbyterian missionaries to Siam, living in Bangkok until 1865.

Described by a Bangkok friend as "very distinguished people, educated, helpful and kind with impeccable manners," the Mattoons became favorites of the progressive King Maha Mongkut, to whom Mattoon was useful as interpreter in the negotiation of treaties both with the United States and England. "Mrs. Mattoon," according to one recollection, "was one of three American women invited by King Mongkut to come into the forbidden area of the palace and teach the women of his household. . . . Mrs. Mattoon frequently went to the palace with her two little girls, Mary and [Emma] . . . to visit with her friends among the king's numerous wives." Serving also as first American Consul, Mr. Mattoon presented the king with scientific books and instruments sent as gifts by President Buchanan. So interminable was the voyage from Siam to America that it was President Lincoln who received Mongkut's return present of a sword and two elephant tusks along with his cordial letter offering to send "young male and female elephants . . . one or two pairs at a time," with instructions for their care and their early release in "some jungle suitable for them" in America.*

Mr. Mattoon translated the Bible into Siamese. The Mattoons would later receive glowing mention in *Anna and the King of Siam.* After the family's return from Siam in 1865, Mr. Mattoon soon rejected the quiet life of an upstate New York Presbyterian parish and courageously accepted the presidency of Biddle University, a Presbyterian institution for Negroes in Charlotte, North Carolina, later renamed Johnson C. Smith University. Here Emma and her sister endured ostracism as daughters of a Yankee carpetbagger who "taught niggers." Emma went north to Elmira College, where she earned a degree, and it was in Elmira that Welling Thomas, visiting a sister there, met her. In 1881 they were married and she accompanied him to Ashley. In 1884, only two months before Norman was born, they moved eighteen miles northwest to the "big" town of Marion.

Norman had several close calls with croup. The family grew with the arrival of three brothers, Ralph, Evan and Arthur. After a pause it grew still more with the advent of two sisters, Agnes and Emma. The meals to prepare, the dishes to wash and the Saturday night baths became formidable. Norman, a bright boy, found his lessons easy and spent his spare time reading the wholesome St. Nicholas Magazine and Youth's Companion and luxuriating in Scott and Dickens. But his parents did

---

*Lincoln, both impressed and entertained, replied February 3, 1862, courteously accepting sword and tusks but regretting that the American climate did not favor "the multiplication of the elephant" and that "steam on land, as well as on water, has been our best and most efficient agent of transportation. . . ."

not see frailty as an excuse for coddling. They expected industry and enterprise. He earned money soliciting subscriptions for church papers (getting so many that he won a bicycle), distributing books to members of a book club and picking berries at a wage of a penny a quart.

The Thomases gave more than usual attention to family ties and cultural pursuits. In 1893, the eight-year-old Norman spent several exciting days with his mother at the Chicago World's Fair, where Marion's threshers won prizes. There was a trip to Charlotte, where Norman for the first time saw that blacks, so rare in Marion, could outnumber whites. There were journeys to the Saratoga country where Mrs. Thomas had been born, on one of which Norman was taken home roundabouts by way of New York and Philadelphia. And there were trips to Mr. Thomas's birthplace near Wyalusing, in Bradford County, where his white-maned, patriarchal father, who had maintained his proficiency in Welsh although not called upon to use it, tended his great vegetable garden with the same authority with which he guided his churchly flocks. The "rich relatives" were Uncle Frank and Aunt Anna Welles, the latter being Mr. Thomas's sister. Uncle Frank, a native of Bradford County and a believer in capitalism who ridiculed opposing social theories, was European representative of the Western Electric Company. The Welleses lived in Paris with their four children, but they too attended at least two of the Pennsylvania family reunions. They caused Norman great humiliation by presenting him with a beret, a headpiece common enough in France but heretofore unseen in Marion. Nothing must be wasted! The Thomases required him to wear it despite the hoots of his friends.

### 3. Only Morals Counted

The great event of '96, which Norman never forgot, was the resounding speech of William Jennings Bryan to a huge crowd from the courthouse steps—so successful that he carried the county although the Thomas favorite and fellow Ohioan McKinley was elected. More fascinating locally was the career of Warren G. Harding, now editor of the Marion Daily Star. Since Norman served for a time as a newsboy for the Star, he had a legitimate interest in the boss. Harding's odd romance with Florence Kling DeWolfe had run the gamut of talk in Marion, for he had a reputation as an amiable rake and she had suffered a social setback as well as her father's rage in her disastrous earlier marriage to a local drunkard. After divorcing DeWolfe, she strenuously courted the six-years-younger editor, whose efforts to escape (so went the talk at the Presbyterian Church) had weakened both because of her determination and his thoughts of the Kling money and prestige. The latter was denied him, because Kling's opinion of Harding was no better than his opinion of DeWolfe. After the marriage the bitter old man disowned his daughter for years and publicly cursed Harding when he met him on the street. Norman later gave his own measured appraisal of the Harding couple:

> Mrs. Harding, in those days, ran the show. She was a woman of very narrow mentality and range of interest or understanding, but of strong will and within a certain area, of genuine kindliness. She got along well with newsboys . . . in whom she took a kind of maternal interest. It was her energy and business sense which made the Star. . . . Her husband was the front. He was . . . very affable; very much of a joiner and personally popular. He was a fine small town or city booster. . . . He used to loaf around his office in shirt sleeves and, if memory serves me, very often with a chaw of tobacco in his mouth.

By the time he entered high school, Norman's terrifying attacks of croup had subsided and he began to enjoy, years behind schedule, friendship and games with other boys. The family doctor, skeptical until then, congratulated Mrs. Thomas on pulling him through. He was forbidden to go to the abandoned rock quarry pool where other boys swam, it being considered dangerous, though he could join in outings on the Little Scioto River a few miles from town, where the catfish were plentiful, but of course not on Sunday. One friend recalled that kissing games were popular at high school parties but could not remember Norman taking part in *that,* nor that he showed interest in any girl. But far from suffering the inner damage sometimes seen in weaklings after years of isolation or babying, he entered easily into the life of his classmates. Although he remained skinny, grew too fast and never adopted the heroic methods of body-building chosen by that other childhood pipsqueak, Theodore Roosevelt, he did undertake athletics in his own way. He tried hard, and his earnest effort was appreciated although he was so awkward that he could seldom catch a ball. He could swim, and he tried basketball and even boxed occasionally with a group of friends who had founded the Tiger Athletic Club. Although he would later exhibit what must have been a bred-in-the-bone trait of physical fearlessness, his technique at fisticuffs was much inferior to that on the flute,

7

which he played under the instruction of a member of his father's congregation. The Thomas household reverberated with trills and arpeggios, for Ralph was taking piano lessons. Norman had embarked on a lifelong love of music, with a special ardor for singing that came honestly from the Welsh and from his mother's hymns.

In this dynamic family circle, busyness and industry were taken for granted. The oldest son was expected to keep an eye on the younger children as well as to beat rugs and mow lawns. He cared also, with Ralph's help, for the chickens and milked the cow that supplied the family more cheaply than the milkman. There were quarrels about the cow, Ralph claiming he could not learn to milk her, Norman insisting that his inability was intentional. Norman joined the Whittier Literary Society at the high school and took part in "speakings" and debates held there every Friday afternoon. His hunger for information and controversy led him to The Nation and The Independent and such highbrow fare as the books of Gibbon, Motley and Lord Bryce. Edward Bellamy's *Looking Backward* displayed an attractive world of Socialism to him at an age when few boys take an interest in social change. He was excited in a different way by Jesse Lynch Williams's glamorous *Princeton Stories* which, he wrote, "gave me a mighty yearning for Old Nassau."

As he later looked back over his years in Marion, he had both praise and blame: "My father spoke in cordial terms of the benign but zealous Catholic priest . . . and was suspicious of the activities of the [American Protective Association], the militant anti-Catholic society of that day. As for anti-Semitism, I did not know what it meant . . ." Yet he thought his parents' code inadequate: "It made them think too much of the goodness or badness of men and far too little of the essential nature of the social system which held even the best men in its toils." And his sense of Marion's narrowness was that of one never satisfied with comfortable backwaters, always seeking instead the rush and challenge of the mainstream. "Marion might have served about as well as Muncie, Ind., as the original of *Middletown*," he reflected. He knew that the easy romancers of the psyche could find in his background reason for repressions, hatreds and the twisting of character: "What a setup for the modern psychologically minded biographer or novelist! A study of revolt born of reaction from Presbyterian orthodoxy, and the Victorian brand of Puritanism in a Middletown setting! The only trouble is that that isn't what happened."

There would be revolt indeed—perhaps a shade more than he thought—against his Presbyterian-orthodox background, but most of all against injustices which the accidents of time and place had hidden from his parents. He could justify them a trifle defensively:

> We children probably lost something because as my sister once said, "In those days only morals counted." The moral code was too narrow, for example, in its Sabbitarianism [sic]; it had both its blind spots and its overemphases. Yet even so, I challenge any Freudian to show that it led to as much nervous disorder, instability, or more unhappiness than the current laxity of standards. I am so old-fashioned as to be glad that I lived in a home, a time, and an environment in which sin, yes and moral vices, were realities to be forgiven and cured but not condoned. . . . It has been good to get rid of some prudery and its attendant repressions. The Victorian attitude toward women had its ridiculous and hurtful side. But I confess I liked better the novels of my youth—yes, we read them in good Presbyterian homes—where the man was always the aggressor in seduction than the current crop wherein it is always the woman!

In 1900—a year which Marion hailed with elaborate ceremony as the opening of the twentieth century—Bryan again carried the county against McKinley while the Socialist candidate, Eugene V. Debs, polled just one vote. Norman rebounded from a severe attack of scarlet fever to become president of the senior class of 1901—a sure sign of appreciation for the boy who had the disadvantages of being an acknowledged "brain" and who was athletically laughable. His classmate Homer Waddell observed that Norman would often stump his teachers with religious or philosophical questions—not to display his brilliance, Homer was quite sure, but because he really thirsted for knowledge. Norman corresponded intermittently with Homer all his life. At graduation time the school superintendent, Arthur Powell, decreed that each of the forty-three graduates should make a short speech at commencement. Because Powell was dictatorial, a big man who had among other duties the job of disciplining refractory boys whom the women teachers could not handle, Norman joined in his first of many civil liberties struggles. The class met under Norman's leadership and voted instead to invite an outside speaker, Powell answering by banning further meetings in the school building—an act which made the opposition a crusade. ". . . [We] stuck together," Norman recalled, "appointed committees, met off the school grounds, and campaigned for support from our parents, the town and members of the School Board. We won." It was a triumph even though the commencement speaker, a Cincinnati lawyer, carried on for more than two hours of deadliest boredom.

That summer, Mr. Thomas "accepted a call" to the First Presbyterian Church of Lewisburg, Pennsylvania. The Marion church fathers then begged him to stay, offering a bigger salary and other inducements he was happy to be able to refuse. "I . . . can still recall the pangs I felt when we all sang 'God be with you till we meet again' on my father's last Sunday in the church that he had built," Norman wrote years later. The children were consoled by the promise that they would see the Buffalo Exposition and then visit at Grandfather Thomas's on the way to Lewisburg.

The job of moving the family of eight—Emma had just turned two —was undertaken with Christian zeal. At Wyalusing there was a great and prolonged family reunion. Grandfather Thomas, now eighty-nine and widowed, a little deaf but still the man of God and the grower of unequaled vegetables, was surrounded for the last time by all of his five children and nineteen grandchildren, including the Welleses from Paris. Norman, almost seventeen, was powerfully affected by this coming together of the clan with the old man as centerpiece. Decades later, although he had lost the faith of his fathers, he described the scene with tenderness:

> With the years the benediction of peace and sure confidence settled about my grandfather's snow-white head. He, a man of few words, of simple devotion to a stern Calvinist creed, was "father" to a whole countryside. . . . However far his grandchildren have wandered physically and spiritually, I do not think we shall ever forget family prayers about his chair nor shall we think of them as perfunctory superstition or an insincere rite. As we sat quietly around him, with his large-type Bible in his lap—one of his few concessions to advancing age—dimly at least we understood from him the sources of light which gave meaning, yes and glory, to the humdrum task, and all the vicissitudes of the year, a light which bathed . . . the cottage and the cherished garden in which this Preacher of the Word lived out his days.

### 4. Meeting Woodrow Wilson

Norman later said that he "arrived in Lewisburg with Emma under one arm and a box of . . . father's sermons in the other." Hilly Lewisburg, barely half as big as Marion, was on the Susquehanna sixty-five miles southwest of Grandfather Thomas's. The Federal high-security prison that would be in the news when Alger Hiss was sent there had not yet been built. The town's two biggest institutions were its chair factory and the coeducational Bucknell University, where Norman matriculated in the fall of 1901. Although it was Baptist, going to college there saved him board and room, something the family had to bear in mind with six children to educate. Unlike flat Marion, where houses all had front lawns, here the houses fronted directly on brick sidewalks in the Pennsylvania style, with lawns and gardens in the rear. The fine old Presbyterian church on Market Street, however, was set back on a tree-shaded lawn with the town library on one side and the Thomas parsonage on the other, an arrangement Norman enjoyed, an added advantage being several good apple trees behind the house. Again there was a family cow whose care was vested in Norman and Ralph.

The third son, Evan, was now taking cello lessons. Mrs. Thomas, always the cultural organizer, got the fourth son, Arthur, interested in still another instrument, so that with Norman's flute and Ralph's piano they could form a small family ensemble. Although this project never wholly materialized, the household nevertheless was a place often filled with music and singing.

Norman soon was dissatisfied with Bucknell. He had such a promising bass-baritone that one of his professors wanted him to study for opera, and he enjoyed playing in the Bucknell band, but he found the academic standards low. He was also distressed because his most active and compelling instinct, his sense of fairness—which would drive him all his life—was violated. Proctoring was so lax that cheating at exams was common. "It didn't need to be a fine art," he noted. "Some of the students destined—and subsidized—for the Baptist ministry were proficient at it." One of the foxiest of the cheaters, he observed, later became a prominent clergyman who, Thomas trusted, had by then reformed. He was overjoyed when his rich uncle in Paris, Frank Welles—who perhaps owed some atonement for the beret—offered him $400 annually to help him switch to Princeton in his sophomore year. Knowing that he had skidded scholastically, he spent the summer of 1902 boning up. When he left for Princeton that fall, tall and skinny and inclined to slouch, his mother poked him in the back and said, ". . . stand up straight and look people in the face."

This leavetaking proved to be more final than expected for, aside from brief holiday visits, he thereafter saw little of his parents and his brothers and sisters except for Evan. His summers were devoted to earning money. Although all three of his brothers also went to Prince-

11

ton, aided by the generous Uncle Frank, Ralph enrolled there after Norman graduated, and Evan and Arthur came later. As for the sisters, Agnes and Emma, neither was as yet in grade school.

"I still remember a sort of surprise that Princeton boys were just like other folks," Norman recalled, "only at that period rather worse dressed in corduroys and jerseys often stiff enough with dirt to stand alone." He found a cheap room off campus and took meals at the unglamorous boarding house of "Mother" Zane for only three dollars a week, though he ate like a horse. Princeton was huge after Bucknell, but it was beautiful too and for all his initial loneliness and intimidation he was beginning a love affair with the university that endured except for one long and tragic estrangement. His entrance exams left him with conditions in math and German which he worked furiously to correct and which he cleared in his first semester. Thenceforth, during his whole three years there, he never got a grade under "first group," the equivalent of A.

The young man who had carried papers for Warren Harding arrived at Princeton the year Woodrow Wilson was elevated from his professorship of politics to the university presidency. Norman could not make the football team or any other athletic team but, unlike the intellectual type of non-athlete who therefore scorns athletics, he appeared at games to cheer the Tiger on. He sang bass in the glee club, played flute in the orchestra at home concerts (he was not good enough to go along on expensive tours) and was on the varsity debating team for three years running. Known as Tommy, he was active in the Philadelphian Society—the college YMCA. Although he neither drank nor smoked, he was not sanctimonious and enjoyed campus beer parties and bull sessions. He soon had many friends, including Raymond B. Fosdick of Buffalo, Dumont Clarke and Tom Carter of New Jersey and Alfred T. Carton of Chicago. He tutored other students and did odd jobs to make ends meet. During one summer vacation he worked at Lewisburg's non-union chair factory—a labor experience he was glad to have—and during another he sold aluminum ware from door to door on Long Island. In their junior year, he and Fosdick were so poor that, unlike almost every other student, they could not afford to go to New Haven for the biggest football game of the year, with Yale. The campus was deserted. They talked dolefully. But when word came that Princeton had won, they rushed to Nassau Hall and rang the bell until they were tired.

Thomas and Fosdick sat at the feet of Wilson, then forty-six, who continued to teach a few courses in politics despite his presidential duties and who also took a special interest in the debating team, of which both boys were members. A brilliant lecturer, he lacked the gift of doffing his dignity. "Wilson" was the name of a cheap whisky widely advertised with the slogan "Wilson—That's All." His sensitivity about any confusion of the two Wilsons was as great as some students' enjoyment of it. As president he sought to further raise Princeton's standards, which meant flunking more students. Wilson, asserted the college humor paper, The Tiger, would make Princeton so difficult as to exclude students entirely. It ran a cartoon showing him sitting disconsolate and alone at the entrance to Nassau Hall, whose doors were choked with cobwebs. The caption read, "Wilson—That's All." On one occasion, Thomas took part in one of the more important annual debates, donning the academic gown customary for this function over gray flannel trousers. Wilson, who presided, let his cool, spectacled gaze run down Thomas's lank figure and said, "Mr. Thomas, it is more usual to wear dark trousers."

Forever after, Thomas remained ambivalent about Wilson, praising his intellect but lamenting his lack of warmth and the Olympian heights from which he gazed down on other men: "All his public life he was inclined to take strong opposition or criticism as a sin against the Holy Ghost."

Not yet interested in politics, Thomas soaked up academic knowledge, never satisfied with his comprehension of the world around him, irked because his courses in German and French did not enable him to *speak* German and French. He complained, "I got a first group in history of philosophy with scarcely the foggiest notion of what it was all about . . ." The history professor, Robert McNutt McElroy, was a nice fellow but he "scarcely added anything to what I'd had in high school." It was true, as he later pointed out, that Princeton at that time had no one in philosophy or psychology of the stature of Harvard's Santayana, James and Münsterberg. Still, he enjoyed English under the starchy Presbyterian Henry Van Dyke, a hard-headed course in economics given by Professor Winthrop M. Daniels and another in Socialism under Professor Walter Wyckoff who, though sympathetic to Socialism, demonstrated that it would not work. But Wilson was the lecturer who could build, sentence by sentence, an edifice of logic beautiful to contemplate. Thomas could also applaud his drive for endowments that would attract more distinguished professors, and understand the disappointment he could not hide when Andrew Carnegie gave money for the artificial lake then being created on the campus. "I asked him for bread," Wilson said, "and he gave me a lake."

Wilson's other identity as the Holy Ghost was well known. Feeling that the privacy of his rambling old presidential mansion was encroached on by McCosh Walk, he used the summer vacation of 1904 to have a high iron picket fence built to keep walkers at a distance—a move a less imperious man might have made without arousing protest. The returning seniors reasoned that the fence encroached on McCosh Walk. The class parade that year satirized the Wilson fence. The tallest seniors, of whom Thomas was one, draped themselves in black with pointed black paper hats and marched in a hollow square to imitate the picket fence. A small pig was trundled in a cart within the "fence"— a terrible indictment of Wilsonian aggrandizement. The seniors carried signs such as "Picket Lane—Formerly McCosh Walk," and "The Fence Must Go." It was a harmless and indeed sophomoric demonstration that furnished mild amusement and was played up in the Daily Princetonian, but scarcely a mortal affront. Wilson was away at the time. On his return he made known his displeasure to the class officers and later refused to deliver the baccalaureate. Some eighteen years later, after Wilson's career was ended, Thomas chanced to be introduced to one of the ex-President's daughters, Mrs. Jessie Wilson Sayre, at a wedding reception. She eyed him coldly, mentioning that they had already met, as Thomas was aware, though he didn't know the reason for the chill.

"What class were you in Princeton?" Mrs. Sayre asked.

"1905," Thomas replied in mystification.

"Oh yes," she said. "I thought so; that was the class that was so cruel to Father."

In his junior and senior years Thomas lived with two roommates in Old Reunion Hall in diggings often crowded with collegians arguing the issues of the day. He delighted in analysis and talk. His pleasant bass voice had a room-filling timbre even when lowered, and his shout could threaten all but firm construction. Front-row collegians jokingly held their ears when he debated. When the Wright brothers made their historic flight at Kitty Hawk, Thomas and Fosdick gave extemporaneous Whig Hall talks about it, agreeing that the airplane was a novel machine of no practical use. When he went home to Lewisburg for holidays he would toss his little sisters into the air, amuse them with studied absurdities and often would stride the floor discussing philosophical questions as he devoured apple after apple. His parents expected him to join the clergy but did not press the subject, and indeed he had not yet made up his mind. His father, who was chary of praise, softened in congratulation when the Princeton debaters, led by Thomas and Fosdick, beat Harvard. His mother, seemingly tireless, headed the Lewisburg school board and helped various of her children with algebra or Latin.

Having to mind his pennies, Thomas never expected to be elected to an upper-class club. In his senior year he was worldly enough to be delighted when the Colonial Club made him a member, an event he was to recall with ingenious logic: "It didn't make a snob out of me, but it did in later years give me a curious confidence that if I espoused unpopular causes it wasn't some personal incapacity for ordinary social success which drove me to them."

In the spring of 1905 he graduated *magna cum laude* as valedictorian, with membership in Phi Beta Kappa, high honors in politics and a first prize in history. He was yet able to ridicule the trick of studying for exams: "It's the art of remembering [facts] long enough to write them down and not deeply enough to stay, and I rather regret the facility in some ways."

# II

## 1. Discovering Degradation

If his parents leaned toward sacerdotalism, Thomas's own convictions veered toward the secular and rationalistic—a trait that would bring him torture. He believed fervently that any man of character, whatever his calling, owed the world an effort to improve it. He listened but he failed to receive that direct and awesome command from the Almighty that so inspired many young candidates for the pulpit. God did not say, "Norman Thomas, I want you." As he put it, "I had no mystical sense of call but a strong sense of duty to some form of missionary work at home or abroad." The do-gooder instinct in him was powerful, linked as much to his ethical sense of fair play as to holy writ.

Joining the clergy would mean smooth sailing. With his Princeton record he could easily go through theological seminary on scholarships and part-time jobs that would be offered him. His fine appearance, speaking ability and talent for getting on with people—gifts of which he could scarcely have been unaware—might take him high in the church. But he was developing a new interest in politics, another career in which one could better the world. Law was an avenue to politics, and he had connections that would virtually assure him a post with a respected New York firm after he had completed his law studies. His friends Fosdick and Carton were both going into law. While he pondered, he joined his classmate Dumont Clarke in attending a Young Men's Christian Association conference at Northfield, Massachusetts, the religious retreat founded by Dwight L. Moody.

Clarke had been president of the Philadelphian Society in his senior year, and Thomas an active member. At Northfield they met young men from many other colleges in the typical YMCA blend of hearty muscular games and wholesome religiosity, Thomas noting, "It wasn't very intellectual." He heard from another Princeton friend, Tom Carter, who had graduated a year earlier and planned to become a missionary. Carter had spent the year in social and religious work at the Spring Street Presbyterian Church and Neighborhood Center on Manhattan's lower West Side. He was staying for a second year. He urged Thomas to join the staff, as did the pastor, the Reverend H. Roswell Bates.

The thirty-four-year-old bachelor Bates, an upstate New Yorker out of Hamilton College and the Auburn School of Theology, was a true eccentric, very neurotic and subject to sudden illnesses, but devoted to his parish. It consisted mostly of noisome slums in an area between Varick Street and the Hudson River docks that would later be rehabilitated as part of Greenwich Village. Bates contended with his inadequate budget by coaxing young college graduates with clerical ambitions to work for him for a small salary on the ground that the experience was valuable. Dozens of collegians had got their first taste of what was called "active Christian service" in this way. Thomas took an instinctive liking to Bates. He joined at $500 a year plus cheap cooperative meals and free sleeping quarters in a semi-renovated tenement adjoining the church.

The choice affected his whole life. He went to Spring Street an idealistic small-towner accustomed to the mores of Marion, Lewisburg and Princeton. Abruptly he was plunged into big-city poverty, ignorance and degradation such as he had never dreamed existed. The Lower East Side district only a mile across town was almost as poor, but was peopled by Jews whose solidarity, intellectual and social vigor and determination to succeed would eventually lead them out of the ghetto. The Spring Street parish was a polyglot of Gentiles crowded into reeking tenements—laborers, teamsters, dockworkers, the unemployed, many of them beaten into an apathy relieved only by drunken sprees. The Phi Beta Kappa Colonial Clubber recalled his visits to such households, "sitting gingerly on a broken wooden chair while I talked to a sick woman on a filthy bed around which dirty toddlers played." One Sunday a terrified boy came running to Thomas, crying, "Come quick; Papa's killing Mama!" He followed the child into a tenement where a drunken longshoreman was threatening his ailing wife with an axe. Thomas's knees were knocking but he summoned up a kind of persuasion better even than that which had beaten the Harvard debaters, and managed to win over the man and get him to put away the axe.

Little was being done for social improvement. The Spring Street church had only one nurse on its staff, an overworked woman who could attend only to the most desperate cases. The city did not even enforce its health and tenement laws. Thomas and Carter had their hands full, sometimes aided by other young men aiming for the clergy. Among them were two Harvard graduates, Charles W. Gilkey and Ralph Harlow, who, more than Carter, remained lifelong friends. Gilkey and Thomas walked the mean streets after work discussing the human debasement all around them. It offended Thomas in that most sensitive part of his being, his sense of fair play. In this treadmill world of hopelessness, children seemed fated to repeat the ignorance and misery of their parents. Why should such conditions exist? *It was not fair.* Thomas worked such long hours in his efforts to right the parish wrongs that when he paid a visit to Carter's home in fashionable Montclair, New Jersey, Carter observed, "Mother thought you were going all to pieces when she saw you."

Idealism was useless unless put into practice. It did little good to put the axe away when tomorrow's spree might bring it out again. The problem was to improve working and living conditions so that workers and their families would be contented instead of despairing. Thomas, in charge of the poorly attended men's club at the church, found the men gripped by a similar apathy, unwilling to try for political action: "Tammany Hall was good enough for most of our neighbors . . . even when [William Randolph] Hearst was running on a radical platform for Mayor." But one member of the club was a single-taxer also interested in Daniel De Leon, the Socialist Labor Party leader, and his paper, The Weekly People, which Thomas read for the first time with skepticism. In the summer of 1905, however, when Bates was on vacation, the young Socialist Albert Rhys Williams filled the pulpit and was persuasive enough to encourage Thomas to take more interest in Socialism.

One effect of Spring Street was to turn Thomas categorically against the law career which he had contemplated. In his efforts to get stevedore breadwinners out of jail, to help unwed mothers and to encourage boy gang members to constructive pursuits, he encountered a breed of pettifoggers who filled him with lasting contempt. Lawyers—and indeed the law—were doing nothing for the parish. The church *was* doing something, if by no means enough. He decided on the clergy— a clergy which itself needed incitement to do more. He was filled with a characteristic impatience to get at the job, to begin his seminary work in the fall of 1906. He put it off because Carter left for Auburn Seminary, Bates's health was shaky and the parish would suffer if Thomas left too. Although Princeton now offered him an instructorship in English beginning at $800 annually—an offer hard to refuse—he stayed on at Spring Street for a second year. Among those on the new staff was young Theodore F. Savage (Harvard 1906) from Orange, New Jersey, who also aspired to the clergy and wanted a year of experience before entering Union Theological Seminary.

In the summer of 1907 a lucky chance kept Thomas and Savage out of the seminary for most of another year. Bates, having a comfortable inheritance and deciding that a trip around the world might improve his health, got a substitute pastor and persuaded Savage and Carter— the latter having finished his first year at Auburn—to accompany him. Bates also arranged privately with Thomas's Uncle Frank to pay Thomas's expenses, and sprang it as a surprise. Although Bates could be difficult when in the grip of ailments that seemed in some part self-induced, this was too good for Thomas to miss.

The four sailed from Seattle in July to visit Japan, Korea, China, the Philippines, Siam, Burma, India and Egypt. Although busy with the ailing Bates, the indefatigable Thomas described the trip in closest detail in regular letters to his parents which—with two exceptions— were later destroyed when the cellar in the Lewisburg house where they were stored was flooded. Aside from these letters, all that is known of this heroic adventure is from his three-paragraph account in his "private autobiography" and an occasional reference in later letters.

Through Bates's arrangements with American missionaries, they found shelter in places remote from tourist itineraries. From Pyongyang, Thomas wrote his father that while Pusan was "wretchedly dirty" and "the native crowd at the station positively smelled unto heaven," Seoul was "delightful." There and in Pyongyang, the "power of the Gospel" was shown by the rapid growth of Christianity, but despite the people's "many virtues they lack aggressive industry." After Peking and Nanking, the wayfarers traveled by boat and mule into Anhwei Province in China, where they stayed for some time at the Hwai Yuen Presbyterian mission, all of them aching from their mule ride except Bates, who had been carried by coolies in a sedan chair. Here Carter stayed, deciding to spend the rest of the year at the mission to further his study of church programs in China. The Thomas magnetism is evident from a later letter from one of the young missionaries, who wrote him, "It seems hard to have you come within hailing distance this way and make me want tremendously to know you well and then have to see you go sailing on your way, putting many seas between us."

The party was reduced to three as they headed south, and Thomas and Savage cemented a friendship. They recalled this journey in letters forty-four years later. Bates was a continuing problem to his companions and to missionary physicians, suffering for a time what Thomas described as "recurring melancholia during which he would beg me to watch him lest he commit suicide." Despite its hardships the tour was of enormous value to Thomas. "China and the Chinese I liked best of all," he noted, "and my blood boiled when I read the famous sign in Shanghai parks: 'Dogs and Chinese not allowed.'"

He stayed in Bangkok for a few days in November while Savage and Bates went on to Burma. Here was where his maternal grandparents had made their mark—the place that had been his mother's home until she was eight. The stories he had heard in his boyhood about Siam had whetted his already strong familial interest, and he had a passionate curiosity about the world. His mother had given him questions to answer. The loving son addressed himself to this duty by making daily tours beginning at dawn and by writing his observations carefully each night so that he would forget nothing. This added up to a thirty-six-page letter, the other surviving one. At twenty-three he showed in his writing a command of detail and a facility for narration that demonstrated acute observation and an orderly mind. Despite the inroads of steam trains and launches, he wrote her, the old "Venice of the East" must in many respects be the same as when she had been there:

> ... the old wats still stand and the old graceful pagodas still point upward with only a few more bricks or tiles fallen off. .... Here by the river you might remember . . . Wat Poh where lies the great reclining Buddha— who but an Oriental and tropical people would imagine the God lying down asleep? I sent some postals which will illustrate some of these things. . . . The palace, [however,] has been rebuilt. .... We could not enter nor could we even see the little city of the women where grandmother used to go.

By tram, ferry and train he visited the places made memorable by their connection with his grandparents before and during the American Civil War. He stopped with Dr. and Mrs. J. D. Dunlap, current Presbyterian missionaries, who well knew the story of the Mattoons and took him to the stone Christian church whose construction Stephen

Mattoon had supervised. Now, Thomas wrote his mother, its pastor was a Siamese Christian, Crew Nan.

> [The church's] foundation made of the stone ballast grandfather begged from ship captains is as firm as ever, but its old white walls have begun to bulge. The people plan to build on the old foundations. . . . Alas, your old house is torn down. . . . [The congregation asked Thomas to speak.] Many knew some English but Dr. Dunlap interpreted. I tell you I felt much moved at speaking from my grandfather's old pulpit. . . . Crew Nan spoke. . . . He said Dr. Mattoon received him when he first came to school. With his own hands he gave him a bath. It much impressed the boy that so great a man should do this.

Living near the church was Ma Esther, the young Siamese woman, now a grandmother, who had been governess for the two Mattoon girls and had traveled back to New York State with Mrs. Mattoon to be present at the birth of Thomas's mother in 1857. Overjoyed at meeting him, she invited him to dinner.

> On the wall hang pictures of grandfather and mother painted by a Chinese painter from photographs. Esther says unless her children prize them she will have them put in her coffin with her. . . . She came to see me one morning. A little woman dressed in Siamese dress, spotlessly clean, with bare feet. She is still erect and her hair black. Her manner and her English would be a credit to the finest lady and her face is expressive of great character. Her joy at seeing me was touching. She said I was her grandson. Over and over she told me how she loved my grandparents and how she owed everything to them and she sends her undying love to her dear Emma and Mary. . . . She has an old photograph of you and Aunt Mary. You look much like little Emma. She says: "Emma was a little mischief, always running around but Mary was very good. . . ."

He took pictures of Ma Esther with his box camera and she gave him gifts to take back to his mother. The fame of the Mattoons was still so great that he was assured that he would have been invited to the royal palace but for the absence of the king. As it was, he met noblemen of several degrees, remarking that "even princes are thicker than colonels in Kentucky. Why, a little barefoot boy playing around a wat was the grandson of a king—one of the results of many wives." He attended the Christian wedding of a young Siamese couple. He thought the people friendly and charming but so indolent that Chinese had been imported to do the work: "The trouble with Siam is the Siamese. They won't work and they don't starve while bananas are plenty." He described in detail the lavish decorations and fireworks arranged for the return of the king. He traveled south by train to Petchaburi, met the local missionaries, Dr. and Mrs. Eakin, and went mountain-climbing with them and their friend, a Miss Bruner, whom he described without conspicuous masculine excitement as "good company." He attended a meeting of the Siam Society, an intellectual group composed of Americans, Britons, Dutchmen and a Japanese educated at Yale. He met the United States Consul, a man named McMurray, and was delighted to find that he was Princeton '02 and that they had mutual friends.

"Just think—the Yale game was last Saturday!" he wrote. ". . . You can guess how glad I was to see a man with whom to talk Princeton!" "How I wish you could have been [here] with me," he wrote as he sailed off to Singapore, where he would board another vessel for Rangoon, "for despite the climate and the mosquitoes I believe it would have made you a girl again to see old Bangkok and your devoted Esther and to hear even after the lapse of 40 years, all the words of veneration and gratitude to your father and mother."

In India, after rejoining his comrades, he was sufficiently influenced by Kipling and by the assurances of missionaries with whom they stayed to accept the belief that British rule was necessary and benign. Yet he was shocked when on a Calcutta tram he saw a British civilian slap a native conductor because there was dust on the seat. "The blow was light, the affront grave," he wrote, "and I began to understand that men could more easily forgive injuries than insults born of arrogance." Sherwood Eddy, already a missionary with long experience in India, took them to see a village of outcasts. They visited a home for lepers. They took the long train journey to Allahabad, where Carl Thompson, a Thomas classmate of 1905, was teaching; he gave them a Princeton welcome. Then on to Moslem Lahore, where the scant record of their eight-month expedition ends. Egypt was the last stop on the Bates itinerary. Somewhat improved, Bates sailed home with Savage as his companion while Thomas spent what he described as "a little while longer" in Europe, where he surely must have visited the benevolent Welleses in Paris. He reached New York alone in March 1908 with decisions to make.

## 2. *Fifth Avenue and Hell's Kitchen*

At Spring Street Thomas found that he had two attractive part-time job offers, either of which would finance his seminary course. One, discovered for him by the Auburn graduate Bates, was as assistant to Dr. Allen Marcy Dulles at the Presbyterian church in Auburn, where Dulles also taught homiletics at the nearby seminary. (Dulles sent his oldest son, John Foster Dulles, to Princeton, where he was a year ahead of Thomas's brother Ralph.) The other was as assistant to Dr. James M. Farr, another Princeton man, at Christ Church in Manhattan. Hence the choice of jobs also involved the choice of which theology school Thomas would attend, since if he worked in New York he would of course go to Union Theological Seminary.

There began a tug of war. Bates loyally favored Auburn, as of course did Tom Carter, all the way from China. Dumont Clarke thought Auburn inferior, writing Thomas: "Can a man of your well-proven intellectual caliber—a man who is not at the same time dominated by his intellect—can such a man as you afford to sit under anything less than the deepest thought of the day?" Thomas consulted with his warm Bostonian friend Charles Gilkey, who, being two years older and having postponed world travel until later, was now at Union and would graduate in the spring. He praised it. Ted Savage was going to Union in the fall and would be a classmate, as would Clarke. Thomas, having experienced the backwaters of Marion and Lewisburg, saw Auburn as another backwater and was stimulated by the intellectual ferment of the metropolis. His admired older friend William Sloane Coffin, a backer of the Spring Street program, was Sunday-school superintendent at Christ Church and urged him to accept the post there. But Thomas's parents strongly opposed Union, which had a reputation for liberalism not shared by the seminaries at Auburn and Princeton. It will be remembered that Thomas's father had attended Union briefly before transferring to Princeton as being more orthodox and to his liking. Norman's revolt against Superintendent Powell in Marion had not been the only evidence of an independence of mind which—despite the fact that he, like his father, voted for William Howard Taft that fall— aroused parental fears that he was moving away from safe theological conservatism. They had been made uneasy by a few of his "advanced" opinions and by letters in which, for example, he questioned the accepted concept of hell.

It was perhaps a measure of the general feeling that Thomas had a brilliant career ahead of him that so many sought to help and advise him. Clarke's appraisal of him as an intellectual with a warm heart—a rare and attractive combination—was a true one and did much to explain his popularity. Thomas chose the Christ Church job and Union. Union was a center of the Social Gospel movement largely founded by the Socialistic-minded Walter Rauschenbusch, a doctrine suspect to many older-line theologians, among them Thomas's parents. The Social Gospel was a radical departure from the traditional view of Christianity as a ticket to heavenly bliss that would more than repay the multitudes for their misery on earth. It saw Christianity rather as the road to a just and equitable society on earth, here and now, minimizing metaphysics in favor of a code of ethics that would allow for practical blessings in this life. To Thomas, after Spring Street, this made sense despite his mother's protests. ". . . [She] was much opposed to my going to Union Seminary," he recalled, "and argued with me against it far more earnestly than Father, but mostly on the grounds of loyalty to him. I came to suspect that her orthodoxy was less questioning than Father's, and far more inspired by her loyalty to her own tradition and to him—and by fear [of] where questioning might lead her."

He began immediately at Christ Church, a "poor relation" church on West Thirty-sixth Street near Ninth Avenue, bordering on the roughneck Hell's Kitchen district. Its financial support came from the wealthy parishioners of the fashionable Brick Church on Fifth Avenue and Thirty-seventh Street. Once again Thomas worked, as he preferred, in a neighborhood of poverty, though not as squalid as Spring Street; he lived uptown at the seminary, then at Park Avenue and Seventieth Street. He derived such pleasure from church music that no matter how busy he was, he always sang in the choir.

Until then his experience with girls had been scarcely more complicated than his brief encounter with Miss Bruner in Siam. Probably he had had a few dates (a subject he eschewed in his autobiography), but girls had never been a serious factor in his life although he was nearly twenty-four. He had delayed his seminary work two years, time was important to him and romance was such a time-consuming distraction that it would take someone unusual to divert his attention. The unusual appeared in the form of two sisters, Mary and Frances Violet Stewart. Mary, the elder, taught Sunday school at Christ Church, while Frances Violet served as a nurse in this parish where squeamish ladies might easily encounter vulgarity. Frances Violet had organized at the church the city's first class for instruction in the home treatment of tuberculosis —a praiseworthy and even risky enterprise, although medical opinion soon turned against home treatment. She was petite and blue-eyed with chestnut hair, Mary being taller and a redhead. They were longtime family friends of the Coffin brothers, William Sloane and Henry Sloane, both of whom were mentors and friends of Thomas. Mary, partially deaf as a result of childhood scarlet fever, could read lips. She was a writer of children's stories and soon published *Tell Me a True Story,* her first of a half-dozen children's books.

While Thomas liked them both, it was the younger sister, always called Violet (a name he thought adequate for a flower but not for a young woman), who captivated him. She was three years older than he. A bluestocking and poetry lover with a mind the cautious Theodore Savage later classed as brilliant, she was utterly fearless at a time when women were expected to be timid. She had a wit fully as quick as Thomas's own. Thomas had now attained his ultimate height of six foot three. Her head reached a point below his shoulder, so there were always witticisms to the effect that he should sit down or remain on his knees while talking with her so that they could be at eye level.

According to his own account, he was admiring rather than headlong in his courtship, being terribly busy, out of pocket and perhaps intimidated by the prominence and wealth of her family—though he was not one easily intimidated. The Stewarts were listed in the Social Register. His own family tree had true distinction, but not the kind recognized on Fifth Avenue. While his impecuniosity might be forgiven, there was the question of philosophical and political rapport. If Thomas was growing too radical for his own parents, how could he be acceptable to the conservative Stewart family?

Of course they did not yet know how radical he was, nor could they know any more than he how much more radical he would become. Violet's venerable grandfather, the great sachem of the tribe, was John Aikman Stewart. Born in New York in 1822 and still vigorous, he had planned the organization of the United States Trust Company, the nation's first. Being almost a half-century old when the Civil War began, too old for combat, he had served as Assistant Secretary of the Treasury under Lincoln and had later held the same post under Grover Cleveland. In the interim he had continued as president of the bank until 1902 and in fact was still, at eighty-six, chairman of the board. Although he was a Columbia graduate, he had for many years been senior trustee of Princeton and so far from seeking retirement that he later served as the university's president pro tem while a replacement was found for Woodrow Wilson. He had the unusual distinction of having known Lincoln (with whom he had dined a few days before his assassination) and Cleveland and now being a close friend of Wilson. When Stewart's first wife died he was a robust sixty-seven, and in 1890 he had married a Baltimore belle less than half his age, with whom he now occupied a mansion at 16 West Fifty-third Street. One of his sons by his first wife, W. A. W. Stewart, was Violet's father, a Princeton man, attorney and ardent yachtsman. On March 10, 1888, when Violet was only seven, he had sailed from New York in his yawl *Cythera,* bound for the West Indies on a voyage which he hoped would improve his flagging health. March 11 was the day of the gale and blizzard of '88 that paralyzed New York. The *Cythera* was never seen again. Stewart and his crewmen were presumed lost at sea, and the probate court eventually awarded his estate to his widow, Frances Gray Stewart. One executor was the late yachtsman's law partner and close friend, Edward W. Sheldon, who also became guardian of the children. Violet's mother, though a peppery woman of old Boston antecedents, wore mourning every day of her life after the tragedy. There was talk that even her undergarments must be black, but a niece later peered into her bedroom and discovered them to be pink. Mrs. Stewart also had two sons, both Princeton men, each outstanding in his own way. She had bought a house in Princeton for their convenience and also to be near them, and the college town was still one of the places around which the family life revolved.

Clearly, Thomas's Princeton and Presbyterian background was in his favor. Perhaps also, in the hard statistical outlook, was the fact that Violet was twenty-seven, an age then considered as bordering on spinsterhood. She had been educated at the Brearley School in New York, a private school for the wealthy, and had later studied nursing largely on her own. She had traveled in Europe and Asia. She lived in quiet affluence with her mother and sister at 27 East Thirty-eighth Street, was accustomed to a staff of servants and to mention in the society columns, and had an elegance of manner that could occasionally be mistaken by the undiscerning for hauteur.

Thomas was reading Rauschenbusch and growing more critical of the social establishment. But his distaste for Tammany made him lend support to city Republicans. Letters from Savage and Gilkey, both in Europe, indicate that Thomas was pumping them for information about Socialist trends across the Atlantic. Savage, in a summer study of settlement work in the East London dockyard slums, wrote of Socialism's spread among the dockers, adding, "Most of the people in settlement work are Socialists, and a great many of the prominent ministers." As for himself, "I have not announced myself as a convert yet, but am heartily in sympathy with the general principles of Socialism." Gilkey, recently arrived with a friend in Germany for a year at the University of Berlin after touring Western Europe, found Thomas's "splendid letter" a spur to his conscience and wrote to Thomas:

> For ten weeks we [have] been living a very selfish existence, as if we were really of the "predatory classes"—earning nothing and spending not a little and doing exactly as we pleased. To be sure, we heard a street Socialist speaker the first night ashore in London, and in High St., Edinburgh, on Saturday night more open drunkenness and degradation, both men and women, than I ever saw before in any city of either New or Old World; but still, we lived for the most part in an ideal world, where the only poverty that really "impinged" was that of our own pocketbooks. . . . Your letter was like a call back to real hard life, from a man who had been really doing something. . . . [He had taken the trouble to read Werner Sombart on Socialism, described the contending Socialist groups in Germany, and feared that the system, despite good intentions, might lead to a "dead-level society":] Personally, I am less and less of a Socialist. I believe the great truth and service of Socialism lies in the just protests against deep-rooted evils.

Dumont Clarke, writing to Thomas from Madras, said not a word about Socialism but told of his study of Young Men's Christian Association work in India, adding, "I am waiting to hear from you about your life work in Seminary. Your old face is looking down on me from the wall."

It was a time-saver for Thomas that he and Violet met occasionally in the course of their church work, since he invariably accepted more responsibility than was thrust on him. And his courses at Union required attention. In classes under such men as Dr. William Adams Brown and Dr. Henry Sloane Coffin, his work was outstanding. He took Violet for walks, and they went canoeing several times near Princeton. Rarely could he afford concert or theater tickets. He got along famously with her mother—his ability to attract women would always equal his influence over men. Mrs. Stewart possessed, along with her firm Presbyterianism, an active intellectualism and had learned Greek by herself, on a whim, long after her children were born. Now and then Thomas had

Sunday dinner at the Stewart home. A gauge of the Stewart dash was their ownership of at least one automobile at this time when owners of such machines were still widely regarded as adventurous if not foolhardy. Thomas's parents viewed his growing attachment uneasily, not certain whether marriage into wealth would be "good for him." He may well have had his own speculations about the wisdom of a union with the daughter of a family representing the conservative tradition of which he was critical and who, on their part, might be more critical of him as they became aware of his thinking.

### 3. An All-Around Sport

In September, 1909, Violet Stewart and Miss Gertrude Smith, a nurse and colleague from the Christ Church staff, set sail for India with the dual purpose of studying the public health programs at Presbyterian missions there and offering their help where needed. The project seems to have originated in New York rather than being the result of entreaties from India. This circumstance might suggest that it was a device of Violet's mother or her guardian to get the young lady away from Thomas for a few months—the approved method of giving romantic heiresses time to reconsider. But Violet's character, by itself, is virtual proof to the contrary. She was impulsive, adventurous, strong-minded and strong-willed, a planner and doer, as she would prove all her life. Decidedly she was not one of those fragile and pliant women subject to manipulation. It seems likely that the India project was her own.

Certainly Thomas was among those who saw the pair off. He had written ahead to various missions in India to announce their errand and request cooperation. He had also written Tom Carter in China, and probably other friends, asking them to write to Violet and give advice and companionship on the long voyage.

While Thomas liked Dr. Farr, pastor of Christ Church and his boss, he thought Farr fell short of Bates in dedication to his needy parish. As a result, Thomas worked too hard himself. No sooner had the women sailed than he took a short vacation at the Saranac Lake place of Cleveland H. Dodge (Princeton '79), the mining and railroad magnate, a confirmed YMCA supporter active in Princeton's Philadelphia Club and a friend of Dumont Clarke's. The Adirondack air so restored Thomas that he led the Dodges in singing and distinguished himself by eating thirteen pancakes at one sitting.

# NORMAN THOMAS

"We the undersigned hereby affirm that the Rev. Norman Thomas has behaved himself wisely, seemly and politely . . . and has not been known to have overeaten . . .," the Dodges later wrote him. "He has proved himself to be a first rate guide, all round sport, high class singer and a jolly good fellow."

The Misses Stewart and Smith spent almost a fortnight in London, where Violet, who knew the city well, led visits to galleries, museums and theaters. They then traveled by train through France, Switzerland and Italy, boarding a steamer at Brindisi and sailing through Suez with first-class passengers most of whom were British officers and civilians of the Indian service. While Violet's letters all began very properly, "Dear Mr. Thomas," the formality ended there.

"This is in answer to your Port Said letter," she once wrote. "Not that I have gotten it yet." She did get one from him there, and although his are missing, hers were long and ran the gamut from the bubbly to the philosophical. "Do you have time for my ramblings or do they interfere awfully with Christ Church and Seminary? I can't help it. I told you I made use of my friends and of you especially." She remarked that he had come through the Red Sea and the canal only the previous year: "It's fun to think you have been here and won't we have fun talking about it?" Her British shipmates were kindly but they had stuffy ideas about the way Indians should be handled. They were sure that the Hindu religion—much older than the Christian—satisfied the natives, and Christian missionaries only stirred up discontent.

"I need a pastoral call . . .," she wrote Thomas. ". . . I do wish you could have helped me talk to this very nice old colonel who has been throwing bombs at all my Indian ideas." "If you knew how glad I was to get [your letter] you'd be glad you wrote it." She enjoyed Bombay, where they stayed at the YWCA, except for a jolting ride in a bullock cart: "If I go on any bullock cart trips the bullocks must walk, or I will." They found that while they were welcomed at Indian mission stations, their services as nurses were not in great demand except at places where Thomas had sent letters of introduction. In Delhi, Violet came down with a fever for a few days and was in the care of a British civil surgeon. Much as she enjoyed India and delighted in the food, she feared that the British had a problem with native discontent: ". . . I'd hate to be England just now with such a responsibility. I just feel that the people hate us . . . and the looks they throw after us are not the same as the salaams with which they face us." Her first letters ended with the prim "Sincerely," but from Delhi she wrote recklessly, "Yours."

They planned to spend Christmas in Calcutta and to go on to Burma, but Violet's remaining letters are lost and these adventures go unrecorded. Thomas meanwhile invited Woodrow Wilson to address a ministerial conference he had organized, getting a courteous refusal: ". . . the truth is I have planned to be out of the country during February. . . . but if I were to be in the country I should certainly find it hard to decline your very cordial invitation."

By February, 1910, Violet was back home and Thomas soon thereafter was in Presbyterian Hospital for minor surgery. Expecting to be out in three days, he did not tell her about it. Instead, he developed phlebitis and stayed on. She wrote him (it was "Dear Norman" now) to relay her mother's insistence that he could not recuperate at the Union dormitory but must be their guest: "We'll not make a fuss over you if you don't want. . . . I won't even tell you more than half the exciting things that have been happening. . . . Don't . . . say you'll be a trouble . . . for you are quite sufficiently popular with Kate and Annie to have them enjoy bringing you trays, to say nothing of me. And Minnie will fix you whatever you like to eat." She called on him at the hospital. "I was very much in love," he later admitted, "but I had never intended to propose from a sick bed. But alas for noble resolutions, I shamelessly took advantage of pity. I decided, and even, I think, said, that I wouldn't go unengaged to Mrs. Stewart's house. At any rate just after I proposed, in marched a nurse to take my temperature pending which all conversation and action were held in suspense."

His temperature held firm and he went to the Stewart place betrothed. There, for several days, he enjoyed Violet's proximity, the ministrations of Kate, Annie and Minnie, and could observe at leisure the amenities taken for granted by a wealthy family, one of them being a piano that played automatic music from a paper roll with mysterious piercings. Meanwhile the pastor of Brick Church died and his place was temporarily filled by Henry Van Dyke, Thomas's English professor at Princeton, who had held that pulpit ten years earlier. Since he continued to teach at Princeton and preached only part of the time, he needed a readily available assistant, and offered the job to Thomas. (Certainly the young man's link with the Stewarts did him no harm.) The kindly, undersized Van Dyke, a poet and essayist whose renown would soon fade, was also an eccentric whose vanity drove him to such flourishes as wearing his doctoral hood in the pulpit.

Although the handsome Brick Church overlooked a portion of Fifth Avenue where trade was beginning to edge out the mansions of the mighty, it was one of many fine buildings between the stupendous Waldorf-Astoria at Thirty-fourth Street and the new library at Forty-second. The Stewart home was only a block north and a block and a half east, although the family illogically were members of the Madison Avenue Presbyterian Church far uptown. Most young clergymen would have regarded the summons of the Brick Church as a dream too grand to be realized. Thomas was anything but unaware that the church offered the kind of "opportunity" to its pastor that getting in with the right corporation offered a young businessman. The substantial salary was important because it would enable him to marry Violet before he finished seminary. He accepted.

Still wobbly from his illness, working hard to catch up on his seminary courses, he was not without stage fright as he preached his first sermon to this genteel, well-dressed congregation—no scuffed brogans, no patches, no calluses. And soon after, it devolved on him to preach on Palm Sunday, a "great day" on which Van Dyke was supposed to officiate but refused because of a disagreement with the elders. Thomas faced the eternal trepidation of the understudy suddenly replacing the headliner. He preferred not to read from a fully prepared manuscript, feeling that it broke a necessary communication of the pastor's eyes with the congregation and produced sleep. As he spoke he liked to gaze directly first at one listener, then another, even if in so doing he might occasionally grope for words. Hence he made only rough handwritten notes for his Palm Sunday sermon, his second and most important so far. He was in a sense an envoy from Hell's Kitchen to the communicants of Brick Church, many of whom had their coachmen or chauffeurs waiting outside with broughams or motorcars. With a generosity easy for the wealthy, they had achieved a churchly segregation, supporting down-at-the-heels Christ Church while avoiding the people of Christ Church. There must have been some temptation to preach safely and pleasingly. Thomas did not. (Was Violet, who would scarcely miss such an occasion willingly, facing him from a front pew? The records do not say.)

Some of the more complete passages from his notes for that sermon underline his acceptance of the Social Gospel, his conviction that religion dealing with heaven and hell with no effort to meet the immediate needs of places like Hell's Kitchen was not far from fraudulent:

> Some years ago I talked to a very intelligent man who was hard at work trying to uplift the poor & get justice for the toilers. He thought . . . that the teaching of the church about heaven had literally cursed the world.

"Why," he said, "the church has gone to the slaves and it has said 'Never mind, this life is only a little thing, you'll be all right in heaven.' It has said to the rich & powerful 'Don't worry about the poor. They are meek & quiet & trust in the teachings of the church [that it will be made] right in heaven.' Such teaching has delayed human progress for centuries."

One communicant whose eyes Thomas met with special intensity and whom he hoped to jolt with his message was a rich businessman whom he considered one of the worst of the "malefactors of great wealth." He continued:

... It is true that there has been a conception of immortality that has been a curse. Listen to Napoleon's views: "How can a state be well governed without the aid of religion? Society cannot exist save with inequality of fortune, & inequality of fortune cannot be supported without religion. When a man dies of hunger by the side of another who is gorged, he cannot accept that disparity without some authority shall say to him: 'I have decreed it thus; there must be rich & poor in the world; but in the hereafter & for all eternity it will be the other way about.'"

This was revolutionary stuff for this hard-shell congregation and he expected disapproval. On the contrary, parishioners came up to compliment him. The ultimate accolade came later when Violet's aged grandfather, who was a member of Brick Church and who knew the malefactor in question, congratulated Thomas, saying that the gentleman had praised his Palm Sunday sermon and urged that he be appointed permanent assistant so that he would ultimately succeed to the senior post. The surprised Thomas, sure that his audience had not been dozing, concluded that a pastor could safely utter iconoclasms from the chancel that might get him clapped in jail if spoken in Union Square. This raised questions that would trouble him: Had comfort-loving Christians changed the function of a church service from its great mission for mercy and conscience into a ritual conveniently shutting out the real world? Had the pastor become an actor in a stately and painless drama, his words shorn of meaning?

A few weeks later, nineteen-year-old Sidney Lovett arrived at Christ Church and immediately felt the Thomas magnetism. A Bostonian who had just finished his first year at Yale, Lovett intended to be a clergyman and sought experience in social work during the summer vacation. "Here was this tall, handsome young man named

Norman Thomas who was in charge of the church for the summer," he recalled. "I was delighted with him. Nights were hot so we put cots on the church house roof and slept there, and talked." Soon introduced to Violet Stewart, he watched with interest as the courtship moved toward matrimony.

That summer, Thomas and Violet established a big vacant-lot vegetable garden in Hell's Kitchen for children who had never seen a radish grow. They also took the train to Lewisburg, where the Thomas family looked over Norman's betrothed with attention. To the small-town Thomases, the petite but dynamic Violet must have seemed startling with her air of elegance, her speech accented in ways surprising to the Lewisburg ear, her touch of imperiousness and even her irrepressible humor. Horror of horrors, she and Norman openly held hands as they walked down the street, and they were criticized in Lewisburg for this impropriety. The Thomases were concerned that their first-born son, so full of bright promise, should make the "right" marriage, one that would fulfill both his career and his personal aspirations. It was all very well for a clergyman to have a competence, but the Bible itself said, "It is easier for a camel to go through the eye of a needle, than for a rich man to enter into the kingdom of God." Furthermore, Norman had troubled them with letters in which he admitted that he could not swallow such doctrines as the virgin birth.

His brother Ralph, just out of Princeton with Phi Beta Kappa honors, sent a letter of congratulations which also expressed Ralph's heartfelt homage to their family background: "I appreciate my home more & more all the time. Isn't it a wonderful home & oughtn't we to am't to something with such training?" Gilkey, now studying at Oxford, a consummate and kind-hearted religionist, expressed to Violet sentiments that would not be entirely realized:

> ... The fact that I haven't met you yet is a misfortune from which I hope
> to escape at the earliest possible moment. But I do know Norman—and
> I think he would let me say, rather well. . . . When I think of what you
> have in Norman, I am moved to congratulation as unusual as it is sincere:
> But when I think of what you two will be able to do together for the
> Kingdom of God, I am moved to a prayer of thanksgiving. . . .

The couple were married by Dr. Henry Sloane Coffin on September 1, 1910, at Madison Avenue Presbyterian Church. Coffin, in addition to being one of Thomas's professors at Union and a family friend of the Stewarts, was a "liberal" religionist who would come to feel that

Thomas carried liberalism too far. The Reverend Welling Thomas came down with a mild case of typhoid which kept him, Thomas's mother and his two sisters and youngest brother in Lewisburg, but they would not hear of a postponement of the wedding. It was genuine typhoid, not an excuse. Thomas's brothers Ralph and Evan (the latter just starting at Princeton) were among the ushers. The others included men who would continue through the decades as friends (some not without consternation)—Gilkey, Theodore Savage, William Sloane Coffin and Thomas's classmate Alfred Carton, now a rising attorney in Chicago. Dumont Clarke was best man. The reception, held at the Thirty-eighth Street house, was attended by a whole platoon of Stewarts from the old sachem on down and other guests, including the Cleveland Dodges. Both The Tribune and The Times referred to Violet by the nickname given her for her good works, "the angel of Hell's Kitchen," The Tribune adding that the bride "is wealthy in her own right." This was not true in the sense that Violet had money available for every whim, for it was under trust-fund restrictions. If the Stewart family offered largesse, it was not visible. Violet's honeymoon with Thomas consisted of a bicycle-and-canoe trip near Princeton. Their first home was a ground floor and basement apartment on West Forty-second Street near Ninth Avenue, far from the streets of splendor—a place where remorseful drunks sometimes pounded on the door of a Saturday night, confusing it with a priest's domicile adjoining the nearby Catholic church and wanting to take the pledge.

There was no Kate, no Annie, no Minnie. Violet disappeared from the Social Register and never appeared in it as Mrs. Norman Thomas.

Thomas was three months short of twenty-six and he still had his second year of seminary to finish. He was confronted in some respects by the classic moral dilemma between love and honor. Should he buck for the Brick Church job permanently, with its prestige, comparative ease, clean fingernails, security, and above all its association with the cultivated and well-heeled class typified by the Stewarts? Or should he follow duty into the slums? It was one thing for Violet to live on Thirty-eighth Street with maid service and breakfast in bed, spending her leisure time being an angel. It was quite another to remove her entirely from her milieu and require her to be an angel full-time—in effect to reduce her mode of living drastically. And Thomas himself would scarcely have been human had he been free from vanity and ambition, from enjoying the society of the well-bathed, well-educated, wealthy and famous who were opening the door for him.

# III

## 1. In Little Italy

Thomas would demonstrate that honor and love could be reconciled. And he displayed the powerful self-confidence of a man sure of his principles, a man who had not merely succeeded but excelled at everything he had tried since he entered college.

Because Dr. Van Dyke spent most of his time at Princeton, and regulations required that the Brick Church have an ordained minister at hand at all times, Thomas's ordination—a ceremony normally taking place at the end of seminary—was advanced to January of 1911. Conservative clergymen were then much concerned about the erosion of Calvinist orthodoxy. When Thomas appeared before the presbytery for his oral examination, the orthodox were led by the correct Reverend John Fox, who questioned him narrowly about his views on such subjects as the virgin birth and the resurrection of the body.

Thomas, having seen more misery in his three years in the slums than most clergymen did in a lifetime, subordinated textbook dogma to his strong concept of the social duties of the church. He was not sure even then that he believed literally in the biblical miracles. What he was sure of was that such speculations were irrelevant to human need. Dr. Fox and his group, not getting answers straight out of the Westminster Confession, pressed him hard.

"I had been well schooled at Union," Thomas recalled, "in the arts of interpretation and verbal reconciliation of opposing theories . . . so that I was accepted after a rather long examination without much difficulty." Yet he came to regret what he saw on reflection as an evasion rather than an open confrontation on this issue which would ultimately play a part in destroying his clerical career: "I was then very sincere in

35

what I believed was basic Christianity, I had strong ties to the Presbyterian Church and an earnest conviction that it should be more inclusive in its ministry . . . Nevertheless, the process by which I and a lot of other seminarians, not all of whom were caught by a rigorous questioner, accepted the Westminster Confession was decidedly less than straightforward."

He won his license to preach despite the protests of Fox and seven other clergymen, by whom "Mr. Thomas was charged with not accepting several of the beliefs of the Church." Cleveland Dodge congratulated him on passing "through your trying ordeal," but his father in Lewisburg wrote the New York Presbytery in some anguish: ". . . . These sensational rumors are exceedingly painful to me, who am conservative in my views and anxious that my son be not made to appear more liberal than the facts warrant." His son was so well liked at Brick Church that its members ignored the dispute. He continued to preach there while he finished his work at Union.

When he graduated in the spring of 1911 as a Bachelor of Divinity with his inevitably superior grades (highest in his class), a Presbyterian red carpet was unrolled before him. He won the Union Seminary traveling fellowship for advanced study but, as he put it, "it did not appeal to me." Sidney Lovett, who by this time saw him not only as an older friend and counselor but as an extraordinary human being, noted that "Brick Church wanted him badly." Acceptance there, if he could also accept its comfortably Victorian concept of religion, meant not only prestige and security but continuation in the social circles to which Violet was accustomed. The birth of their first child, Norman Thomas, Jr., on August 22 might have been expected to make security a stronger factor. But his confidence ruled out worry and he knew very well that Violet did not need Fifth Avenue. "It was not the sort of ministry in which I thought I could be most useful," he said. He had in fact been inspired by the devotion of Dr. Bates, for all his eccentricities, to his parish, so needful of devotion in a way that Brick Church was not.

". . . I am overwhelmingly distressed that you felt it your duty to give up your position just now," wrote one of the church elders, A. R. Ledoux.

Lovett knew that Thomas wanted to be useful rather than merely successful and that he was looking for "a very difficult and challenging job in New York." He found it in tough, poverty-stricken East Harlem, then a polyglot white community with colonies of Italian Waldensians, Hungarians, Slovaks and a few Swedes, many of them immigrants who spoke little English or none at all. The district had the highest homicide rate in New York. Thomas had a church of his own to run—the East Harlem Church on 116th Street between Second and Third Avenues, whose previous pastor had given up the struggle. He was also in charge of a federation newly organized by the Board of Home Missions called the American Parish, which included the Church of the Holy Trinity (Italian Presbyterian) on East 153rd Street, the Church of the Ascension (also Italian) on East 106th Street (just across from the headquarters of the Mafia) and the Friendship Neighborhood House near the Harlem River on Pleasant Avenue. Thomas's own sizable East Harlem Church housed not only his English-speaking flock but a Hungarian congregation and a Swedish Sunday school. The salary was $2,500 a year.

The Thomases moved to a three-story brickfront at 221 East 116th, directly across from their church. To the north of them were pockets of Central European and Balkan peoples, to the west a largely Jewish district, and surrounding them and to the south was the largest Little Italy in America. Refuse, stray cats, hordes of children chattering in accents brought from Sicily or Calabria, and rock-throwing street gangs using garbage-can covers as shields made the previous Thomas neighborhood on Forty-second Street seem modish. One street after another of closely packed tenements teemed with life, noise and a thousand odors, with smiling and gesticulating people, many of them barefoot until winter because of the cost of shoes—streets where merchandise was sold on the sidewalks, fish peddlers shouted their wares from carts and others hawked salami, cheese, pasta, olive oil and wine. Hard-liquor saloons were few among these people brought up on the grape. No organ-grinders came here—there were too few pennies to spare. The Thomases were scarcely unpacked before the visible need all around started them, Violet as well as Norman, on a religious effort that included the sending of coal to freezing communicants, the last-minute payment of rent to prevent families with many children from being cast out on the street, the dispatch of nurses or doctors to the ailing poor and the discouragement of drunkenness, prostitution and crime. Church clubs were formed for groups of boys, some of whom were stickup artists, and for girls of all shades of morality. Athletics and the domestic sciences were promoted for the young, speaking programs and discussion groups for the mature. It was a working-class district with considerable unemployment and low wages for those employed. There were the hopeless and the helpless, and there were also sturdy and devoted people on whom the Thomases could depend.

Both of them loved the work—"the kind of a job," as Thomas described it, "which was literally never done." They were solving human problems every day, implementing the Social Gospel. The congestion was incredible—5,000 people crammed into some blocks. A few doors down the street from the Thomas home was an Irish-dominated Tammany club joined by Jews who, Thomas observed, "united with the Irish in cursing the Italians when they first began to break in." His basic church expenses as a "missionary" in this district were paid by the Board of Home Missions as if he had been in China. He nevertheless found very soon that more money, more resources, were needed. He made an arrangement with the Union Settlement on 104th Street to help handle hardship cases and he began a lifelong routine of wheedling money out of the wealthy. He and Violet helped open workrooms where the unemployed earned fifty cents a day making simple baskets and cement products.

The Thomases soon gave a dinner for the Reverend Ladislas Harsanyi, pastor of the Hungarian flock, and the elders of that congregation, all of the latter rough immigrants of peasant stock. Difficulties arose because Harsanyi, though a graduate of the University of Berlin and familiar with a half-dozen European languages, spoke no more than a few words of English. The same was true of the other guests, so that for the Thomases communication was limited to the necessities. The dinner, served beautifully with fine china and silver, won the Hungarians' hearts but included dishes unknown to them. They would ask Harsanyi in Hungarian how they should be eaten. Thomas thereafter met with Harsanyi (they were immediately "Ladis" and Norman) from eight to nine every morning and taught him English. "No one could ever describe the kindness of Norman Thomas," Harsanyi said years later, recalling the occasion when his child contracted typhoid. Thomas called at once and arranged for a nurse—very hard to find at the time. But then Mrs. Harsanyi caught typhoid and it was necessary to send both her and the child to a hospital—something Harsanyi's modest salary could not stand. Thomas appeared again and, without saying a word, put the needed money on the table.

# NORMAN THOMAS

## 2. Blessed Be the Tie That Binds

Thomas was supremely optimistic that Harlem and all such pockets of poverty could be lifted into middle-class responsibility and contentment by good leadership and the vast wealth implicit in America's resources and technology. The wealth was there, and only needed to be produced more efficiently and distributed more equitably. Ignorance and selfishness were the obstacles, and they could be beaten. He confidently looked forward to seeing his parish rise from blight to beauty. (It is today more than ever blighted.) "I was of a generation of Americans . . . who had no doubt about Progress," he later admitted, ruefully using a capital P.

He took Italian lessons from his colleague, the Reverend Giovanni Tron, but never got far because emergencies usually intervened. His office, on the ground floor of his house, was a bedlam of crises. On Sunday he preached a God who would reward righteousness on this earth even if at times he seemed to take overly long getting around to it. His congregation began as a handful and grew steadily, and he was encouraged by the progress of the parish work in the satellite churches and the settlement house. Home Missions saw that the Thomases hit it off in this community—were admired and loved because they gave themselves without stint, smiled easily, were firm on matters of principle and would not be pushed around. An important part of Thomas's effort aimed to reduce native clannishness among immigrants and their children and to instruct them in their duties and rights as Americans —a process always verging on politics. Like Walter Rauschenbusch, who had done the same work among German immigrants in the metropolis thirty years earlier, he saw ignorance holding his people in slavery—saw employers exploit ethnic jealousies to prevent the formation of unions and keep wages low. "They would play off Slovaks against Hungarians," he observed, ". . . and both against Italians." He went further than most men of the cloth to remind the Slovaks, Hungarians and Italians that their wages would not rise until they dropped Old World animosities and unionized. The recent nonunion Triangle Waist factory fire, in which 146 workers died—most of them young Italian and Jewish girls—and scores were disfigured, was an example of the kind of working conditions that could be expected so long as there was no determined opposition.

Moving gradually toward the left, he was in 1912 an enrolled Bull Mooser who deserted Theodore Roosevelt to vote for the Princetonian Wilson. He was skeptical about the ability of Eugene V. Debs, who polled 901,000 Socialist votes that year. He attended a few Socialist meetings and was not impressed. His affection for his alma mater was overflowing. To Princeton's role as his university was added the college's connection with his romance and marriage—the happiest event of his life. He served on the graduate board of the Philadelphian Society, was desolated if work kept him from class reunions, and with Violet even attended a football game occasionally, singing and shouting for old Nassau and hailing old classmates. This did not prevent him from reminding them of their obligations toward the less fortunate. In one of his class letters he wrote:

> With all my love for Princeton I sometimes think, unjustly of course, that my education really began when I left there and that not the smallest part of it has been the life here in this district. It is a sort of school which sets hard lessons and asks some difficult questions. What is our democracy worth? How shall we make it apply to our social, industrial and political problems? Are we preparing well . . . when so many of our workers cannot even under favorable conditions make the proper living wage? I wish more Princeton men were students in this school—but that is preaching, which is against the rules in a class letter.

His warm, idealistic brother Evan, heading also for the clergy, finished Princeton and entered Union Seminary. Six feet five, two inches taller than his tall brother, he lived part of the time with the Thomases, helping with the parish work. When the youngest brother, Arthur, now at Princeton, came to visit, Violet was microscopic among them, for Arthur was Norman's height. The middle-sized Sidney Lovett, also at Union, arrived to help with the boys' club work. He found the American Parish lively, since there was sporadic gang warfare and the boys were apt to carry short lengths of pipe or brass knuckles—some even knives or guns. Once, failing to persuade one of his charges to give up his gun on the ground that it was iniquitous, he bought it from him and dropped it in the river—an extravagance, it turned out, for within a year the young man was in Sing Sing for armed robbery; both Lovett and Thomas visited him there. Another young church club member came in on Christmas Day to announce a belief in God that had not previously been evident. He explained that he had held up a man on 122nd Street, taken seven dollars, and then had been importuned so touchingly by his victim, who pleaded it would mean that his wife and three children got no Christmas gifts, that he gave the money back. "God bless you!" the man cried. "And God did bless me," the young puppy affirmed. "I went over to Mount Morris Park and stuck up a guy for almost $100."*

Other club members showed promise in better directions. Thomas managed to get scholarships for several of them at Mount Hermon School, where he spoke occasionally. Decent education, wages and living conditions seemed to him the answer to anti-social behavior in Harlem or anywhere else, and who could say that President Wilson or Norman Thomas himself, if reared under the worst Harlem conditions, might not have packed guns?

The Thomas family grew with the arrival of a second son, William Stewart, in 1912, and their first daughter, Mary Cecil, in 1914. The Stewarts still regarded Thomas fondly, for all his wild and impracticable social views. They did not extend this to making frequent familial trips to grubby Harlem, but Violet often traveled downtown to visit them, Thomas joining her when he had time and always thoroughly welcome. Violet's sister Mary came up to Harlem whenever a play, which she would help direct, was planned by the children at the Neighborhood House. Violet was physically fragile, subject to colds and other infections, and what with the children and the church work it was essential for her to have servants. The Thomases spent much of their summers with the affectionate Grandmother Stewart at her grand old Georgian brick country home, Stornoway, near Ridgefield, Connecticut. As the family grew and filled Stornoway with clamor, Violet's mother built the Thomases a handsome frame house of their own on the acreage. While the Stewart money was by no means showered on them, Thomas's family now lived in a style that pricked his conscience when he saw so many of his own parishioners undernourished and living in rags in tenement hovels.

They were at Ridgefield in August, 1914, when European ultimatums led to a war which Thomas deplored, though he felt sure the Allies would quickly win. Hostilities flared also in his parish, especially after Italy entered the war and Harlem's Italians and Hungarians instantly assumed their European enmity. Rocks thrown by Italian children broke Hungarian windows, and vice versa, and there were street fights.

*This story became a Thomas favorite. It was told to the author (of course with variations) by eight people interviewed, who had heard it from Thomas.

The sexton of the Church of the Ascension, presided over by the Reverend Francesco Pirazzini, was shot in the leg mysteriously one night as he was locking up. Thomas, who had won over some of the less lawful people of the district, received a letter, unsigned, assuring him that the shooting was accidental. Nevertheless, the plump Pirazzini, who also had the Mafia across from his church, took to carrying an automatic pistol for protection. He was embarrassed at a parish meeting at Thomas's house when the gun slipped from his pocket and clattered to the floor. A temporary coolness existed between Pirazzini and Harsanyi, each of whom naturally sided with his own countrymen. Harsanyi, however, suggested forming a children's band of all nations as a unifying influence, an idea Thomas cheered.

A Thomas characteristic was his eagerness to carry promising proposals into action. Since it was out of the question to expect local families to buy instruments, he begged money from the Presbytery and from prosperous friends. A forty-piece band was organized under the direction of the church organist, an accomplished musician named Louis Serly, with enough success that outdoor concerts were given in the summer and the group once played at Town Hall. While it could not be said that conflict instantly ceased, the flow of blood was reduced.

Thomas's Neighborhood House, near the junction of the noisome Harlem and East rivers (where local boys swam joyously in filth), had its own problems. Catholic boys were free to join in the basketball and punchball played on the outdoor court there, and to drink from the water fountain. Vito Marcantonio, a Harlem boy who later became a leftist Congressman, recalled that the priest warned them that they would go to hell if they drank from the fountain, but they all risked it because it was the only playground around and naturally they got thirsty. Thomas, Marcantonio said, was admired because by importuning toy wholesalers and dealers he managed to see that at Christmas time every child got a present at the parish party, and because he made the Neighborhood House a thriving community center (it expired soon after his departure). Fighting was of course a normal outlet. Two of Thomas's Italian Bible clubs supervised by Lovett broke into savage battle during a close basketball game but were coaxed at its end to hold hands in a circle and sing "Blessed Be the Tie That Binds." No sooner had they left than the tie snapped and a street fight ensued during which someone produced a length of pipe; "and there was Walter Bruno," Lovett recalled, "on the sidewalk with a great gash in his head."

### 3. *Testing the Faith*

Thomas published a monthly paper for his congregations, brought in guest preachers, including Theodore Savage (now pastor at Christ Church) and the already noteworthy Harry Emerson Fosdick (elder brother of Raymond), inaugurated a training program for social workers in the slums, raised money for an extra visiting nurse, founded a summer camp in New Jersey for his Harlem youngsters, conducted a contest for designing a camp emblem, sponsored outings for mothers with infants, enlarged the Swedish Sunday school, increased the religious work among the Slovaks at the Neighborhood House, and attended with representatives of his Hungarian congregation a Magyar conference at Wilkes-Barre. His three subordinate pastors were astonished by the inexhaustible Thomas energy, expended also in routine details.

"I enclose check for $49," he wrote his parish treasurer. "Of this $15 is Mrs. Thomas's payment of subscription to date, but please notice that of this $34, $1.19 is the Sunday School's payment toward missions." He ordered coal for his several buildings: "Egg coal is better there for our furnace, not broken unless the broken is about as small as egg." He and Violet visited his well-heeled friend Dumont Clarke, now married but not yet embarked on a career, and got a $1,000 donation from him. The Thomases were skilled at coaxing butchers and grocers to be patient with needy debtors, landlords to hold back on evictions, and doctors to cut their charges or in many cases to give treatment free. They were incensed at the huge fees charged the poor by rich funeral directors. Thomas's own $10 fee for presiding at a funeral—charged only when it would not cause hardship—went automatically into the church fund.

He brought in the handsome and dedicated Reverend John Whittier Darr, an Ohioan from Bucyrus four years younger than himself, as his right-hand man. Darr arrived straight from his graduation at Union, was ordained at East Harlem Church and, like Lovett, would come to find his whole life influenced by Thomas. The addition of young college men and women part-time brought the number of parish workers to about forty, a considerable organization. When Thomas joined the local school board—a post fated to be the only public office he ever held—it took more of the hours which in all his life would never be enough. He won generous praise for his work from his former teacher at Union, Dr. William Adams Brown, who had been educated at Yale and at Union and who was now head of the Presbyterian Home Missions Committee.

The Thomas household was already so busy that the arrival of the fourth child, Frances Beatrice, in 1915 could scarcely make a visible difference. From his father in Lewisburg, Thomas heard that the war was causing difficulties for Frank and Anna Welles. "Frank was arrested for a German spy on his way from Paris to Bourré," he wrote, adding that it took some time before he was identified and released. ". . . Today's war news looks bad for England and France. . . . It is a time that will test our faith as it is seldom tested." He spoke more truly than he knew, for it would test and then explode the faith of two of his sons. Welling Thomas died November 16, 1915, his last undelivered sermon questioning the war which many Americans already believed was a holy struggle against German barbarism.

The widowed Mrs. Thomas moved to Baltimore with the two teenaged girls to live with Ralph, who was still unmarried. After finishing Princeton, Ralph had spent two years at the Massachusetts Institute of Technology and was employed by a Baltimore power company. Evan Thomas, whose independence of thought equaled Norman's and whose religious doubts were growing, had gone to Scotland to enlist in Young Men's Christian Association work in war-gripped Edinburgh, where he faithfully read The Literary Digest and The New Republic. "I cannot realize that Father is really dead," he wrote Norman. "I had just mailed a long letter to him before your letters arrived. . . . I would give a very great deal to be able to think that my relations with Father during the past year had been more in accord with his thought. . . . Mother's letter was perfectly wonderful. . . ."

Thomas's own letters reveal a man whose assumptions about social progress and even about religion were being tested. His admiration for Wilson waned with the President's intervention in Mexico and toughness toward Germany. At home, he sided strongly with the striking city streetcar workers: ". . . some of my friends who are very philanthropic and genuinely sorry for the sufferings of the poor can always be trusted to be on the side of the capitalists in any specific quarrel. They utterly fail to understand the strength of the case presented by the Street Railroad men . . ." Aghast at the carnage in Europe, he ignored the Socialist candidate, Allan Benson, and voted with misgivings for Wilson in 1916, hoping that he would indeed "keep us out of war." To him, the war was a selfish struggle between rival imperialisms from which America must stand strictly aloof. He carried on an epistolary debate with Ralph, who favored military preparedness and was also impressed by the preaching of Billy Sunday. Sunday's flag-waving revival meetings were bringing in converts in high numbers but of questionable staying power, as would be done decades later by those of Billy Graham.

". . . I think his sweeping condemnation of the theater and of dancing is likely to do more harm than good," Thomas wrote Ralph. ". . . . if all of the people whom Billy condemned to the bottomless pit are really going there, the company will be pleasing. In all sincerity I should prefer it to that of most of Billy's converts."

To Thomas it became obvious that it was ignorant, easily led Harlem —all the world's poverty-stricken Harlems—whose exploitation supported all the magnificent Fifth Avenues. It was the guileless men of the Harlems who fought and died by the thousands in all the wars. At the well-furnished East Harlem manse, which in summer was not always free from unlovely street smells, Darr and Lovett, each with his young bride, joined the Thomases in late-night discussions. Thomas, striding the floor, head bowed in thought, would lead the talk. Each of the two younger men fell in line wholly with his pacifism and absorbed some of his radicalism. Darr in 1916 left to become pastor of Spring Street Church (the Reverend Bates, on another health-seeking tour, had died in Peru), but Jack and Vera Darr remained friends for life. Lovett and his Boston-born wife, who lived near Union Seminary, managed an American Parish summer camp in 1916. "Norman and Violet were almost like mother and father to us both," he recalled. Shattered when Rebekah Lovett died in childbirth in September, he found in the Thomases his greatest comfort. Thomas accompanied him to Andover for the funeral, and Lovett soon moved into the manse as Thomas's assistant while he finished at Union. (The Thomases named their next daughter, born in 1918, Rebekah Lovett Thomas.) Lovett called Violet "Mom" as long as she lived.

### 4. Getting Out of Hand

Among those who knew Thomas and were aware of his many talents, there was no doubt as to the gift that drove him to exertions beyond most men's stamina. It was his capacity for indignation over injustice. The injustices done the ignorant and defenseless masses could be traced to the compact minority of the rich, the educated, the well-connected, the shrewd, the aggressive and expedient. They were often admirable people—consider the Stewarts—but they lived in a world apart from the masses, did not understand them and were either the believers or the exploiters of that easy rationalization, "The poor are always with us." For years Thomas's indignation had made him a crusader for measures against poverty. Now he had a new and allied cause in the threat of American entry into the war—a threat which came from that same influential and affluent minority. An enormous advantage, possessed by no other proletarian leader to the extent that he possessed it, was his connection with that affluent minority. Being almost as much at home on Fifth Avenue as he was in Harlem, feeling in his heart that Fifth Avenue was basically good even if at fault, he was saved from the rancor and animosity that spoiled the efforts of many friends of the masses. He saw himself as an educator of both classes, and his lectures were animated with an understanding and a humor that made his barbs tolerable.

He joined the American Union Against Militarism, which fought military preparedness on the ground that it would lead inevitably to American participation in the war and used in parades a huge effigy of a dinosaur, meant to symbolize aggressive brainlessness leading to extinction. He spoke at street meetings, in public schools and public halls. He caught trains to speak at colleges and clubs in the East and Midwest, usually without fee except for expenses. For addressing the Young Men's Christian Association at Wesleyan University he received $5.16, the price of his round-trip rail fare. He was employing an art at which he had excelled at college and which had improved ever since. His speaking voice was vibrant, musical, appealing, an instrument he manipulated with subtlety, yet capable of such volume that he could be heard on street corners over the thunder of the elevated railway. His height and impressive appearance, his obvious decency and kindliness, his mobile face and warmth of expression, his skillful marshaling of points, his quick smile and mastery of humor, combined to hold audiences. Listeners invariably had the impression of a learned but compassionate man uttering indisputable truth. Sidney Lovett heard him debate preparedness with a downtown lawyer before a crowd at a Harlem school. "The other man was an able speaker," Lovett recalled, "but Norman picked up a few of his opponent's last points, swiftly demonstrated their absurdity by putting them in a different context, and destroyed him. The audience was so enthusiastic that they surged around Norman to shake his hand or just to touch him."

There were immigrants there, Lovett saw, who could speak little English but had come for the excitement and who understood Thomas's compassion, knew he was with them. It reminded Lovett of the gospels, of poor people gathering around Christ to touch the hem of his garment. It was experiences such as these, he felt, that convinced Thomas of his power and persuaded him that he could be useful in a wider arena in advancing his ideas of social justice.

Late in 1916 Thomas joined the Fellowship of Reconciliation and pushed its Christian pacifist message with his Union classmate, the Episcopalian Reverend John Nevin Sayre, whose older brother Francis had married President Wilson's daughter Jessie. Other leaders were the intense Reverend A. J. Muste, Emily Greene Balch and Thomas's good friends John Darr, Dumont Clarke and Ralph Harlow. Thomas was so busy that he regretfully declined an invitation to teach a once-a-week course in American missionary problems at Princeton—a refusal the university later was thankful for. He soon became co-chairman of the Fellowship of Reconciliation and then head of the new No-Conscription League, organizing the efforts of anti-war people including Rabbi Stephen S. Wise, the Reverend John Haynes Holmes and James A. Farley. He taught a graduate course at Columbia's nearby Teachers' College on the problems of immigrants. By the end of 1916 he was a member of a score of committees, pouring out his energies for many if not all of them. In his work against war he joined forces with people then or later to become widely known, including Jane Addams, Upton Sinclair, the left-wing Socialist Max Eastman and his sister Crystal, Scott Nearing, Oswald Garrison Villard, Lillian Wald, A. A. Berle, and that Harvard-bred wit, sage, bird-lover and fighter for civil liberties and lifelong friend, Roger N. Baldwin. Many of the Irish, such as Farley, whose anti-war sentiments contained some anti-English tincture, admired Thomas's stand for Irish freedom despite his lack of Irish blood.

But when Germany announced unrestricted submarine warfare, American feeling rose against those still favoring peace. Thomas, the devoted '05 man, sustained a volley of savage criticism at a Princeton class dinner, judging from the handsome written apology (". . . that meeting got rather out of hand . . .") he received from his classmate W. Seaver Jones.

Workers for peace were soon being called pro-German, and not only by hotheads like Theodore Roosevelt. Thomas's mother in Baltimore, cautious for one who as a child had frequented the harem of the king of Siam and inclined to agree with the patriotic Ralph, worried about the nonconformism of Norman and Evan. Norman stopped in with her occasionally when speaking in the area or calling on some Congressman in Washington. His speeches were generally regarded as radical and his errands always seemed opposed to the administration. Invariably in a hurry, he usually forgot something. "You left these and other papers on the mantel—I'll try to send them all," she wrote him. ". . . . I'm sorry you had to rush so—thank Violet for her wanting me."

She and Ralph attended the Brown Memorial Church in Baltimore, whose pastor, the Reverend John McDowell, Norman knew as a Princeton man and Philadelphian Society adviser. Through McDowell, Norman had found a Baltimore church post for the Reverend James J. Coale, who had been forced out of his Lackawanna (New York) church by the all-powerful steel corporation in that company-controlled town because he had testified, truthfully, that the steel company worked its immigrant laborers twelve hours a day, seven days a week, in violation of state law. Norman obviously had an affinity with radicals, while Evan in Scotland, though trying not to upset his mother, could not conceal his real feelings from her.

"I am sick to death of hearing people resignedly talking about the death of their sons or friends in this war, submissive to God's will," he wrote her. "They ought to be up in rebellion against such a God." He had renounced the churchly career for which he had been trained and was considering teaching or journalism: "If only I had not spent so much time on theology! That is the one thing that makes me most impatient —that I should have dawdled around in those death tombs of theological colleges so long. . . . I mean no criticism of any individual, least of all my own Father, whose life will always be an inspiration to me." He had conceived an admiration for Bertrand Russell and H. G. Wells as strong as his aversion to Roosevelt. To Norman, to whom he could write with more frankness than to his mother, he railed against both the war and the church, writing, "What God the church does have is mostly tin."

While Norman never referred to tin gods, he was fighting a church and an administration and an upper crust that were moving inexorably toward war. He protested that the American Federation of Churches itself was "working for war and not only for war but for conscription. . . . It is this which tempts me to despair for the future of the church." He regretted that President John Grier Hibben at Princeton, whom he knew as a fellow member of the graduate governing board of the Philadelphian Society, had refused to permit the pacifist David Starr Jordan to speak on the campus, whereas Jordan had addressed a large audience at Yale. He wrote Hibben to protest this and also in criticism of a meeting at the Princeton Club in New York where A. A. Berle had spoken against conscription and had been attacked in reply by the firebrand General Leonard Wood, who called his reasoning "degenerate"—an attack Hibben, who was present, did not disavow. In writing to Hibben, Thomas used a tactic characteristic of both his fairness and his diplomacy, one he would use throughout his life. After three paragraphs of respectful criticism, he ended with a compliment on another subject: "May I express my deep appreciation of the stand you have taken with regard to the club situation at Princeton? I think that in this matter Princeton has shown more idealism than any university I know of." Hibben replied courteously but seemed more aware of the first three paragraphs, saying he thought Jordan's point of view "wholly unpatriotic" and permitting himself to mention "pacifists" and their "crowd," a crowd including Thomas.

Thomas thought the anti-war movement so urgent that he sought to lighten the load of his routine parish work. It was even more important to spur a campaign that might save thousands of young Harlem lives than to aid individuals in the district's mean streets. He had to spend some of his time 102 city blocks south at the office of the No-Conscription League on East Fourteenth Street, and more time at the Fellowship of Reconciliation office on East Twenty-eighth Street. He could not have been getting enough sleep, although he could do with little. He had managed to get the Reverend Harvey E. Holt of Cleveland to fill Darr's place. He thought seriously of hiring another pastor, one experienced in immigrant work, to take his own place while he went on leave to concentrate on his efforts against the war, but the plan was not feasible.

A random example of his response to individual need was his aid in getting his parishioner, Ricardo ———, examined without charge by a doctor who diagnosed Pott's Disease of the spine and lungs and hurried him to a hospital, whereupon the sheriff came, vowing to evict the wife and family for non-payment of rent. The Charity Organization Society had promised Thomas they would handle this but had failed, and Thomas paid the rent in time to save the day. He inspired such trust that he was asked to solve intimate domestic dilemmas:

Just before the Baby was born, Mr. Thomas, my husband went out one night to go to a smoker, he said. He . . . didn't come home until after 1 o'clock in the morning. Something told me he did not go to a smoker and it's been telling me ever since. Last night he told me the truth. He was out that night with women to a burlesque show and then they all went to a cabaret show. . . . I am broken hearted, Mr. Thomas. . . . Can you please come over and help me or advise me what to do?

He replied immediately, counseling patience, which the lady agreed to try "for the sake of my Baby."

# IV

## 1. You Are My Enemy

Thomas got along splendidly with his boss, Dr. William Adams Brown, except that Brown was pro-war, telling Thomas that preparation for war was having the effect of a "great revival on the life and spirit" of the men at Yale, his alma mater. "I mistrust war in general as an agent for national regeneration," Thomas wrote Darr. ". . . I [told him] that if so it was a revival which all history showed was followed by a terrible reaction." He cited among other examples the decline of English morality after the Napoleonic struggles and the triumph of corruption after America's Civil War.

He got little help for the peace cause from the institutions that might be expected to give support in great moral crises—the churches, the colleges and the political parties. Well, there was an exception, the Socialist Party, which doctrinally opposed capitalist war. This was taken by some as a joke, considering the way in which European Socialist parties, all "internationalist" and uncompromisingly against capitalist war, had rallied to the capitalist colors when capitalist war was declared. French and English Socialists were killing German and Austrian Socialists in the name of freedom just as French and English Christians were killing German and Austrian Christians for the glory of God.

The United States Socialist Party, determined to plot a specific course in advance, called an emergency convention in Saint Louis for April, 1917. But German U-boats worked even faster. When the convention opened April 7, the United States had already been one day at war. Nevertheless, the leader of the New York Socialists, Morris Hillquit, presented a resolution calling the United States declaration of war "a crime against the people of the United States and against the nations of the world." It was passed 140–36, whereupon the Party began to disintegrate. Among the influential members who resigned or denounced the Party, or both, for its treason were John Spargo, William English Walling, the millionaire J. G. Phelps Stokes, Charles Edward Russell and Upton Sinclair. The California Socialist leader W. J. Ghent wrote his old friend Hillquit in outrage, ending his letter:

> You are my enemy, and I am
> Yours,
> W. J. Ghent.

The actuality of war aroused an American "patriotic" intolerance which reached such extremes as the denunciation of dachshunds, sauerkraut and Beethoven and the abrupt cessation of German courses in high schools, along with the dismissal of many teachers guilty of giving instruction in that language. One quick disillusionment for Thomas was caused by the eloquent Rabbi Wise, who at a Carnegie Hall peace rally had told the audience that he had brought his son to hear him say he would never support this war. A few weeks after war was declared, without mention of his son, Wise denounced Thomas and all his former peace brethren as pro-German because they were not supporting the war.

So the brave stand for peace was reduced to a rearguard effort to keep American participation within reason and to defend civil liberties already under heavy attack. The pressures and haste under which Thomas worked were evident in his otherwise admirable form letter on policy to members of the Fellowship of Reconciliation, in which "difficult" appeared as "fiddicult." With Jane Addams and Lillian Wald he called on Secretary of War Baker to urge an enlightened policy toward conscientious objectors. With Jane Addams, Villard and others he signed a letter to President Wilson warning him about bills before Congress which menaced democratic safeguards:

> . . . Even by this time we have seen evidence of the breaking down of immemorial rights and privileges. Halls have been refused for public discussion; meetings have been broken up; speakers have been arrested and censorship exercised, not to prevent the transmission of information to enemy countries, but to prevent the free discussion by American citizens of our own problems and policies.

Pulling every visible string, he telephoned Nevin Sayre, whose church was in nearby Suffern, New York, and persuaded him to write his brother Francis, the President's son-in-law, and also direct to Wilson himself, protesting excesses in the proposed conscription bill. Thomas wrote Senator George Chamberlain, chairman of the Senate Committee on Military Affairs, urging a more liberal exemption of conscientious objectors than the one proposed, which exempted only members of pacifist sects: "To exempt the members of a certain sect is to recognize the principle of the rights of conscience even when the nation is at war. Is it not fair to make this an individual matter?" For The Nation, owned by the flat-out pacifist Oswald Garrison Villard, he wrote a long letter —in reality an article, "Conscience and the Church," attacking the concept that one's conscience could only be effective or recognized if linked to religious dogma:

> Conscience is individual and not corporate; not all conscientious objectors are Quakers. When the Church countenances the denial of this fact she is cutting the ground out from underneath her. Her Bible was written by men who were in small minorities. . . . The claim of the state to coerce conscience is a blow to that freedom of religion which has made America great . . .

To Thomas, a rank atheist might well have God-given ethical objections to war which would be as sacred as those of any religionist. Objectors could be useful on the farms. Far better that a few slackers should escape the army net than that the holy conscience of honest men be denied. Thomas had enormous respect for sincere conscientious objectors, as he did for all men who had principles and stood by them. He would encourage objectors, fight for their rights through the Fellowship of Reconciliation and other organizations and would write a book about them. He was thinking in political as well as evangelical terms, seeing in the CO's an elite cadre of anti-war people who could perhaps be enlarged in a political struggle for the pacifist ideal. But when the sporty Max Eastman, editor of The Masses, wanted to borrow The Fellowship of Reconciliation's mailing list in the hope of selling his magazine to its members, the answer was No. Though The Masses was Socialist and anti-war, and Thomas was looking for allies, Thomas thought its capitalization of sex and shock diluted its political message and that the religion-oriented Fellowship of Reconciliation people would resent any fraternization. He wrote Eastman so eloquently urging a more mature political approach that Eastman thanked him for his gentle criticism but defended The Masses and said it had to go its own way.

In Max Eastman, one year older, were a background, a brilliance, an independence and an energy that paralleled Thomas's, along with a hedonism Thomas did not share. Thomas was handsome, but Eastman was beautiful. Upstate-born son of both a preacher father and a preacher mother, Phi Beta Kappa at Williams, facile poet, former teacher at Columbia, already respected for his *Enjoyment of Poetry* (1913), Eastman was as well known for his frank sexuality as for his politics, which were then much to the left of Thomas's. Though they were never close friends, they appeared on speaking platforms together and their careers and thoughts touched intermittently for decades and ultimately threw sparks.

Thomas's anti-war support was dwindling. The Young Men's Christian Association almost immediately became a war machine—which included Princeton's Philadelphian Society and all his friends there including Cleveland Dodge. The Presbyterian Church was waffling. Ralph Harlow, once so strong for the Fellowship of Reconciliation, now wrote of his fears of Prussian world conquest and of his own "confusions of mind." Thomas's Princeton friend in Chicago, Alfred Carton, read Thomas's Nation letter and wrote him in rebuttal, declaring that freedom of conscience had been sufficiently won in the United States, that military force was essentially an external extension of internal police power which everybody approved, that if Thomas opposed police power he was an anarchist. There was a large group whose opinion Thomas had to respect—Henry Sloane Coffin and Harry Emerson Fosdick were among them—who had fought hard against war but at last had agreed with Wilson that war could not be avoided.

Among the opposition were Thomas's own family and in-laws. His brother Ralph enlisted in the engineering corps almost immediately, and Arthur was debating which branch of the service to enter. Violet's grandfather, now ninety-five, the friend and admirer of Wilson, was incensed at Thomas's stand, and Violet's brothers could not be said to be enthusiastic about it. Ralph was in training at Plattsburg. The widowed Mrs. Thomas visited during that summer of 1917 with Violet, Norman and the children, spending some of the time at Stornoway. The visit was not without tension, for Mrs. Thomas was unhappy about the trend of Norman's thinking—he said, for example, ". . . I agree very nearly with many of [the Socialist Party's] fundamental doctrines." Violet was with him every inch of the way.

Sidney Lovett, just graduated from Union, knew that his own scruples against war would bar him from being ordained until the war was over. With Thomas's blessing he moved on to take the Maverick Church in

Boston, a workingmen's church not unduly exercised about ordination. Soon his place in the American Parish was taken very temporarily by another pacifist, Evan Thomas, who stopped in Paris with his aunt and uncle on his way home. He wanted to challenge the draft he could have escaped by staying in Scotland.

To Carton, Thomas wrote, "I think your letter is a very clear statement of what is perhaps a dominant position today and I like your honesty in admitting that nationalism and 'my country right or wrong' are your guiding principles." He had already dealt with the confusion of police force and war, seeing conscience again as the key:

> [War] makes me give over my conscience to my superior officer. I am no longer to judge the measure of force to be applied . . . I must obey! In the use of police force . . . killing is only resorted to in the very last extremity after other things have failed. In war there is nothing else to do but to kill. . . . When I use police force I can establish personal relations even with the criminal and having restrained his violence it is my duty to do all I can to redeem him. . . . In war, my relations are either hideously impersonal or inspired by hate and I have no chance to redeem the enemy. In war, I do not deal directly with criminals but with their dupes who seek my life as I seek theirs. . . . [P]olice force is consistent with law and measurably consistent with love to a degree that war cannot be even when it is undertaken for ends which men think must be noble. . . .

From Ralph Harlow, now in Boston as an official for Armenian and Syrian relief, came two more letters in which Ralph caved in remorsefully. He had seen Armenia despoiled by the Turks, thought the Germans equally bad, felt that idealism and democracy were on America's side and, after terrible soul-searching, admitted that he could no longer oppose the war. He wrote Thomas in fear that their friendship might be ended. Thomas's immediate reply suggested a patience growing thin:

> There is no denying that I am disappointed at your letter. Yet . . . had I been in Armenia with you I might very likely share your views.
>
> Aside from the fundamental Christian question I think you are wrong in your high estimate of the idealism involved in this war . . . I am not even sure that President Wilson's idealism measures up to his words. I am quite sure that the country at large like all other countries is fighting not for idealistic motives but for certain deep instincts for combat and for that most complex of motives known as patriotism. . . . It is, however, absurd

to say that we as a nation are animated in this war greatly by love of democracy when we adopt motives that are the denial of democracy. Do you really believe that our great papers like the "New York Times" which prate about war for democracy when they have devoted all their strength to oppose political and industrial democracy at home [*sic*]? Do you think theirs is a pure love of humanity when they have been the open defenders of a system which produces the unnumbered inhumanities of our industrial life? Can we think Americans in general with their shameful record in race riots are purely disinterested redressors of the crimes to Belgium and Armenia? Do you think the whole system of military autocracy will be a training school for the democracy we need? . . . Here are men of America being drafted for a war for which great numbers of them would not have voted. . . .

At the very least you earnest men who take the position you point out are charged with an enormous responsibility of working to bring about the day when Christian men can make a Christian choice and are not shut up to a choice between evils . . . what have you to say for your religion which leaves its followers with only a choice between evils? Does it sound like the faith that will overcome the world?

## 2. *"Democracy Is Endangered"*

Roger Baldwin, who had the help of Thomas and a few others at this time in founding the National Civil Liberties Bureau (later the American Civil Liberties Union), was beginning a half-century of collaboration at whose end he would call Thomas "my lifelong colleague and friend in every cause that mattered to me." The slightly-built, puckish, non-religious Baldwin well knew that a religious-moralist reformer losing a battle to immorality could be dreadfully dull if he was also lost to humor. His discovery that Thomas's occasional weakness for pontificating was relieved by "wit and infectious gayety" helped make the half-century enjoyable. Thomas was so susceptible to the comic that even while developing a serious argument he could discover a bizarre sidelight that brought out his quick, hearty laugh. His height, thrusting his distinguished and expressive face above others in a crowded room, gave him a presence that made people ask, "Who is that man?"

By 1917, more and more people knew who that man was and disliked his policies. Even in his own American Parish, some of his Italian-Americans were unhappy about his opposition to the war in which Italy hoped for vast territorial gains as a reward for joining the Allies. Many of the younger Italians were enlisting, to find themselves better fed and clothed than they ever had been in Harlem—"a sad commentary," Thomas observed, ". . . that good food, clothing and some sense of comradeship depend on being sent to a military camp to be trained for the business of war."

Violet's susceptibility to illness troubled him. So did his realization that he had been naive in his certainty of progress. He felt now that the great gains he had made in his parish church rolls—an increase from 487 members in 1911 to 1,582 in 1916—were mostly numerical, that otherwise he had barely held the line in matters of human need and moral improvement. He could speak of "the futility of many of our measures of amelioration." He had in hand a letter from a California clergyman and Fellowship of Reconciliation member protesting the church's warlike spirit: ". . . churches are almost turning into recruiting offices . . . Epworth Heralds are shouting for recruits; theologians are showing that God is a God of war and Christ a military hero. Twenty-five hundred brother pastors of California . . . have consented to advertise Liberty Bonds from their pulpits tomorrow." To the New York Presbyterian Church Thomas himself protested a Sunday-school poster for children "which has as its main picture men firing off a gun and its dominant sentiment 'Peace with Honor and Peace with God.' "

His conviction that the church had failed the people was plain in his letter to Harlow. With his inner need for improving the lot of mankind, he rejected Tolstoyan asceticism and non-resistance to evil and looked for agencies that might do better than the church. One of those was the National Civil Liberties Bureau, dedicated to saving the Bill of Rights from all passions including those of war. Another was the Socialist Party. By August Thomas was writing, "I myself am constantly troubled with this problem: I acknowledge that the hope of Christianity is in the search for a new social order . . ." Since few other churchmen would acknowledge this need, there was trouble ahead. The Socialist Party had done precisely what the church had feared and failed to do— renounced nationalism and condemned the war. Thomas had to admire forty-eight-year-old Morris Hillquit, born Hilkowitz in Latvia, the chief author of that courageous resolution. In 1917 Hillquit ran on the Socialist ticket for Mayor of New York City against the spread-eagle incumbent, John Purroy Mitchel, and Hearst's candidate, John F. Hylan. On October 2, Thomas gave to the press his letter to Hillquit:

I should like to assure you of my personal support . . . For various reasons I have not seen my way clear to join the Socialist Party but I am behind you in this campaign for these reasons:

I believe that the hope for the future lies in a new social and economic order which demands the abolition of the capitalistic system. War itself is only the most horrible and dramatic of the many evil fruits of our present organized system of exploitation and the philosophy of life which exalts competition instead of cooperation. . . . I am convinced that the hope of peace lies not so much in statesmen who have already shown themselves largely bankrupt of ideas but in people of all countries who demand the cessation of war in which they pay so horrible a price. To vote for you is to voice that demand. . . . I cannot believe that democracy is a garment that can be taken off and put in moth balls for future use or that you can secure democratic ends by Prussian methods of which the latest example is the legislation which makes the Postmaster General judge of what the American people shall read. . . .

His letter was a shock to friends and relatives who subscribed to Theodore Roosevelt's charge that Hillquit was a traitor, a "Hun within," and to the advice of Thomas's old professor and pastoral mentor, Henry Van Dyke, that the best way to handle the situation was "by hanging the Socialist candidate for Mayor." From Thomas's mother in Baltimore came a protest that he answered at length:

I did not know you would be so surprised at my supporting Hillquit. . . . When you were here last summer the issues of the campaign were not drawn. Mr. Mitchel had not called every man a traitor who disagreed with the most violent pro-war party nor had the campaign of suppression of free speech and assemblage gone so far. . . . I believe that the struggle for the preservation of freedom of speech and assemblage is absolutely vital. . . . [D]emocracy is endangered in America. The action of the Post Office Department in repressing radical papers is tyranny pure and simple. . . . I cannot see why we should have a splendid municipal system for the supply of water and leave the equally important matter of milk supply to competing companies . . .

. . . I do not see that Mr. Hillquit's position is treasonable. . . . As for the church I believe I am doing her the highest service by . . . trying to prove that she is catholic enough to make room for social radicals. The strife between radicalism and conservatism is the battle of the future. . . . For myself I believe that Christian ethics are impossible in the present order of society. . . . Whether the church will tolerate me or not is for it to say.

I hope it will. . . . I am perfectly aware that the stand I am taking is costing me many friendships. . . . Dr. Brown, while he disagrees with me, is a believer in liberty. The danger will come from the pressure of respectable church folk with money. . . .

At Plattsburg Ralph was shocked by bayonet practice which, he wrote, "in stark brutality of methods . . . seems to transcend anything we have known." The realities of technique were also stressed by a YMCA man's manual on hand-to-hand fighting: "Never miss an opportunity to destroy the eyes of the enemy. In all head holds use the fingers on the eyes. . . . The eye can easily be removed with the finger. . . . Neck: It is easy to strangle a man with any of the neck holds, but the chief weapon of attack with the neck is the foot. . . . Don't kick but jump on it with the full weight of the body." Thomas campaigned strenuously for Hillquit, one of his listeners writing him years later:

> . . . I have a very vivid recollection of you talking during World War I from the tail of an auto, at the corner of 96th Street and Broadway, against . . . the war. And when someone asked you whether you would buy Liberty Bonds, instead of dodging, as some very courageous radicals and anti-war people did . . . you frankly said you wouldn't. . . . At first [the crowd was] hostile but your calm reasonableness and your utter frankness had them eating out of your oratorical hand in the shake of a lamb's tail.

Thomas had a new thrill, being one of those who addressed a huge rally for Hillquit at Madison Square Garden. His appraisal of Dr. Brown and the "respectable church folk with money" hit the mark squarely. Brown, who applauded Thomas's work and liked him personally, summoned him to the church offices at Fifth Avenue and Twenty-second Street. As Thomas recalled it, "It was bad enough, he said, that I should be a pacifist, but to be also a Socialist . . . ! . . . . He told me how hard I had made the financial situation." Contributions both to the church and to Thomas himself from wealthy benefactors had indeed withered, and one prosperous merchant who gave annually a supply of Christmas toys for Harlem's children said there would be no more of that with Thomas in charge. Thomas resigned.* Brown, immensely relieved, then prevailed on him to stay a few months until his successor could

---

*Twenty years later, when Thomas met Brown on the street, Brown forgot that he had virtually demanded his resignation and said, "Oh, Norman, Norman, why did you ever leave?"

take over—an arrangement Thomas wryly regarded as a victory of convenience over principle, allowing him to corrupt the parish for many more weeks.

Hillquit polled 145,000 votes, the largest number ever received by any Socialist candidate for the post, and eighteen Socialists were elected to city and state offices, a local showing that did not reflect the party's national decline. Thomas, not without sorrow in leaving the church at thirty-three after thirteen years in its service, was already planning the first issue of The World Tomorrow, a new publication sponsored by the Fellowship of Reconciliation of which he would be editor in chief. He now had five Harlem Italian boys on scholarship at Mount Hermon School, and somehow managed to write them occasionally. At least three of them, Bruno, Tony and Romeo, wrote him with evident affection and regret at his resignation.

"This war is beginning to seem like the statement Sherman said it was," Tony wrote, adding, "Remember me to Mrs. Thomas and all the 'Boys,' also your brother Evan." The Mount Hermon gym was closed and other buildings chilly due to the wartime coal shortage, but football was not dropped and three of the five had won letters in that sport. Romeo wrote in part, "I am very sorry to hear that you are leaving that real country, Little Italy. . . . It is indeed grateful to me to compare myself with some of the [Harlem] 'tough guys' and to see a real difference; all because you have been kind enough to devote your lives in Little Italy."

### 3. Indecent Display

While no one yet urged for Thomas the hanging Dr. Van Dyke recommended for Hillquit, he had lost many friends and he had lost his beloved alma mater. The sympathetic secretary of the Philadelphian Society, T. S. Evans, was watching developments for him there. Evans had written him earlier, "I have not seen any indications that a pacifist is unsafe on the Campus," but the climate changed after Thomas supported Hillquit and Evans now wrote, "Judging from some hints which have come to me from some members of the Board, I rather feel like advising you to resign." Thomas resigned the next day, and later resigned from the Colonial Club. Quitting these college organizations which had been dear to him since 1905, and being shut out also from class dinners and reunions, was infinitely painful. He also felt obliged to resign from the Harlem school board and from the Theta Club, a valued New York City discussion group. From Tom Carter in China came a letter saying he had heard rumors about Thomas's pacifist efforts and expressing thanks to God that we were fighting the Germans. Meanwhile young Arthur Thomas had enlisted in the air force, while Ralph sailed for France with his engineering outfit "singing and shouting," as he described it, adding with brotherly understanding to Norman: "I am sorry we don't agree in this, the biggest affair of our lives, but you know I respect your courage of conviction and idealism."

Evan had recently returned from Europe to stay briefly with Violet and Norman in the manse they were about to abandon. The tall brothers were "talkative and walkative," pacing the floor as they argued, passing each other as they talked. Norman's admiration for Evan's ideals was mixed with worry about his absolute fearlessness in acting on principle. Evan soon was drafted and sent to Camp Upton, where he announced his refusal to take part in killing. Late in April, 1918, Norman and Violet moved from Harlem with their five children.* They had rented a house at 221 East Seventeenth Street at $100 a month, but pending its refurbishing they stayed with Violet's mother on Thirty-eighth Street, a port never closed to them whatever the storm. The Seventeenth Street location was convenient to Thomas's Fellowship of Reconciliation office on Twenty-eighth Street, where he served as both executive secretary of the organization and editor of The World Tomorrow, and to the Friends' Meeting House on Gramercy Park, where the 200 members of FOR's New York organization met.

The tyranny that disgraced the Wilson administration was only beginning. The Socialist Call was banned from the mails. The Masses was suppressed and Max Eastman, Floyd Dell and other editors were on trial as conspirators. The Nation got into trouble over a story criticizing Samuel Gompers. Jack Darr was under suspicion and writing Thomas, "you may be in jail long before I am!" The peppery Elizabeth Gurley Flynn and 160 other Wobblies were arrested for sedition. Thomas helped raise bail for Scott Nearing, who had been jailed because of anti-war sentiments expressed in a pamphlet published by the Socialists' Rand School. He jousted with the city department of education in behalf of Isabel Davenport, a high school teacher harassed when she refused to sign the city administration's loyalty pledge, Thomas arguing

---

*The move cost them five dollars per hour for a van and four men, regarded as an inflated wartime price.

that this "was precisely the Prussian policy against which we are at war." Thomas himself was politely eased out of his part-time professorial post at Teachers' College because he caused "embarrassment to the College," and his suggestion that Emily Greene Balch (later to win a Nobel Peace Prize) be given the post was rejected because her own pacifist attitude was as "objectionable." He did not fight his ouster, being as busy as he was enthusiastic over The World Tomorrow (its first issue was called New World), which surveyed the current scene critically from the pacifist point of view in articles by such contributors as John Haynes Holmes, Oswald Garrison Villard, Willard L. Sperry and Thomas himself. The New York Postmaster had a battery of readers searching for subversive material. Thomas was in immediate trouble. The New York censors found fault with his first issue and every one of nine successive issues. Various articles in various issues were condemned because:

". . . [The] writer charges . . . that the government has discriminated against the colored soldiers. . . ."

". . . [The] writer (presumably the editor) . . . is in sympathy with the Christian Pacifists who . . . were found guilty at Los Angeles . . ."

". . . [This] article is virtually a defense of the I.W.W."

"[In the book reviews there are] strong pacific anti-war ideas and views."

". . . [The] writer, Norman Thomas, indulges in . . . criticism of the Espionage law."

". . . [No] mention has been made of Liberty Bonds, War Savings Stamps or other war measures . . . this publication is pro-German and anti-American."

"Note the editorial defending Debs."

"[The article] is written by some ass of a pacifist person. . . . it preaches disruption on every page."

Thomas, aroused at the muzzling of a large American minority, helped to undo his own reputation at his alma mater by urging Princeton to sponsor a debate on the question, "Resolved, that the government should limit the free expression of opinion." The proposition was rejected, whereupon he was again nailed by the censors for writing in the magazine:

When universities refuse to permit or discuss free speech, when mobs beat or kill agitators, when the government prosecutes critics of the war, it is liberty itself which is the chief victim. What shall it profit us to defeat Prussia if we prussianize our ownselves?

The World Tomorrow was regarded as so subversive that the New York Post Office people alerted Military Intelligence, who replied ominously: "We feel that this [magazine], particularly the editor thereof, Reverend Norman Thomas, is only a shade removed from questionable public utterances as compared with Roger N. Baldwin . . . now under investigation by the Department of Justice, and should be glad to keep this subject under continued observation." The office of Postmaster General Albert C. Burleson, the Texas politician in whom was vested authority to forbid all but "patriotic" publications, was less excitable than the New York officials. Twice in 1918 Thomas managed in trips to Washington to have the ban on his magazine lifted, but his September issue drew the heaviest censure of all. It contained an article by Holmes, "The Search—A Parable," in which a hunt for Hate failed to find it in such likely places as the trenches but found its source at an elegant table at which were seated "an old, old man, a childless matron and a curate." Even worse was an article by Thomas himself, "The Acid Test of Our Democracy," which criticized American military intervention in Soviet Russia and of which two Post Office critics reported in small part, "Norman Thomas's article . . . is pro-Bolshevik and teems with anti-Japanese sentiments utterly vicious . . ." "[It] even questions the good faith of the expedition—suggesting . . . that it is for the benefit of capitalistic interests."

Thomas and John Nevin Sayre, his colleague in the Fellowship of Reconciliation, hurried to Washington and were denounced by an angry Burleson. "If I had my way," he said to Thomas, "I'd not only kill your magazine but send you to prison for life." He ultimately agreed to drop the ban if Thomas promised to "behave" thenceforth—a proposition Thomas icily declined. They were shown the door. Thomas then urged Sayre to try to see the President, which he did despite reluctance to capitalize on his relationship with him. Wilson turned out to be in lenient humor. He looked over the proscribed magazine, said he did not think it seditious and added, "But you go and tell Norman Thomas that an English historian once said, 'There is such a thing as indecent display of private opinions in public,'" which seemed equivalent to Dr. Brown's suggestion that free speech was nice to have providing that one did not use it. Wilson wrote Burleson:

I know the principal writer for this paper, Norman Thomas. He was once a pupil of mine at Princeton. I have just had a talk with Nevin Sayre . . . which I hope and believe will alter the policy and, to some extent, the point of view of men like Thomas . . . I know they are absolutely sincere and I would not like to see this publication held up unless there is a very clear case indeed.

Burleson, however enraged, heeded the omnipotent and again the ban was lifted. But the very next issue incurred new wrath which Thomas this time escaped by writing a long letter to the President's secretary, Joseph P. Tumulty, defending the magazine's tone and adding, "In these stirring times the fate of a little magazine like The World Tomorrow may not be very important. But the fate of civil liberties is important." The magazine was banned in Canada, causing one New York censor to write, "The Canadian Government at least seems to have sensed the true spirit and attitude of this thoroughly unpleasant sheet." And there would be further objections.

An era of secret federal agents—an arm of the law strange in America, upholding the Espionage Act and operating under the comfortingly named Department of Justice—got under way. Another group of agents representing New York State's own watch over "seditious activities" was abroad. Thomas, considered quite dangerous, seems to have been under the surveillance of either or both of these groups whenever he made a speech—a surveillance that continued long after the war was over. One of those assigned to watch the Rand School* was Agent 22, a woman later identified in the files of the state's Joint Legislative Committee Investigating Seditious Activities as Betty Thompson. She took notes on speeches and lectures Thomas and others made there and reported to her superiors. Two male agents were on hand when Thomas addressed the Irish Progressive League, noting that among the things he said there was, "If you want to free Ireland, you want to free ourselves first [sic]." The agents reported that "The only speaker whose remarks can be construed as distinctly un-American was N. Thomas." Someone else unnamed was listening when Thomas (along with Elizabeth Gurley Flynn and James Weldon Johnson) spoke warmly but hardly seditiously at a Harlem meeting sponsored by the Committee on Justice to the Negro. His speech was judged so dangerous that it was stamped "Not to be released for public use until after September, 1969," that being fifty years after its delivery.

Thomas was so well aware of the spying that Agent 22 (whom he perhaps came to recognize for what she was) observed that he made a sardonic practice of stopping a remark in mid-sentence and saying, "Oh

*New York's Rand School, supported by the Socialist Party, also taught workers such courses as English, grammar and history.

no, I mustn't say that for the [agents'] pencils are already waiting to take this down."

Public hysteria against deviations was whipped up by politicians, civic leaders and the press. Meetings of the Socialist Party, Industrial Workers of the World, Nonpartisan League and the International Bible Students were "attacked and broken up from one end of the country to the other." The anti-war Charles A. Lindbergh, father of the as yet unknown airman, was so harried as candidate for governor of Minnesota that he had to hold at least one meeting across the line in Iowa. Six Texas farmers were beaten bloody because they would not subscribe to the Red Cross. The Socialist Rose Pastor Stokes got a ten-year sentence for writing a letter to a Kansas City newspaper against war profiteers. The Reverend Herbert S. Bigelow of Toledo was for the war, all right, but was kidnaped and horsewhipped "in the name of the women and children of Belgium" because he opposed hatred of the Germans. In Butte, Montana, Frank Little, an anti-war IWW organizer—a cripple—was seized by masked men at night and hanged from a railroad trestle. Gus Lindin, a Socialist of Duluth, was tarred and feathered by a group describing themselves as "The Knights of Liberty."

The ridiculous joined with the outrageous and violent. Waldemar Czapanski of San Francisco spent ten days in jail for laughing at rookies drilling at the Presidio. A New Yorker drew ninety days for spitting on the sidewalk near some visiting Italian officers. The famous German conductor Karl Muck was forbidden to conduct a symphony in Baltimore. At a Socialist meeting in New York's Lower East Side at which the war was not treated with full respect, a patriot leaped out of the crowd and stabbed the speaker, Isidore Cohen, inflicting serious wounds. Scott Nearing managed to escape conviction but the Rand School directors were fined $3,000 for publishing his pamphlet, and strong government efforts were made to close the school by injunction. Professors J. M. Cattell and H. W. L. Dana of Columbia University, both known to Thomas, were dismissed for criticizing government policy, at which Professor John Dewey, though thoroughly pro-war, protested in vain and Professor Charles A. Beard resigned. Five anti-war national officials of the Socialist Party including Victor Berger of Milwaukee were found guilty under the Espionage Act and sentenced to twenty years at Leavenworth Prison. Judge Kenesaw M. Landis, who tried the case, said, "It was my great displeasure to give Berger 20 years at Fort Leavenworth. I regret it exceedingly because I believe that the laws of

65

this country should have enabled me to have Berger lined up against a wall and shot."*

### 4. Evan Imprisoned

Doubtless Landis would have said the same about Evan Thomas, who suddenly was in serious trouble. He had been shipped with many other conscientious objectors to Fort Riley, Kansas, where they were treated like criminals, occasionally beaten, subjected to more cunning cruelties and threatened with life imprisonment. His mother wrote Norman asking his advice and also imploring him not to talk of pacifism in a speech he was to make in Baltimore lest it damage Evan's case. "I assure you I was not going to make any pacifist speech," Norman replied, ". . . but only an appeal for civil rights"—a distinction that probably did not relieve her overmuch.

The plight of the objectors—most of them men of principle suffering for their beliefs—presented propagandist opportunities he wanted to exploit to the utmost before Congress and the people. He was anxious that Evan and his fellows make a case for themselves that would elicit public understanding and sympathy. But the impulsive Evan lived by principle and cared nothing for politic appearance. Ordered to do menial labor, he refused, not because of objection to labor but because to accede would be "to become part of the army machine." He would of course be viewed by the public as that loathsome creature, a slacker who refused even to work while patriots were giving their lives. Norman wrote him to urge that he could work without violating his pacifist conscience.

"Never will I work to keep myself a slave," Evan replied with some heat. He and two others of his persuasion then went on a hunger strike against foul food and other deliberately maleficent conditions at the camp. To his sister Agnes, who sent him goodies, he replied with thanks, adding, "Unfortunately they arrived after we had started our hunger strike. As we mean this strike to last a long time I gave the candy & nuts to some of the other men in our tent who are eating. They tell me it

*The Berger convictions were later set aside by the Supreme Court, but Berger, who had been elected to Congress, was removed from Congress by the Court. Rose Pastor Stokes's sentence was also set aside, but she was harassed again and again by repeated arrests, often with large bail requiring imprisonment until paid.

is great. . . . We are ready for what comes having already gone 3 days . . . Hunger striking is quite an experience. . . . The gnawing hunger has begun to leave me."

Norman, fearful of Evan's determination, wrote him hastily, ". . . I wish you could see your way clear to abandon this hunger strike plan. . . . From this distance I can't see that your course is demanded on principle or that it is technically advantageous for the cause you love. Naturally I am concerned on Mother's account for I fear I cannot make her understand. . . . You and your comrades are needed by this generation, which is one reason I care so much that you should make your protest in the best possible way, and not inadvisedly risk life or health."

Norman—himself under suspicion as editor of an "unpatriotic" publication—and his mother left by train for Junction City, Kansas, the town nearest Fort Riley. They found Evan in bed at the base hospital. Always a beanpole, he was more gaunt than ever and there had been actual fear for his life. Because of his extensive education and warm personality he was rightly regarded as a leader of the dissidents. The night before, on an order from the medical officer, enlisted men had roused him and scrubbed him with stiff kitchen brushes fit to render him raw and bloody, but he was so likable that they had gone over him only lightly, leaving him merely sore. Later he had been roused again and told that he would be forcibly fed. It is not likely that his principle had surrendered to hunger, but Evan was subject to philosophical deflections. He decided that passive acceptance of forcible feeding would not violate his anti-military vow. Hence when Norman and his mother saw him he had had his first real meal in almost a week. Norman talked with the medical officer who, he wrote Roger Baldwin, "cursed [Evan] forward & backward & up & down—said he'd land him in a straight [*sic*] jacket."

Mrs. Thomas was enduring terrible stress. While the fate of Evan might vary between anything from starvation to a long prison term and lifelong disgrace, and Norman was persisting in "seditious" activities, Arthur was flying egg-crate training planes in Texas and had just seen his best service friend killed in the crackup of such a plane. Now, at Fort Riley, she received a War Department telegram saying that Ralph, a captain of engineers, was seriously wounded in France.

Norman talked with many of the objectors. "Really these are remarkable men," he wrote Baldwin. ". . . . I have rather urged that not to resist forcible feeding makes their position stronger . . ." He had intended to publicize their plight in the New York papers and news services, but could not do so because his mother would resent it:

Even your tact & skill would be strained by my position: a somewhat
suspicious military; a Mother who is a brick & who sees daily, yes hourly,
more of our point of view but still thinks hunger striking almost suicide
and morally wrong . . . Inside of me struggle admiration for the men
. . . a desire that their struggle thus far be not in vain, hatred of this vile,
cruel & stupid religion of the State whose creed of conscription makes it
the modern Moloch, and a feeling of dislike for hunger striking and doubt
of its tactical value.

He asked Baldwin to pass the facts on to his own World Tomorrow
and also to Villard's Nation. Ironically, on that same day, federal agents
were raiding Baldwin's Civil Liberties Bureau in New York and im-
pounding its records as evidence for prosecution, in the belief that an
organization devoted to the protection of constitutional rights was seditious. Norman hurried back to New York to defend the Bureau, with
Evan's ordeal far from over. As for Ralph, shrapnel had punctured a
lung and injured a leg but he was mending at the best of all places, the
villa of Aunt Anna and Uncle Frank.

Soon after Mrs. Thomas returned to Baltimore, she received a cheerful note from Evan ending, "Address me c/o Guard House, Ft. Riley,
in the future." The next word she got showed that the army did not take
conscientious objection lightly. Evan had been court-martialed and sentenced to dishonorable discharge and life imprisonment at hard labor
—a staggering penalty. Then mail from him ceased to reach her. She
heard from relatives of other objectors that Evan and fifty other prisoners had been put in solitary confinement for some new infraction and
refused communication with their kin. She wrote the President a long
letter in behalf of all the objectors, soundly constructed and argued—
a talent all the Thomases seemed to have. She did not fail to butter him
lightly, saying that all four of her sons ("all twenty-five feet of them" was
a term she often used, since they totaled that length) were Princeton
men, that "your influence over them was as strong as that of any teacher
in their lives," but that two were sincere pacifists while the other two
as sincerely favored the war. She managed to see Secretary of War
Newton D. Baker, who simply denied that conditions such as she described existed at the CO camps.

Transferred to Fort Leavenworth, Evan discovered that members of
the small Molokani sect were imprisoned there although their religious
scruples against war were as rigid as those of the Quakers. They were,
unlike the Quakers, totally without political influence. Evan thereupon

sent a written complaint to the commandant, got no satisfaction, refused to obey all orders and was placed in solitary again. A fortnight after the war ended, Mrs. Thomas received a letter from the commandant regretting the necessity of disciplining her son:

> While in confinement, his hands are fastened in such a manner as to make sure that he will stand up during the working hours (nine hours per day), that is to say, he is handcuffed to the bars. . . . He is visited each day by a physician. . . . You may rest assured that if he breaks down in any way —and it is not anticipated that he will—he will be given proper medical care and removed to the hospital if necessary.

If kindness motivated the letter, it was a strange kindness. From France, Ralph wrote, "The [news] about Evan hit me harder than anything I have heard. I feel ashamed of myself to be having a good time in Paris and classed as a young tin hero because through no fault of mine a Boche shell dropped beside me. Much as I may disagree with him, I must say Evan has what in college we called guts."

### 5. Stand Up and Be Counted

Thomas had hesitated about joining the Socialist Party, telling Algernon Lee, the head of the Rand School and a Party official, that he was not an organization man and feared Party discipline. It would have been better, Lee later said bitterly, if he had just said thank you and dropped the matter. But Hillquit liked Thomas and saw him as a means of bringing more Gentiles into the New York Party, which was overwhelmingly Jewish. In the fall of 1918, while Evan was enduring his ordeal in Kansas, Thomas wrote the membership secretary, Alexander Trachtenberg:

> I am sending an application for membership in the Socialist Party. I am doing this because I think these are days when radicals ought to stand up and be counted. My belief in the necessity of establishing a cooperative commonwealth and the abolition of our present unjust economic institutions and class distinctions based thereon [sic].
>
> Perhaps to certain members of the Party my Socialism would not be of the most orthodox variety. As you know, I have a profound fear of the undue exaltation of the State and a profound faith that the new world we desire must depend upon freedom and fellowship rather than upon any

sort of coercion whatsoever. I am interested in political parties only to the extent in which they may be serviceable in advancing certain ideals and in winning liberty for men and women. My accepting of the Socialist platform is on the basis of general principles rather than of details. If I were a farmer and lived in certain states of the Middle West, it is quite likely that I should be a member of the Nonpartisan League . . . Though I am a staunch pacifist, I should not have voted for the preamble of the St. Louis platform. . . . I shall be glad to answer any questions that you may have to raise. If this statement is satisfactory I shall look forward to the fellowship of the Party as a real privilege.

He was accepted as a member, as was Violet, the granddaughter of the old sachem.

## 6. *A Little List*

"We have four cases of influenza in our family," Thomas wrote at the height of the epidemic, and Violet had one of her heavy colds. Not only because of the intermittent family infections, the hospitable Thomas home was avoided by many who once had been regular callers. This was hardest on Violet, since the absentees included some of her own family. There were friends in a middle category whose friendship continued but on a cooler level, and who wrote Thomas about "your new theories" and whether "they are going to help bring about the millennium." There were others who crossed the street to avoid meeting the Thomases. "In all this sudden break with old friends," Thomas later observed, "there lay . . . possibilities of considerable emotional shock and strain. That they were not greater is due to the closeness of new friendships of fellow protestors, the confidence that we then had that the future would be with us, and above all, Violet's steadiness who took what befell in her stride."

If their growing children suffered occasional rebuffs from playmates whose parents detested the Thomas heresies, there was never any pall hanging over the household. Violet, chatty and gay, had a gift for humorous exaggeration. She could also recite Shelley and Keats from memory with scarcely a pause. Thomas, disillusioned though he was with the church, occasionally took the children to services "and embarrassed us," his daughter Frances remembers, "because he sang the hymns so loudly."

The friendship of the Darrs, the Sayres, the Villards, of Roger Baldwin and John Haynes Holmes was all the warmer because they were under the same cloud. Holmes was one of the few pastors who had steadily opposed the war and by an eyelash managed to hold his church and congregation with him. The Darrs, who now had two children known as the Darrlings, were made uncomfortable at Spring Street and Darr soon accepted a call to Northampton, Massachusetts. Baldwin, when called by the draft, refused to serve and was promptly imprisoned for a one-year term (on Armistice Day) but was treated as a distinguished guest by the Irish warden who abominated the Englishmen's war. Sidney Lovett was a true friend in Boston, as was Dumont Clarke, now teaching at Andover. Charles Gilkey at the University of Chicago, not a rebel against the war, nevertheless understood and cherished the Thomases.

On Friday afternoons the Fellowship of Reconciliation staff would meet at the Thomas home for prayer and tea. The living room was also the scene of meetings of such radical groups as the Women's International Party, known before the war's end as the Women's Peace Party. Thomas, a compulsive worker who put in ten-hour days and many evenings as well, had the gift of inspiring others. "I cannot close without telling you how much you have meant to me . . . ," wrote his friend, the Reverend E. B. Chaffee. "Your fearlessness and your determination . . . have been an inspiration." As a new member of the executive committee of the Intercollegiate Socialist Society, Thomas sandwiched college speeches into schedules that had him racing for trains. The subway took him into darkest Queens or Brooklyn to address Socialist meetings or denounce the treatment of CO's. Still worrying about his Harlem people, he wrote the tuberculosis specialist Dr. James A. Miller to ask for help for one of his former parishioners: "Several of her family have died of tuberculosis, and now this youngest daughter seems to have it. She is only recently married and has a baby five weeks old. The family is one of the best in my old parish . . . and will pay what they can, but that is little enough." He secured the free services of his friend and co-worker for Irish freedom, Dr. William M. A. Maloney, in similar cases.

To "Dear Charley" Gilkey he wrote, "Are you likely to be in New York soon? . . . I have got too much to say about economic conditions, civil liberties, political prisoners and the state of the Church to begin to write, but I am most eager to talk." To Dr. John R. Mott, his onetime friend and now head of the Young Men's Christian Association, who sidestepped a meeting with him about conscientious objectors, he wrote icily, "I recognize the multitude and vastness of your affairs," adding, "I beg you to believe that Christianity's hope of reaching a growing multitude of unchurched radicals depends in no small measure on her handling of these problems."

After the 1918 Christmas holidays, with the war six weeks over, he and Violet took the two boys, Tommy and Billy, to Baltimore to visit his mother and two sisters. By now the liberal weeklies and some of the newspapers were criticizing the treatment of CO's, one of them being The New York World, which at Thomas's urging had sent a reporter to Kansas. The War Department promised to abolish the manacling of prisoners. Evan and some others had been released from solitary at least temporarily—improvements which Thomas ascribed to "Evan's heroic action." He wrote Ralph, "Major General Leonard Wood in his mercy reduced [Evan's sentence] to 25 years. . . . I can hardly keep the engagements that come to me to speak at forums and elsewhere on the ferocity of their prison sentences and the need of a general amnesty. . . . [We] had a good visit to Baltimore, where Mother bears up better than I feared."

Soon a review board found an error in Evan's court-martial. As if glad to get rid of such a trouble-maker, the army freed him on a "dishonorable discharge" on January 14, 1919, illogically leaving hundreds of others no more guilty than he behind bars.* Ten days later, a United States Senate committee investigating German propaganda authorized the publication of the names of sixty-two men and women, including Norman Thomas, who had been most active in movements "which did not help the United States in the war." Archibald Stevenson, a New York lawyer employed by Military Intelligence, had testified that the sixty-two had been under surveillance and held "dangerous, destructive and anarchistic sentiments." The list included twenty-six educators, ten clergymen and a scattering of professional people, all belonging to organizations that had opposed United States participation. "Can there be any question but what these organizations contributed to the cause of Germany . . . ?" Senator King demanded in a spirit that was growing

---

*Evan, outraged that others were still imprisoned, returned to live with Norman and Violet. He rediscovered an old ambition to be a doctor, but was rejected at medical school because of his "war record." He tried odd jobs, worked for a time for a textile union, then, in disgust with his own country, sailed for Ireland to seek a medical fellowship at the Catholic University in Dublin. He could not qualify, became an ordinary seaman for a time and was a worry to the Thomases until 1922.

rather than subsiding now that the war was won, and which would recur three decades later. "In the universities there has been a festering mass of pure atheism . . . We ought to weed out and drive out these pernicious teachers."

Although they were not accused of lawbreaking, turpitude was implied when their names made front pages nationally in a listing described as "A Who's Who in Pacifism and Radicalism." The New York Tribune and Times each ran well over two columns on the story. There was a feeling among radicals that since prosecution was impossible, this was an effort of the Senate to take vengeance by heaping shame on the sixty-two and if possible to injure their careers by causing them to lose their positions and make it unlikely that they would find other employment. Thomas of course had already damaged his promising church career and his presence on The List was no more apt to bring Presbyterian forgiveness than to please his mother and the Stewarts. He was one of the leaders in the number of "disapproved" organizations to which he belonged. Almost all of the sixty-two were his acquaintances and many were close friends. With few exceptions they were people of high character and abilities whose criticisms had been thoughtful and whose contributions to the nation would (if they had not already done so) outshine those of their detractors. They included Roger Baldwin (now chafing in prison despite good treatment), John Haynes Holmes, John Nevin Sayre, Morris Hillquit, Eugene V. Debs (under sentence of ten years in prison), Oswald Garrison Villard, Jane Addams, Emily Greene Balch, Elizabeth Gurley Flynn (out on bail), Jessie Wallace Hughan, Agnes Brown Leach, Charles A. Beard, Alexander Trachtenberg, Rabbi Judah Magnes, Scott Nearing, David Starr Jordan and the saintly head of the Quakers, Rufus M. Jones.

Inevitably, the radical rank-and-file looked with respect on those who were on The List. Some, such as the Reverend A. J. Muste, must have been inclined to demand inclusion on it in view of their own earnest anti-war efforts. The List came to be regarded almost as an exclusive club, some of whose members lived on to oppose other wars and other ferocities and to be included on other lists.

When Thomas said that the Fellowship of Reconciliation ought to "summon men to achieve a revolutionary change in social and economic conditions without recourse to the self-defeating methods of violence," he could as well have been talking about his hopes for the

Socialist Party. His own comparative affluence remained an embarrassment. However simple his own tastes and however modest the Thomas scale of living compared to what Violet had been accustomed to before marriage, the fact remained that they were well off because of her inherited income. While it never exceeded $10,000 a year, that was far more than his own earnings and was a substantial sum at the time. Against this income had to be balanced her physical frailty and the fact that Thomas's income could not buy the luxuries to which she was accustomed. The Thomases were well housed, fed, clothed and schooled. Thomas himself, uninterested in clothes, got his suits at Brooks Brothers at Violet's suggestion and received the customary discount for the clergy. He was usually rumpled and his hat battered. Violet, who dressed beautifully, looked like a jewel beside his often picturesque dishevelment. The children were sent to the Friends' School—the Thomases admired the Quakers—on Rutherford Place, only two blocks from their home, instead of to the free public school. The family's most obvious departure from middle-class custom was in their employment of several servants. These were essential because of Violet's health. One could not unilaterally renounce the American capitalistic system even while trying to change it. Nevertheless, Thomas, who when confronted by a sticky moral problem liked to put his thoughts in writing, did so shrewdly on the question of the family life style:

> . . . My own feeling is that there is no particular virtue in not eating cake unless it helps my brother to have bread. There is a luxury which under any social system will be enervating and vicious. . . . Nevertheless, I personally am interested, not in austerity but in abundance of life, in the multiplication of beautiful things, and in the increase in the opportunity and capacity of mankind to create and to enjoy them. The ascetic ideal as such makes no appeal to me. The question, as I see it, is the extent to which our denial may help others. . . . I am persuaded that a man is scarcely justified in making his wife and children pay the chief price of his renunciations. There are crises in history, such as the war . . . which may compel us to say "I must stand by this principle regardless of consequences to anyone." I do not believe there is any such clear ground of right or wrong in regard to the scale of one's living. . . .
>
> . . . . My wife has a leaky heart. If she can be kept from overwork, the doctor said that she may hope for a reasonably long and useful life . . . I have five children, and I think it is a dubious service to society not to bring

them up as well as I can, in health of body and mind. . . . Both Mrs. Thomas
and I felt during the war that we could not keep still about our principles,
even if it meant jail. . . . We feel now that there are certain things we
cannot keep still about regardless of consequences. We do not feel however that to cut off some hundreds from our scale of expenditures falls
. . . into this class of imperative duties.

He nevertheless wrote The Fellowship of Reconciliation that "my
resignation is at your disposal" if it was felt that the Thomas mode of
life was too fancy. It was rejected.

# V

## 1. Every Home a Sentry Box

Since Socialists had to be rebels in order to be Socialists, and took their politics seriously, they quarreled incessantly among themselves, sometimes over points so tenuous that Republicans or Democrats could scarcely understand them. With the war over, the Party settled down to such bitter feuding about its policy in relation to the Soviet government under Lenin and to the Third International that Thomas's attendance at meetings was irregular. Naturally the spectacle of what was believed to be a workingmen's republic was an inspiration to everyone in the Party, which was unanimous in execrating the presence of American and other armies in Russia, and the more revolutionary were so ardent as to believe that the time was ripe for the overthrow of American capitalism. As Roger Baldwin went to prison for a year, the firebrand John Reed assured him that the revolution would free him well before his term expired. But conservative evolutionary Socialists accused the revolutionists (or Communists) of seeking to attach the Party to the Soviet kite. In 1919 the angry Communists left the Socialist Party and formed their own party. Among Thomas's friends who left were the motherly organizer Ella Reeve Bloor and a sharp young man named Jay Lovestone. Alexander Trachtenberg and others soon joined them.

Thomas watched the Russian experiment with great sympathy and with the dislike of the libertarian for the suppression of ideas. When two propagandists for Soviet Russia, Ludwig Martens and Santeri Nuorteva, were denied a public hall in New York, they addressed a large audience at the Thomas home. American "secret agents" were present to guard against subversion.

Thomas was now horrified at his own unenlightenment at the time

76

he visited India. He joined the scholarly Robert Morss Lovett, Sidney's older brother, in forming the Friends of Freedom in India—a cause that would grow in importance for him. His assumption that the war's end would quickly restore civil liberties proved mistaken. The discouragement of religion in Russia, an increasing number of strikes in the United States and the dispatch of several dozen bombs through the mails brought America close to being a police state. The bombs were addressed to thirty-six individuals—all of them objects of leftist dislike—ranging from Judge Landis and Attorney General A. Mitchell Palmer to J. P. Morgan and John D. Rockefeller. The fact that all the parcels were luckily intercepted and no one was hurt did not mitigate the senders' violent intent. A month later a bomb destroyed the porch of Attorney General Palmer's home in Washington. Palmer, whose eye was on the White House, thereupon stepped up the raids on private homes and "radical" gatherings forever to be linked with his name. Spies and agents provocateurs sifted into labor and leftist groups. John Doe warrants were issued wholesale. Some 6,000 suspected "traitors" were arrested, most of them later found to be innocent, and about 550 radical aliens were deported to Russia. All of this had the support of all but a minuscule portion of the capitalist press.

New right-wing organizations which burgeoned after the war differed in some respects but were alike in recommending the muzzling or jailing of critics of the status quo. Among them were the National Security League, the United States Flag Association, the American Protective League, the American Defense Society, the Better American Federation and the National Association for Constitutional Government. There were the new Sentinels of the Republic, whose motto was "Every Citizen a Sentinel, Every Home a Sentry Box." Long-established organizations still doing strong work in the same field were the Daughters of the American Revolution and the National Civic Federation. A new one which would outstrip them all in the sentry business was the American Legion. Since the Socialist Party had long had its far-left fringe of Communists, there was a tendency to lump all Socialists together as Bolshevists. In the staid New York Times magazine section, an article, "Socialism as an Alien Enemy," bore without explanation, as if it were the most natural thing in the world, the byline "By a Government Agent." The Government Agent said of the typical Socialist that "His head is full of Bolshevism," added, "We can remember . . . the time when a man could consider becoming a Socialist without first wiping his feet on America," and spoke with praise of American

Legion stalwarts who had prevented the Socialist Irwin St. George Tucker from speaking in Reading, Philadelphia and Hartford. Loyal Legionnaires also prevented Scott Nearing from speaking in Troy and elsewhere, and broke into the Cincinnati Socialist office and burned the Party's "seditious literature." The Young Peoples' Socialist League (called the "Yipsels") was described as a plot "to inculcate Bolshevist theories and morals into children." On May Day, 1919, about 700 Socialists with their wives and children were the guests of The New York Call, a Socialist paper, to celebrate the opening of its new office on Fourth Avenue. ". . . About 400 soldiers and sailors stormed the offices," the Times noted. ". . . The remaining soldiers and sailors formed a semicircle in front of the building, and as the people emerged, the men in uniform struck them with clubs. Seventeen persons, it was said, had to be treated for injuries." In Cleveland on the same day a Socialist parade was broken up by two-fisted patriots who precipitated a riot in which a man was killed, scores were injured and the Socialist headquarters was wrecked, its furniture and typewriters flung out the windows into the street.

Some of the sentinel organizations sent out speakers to warn the public of subversion, and broadcast ominous publicity releases which in turn were published by the papers. S. Stanwood Menken of the National Security League said there were 600,000 Communists abroad in the land—a figure inflated not merely by ten but several times ten. Theatergoers were warned to shun the Soviet propaganda oozing from the performances of Fyodor Chaliapin and the Moscow Art Theater. Norma Talmadge and Will Rogers, too, were suspect. Secret agents went through the waste paper in Max Eastman's trash barrel. The Better America Federation attacked *Main Street* as a libel on the nation and its solid patriots. The Socialist Rand School, which had 5,000 students, a bust of Debs and a library including Marxist works, was raided. Professors Felix Frankfurter and Zecharia Chafee of Harvard, Max Mandell of Yale and John Dewey of Columbia were among many who fell under suspicion because of liberal utterances. The staff of The Nation held a party to celebrate the publication's listing as "subversive" by the Daughters of the American Revolution. Schools and colleges, as well as textbooks, were watched closely, and Wilson's Vice President, Thomas Marshall, spoke out against the radicalism which permitted girl debaters at Radcliffe to take the affirmative in a debate on the subject, "Resolved, that the recognition of labor unions by employers is essential to successful collective bargaining." Unionization itself was regarded as unpatriotic, the open shop being called "the American plan."

Attorney General Palmer, being a member of the Friends, was called the Fighting Quaker. Radicals referred to him as the Quaking Fighter or the Faking Quitter, but he was the hero of the hour as federal and local law abandoned constitutional rights. In Hartford, for example, while suspected Communists (many of them later found to be non-Communists) were held in jail, people who visited them were themselves promptly jailed on the theory that only a Communist would visit a Communist. Some municipalities took the cue and forbade any speakers but those of conservative line. Since to oppose these repressive measures could get one into serious trouble, it is likely that many people of ordinary courage loathed the repression but said nothing.

Thomas was not alone in reasoning that if this suppression went unopposed, free speech would be gone. To fight it was essential. When the New York suburb of Mount Vernon welcomed Republican and Democratic speakers in the 1920 elections but forbade "radicals," the American Civil Liberties Union furnished the opposition. Three ACLU activitists, Thomas, John Haynes Holmes and Rose Schneiderman, who was also an organizer for the Women's Trade Union League and was running for the state senate, drove to Mount Vernon in an open car. They stopped on the main street, where Holmes rose in the back seat and began reading the Constitution. ". . . before I could get to the opening words, 'We, the people,' " Holmes recalled, "I was placed under arrest and carried to the station house." Thomas immediately began reading the Constitution of the State of New York, whereupon he was also arrested, as was Miss Schneiderman when she uttered a few words. They were booked, released on $200 bail and found guilty by a local judge the next day. A higher court soon reversed that judgment and, Holmes noted, "The streets of Mt. Vernon were henceforth free to speakers of all parties."

Earlier in 1920, Thaddeus Sweet, the Republican Speaker of the New York State Assembly at Albany, summoned to his rostrum the five Socialist Assemblymen, Louis Waldman, August Claessens, Samuel A. De Witt, Charles Solomon and Samuel Orr. This was just two days after the Times article about subversive Socialism. Before the entire Assembly and many guests, Sweet treated them like prisoners in the dock. "You are seeking seats to this body," he said, "you who have been elected on a platform that is absolutely inimical to the best interests of the State of New York and the United States." The Socialist Party, he said, was a "subversive and unpatriotic organization." He summarily suspended them although they had been duly elected from districts in New York City. All five except De Witt had served in the Assembly before— Socialists had served in that body for years—and the Socialist Party was a legally recognized party under the election law. But the men were hustled out of the chamber by the Sergeant-at-Arms, thus in effect disfranchising some 60,000 voters in New York City. The five were forbidden to attend sessions until such time as they could prove their fitness to serve—a classic case of sentence before trial. The Assembly backed up the Speaker 145–2. Charles Evans Hughes and the New York Bar Association said they regarded "with deep anxiety" the suspension of Assemblymen simply because they were Socialists. Hughes and the bar association were charged with disloyalty and pro-Germanism for their pains. The "revolutionary" Nation and New Republic denounced the ouster, but there was little sense of immediate affront among the big daily papers of New York City, which came around to opposition more slowly than did some liberal pastors including Thomas's trinomial friends Henry Sloane Coffin, William Adams Brown and Harry Emerson Fosdick.* Even the National Security League startled libertarians by opposing the ouster, but the Assembly was undaunted.

Morris Hillquit went to Albany to perform the strange duty of serving as attorney for the "defense" of men whose crime was opposition to capitalism. "To prove that Socialism was not hostile to religion and did not seek to disrupt the family ties," Hillquit wrote, "the defense called a young Presbyterian clergyman, Norman Thomas . . . who deeply impressed the audience by his idealism and candor." Not deeply enough. Thomas deliberately and smilingly went on exhibition to show qualities which no Democrat or Republican was required to show—his Christian credentials, his happy family life and his five children. The Assembly stood fast. Waldman and Claessens were charged with "intemperate speeches" which "breathe in every word the spirit of treason and revolution." Claessens was also guilty of teaching at the Rand School, and a seventeen-year-old stenographer witness affirmed that she had seen Solomon, at a Socialist meeting, "spit on the flag." In the end the Assembly voted overwhelmingly to expel three of the five Socialists, and the other two walked out in protest. Assemblyman Claessens, a humorist, said on parting, "Gentlemen, we are coming back. Like the old cat. But next year, with kittens." (As it turned out,

---

*"Norman Mattoon Thomas" sounded fancy too, but Thomas was content to remain binomial all his life.

in 1922 Claessens was the only Socialist elected to the Assembly.)

"All the religion the Albany legislature has," Thomas said, "is an idea of God as a big policeman who is going to hit someone over the head."

Had Thomas's appearance been delayed a few months he could have boasted of six children instead of five because of the arrival on Bastille Day of a third son, Evan. Meanwhile Violet's older sister Mary had fallen in love with Colonel Raymond Sheldon—both of them being well into the age of discretion—and a family problem arose with the wedding plans. Colonel Sheldon, nephew of Violet's guardian, Edward Sheldon, was an army career man who had spent years in the Philippines and was now commandant of Governor's Island. He resented Thomas's politics during and after the war. Many of the guests at the wedding reception would also be army officers and their wives, equally disapproving. Violet's mother, who had truly loved Thomas, had recently died, but he had a champion in Mary herself, always a good friend.

Still, how could this anti-militarist anti-capitalist mingle with the dress uniforms without provoking a quarrel or even a duel? Would he not at the very least throw a pall over what should be a joyous event?

The senior participants wrestled with the issue. The reception was to be at the home of Mary and Violet's brother, W. A. W. Stewart, at 1 Washington Square. Violet and Norman could of course be invited conjointly only to the church ceremony, from which Violet would go to the reception and Norman could go where he pleased, so long as it was not to 1 Washington Square. But this would surely wound Violet. Besides, Stewart, though he was a confirmed capitalist whose clients included members of the Gould family, liked Thomas. "I'll be damned if we can't invite Norman," he said.

A strategy was worked out. Thomas was invited along with Violet to the reception, which was held in the huge Stewart dining room. But the dining room was, in military parlance, out of bounds for him. He was given the freedom of an adjacent parlor, where he talked cheerfully with his own older children and those of some other guests while the music and the toasts wafted in. Violet dropped in occasionally to show her solidarity. Stewart's daughter recalls that one of the women guests looked into the parlor and asked, "Who is that nice man with the children?"

## 2. The End of God

Thomas, now identified by the newspapers as "the Socialist clergy-man" or "editor of The World Tomorrow and member of many radical societies," was encouraged by the growth of the Labor Party in England. In one of his lectures, "The Disintegration of the European Capitalist System," he prophesied that "a similar process is slowly but surely going on in this country." He campaigned in 1920 for the imprisoned Socialist candidate Debs for President against his own fellow-townsman Harding and the Democrat James M. Cox ("Cox and Box," Thomas called them), but realized that Debs's total of 915,000 votes indicated that the disintegration of American capitalism was marked more by slowness than sureness.

Thereafter, for several years, Thomas was so preoccupied with sickness in his own family that he receded from politics and had trouble enough keeping The World Tomorrow going. All six of the children were stricken with streptococcus infections, emerging from one siege only to fall prey to another. The oldest, nine-year-old Tommy, a promising boy who wanted to be a physician, suffered successive infections, was weakened by a mastoid operation and died of meningitis—a tragedy that brought Sidney Lovett down from Boston. Violet herself was hospitalized at times, her heart condition aggravated, and Thomas himself seemed the only healthy member of the family. Germs became frightening realities to them. On the advice of Dr. Maloney they left the city and lived for more than a year in a house in suburban Hartsdale which had capacious fresh-air sleeping porches.

In 1921 Thomas, proposed as a candidate for Mayor, withdrew his name because of his family's illnesses. During this time he called on President Harding twice, once with a committee and again with Villard, to plead for the release of the aged and ailing Debs, whom Wilson had kept in Atlanta prison, and to ask for a general amnesty of Espionage Act prisoners whose crime had been mere vocal opposition to the war. Harding had none of his predecessor's vindictiveness and on the second occasion reminisced genially about Marion with his former newsboy. But he had no visible idealism either. He made it plain that Debs was purely a political consideration with him and that he would go free only if it could be shown that public sentiment favored it. The Socialist Party and other groups were able to show that there was enormous national sympathy for Debs, so he was eventually released (over the protest of the American Legion), though without restoration of his civil rights, and there was no general amnesty.

Violet, for all her fragility, was anything but an invalid. Although she was a slow starter who invariably had breakfast in bed, her energy thereafter was considerable. She did not fit any stereotype, least of all that of clubwoman. A perfect hostess who served tea beautifully and could have won social eminence in Hartsdale, she candidly loathed the suburbs. The Thomases had a new Model T Ford which she would jump into at every opportunity and drive to the city, manipulating the spark and gas levers and the planetary transmission with skill. Once, after a group of Hartsdale ladies had called on her, her children found her in tears—tears of laughter, it turned out, for the women had invited her to membership in their Giraffe Club, so named because they "nibbled only at the higher leaves of culture." Thomas, in tune with her, responded to her nonconformities and unpredictabilities. Her weak heart was a worry which he seldom mentioned, but when he was away as long as twenty-four hours he wrote to her. The household that could have been dominated by gloom was later remembered for its laughter. At Christmas, Violet had a stocking over the fireplace along with all the children, and despite the expensive gifts she received from wealthy relatives, the important one was a letter from Thomas, placed in her stocking, telling in new words each year of his love for her. At the toe of each child's stocking was a twenty-dollar gold piece from their great-grandfather, who reached 100 years of age in 1922 and received messages of congratulation at his Morristown country estate from celebrities including John D. Rockefeller. The gold pieces were due to the attentions of Violet, who liked her grandfather and visited him with the older children, chatting gaily into his ear trumpet.

Old Stewart was understandably making something of his friendships with Presidents—Lincoln, Cleveland, Wilson, and now a long visit with Harding—and some felt that the decades had improved his tales of White House tête-à-têtes. But he stayed this side idolatry, saying of Wilson, "If you disagreed with him you were wrong and he was right, and that ended it."

With this criticism Thomas would have agreed and then some. If he had been disenchanted with Wilson during the war, his reaction to the President's postwar neglect of civil liberties and toleration of police-state tactics was one of shock. The discovery that democracy could be violated by a former Princeton professor who made democracy his worldwide slogan and who was venerated internationally for his presumed defense of it—and that the neglect could be urged and supported by leading Democrats, Republicans, Presbyterians, Catholics and Jews—profoundly affected Thomas's later life. These years that revolutionized his politics and disillusioned him with the church brought the greatest wrench of all—a growing doubt and final rejection of the God of his fathers, whose performance seemed no better than that of the church. The practical test of God's effectiveness and credibility was his toleration of evil on earth and the suffering of mankind, and his indifference to the hope and fate of the individual. The illness in Thomas's family and the death of Tommy—a loss he felt for years— doubtless were factors. His change in religious outlook, though not on the same plane as his political change, stemmed from the same inordinate concern for humankind. The individualist Thomas, whose faith in biblical miracles had been too doubting for the orthodox, nevertheless had believed in a loving God whose eye was on each of his children individually, a God who did not view humanity as so many armies, votes or chessmen. As he defined it:

> I cannot discover a God who is love and at the same time omnipotent. I cannot accept any theory of Theism or pantheism which postulates an all wise, all powerful, and all good God. I can easily walk in humility and awe in our marvelous universe. I am inclined to find design in it. But not that perfection of creation or that loving care for each of us as individuals which I crave and which I once found in Christian doctrine.

"Crave" was the exact word. Even after his doubt made him cross that momentous spiritual divide forever, he missed the God who had comforted him, he sang the old hymns he loved and he would veer from sarcasm at empty sermons and scorn for the perfunctory oblations of preachers who, he was sure, had no faith but their own good living, to occasional deep reconsideration of his own logic to make sure he had not missed something. As for Violet, whose religion had never been more than simple humanitarianism, she suffered no wrench at all. Thomas was never thereafter offered a church, nor would he have taken one, although he spoke in churches hundreds of times. His brother Evan had also rejected the church, whereas his two other brothers were devout lay leaders. Evan, after his seagoing, had landed in New Orleans, worked in lumber camps and wheat fields and finally, at the entreaty of Violet and Norman, returned to live with them in 1922 and took a job as laboratory technician at Roosevelt Hospital which Thomas arranged through Dr. Maloney. As Sidney Lovett saw it, it was Norman and Violet who "brought Evan back" to equanimity.

### 3. Riga, Vilna and Minsk

Thomas reluctantly resigned the leadership of the religion-oriented Fellowship of Reconciliation and the editorship of The World Tomorrow. The end of his Social Gospel phase and the collapse of hope for transcendental aid put man's fate squarely up to man. To Thomas that meant chiefly the Socialist Party which, contrary to conservative fears, had dwindled from 108,000 members in the forty-eight states in 1912 to 26,766 in 1920. It soon amounted to less than that, because of another Socialist split with revolutionaries who left to join the Communists. The prospect was bleak but Thomas, who seemed to err on the side of optimism, saw hope in a plan of cooperation and eventual political consolidation of the Party with labor, farm and progressive groups. He was thinking of what had been done in England. His underlying toughness and buoyancy were proved by his emergence whole from a spiritual struggle that could easily have crushed and embittered a man who had been nurtured in Christian devotion and followed it into early middle age.

His abilities boosted him swiftly—dangerously swiftly—in Socialist councils. He was appointed co-director of the reorganized, refinanced and renamed Intercollegiate Socialist Society, now called the League for Industrial Democracy, with offices at 160 Fifth Avenue, next door to the Presbyterian Church offices at 156. His salary was $5,000 a year. His co-director colleague was the Wesleyan-and-Columbia-educated Harry W. Laidler, a veteran of the organization and a leading Socialist theoretician. Laidler, five feet six and squeaky of voice, looked like a midget next to Thomas and there were the inevitable remarks about Mutt and Jeff. Although Laidler could not have been overjoyed to see a newcomer leap into equality with him at a single bound, the two worked together harmoniously for decades. The League, organizationally separate from the Party, was a day-by-day promoter of the Party which itself only became aroused at meetings or elections. It had a promising ("frightening," conservatives called it) membership in colleges all over the country, which Thomas, who spent most of his time speaking, set out to enlarge. From the start, and through every year of his long life, he pinned much of his faith on the education of the young who had not yet fallen into Babbittry. He saw things wrong with America other than smug respectability, cultural poverty, political ignorance and blind prejudice just then being pilloried in Harold Stearns's *Civilization in the United States* and in Sinclair Lewis's examinations of Gopher Prairie and Zenith. In the prosperous twenties, the Era of Wonderful Nonsense, the number of million-dollar-a-year incomes rose from 65 to 513, men's silk shirts sold fast and automobiles became common, but there was never less than 10 percent of the labor force unemployed, more than 42 percent of the population got along on incomes under $1,500, and miners were regularly killed at their hazardous occupation without public outcry.

Thomas was friendly with Morris Hillquit who, recovering from tuberculosis, was one of the leading successors to the imprisoned Debs in Party prestige—a distinguished man and an effective speaker. He came to know the Party's steadiest donor, a Yiddish-language newspaper, the rich, 200,000-circulation Jewish Daily Forward in New York, edited and led by the Vilna-born Socialist Abraham Cahan. The slim, short, fiery Cahan had once likened the Socialist message to "the giving of the law on Mt. Sinai." When the Party needed cash, as it always did (it had been able to spend only $50,000 nationally in the 1920 campaign), it knocked most confidently at the door of the Forward in the Lower East Side although other angels were constantly importuned. The Forward also gave it $500 a month year in and year out for operating expenses, a subsidy that barely kept the Party and its national office in Chicago going. The business manager of the Forward, the charming, poetic, Minsk-born B. Charney Vladeck, a revolutionary Socialist who had spent time in European jails, became Thomas's good friend. Vladeck, seeking to spread New York Socialism from its Lower East Side and garment-district Jewish milieu, saw Thomas as a means to this end.

For one of the Socialist problems was that these three men, respectively from Riga, Vilna and Minsk, all spoke English with heavy accents. Austrian-born Victor Berger of Milwaukee, the first Socialist Congressman and the Midwest equivalent of the three, had a thick German accent and was almost as old as Debs. With the Inquisition still going strong, there could scarcely be a greater handicap for an aspiring politician than for chauvinistic 100-percent Americans to connect him by origin and accent with Lenin's Russia or with Germany.

Not surprisingly, Thomas, born in Ohio of an old American family, with unexceptionable reputation, speaking unaccented English with telling effect, still bearing the disarming status of the clergy,* splendidly educated, intellectual but seldom stuffy, a man who had sacrificed his career to principle and had won high position on The List, a home-loving father of five, handsome and distinguished in appearance, afraid of nobody, friendly and approachable, mingling with equal aplomb among bankers, society women and stevedores, generous with his own home for Party functions, a workhorse for the cause—not surprisingly, many spoke of him as representative of the "New Socialism."

There were disadvantages and criticisms too, which would enlarge into political perils. Still, no one else in the Party could have done what he did in a public debate at the National Republican Club in New York, where he picked apart the arguments of State Senator Clayton R. Lusk, head of the committee that had sponsored repressive laws including the licensing of schools and the establishment of a network of spies who had watched Thomas, among others. Thomas ridiculed Lusk's effort to enfold himself in the Constitution and to deplore violence:

> I have heard Republicans who did not speak with the utmost respect for the 18th Amendment, and Democrats who did not admire the 14th and 15th. . . . There are gentlemen in this room famous for their zeal in behalf of constitutional government who never raised their voices to protest when Mussolini quite unconstitutionally captured power in Italy. . . . Mussolini has been blessed by the very men who denounced the Bolsheviki for the self-same crime. . . . No one here can disbelieve in violence more than I . . . but those who justify organized violence in their own cause, who glory in the spies and Secret Service agents of corporations and Government and in political prisoners confined for opinion are in no position to denounce violence.

After leaving the Fellowship of Reconciliation, he became an associate editor of Villard's Nation (classed as "revolutionary" by the American Defense Society, as were The New Republic and The Freeman). With Roger Baldwin and others he was on the board of the Garland Fund, financed in 1922 by one of the most incredible but unsung young men in all history. Charles Garland, not long out of Harvard, inherited more than a million dollars from his stockbroker father, decided he did

---

*A handicap to the Socialists was the widespread belief that they were avowedly godless —untrue, for Party rules held that religion was a matter of private conscience. However, the percentage of unbelievers in the humanistic and nonconformist Socialist Party was surely higher than among the bourgeois major parties.

not deserve all that and gave $900,000 to be used for liberal enterprises. The money, invested in the bull market, was spent by the hundreds of thousands in radical causes, and yet the fund grew to almost $2,000,000 and lasted several decades. In 1923 it supplied some $50,000 to help found a strong labor newspaper, to which left-wing unions including the International Ladies' Garment Workers and the Amalgamated Clothing Workers added enough to make a total of $125,000. Thomas was urged by Hillquit, long the attorney and adviser for ILGWU, to take the editorship.

The paper, a daily called The New Leader, was to replace the old Socialist Call, whose circulation had fallen below 10,000. It was to be officially non-Socialist, a labor paper aimed at creating political unity among the New York workers. It was planned not as a mere propaganda sheet but as an all-around daily paper with full news coverage and features so that it could serve as the family newspaper, unlike the Party-lining and virtually newsless Call.

Thomas accepted with enthusiasm. For all his writing and editorial experience, his closest acquaintance with daily newspaper operations had been to deliver papers in Marion, so Heber Blankenhorn, a veteran of The New York Sun, came in as managing editor and a staff was gathered. Others of more than ordinary talent were the city editor, Herbert Gaston; Ed Sullivan, sports editor, later famous as columnist and television star; the cartoonist Edmund Duffy, twice later a Pulitzer Prize winner; the former United Press man Paul Sifton; Howard Brubaker, later of The New Yorker; and several loyal Socialists including the labor reporter Edward Levinson; the former Sun man and friend of Debs, McAlister Coleman; and William Feigenbaum, a former State Assemblyman from Brooklyn. The business manager was Evans Clark, once a Princeton economics professor, who had been included on The List.

The New Leader got off to a good start on October 1, 1923, with competent handling of domestic and foreign news and most of the attractions offered by other daily papers. Murders received due attention, it covered the entertainment field, its sports pages ran the gamut from horse racing to the McTigue-Stribling bout to the World Series, and the thoughtful editorials (many written by Thomas) were far removed from the partisan blasts of The Call. The paper's circulation leaped ahead for a short period when a pressmen's outlaw strike closed other newspapers, but slumped when the pressmen returned. Its advertising income naturally was minuscule in its infancy, it was losing money every day, and its cantankerous labor audience was dissatisfied with its policy of objective reporting. Its circulation never reached 30,000 although the unions "supporting" it had more than 300,000 members. There was at the time a bitter struggle within the International Ladies' Garment Workers' Union, which a Communist minority was trying to take over. Complaints came from one side that the paper was anti-Communist, from the other that it was pro. There were quarrels between the two big unions which had contributed most about how the paper should be conducted.

The Leader's starting capital, which seemed large to Socialists, actually was minute in the metropolitan newspaper field. The necessity to pay off The Call's $50,000 debt and to keep that paper going until The Leader got under way was another handicap. After only six weeks, Thomas, preoccupied with editorial policy, was staggered when Clark announced out of the blue that they were broke. Even so, the prosperous unions could have saved the paper if they had been willing. They were not, and in fact the factionalism in the unions made them poor sponsors for any but a factional press. The Leader closed, and as McAlister Coleman left the building he saw a sign man gold-leafing The New Leader lettering on the door. Thomas was thwarted even in his effort to organize a union of newsmen, the Press Writers' Union, which was denied an American Federation of Labor charter and expired.

This did not mark him as gifted in business. It provided a fiscal lesson he never forgot. "My own spirits were at low ebb," he confessed. "Here I was almost 40, father of a large family, well trained for a profession I couldn't honestly follow, a failure in meeting the great opportunity which had come to me." He was relieved that his staff quickly found other jobs, while he returned to his League for Industrial Democracy post. The Thomases had moved back to the city, living in an apartment until they bought and refurbished a run-down but spacious four-story residence at 206 East Eighteenth Street, hard by the Third Avenue elevated railway. He was busy enough so that he did not attend the 1924 Socialist state convention at Finnish Hall in Harlem, from where a telephone call informed him that he had been nominated for Governor if he would accept. He accepted.

### 4. Thomas for Governor

In a February joint meeting in Saint Louis, which Thomas covered for The Nation while also being an interested spectator, the Socialist Party, the Farmer-Labor Party, the Nonpartisan League and several union groups had agreed to join in nominating and backing a third-party slate of national candidates. Their adoption of a largely Socialistic program of public ownership and anti-militarism increased the enthusiasm of Hillquit, Thomas and other Socialists whose "labor party fever" had been growing for several years. As Thomas pointed out in an article in The New York Times—his first in that paper—the Democrats were tainted, if not as badly as the Republicans, by the Teapot Dome scandal, Progressive Senatorial candidates had won in seven western states, and "All this makes for a third party." He conceded also that there were "divided counsels and partisan jealousies" among the third-party people—a judgment time would emphasize.

Senator Robert M. La Follette of Wisconsin was the unanimous Presidential choice of the coalition. La Follette accepted the nomination but declined their third-party designation, insisting that he would run as an independent though he predicted that a third party would arise in strength from the election. Some Socialists were chagrined at the less than worshipful treatment the Party got, expecting at least that La Follette would name an eminent labor man as his running mate, and were disgruntled when he picked the Progressive Democratic Senator Burton K. Wheeler of Montana, for all Wheeler's prominence in exposing the scandals. Others said that Socialism was a sacred entity that could not be watered down or compromised and that it was up to others to rally to *their* standard. But the fact was that beggars could not be choosers. The Party had suffered terribly from the beating it had taken during the war and since at the hands of the spread-eagles, and had lost numerically by the schism with the Communists. Heroic measures were essential. Coalition had worked wonderfully in England. The divisive and conspiratorial Communists, who now wanted to jump aboard the La Follette bandwagon, were firmly driven off. The American Federation of Labor, always so conservative, endorsed La Follette.

Although both the Farmer-Labor Party and the Nonpartisan League had far greater numbers than the Socialists, both were regional. Only the Socialist Party had a national organization of sorts, which it whipped up in the service of the Presidential ticket. The nation knew of La Follette as the Progressive candidate and was not acutely aware that the Socialist Party was behind him, much less that it had had an important role in forming the coalition. The Progressives nominated no state ticket in New York, so it was up to the Socialists to name their own— hence the Finnish Hall convention where Thomas was nominated after Hillquit declined. Hillquit admitted hoping that the Saint Louis coalition would be so successful that its delighted members would swell Party rolls and give it new national scope and authority. To this Thomas said amen. He saw in the Party the intellectual and inspirational force for a great new mass movement. If the millions of workers and farmers who now voted Republican or Democratic could be won to a party really representing their interests, what a third party it would make!

On the other hand, the Party itself had to make a decent showing or it might disappear entirely in the hubbub. Thomas's task would have been formidable had he been running against a notorious grafter inimical to labor. His opponent was, alas, that gifted trifler with syntax, Governor Alfred Emanuel Smith. Smith had been a good Governor, fair to labor, strong for civil liberties. His popularity was immense. Many New York Socialists and labor leaders favored his reelection. Much as they may have liked Thomas, he obviously could not win, and there was fear that he would divert enough votes from Smith to insure the election of the Republican candidate. The latter was young Colonel Theodore Roosevelt, son of the late castigator of the Huns, of whom Thomas said rather cruelly, "he is best known as the son of his father." Smith's friend Joseph Proskauer visited Thomas to urge politely that he drop out, or at least make only a token campaign. Thomas, backed by Hillquit and the Party committee, rejected the proposal. His duty was to make a showing for the Socialists. He loved public speaking, the heat of debate and the excitement of the hustings, and was coming into greatness in the magic he could exert over an audience. He was thrilled by his nomination for the Governorship of the Empire State even under such adverse circumstances. But it soon appeared that the Socialist organization forgot its own state ticket in its anxiety to push La Follette and Wheeler. Joseph D. Cannon, the Socialist Party New York campaign manager, might have been working for Smith by the tone of a New York Times story beginning:

> After an exchange of letters for several weeks between Gov. Smith and the Rev. Norman Thomas, in which the Socialist candidate for governor

conceded the progressive nature of the Governor's record and program in labor and social welfare matters, it became apparent yesterday that the Socialist Party had abandoned all intention of making any serious contest on behalf of Mr. Thomas against Gov. Smith.

Cannon next day disputed the story, calling it a "misinterpretation," but still failing so visibly to come out strongly for Thomas that readers were justified in believing the first account. If the Party itself was not pushing Thomas, Socialist voters fearful of causing Smith to lose the Governorship would scarcely feel duty-bound to vote for Thomas. Thomas had a moment of glory when 14,000 people packed Madison Square Garden and 6,000 more listened by means of amplifiers outside in the park—the biggest Garden crowd in history—when La Follette spoke in New York, preceded by a brief speech by Thomas which was "wildly cheered." But he was of course restricted to booming La Follette and could say nothing about his own candidacy. After that, things went downhill. George Berry, head of the Pressmen's Union, came out for the Democratic Presidential candidate, John W. Davis; John L. Lewis of the Miners announced for Coolidge; and on the state level, Thomas's opponent Smith got the support of the Central Trades and Labor Council (not to mention the young and energetic Mrs. Franklin D. Roosevelt, whose husband was incapacitated by polio). The influential Dudley Field Malone came out for La Follette and *Smith*. The railroad unions disowned the Socialists. The Jewish Daily Forward put most of its money and headlines on La Follette, and the persuasive Hillquit was so taken up by the Presidential race that he seemed to forget Thomas. Thomas got to know two men who would reappear in his future. One was a colleague, the Socialist candidate for Attorney General, Louis Waldman, born near Kiev, who had been one of the five ousted Assemblymen and who now said, "After the election there will be but two parties left in the state, the Progressives and the Reactionaries." The other was Senator Wheeler, who shared the rostrum with Thomas at several places including Dickert's Grove in the Bronx. For the rest, although John Haynes Holmes, Walter Frank, McAlister Coleman and others formed a committee and loyally did what they could for him, he was mostly on his own.

During the campaign, General Plutarco Elias Calles, recently elected President of Mexico, visited New York. Since he proclaimed himself a Socialist (later he became a Fascist), he was feted by the Party and the Thomases had him and his small entourage for dinner. It was a convenience for the Party (although some Socialists grumbled about the Thomas grandeur) that it had in the Thomases a graceful hostess and host with the requisite elegance of household and with servants for distinguished guests. The eldest daughter, Mary (always called Polly), then ten, noticed with amusement that a Tammany election parade headed by a band passed by, delighting Calles, who assumed it was in his honor. Neither Thomas nor Violet saw any need to correct this pleasant error, and Violet assured Calles that all her children were studying Spanish, which was not strictly true.

Thomas went on to electioneer from Long Island to Buffalo, spending a grand total of $895. Often the state organization failed to pave the way for him. On numerous occasions he arrived in a town to find that no meeting had been prepared, and he discovered that some upstate La Follette leaders were strong Smith men and ready to disown Thomas. Even in 1924 he still appeared on hate lists published in newspapers, one of them being "The Spider Web," compiled by one Charles Norman Fay, which showed the tendrils connecting Thomas (and some of his best friends) with "disloyal" organizations. Among them were the Fellowship of Reconciliation, described as "Yellow, Pacifist, Internationalist, Pro-German"; the La Follette Campaign Committee and the National Child-Labor Committee, listed as "Pink, Progressive, Collectivist"; the League for Industrial Democracy, said to be "Red"; and the American Civil Liberties Union, the Garland Fund, the Rand School and the Socialist Party, all four of them "Red, Radical, Communist, Subversive." The difficulties inherent in leftist politics were dramatized by the irrepressible August Claessens who, addressing a crowd in the Bronx, saw a runaway team of horses coming directly toward his audience and warned them to run. "As the horses came near me," he recalled, "they must have sensed that it was a Socialist meeting and they swerved off to the right."

Thomas boosted the national ticket, saying at Albany, "the supreme issue in this campaign is the building of a new party," but by this he did not mean the immolation of the Socialists. "The State Committee," he later recalled, ". . . sent me to meetings for La Follette where it was stipulated that I could not refer to our own state campaign. At one Syracuse meeting, the chairman, a local labor skate, when I had finished, got up and said that all my reasons for supporting La Follette should make the audience vote for Smith for governor." In the end, La Follette's total in the state was 467,293, while Smith won the governorship with a plurality of more than 100,000 over Roosevelt, getting a total vote of more than 1,600,000. Thomas's vote was 99,854. Smith's split-ticket profit at the expense of Thomas was shown by the fact that Thomas ran 25 percent behind his own ticket, something that would happen to him only one other time in his life.

Thomas, despite his own setback, was encouraged for the coalition, as was Hillquit. La Follette, though untruthfully linked with the Communists by the Republicans, many spread-eagle organizations and the Saturday Evening Post,* had totaled 4,826,471 votes nationally—about five times larger than the biggest vote ever received by any Socialist Presidential candidate. But the patience necessary for building a new party was lacking. Some Socialists felt that they had sacrificed their own party without reward, the American Federation of Labor was disgruntled and the coalition fell apart in a later Chicago convention. "Labor and the political amateurs . . . were unduly discouraged after having put their hopes fantastically high," Thomas reasoned. The Socialist Party was left scarcely breathing.

## 5. The Man from Mars

In the spring of 1925, Thomas took his twelve-year-old son Bill with him to Princeton, determined to celebrate the twentieth anniversary of his graduating class whatever the hostility. He was pleased to be accepted even though there was a chill around the edges. While John Grier Hibben, still president, was downright fearful of Socialism, he was a courteous man and Thomas had got used to making do with attitudes in which courtesy masked suspicion. Theodore Savage, now a rising Presbyterian official and a Republican, later could not understand how Thomas escaped bitterness over his treatment in the twenties.

Although the Thomas children were still subject to illness and Violet had an occasional heart attack that gave them all a scare, the ménage on Eighteenth Street was a cheerful and noisy place—so noisy that now and then Violet would take to her bed and close the door to escape it all. Part and parcel of the family was Evan Thomas, called "Unk," whose charm and warmth exceeded even those of his older brother and who was a favorite with the children. By now young Bill was going to Gilman

---

*Middletown, the survey of a Midwestern town, noted that people who admitted voting for LaFollette were looked down upon, and "strong heretics—religious, economic, political, social—are increasingly frowned upon."

School in Baltimore, and there were plans to send away the other children, who still went to the Friends' Seminary. The home atmosphere was neither religious nor anti-religious. The Thomases had never been family-prayer or table-prayer people, though the children when small had said prayers at bedtime, and Sunday school was optional. There was a balance not present in households where an ailing mother retires from the scene, for Violet, not one to retire, remained a vivid influence.

Roger Baldwin, whose American Civil Liberties Union had Thomas's hearty support and was growing in strength, was never a Socialist and indeed not a political organization man at all. He noticed that Violet and Thomas were still, and would remain, as affectionate as a honeymooning couple. She was a dues-paying member of the Party, went to some of the more important meetings and had some of them in her own home. She came to know the Party leaders and others she would never have met in her Stewart family circle. They ranged from the ponderous Marxist Algernon Lee to the mustachioed and knife-scarred Carlo Tresca, whose career was already wildly improbable. Born to wealth in Italy and embracing Socialism, he had fled the country because of his politics, quarreled with the then-Socialist Mussolini in Switzerland, then come to America and fought labor's battles so vigorously that he had been wounded and jailed repeatedly. He was famous for his earlier passionate romance with Elizabeth Gurley Flynn, his anti-Fascist weekly paper Il Martello (The Hammer), and for the year he had spent in Atlanta Prison for publishing a prim advertisement for birth control which had been ruled a "criminal obscenity." "Everybody like me," he would say. "I like everybody. Jeez Christ, I canna keep no enemy."

Tresca was a member of the world the Thomases now inhabited, so different from the cloistered one that would have been theirs had they stayed with Brick Church. Thomas was so enwrapped in this colorful Party, that he had few hobbies. There was a crank-up Victrola in the parlor with the Red Seal records of Caruso and his contemporaries but it was seldom played. In fact his musical talent did not go far beyond the simple hymns he loved, nor did he have any discriminating appreciation of art; and his enjoyment of the theater had surrendered to Party demands on his time. His robust relish for gossip—an interesting quality in a moralist-reformer—was devoid of malice, an extension of his sense of humor applied to human foibles. His knowledge of the mode of life of Elizabeth Gurley Flynn and Carlo Tresca did not impair his appreciation for these valued activists, with both of whom he had profound political disagreements combined with great lifelong affection.

He wanted his children to have every reasonable opportunity for success and contentment and to make the most of them. He made it a rule not to preach Socialism to them, remembering his own parents' sometimes excessive Presbyterian exhortations, but the rule was often honored in the breach. So articulate a man could hardly be expected to keep quiet about what had become his religion. The Thomases now had a summer and weekend place far out on Long Island at Quogue, where the children were encouraged to swim, sail and play tennis and Violet had started to raise cocker spaniels. Thomas liked to swim and garden when he had a chance. An omnivorous reader of novels, histories and books on politics, he read also the "intellectual" weeklies and the newspapers with great speed and retention, enjoying also the sports pages. He relaxed with light reading, above all P. G. Wodehouse, and at times was torn by moral doubts of his right to take such pleasure in the odd doings at Blandings Castle. Like the place in New York, the Quogue cottage was noisy and sociable, with children and friends coming and going, always with animated discussions at the dinner table—sometimes several discussions at once, with laughter or disputation enough to hurt the ears, whereupon Thomas's mighty platform voice would rise above the clamor: "This has got to stop!" But discipline was scarcely rigid. On a few occasions in New York, when the family uproar threatened the composure of both parents, Violet and Thomas used the strategy of retreat. They put on their hats and coats and left to spend the night in a quiet hotel, leaving the children in the care of the servants.

Whereas in 1924 their father ran for Governor, in 1925 he ran for Mayor of New York. He was nominated by the Party at Beethoven Hall on East Fifth Street, following a free-for-all in which a group of Communists who wanted to participate were ejected forcibly. Thomas, the Times said, was "cheered for several minutes":

> He said he was reluctant to run for Mayor this fall and that family and health reasons might yet make it necessary for him to withdraw. He hoped, however, to remain in the fight and if he did he promised a lively scrap.

The divisions of the La Follette campaign and its use of the Socialist Party national organization for non-Socialist candidates had cut total paid-up membership to barely more than 10,000. The national secretary in Chicago, William Henry, was a Hoosier who had devoted his life to the cause but was semi-illiterate, disorganized and out of his depth in this office that should have been the pulsing heart of American Socialism. The Socialist David Karsner had called the Party "a ghost" before the La Follette campaign, so that it was now the mere shadow of a ghost. Thomas, who could have been a successful politician in any party he chose, stayed with the ghost, believing in it. The once-huge New York City Party organization was still sizable, but there and nationally the prospect was one of laborious rebuilding for those who still had hope. "I was not launched in Party leadership at an auspicious moment," Thomas reflected, while other Socialists put it, "Norman came in when everybody else was leaving." He hit the speechmaking trail regularly for the Party, having gained such a reputation as a debater that some potential opponents dodged him. The Progressive Club at Northampton, Massachusetts, found an opponent in a General Electric representative whose specialty was addressing women's clubs on the wonders of electricity and who had never heard of Thomas. When Thomas began impaling him on statistics and finding humor in his replies, Granville Hicks, who was in the audience, noted that the GE man "announced that he had to catch an early train" and ran down the aisle with Thomas pursuing him, saying, "I have another question, I have another question."

His Democratic mayoral opponent was to be the winner of a primary between Hearst's man, Mayor John F. Hylan, and the debonair State Senator Jimmy Walker. Crystal sets and peanut-tube radios were coming in, the city had its own station WNYC, and Thomas denounced Hylan for reserving it, as well as city bandstands, for his own electioneering. "[The station] ought to be made an important means of the political education of the people," he said—a new thought at the time. His ridicule was amusing but he also had a positive platform for city improvement, including better schooling and transportation and, above all, new housing to replace noisome tenements—another novel idea. The Progressive Congressman Fiorello La Guardia, a man of similar bent, backed him publicly as "best qualified," saying, "He is the only one who has a platform that is constructive and means something."

Before the campaign got under way, he gave the sermon at the Madison Avenue Presbyterian Church, the church where he and Violet had been married in what seemed another century but was only fifteen years ago, the church which now thought him a woolly-headed idealist-consorter-with-bomb-throwers, the church of the Stewarts, the church that epitomized his unmendable break with the old easy past, but where Henry Sloane Coffin was still reasonably friendly and needed someone to fill in on a hot July Sunday. A man from Mars, Thomas told the congregation, entering an American church, would hear so much about love, truth and freedom that he would be impressed at the perfection that must exist on this planet. This talk of love, truth and freedom, Thomas suggested delicately, was hypocritical: "But let [the Martian] go out into the world and see it as it is and then he would wonder where is the love in which men believe. . . . Perhaps after hearing about love and truth and all the other things he would observe the tenements, the slums and the shacks in the country and wonder whether we strive for love and truth."

Thomas was himself the man from Mars, taking people at their word and seeing earthly events as they were, not as they were painted. "I was very innocent of course in those days," he said thirty-five years later.

### 6. The Literal Man

Wrinkled old Eugene Debs, the living saint and figurehead of Socialism, came to speak for Thomas at Carnegie Hall to an enthusiastic assemblage—except for the Communists packing the galleries who booed Morris Hillquit, chairman of the meeting. The fearless old warrior was not fully aware of the "new Socialism" Thomas sought to build. Debs had an occasional weakness for making pronouncements embarrassing to the Party. In 1919 his impulsive declaration from prison, "From the crown of my head to the soles of my feet I am a Bolshevist and proud of it," had delighted Max Eastman (who plugged it on the cover of The Masses), overjoyed the Communist element that was breaking away and chagrined the more conservative Socialists in whose camp Debs had remained. Thomas and Debs had talked far into the night after a meeting at Poughkeepsie a few years earlier. As a speaker seeking improvement, he had studied Debs's oratory, thought it a little florid and dated and, while admiring his courage, thought him at times unwise. Now at Carnegie Hall, Debs shouted, "Not only the political parties but the press and the churches have become frank agents of capitalism. . . . just let Wall Street get us into a new war tomorrow and see how every preacher in the country will yell for blood!"

While Thomas believed that this was all too true, it was the kind of talk that had given Socialists their "godless" reputation, that had made people equate them with Communists and had required Thomas's presence before the Albany Assembly as a clergyman and family man in 1920. A party with 10,000 members, some of them religious themselves, could not afford to alienate either the religious or the press. For all Thomas's own sentiments, he cultivated the press. He respected the unfulfilled ideals of religion just as he respected his own deeply religious clerical friends—Holmes, Lovett, Sayre and Gilkey were only a few—and he wanted every Protestant, Jewish and Catholic vote he could get. His agnosticism was his own, not the Party's. He kept it to himself. He would chide or even censure the church but would never condemn it out of hand. When forty churchmen attending a conference at Union Theological Seminary toured the headquarters of the four radical parties—the Socialists, Communists, Wobblies and Anarchists—it was the Socialists who got constructive newspaper publicity out of it because of Thomas's tact and sense of the newsworthy:

> Norman Thomas, addressing the visitors at the Rand School of Social Science, declared that unionism had really done much that the pulpit had sponsored in theory. While placing before them the beliefs of Socialism he also took occasion to compare the actual achievements of Socialism with whatever [religion] his guests represented.
>
> "Take child labor as an instance," he said. "It is not necessary to go over again the conditions that have existed in industry here as compared with conditions now. But what did Christianity . . . have to do with the abolition of child labor? . . . The fact is that the labor unions brought about the clearing up of that sore. . . . It is through Socialism and not through the churches that our great social progress has been made. Christianity is doing something, but Christianity can do a lot more."

He gave each visitor a copy of The New Leader, which had been revived as a weekly, and sent them away friendly but thoughtful. He could not have done other than wince at Debs's blunderbuss anti-religion and wonder how many votes it would cost the Party. His Tammany opponent turned out to be Jimmy Walker, who never alienated the church and who promised solemnly to "drive the crooks and stickup men right out of town." His nonchalance infuriated a clubwoman supporter of the Republican candidate, the fountain-pen king Frank D. Waterman, who said in a speech, "I tell you this, Mr. Walker, that every woman in New York knows that the underworld will vote for you to the last stickup man." This in turn upset Eleanor Roosevelt, whose husband had just returned from Warm Springs. Although she was already socially conscious enough to be a member of Rose Schneiderman's Women's Trade Union League, she was a loyal Democrat. Her letter to The Times praised Walker and reprimanded his slanderer: "She has, of course, no knowledge, only a desire to make a telling statement."

Thomas had the usual nonpartisan committee supporting him, including the Reverend Chaffee, Freda Kirchwey of The Nation, Arthur Garfield Hays and the loyal John Haynes Holmes. He also had an opponent in Benjamin Gitlow, the Communist would-be candidate for Mayor, who later admitted that his orders came from Moscow. "Needless to say," he wrote, "I entertained no hope to be elected . . . One of the main political purposes was to throw mud on the Socialist Party and its standard bearer, Norman Thomas." Gitlow was barred from the ballot because he was in jail for "criminal syndicalism." Thomas, who had opposed his jailing in the first place, now opposed his exclusion from the race, saying, "The fact that Gitlow has been convicted of a political offense . . . does not indicate that he is a criminal." While he defended Gitlow, Gitlow continued to assail him, terming Thomas and all Socialists "betrayers of the movement" and Thomas himself a "sky pilot" who was "unfit to lead labor," and inviting Socialists to see the light and join the Communist Party. Thomas—the most active board member of the American Civil Liberties Union—was upholding his principles against political imprisonment and also seeking the return of Communists, some of whom he knew well, into the Socialist Party. Gitlow was practicing the regular Communist tactic of the "united front from below" —the systematic blackening of a Socialist leader accompanied by extending inducements to Socialists to become Communists.

When Walker won in a landslide with 751,000 votes to Waterman's 360,000 and Thomas's puny 40,000, The Times editorialized about "The Socialist Decline," since Hillquit had polled 145,000 votes for the same office in 1917. Not a Socialist was elected even to minor office, and The Times declared without regret that the "party of protest" was now too infirm to fulfill any function of protest.

### 7. Christian Ethics

Thomas went on to Pittsburgh to make a League for Industrial Democracy speech (despite the election, illnesses and other interruptions, he spoke on twenty-nine campuses that year and edited the LID's bi-weekly news service) and to meet a knot of Socialists there, including the insurance man Sam Oshry. With a group, among them Oshry's

# NORMAN THOMAS

young daughter Eleanor, he rode to a coal mine where the miners had been locked out and were suffering privation. He moved among them, talking with them and observing their appalling living conditions as the Socialist group passed out sandwiches, apples and cookies. He seemed so sincerely interested in these crude miners as individuals, and made such an impression of kindliness and intelligence on Eleanor Oshry, that later, when she moved to New York, she joined the Party and renewed the acquaintance. Thomas noted a persistent pattern in industrial strikes: The workers got a wage insufficient for decent living; when they organized and struck, they soon lost their civil liberties because the local government, and usually the church, were entirely aligned with capital; forbidden to assemble, penniless and hungry, they lost the strike and went back to work under the same wretched conditions. Some of the weapons used against them were illegal. As with the suppression of free speech in Mount Vernon, this illegality had to be fought. When he saw the pattern repeated as 13,000 struck the huge Botany textile mills in Passaic and adjacent Garfield, New Jersey, Thomas moved in, with the League for Industrial Democracy and the American Civil Liberties Union behind him.

The strike had been unwise in the first place, begun under Communist leadership in mid-winter to protest a pay cut at a time when the workers were too weak in organization and resources to have even a fair chance of success. Its brutal suppression was nevertheless illegal. Thomas helped form a committee to send food to the strikers and addressed several of their meetings. By spring the operators brought in workers from outside ("scabs," in labor parlance, a term Thomas disliked because they were poverty-stricken human beings too) and hired detective-agency gunmen to protect them; and the police raided strike headquarters. They jailed Albert Weisbord, the young Harvard-trained Communist organizer of the strike, in $30,000 bail and banned all strike meetings. Sheriff George Nimmo publicly read the riot act and thereafter enforced what amounted to martial law. Hoses were turned on strikers in freezing weather. New York newspapermen were beaten and their cameras smashed, a circumstance that brought the press around a trifle to the strikers' side. Nimmo broke up all gatherings. The League rented a vacant lot in Garfield and Thomas arrived to speak from this sanctuary, accompanied by the Reverend Chaffee, Freda Kirchwey, Lillian Symes, McAlister Coleman and Forrest Bailey of ACLU.

Thomas, who later admitted "much apprehension," mounted a low

101

tree stump to address some 150 strikers as armed deputies and strike-breakers with shotguns watched. "This is the first stump speech I've ever made from a stump," he said. "We have come here to test our rights as American citizens to hold a peaceful meeting. . . . Yesterday, Thomas Jefferson was born [*sic*]. You may have heard the name. His birthday is being celebrated in Passaic by a shameful desecration of the cause of liberty . . . I want to urge upon the strikers here that they continue their fine record of peaceful endeavor to win their just demands. . . . This has been a legal and orderly strike. Your leader, Albert Weisbord, is in jail . . . in $30,000 bail. This excessive bail is a mockery of American justice."

A whistle blew, the gunmen closed in and Thomas was manhandled into a car and driven away at high speed. He was taken to the county seat at Hackensack, where Justice of the Peace Louis Hargreaves, a salesman in private life, was at first uncertain how to charge him but then received instructions from the prosecutor's office. Though his speech had urged the opposite, Thomas was charged with inciting to riot and bail was set at $10,000. Not having $10,000, and being denied an opportunity to consult an attorney or telephone his friends, he spent the night in jail while colleagues searched for him. Bailey of ACLU, who said it "looked like a case of kidnaping," did not find him until morning, when bail was raised for him. An effort was made to keep him in jail another day on a technicality but, said one reporter, "The presence of Mrs. Thomas, who rose from a sickbed to call on her husband, apparently softened the sheriff's representatives." The Thomases went home. More local toughs were sworn in as deputies to patrol the streets of Garfield and "order strangers out of town." It was discovered that Mayor William Burke of Garfield, who had asked the sheriff's help, was a Botany employe. The rip-snorting Elizabeth Gurley Flynn, always an admirer of Thomas although she was a Wobbly, stood just across the city line from Garfield and exhorted the strikers to stand firm. Bail at last was raised for Weisbord and he was freed. John Cashman, a speaker for the National Security League, told the local Lions that Thomas had brought college students with him to Passaic "to instil in them the seeds of revolution." Thomas, angrier than he had been in a long time, promptly sued him for slander. Rabbi Stephen B. Wise found a rostrum in a Passaic Catholic church, said that he and his associates were no more Communist than the mill owners and spoke for the strikers. Station WEAF in New York canceled a Thomas broadcast because he was "controversial," or, as Thomas phrased it, "Of course my character has suffered from recent events."

Five days after his arrest, Thomas attended a meeting of the county Presbytery at the Passaic Presbyterian Church and asked permission to speak. There was heated debate among the clergymen, who were generally opposed to the strikers or unwilling to be lectured by an outsider, before they voted down a motion that he be heard. In his anger the man from Mars almost forgot his policy of tact toward the church. His "elevated railroad voice," ringing with emotion, defeated the vote, for they heard a part of what he wanted to say:

> The 10,000 [*sic*] men and women who are on strike here may be successful [or] they may be defeated. . . . If they are defeated they will always bear in mind that the Protestant churches here have stood by while methods were invoked against them such as prevailed in the Russia of the Czars. . . . [W]hile you talk of Christian idealism, you did nothing. On the other hand, a Jewish rabbi went so far as to discuss the situation in a Catholic church. [He cited figures to show Botany's gratifying profits.] Christian ethics demand that you pay attention to this! . . . . The church must properly consider a Christian wage. You gentleman are aware that I am a Socialist. Under some conditions it is easier to be a Socialist than a Christian.

Here he was shouted down. The Hackensack board of education refused to let him speak at a local high school next day—a lecture that had been arranged long in advance. The ACLU meanwhile sought an injunction against Sheriff Nimmo's arbitrary ban on peaceful meetings. A week later Thomas, with John Haynes Holmes and Miss Flynn, appeared at Belmont Park Hall in Garfield, which was owned in full by the Magyar association of textile workers. They and the workers were denied admittance: "Sixty police and deputy sheriffs with shotguns on their shoulders held a crowd of more than 2,000 textile workers at bay . . . At 5 o'clock the impasse ended abruptly. Injunction papers were served on the sheriff . . . Dramatically the sheriff and the police gave way and the cheering strikers poured into the hall."

So Thomas, Holmes and Miss Flynn addressed them—in itself a victory of sorts. The case against Thomas was dropped. But after all this effort, the workers—some of them starving—could not hold out and they lost the strike. Four months later the Passaic board of education barred Thomas again from speaking at a local high school.

## 8. *The Russian Enigma*

In any Socialist gathering, one could start a fight by bringing up the subject of Russia. Party feeling had swung from almost unanimous enthusiasm at the time of the revolution to bitter contention a few years later. Thomas's interest in the first Socialist government in history had developed greater sympathy because of the quickness of American and European conservatives to condemn it out of hand and to send armies against it. No such condemnation had fallen on Mussolini, whose revolution had favored the ruling class. Few could have been more aware than Thomas of the conservative and churchly control of American propaganda which stirred up fear and hatred against the Communists (and Socialists). The shortcomings of American religionists who drew back in horror from Soviet anti-religion were scarcely lost on the deviant clergyman who had found both God and the church wanting. The Babbitt tendency to believe all leftists subversive was as suspect to him. The brutalities of the true patriots had been seen in A. Mitchell Palmer, the Albany Assembly, the New Jersey mills and elsewhere.

There were still left-wing American Socialists who sought reunion with the Communists, and the United States Communists would have been happy to swallow the Socialists whole. Thomas, though never possessing the starry-eyed faith in the Soviet millennium of John Reed and Emma Goldman, was inclined to give it the benefit of too few doubts. He saw it as a great social experiment that should be given every chance for the success he hoped it would have. He walked a careful line as he waited for more evidence to trickle out of Russia. He was, he later conceded, over-optimistic. In 1925 when Alexander Kerensky, Russia's last democratic premier and a butt of Communist invective, visited New York, Thomas criticized the anti-Soviet Jewish Socialist Verband for staging a rally to welcome him. Kerensky deserved to be heard, he agreed, but it was unwise for Socialists to lead cheers for him: "The Socialist Party can well afford to be generous in praise of Russian achievements even while it pleads the cause of Russian political prisoners. Do not forget that the average worker would regard the collapse of the Russian experiment as the collapse of Socialism as well as Communism."

He was dismayed by the news of tyranny in Russia even if, as the apologists said, it was less than the tyranny of the czars and justified as a temporary measure in building a truly Socialist state. But if the drift of thoughtful Socialists such as Max Eastman and Scott Nearing into Communism had any influence on him, it was countered by influences in the other direction. The bowing and scraping the United States Communists did before Russia, and their slavish imitation of Russian precedents, was offensive to him. He hoped that many United States Communists would tire of this servile rigmarole and come back wiser to the Socialist fold. The door should be held open for them. Although he had warned the Jersey mill owners and churchmen that their callousness was the sort of thing that drove workers into Communism, he was not a Communist-denouncer. This restraint was notable because of the vitriol the Communists poured on him as being bourgeois and soft-headed in his opposition to violence, his faith in constitutional and evolutionary change. Were the capitalists who owned everything going to hand it over without a struggle? Had not George Bernard Shaw said that a Bolshevik was "nothing but a Socialist who wants to do something about it"?

For all that, Thomas (and the American Civil Liberties Union) fought for the rights of Communists as American citizens. He defended the Communist Gitlow, he debated amicably enough with Communist Earl Browder in the Bronx, he denounced the imprisonment of Albert Weisbord, and he, along with other Socialists and Communists and 10,000 trade unionists whom both the Socialists and Communists sought as members, met in Madison Square Garden to protest the Sacco-Vanzetti convictions.

Thomas was deeply impressed by the journey of three friends to Russia in 1927. One was James H. Maurer, a Party leader from Reading and president of the Pennsylvania Federation of Labor, in whose judgment he had great faith. Heading a trade-union delegation, Maurer had left with cautious reservations and returned full of enthusiasm: "If what they have over there is Communism, I don't care if they call me a Communist." The Socialist-leaning Paul H. Douglas, economics professor at the University of Chicago, had also been impressed: ". . . there is a real community of belief, a national ideal and moral unity, which is the solid basis of the new Russia." Soon after, Roger Baldwin returned after three months in the Soviet Union to write a book so hopeful about freedom there that it later became an embarrassment to him. There were others who came back from Russia glowing, but certainly the considered opinions of these three buttressed Thomas's own inclination to give technologically backward Russia time to round out its complex task of spreading the new order among many races over vast areas.

His attraction to Socialism had nothing to do with Marxism as revelation but was grounded on his pragmatic belief in its egalitarian aspects, first and foremost being production for public use rather than private profit. He was independent enough in thought to offend down-the-line Marxists. It seems uncertain that he ever studied Marx with quite the ardor with which he read Wodehouse. This was something it was not politic for a Party leader to confess, although no one could rub elbows with such doctrinal experts as Hillquit, Laidler and Lee without hearing much of Marx's gospel. The clergyman who had taken the biblical miracles with salt was not likely to idolize Marx. His initial delay of some two years in joining the Socialist Party despite his support of its practical aims was significant, as was his statement to Trachtenberg on joining:

> As you know, I have a profound fear of the undue exaltation of the State and a profound faith that the new world we desire must depend upon freedom and fellowship rather than upon any sort of coercion whatsoever.

### 9. Strong Medicine

The power with which the yearning to combat evil and do good for mankind seizes some unusual individuals has always inspired among their ordinary brethren curiosity, ridicule, hatred and in some cases ultimate veneration. Thomas in his lifetime would arouse and experience them all. At Union Seminary he had studied the saints and knew in detail how all of them, ranging from John the Baptist to St. Francis and right down to Eugene Debs, inspired among different listeners contempt, loathing or acceptance. To reduce the loathing and increase the acceptance he made studied use of his quick wit and appreciation of the absurd, giving a pleasant flavor to his strong medicine of reform. The desire to help, to improve, was of course the cause of all human advancement, and ignorance or apathy was its enemy. Always in his mind's eye were the Harlem slums, the Appalachian hovels, the pinched, big-eyed children of the textile towns. These things hurt him personally. His own children grew inured to his constant adjurations that any decent person must make some improvement in a world that so badly needed betterment.

# NORMAN THOMAS

The Thomas-Baldwin-Muste reformist trio, all born within a few months of each other, would collaborate in many causes for a half-century despite great individual differences. Baldwin was cool and detached in his approach, whereas Thomas and the serious Muste would be gripped by indignation, though different in their expression of it. Thomas admitted that he was an incurable evangelist. He knew he was eloquent and had a human enjoyment of applause, but those of his critics who thought him a mere seeker of ovations totally missed the urgency and passion of the do-gooder in him, the deep anguish it brought him to see America in what he construed as error, and the absolute necessity it created in him to oppose, to speak, to teach. As he would disclose in some of his more private writings, and especially in a later diary, injustice or error so disturbed him mentally and emotionally that he was compelled subjectively to speak out against it. This reduced the terrible inner pressure and made him feel better even in instances where he knew his speeches did little if any objective good, somewhat as one in a temper writes his boss a savagely critical letter and then tears it up, feeling relief at merely articulating his thoughts.

People of such intensity are not usually easy to live with, however strong their familial love. It was a tribute both to Thomas and his family that on the whole, with few exceptions, they got along very well. Thomas's own brother Evan was a moralist and humanitarian in his own right, but he thought Socialism materialistic and unfeasible, saying, "Norman, it's a pretty dream that will never work." Both loved philosophical and political debate, but eventually they reached a mutual understanding of the uselessness of argument about Socialism. For Evan to be able to disparage his older brother's profoundest beliefs without incurring bodily injury and indeed for them to have remained deeply attached argued some flexibility on the part of the elder.

# VI

## 1. The Darkest Stain

Thomas's nomination for the comparatively humble job of State Senator from New York's Lower East Side in 1926 did not signify any fall in his Party importance. He wanted to run for an office he thought he had some chance to win, and he was quite willing to let the Socialist Judge Jacob Panken shoulder the burden of running for Governor against Al Smith. Although Panken, born in Eastern Europe and possessor of a foghorn voice, was top man on the ticket, Thomas got more newspaper attention. He gave much of his speaking time to promoting Panken, and while he conceded Governor Smith's good character, he attacked his claim that he deserved labor support:

> Al Smith is a jolly good fellow, he was brought up on the sidewalks of New York, he is a wet, a Catholic, and he has done some things in an executive capacity that the New York Times likes. But what has he done for the laboring man? Nothing.

Smith inundated them all, Thomas losing again. In Chicago, Eugene Debs died at seventy, and New York Socialists who planned a great memorial meeting discovered that the Communists sought to take Madison Square Garden for the same purpose, ready to exploit in death the man they had abused while alive. The Socialists had to do some fast talking, backed by money from The Forward, to hire the Garden away from them. Thomas traveled to Debs's home town of Terre Haute to address a throng from the late leader's front porch at the funeral service. It was one of the 175 speeches and lectures he made in 1926, most of them at colleges and universities, most of them under League for Industrial Democracy auspices, only a few being private lectures for

108

which he kept the fee. Some Socialists thought he made a good thing out of the LID. While it was true that his travels for the organization helped spread his fame, the LID made a good thing out of him financially since the fees he remitted to it annually totaled as high as $14,000, almost three times his salary. Although in his private lectures he said he expected a fee equal to that of other lecturers of similar note, he was a soft touch for any college or group representative who pleaded poverty and he often traveled by night in drafty cars to address a group paying only his expenses. He loved to lecture, to explain, teach and analyze, and it is not impossible that by now he had political office in view as an actuality rather than as a Socialist "showing." One of his speeches was at Edgewood School in Greenwich, Connecticut, where both his older daughters, Polly and Frances, were students. It was a talk in part on politics which both daughters remember as making sense and favorably impressing even those few of their schoolmates who thought of Socialists as dangerous people.

In 1926 the old sachem, John Aikman Stewart, died at 104. He had a grown and married son and daughter by his second marriage, and his first marriage, which had produced Violet's father and three other children, was so far back in antiquity that the long New York Times obituary failed to mention it. All of the flags at Princeton sank to half mast. His death brought a bequest to Violet, who was enlarging her kennels and beginning to make a modest profit at raising spaniels.

"In 1927," Thomas recorded, "I was somehow induced to run for Alderman in part of that same district. . . . And lost." That made four consecutive years of running and losing, a grind that he could not look back on with unalloyed cheer. Yet in the following year he was again a candidate, this time for President of the United States—probably the first man to jump in one year from aldermanic to Presidential aspiration.

This was against his own wishes and judgment. No equivalent of the La Follette coalition had emerged, so he was the candidate of the lone little Socialist Party with some 8,000 paid-up members. "We were not rich in available Presidential material," he recalled, describing himself as "Hobson's choice." Debs was dead, neither Berger nor Hillquit could be candidates because of their foreign birth and the popular Socialist Mayor of Milwaukee, Daniel Hoan, preferred that secure job to running himself into unemployment on a Presidential ticket. "Mr. Thomas received an ovation as he rose to speak" at Manhattan Opera House where the convention was held, said The Times, but the Presidency was so far out of reach that Hillquit had to plead with him for two days before he accepted the nomination as a Socialist duty. His campaigns in New York had made him known in that state, his support of civil liberties, as in the Botany mills case, had made favorable Socialist news, and his itinerant speechmaking had introduced him to liberals at a hundred colleges east of the Mississippi. In the Far West he was unknown. Alas, he would be running against the Democrat Al Smith and the Republican Herbert Hoover.

President John Grier Hibben thought it "the darkest stain on Princeton's escutcheon" (or so Thomas later described his attitude) that a son of Old Nassau should run for President on the Socialist ticket. Not so the Daily Princetonian, which congratulated him on his candidacy and also on his gradualism:

> The Princetonian does not expect that Mr. Thomas will be elected and the candidate himself has subscribed to that belief, but we are glad that he is in the running. . . . He is whole-heartedly and sincerely for the party platform, but he believes that any except the most gradual change would be disastrous.

Thomas's running mate was the salty, self-educated James H. Maurer. The national Party office in Chicago was hopeless as a campaign organizer under William Henry, whose loyalty had made him so many friends that to fire him would have raised a storm. Thomas all but gave up on Henry and toured the country making speeches largely arranged by his own aides, usually accompanied by August Claessens or McAlister Coleman or both. Coleman, the press secretary, had to give most newspapermen simplified instructions on the differences between Socialism, Communism and Anarchism. Claessens, for fourteen years a member of the New York Assembly, often addressed smaller crowds and had his own way of illustrating Socialism. In Memphis—this was only three years after the Scopes trial—he told a crowd that Darwin was terribly wrong in suggesting that men evolved from beasts:

> Take the woodchuck. . . . As the summer grows, the woodchuck . . . gets fatter and fatter. By autumn he is so obese he can hardly run. The first frost nips his tail and he hurries to his hole, goes in and takes all the fat with him for his winter's fuel and feed. Were the woodchuck a man, he would hand over the fat to the capitalists, vote the Republican ticket, go down into his hole and starve. . . . We are no kin to the beasts.

Sometimes, when seating arrangements permitted, Claessens asked the audience to throw money at him on the stage. He did this in Spokane, forgetting the prevalence of silver cartwheels there and, Thomas observed, "did some mighty active dodging to avoid dollars aimed at his shiny bald head."

The country was at its height of prosperity, although some four million were unemployed. Thomas was proceeding on an utterly new plan, seeking to broaden the base of the Socialist Party by moving away from the old insistence on immediate nationalization of basic resources and industries, hoping to tap a large constituency of middle-class liberals. The existence of such a constituency was suggested by his extraordinary popularity at colleges and universities among students and professors and a fringe of college-town intellectuals. Scores of Thomas-for-President clubs sprang up in the colleges. Among educators actively supporting him were Paul Douglas and Robert Morss Lovett of the University of Chicago, Jesse H. Holmes of Swarthmore, Thomas's friend S. Ralph Harlow, now teaching religion at Smith College; and Reinhold Niebuhr and Harry F. Ward of Union Theological Seminary. Now, as in his speaking for the League for Industrial Democracy, he made vigorous use of the question period following his address, and was himself the questioner when opportunity offered, sounding public opinion. Earlier that year he had visited the University of Kansas at Lawrence for the first time and had addressed some 4,000 there. Afterward he walked around the campus with Paul R. Porter,* a senior student who was president of the Young Men's Christian Association, editor of one of the college newspapers and leaning toward Socialism. Porter was charmed by the older man's personality and also impressed by the many shrewd questions he asked about local thought, political and otherwise.

So Thomas campaigned not for Marxism but for Progressivism, not for revolution but for reform. His sisters Agnes and Emma meanwhile had graduated from Goucher College, near Baltimore, and it was at Goucher that his youngest brother Arthur, now a labor relations specialist in the textile business, met his bride-to-be. Violet attended their wedding, Thomas begging off because of his electioneering. He made 150 speeches from coast to coast during the 1928 campaign and spoke three times over radio networks. The Socialist Party had straddled the

*Porter, who was instrumental in arranging the address, after graduation became an LID worker under Thomas in New York and was on his way to becoming a Socialist leader.

liquor issue and in Milwaukee it was plain that the important Socialist Presidential vote in this beer-loving state would go to Smith. The city was hung with signs, "VOTE SOCIALIST AND WET," and at a convivial luncheon for Thomas at Victor Berger's home (three cocktails plus whisky washed down with beer), Berger told Coleman that Wisconsinites would split their ballots and vote for Smith nationally. The Party had just under $100,000 to spend on the campaign—a shade more than Debs had had in 1920—and little of that came from union labor, which was heavily behind Smith. Thomas and his aides were so pressed for money that they passed the hat at smaller meetings. "It was, I think, in Arkansas," Thomas later wrote, "that [Coleman] reported that when he went to pay a hotel bill with a lot of small coins such as we had to depend on in collections . . . the hotel proprietor wanted to hold him for investigation, thinking him the man who had [just] robbed a Sunday school. . . . Between you and me, I always took the story with a grain of salt."

And in the end, crushing defeat. To Hoover's 21,000,000 and Smith's 15,000,000, Thomas polled only 267,420 votes. It was the Party's worst Presidential showing ever.

Yet it was not without promise, if one could muster that upside-down optimism some Socialists—and even Thomas—called to their aid when things looked black. For one thing, almost a quarter of Thomas's votes came from New York City, which showed poor organization in the rest of the country but demonstrated that he pulled votes from people who knew or heard him. For another, he polled only 18,000 votes in strongly Socialist but "wet" Wisconsin, whereas the wet Milwaukee Socialist Berger polled 42,000 in a single district—though even he lost his Congressional seat. Conversely, it also seemed clear that throughout much of the country, fear of the Catholic wet Smith had deprived Thomas of much of the liberal dry and Protestant vote, which went to Hoover. Besides, the decline in Party membership had been stemmed. It was inching upward. Socialists, accustomed to adversity, could find cheer in small things. Wait till next year! A few days after the defeat, Thomas spoke before a group in suburban Englewood, New Jersey, so impressing a women listener that she came up afterward, said it was the best speech she ever heard and that if Mr. Thomas ever ran for President she would surely vote for him.

## 2. Made in Heaven

In 1929 the intrepid Violet Thomas took her fourteen-year-old daughter Frances with her to Paris to visit Violet's elderly aunt, long a resident there. Violet had a heart seizure while there, took medication and a few hours' rest and seemed as well as ever. Most of her attacks were deceptively moderate so that the children not aware of their seriousness, were no longer upset by them. "Norman and Violet knew how serious it was," Roger Baldwin observed. "His heart was on his sleeve when he was with her." Baldwin was a frequent visitor due to the American Civil Liberties Union connection, whereas Raymond Fosdick, now a capitalist attorney, was only a few times, with his wife, a guest at the Thomas town house—enough for Fosdick to notice that the Thomas marriage seemed "made in heaven."

The Thomases that year sold their place at Quogue, inconveniently far from the city, and bought five acres on Goose Hill Road in Cold Spring Harbor on the north shore of Long Island, an hour's ride from New York. Here they built a handsome fourteen-room house, entirely designed by the remarkably gifted Violet without benefit of architectural training. It was U-shaped, with several French doors opening on a court inside the U. In keeping with the fresh-air, germ-defeating precept, every bedroom had at least two, and some had three, windowed exposures. The floors of several downstairs rooms were tiled, against spaniel errors. Well to the rear were Violet's enlarged Blue Waters Kennels, tended by a hired man under her supervision. There was also a poultry house and a cow barn which usually contained a cow, either rented or owned, and which Thomas milked expertly when he had a chance. On one occasion when the cow was lost, he posted himself at the barn and mooed with such verisimilitude that she immediately returned.

If Thomas worried about Violet, she in turn worried enough about his hurry-up, train-grabbing, sandwich-bolting, speechmaking, Socialist-meeting-until-eleven-and-then-talking-into-Dictaphone-until-two routine that there seems to have been an agreement that the Cold Spring Harbor place was strictly for relaxation. Political problems so concerned him that she asked the League for Industrial Democracy office staff to keep from him the less important ones. The Party, which often invaded the town house several nights a week, was barred from Cold Spring

Harbor. Thomas was able at last to have the big vegetable garden he had always wanted—his only hobby other than reading—one almost as ambitious, with perennial rhubarb and asparagus and other vegetables ranging from small row crops to corn, as his paternal grandfather's great garden in Pennsylvania. He got out to Cold Spring Harbor only on weekends, when he would work up a sweat with a hoe or a wheel cultivator. The children—young Evan was now nine—were expected to put in a few hours a week on the garden. In front of the house were a dozen apple trees which eventually furnished fruit which the apple-loving Thomas relished and the whole family enjoyed. By now Bill Thomas was sailing a small boat. He would take his father and a sister or two along for ballast while Violet, not forgetting the fate of her father at sea, simmered in nervousness but never complained. Thomas himself tried sailing but was so awkward that he gave it up. He was almost equally maladroit at the wheel of a car, although no one told him this because it would have nettled him, and his family worried because of the apparent inevitability of a nasty crackup.

The Thomases thus maintained two commodious year-round establishments involving considerable expense—the kind of town-and-country luxury enjoyed by, say, bankers or brokers, whose contributions to society Thomas could not approve. To Frances, the most socially conscious of his children, who remarked that it did not seem right for them to live in such comfort and to drive a Buick while there was so much poverty abroad, he had to explain that he could not as yet alter the fact that they lived in a capitalist society. Yet his affluence tugged at his conscience although the Party was far from excluding Hillquit, Waldman or Cahan because of their prosperity, or Professor Albert Sprague Coolidge of Harvard and Alfred Baker Lewis of Boston because of their riches. Thomas could not make public capital of the facts that put him in quite a different category: The money was not his but Violet's. Violet fully expected that one of her heart attacks would kill her—a judgment which time confirmed. Her sudden death was a possibility he had to face. She had sacrificed much to his politics; he could hardly ask more. Despite his deep sense of privacy, in later years he forced himself to make occasional frank acknowledgement that he had been deprived of the indigence which Socialists were rather expected to face.

Now, in 1929, both he and Violet were delighted that Uncle Evan, at the age of thirty-nine, was at last accepted at the New York University medical school and began studying anatomy alongside young men half his age. And it was no surprise to the family that Thomas, for the fifth successive year, was a candidate for office.

### 3. The White-Haired Boy

There were factors other than Thomas's ability, magnetism and energy which were propelling him into rivalry for the Socialist leadership with the respected and powerful Hillquit. As a busy attorney (he was criticized for taking occasional capitalist clients), Hillquit did his Party work in his spare time. He was fifteen years older than Thomas, his health uncertain and his energies on the wane. Thomas worked full-time for the League for Industrial Democracy and was in constant touch with Socialist and liberal groups in New York and much of the country. His preternatural dynamism made his partner in LID, Laidler, seem sedentary. Several key appointments in the Party and the LID, while certainly not made by Thomas alone, involved people who soon saw him as the coming leader, came to admire him personally, and cheerfully slaved for him at salaries around twenty dollars a week.

Thomas had exerted much of the pressure that at last forced the resignation of the incompetent William Henry as national secretary and his replacement by the twenty-seven-year-old Clarence Senior, another graduate of the University of Kansas, where he had been a year ahead of Paul Porter and a fellow member of LID. Since his graduation, Senior had moved to Cleveland in an adult education post and had helped revitalize the Party there. In the largely Jewish New York councils of the Party, the six-two Senior and the six-three Porter became known as the "Kansas goyim." The older Paul Blanshard, a native of Ohio who had become a valued LID representative, had been a Congregational clergyman out of Harvard, had become an agnostic and a Socialist union representative, and had served a month in jail in Utica for excessive sympathy with striking millhands there. A new recruit was New York-born John Herling, who possessed a 1928 Harvard degree in philosophy and the classics and had been an LID member there and active in such things as the Sacco-Vanzetti protest. All four were intellectuals and activists in the Thomas mold and implied some movement of the Party away from the old Debs working-class Marxism in the direction Thomas wanted it to move—toward middle-class Progressivism rather than revolution, toward the building of a liberal coalition that could win. A further move in this direction was Thomas's success, despite considerable opposition, in removing the requirement that applicants for Party membership affirm their belief in the class struggle. The English Socialist leader A. Fenner Brockway, who called on Thomas and spoke for LID during a visit to America, mentioned his "open and continually developing mind" and described him politically as a conservative, "a typical Social Democrat of the Centre." Thomas, he said, sounded somewhat as if he were addressing an audience even in private conversation—not surprising, Brockway agreed, because Thomas usually *was* addressing an audience.

Other signs of the Thomas influence were such things as the membership on the LID board of wealthy Mrs. Ethel Clyde, widow of the Clyde steamship lines mogul. She had a summer place on Long Island and was driven by a chauffeur in a limousine flying the Clyde flag. Not a Socialist but liberally inclined, she furnished advice and that vital ingredient, money.

That Thomas could have a hand in accomplishing all this without offending old hands such as Hillquit, Waldman and Lee was scarcely possible as human affairs are arranged. Possibly the annoyance was not mitigated by their knowledge that in him they had their only good front-line campaigner and candidate.

Senior took over the national Party office in a warehouse building at 549 Randolph Street, next to the Northwestern Station in Chicago. Herling became membership director of LID at the Fifth Avenue office. Porter, though traveling extensively as LID field secretary, had an odd encounter with Sinclair Lewis and Dorothy Thompson in New York. Lewis, planning a labor novel, had a long conversation with Thomas in his search for background material. Thomas told him he should join the Party himself—a suggestion Lewis did not reject outright, and he did help write a Party pamphlet. By way of thanks, Thomas sent Porter to the Lewis-Thompson home on West Tenth Street bearing a Socialist membership card made out to Lewis. The Lewises prevailed on Porter to stop for a drink. Porter and Mrs. Lewis each nursed along one drink while Lewis laid waste six or eight, talking enthusiastically about his labor novel until his speech blurred and he was beyond locomotion.* Mrs. Lewis said with vexation that he was in no condition to take her to dinner. Porter, feeling somewhat responsible, gallantly offered to take his place. She led him, however, to a fancy

---

*Lewis, though he also consulted James Maurer, Tom Mooney and others, never did write the labor novel.

Village eatery where the bill was far beyond his thin LID wallet. He had to confess this, whereupon she paid without a murmur, Porter suffering a humiliation he was unable to repair until years later.

When Hillquit declined the Socialist nomination for Mayor of New York in 1929, Thomas accepted the candidacy "very cheerfully." He had studied municipal affairs ever since his tenure on the Harlem school board, a study heightened since his trouncing by Jimmy Walker in 1925. Now he was running against Walker again and against his friend Fiorello La Guardia, who had hoped for fusion support but had been nominated only by the Republicans. Prohibition-era gangsterism flourished so openly alongside official corruption in the easy Walker administration that it was hard to draw a line between them. The same open sympathy and honesty which had made people in Harlem bring their private troubles to Thomas now brought him civil servants, union members or criminals with tales of injustice or fraud. "Mostly my informants were frightened," he recalled; "sometimes they were clearly unreliable, often they were neurotics and dope addicts. One dared not depend too much on them, yet there was a large residuum of truth in what they said." It happened that one of his informants produced evidence that a certain hoodlum was occasionally in the employ of the Amalgamated Clothing Workers. There was no evidence that Sidney Hillman, the powerful president of the union, knew of this. Hillman, however, heard a garbled story of the interview and was thenceforth a bitter enemy of Thomas—a hatred that later had serious consequences.

Thomas's speeches, which could bite with literate irony, could also touch on the poetic and sometimes exude a whiff of the pulpit: "We Socialists look at this city of great luxury and greater poverty, a little beauty and immense ugliness, this market place where everything, even justice, is bought and sold and we say: Nevertheless those who toil with hand and brain can, if they will, by intelligent, collective action; by building their own party make this marvelous city the dwelling place of comfort and beauty, justice and peace." As always he pushed a concrete program for city betterment—not of socialization, which had in the main to be a national undertaking—calling among other things for unification of the patchwork transit system, rent controls, the merit system for appointments, and emphasizing his everlasting appeal for the razing of slums and the municipal erection of housing. Walker had started his career as vaudeville gagman and composer, his best-known song being "Will You Love Me in December as You Do in May?" He was as notable for his absences from City Hall—he had taken seven

117

vacations in his first two years in office for a total of 143 days—as for his considerable malfeasance. But he was a magic figure of the Roaring Twenties, as winning as he was irresponsible, loved by a thoughtless public for his Irish smile, his wisecracks and the carnation on his lapel. Even Thomas the moralist privately called him "personally likable," at the same time attacking the Walker scandals, including the unsolved murder of the racketeer Arnold Rothstein, and daring to name several Walker magistrates whose illegalities later removed them from office. Nor did he spare La Guardia despite his liberal record. Thomas had long been irate at the practice of city Republicans—he called that party the "kept woman of Tammany"—of collaborating with the Tiger for a part of the loot. He accused La Guardia of running "with a bunch of militant conservatives," added, "He has openly promised jobs in event of victory to district leaders," and taxed him with having no program. After one encounter with Thomas on the same platform in Brooklyn, La Guardia buttonholed him and pleaded, "Now, Norman, you know I only have the Republican nomination. How can you expect me to make a program?"

On October 24, 1929, a week before the election, the period so well typified by Walker began collapsing with a plunge of the stock market —a phenomenon not given due weight until months later.

The Thomas forces gathered by seven each evening at his Eighteenth Street home. They were given, like all candidates and their aides, a police motorcycle escort with shrieking sirens—an exhilaration Thomas enjoyed perhaps a trifle more than a Socialist should—from one speaking place to another, five or six of them every evening until they returned to the Thomas place after midnight. There the weary campaigners would be met by Violet with tea and coffee—not a drop of illegal alcohol. (Thomas himself was not a total abstainer but declined to break the law.) For the first time he had the support of one New York newspaper, the smallish Telegram, but he was also given serious attention by the Times, Herald Tribune and World. Walker did little campaigning, spending much of his time with his new mistress, who was then rehearsing a Broadway play. Walker won easily, to be sure, and La Guardia came in a poor second.* But Thomas was a respectable third with 174,931 votes, well over four times his total in 1925, exceeding even Hillquit's total in 1917 and in fact the biggest vote a Socialist had ever drawn in the city. Analysis showed that much of his vote had come from

*Walker received in round numbers 865,000 votes, La Guardia 368,000.

middle-class rather than Socialist elements. There was rejoicing at Socialist headquarters. The upward turn was marked also by an increase of more than 500 in Party membership in the city alone—a sizable gain in a party that had recently numbered only 8,000 nationally. As of that moment, Thomas was the white-haired boy of American Socialism.

## 4. A New Party

Before the crash, Thomas had expounded his favorite theme in one of his magazine articles, "Why Not a New Political Party?" in The North American Review. He told his readers that they were not quite correct in believing that they enjoyed democracy, since democracy implied choice:

> ... the two major parties ... have no clear cut difference between them. ... Obviously the choice between two parties which do not divide on basic principles, which belong to the same general set of interests, which fight for office and discuss at election time only irrelevant or secondary issues, is next door to no choice at all. We might as well save the expense of an election and draw lots for our rulers. ... [Royal Copeland] started as Republican mayor of Ann Arbor, Mich.; he has just been reelected Democratic Senator from New York; all he ever changed was his address.

The article pointed up Thomas's value to the Party as a showpiece and propagandist to the middle and upper classes. No haranguer or quoter of Marx, he wrote with an urbanity, wit and common sense that made him welcome at the Review, decidedly not a working-class magazine. No one else in the Party had such talents. He could both speak and write to reactionaries and hold their attention. In this article, as in many of his speeches and writings, he poked fun at the similarities of the two old parties with arguments that remained applicable decades later: "No wonder your General Motors and Du Pont officials, your bankers and others, so nicely [divided] up their financial support [between the Republicans and Democrats]."

To people who equated Socialism with rioting in the streets, he was the gentleman personified, the man you would be proud to have living next door, soft-pedaling Marxism and making nationalization sound sweetly reasonable. Were not the highways, the schools, the water systems already publicly owned? And would anyone want it otherwise? Now the discovery that the Wall Street crash was real, that the Republicans and Democrats were identical also in their inability to stop the terrifying economic collapse, offered the Party a golden opportunity. Capitalism, which had enabled the luckier workmen to buy silk shirts and Fords, now could not find them jobs. Thomas and the Party had new weapons in attacking the problem that had frustrated them for years: how to attract the labor and farm vote (as well as the middle class) away from the two major parties. Thomas's fine showing for Mayor was made despite the opposition of most of organized labor. The city Central Trades and Labor Council, representing the majority of the American Federation of Labor, had endorsed Walker, and Thomas had gotten support only from some of the local needle trades. Under William Green the AFL was continuing the Gompers policy of flinty disdain for the Socialists and support for one or the other of the major parties in return for minor services to labor. But now, with both Republicans and Democrats discredited by their helplessness in the face of economic ruin, the Socialist Party should finally come into its own.

The desire to make it more inclusive caused a minor dispute about its name. The Red Scare of the postwar years was not forgotten. Despite the separation of the Socialist and Communist parties and the fact that they were now bitter enemies, the public continued to confuse the two or lump them together. Since both parties owed their original ideology to Marx, celebrated May Day and called fellow members "Comrade," many middle-class voters thought them the same and shunned them both. At a rally celebrating Thomas's fine showing in the mayoral race, John Haynes Holmes urged that the Party should drop its Socialist tag so that Thomas could become the "Moses" of a "general nonpartisan mass movement of righteousness in New York." Holmes even recommended that the Party drop some of the Socialist dogma that intimidated outsiders, bring in the masses and *elect* candidates instead of offering them up for sacrifice. The fundamentalist Hillquit rejected the idea: "We . . . have undertaken to reorganize society from the bottom up." Thomas, however casual his Marxism, believed firmly in nationalization and production for use. Speaking from the audience, he said he was not adamant against changing the Party's name: ". . . I put myself in the position of a young lady. I would fain change my name, but before doing so I would want to know something about the gentleman. I would at least want to know his name."

Holmes said incautiously, "the Socialist Party lacks the intellectual leadership worthy of its candidate, Norman Thomas"—undiplomatic talk in the presence of Hillquit and Waldman. The dapper Waldman, eight years Thomas's junior, was driving hard for Party leadership and his intellect was good. He had gone to work in a clothing sweatshop on arriving from Russia at seventeen and finished high school at night. He continued nights at Cooper Union while cutting clothes by day, became a civil engineer in five years and went to work building subways. But again he went to night school and learned the law, which he liked better. His Socialism had sprung from the garment workers and the subway laborers. He had become an Assemblyman while still in his twenties, and since then had built a good law practice, much of it for the unions. The man from Princeton had come to Socialism by a different route, and there were breakers ahead for these two. As for the Party's name, Thomas may later have regretted that it was not changed, for the Socialist name would always be an albatross.

Meanwhile Thomas was prime mover in forming an offshoot of the League for Industrial Democracy called the City Affairs Committee, a nonpartisan group nominally led by Holmes, Rabbi Wise, John Dewey and others. Its job was to investigate corruption under Walker, suggest methods of reform and win middle-class voters to the side of the Socialist drive for honesty. Its vigorous director was Thomas's close ally, Paul Blanshard. Thomas also joined with Paul Douglas, who was forming the League for Independent Political Action, aimed at founding a Progressive farmer-labor coalition of the La Follette type but with more advanced economic plans. Douglas was impressed by the Minnesota Farmer-Labor Party's election of two United States Senators and three Congressmen in the space of six years—a success in contrast to Socialist failure. Douglas, like Holmes, was wary of far left-wingers and aware of the public fear of "Socialism," but totally approving of Thomas's moderate course. Other leaders in LIPA were John Dewey, W. E. B. Du Bois, Oswald Garrison Villard, James Maurer and Reinhold Niebuhr, the latter also serving as an editor of Thomas's old brainchild, The World Tomorrow.

Blanshard observed that in New York City "the Socialist Party had come to occupy a special position [in part] because of . . . the great personal prestige of Norman Thomas, who had become a kind of civic conscience for the middle class. . . ." Thomas and Blanshard, who were co-authoring a book, *What's the Matter with New York?,* kept a sharp eye on the Walker administration. "We often attended Board of Estimate meetings together," Blanshard recalled, "and we objected so strongly to the visible corruption that once or twice we were ejected." Thomas seemed the converse of the political innocent often seen in the preacher-turned-politician. Meeting and talking with people ranging from laborer to Mayor, he knew more than a little about the half-world where politics and crime joined hands. He was, for example, aware of suspicious activities on the part of the Tammany leader Jimmy Hines years before Hines was brought to book.

In 1930 Thomas ran for Congress from a Brooklyn district with LIPA as well as Socialist support. His 21,983 vote (though he still lost) was almost three times that of the 1928 Socialist candidate. It appeared that more voters were emulating the wisdom of the woodchuck. But dissension was beginning to split the Party at a time when its promise seemed the brightest in years.

# VII

## 1. The Crash

To the sad clichés of the Great Depression—the ruined investors leaping from windows, the hollow-eyed apple-sellers and shoe-shiners —were added the dolorous tales of what success had descended to. Most college men doffed their baccalaureate caps and gowns to sink into unemployment. One Dartmouth honor graduate was envied because he had secured a job in the new but as yet unoccupied Empire State Building, flushing toilets. It was necessary to do this once a day to prevent chemicals in the water from marring the finish. He spent his hours striding down echoing corridors on floor after floor, entering swinging doors and manipulating hundreds of identical levers, becoming expert at a job that made little use of his education and offered no future but provided the blessed advantage of a weekly paycheck.

Thomas, in his travels, talked with collegians about to leave school for lack of money, with professors who were discharged or whose salaries were cut to the bone, with college presidents who wondered whether their institutions might have to close down. He saw breadlines, boarded-up businesses, foreclosures, sheriff's sales watched by gaunt unemployed hangers-on. "I did much traveling," he recalled, "in that black winter when . . . a bushel of corn sold for a price barely equal to the cost of a corncob pipe." His brother Arthur, now directing labor relations for a textile mill in nearby Garnersville, New York, and Ralph, with the power company in Baltimore, had stories to tell of the crises both for capital and for labor.

He heard a depression joke he thought funny in a morbid way. It concerned a jobhunter who was approaching an Omaha packing house when he heard a man crying for help from the nearby Missouri River.

123

He rushed to help the man struggling in the water, then checked himself and asked, "Who are you and where do you work?" With his last breath the drowning man replied, "I am Tom Smith and I work in that packing house." The inquirer let Smith sink and rushed to the packing house to apply for the job. "No opening," he was told. "But I just saw your man Tom Smith drown in the river." "Oh, yes—that job's filled by the man who shoved him in."

Outside of that, Thomas could see no humor in the depression. He worked for the jobless as if they were all dear relatives. No one so steadily urged, entreated and harangued Mayor Walker, Governor Roosevelt and President Hoover to create jobs for the unemployed and to furnish adequate relief for those who could not be employed. With Blanshard he visited J. P. Morgan's right-hand man, Thomas W. Lamont, gave him a "quiet but stern lecture about the terrible plight of the poor and told him that something must be done." Blanshard felt that this was Lamont's first inkling of the immensity of the disaster and that thereafter the business community was a trifle more understanding. Thomas's importunings to the Mayor, Governor and President were endless. A perpetual tribune, he insisted that government had a responsibility to help the helpless—an idea then not only uncommon but suspect in the United States. He asked for a legislative inquiry into milk and food profiteering in New York City. He pressed both the state and the city to open free employment agencies. He clashed repeatedly with Mayor Walker at City Hall meetings over Walker's lack of urgency about unemployment. He entreated Walker to push subway and paving projects to create jobs. With Rabbi Wise and John Haynes Holmes, his colleagues on the City Affairs Committee, he compiled statistics on the growing number of jobless and urged the Mayor to act. Walker grew impatient with the Thomas-Blanshard assault. He once reminded Blanshard that he had "done a bit"—meaning his sojourn in the Utica jail during the strike troubles—and again suggested that Thomas was starting on his next political campaign. Walker later moved to Long Island and bought a dog from Violet, at which time he and the Thomases met on a friendly basis, but as Mayor he drew steady Thomas fire. With Nevin Sayre and others, Thomas visited Washington to meet with Senators Burton K. Wheeler and Lynn Frazier and request President Hoover to call a special session of Congress to evolve measures for relief. He felt keenly the misery of unemployment and was a soft touch for a dollar, but he knew the uselessness of that kind of help. He was one of the first to talk big money, advocating the immediate appropriation of

$500 million for relief and $3 billion for public works.

Hoover denounced the public works plan as unsound because it would unbalance the budget—a kind of reasoning not influential with Thomas, who thought that to have millions in want was worse than unsound, specifically, inhuman. He made repeated trips to Washington to besiege Congressmen who might help. Repeatedly he wrote the President to assail a policy which left the unemployed "to subsist on patriotic oratory. . . . The United States is offering them a standing invitation to riot or starve." And he attacked Hoover's use of troops on the bonus army: "It is a characteristic climax to the policy of a man who promised prosperity to us all but has fought off every dole except a dole to bankers [the Reconstruction Finance Corporation]."

## 2. *Wintergreen for President*

Thomas was so dissatisfied with the progress of the Party that he wanted very gently to depose Hillquit and name a more satisfactory chairman. He had run for office eight grueling consecutive years (in 1931 he was a candidate in a special election for Borough President of Manhattan) and perhaps felt in danger of taking on the Debs latter-day status of figurehead and crowd-pleaser without real authority. Kirby Page, reviewing Thomas's latest book, *America's Way Out,* in The World Tomorrow, had different feelings about Debs: ". . . the mantle of Debs has fallen upon Thomas and he has become the acknowledged spokesman of American Socialists."

Perhaps Hillquit was less ready to acknowledge this. Charney Vladeck reviewed Thomas's book in The New Leader, giving it generous praise ("a landmark in the history of American Socialism") but admitting that in showing the Party's past failures and charting what he felt to be a wise future course, Thomas trifled with its scriptures. He "dispenses with the whole Socialist terminology," Vladeck wrote, and uses "hardly a quotation from any recognized Socialist authority. . . . In fact, any Rotarian can understand him." Thomas of course hoped to win Rotarians to Socialism. He doubted that Socialism could be scientific. He rejected a purely economic interpretation of history and the materialistic philosophy that was a cornerstone of Marxist Socialism. In the theory of class struggle he saw organizational value instead of certain revolution. To Socialists who he felt were bemused by a dream of overnight social revolution, he wrote, "Emancipation is a process, not merely a dramatic act." Such heresies, Vladeck observed, would once have jeopardized his standing in the movement, but not any more, as was shown by the fact that the book was on sale at the Rand School bookstore for $2.50 and advertised in The New Leader.

Party friction was growing in 1931 when Thomas took a belated step: He formally demitted the Presbyterian clergy, having awaited the death of his mother to spare her feelings. The church sent Theodore Savage, now secretary of the Presbytery, to urge him to stay in the fold, but the forthright Thomas could not honestly do so and did not wish to. A few months later occurred a joyous event. At the urging of Raymond Fosdick, now a trustee, Princeton offered Thomas an honorary degree, although Hibben was still president—a sign of the more favorable treatment he was getting in the press and of his acceptance into something approaching respectability. In Socialist circles he had always played down his Ivy League background as something antipathetic to proletarians. "Norman didn't know whether he should accept," Herling recalled. "He thought it might be considered too fancy-schmancy for the Party." When Fosdick, the kindliest of men, urged him to accept, Thomas argued that it would scarcely help him with the Party—a view showing his concern for his Party standing, since nothing trivial could have made him decline such a pleasing reconciliation with the college he loved. To this Fosdick replied that he had not urged it for Thomas's sake so much as for Princeton's. It would do the place good to recognize radicalism for a change. This, Fosdick thought, was the argument that won him over.

Violet accompanied him to the open-air ceremony, sitting in the audience while he joined the group on the stage. The function took place not far from Old Reunion, where he had lived during his junior and senior years a quarter-century earlier. Without question he was deeply moved. He watched while others were honored with degrees. Then he (and Violet) felt consternation when the president announced, "And finally, Benjamin Nathan Cardozo." He had passed over Thomas, who wrote of this:

> My wife, sitting in the audience under the trees, heard a neighboring lady
> say triumphantly to her friend: "There, I told you they'd never give *that*
> man a degree."

But the error was noticed at once and Thomas was invested with the hood of a Doctor of Letters. He said nothing about the degree to Party brethren, though he could scarcely quell his phenomenal smile. This smile, quick and dazzling, seemed to light up a room. It was described variously as a million-dollar smile, a thousand-watt smile or as something the beholder took in with his eyes and felt all the way down to his toes. Those who disliked him, such as Algernon Lee, thought it was a total fake and that he used it with calculation and for effect. Admiring co-workers said it was the most natural of smiles, that it was not overused and that he also had a potent frown. Thomas would have disputed the idea that there was anything deceptive in learning something of the art of public speaking, which was taught at all colleges and theological seminaries and included a reasonable control of facial expression along with the wave of the arm, the pointed finger and the crouch of the body in aid of the voice. A speaker owed his audience some skill with his craft and also owed it to himself if he expected to drive home his points. An occasional smile built better rapport than a steady scowl, just as an endless grin would be cloying. He was, at forty-six, one of the most seasoned and skillful of speakers, but he still was nervous at the beginning of a speech, gaining complete confidence as he warmed up. His great success over radio argued no dependence on eye-catching props.

He was the parfit gentil knight to the staff of the League for Industrial Democracy, whose offices had been moved to 112 East Nineteenth Street in the same building where the City Affairs Committee was based, near Gramercy Park and only three blocks from Thomas's home. He was always called "Norman," never "Mr. Thomas," except by female younglings too shy for such familiarity. He called them by their first names. The people there, who were all underpaid and overworked, did not bewail their lot because they had jobs in this time of joblessness, they were workers for a cause and they knew that he was also underpaid and overworked. He worked with the intensity of a man who can never catch up and was said to be able to do two things at once—for example, to polish off his weekly piece for The New Leader while he carried on telephone conversations. He dictated letters at high speed, often while pacing the floor with the pretty stenographer Hattie Ross trotting alongside him with her notebook. One day he arrived bubbling after he and Violet had gone to the theater—a rarity for them—and had seen the Gershwin-Kaufman-Ryskind musical comedy "Of Thee I Sing."

"We'll all go together, at office expense," he said.

He and Violet escorted the LID and City Affairs Committee workers to the Music Box Theater and saw it a second time themselves. Thomas's booming laughter was audible all over the house. For days thereafter the two offices rang with whistled renditions of "Wintergreen for President" and "Posterity Is Just Around the Corner," the latter held to be rich satire on Hoover's promises. But the Party was fated not to emulate John P. Wintergreen in campaigning on a platform of love.

### 3. Marx and Calvin

Hillquit was chieftain of a powerful party-within-the-Party—the New York local—which Thomas was convinced exercised an unhealthy sway over the national Party. Behind the New York local were the money and influence of Cahan and The Jewish Daily Forward, which also helped subsidize the Rand School, the Socialist radio station WEVD, the Party summer camp in the Poconos and the national Party itself. It even contributed enough to keep afloat the losing Milwaukee Leader, the only official Party paper of consequence west of New York. Among Hillquit's loyal lieutenants in addition to Waldman were the sixty-five-year-old, Dubuque-born Algernon Lee, for two decades director of the Rand School; the aging Julius Gerber, a sheet-metal-union leader long secretary of the New York City party; pipe-smoking, Indiana-born James Oneal, editor of The New Leader; Charles Solomon; and Judge Jacob Panken. The New York local leadership was largely composed of officials and members of, and lawyers for, the powerful American Federation of Labor needle-trade unions headed by David Dubinsky (born in Poland) and Sidney Hillman (born in Lithuania) and which had a defender in The Daily Forward (except for the occasional maverick Vladeck). Both Hillquit and Waldman often had unions as their clients. The local was relatively prosperous and inbred, composed largely of foreign-born or first-generation Americans, mostly Jewish, who still were more preoccupied with events in Vilna or Vienna, where they had relatives, than in Bangor or Broken Bow, and who tended to regard members west of the Hudson as hicks without understanding of Marx. Paul Blanshard felt that Local New York was so solidly Jewish that Thomas, as a goy, for all his racial impartiality, was at a crippling disadvantage.

Local New York, with its many branches stretching from the Bronx to the far reaches of Brooklyn and Staten Island, comprised some 16 percent of the total national membership but swung far more than 16 percent of the influence in the national Party. Its Old Guard leadership was concerned with local union problems to the detriment of its national overview, Thomas thought, so that money and solidarity rather than broad national policy supplied its power. He thought it shared the ideology, complacency and weaknesses which were even then leading the once-powerful Social Democrats of Germany into ruin at the hands of Hitler. Thomas, who got along well with Dubinsky but not with the autocratic Hillman, was unhappy about the union methods of the AFL —only a fraction of whose membership was Socialist—of which he later wrote, "Its leaders hated Communism and distrusted Socialism rather more than they hated or distrusted Wall Street." Thomas believed that the Russian Revolution would yet turn the economic corner that would enable it to stop its "transitional" tyranny (a term he used), and that American Communists might turn a similar corner and help the Socialists rather than hinder them. For this he was regarded with something like horror even by Old Guardsmen who admired him in other ways but who had more experience in dealing with Communists than he. For his part, he thought the Old Guard's loathing for Communism exaggerated, motivated less by principle than by the competition the AFL was getting from some Communist unions.

Thomas was far and away the top expert on Party affairs in all their aspects throughout the nation, friendly with leaders and members in virtually every state, aware of regional interests, opinions and bias. He had some reason to see himself as capable of installing a leadership that would draw the Party's elements together as Hillquit's group could not.

His difference with Hillquit came into the open when Hillquit served as counsel for the Standard Oil and Vacuum Oil companies in their lawsuits to regain oil lands which had been nationalized by Soviet Russia. The nationalization of such resources was a Socialist concept which Thomas earnestly hoped would come to pass in America. For Hillquit to challenge the principle in behalf of two giant American corporations so angered him that he created a sensation by criticizing Hillquit openly in his column in The New Leader. Indeed, criticism was so widespread in the Party that Hillquit ultimately withdrew from the case. Ideological differences, including Marxist purity but also including issues much beyond that, were at the center of the quarrel. Thomas admired Hillquit for sacrifices he had made for the Party, saying that he would surely have won a judgeship had he been willing to turn Democrat. But Thomas thought it ridiculous to allow the Party to be in bondage to nineteenth-century thought. He saw great principles in Marxism, which he felt should be modified pragmatically to fit current conditions. His article "Why Not a New Political Party?" did not portray one that would have suited Marx, and his second book in two years, *As I See It*, again was "full of the most awful heresies in Marxian theology," as Charney Vladeck, who generally praised it in his New Leader review, pointed out. Again Thomas was more critical of the American Federation of Labor than the local comrades thought permissible. He denigrated the ideas of class struggle and the economic interpretation of history, writing, "we cannot work in the laboratory of life as we work by scientific laws in chemistry," and "Let us not make Marxism a kind of slogan of salvation which men must accept in our precise formula before they can make Socialism the alternative to disaster." For the Old Guard's taste, he was also much too tolerant of the Soviets, writing, among other things, "Russia is disproving the fallacy of the necessity of the worship of the profit motive to make men work and work hard." For these and other heresies he was called up before a panel of three younger members appointed to examine him for correctness of theory. This interrogation—so characteristic of Socialist portentousness and perhaps in this instance a deliberate attempt to humiliate him—made Herling and other Thomas partisans seethe at the idea that such pipsqueaks should be considered capable of instructing him.

"It's unimportant," Thomas said to Herling, shrugging it off. But for him to be catechized on his Marxist orthodoxy he considered as pointless as the Presbyterian suspicions once felt about his view of the virgin birth. More important, he believed that Hillquit had reverted to thinking largely in terms of a labor party. In Thomas's opinion, the Party had held out so many inducements to labor for so long and with such uniform failure that new methods had to be tried. He now felt that labor would come in only on the heels of a great middle-class influx. He wanted the Socialist Party to be "inclusive"—a word he used often— inclusive enough to take in all good Marxists but to add also other deviating leftists and middle-class liberals plus new thousands of voters estranged from the old parties by the disastrous state of the country whether or not their conception of class struggle and production for use went by the book. The Republicans and Democrats were successful because millions of their voters had no idea what they were voting for. With the nation sinking into deeper distress with every week that passed, with banks closing and ten million Americans unemployed, and with neither the Hoover administration nor the Democrats in Congress offering any substantial relief, he thought it time to move Karl Marx to the rear of the Socialist display window and strike hard for a truly liberal, inclusive third party.

# NORMAN THOMAS

Hillquit, since the death of Victor Berger, was the grand old veteran of Socialism. In 1897, when he was only twenty-eight, he had led the conservative Socialists in revolt against the radical Daniel De Leon, and ever since had been a force in building up the Party. For three decades he had been its leading theorist and tactician, representing it also at the Socialist International, his prestige enhanced by three books which serious Socialists were supposed to own and read, *The History of Socialism in the United States* (1903), *Socialism in Theory and Practice* (1909) and *From Marx to Lenin* (1921). He was fluent in five languages, had a distinguished presence and a sense of humor and was an excellent speaker, particularly in New York where foreign accents could often be more of a political help than a hindrance. With radio now a large factor, some felt the airwaves unkind to him when they reached out of the city. He and Mrs. Hillquit and Thomas and Violet had mixed socially, friendly notes had passed between them, and the two men had worked together politically for more than a decade. There was respect between them but there was also more than the usual differences common to men of strong wills and beliefs. From the very beginning, before Thomas joined the Party in 1918, he had let Hillquit and Lee know that he was not an "organization man" and had reservations about being able to subscribe to "party discipline" and "coercion." He had been admitted despite all this and had never really become a conformist. He had gradually been placed by the Party hierarchy in an odd category all his own—a member at once suspect because of his divagations and valuable because of his energy, popularity and talents as a propagandist and candidate.

He was in line for the Presidential nomination again in 1932—something he wanted to undertake with a progressive political program and without being hobbled by a Party discipline which meant—not defeat, which was expected anyway, but the hindering of ultimate victory. The Old Guard for its part saw him as a good candidate but an impossible Party leader. He was considered a dreamer-idealist with his feet always somewhat above the ground. His clerical background, and that of some of his supporters—Paul Blanshard, Holmes, Niebuhr, Franz Daniel and others—was rather disdained. His popularity among young New York Party members, including many who thought the Old Guard archaic, underlined the suspicion that *he* thought them archaic. Although he was probably the best-informed member on current events, he was believed to be poorly read in Socialist literature. Unlike some who had been virtually born into the Party, he had not joined until he was

131

thirty-four and had risen too fast for the conservative. Hillquit and Lee had been working Socialists when Thomas was still in knee pants. He knew no trade, had no calluses. His wife had never seen a sweatshop nor manned a picket line. His talent for speaking instantly and persuasively on almost any subject had plenty of admirers, but there were also those who said that Thomas was too fond of the sound of his own voice.

His peculiar Party status, of being at once accepted and suspected, could only continue unchanged so long as he did not challenge the top leadership and seek to institutionalize his heresies, which he was now about to do.

## 4. Sewer Socialists

When the Party met for its 1932 national convention in Milwaukee, the Thomas group had more delegate strength than Hillquit, including support from Centrists and Militants and from one highly influential member the Old Guard took for granted as an ally, Vladeck of The Forward. Thomas's intention was to remove Hillquit from the Party chairmanship, do him honor for his long service and elect him to the National Executive Committee. His place as chairman would be taken by fifty-year-old Daniel W. Hoan, a University of Wisconsin graduate and attorney who had served for sixteen years running as Mayor of Milwaukee and had compiled a splendid record of honest and efficient city government. Hoan had another important qualification: His neutral status was unblemished, for he had avoided involvement in the Militant–Old Guard quarrel. He had crossed swords with Hillquit while working under him during the 1924 campaign and found him "woefully weak on matters of organizational tactics," but refused to run for the chairmanship until Thomas convinced him that only he could beat Hillquit.

The Hillquit forces knew they were in for a battle. The fickle vagaries of politics were illustrated by the apparently minor error that defeated Thomas. That even his factional foes recognized him as the only viable Presidential candidate was shown when he was placed in nomination by Old Guardsman Waldman and won without a fight, Maurer being again his running mate. But Hillquit was in no mood to be retired, and a rancorous struggle broke out when Hoan was nominated for the chairmanship by Heywood Broun, then a Party member, and by William Quick, a Milwaukee delegate. Quick, in extolling Hoan, spoke of the need for an "American" chairman. As a politician who surely sought not to lose but to win votes, it seemed that what Quick meant was Hoan's advantage of unaccented speech, Wisconsin birth and location in mid-America, in view of the known bias of many western Socialists against New York. Hillquit's followers, however, immediately inferred that Quick's meaning was not only nativist but anti-Semitic. Quick later swore to Thomas that this was furthest from his meaning. But the dispute made the front page of The New York Times, which said the convention was "rent asunder in one of the most bitter factional battles in the history of American Socialism"—hardly an exaggeration when Waldman, Solomon and Lee all charged Thomas with bringing race and sectionalism into the Party under the guise of Americanism, and with trying to "destroy 'orthodox' Socialism in the United States."

As Thomas later put it, "Once the anti-Semitic issue was raised, even though unjustly, I was inclined to think it best that Hillquit won." Hillquit, the resourceful attorney, rode the point rather hard in his speech: "I apologize for being born abroad, for being a Jew, and living in New York." He was reelected chairman 108–81, although the greater strength of the Thomas faction was shown when it elected a majority to the National Executive Committee (including Thomas himself for the first time) and hence won nominal control of Party machinery. The New Leader sought to paper over the dissension with a photograph of Thomas covering its entire front page and a story of the convention headed "Socialists! to the Battle!" which made no mention of the anti-Semitism issue and soft-pedaled Hillquit's angry speech in which he criticized Thomas's deviations from Marxism and the provincial Hoan-Milwaukee brand of Socialism which consisted of "providing clean sewers" for the city. The underlying anger was better shown by the treatment of Vladeck, who was thereafter regarded by many in the Old Guard as a traitor. He was privately censured by his employer, the association holding ownership of The Jewish Daily Forward, and the hot-blooded Abraham Cahan never spoke to him again as long as he lived although they worked in the same building and met repeatedly.

## 5. War on Poverty

So the Party was quarreling internally as it fought the 1932 election. Hillquit, a generous mediator, labored for unity but failed. Rumors spread that Thomas, a man remarkably free from racial bias, was anti-

Semitic. National Secretary Senior slaved with his small staff for solidarity and sent out streams of campaign literature. Thomas's fear of a Fascist takeover was so real that he thought someone like Huey Long might have tried it already but for the difficulties imposed by the sprawling size of the country. The Socialist Party now claimed 25,000 members, probably an inflated estimate, triple the 1928 number. There were almost 1,600 Socialist locals in the United States—a number, however, disclosing that many locals had only a dozen or so members. In some states, including important Illinois and Ohio, reactionary legislators had framed laws making it difficult for candidates to get on the ballot, so that Socialists could not vote for Socialist candidates.

Thomas was forty-seven, in his prime, his silvery hair receding, his blue eyes alternately benign and fiery, his clothes usually baggy. He had scrupulously told Brooks Brothers that he was no longer a clergyman but they nevertheless insisted on giving him the same discount even though he was so irregular in getting his suits pressed that he seldom made a good advertisement for them. Violet, successful in her kennel enterprise, had astonished everyone by opening a restaurant in a building she owned at 71 Irving Place, a block south of Gramercy Park. Their children were growing. Nineteen-year-old William, after a whirl at college, worked for a power company; eighteen-year-old Polly had finished her second year at Vassar and, being in love with a Yale man, had taken a salesclerk's job at Gimbel's pending her marriage; Frances, now seventeen, worked in her mother's restaurant and was to enter Barnard College in the fall; fourteen-year-old Becky was on vacation from Milton Academy as was twelve-year-old Evan from Edgewood School. They all firmly preferred the pleasures of midsummer Long Island when Thomas attended a gathering of 15,000 Socialists at Ulmer Park in Brooklyn. There was band music and a free show by Broadway performers while Socialist families ate picnic lunches, then heard Louis Waldman, who was running for Governor, and finally the principal speaker, Thomas. There were, he said, between ten and twelve million unemployed in the nation—200,000 in New York City alone without either work or relief:

> Men and women search the garbage cans . . . competing with rats and stray cats. . . . That's how the celebrated law of supply and demand works under capitalism. . . . Next winter [may see] a complete breakdown, made more terrible by riots and actual starvation.
>
> No hope? No hope unless we declare war on poverty with the energy

with which we warred on Germany. No hope, unless we seek to repeal unemployment with a hundred times the fervor and intelligence men seek to repeal the discredited 18th Amendment. . . .

Here is where our Socialist plan begins. . . . We intend to subsidize consumption instead of letting the subsidies all go to producers seeking profit. . . . The Federal government should grant emergency subsidies to unemployed families on a weekly basis. . . . We must begin to think in terms of ten billions. . . . The next great Socialist principle is the five-day week. . . . A system of unemployment insurance must be set up. . . . There is no conceivable physical reason why every American family should not be well fed, well clothed, well housed, possessing its own radio and automobile and, above all, free from that dread fear of tomorrow which is the tyrant of our waking and sleeping hours.

The Party platform, which Thomas had a large part in shaping, favored public works, a shorter work week, agricultural relief, unemployment insurance, the elimination of child labor, old-age pensions, slum clearance, low-cost housing, higher taxes on corporations and the wealthy, and the nationalization of basic industries—all Socialist measures which capitalist America would condemn but would ultimately adopt, every one but the last.

The Old Guard, controlling the city and state machinery, gave its money and enthusiasm to Hillquit's candidacy for Mayor and Waldman's for Governor. It complained about the employment of two Militants, Mary Hillyer and Amicus Most, in the national office for campaign work. Although the state organization did little for Thomas, it objected sharply when the national campaign committee organized a Thomas-for-President committee in the state. Thomas had and needed badly the support of the League for Independent Political Action, which had its nonpartisan Thomas office in the same Nineteenth Street building as the League for Industrial Democracy, sponsored by such men as Douglas, Niebuhr and Villard and operated by Mary Fox, a Vassar-educated LID worker. Times were so hard (and the Old Guard so close-fisted) that Thomas had to make do with $26,000 in campaign money collected by the Party—barely more than a quarter of its 1928 fund—plus $17,000 collected by the independents. It was, as always, small change compared with the millions spent by the two big parties even in that time of hardship, nor did Thomas have any Gus Claessenses or McAlister Colemans as aides. He electioneered across the country usually alone. Though he had to watch every dollar, he nevertheless splurged on a dashing campaign photograph taken by Pirie Macdonald. His crowds were huge. Instead of a few hundred at meetings, he had thousands. More than 20,000 packed the new Madison Square Garden (no longer on Madison Square) to hear him, 14,000 heard him in Milwaukee and great throngs in Hartford, Indianapolis, Los Angeles and elsewhere. In Philadelphia, Republican city officials forbade Thomas and Maurer to speak at Rayburn Plaza on the pretext that only educational meetings were permitted there—an obvious discrimination, since Hoover was scheduled to speak there. The Socialist Party announced that "Professors Thomas and Maurer" would lecture to classes in history and politics, and the city fathers were ashamed enough to withdraw the ban. Violet often accompanied Thomas on the shorter tours, advising him on audience reaction (including her own) to his speeches and deprecating his habit of leaving things behind him. ("Norman is being demagogic about Hoover," she noted during one address.) On one occasion Frances was with them in their car in New York State and drew a sharp rebuke from her father on discovering that she had left her coat at the previous night's hotel, his reproof fading when he found that he had left his watch there and had to turn back anyway.

As always, his speeches came to grips with current issues which his opponents evaded with generalities. He appealed both to the intellect and the sense of humor.* He hammered at the Democratic-Republican sameness and the absence of choice, saying the two parties were "merely glass bottles with different labels, and both of them empty of any medicine for the sickness of our times." Thomas was endorsed by forty-six Harvard faculty members, had strong support at colleges all over the country, and was actually praised by Vanity Fair ("his leadership has brought new vigor and dignity to the Socialist Party"), The Christian Science Monitor and Christian Century. A Literary Digest poll predicted two million votes for him. Most flattering of all was his appearance on the cover of that cheeky magazine Time, run by another man of churchly Presbyterian background, Henry Robinson Luce, accompanied by a story so largely fair and complimentary that it may have been what started Thomas as a regular reader of Time.

Possessing an indestructible vocal mechanism, he often spoke five

---

*I heard Thomas at the University of Minnesota that fall. He bounded to the rostrum and spoke with a vigor, fluency, conviction and charisma that lingers in my memory forty-four years later. I was a Socialist at the time, but Thomas may have got my vote even had he been a Bolshevist or Falangist.—Author.

times a day every day in the week. Since he had to compete with Roosevelt for voters protesting against Hoover, he trained most of his guns on the former, at whom he was indignant anyway over his expedient delay in removing the discredited Mayor Walker. Thomas's thrift was unpresidential. With Violet he campaigned by automobile through New England for ten days at a total cost of $55.45—lodging and meals, $16.20; ferry charges and tolls, $6.25; gasoline and oil, $22.65; repairs and grease, $4.85; public stenographer, $4.00; and incidentals, $1.50. He would have been satisfied to fulfill the *Digest's* prediction of two million votes. If his crowds were good, there were also disturbing signs—too many people like the woman in San Francisco who told him she agreed with everything he said: "But . . . I'm not going to vote for you. This year we've got to get that man," meaning Hoover.

Late in October he returned on a day coach from a thirty-eight-state speaking tour and was delighted to be met at Pennsylvania Station by Violet, his son William and daughter Frances, and 2,000 Socialists, Yipsels and Thomas-for-President collegians from Columbia, New York University and City College. They cheered him, surged about him and sang, then followed him to the Nineteenth Street building, where he mounted a big packing case and spoke. He predicted a good Socialist vote, "probably the best we ever got. . . . And I believe that if we keep it up, and I think we will, we'll have a pretty big delegation in Congress two years from now."

Again, disappointment. In the Roosevelt landslide of almost 23 million votes and Hoover's more than 15 million, Thomas polled only 884,781. Nor was a single Socialist Congressman elected.


### 6. Do You Really Believe?

To admirers who told him it was better to be right than President, Thomas always replied, "I am quite willing to be both." In an election statement he declared that Roosevelt obviously had got the entire anti-Hoover vote and added, "This tendency of the human herd to stampede in order to express not its hopes and plans but its hates is a terrible danger to democracy." But he saw hope for the Congressional elections of 1934 if the Party could hold and increase its influx of young people. He had only to compare the vote he got in the Old Guard stronghold of New York City (122,565) to Hillquit's stupendous vote for Mayor

(251,656, a Socialist record) to realize that if the Old Guard had not precisely sabotaged him there, they had scarcely helped him. The anti-Semitic talk had done him no good. His national vote had been cut, too, because of the three states (Oklahoma, Louisiana and Florida) in which the Party had been unable to get on the ballot, and because of the notorious laxity of pollworkers elsewhere who often did not bother to tally Socialist votes. One encouragement was the fact that after the election the Socialist membership, instead of slumping, kept up a modest but steady climb—a paradox Senior laid to Thomas's impression on listeners during the campaign.

Thomas was confident that the half-measures Roosevelt could be expected to use—he had promised to balance the budget—would fail to save the nation. He decided that in 1933, for the first time in nine years, he would not run for anything, even keeper of the pound. ". . . If the unusual makes news," he wrote, "it ought to be news that this year I am not a candidate for anything." He wanted to travel, to learn, to think, to write. He wanted to visit Russia to see if some inspiration for administrative efficiency could be found there. A left-wing politician was hardly in the swim if he had not glimpsed the Kremlin with his own eyes, but Thomas's curiosity was vast and genuine. This would take money. The Thomases had children to educate, their living expenses were high and Violet's kennel and restaurant enterprises testified not only to her lively nature but also to the fact that the money would come in handy.

Despite Thomas's busyness he had kept in touch with Sidney Lovett in Boston, Ralph Harlow at Smith College and Charles Gilkey, now dean of the chapel at the University of Chicago. Harlow was a confirmed Socialist, Gilkey a League for Industrial Democracy board member and Lovett was, at any rate, still a pacifist. Thomas and Violet were delighted that Lovett, who had remarried, was now back at nearby New Haven as chaplain at Yale, and Thomas had a date with Gilkey to speak at his chapel in December. Gilkey urged him to bring Violet, who had half promised to come: "I do hope there will be time for a good walk and talk such as we had last time . . ."

Gilkey wrote this although, as a staunch believer, he felt that Thomas had been in religious confusion since leaving the church. Thomas, on his part, thought the illogic of transcendental religion so evident that it was his opinion (substantiated by some specific cases) that many clergymen ultimately became unbelievers but continued in the pulpit because their congregations "needed" religion and it made a comfortable living for ministers past the age when a new career could easily be undertaken—a personal revolution Thomas himself had achieved. Gilkey thought Thomas basically religious, and yet Thomas and Violet had asked him a few careful, friendly questions which came down to: Do you still really believe?

# VIII

## 1. Pink Tea for Pink Socialists

On Roosevelt's inauguration day, Thomas and Violet were the guests in Chapel Hill of President Frank P. Graham of the University of North Carolina, where Thomas had addressed a student audience. Both Graham and Thomas were impressed by the new President's speech, which promised at least some of the decisive action which Thomas had demanded. On March 14, 1933, Thomas and Morris Hillquit were greeted by Roosevelt in the White House with a geniality not usually accorded Socialists. Both had met him in Albany, had followed his career and found little in it to prepare them for his bold step in closing the banks. They urged on him a $12-billion bond issue for relief and public works as well as the nationalization of the banks he had closed, were given an attentive hearing though not entire agreement, and left well impressed. As weeks went on, Thomas, to his own surprise, was enthusiastic about most of Roosevelt's program which, he said, "far more nearly resembled the Socialist . . . than his own [Democratic] platform."

Thomas was the leading speaker at that annual occasion for Marxist muscle-flexing, May Day, with David Dubinsky as grand marshal of the great parade that wound through the Seventh Avenue garment district before homing on Union Square, a dozen bands joining in playing the International. Some 30,000 were said to be there, and their combined singing voices shook the windows of surrounding buildings:

*It is the Final Conflict;*
*Let each stand in his place.*
*The International Party*
*Shall be the human race!*

Socialists who did not attend with their families and as many friends as possible were considered slackers. The turnout, which included many workers who were not Party members, was a measure of Socialist success in the rivalry with the Communists. It was watched narrowly for annual increase and attendance was always exaggerated by the faithful. The two parties had agreed to avoid skirmishes by keeping their celebrations separate, the Socialists taking over Union Square until 3:30, then clearing out for the arrival of the Communists at 4:00. The Socialist crowd was easily the larger. Thomas, asked about the united front the Communists were beginning to urge, gave a reply that would become standard and which was condemned by the Old Guard, whose answer was always a sharp No: "The basis for any united front is good faith, isn't it? The Communists don't seem to have displayed much good faith in the past."

He sent identical letters to Scribner's and Harper's magazines, The Forum, Collier's Weekly and the Scripps-Howard newspapers inquiring if they would be interested in articles about Russia. Although, he said, he realized the limitations of the six-week tour he planned for the summer, he would be accompanied by a man (whom he did not identify) who was born in Russia, had been there recently and spoke the language well: "We shall go off the beaten highways and I think my impressions as an American Socialist, not a Communist, disposed to be friendly but by no means uncritically friendly of Russia might have a certain value."

Both Scribner's and Harper's expressed interest. The theft of fifty Plymouth Rock hens from his Cold Spring Harbor coops made him that much poorer and Moscow that much more distant. But either he was not granted a visa—a good possibility in view of the American Communists' enmity toward him—or some other hitch developed, for there was no tour of Russia that summer. Instead, the travel-loving Thomas planned a cross-country tour with Violet in the fall which would enable him to give lectures as he saw how the country reacted to the Roosevelt measures. Through his New York agent, the Socialist Roxanna Wells, and another in Los Angeles, he arranged lectures beginning in Cleveland and continuing all the way across the country to California. Meanwhile his brother Arthur lost his textile job because of the depression and moved with his family to York, Pennsylvania, where he became a relief specialist as head of the Family Service Bureau there. Arthur, who was pleased at Roosevelt's beginning, had heard from that capitalist benefactor of all the Thomases, Uncle Frank Welles in Paris. Uncle

Frank agreed that it might be necessary to give Roosevelt credit for good intentions, with which the road to hell was said to be paved, but: "Whenever a Socialist experiment breaks down, as they all do in the end, there is an immediate and automatic return to capitalism, the only practicable working basis, as human nature is constituted." Arthur sent a copy of the letter to Norman, who replied equably:

> It is an excellent statement of the position of a thoughtful conservative, and it has a certain weight even with Socialists like myself. . . . In general I think that Uncle Frank wants to do what the march of events makes impossible: namely, to keep a laissez faire economic order which has already committed a virtual suicide.

But blows, problems and irritations harassed him. He was badly hurt that summer by the resignation of Paul Blanshard from the Party. Blanshard had toured Germany, heard the fanatical Nazi orations, seen the Hitler youth and the anti-Semitism. He was shocked into the reflection that the Socialist Party, which with a fine candidate in 1932 had got only 2.5 percent of the vote, was "too feeble an instrument for dealing with such a threat as Hitler." There was a special affection between Thomas and Blanshard, who in his autobiography would recall Thomas as "the noblest human being I had ever known . . . never mean or unfair or petty." In his announcement that he would support La Guardia for Mayor, Blanshard paid tribute to Thomas, for which the latter thanked him but wrote, "In some ways . . . that makes your repudiation of the Party more devastating . . ."

Mary Hillyer, a handsome native of Topeka who had moved from Young Women's Christian Association work to Socialism and who organized Thomas's lecture tours for the League for Industrial Democracy, was such a loyalist that she would scarcely speak to Blanshard after his defection. Later she became his wife. Thomas also disagreed with John Haynes Holmes, an admirer of La Guardia, who thought the Socialist Party should join the fusion movement and help elect an honest Mayor instead of running its own token candidate. But La Guardia had Republican backing, about which Thomas commented: "Whatever may be true about individual Republicans, the party as a whole is worse than Tammany in the sense in which a jackal is worse than a tiger." A reminder of the Socialist Party's internal wrangling came from the young Militant Amicus Most, who urged that the Party should maintain more rigorous discipline over the somewhat lordly Old Guard. Thomas replied:

. . . it is emphatically bad theory and bad tactics for the Socialist Party to try to emulate the Communists in the severity of its discipline in matters of detail. . . . To be perfectly frank, for a party doing as badly as ours is now . . . to enforce a rigorous conformity . . . would simply disrupt the Party and lose our immensely valuable members.

He was embarrassed because two girl waitresses who did not meet Violet's standards at her tea room and were fired, were "reached" five weeks later by the Communists, who spun the incident into a two-part drama of capitalist oppression of the working class in The Daily Worker. "Mrs. Norman Thomas," it began, "owns an exclusive tea room for select persons at 71 Irving Pl. Here she serves pink tea to pink Socialists." The Worker gave it a four-column headline, "Mrs. Norman Thomas Fires 2 Workers," and devoted some 3,000 words in two issues to her high social station, her utter cruelty and the bleak future confronting the two girls, "facing the winter without food or lodging, in a strange city, with no friends. . . ." They had, however, found warm friends among the Communists, for the story ended:

Workers are asking themselves many questions about . . . the "Socialist Party." These questions give them only one answer. The answer that Louise and Frances Dunlap found—aligning themselves with the militant workingclass movement under the leadership of the Communist Party.

This was bad Party publicity. Violet, still not breaking even in the enterprise, had to explain the situation to Julius Gerber. More pleasing to Thomas was a letter from the S. Wrens of Massillon, Ohio, who had heard him speak there in 1932 and had named their recently born only son Norman Thomas Wren; and one from Mrs. H. G. Showers of Reading, Pennsylvania, whose son, though born on Columbus Day, was named Norman Thomas Showers. Thomas, rushing to complete his affairs so he could get off for the West with Violet, left little signs on his trail such as an unexplained voucher in his records showing that he paid $2.70 to the Bowery Branch YMCA for nine meals for one James Brown. He was irked because he gave so much of his time to the Socialist Party that some Party people expected all of his time. He wrote the Party secretary in California:

Given the necessity I am under to earn my daily bread, I have done the best I can for the Socialists of California. . . . I give far more time to free speaking for the Party than to paid speaking in the course of a year. . . .

Both he and Violet were eager to visit their old friends the Darrs, now in Claremont, California, where Darr taught religion at Scripps College —another religionist who still believed. Thomas was to speak at Scripps but his schedule was already so tight that he and Violet would have time only for dinner with the Darrs before they left for Denver. The day before they were to leave New York, Thomas was at City Hall with the Citizens' Committee on Unemployment, asking the Mayor for relief funds more than just "enough . . . to keep us from being shocked by seeing the unemployed die of starvation in our streets." The Thomases got away October 7. After speaking in Detroit on the ninth, Thomas got word that Morris Hillquit had died in New York. He telegraphed to Herling a statement for the press commenting magnanimously on Hillquit's career and ending ministerially, "IT IS FOR US TO CARRY ON THE STRUGGLE FOR THE GLORIOUS END FOR WHICH HE GAVE HIMSELF SO GENEROUSLY."

He and Violet went on to Chicago, where he hoped for time to attend the Century of Progress exposition held ironically when progress seemed to be retrogressing. (In Chicago, too, Thomas always telephoned Gilkey if he did not have time to visit him.) But while lecturing, he found it hard to refuse on-the-spot requests to address another group at lunch or in the afternoon or evening, so that often a one-speech stop would become a hectic race from one engagement to another—what his New York colleagues came to know as the Thomas Track Meet. It does not appear from the records that the Thomases got to the exposition. They traveled west and spent nine days in California, where Thomas debated with Lincoln Steffens in San Francisco, talked with Tom Mooney at San Quentin Prison, dined with President Robert G. Sproul of the University of California at Berkeley, noted the poverty and peonage of the migratory workers in the San Joaquin Valley, and ran a "track meet" among dozens of Socialist meetings where he spoke free, and non-Socialist ones where the fee was usually no more than $100. (He avoided one Lions' Club meeting where he did not want to speak by asking a $200 fee.) He lunched in Los Angeles with John C. Packard, head of the state Socialist Party, and, amid a blizzard of engagements, saw the Darrs and talked with their friend Jerry Voorhis, a Socialist of San Dimas who later suffered political injury at the hands of Richard Nixon. Voorhis felt the condition of the Party in California to be "nothing short of deplorable" and was worried, as was Thomas, because the Socialist Upton Sinclair had just made the startling announcement that he would seek the *Democratic* nomination for Governor on a "Socialist platform"—as if a Presbyterian were seeking an alliance with Cistercians.

Sinclair's move—which he had made despite Thomas's strong advice against it in earlier correspondence—was, like the Blanshard resignation and the Holmes stand on La Guardia, another sign of Socialist despair, confusion or splintering in the face of national problems and political alignments never encountered before. Still another came to Thomas's attention in Denver, where the loyal state Socialist leader, the attorney Carle Whitehead, and other local members were so attracted by Howard Scott's claims for Technocracy that they urged the Party to support Technocracy. Technocracy had suddenly become a national craze, discussed in the newspapers and magazines, and Thomas was deeply suspicious of it. Whitehead brought another item to his attention: One of the attractions of the Fanchon & Marco vaudeville offerings was a group of black musicians called the Norman Thomas Quintette. Were they not capitalizing on his name, and should he not take legal steps? Thomas replied:

> I think that there really is a Norman Thomas who has that Quintette. Anyway, he has been using the name so long that he is entitled to it. I have had some amusing experiences about the aforesaid aggregation. Unfortunately I have never heard them in action but I understand they are pretty good.

### 2. Educating and Laying Foundations

The Thomases returned to New York in time to vote for the Old Guard Socialist candidate for Mayor, Charles Solomon, one of the ousted five Socialist Assemblymen of 1920. In the La Guardia victory that gave the city honest government for the first time in years, Solomon polled only 63,450 votes. Obviously many Socialists had voted for La Guardia, as if responding to Dr. Holmes's earlier urging that the Party join the La Guardia fusion. Thomas declined La Guardia's telephoned offer of a city post—unspecified but sure to be important. Blanshard became Commissioner of Accounts and several Socialists accepted La Guardia jobs at the same time as other Socialists became supporters of the New Deal.

"[The vote] was the worst we have had for years," Thomas wrote Senior in Chicago, "and raises very serious questions of our future."

He was alternately punched on the nose and patted on the back, for his admirers were warm. "Don't give up your missionary work whatever the discouragement," a pair of them wrote. "You are educating the people and laying foundations. We are grateful to you in your self-sacrificing Herculean labors. Enclosed find $100 for what you will. . . ."

He had indeed been trying to educate people and lay foundations ever since that momentous Palm Sunday sermon at Brick Church when he inveighed against the Napoleonic idea of religion. He had sought to educate people and lay foundations for seven years in East Harlem. And he had tried to educate people and lay foundations with larger audiences since he joined the Party in 1918. His hundreds of League for Industrial Democracy speeches over the years to many tens of thousands of collegians had aimed at laying foundations, but where were those collegians now? And his political campaign speeches to millions of listeners all over the country in person and by radio had been intended as educative.

What had become of all that education and foundation-laying? He knew much of the answer. At the very moment when the disruption of the capitalist system should have paved the way for Socialism, along came Franklin D. Roosevelt, Fiorello La Guardia and Upton Sinclair—all men of ability, charm and principle—to give the old order oxygen just as it seemed about to breathe its last. And it appeared that one of those warm and inspiriting Roosevelt fireside chats, reaching virtually everybody in the country with the full prestige of the White House behind it, could undo years of Thomas education and foundation-laying. Even so it was a time of confusion, with Roosevelt and the old order still in doubt and being attacked or importuned by other educators and foundation-layers—Huey Long, Father Coughlin, Dr. Townsend, Technocrats, Minute Men, Silver Shirts and shirts of other hues.

But it was discouraging, for example, to see Dr. Francis E. Townsend, unheard of before 1933, gather millions of followers in the space of a few months through his plan which offered $200 a month to people over sixty. The Socialist Party, by dint of years of effort, had advanced to 18,548 paid-up members in 1933 and was disintegrating in disaffection and fratricidal warfare.

### 3. *The Gathering Storm*

The graduation of Evan Thomas from medical school at forty-two had been a great event of 1933. Though he specialized in syphilology, a subject that made Violet wrinkle her nose, it was nevertheless reassuring to have a doctor in the household (or at nearby Bellevue Hospital where he interned) against her heart attacks. Evan's failure to become a Socialist was forgiven on the score of his general benevolence, liberalism and absolute pacifism. Perhaps once a year he would go with Violet and Norman to a Princeton football game, at which the diminutive Violet would astonish nearby spectators by shrieking, "Kill him!" and Norman would drop all pretense of the dignity of a two-time Presidential candidate and a Litt.D. The Thomas place kept the servants busy, what with a half-dozen cockers underfoot and the children bringing friends home from college for weekends. Its use as a hotel for relatives visiting New York and for the Socialist Party added to the commotion. Clarence Senior and his wife were among the many who, arriving on Party errands, saved the Party money by putting up at the Eighteenth Street house. The Thomas girls were not afraid of "menial" work, Polly still clerking at Gimbel's and finding it absorbing and Frances waiting on tables at her mother's restaurant in her spare time. A regular patron was young John W. Gates, a Tennessean and recent Princeton graduate, now working for the Bank of Manhattan. When he and Frances began dating, Thomas disapproved because a banker, even with a Princeton background, was a barnacle on society. (Thomas had recently urged the Board of Estimate to increase a $5-million bond issue for relief of the unemployed to $15 million and, on being told it was hard enough to float the smaller issue, replied, "You have been dictated to by the bankers. It is time for you to dictate to the bankers now.")

Violet tried a New York dog-training academy by enrolling one of her cockers there and was indisposed when the training period was finished, so Thomas drove over to get the animal. He discovered that he was attending a graduating exercise for a whole troupe of dogs of various breeds. He and the other owners were required to walk around in a circle, holding leashes while the dogs demonstrated their training, after which the headmistress of the school said, "Mr. Thomas, would you mind giving the commencement address?" He had given many such addresses at high schools and colleges and could go along with a joke. To the assembled well-brushed canines more than to their owners he gave one of his shorter speeches, urging on them dogged effort to attain their ideals, warning them against barking up the wrong tree, congratulating them on their renunciation of private property and wishing them all a doggone good life.

He needed an occasional flight of fancy, for the Party was scarcely a happy family. After Hillquit's death, the Old Guard was so fearful that Thomas might seek the post of national chairman that they urged Hoan (whose "sewer Socialism" they had derided) to bid for it. Hoan was not interested, nor was Thomas, and Leo Krzycki of Milwaukee was elected although he was farther to the left than either Thomas or Hoan. Krzycki (pronounced Krisky), a vice president and organizer for Sidney Hillman's Amalgamated Clothing Workers and a former Milwaukee undersheriff, was called a "pet Pole" by those who saw union or political advantage in his ethnic background. To the Old Guard, who did not forget the Polish record of anti-Semitism, he was satisfactory only because of their anxiety to exclude Thomas. When President Roosevelt recognized Soviet Russia, Krzycki made a public statement applauding the Soviets so enthusiastically that it infuriated the Old Guard and even took Thomas aback:

> . . . The next step that must follow government recognition [is recognition] by the American people of the Russian ideal—an economic order without private profit. In 15 years Russia has built herself up from a weak and poverty-stricken nation to a strong and prosperous one by concentrating on one principle—the elimination of private profit. . . . Because their electorate was uneducated and untrained in democratic methods, they had to exercise that control not only against the dispossessed aristocracy, but against those members of the working class who had not enough vision to understand what they were doing. . . .

Thomas wrote Senior:

> The picture of wellbeing in Russia is overdone. . . . Much more serious . . . is the statement that Russian leaders had to exercise a control not necessary in America "against those members of the working class who had not enough vision to understand what they were doing." The average man in the street or in the factory is bound to think that this is not merely a justification of dictatorship in Russia but of the extraordinary terror which unquestionably has been directed against Russian radicals. . . . We are on mighty dangerous ground when we give that impression.

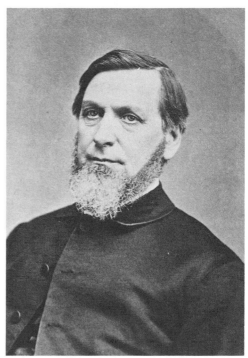

1. Grandmother Mary Mattoon sowed
Christianity in Siam starting in 1848.

2. Grandfather Stephen Mattoon served
as missionary and consul in Bangkok.

3. Norman Thomas's birthplace in Marion, Ohio. As a boy he milked the cow, delivered Warren Harding's newspaper and read avidly.

4. Norman was puny at age seven.

5. At age fourteen, still skinny.

6. The whole family—Emma and Welling Thomas with (*from left*) Emma and Agnes, and Arthur, Ralph, Norman and Evan. The latter four added up to twenty-five feet.

7. Norman Thomas rides Chinese rickshaw during world tour in 1907, aged twenty-three. White mistreatment of Asiatics appalled him.

8. Going to college, not yet—

9. —acquainted with Violet.

10. John Aikman Stewart (at age 101) knew Lincoln, Cleveland and Wilson.

11. Thomas would ever remain ambivalent about Woodrow Wilson (shown at Princeton with Andrew Carnegie).

*Left and opposite.*
12. Handsome Brick Church, a temple for the wealthy, offered Thomas a brilliant and comfortable clerical career. But he declined the prestige and silk hats of Fifth Avenue and accepted a parish in a slum area.

13. Charles W. Gilkey sent Thomas news of Socialism while in Europe.

14. Sidney Lovett helped Thomas deal with Harlem poverty and crime.

15. A. J. Muste, often a Thomas collaborator for more than fifty years.

16. H. Roswell Bates gave Thomas his first experience in slum church work.

17. Morris Hillquit, whom Thomas set out to oust as the Socialist chairman.

18. Louis Waldman, Hillquit's ally, looked on Thomas as a Party traitor.

19. Eugene Debs had become more a Socialist saint than a Party leader.

20. Upton Sinclair galled Thomas by running in California as a Democrat.

21. Abraham Cahan and his Jewish paper were the Party's bread and butter.

22. B. Charney Vladeck won Cahan's enmity by joining Thomas's "treason."

23. Algernon Lee was sorry Thomas had ever been admitted to the Party.

24. James Oneal tried to heal wounds by getting Thomas named for the Senate.

25. 1932, Madison Square Garden, an applauding throng: it was Thomas's high-water mark as a Presidential candidate. The charisma, energy and political confidence so evident here were to be frustrated by growing Party factionalism and disaffection.

26. Dr. Townsend lured millions while Thomas's following steadily dwindled.

27. Max Eastman (*left*) turned leftward, later flipped, embraced capitalism.

28. Thomas thought Huey Long quite capable of launching a coup.

29. Jack Herling (*upper left*) and Mary Fox (*above*), firm Thomas workers, saw his party unity crumble. They later married.

30. Mary Hillyer upbraided Paul Blanshard (*shown with her*) when he quit Thomas to support La Guardia. She later married Blanshard. They remained lifelong Thomas friends.

31. Angelica Balabanoff had worked with the pre-Fascist Mussolini, then with Lenin until the revolution disillusioned her. She found in Thomas her ideal of political integrity.

32. The starvation and despair of the Great Depression triggered a Thomas drive for relief from the dapper Mayor Jimmy Walker (*right*). But Thomas's prescriptions were national in scope, and many were borrowed by Franklin D. Roosevelt.

33. May Day was the day when hostile Socialists and Communists paraded and fought as each sought to win labor members.

34. The fiery Elizabeth Gurley Flynn, always a Thomas friend whatever her politics.

35. Earl Browder did clever work in exacerbating the Thomas–Old Guard split.

36. Thomas joins in singing the International after his 1936 nomination for President in Cleveland—a campaign that ended in disaster. Mayor Daniel Hoan of Milwaukee is first man with moustache to left of the nominee's upraised arm.

37. Sidney Hillman was not one of Thomas's favorites.

38. David Dubinsky joined Hillman in the labor coup for Roosevelt that worsted Thomas.

39. In Arkansas, Thomas addresses sharecroppers whose rights were virtually nil until he helped them organize. His "man on the spot" was H. L. Mitchell (*right*), who endured manifold perils.

40. Thomas and Violet (*met by son William*) return from 1937 visit to eleven European countries including Stalin's Russia and warring Spain. While Thomas had sharp criticism for Russia, he still saw it as a bulwark against rising Fascism.

41. Louis Mayer works on Thomas sculpture which provided years of discussion.

42. Violet Thomas was dog fancier, architect, wit and victim of an ailing heart.

Thomas mended matters somewhat by joining Louis Waldman in a more politic message of congratulation to Roosevelt. If the injudicious Krzycki was nominal chairman, Thomas was the leader of the Party in prestige and authority everywhere but in his own city and state of New York, where the Old Guard and The Forward ruled. Here much of the authority of Hillquit had descended to the ingratiating but egotistical labor lawyer, Waldman, who was state Party chairman. Foremost among his allies were Algernon Lee, James Oneal and Julius Gerber. One difference, in which Thomas later admitted that the Old Guard was more nearly right than he—though, he felt, for the wrong reasons —was in their flat-out repudiation of Communism. They had had enough of Communists in New York or in Moscow. They barred absolutely any negotiation with them. Thomas, despite the invective the American Communists heaped on him—"Social Fascist sky pilot" and "sniveling, yellow Socialist faker" were two of their gentler epithets— wished to leave the door ajar for possible future cooperation. He was haunted by the failure of left-wingers to unite in Italy and Germany, clearing the way for Mussolini and Hitler.

His suspicions of the Old Guard's anti-Communist motivation held strong. He was not grappling with Communists on a day-by-day basis, and he perhaps underestimated the ferocity of the Communist raids on Dubinsky's International Ladies' Garment Workers' Union a few years earlier, but neither was he ignorant about the infighting in the unions. Because his honesty and fairness were universally known, he was often called on to mediate union disputes in New York. (He was even urged by Chicago union people to go there and solve the gang-style murder of Comrade G. Pippen of the Italian Bread Drivers' League.) In his investigations of the Taxi Drivers' Union, the Fur Workers' International, the Fancy Leather Workers, the Motion Picture Operators and others, he found that in many cases vicious and even racketeering practices in American Federation of Labor unions were winked at by the Old Guard or their union supporters while they denounced the same practices in Communist unions. Thomas protested against this to the city leadership without result. As a firm moralist, he thought the Old Guard–AFL–Daily Forward alliance was morally shaky.

On their part, the Old Guard thought Thomas still relatively innocent about the Communist policy of deliberate treachery, an incurable clergyman unfit for practical politics. His invasion of what they considered their own turf, New York, united them in resentment. Certainly his very articulateness burned them up. In 1934 he published his third book in three years, *The Choice Before Us,* all three giving his analyses of and solutions for current problems. His books, invariably gathering together inside one cover his thoughts expressed in speeches and articles, had received respectful attention in leading newspapers. That this Johnny-come-lately tinkerer with Marxism should regard himself—and should be regarded—as the spokesman for Socialism goes far to explain the vindictiveness felt by some old-timers like Lee.

The Old Guard saw National Secretary Senior as Thomas's "man" and sought vainly to have him fired. It was true that Senior agreed in most questions with Thomas, that they were personally friendly and carried on an extensive correspondence, and that Senior had the Westerner's objection to the tight and parochial New York knot of power. But he clearly had at heart the well-being of the Party all over the nation, and he came to doubt Thomas's wisdom in some matters. Another problem was the Old Guard's control of the Party's national organ, the weekly New Leader. It was edited by Oneal, assisted by the state committeeman, William Feigenbaum, in the Rand School building. It gave accounts of Party controversies which Thomas thought sometimes so biased that he withheld his weekly column, "Timely Topics," in protest; and in 1933 the National Executive Committee (now usually having a Thomas majority) ordered it to cease advertising itself as an official organ of the Party—an order the paper ignored.

Each side in this struggle had its own fortress and army. The Old Guard had long been entrenched at the Rand School at 7 East Fifteenth Street, off Union Square—the address also of the state headquarters headed by Waldman and the city Socialist Party headed by Gerber and Lee. Daily Forward and union functionaries manned its big guns. Thomas was dug in four blocks north and farther east of Fifth Avenue in the 112 East Nineteenth Street building, always known as "112." Laidler, his associate director of the League for Industrial Democracy, leaned toward him but tried to steer a middle course. The staff, composed of such people as Paul Porter, Mary Fox, Jack Herling and Mary Hillyer, were all firm Thomasites. (Porter, recently stricken by tuberculosis, had been taken in hand by Thomas's friend, Dr. Miller, and sent to the Trudeau sanitarium in the Adirondacks, most of his expenses being handled by a special fund drive Thomas started.) Violet's restaurant, known as the Tea Room, an attractive place with an open garden at the rear for summer use, was just around the corner from 112 and a spot where tactics were discussed over London broil or tomato and bacon sandwiches. The League was so largely dominated by Thomas that the Old Guard looked on it as a competing rather than a cooperating organization. If the Old Guard controlled the Daily Forward and New Leader, Thomas had his own propagandist aid in his speechmaking; his New Leader column (which still persisted though in unfriendly terrain); his frequent articles in The World Tomorrow which, though not officially a Socialist publication, had his fellow Socialists and friends Devere Allen, Reinhold Niebuhr and Kirby Page as editors; and his articles for The Nation and other publications.

The collision of the two factions would not have been so explosive but for a culminating event that brought real fright to American Socialists on top of the Italian and German disasters. This was the February 1934 uprising of the Austrian Socialists—the nation's biggest party—against the Fascist Chancellor Dollfuss, and Dollfuss's ruthless military crushing of the Socialists and installation of a dictatorship.

On February 16, while the battle in Vienna still raged (and while Thomas was on a speaking trip), the Socialist Party and a group of labor unions staged a great rally at Madison Square Garden to voice their solidarity with the Austrian workers. The New York Communists introduced 5,000 well-coached members into the crowd of 20,000. Scheduled speakers included Mayor La Guardia, David Dubinsky and Matthew Woll of the American Federation of Labor. When the chairman, Algernon Lee, opened the meeting, the Communists, led by Clarence Hathaway and Robert Minor, began organized booing and jeering. Socialist ushers tried to stop them. Fights broke out in the aisles. Speakers tried to make themselves heard but failed, and the fistfights spread as the clamor rose. "Chairs were flung from the balconies," The Times noted, "and shrieks of women, mingled with boos, yells and catcalls drowned out the voices of speakers on the platform." Hathaway, editor of The Daily Worker, mounted the platform in an effort to capture the meeting as the Communists chanted, "We want Hathaway!" The Socialists did *not* want Hathaway: "Several men leaped on Hathaway, struck him with fists and chairs, rushed him across the platform, and threw him over a railing to the floor." Others seized him there and propelled him, his face bleeding, out the door to Forty-ninth Street. Most of the twenty injured were Communists, but they succeeded at least in breaking up the rally, an action which for a time went out over the air—one of the most violent and unrehearsed of radio broadcasts.

"New York learned at first hand how it was that Hitler came into power," said The New Leader in its account of the "deliberate and planned action by the gangs that call themselves the Communist

Party." The riot caused a special touch of embarrassment to Thomas, for in his latest book, *The Choice Before Us,* not to be published for another month, he discussed the Communist strategy of falsehood but concluded, "what hope there is in America, and probably in Europe, lies in the pressure of sheer necessity that Socialists and Communists act together in certain matters unless they wish to be destroyed separately."

The Austrian onslaught convinced many Socialists that America would be the next scene of a Fascist coup. The summary elimination of the unprepared European Socialists seemed a warning of what could happen here. The gentlemanly parliamentarian methods of Socialism were obviously ineffectual against machine guns. Thomas was surrounded by Party comrades, most but not all of them of the younger generation, who said in effect that the nice-Nelly American Socialists had better put away their crocheting in favor of firearms against Fascists who would otherwise mow them down as they had the workers in Vienna. One young, thoughtful New Jersey member, Robert J. Alexander, wrote him:

> That Austrian collapse is the food for much thought. . . . When the most active and energetic Socialist Party in the world [is wiped out] in four days' fighting, something is wrong. . . . things are happening so fast now that we do not know what will come next. The Socialist idea is slow education and organization. That sounds well, but will the times wait for us to become organized, and let us convince the majority of the people[?] It does not look as if the American capitalists will shy away from Fascism any more than those of Europe did. . . .
>
> I believe that we should change our outlook to the extent of being willing to set up a forcible dictatorship here, if, when and if we are elected, the capitalists try to keep us out of power. . . . The Fascist movement in this country is nothing to be sneered at. The Khaki Shirts in this county claim a membership of 2000 people, while the Socialist Party membership is 250 at the most.

### 4. The Question of Violence

Thomas himself was concerned over the events in Europe and the deteriorating situation in America—recovery lagging, unemployment persisting, capitalism being nursed and favored, Roosevelt pushing a big-navy program. Thomas had never seen the New Deal as anything more than a transitory phase, fending off despair but unable to revive capitalism, which would inevitably be succeeded either by Fascism or some form of Socialism. The growing strength of Huey Long, Father Coughlin, the Technocrats and several of the openly Fascist march-and-salute mobs raised the specter of violent takeover. There was talk of a group of Wall Street brokers plotting a right-wing military coup. The speeches of the plausible Lawrence Dennis pictured a polite and cultivated Fascism in America. Popular magazines featured articles with such titles as "Is Fascism Coming?" Thomas took special note of a Liberty Magazine article by Assistant Secretary of War Harry Woodring which bristled with militarism and favored the immediate incorporation of the supposedly civilian Civilian Conservation Corps into the army. He wrote Secretary of State Hull to protest against the propagandist activities of the visiting Fascist diplomat Pierro Parini. He was curious enough to write the Technocrats and ask bluntly how they intended to take power in order to install their "system." An underling of Howard Scott, the military-minded chieftain of Technocracy, replied for Scott: "He begs me to advise you that the matter of tactics must still remain the private property of GHQ, Technocracy, Inc."

The Communist Party and the Trotskyites, frankly espousing violent revolution, had drawn to their ranks members or fellow travelers as famous as Theodore Dreiser and John Dos Passos and of such intelligence and judgment as Granville Hicks, Max Eastman and Scott Nearing. Dos Passos's remark that to a red-blooded Communist, Socialism was "like near beer" stung young Socialists into a demand for a stronger brew. It appears that by this time the Communists and/or some of their splinter groups, especially the Lovestonites, had infiltrated the Socialist Party with young members dedicated to sowing dissension. Thomas's chief support in New York came from the younger Centrists or Militants, who were moving toward or already espoused Socialist violence if necessary to counter Fascist violence and some others who aped the Communists in their demand for Socialist violence as an essential part of the revolution. Thomas, though not agreeing with the hotspurs, viewed the argument as largely academic in a party so small, and was willing to stretch a few points in order to hold young members threatening to move into the Communist Party—members who would grow more conservative in a few years. His own loss of formal religious belief and his experiences with capitalism had removed violence as well as war from the category of the unthinkable in his philosophy. The brutal force he had seen in Passaic—the use of the fire hose, of beatings and arrests and the terror of shotgun-carrying goons—and the wounding and killing of dozens of textile strikers in the Carolinas made him impatient with innocents who thought American capitalist society non-violent. In his latest book he had written:

> If a small handful of Socialists are Tolstoyan, most of them are fully aware that the working class cannot renounce all right to use of violence in the face of an owning class which uses it habitually. But Socialists intend to emphasize that there is effective struggle which falls short of the mass murder of civil war or terrorism, and they present Socialism as an alternative to widespread violence of this order, not its doubtful consequence.

Hence, of all the forces that could change the American system as Thomas had no doubt it was destined to be changed, Socialism would bring it with a minimum of violence, if any at all. Now he expressed similar feelings as he sought to hammer out a Party policy that might unite the warring factions at the coming convention in Detroit. His draft was exploratory, for the purpose of testing the reactions of certain members. While it admitted the possibility of a necessity for violence, he stressed warnings against it rather than a prescription for its use:

> . . . America with its lynchings, its third degree, and its criminal gangs, is peculiarly a sadistic country, wherein to unleash great violence is far more likely to invite chaos and dark night than any constructive revolution. . . . To say this is not to assert that workers can at all times avoid violence or preparation for it. . . . At the very least, what is needed is a . . . critical analysis of the kinds and degrees of violence and the circumstances in which its use may possibly be surgical rather than purely destructive. . . .
>
> . . . I believe that today a Socialist program for America should seek to minimize violence. . . . [Socialism] believes no violent act and no dictatorial power can do more than remove ancient abuses. A new life will have to be planned and guided. And if that life is strong enough its struggle for power will not involve catastrophic destruction. It will come to fulfill and not to destroy the dreams of those Americans who have held that all men are entitled to life, liberty and the pursuit of happiness.

He sought a middle ground that would satisfy the firebrands without alienating the Old Guard—perhaps an impossibility. He showed the draft to young Joseph Lash and Kenneth Meiklejohn, who worked in the college department of the League for Industrial Democracy. Each thought it too namby-pamby, feeling that many young Socialists would think that it overemphasized the danger of violence. He sent it to Paul Porter at the sanitarium, who thought it virtually right-wing. And there was the self-styled Revolutionary Policy Committee to worry about. This fiery group of Socialists, at the extreme Militant left, frankly favored the violent overthrow of the government and were in fact so forgiving of the Communists that they thought the Socialists shared the blame for the Garden riot.

## 5. Never Speechless

As the time approached for the Detroit convention, at which an irresistible force (the Militants) could be expected to strike an immovable object (the Old Guard), Thomas attended to duties small and large that seemed disconnected but were mostly in the cause. He wrote President Roosevelt in behalf of Tom Mooney, aware that only Governor Rolph could pardon him but that "I have such confidence in your combination of boldness and shrewdness that I think you may find a way...." He finished reading and correcting the manuscript autobiography of Morris Hillquit, which he had agreed to do for the publisher; the work treated Thomas with respect and ended with optimism for the Party. He wrote Secretary of Labor Frances Perkins in support of the request of the Cumberland Mountain Workers' League in Tennessee for an increase in wages for cutting wood from sixty to eighty-five cents a day—ten hours' work constituting a day, so that the raise would be from six cents to eight and a half cents an hour, if granted. On a later visit to Tennessee and Mississippi he was shocked by the privation of the sharecroppers, not speechless (Party colleagues joked that he was never speechless), but into a crusade against New Deal inaction.

He attended the wedding of his son William to Mary Campbell of Huntington (Cold Spring Harbor was a part of Huntington Township), at the Presbyterian church in that town. (Thomas was still believed in some quarters of the upper crust to be so disreputable that when the reporter Inez Robb called on the mother of the bride-to-be, she burst into tears and cried, "It's bad enough as it is! Do you have to put in in the newspaper?") He invited the black Socialist George Streator to dine with him at the Thomas home (a fairly daring social departure at the time) to discuss Streator's suggestion that some Party locals in Harlem be exclusively for Negroes—an idea Thomas opposed, writing, "I hate to see locals formed on the express basis of difference in race when there is no difference in language," and mentioning, "I have to speak at the Rand School at 8:30 P.M., but then I have to speak somewhere every night." He spoke weekly over New York's small 1,000-watt Socialist radio station, WEVD, and not infrequently over big 50,000-watters such as WEAF and WOR, on the latter besting Donald Richberg in a debate about Roosevelt's National Recovery Administration. He began a new book about human exploitation, with research help from Jack Herling and from Paul Porter at Trudeau.

He wrote to the officers of a union publication in Illinois, The Progressive Miner, to protest its frequent anti-Semitic opinions and references, such as to "the frozen people," and heard in reply that The Progressive Miner felt the Jews unfair in their attacks on the Nazis and that "I have positive proof that [an international Jewish organization] is attempting to set up a military dictatorship in every country in the world." The Party had troubles enough without numbering Nazis among its members. Thomas kept on trying to educate The Progressive Miner.

Leading 300 members of the Young People's Socialist League, he picketed Macy's in New York for its commerce with the Nazis, carrying a sign, "Don't Buy German Goods." On a swing through New England he spoke at Smith College, where his daughter Frances was now a student after a year at Barnard, and where Ralph Harlow was known as "Professor of Socialism" because he often dwelled on that subject in his classes in religion. By now Thomas had become the all-American circuit rider, well known on most campuses, friendly with many college and university presidents who were flattered to have him dine with them and often gave him a room overnight, trusted as Socialists never used to be trusted, able to speak freely in the free-speaking depression years, and almost invariably bringing down the house. To the power and grace of his "set speech" was added the question period afterward, which he handled with urbanity and zest. He was now so popular that it was usually essential to book him a year in advance. Fully one-fifth of his hundreds of outgoing letters were regretful declinations because of lecture dates already crammed, and he had every reason to believe that he was "educating and laying foundations."

Thomas urged Roosevelt to push the restoration of political rights to some 1,500 people from whom they had been divested by ultra-patriotic state laws during the world war, now fifteen years past, adding, "I might have been one of them had I lived in some small hysterical community instead of in New York City." The Socialist Sir Stafford Cripps arrived from London and spoke at the Rand School (Julius Gerber had never heard of Cripps and Louis Waldman addressed him as "Sir Cripes"); he dined with the Thomases and invited them to England for the fall. Thomas, however, was already tired of his one-year hiatus in being a candidate and planned to run in the fall (if the Old Guard would let him) for the United States Senate against the address-changing Royal Copeland, not hoping to win but to build up Party membership in upstate New York. He concerned himself also with the arrival in New York of Margharita Sarfatti, a friend of Mussolini's and of Fascism who was said to be spreading propaganda successfully even at the Italian department of Columbia University. Still working for a third-party coalition, he wrote Governor Floyd B. Olson of Minnesota to congratulate him on the adoption by the Farmer-Labor Party there of a largely Socialistic platform. He hoped to draw Governor Olson out on the prospects for a coalition, but Olson's reply was disappointingly short and noncommittal. It seemed always that any group seeking coalition must act toward other similar groups as if it were doing fine by itself, didn't really need coalition and would be doing the other groups a favor.

Thomas was embarrassed because, being incurably soft-hearted, he had signed a note for a Socialist friend who had failed to pay up so that Thomas was being dunned. From a Party leader in Clovis, New Mexico, he received an ultimatum: "Comrade Thomas, you do NOT belong to the East. You belong to the entire American Socialist movement. New Mexico is entitled as a matter of right to some of your time." Thomas, however, was only one man. He used the airplane when possible to save time, the dean at Bowdoin College, where he was to speak, writing to him, "I hope also that . . . you can come on a Christian train and return on another Christian train instead of making it all a fly-by-night arrangement."

To Clarence Senior, who wrote to him in January urging him to crowd in more speaking dates, Thomas demurred, telling him confidentially, "I am more alarmed than I have been for months about Violet's heart. . . . I am . . . a rather badly scared person at the moment. . . ." But Violet recovered as she had so many times before. In February she accompanied him to Tennessee, where he gave a series of speeches, but was called back from Nashville by a death in her family. Thomas, as he never failed to do even when the amount was only a dollar or so, later wrote to the capitalist railroad company and received a refund for the unused portion of her ticket.

### 6. Prosperity Through Starvation

His attention was called to the plight of the sharecroppers by a husband-and-wife team of Socialist organizers, Edward and Martha Johnson. They urged him to see for himself.

"[The sharecroppers] cannot vote out the poll tax since they can't pay a poll tax to vote," Mrs. Johnson wrote from Arkansas. "Political bosses in these tiny towns pay the poll taxes and then carry the voters to the polls. A revolt and bolting vote is impossible, for everyone knows everyone else. . . . We MUST have a Socialist program for sharecroppers."

Thomas had already found serious fault with the New Deal. He wrote to General Hugh Johnson to give him specific examples of "the way in which minimum wages set by the [National Recovery Administration] code tend to become maximum." He saw the NRA as a potential back door to Fascism. But to him the New Deal's greatest enormity was the curtailment of crops and stock under the Agricultural Adjustment Act when people were ragged and starving—a program to save capitalism at the expense of the poor, which he called "subsidizing scarcity" or "prosperity through starvation."

He was solidly booked as usual but he arranged a Track Meet side trip to Memphis and eastern Arkansas for February, 1934, although it meant that he would get little sleep. In Tyronza, Arkansas, he met H. L. Mitchell, the proprietor of a small dry-cleaning shop, who had become a Socialist after reading Upton Sinclair. Mitchell said the croppers were desperate and that Huey Long's share-the-wealth propaganda would win them over unless the Socialists got a move on. He took Thomas on a tour of nearby cotton plantations where Thomas talked with the croppers as well as the owners. He had attacked the system in *The Choices Before Us* but this was his first actual view of it and he was utterly shocked at the workers' rags, their hovels, their hopelessness. His speech at the local high school was heard by planters who glowered under his denunciations and by croppers who saw in him a hero, a man indeed from Mars. Before he left Tyronza he promised Mitchell all aid in protesting to the administration about these conditions, while Mitchell was to start forming a sharecroppers' union as well as a drive for the Party.

Thomas also spoke across the river in Memphis through the cooperation of Professor William R. Amberson, a Party member and research physiologist at the University of Tennessee at Memphis, who reminded him that the word was not "crop-sharers" but "sharecroppers." While the contracts sponsored by the government specified a division of the plow-under payments between the plantation owners and croppers, the program was administered locally by the planters. Some of the croppers had no understanding of the matter. In many cases the workers never saw their portion and lost their jobs in the bargain because less cotton was planted. Amberson agreed to take a chance on losing his professorship by supervising a study of nearby plantations to determine the Agricultural Adjustment Act's precise effect on the croppers. Thomas hurried on to speaking dates at Baton Rouge, Oklahoma City and Saint Louis.

His indignation was aroused as it had seldom been. The slavery and degradation he had seen in Arkansas was shared by a million and a half farm families all across the South. The average cropper annual income for his whole family was nearer $250 than $300. Many were illiterate and suffered from pellagra. "The sharecroppers in no true sense are free men," Thomas wrote. "They are virtual slaves to the landlord and to his Commissary, and the terrible rate of interest they pay . . . is one of the chains which bind them." He had met Secretary of Agriculture Henry A. Wallace when the latter was still in Iowa and had a good opinion of him, but by the time he reached Wichita he could no longer wait to write Wallace sharply about "one of the most abominable and indefensible systems of landlordism in the world." He knew Wallace's good intentions, he wrote, but his plan embodied errors causing appalling want:

> Now, under the operation of AAA hundreds of thousands of [sharecroppers] are either driven out on the roads without hope of absorption into industry or exist without land to cultivate by grace of the landlord in shacks scarcely fit for pigs. . . . Has the Administration any plans . . . other than pious hopes . . . ? Shall they starve quietly so as to not interrupt our much predicted return to "prosperity"?

Wallace replied that his department was aware of the problem and was "investigating." But Wallace was an odd one who had once told a complainer in another matter, "I'd rather sit under a tree and let the cycle of time heal the situation." An AAA representative did visit Tyronza and talk with the planters but, as Mitchell reported to Thomas, talked with no croppers. As he was leaving, he saw Mitchell and "requested that there not be any more complaints . . . and also that since the 'landlords are all your friends and these sharecroppers are a shiftless lot there is no use of being concerned about them. . . .' " The "investigation," Mitchell wrote, was a whitewash, and Dr. Amberson agreed. Amberson's own investigation had turned up evictions of croppers from their shacks, brutality toward them and systematic defrauding of them by some unscrupulous planters in the payment of cotton money. The federal program designed to protect them had aggravated their woes.

Thomas began a systematic effort to see Secretary Wallace, while the Secretary systematically dodged him. Visiting Washington in behalf of the unemployed and the Civil Works Administration workers then being discharged, he did manage to see Wallace's assistant, Paul Appleby, without result. He sent fifty dollars of his own money to Amberson to extend his investigation, and fifty dollars to Mitchell—big money in Tyronza in those times. To aid the willing but inexperienced Mitchell in organizing the union, Thomas persuaded the intense young Socialist Reverend Howard Kester of Nashville, a Methodist clergyman who was secretary of the Committee on Economic and Racial Justice, to move to the Tyronza area for a time. Thomas received letters from sharecroppers who had heard him in Arkansas, such as the following penciled scrawl:

> I have not got any work and no where to put my things I have got my house hold sitting in a wood shed and the rain is runing every thing I have got I though I would write you and see if you help me get a tent or some place to take my wife and things.

Thomas answered such pleas personally and then relayed them to Mitchell, who wrote, "These things are an every day occurrance [*sic*]. . . . If we should start some sort of relief we would be swamped with appeals. . . . We seem to have stirred up a hornet's nest [among the planters]. . . . By the way you have a new namesake down here in Tyronza, a child was born . . . and named Norman Thomas White, it was born in a kind of truck this family is living in. . . ." There was talk among the planters, he added, of reviving the Ku Klux Klan.

Thomas perhaps would have been better off if he could have dropped all else but the task of saving the Party. But the troubles of others were his own. As one colleague observed, it was lucky Norman Thomas was not a woman, for he could not say No. He was juggling other problems and duties. He besought the help of Senators Wagner and Cutting for shipyard strikers in Camden. He spoke over NBC against the Dollfuss tyranny in Austria. He was looking into the case of a convict at Sing Sing who claimed he was wrongly convicted. He led a "march on Washington" of more than 4,000 representatives of the unemployed and addressed them at the Auditorium. He wired Leo Krzycki for help for strikers at the SKF plant in Philadelphia. He wrote Dr. Henry Goddard Leach, editor of The Forum, "I am so stirred up about this share cropper business that I might write an article for you. . . ." Instead he agreed to write one for Current History. He advised his sister Agnes in her search for a different teaching job. In a speech at the Foreign Policy Association in New York he condemned the miserable wages in the textile industry. With a sinking heart he heard from Jerry Voorhis in California that he, who had earlier worried about Socialists supporting Upton Sinclair, after inner wrestling had gone over to Sinclair himself because (though he worded it euphemistically) the Socialists seemed to be finished there, whereas Sinclair led a massive movement. Thomas tried to mediate a new dispute in the Motion Picture Operators' Union. He wrote President Roosevelt to urge his support of a bill providing bigger federal aid "to make more adequate state relief for the aged." He sent a protesting letter to three magazines against the suggestion that the scarcely peaceable Young Men's Christian Association leader John R. Mott be awarded the Nobel Peace Prize. A new subject on his lecture repertoire was the degradation visited on the sharecroppers by the Agricultural Adjustment Act. He replied cogently to The Memphis Commercial Appeal, which scoffed at his idea that his "brief trip" qualified him to speak about sharecroppers, defended the system and said most workers were victims of their own "shiftlessness" and that they "live in poverty and squalor because of lack of pride and industry."

He did not fail to write Norman Thomas White in Arkansas a cordial letter wishing him a better world than that of his parents. He did the same on learning that a Socialist family in Worcester had christened their new son Norman Thomas Sheridan.

He tried to do too much—a failing he would never quite conquer. The joke that he traveled so fast that he was always in two places at once was almost substantiated when he wrote Professor Walter Rautenstrauch at Columbia University to ask for economic information for his current book, adding, "I am enclosing two envelopes addressed to myself at two different places in the hope that one or the other will reach me quickly."

His secretary, the efficient Freda Straus, worked for him either at the

League for Industrial Democracy office or the office he maintained in his home. He rattled off many of his letters into a Dictaphone, sometimes late at night, leaving such notes as, "Miss Straus, *very important.* Do this cylinder first. Note telegram!" And in such cases as those of Mrs. Louise Jessen and Professor Paul A. Schilpp he "shot from the hip," to his own embarrassment. Mrs. Jessen was the spunky secretary of the Socialist Party in New Orleans, where she and her husband had given Thomas lodging on one of his visits. She had been arrested while passing out Socialist campaign handbills on a downtown street—an activity declared illegal—and given a ten-day jail term. The illegality was the kind found and punished only in dissidents, with the aim of suppressing dissidence. Thomas alerted the American Civil Liberties Union to come to her aid, sent her a cheering telegram in jail, and sent to The New Orleans Times-Picayune a blistering opinion of law enforcement in that Huey Long realm. He raised a considerable newspaper storm, and she was released in three days. "The prison was very clean, and I received kind treatment," she wrote Thomas in thanking him.

He heard from Martha Johnson, however, that other punishment was being visited on Mrs. Jessen through her husband Otto, who worked for the federal barge line in New Orleans. Jessen had earlier been told that he would be discharged unless his wife kept out of the papers. Instead —in part thanks to Thomas—she had been on the front pages, and Jessen was given notice of dismissal for reasons of "economy." Thomas, suspecting that the Long spoils system was at work, wrote the presidential secretary Marvin McIntyre about it and received McIntyre's prompt assurance that Jessen would not be discharged for any reason other than economy. Thomas then received Jessen's worried note asking him not to intercede, for he had not been laid off as yet and any protest might worsen the difficulty. Thomas replied with concern, "With all my heart I hope that I have not unintentionally done more harm than good." Alas, a month later Jessen got the gate.

Professor Schilpp, whom Thomas had met twice in California, was the ardently Socialist head of the Department of Philosophy at the College of the Pacific in Stockton. His "radicalism" in such issues as his opposition to the college's participation in Navy Day had earned the enmity of the American Legion and other groups and he had been fired "for reasons of economy" in the midst of the anti-Red wave there. Thomas, hearing of this from a friend of Schilpp's, sent off identical letters to The Nation, The New Republic and The Christian Century commenting that "teaching is a dangerous profession for men with ideas and the courage to express them, in the state of Mooney and Billings." He sent a copy to Schilpp, who was flattered but wrote back to say that sentiment against Socialists being what it was, he had to think of his wife and family and feared that the magazine publicity would make it harder for him to find a new post. Thomas hastily wrote the three magazines asking them not to publish his letter.

But Thomas handled a multitude of details with sympathy and efficiency. While he contended with the Party split and prepared to run for the Senate, he gave incessant attention to the sharecroppers. He read Professor Amberson's careful report on the failures of the system and it was sent on to Secretary Wallace, who continued to dodge him. He sent copies of the report to Congressmen who might help. He sent one of Violet's silky cockers to Amberson by way of thanks. To Mitchell, who needed money and encouragement rather than a dog, he sent money and encouragement.

Mitchell, himself the son of a tenant farmer, had the courage without which idealism would be of little use. With Kester and Amberson he was starting a revolution, at considerable risk to himself and his family. First his dry-cleaning business was boycotted. Then he was given notice to vacate his shop. He received threats. "It isn't very pleasant," he wrote Thomas, "for my family to live in a town where we are completely ostracized by all our former friends. Also my son who is of school age will be taught by the wife of one of our bitter enemies." Still, by July he and Kester had formed the Southern Tenant Farmers' Union in Tyronza, unsegregated, blacks and whites together, a weak but hopeful organization surrounded by powerful foes.

# IX

## 1. The Tear Gas Treatment

Thomas returned early in March, 1934, from a grassroots exploration through nine southern and midwestern states on the same day that two young men seeking snow removal jobs fainted from hunger at City Hall. He had seen some of the country's worst Hoovervilles in his various travels and thought the ones outside Saint Louis and Oklahoma City the most sordid. He foresaw more hunger and perhaps disorder because of the dropping of the Civil Works Administration. "To put it brutally," he said, "you can keep a dog hungry for a good while and he won't bite you, but you'll have an awful time grabbing a bone away from him." The very next day he debated Huey Long before 2,500 at Mecca Temple, defending the affirmative of the proposition that "Capitalism is doomed and cannot be saved by the redistribution of wealth." He felt sure that Long knew this to be true but used his share-the-wealth plan simply as pie in the sky to attain power—an insincerity Thomas did not, for example, believe of Dr. Townsend. Long, who had the advantage of the last word, was at his most puckish. He declared that the lands and flocks of Abraham in the Bible were capitalistic at God's own inspiration and complained that under Socialism a man would not even own his garters. "They'll belong to the government," he said. The Kingfish was a formidable opponent histrionically if not logically, and one reporter said that "a mob of autograph seekers followed Huey out of the building," while another observed, "The unofficial verdict of the audience was for Mr. Thomas."

In April Thomas went with Violet to their Long Island place, where she worked in the kennels while he got the garden started, wrote some speeches and pamphlets and set himself for the Detroit convention.

The convention would start May 31. Thomas, always conserving time and transportation expense, left a fortnight earlier, with Violet accompanying him part way, on a Midwest speaking tour. In Taylorville, Illinois, he sought to speak for Socialism and also for his Methodist companion, the Reverend Douglas B. Anderson, the state Socialist Party leader, who was running for Congress. He asked permission of Mayor J. R. Spreiser to use the town auditorium in the park, which seated 5,000. Spreiser was partial to the huge Peabody Coal Company, whose nearby mines had made the town a scene of labor troubles and whose owners were antagonistic to Socialism. He refused, saying, "There aren't 5,000 people in the state who would listen to you." So Thomas addressed a crowd (including Violet) from the courthouse steps. Some of the listeners broke the law as proclaimed on "Keep Off the Grass" signs. Thomas had scarcely warmed up when he was arrested by Deputy Sheriff Joseph Betterton, who hustled him into the courthouse. Betterton, who was cross-eyed, took some gibes from the crowd, perhaps including Violet. While Thomas was held incommunicado inside, his demands to know what the charge was or to call a lawyer denied, Anderson addressed the crowd outside. Betterton sneaked out of the building by another door. He got around to the windward of the crowd, as the sharp-eyed Violet observed, then tossed four tear-gas bombs that scattered them while Anderson was arrested by another deputy sheriff.

Thomas was almost as angry about this roughneck use of tear gas as about the denial of liberties. When he and Anderson were released after an hour, he was said to have told Betterton, "I'll make you and your cross eyes famous," which he later denied. When he got time he wrote Attorney General Homer Cummings about it and brought suit against Betterton for false arrest, as did Anderson.

Meanwhile he went on without Violet to Rockford, where a week later he was addressing a crowd in a public hall when someone (perhaps someone who had read news stories of the Taylorville incident) threw a tear gas bomb in through a window. "The 400 or more in the audience dashed, choking and blinded, for the doors," one account said. When order was restored, Thomas continued his talk outside.

## 2. *Chips on Shoulders*

The Detroit convention was not for the nomination of candidates but to take stock of events since the New Deal and to compose a new statement of Party policy looking to the forthcoming Congressional elections. Although few could have encountered the difficulties Thomas did en route, all factions seemed to arrive with chips on shoulders and the glinty eyes so characteristic of ideologues of the left. Leo Krzycki, the chairman, was a figure of unimportance. The Thomas effort to unseat Hillquit in 1932 burned hot in Old Guard memories. The Old Guard were themselves divided into two factions varying in conservatism, while their opponents ranged from Centrists to Militants to Revolutionaries. The distance separating them had widened, for a part of the Old Guard was flirting with the New Deal, which the Revolutionaries saw as incipient Fascism.

By this measurement, Thomas was left-of-center but not far left. To him, the Old Guard's handling of the Communist issue was mistaken. He saw the Communists as Socialists who had gone astray, whose tactics were deplorable but who might, some of them, be won over as badly needed and politically knowledgeable allies against the threat of Fascism. It was Fascism, Fascism that haunted his dreams. Deputy Sheriff Betterton and the Peabody Coal Company, and the Southern planters allied with the Agricultural Adjustment Administration, looked much more dangerous to him than the sharecroppers or the overwrought left-wingers in his own party. That American big business might with quick violence seize a government where big business was already predominant seemed to him entirely possible. Yet in the "inclusive" party he wanted, the radical left would be a minority and he had said that in the search for coalition, "those whom we must win are to the right and not to the left of us." But he was so anxious to keep the younger element in the Party and to bring in still more young people that he would accept a modicum of proletarian nonsense if its exclusion meant their alienation. That there were limits to what he would accept had been shown recently by his sharp criticism of what he called the "infantile leftism" of the policy proposals of forty-seven of the Revolutionaries.

The prosperous Old Guard had not endeared themselves to the convention by their failure as yet to contribute more than chicken feed toward a drive for $12,000 to succor the national office in Chicago; it was in such straits that the staff was owed more than $1,000 in back wages. The Old Guard, for their part, felt the national office to be largely a Thomas benefice. They charged that Secretary Senior picked only Militants for Party speech tours (to which Senior replied that he had requested several Old Guardsmen, including Waldman and Claessens, to tour but they were invariably too busy); and that Senior insulted them by failing to mount a large picture of the late Morris Hillquit on the convention platform (a failure Senior blamed on the decorations committee which, he said, was headed by an Old Guardsman, Meyer Schneider).

In formulating a new Declaration of Principles, the Old Guard, who had devised much of the past policy, wanted little change. The younger and more aggressive demanded fireworks. It seems clear that some of the Old Guard leaders saw the convention as an opportunity to reduce the power of Thomas, which Thomas in turn hoped to increase at the expense of the Old Guard, whom he regarded as reactionaries. The committee empowered to write the new Declaration, composed of sharply differing members, had finally given up late in the evening, admitted irreconcilable disagreement, and Devere Allen had been given the thankless task of rewriting it for presentation the next day. The kindly, tousled Allen, forty-three, an Oberlin Phi Beta Kappa who lived in Connecticut, was a Quaker, a pacifist member of the Fellowship of Reconciliation, and had for ten years been an editor of The World Tomorrow. It was ironic that this peaceable man brought the Party conflict to a crisis. He worked all night and came up with a Declaration which seemed to reflect not only the prevailing fear of war and Fascism but also his effort to please all factions. He saluted the Socialist dedication to "peaceful and orderly means" but warned that Fascist violence would not be tolerated and that Socialists would use measures "which will not merely serve as a defense against counter-revolution but will carry the revolutionary struggle into the camp of the enemy." There was praise for the democratic process along with a statement that the Party aimed to replace "the bogus democracy of capitalist parliamentarianism by a genuine workers' democracy." And the traditional Socialist opposition to war, the statement said, would be implemented by "massed war resistance, organized as far as possible in a general strike of labor unions and professional groups in a united effort to make the waging of war a practical impossibility and to convert a capitalist war crisis into a victory for Socialism." It declared elsewhere:

Capitalism is doomed. If it can be superseded by a majority vote, the Socialist Party will rejoice. If the crisis comes through the denial of majority rights after the electorate has given us a mandate we shall not hesitate to crush by our labor solidarity the reckless force of reaction and to consolidate the Socialist state. If the capitalist system should collapse in a general chaos and confusion, which cannot permit of orderly procedure, the Socialist Party, whether or not in such case it is a majority, will not shrink from the responsibility of organizing and maintaining a government under the workers' rule.

Although the wording was vague and subject to different interpretations, it had a heady sound which Thomas and Mayor Hoan wanted to tone down. They agreed to propose amendments. But Charles Solomon of the Old Guard got the floor, argued that there should be no alteration or compromising of the Declaration, and was upheld by the delegates. Solomon evidently felt that it should and could be defeated in toto as a lesson to its backers, while its backers wanted it *passed* in toto.

Hence the draft was treated as a finished product. The protocol intended as a basis for modification became instead an object of warfare. The hall was steaming, delegates sweating, and ill temper took over. Left-wingers attacked the Declaration as not radical enough. They were warned by Thomas against "playing with fire" and giving "a weapon to Fascism." Waldman, the putative successor to Hillquit, was booed as he led the attack with the argument that it was violent and illegal. Thomas, frustrated in his plan to amend it, spoke strongly in its favor. "The issue," he said, "that has been raised this afternoon ought to lift up our hearts." Waldman, no more an unbiased observer than Thomas, wrote ten years later that Thomas was "pale and nervous," adding, "here was a man who, more than any outstanding Socialist, was Presidential timber . . . and here he was placed in the position of acting as leader of a group of political adventurers."

The scene had its grotesquery—a party which claimed 23,000 members, not all of them in robust health, disputing as to whether or under what circumstances they should assume command of the nation's resources and its 125 million inhabitants, "crush the reckless force of reaction" and rescue the United States of America. In the end, Thomas won and the Declaration passed 99–47, with the provision that it be approved by a Party referendum. And after that the Old Guard was further humbled by the defeat of Waldman, Jasper McLevy and other

Old Guardsmen and the election of only one of their number, James Oneal, to membership on the National Executive Committee.

### 3. Secession Threatened

The New York Times reporter who covered Socialist affairs was Joseph Shaplen, a Party member and loyal Old Guardsman who reflected the Waldman-Lee-Cahan point of view. Shaplen at least once earlier had written The New Leader to denounce Thomas for views in his column sympathetic with the Soviet Union. Shaplen had long been condemned by Militants for his bias. Now, in a front-page Times story headed "LEFT WING SEIZES / SOCIALIST PARTY," he wrote that "Norman Thomas captured complete control of the Socialist Party. . . . He thus achieved the purpose which he barely failed to attain in his battle with the late Morris Hillquit at the Milwaukee convention two years ago." The story went on:

> In "right wing" circles of the convention the belief was expressed that the more than 6,000 members represented by the opposition to the Thomas and the "left wing" factions have been placed under the necessity of seriously considering secession from the Socialist Party. . . . Mr. Panken warned the convention that "we are face to face with a definite cleavage in the Socialist movement."

Shaplen did not mention that the Declaration might have been modified had not the Old Guard prevented it, though he did tell of Thomas's efforts to keep the left wing under control. The Shaplen bias added to the Old Guard propaganda advantage in New York already assured by The Daily Forward with its 200,000 circulation and the Old Guard-controlled New Leader. For Socialists to air their private quarrels in the capitalist press had always been taboo. But Waldman, the state chairman, made an immediate public statement on returning to New York, saying, "We repudiate the essential features of the declaration of principles . . . sponsored by Mr. Thomas and his allies. . . . The declaration of principles Mr. Thomas sponsored . . . is perhaps less frank, but not one bit less dangerous, than the doctrines of the Communists." This was followed by a long letter in The New Leader by Waldman's ally Louis Hendin saying that "certain members of the National Executive Committee" (now dominated by Thomas and men friendly to him) might be "disguised Communists." These were fighting words. Two

169

days later came a denunciation by the Old Guardsman Alexander Kahn in The Daily Forward. The founding by the Old Guard of a self-styled Committee for the Preservation of the Socialist Party, dedicated to the defeat of the Declaration in the referendum, suggesting that its proponents were Party-wreckers, made Thomas bristle. So did the Old Guard's issuance of an occasional propaganda paper called The Socialist Voice, opposing the Declaration and its supporters and sent to all members at considerable expense. A special hurt to Thomas, although he knew his old friend's automatic recoil from violence, was John Haynes Holmes's statement in The Voice:

> The Detroit Declaration of Principles is Communism pure and simple.
> . . . I am utter-opposed to the Declaration and hope it will be defeated
> in the referendum. It is foolish and rather pitiful for Norman Thomas to
> say that there must be no split in the Party. The Declaration, of course,
> makes a split inevitable. . . .

Holmes of course was no Old Guardsman but said exactly what he thought. Thomas, in an attempt at conciliation, did write "Dear Louis" Waldman a placatory letter, saying, "I do not forget that twice you nominated me for President of the United States," praising his ability and urging that he make a new statement to the press modifying the unfortunate one already printed. But he had little hope, for the next day he wrote Paul Porter that "we are going to have trouble here in New York," that Waldman was a no-holds-barred fighter and that "In spite of his brains it will probably be a good thing if the Party loses him." This was written before he received Waldman's glacial reply, in which he gave no ground, denounced the Declaration as violent, illegal and closer to Communist than Socialist doctrine and blamed Thomas for it.

One New York militant, outraged by the Old Guard line in The New Leader and elsewhere, wrote Thomas, "I have long been of the opinion that some of the Old Guard leaders were—to put it frankly—sons of bitches, and I knew the fight would be sharp. But I had not expected it to be so dishonest. . . ." Porter wrote to Thomas, "If we lose the referendum, I dread to think of the future of the Party. It will, for one thing, mean a crushing defeat to your leadership."

Thomas was conciliatory in his New Leader column, one paragraph being headed, "There Must Be No Split!" But Vladeck was the leader who worked hardest to mediate the quarrel. He urged Thomas to agree to a revision of the Declaration, adding, "Comrade Thomas, you know how deeply and sincerely I have been attached to you." But Thomas at first was unwilling to retreat before the Old Guard minority: ". . . I can't for the life of me see that we can afford to purchase Party harmony, or indeed that we could get it at all by a policy of knuckling under to a small group armed with a bludgeon, financial and otherwise."

Unprinted charges flew on both sides. Thomas heard a rumor that The Forward would no longer subsidize the losing Milwaukee Leader unless it was "right" on the Declaration. Senior wrote Thomas about talk that the extreme left wing of the Party, the obstreperous Revolutionary Policy Committee, "is at least partially run by Lovestone," meaning Jay Lovestone, now a dissident Communist leader. Senior, a hard worker who hated strife, had lost seven pounds and had to take a rest.

Thomas himself was looking haggard. In the midst of the battle he found time in June to attend the marriage of his twenty-year-old daughter Polly, whom he gave away to Herbert C. Miller of Columbus, Ohio, and Yale. Perhaps the wedding had a softening influence. By June 20 Thomas wrote Senior that "fighting about a few sentences in a Declaration of Principles" was ridiculous and agreed that a compromise should be sought. "You have to be here in New York to appreciate what things are like," he added to Senior. The effort was made but the Old Guard rejected compromise, insisting that the whole Declaration be disavowed—a stalemate that left the issue up to the referendum, which would take several months. Meanwhile Thomas, still hoping to run for United States Senator, faced the formidable problem of getting the nomination at a state convention dominated by the very men he was opposing at the national level.

At the convention, held in New York City July 1, at the time of Hitler's blood purge, the reelection of Waldman as state chairman merely verified Old Guard control. Waldman forced through a resolution condemning the Declaration of Principles. Charles Solomon, despite his poor showing in the mayoral race, was nominated for Governor over the Thomas-supported candidate, Professor Coleman B. Cheney of Skidmore College. One fistfight broke out. Judge Panken attacked Thomas bitterly in nominating James Oneal for the Senate. Oneal could have had the nomination but was still friendly enough to Thomas to withdraw at the last moment on the suggestion of Julius Gerber, for "party harmony." Since there was no time to launch another candidate, Thomas won the nomination if not the blessing of the convention.

"The conduct of the convention was outrageous," Thomas wrote Mayor Hoan, "and the speeches against the Declaration were extreme." Still, there had been generosity enough to permit his nomination. To Senior he wrote, "For myself, of course, the campaign will be in some respects a torture. . . . I expect to give the fall pretty solidly to it. . . . During July and August I have a good many [lecture] dates here in the East and I shall have to work like fury on that rather important book about human exploitation."

### 4. We've Got the Money Too

While the Old Guard was high-handed especially in its refusal to negotiate a compromise on the Declaration, Thomas was hardly without fault. Hillquit was dead, Krzycki was a paper chairman and Thomas was not only the leader of the majority of the Party but far and away the most prominent and influential Socialist nationally. Compromise on the anti–Old Guard side depended on him. It appears that reconciliation could have been achieved (if it was possible at all) only if Thomas had remained above the battle and earnestly continued to work for compromise. Such a course might—just might—have held the great body of the Party together at the cost of losing some few members on the far left and far right. Although Harry Laidler and a few other Centrists labored for compromise, it was Thomas whose influence could have been decisive. As always, he was coping with too many simultaneous problems and could not seem to make up his mind or, in a few instances, to hold his temper. His generous gestures toward the Old Guard were sometimes followed by angry outbursts. While it was Waldman who started breaking Party rules by fighting the battle in the capitalist press, Thomas later did likewise.

Despite his political disagreements with the Militants, he was their hero because he was farther to the left than the Old Guard. Young Militants usually met him at the station when he returned from trips and filled his ears with the latest misdoings of the Old Guard. Laidler and others felt that it would have been politic for him to remain more aloof from the Militants and to drop in at the Rand School building occasionally and nuzzle the Old Guard. Thomas's suggestion to Porter that "it will probably be a good thing if the Party loses [Waldman]" was not in the conciliatory strain. Senior, for all his admiration for Thomas, later thought that only Hillquit (who had kept Waldman and other hotheads in line) could have stilled the quarrel, and Senior was doubtful that even he could have done it.

For the rather superficial quarrel over the Declaration was the outward sign of deep-seated political and moral differences. The question of dealing or not dealing with the Communists was one of them, and in this Thomas would admit years later that he was mistaken and would write, "Even the memory of this educational process is painful." Another was the Old Guard's holy rigidity against accepting younger members who did not walk the line of doctrine. And at bottom, Thomas the moralist thought that if the Old Guard could not precisely be called corrupt, they had at the very least descended to unfairness and expediency in their relations with unions and in other matters. Two of their leaders, Panken and Solomon, had accepted judgeships from La Guardia and had not resigned from the Party (as Blanshard had). Lesser members had accepted federal posts, and in fact the Old Guard were moving closer to the New Deal while Thomas moved sharply away. They had used their money for Party power and now seemed to be withholding it for the same purpose. They were insufferably parochial, prizing their connections with the powerful Hillman-Dubinsky needle-trade unions and giving scant heed to injustice in Arkansas. The personal detestation of some of their leaders for Thomas seemed irreversible. The Old Guard seemed to sit back and say, "We have the money and we have the institutions—the Rand School, The Forward, the radio station, The New Leader, the summer camp. The Thomasites will have to make the concessions."

It appeared at times that Thomas believed the Old Guard to be an impossible deadweight against his design to make the Party more inclusive by taking in members further to the left and right of the present narrow spectrum. There were some indications that his several moves for reconciliation were made more to establish a record of correctness than out of any real desire to bring back an Old Guard that would always be boss in New York, would always suspect him and always block his ambitious plans for the Party's role in saving the nation from Roosevelt.

### 5. Come into My Parlor

Luckily for Thomas, he and Violet had one idyllic interlude in the fall of 1934—one he never forgot—for many things dear to him were going sour. There were war clouds in Europe, Roosevelt raised the military budget and there was a drive for Reserve Officers' Training Corps at more colleges, Princeton included. Labor leaders, instead of becoming Socialists, were joining the New Deal. Thomas was quite right in saying that its leaders hated Communism and distrusted Socialism "rather more than they hated or distrusted Wall Street." The Party piggy bank was almost empty. Paul Porter, released at last from the sanitarium, was appointed Labor Secretary and was to go temporarily to California to lift the sinking Socialist fortunes there. He got as far as Chicago and could go no farther because the Party could not raise his rail fare and expenses in California.

The World Tomorrow, which Thomas had brought to life in 1918 and had loved ever since, died of debt despite his last-minute effort to raise money to save it. The Socialist Party in Oregon (numbering 142 members), believing the Declaration of Principles made them vulnerable to a state law against syndicalism, resigned in a body from the national Party with a parting blast from its leader against the "sky pilots, lawyers and college-kids, who gained their knowledge of the working class while they lounged in easy-chairs . . ."

Ex–Sky Pilot Thomas knew he was one of the targets.* He tried to raise money. Socialist dues had never paid Party expenses so that reliance was always placed on The Forward and on wealthy angels of the left. He had a talent for coaxing money from them, but resistance was rising. Agnes Brown Leach, one of his companions on The List of 1919 and long a generous contributor, had become a Roosevelt admirer and gave the Socialists not a penny. Thomas wrote to Ethel Clyde, he wrote to Frederick Vanderbilt Field, he wrote to John McChesney, Margaret Gage and many others: *"We must lay our hands on $6,000 to finish this year."* His appeals brought in only $1,250. One drain on the Party, instead of a profit as expected, was Julius Deutsch, famous as the head of the Socialist Party in Vienna, who had barely escaped that city with his life. Deutsch arrived with great fanfare, was given a reception by the Thomases and was booked for a six-week tour by Senior's office. He turned out to be a grouch with exaggerated ideas of American Socialist riches. He lived in the best hotels, dined splendidly and spoke unintelligible English so that his crowds were small and his tour a net loss of $270.28 to the Party. His American comrades were delighted to get rid of him when he returned to Europe complaining that he had been underpaid. He was the direct opposite of Thomas, who specified upper

---

*A committee of Socialist lawyers had studied the Declaration of Principles and declared it legal in every state.

berths and stayed at the modest Morrison in Chicago and comparable hotels elsewhere when he was not invited to stay with a comrade. Thomas was now offered regular commercial lecture bookings at $150 to $200 by the agent Thomas Brady and turned them down—too busy for the Party. He had worked so hard for the Party and declined so many agreeable fees that he was pinched at the moment—both he and Violet had made extra Party contributions of their own—and he found it necessary to ask Kent School in Connecticut, where young Evan was now a student, to wait an extra month for its tuition payment. It would be surprising if the man who had always, always been successful had not now been dogged at times by presentiments of defeat.

Earl Browder, joyfully aware of the Socialist quarrel and eager to worsen it, kept writing to him on hammer-and-sickle stationery, urging a united front of Socialists and Communists. Thomas replied that this was unlikely so long as "your party still regards it as primarily a weapon to destroy the Socialist Party." But he did not flatly say No and Browder kept after him like a bulldog with repeated essays of exhortation, one of them covering five single-spaced pages, begging Thomas to walk into his parlor, hurling chunks of propaganda at the graceful prose of Thomas. More violent appeals came from ordinary workers either cunning or outraged:

> Anyone can see that we must have a revolution or economic slavery. Why doesn't the Socialist Party join the Communist and get armed as quickly as possible. . . . I have an invention that will take care of the army tanks and I am ready to fight any time you say, but for God's sake let's get started and do something, what are you waiting for?

Thomas made a flying trip to Ohio in behalf of striking onion-field workers there. Returning, he was off again to North Carolina to aid textile-factory strikers, losing his topcoat while changing trains, stopping in Washington on the way back, hoping to see the President about misuse of troops (several strikers had been killed) but seeing only his secretary, McIntyre. Hurrying back to New York, he spoke over NBC about "Hitlerizing the Textile Strike" and received dozens of postcards in praise from listeners in Providence, Cleveland and elsewhere. Drawing only a few breaths, he flew to Michigan to address the state education association at Petoskey and Escanaba. In the scant intervals he continued a heavy correspondence, coaxed American Federation of Labor President William Green to bring pressure in favor of the onion-field workers, slashed at General Hugh Johnson for permitting "chiseling on the codes" against the textile workers, wrote a 400-word "message" for the Camden Socialist Party publication and penned a swift condolence for the family of a deceased Party member. He returned from Michigan barely in time to begin his own campaign for the Senate. In California, Upton Sinclair had been expelled from the Party upon becoming the Democratic candidate for Governor, even though he said very softly that he was still a Socialist. Thomas wrote him severely that it was of course impossible to institute Socialism in one state of the forty-eight, adding:

> ... with all your good intentions, you are doing an enormous injury to the Socialist cause. . . . I rather suspect you may have occasion to regret this error in judgment almost as much as you regretted your support of Wilson in the "war to end war."

The Socialists had nominated their own candidate for Governor of California, the former Unitarian clergyman Milen Dempster of San Francisco, who of course had no chance. Sinclair followers in the state —some of them Socialists—regarded him as an emancipator and feared that Dempster might draw enough votes to make Sinclair lose. Thomas was pelted by letters from California beseeching him to get Dempster out of the race, accusing Thomas of jealousy of Sinclair and even suggesting that he was being paid by the California Republican forces as a spoiler. A side issue was the public announcement by Dr. Michael Shadid, a Syrian-born member of the National Executive Committee from Oklahoma, supporting Sinclair. This was heresy when a Socialist candidate was running against Sinclair. There was a move to expel Shadid from the National Executive Committee, which died immediately when it was discovered that he was so popular in Oklahoma that the state Party would probably secede if he was expelled.

So the Party disruption was ominous when Thomas began campaigning. He had made a careful study of the record of the incumbent Senator, Royal Copeland. He avoided Old Guard–ridden New York City and campaigned strenuously upstate in the hope of winning that region away from the Old Guard. Violet was his companion and aide on several forays northward in their rumble-seated Chevrolet roadster. As Thomas drove, she sat beside him, portable typewriter in her lap, taking his dictation of letters and speech notes. The affection between them, the autumn glories and the stopovers with Socialist friends made these tours memorable. "It is a joy to be alive," Thomas wrote, "on some of these radiant days with the hills aflame with color." He would be fifty in November, and Violet almost fifty-three. Their life together had had the difficulties inherent in Thomas's independence of thought, and it was seldom free from at least a trace of that dreadful fear about Violet's heart, but their candid joy in each other seemed to triumph over all the rest. They never knew when it would end, but they were together at any rate in these zigzag rambles over country roads in sparkling weather.

"I am working very hard on this New York campaign," he wrote, "and with Violet's help may get somewhere." At Schenectady, Utica, Rome, Herkimer, Binghamton, Ithaca, Canandaigua, Salamanca, Buffalo and scores of other places they stopped and Thomas addressed crowds in high school gymnasiums, in city auditoriums or at factory gates. At the smaller towns he would get up in the rumble seat and speak to groups of 50 or 100, urging them not to stand so far away, assuring them that if Socialism was catching it was beneficial rather than dangerous. The Old Guard was in charge of the state machinery and Thomas, a stickler for efficient staff work, did not think he was getting it:

> I go to towns for open air meetings without even the names of the Social-
> ists in the town. I meet them, if at all, more or less by accident, and this
> in spite of urgent requests for full information. . . . Well, such is life.
> . . . We found a Socialist comrade who rigged up a pretty good sound
> apparatus on his car and Violet and I are underwriting him as a sort of
> advance agent.

He was not nearly as discouraged as was Dempster in California, who begged Thomas to come out and speak for him. And Eli Bourdon, the Party candidate for United States Senator in New Hampshire, implored him to drive over there and speak in five cities for him, which Thomas regretfully refused to do. He was holding his breath for the outcome of the referendum—had written several friends, "I cannot tell you how serious will be the defeat of the Declaration." On October 17 he learned that 5,993 members had voted for the Declaration and 4,872 against it, half the membership abstaining. The Old Guard had been defeated, but by a vote uncomfortably close.

Thomas lighted the peace pipe. He sent so conciliatory a message to The New Leader that its Old Guard assistant editor Feigenbaum cheered him for "taking the lead in helping create a sentiment for unity and harmony." Thomas was still campaigning. A fortnight later he was jolted to read in The Times that Waldman and Solomon intended to confer with labor leaders about starting a labor party. He was already irked by James Oneal's action in circularizing Party members for money for a pamphlet attacking the Thomas wing. He wrote a long and careful open letter to the state committee urging unity, which "means, of course, more than mere avoidance of an open split. It does not necessarily imply that we must all agree. It does imply that there must be a unity of devotion and a comprehensive plan for work." He permitted himself an edge of irony in commenting on the Waldman-Solomon labor party plans: "I believe intensely in a labor party of the proper kind. The relation of the Socialist Party to it or to the initiation of it is primarily a national matter." He went on:

> It should be remembered that Oneal is a member of the National Executive Committee and has never brought directly or indirectly to the attention of that body the charges he now circulates abroad on the basis of an appeal for funds from Socialists who are not adequately supporting the Party or the campaign. . . . None of these things is fatal to the Party. . . . We don't have to agree on everything in order to work together for the cooperative commonwealth. It is for that that we should plan . . . Any split of the Party will be suicide for both factions, or at least it will make the job of rebuilding enormously more difficult. . . .

Thomas got 194,952 votes for Senator against Solomon's total of 126,580 for Governor. While Solomon was not in his class as a speaker or campaigner, a direct comparison was not fair since Solomon had run against the highly popular Governor Herbert Lehman. In California, poor Milen Dempster got a humiliating 2,947 votes while Sinclair polled 879,537 despite a viciously unfair campaign against him, but of course lost to the Republican Frank Merriam. Three days after the election, Thomas was on a train to Portland, with a three-hour stopover in Chicago during which he exchanged Party gossip with Senior. He replenished his bankroll by lecturing in Idaho, Washington, Oregon and California. Shortly before he returned to New York on December 4, his secretary wrote to a Massachusetts Socialist who wanted him to work in a speech in Brockton:

> I hasten to tell you that the New Jersey engagement for December 8th is a banquet given by the New Jersey State Socialists in Trenton and will not be over until late that night. Comrade Thomas plans to catch a train in New York at midnight for New England.
> With four engagements on the 9th and the same number on the 10th

I don't see how he can crowd in a trip to Brockton. On the evening of the 9th he is due at the Methuen Forum and on the following evening he is scheduled for the Worcester Forum. The evening of the 11th he is due in New Brunswick, N.J. If you could see Comrade Thomas's crowded schedule made months ago I'm sure you would realize the difficulty of trying to fit in extra dates.

She neglected to mention that Thomas had promised to lunch with his youngest daughter Rebekah, known as Becky, at Milton Academy near Boston. His good Socialist friend in Boston, Alfred Baker Lewis, saw him in that city and wrote to urge that Thomas "take a holiday" as "you looked pretty tired at the Committee meeting here." Thomas replied by mail, "I don't need a vacation. I just need to see the Socialist Party move along and attend to its main business instead of fighting."

# X

## 1. Population Terrorized

In Arkansas, planters backed by local businessmen, newspapers, churchmen and "law" officers fought the Southern Tenant Farmers' Union with terror. Union members were taken off payrolls, evicted from their shacks and beaten. One of the techniques used to intimidate union members was to arrest them and put them in intentionally foul jail cells with no heat and little food. Mitchell, his business gone, was living temporarily on a stipend furnished by Dr. Amberson and a few other sympathizers in Memphis. Norman Thomas and Reinhold Niebuhr, who headed the Committee on Economic and Racial Justice, had managed to raise a little cash for the battle and to get the American Civil Liberties Union into the fight. A young Socialist preacher from the Ozarks, Ward Rodgers, spent a few weeks teaching illiterate croppers the rudiments of reading, writing and, most important, simple arithmetic, so that they would know when the planters were defrauding them on the contracts. Warned to get out of town, Rodgers lost his temper and said, "If necessary I could lead the sharecroppers to lynch every planter in Poinsett County, but I have no intention of doing so." He was immediately jailed on charges of blasphemy, anarchy and attempting to usurp the government of Arkansas.

C. T. Carpenter, an attorney in the town of Marked Tree, agreed to represent the STFU and its adherents although he was not a Socialist but a Democrat concerned about civil rights and remarkably thoughtless of his own safety. By the time he got Rodgers bailed out, the British author Naomi Mitchison visited Eastern Arkansas with two companions and issued a horrified statement about the croppers who "are being treated worse than animals. . . . They seem to be denied all of their rights." She found that Thomas's status as a superman among them had been raised even higher by an address about the croppers he gave over a nationwide radio hookup. One of them had composed a song in his praise, a small part of it reading:

> *I'm on the way to New York*
> *(I shall not be moved).* . . .
> *Just like a tree that is planted by the water;*
> *Just to see Norman Thomas.* . . .

The verses, she wrote Thomas, were "written by a man who had been badly beaten up—his face showed it—and imprisoned for 40 days. . . . they told me how they'd heard you on the radio." To Thomas, a shining fact of the embattled STFU was that blacks and whites worked together in it in harmony. His outrage over their treatment had brought wry amusement to Walter White of the National Association for the Advancement of Colored People, who wrote that he seemed to forget that blacks had been under Fascist tyranny in the United States for centuries. With Secretary Wallace still dodging him, Thomas talked with Undersecretary of Agriculture Rexford Tugwell and with the deputy administrator of the Federal Emergency Relief Administration, Aubrey Williams. They feared the powerful southern Democratic Senators, but Tugwell felt that, given time, the vast Agricultural Adjustment Administration program would mitigate the abuses. Thomas was less able to take a placid long-run view of people who were suffering and starving in the short run. He was painfully aware that their condition had been made more immediately desperate because of their adherence to the croppers' union, which he had urged on them. He tried in vain to see Chester Davis, administrator of AAA. He was unable to get a hearing at the White House. Through Washington newspapermen he knew, he tried to reach Eleanor Roosevelt about the matter but failed. He sought the help of Felix Frankfurter, who replied in maidenly prose that his intimacy with the President was exaggerated.

Thomas finally was reduced to the extremity of publicizing the sharecropper crisis before the nation even at the risk of getting himself shot. On March 11, 1935, he and Jack Herling arrived in Memphis en route to Little Rock. An anti-Thomas campaign by The Memphis Commercial Appeal had made him unpopular in the area. In Little Rock he asked Governor J. Marion Futrell for protection for the sharecroppers, to no effect; the planters were the Governor's constituents. Thomas then lodged with Attorney Carpenter in Marked Tree and spoke to thousands of croppers, black and white, in nearby hamlets. Some walked many miles to hear him. He was of course called a Communist by local Bourbons—he had indeed been given forty-one lines in Elizabeth Dilling's *The Red Network,* in which Mrs. Roosevelt got only thirty-five—but until his last day in Arkansas it was only name-calling.

One can scarcely imagine Louis Waldman, or for that matter Daniel Hoan or any other Socialist leader, addressing Arkansas sharecroppers under such circumstances. Thomas did so as a Party leader, but he would have done it on humanitarian grounds had there been no such party. His interest in the public welfare went far beyond Party requirements, just as his fame and stature transcended his role as a Socialist. This tour was entirely at his own expense. In Arkansas he was in far more physical danger than he had been in 1926 in Passaic, a few miles across the river from New York, with metropolitan newspapers watching closely. Here he was an interfering Yankee, thirty miles from hostile Memphis, a thousand miles from New York, in gun-toting country. His audiences, so different from the crowds of his New York State campaign, were largely uneducated. He had to use the simplest words and phrases—had to inspire them to hold firm but to shun violence.

On March 15, with Kester and Herling, he reached a village in Mississippi County prettily named Birdsong, though a local wag said "Hogwaller" would be a more fitting name. He had been invited to speak there by black churchmen of the town. As Kester began to introduce Thomas with the phrase "Ladies and gentlemen," he was shouted down by thirty or more planters, described as "armed and drunken," who surrounded the platform. Thomas held aloft a copy of the state constitution, saying that it permitted peaceful assemblage and free speech. They discounted legality, one of them saying, "There ain't gonner be no speaking here. We are the citizens of this county and we run it to suit ourselves. We don't need no Gawd-damned Yankee bastard to tell us what to do."

Herling was struck a glancing blow on the head from behind. Thomas and Kester were jerked from the platform, manhandled into their car and warned to "git." One member of the planters' group was a deputy sheriff who now assumed his official capacity and advised Thomas to get out fast or there might be violence. An Associated Press man who arrived at this moment was surrounded by shotguns and sent off instantly. The Thomas party was followed by several carloads of planters to the county line.

Thereafter the terror was increased with the obvious intention of finishing off the Southern Tenant Farmers' Union once and for all. The Marked Tree cabin of the Reverend A. B. Brookins, the seventy-year-old black chaplain of the union, was riddled with bullets, one of which grazed his daughter's head. Beatings were common. A Negro church near Hitchiecoon, which had been a union meeting place, was burned to the ground. The Reverend T. A. Allen, a black union organizer, was shot dead and there was no investigation. W. H. Stultz, president of the STFU, was so terrorized by night riders that he took refuge in Memphis with his wife and six small children. Mitchell himself was forced to move to Memphis. The high-mettled Mary Hillyer of Thomas's League for Industrial Democracy office went to Marked Tree on her own, addressed a union gathering, then was driven by a mob into Carpenter's office and finally escorted by gunmen out of the county.* Two nights later, Carpenter's home was besieged by an armed band and he was ordered to come out. Carpenter, whose father had fought under Robert E. Lee, got his pistol and warned the marauders to keep their distance. They perforated his house with bullet holes before leaving. The last sentence of a telegram Thomas received from Kester and Mitchell read, "ENTIRE POPULATION TERRORIZED."

"Niebuhr and I," Thomas replied, "are trying . . . to get a really distinguished group of clergymen to risk their necks in Arkansas. We're going to begin on Bishop McConnell." He was aghast at the commotion he had started but there was nothing to do but ride the whirlwind. He sent more letters against the stone wall in Washington, and in another NBC broadcast he urged, "I appeal to you who listen to my voice to bring immediate pressure upon the Federal Government to act." With Senior's help he sought more newspaper publicity. At last he had success, for The New York World-Telegram sent Frazier Hunt to Arkansas for a series of stories, and The New York Times had Raymond Daniell at the scene. One of Daniell's accounts mentioned his meeting in Marked Tree with the Methodist Reverend Abner Sage, who favored the planters and said, "It would have been better to have a few no-account, shiftless people killed at the start than to have all this fuss raised up." Thomas wrote to nine Senators for help against what he called "the most damnable thing in America." He urged The New York Herald Tribune's syndicated Sunday supplement This Week to publish

---

*After her marriage to Paul Blanshard in 1935 (performed by Mayor La Guardia), Miss Hillyer mounted the steps of the United States Treasury Building and startled Wall Street clerks with an impromptu speech urging their unionization.

a story about Carpenter. That courageous attorney, always packing a pistol, fearful for his family, was a pariah in his own town of Marked Tree, filing lawsuits for the STFU in federal court because the local courts would have laughed at him.

Secretary Wallace was as immovable as a tree. He told a Boston audience that the trouble in Arkansas was due to "Communistic and Socialistic gentlemen" who "have gone in to stir up trouble in a sore spot." President Roosevelt again sidestepped Thomas's plea that ". . . I think it is imperative for the honor of your administration before the judgment bar of history and for the sake of all the human values you care for that you should hear at first hand some of the stories that I or others can tell you about the present situation in Arkansas." In May, when Thomas addressed 500 people in New Hampshire in behalf of Eli Bourdon, now running for Governor, Bourdon expressed delight except that he talked less about Bourdon than about sharecroppers.

At long last, when Roosevelt did invite Thomas to the White House, he admitted obliquely that he agreed with Tugwell and Williams about the power of southern Senators who headed important committees, the most potent of them being Joe Robinson of Arkansas, the Senate majority leader and a loyal Roosevelt man.

"Norman, I'm a damned sight better politician than you are," he said.

"Well, certainly, Mr. President," Thomas replied. "You are on that side of the table and I'm on this."

"I know the South," Roosevelt went on, "and there is arising a new generation of leaders in the South and we've got to be patient."

The President was admitting candidly that federal power had its limits. Still, his urging of patience on men in mortal danger seemed unrealistic. But the union began to win through by dint of maintaining the courage to hang on. It now had some 10,000 members needed in the cotton fields. By October, after a strike, they won a raise of 40 percent over their previous average pay of about seventy-five cents a day, causing Mitchell to write Thomas, ". . . we have won the strike and are in a much stronger position than before." To the reporter Frazier Hunt, their struggle was "as inspiring a tale as can be found in the whole history of America."

## 2. Eating Cake

Not surprisingly, Thomas, dealing with sharecropper poverty in the South and with Senior's growing financial straits in Chicago, looked on the prosperous Waldman, Cahan and the rest as gentlemen who were eating cake and not over-exercised about the troubles of others. Senior was doling out five dollars a week in salaries to each of his staff and still getting farther behind in rent and bills. Mrs. Senior, expecting a baby, warned him to put enough money aside to get her out of the hospital. Unluckily, while she was *in* the hospital, the mother of a girl in the Party office died and it took all of Senior's cash to bury her. Through sheer good fortune, a pleasant note from Violet contained a gift check for $35 which, in that depressed time, liberated Mrs. Senior and her child (whose middle name was Norman) from the hospital.

The financial hold The Daily Forward had on the Party—the $500 monthly it paid for running expenses and its liberal special gifts—was essential financially but helpful morally only so long as harmony reigned. Even then it tended to give The Forward and its Old Guards-men a trace of paternalism and authority that had never sat well with less-monied branches of the faithful. Thomas had long since put his finger on this money factor as unwholesome and had sought vainly to find other sources of income—not easy in the depression.

In 1935 the Forward payments lapsed for several months. Senior was torn between poverty and pride. Should he ask for the money? At last he was given the news: The Forward had ceased its payments. The financial pressure swelled along with intraparty resentment. There was a feeling at the Chicago office that the Old Guard was enjoying Senior's discomfiture and betting on how long he could stay open. Meanwhile the National Executive Committee had voted to permit "reformed" Communists who had left that party to join the Socialist Party as individuals if approved by local branches. Ben Gitlow was among those who joined on this basis, causing bitter protest from the Old Guard, who said that Communist elements were plotting to destroy the Party from within. They seemed more correct than Thomas on this score, for Git-low himself later wrote that the extreme left wing of the Party "swarmed with agents of the Communist Party, the Lovestonites and the Trotskyites." ". . . [Our] New York comrades," Thomas wrote the National Executive Committee, "can detect a Communist a mile off but

. . . some of [the comrades] . . . support more or less openly Republican or Democratic politicians." He was sure of his ground, writing to The Times in reply to a Waldman complaint, "It has never been my idea . . . to try to reform the Communists by marrying them," and emphasizing the danger of being "stabbed during the honeymoon." The middle-roading Daniel Hoan, who was trying to mediate between the Party factions, wrote to The Times to protest its distortion of Socialist policies through "a reporter who is vehemently lined up with one extreme faction of the Party." Thomas thought that the Old Guard and the extreme left wing were "both crazy," and he conceded discouragement to Darlington Hoopes, a Party leader of Reading; "the New York situation is a kind of millstone around my neck and terribly handicaps my usefulness." In the fall of 1935 the Old Guard quietly barred Thomas from speaking to the New York Socialist groups under their control. He was getting blistering letters from old Socialists he had known personally and with affection for years. Some accused him of betrayal or of getting rich on his League for Industrial Democracy salary—though on the contrary that job represented a drain on his earning power which he could not possibly have afforded to continue had it not been for Violet's inheritance. One Brooklyn Socialist emulated Zola in a letter headed *"J'accuse,"* which charged him with the following:

"high treason";

"betrayal of the trust reposed in you";

"violation of Socialist ethics";

"flouting of fundamental principles of democracy";

"arrogating to yourself the role of the entire NEC";

"being a party to a dastardly cabal to disrupt our movement";

being a member of "a small vicious group";

having a "lust for power" that "will brook no opposition";

"flagrantly flaunting the prestige that attaches to your name and person";

behaving "like a cheap stage conspirator."

This indictment ended, "I charge you with fomenting a fratricidal war, from which only the vultures of Communism, hovering above the fray in lascivious anticipation of feasting on the carrion, can profit."

At the same time, some of the more ardent of the Militants and left-wingers let him know they felt he was babying the Old Guard. He wrote in stern admonition to Francis Henson, a Revolutionary Policy Committee leader, when that group on its own issued a declaration which was nearly a direct advocacy of armed insurrection—a declaration which the Old Guard seized on as new evidence of Communist infiltration. To Thomas it was not as funny as it was to a Boston paper which chuckled over the idea of a revolutionary Socialist Party:

> Imagine the picture of the gentle Norman Thomas in the shoes of a grim mass executioner like Lenin. And take our local Socialist leaders. Can anyone imagine that prim and precise gentleman, Alfred Baker Lewis, leaving his beautiful Cambridge mansion on the day of the revolution and ordering his chauffeur to drive him to the barricades instead of the office? Or the scholarly Dr. Albert Sprague Coolidge, with all his youthful zeal for the Socialist Party, deserting his test tubes in the Harvard laboratory to shoot down the capitalists in Harvard Square?
>
> No. The revolution here will not be made by the Socialists. If and when the Communists do make it the Socialists will be the first victims of the terror as they were in Russia. Norman Thomas, as the Socialist leader, will have no more chance than Kerensky had in Russia.

This was the kind of toothless and helpless Socialist Party that the vinegary younger hotspurs kept warning Thomas about. From the other side, Feigenbaum kept sending Thomas three- and four-page letters like distress rockets at sea, stressing that Feigenbaum had given his life to the Party and would have nothing further to live for if it foundered ("I am making what may be my last, despairing attempt to . . . stop what is rapidly becoming a sort of mass-suicide.") His letters were moving examples of a kind of old-Socialist love of party that could hardly be duplicated by Republicans or Democrats. From Milwaukee, Mayor Hoan sought to spread balm. He seriously advised Thomas that he was too long-faced about it all, that he should make light of the fracas by saying, for example, "that you are willing to buy boxing gloves so that the leaders can put on a real fight . . ." Hoan noted to other members of the National Executive Committee that "this is getting on the nerves of Norman Thomas. . . ." He reminded the Old Guard that they had started the ruckus in the first place by insisting on leaving the Declaration unchanged when it could have been modified in Detroit.

### 3. Doing Without Lunches

Family concerns gave Thomas momentary relief from his predicaments. In June 1935 he gave away his second daughter Frances when she was married to John Gates at the Cold Spring Harbor house, with

Sidney Lovett presiding. William Thomas and his bride Mary had moved into the fourth floor of the Thomas house on Eighteenth Street. The Gateses now took the third floor, so that the house contained three family layers and was less often available as a hotel. Violet, soon to give up her restaurant, said that it had never made her a profit but at least it brought her a son-in-law. Meanwhile, Polly Thomas Miller, the first married daughter, and her husband were living in New Haven while he completed his medical studies. In September the birth of their son Norman Thomas Miller made Thomas and Violet grandparents for the first time.

Meanwhile the inexorable Party struggle continued in steady strife and with mounting crises and confrontations.

The Socialist Party of Indiana (680 members) split on Old Guard–Militant issues with the Old Guard state leadership preparing to conduct a referendum on questions including that of seceding from the national organization, as Oregon had. This would have contravened the Party constitution. Indiana Militants also charged that the referendum would be unfair, being in the control of the Old Guard. For the national Party to intervene after the fact would mean a costly lawsuit, so Senior, with the assent of the entire National Executive Committee except for Oneal, sent Paul Porter full speed to Indianapolis. There he informed the state leader that their charter was suspended, and the Indiana records were surrendered to him. Oneal and the New York Old Guard denounced the move as "Cheka methods."

Impatient Militants in New York City, including Jack Altman, Amicus Most and Max Delson, demanded the founding of a "nonfactional" Socialist paper in opposition to The New Leader. Thomas opposed this as divisive, but Militant pressure became intractable, and in February 1935 was launched the weekly Socialist Call, whose masthead told the story of Party discord: "Official organ of the Socialist Party of Arkansas, Illinois, Missouri, Ohio and West Virginia. Endorsed by the Socialist Party of the states of Indiana, Massachusetts and Michigan, and by the Young People's Socialist League of America." Julius Gerber warned Thomas that if this move led to Militant victory, it would be a Pyrrhic one. Thomas, whose columns for The Leader had seldom been tampered with, found that in his article for the first issue of The Call, his praise for an anti-Soviet book by Vladimir Tchernavin and his wife had been deleted.

The New Leader did not take The Call's claims lying down. ". . . The New Leader continues to support the Socialist Party of the United

States," it said. "In so doing it does not pledge blind allegiance to Party officials or so-called 'leaders' [the latter a slap at Thomas]. It continues to be the official organ of the Socialist Party of New York State and of the states of Pennsylvania, Maryland, West Virginia and Indiana."

The New York Yipsels protested against the Old Guard refusal to admit them into the Party on coming of age unless they forswore Militant doctrine and subscribed to Socialism as interpreted by the Old Guard. Thomas was so popular with the Yipsels that they had adapted the sharecropper ballad, singing, "Thomas is our leader—we shall not be moved." At the Socialist picnic that summer, forty-odd Yipsels outraged the Old Guard by snake-dancing as they sold copies of the despised Call in Leader country.

Senior and his Chicago staff were now often doing without lunches. Thomas, who was chairman of the finance committee, wrote, "I find it a virtual impossibility to raise money from friendly sources because of the general belief that we are dead or dying." He regretted his still-pending lawsuit against the cross-eyed deputy sheriff in Illinois, on which he had already paid $200 in lawyers' fees, which would have bought a lot of lunches. His desperation was reflected in a somewhat crusty letter to the Reverend Douglas Anderson in Illinois, in which he expressed disappointment that the Illinois Socialists had not made better propagandist use of the case and said, "There's no use crying over spilt milk but I want to know how much more I will have to spill."

The Party, doing little but fighting, was paralyzed in any constructive activities, and with an election year looming. The arguments Thomas got in favor of ditching the Old Guard and starting fresh came from valued and intelligent Militant friends ranging from the experienced Sam De Witt—one of the fabled Assemblymen expelled in 1920—to the young and forceful Paul Porter. De Witt thought the Old Guard corrupted beyond repair because their union connections gave them a profit motive in Socialism and "We must bury the old set-up and start a new Socialist Party right here, using whatever good timber there is left of the old house, but building mainly on the youth for foundation." Porter wrote Thomas, "The National office has taken the worst licking in the whole fight. . . . The O.G. has completely sabotaged it. . . . But unless real money is raised . . . and unless a real Party-building program is seriously undertaken, I am through wasting my time on the Party. And I think Clarence [Senior], too, should resign." Within a fortnight Porter had resigned his "salaried" Party post and become editor of a labor paper in Kenosha, Wisconsin, though still remaining a loyal member.

To raise money and stir things up, the Militant but penniless New York Call arranged a debate in Madison Square Garden between Thomas and Browder. Browder had pushed the idea, knowing the Socialist Party's poverty and making it attractive by offering all proceeds to the Socialists—an offer, it hardly need be said, motivated not by generosity but by the knowledge that the debate would further the split among the Socialists. Gerber and other Old Guard leaders threatened Thomas with expulsion, arguing that to debate with Browder was equivalent to joining a united front with the Communists. The pro-Thomas National Executive Committee voted down that argument and the two men met November 27 before a crowd of more than 20,000. Thomas did not dislike the brisk, haggard-looking Browder, whom he had met intermittently for years. The calumny Browder had heaped on Thomas and the Party had not been as bitter as the invective used by Foster and others. "The Socialists and Communists joined in singing the 'International,' the 'Red Flag' and 'Solidarity Forever,' " The Times said. "At one point Mr. Thomas led the singing." Browder did not really debate. He oozed comradeship, urged a united front against Fascism and complimented Thomas on his opposition to the Old Guard—a blunder bringing a Thomas reply that Browder was "not qualified to be a judge of the factional conflict in the Socialist Party." The Old Guard shunned the debate except for a few spies, so that the Communists and fellow travelers probably outnumbered the Socialists. As if under instruction, they cheered Thomas's camaraderie and his praise for the achievements of Soviet Russia. The cheers died when he rejected a formal united front because of doubt of Communist good faith, and turned to boos when he assailed Communist doctrine and methods and criticized Mother Russia's totalitarianism and her ruthlessness: "Is Russia so weak that it cannot afford, 18 years after the revolution, to grant civil liberties to its citizens? . . . It is by Russian oil that the defenseless Ethiopians are killed."* The affair was not the "love feast" that both Waldman and Lee called it, but a thaw when compared with the Communist-Socialist riot in the same hall eighteen months earlier. It brought in several thousand desperately needed dollars. (And a check for $3,000 from the wealthy and socially conscious Margaret Gage,

---

*Max Eastman later descended to Daily Worker flimflam when (in *Love and Revolution,* p. 584), he cited only Thomas's praise for Russia, giving a totally false impression.

followed by $2,000 more two weeks later, moved Thomas to warm praise of Miss Gage, who could hardly have known that she was helping to save Socialist workers from malnutrition only less serious than that of the sharecroppers.)

### 4. A Misunderstanding

Each faction made undignified efforts to win over Socialists elsewhere in the country who viewed the New York struggle with consternation. Socialist loyalty could be a sacred thing. A Pennsylvania member later wrote Thomas about two comrades "so discouraged over the Party split" that one died of a brain tumor and the other went insane. Thomas had decided that he had no recourse but to fight the Old Guard for supremacy in New York and the nation, writing to Alfred Baker Lewis, "For myself, I feel almost a sense of relief that things have come to a head."

Things came to a head indeed when the Old Guard dissolved twelve pro-Militant Party branches in the city as troublemakers. New York Centrists protested against this and joined the Militants in a coalition that outnumbered the Old Guard in its very own bailiwick. Vladeck warned, as if he knew of a new Old Guard alignment brewing, "Comrade Thomas, mark my word. If the present breach is not healed up there will be no Socialist Party to speak of in New York City, and if one should come, you will not be in it." But there were more like the Centrist Jessie Wallace Hughan, Thomas's friend and ally ever since she had joined him in the formation of the Fellowship of Reconciliation before the war, who wrote to him: "I . . . am declining to stand either for the Right or the Left, but I do stand unequivocally for Norman Thomas and a solid Party behind him in 1936."

The new Militant-Centrist coalition, outvoting the Old Guard, formed a rump party with Thomas's cooperation and declared itself to be the true New York State Party. The new group elected Harry Laidler, Max Delson and Jack Altman to the offices held by Waldman, Lee and Gerber (and which these latter declared they continued to hold). The Thomas-oriented National Executive Committee, which for more than a year had been fairly evenhanded in its efforts to mend the breach, now gave in, revoked the charter of the Old Guard organization and recognized the new Thomasite state party—an act the Old Guard defied. According to New York law, however, control of the state party had to be decided by a primary election, which was set for April 2, 1936. There were so many meetings held at the Thomas home, often with dinner on the side, that Jack Altman later commented admiringly on the Thomas china and silver and said it was there that he learned fancy table manners. It turned out that his birthday fell on November 20 as did Thomas's, and he was presented with one of Violet's spaniels.

"The left wing of the Socialist Party," Waldman said right out in The Times, "has become the conscious or unconscious tool of the Communist Party. Under Mr. Thomas's leadership . . . [it] has lost about 7,000 members, about one-third of the national membership." Thomas replied in the same capitalist medium: "The Old Guard, as a final climax to its adventures in sabotage, has read itself out of any true Socialist Party. There was nothing left for us but to set up a true Socialist Party in New York. . . . What we want is a clean, inclusive, aggressive Socialist Party."

When it became apparent to Thomas that a national majority of Socialists opposed any negotiations with the Communists, he dropped the idea of specific united fronts with them. He kept searching in Washington and Wisconsin for an alliance with farmer-labor groups. Jack Herling opened a press bureau in the National Press Building in Washington which unfortunately cost money but gave the Party skilled representation there. Nominally on Thomas's side were some of the more idealistic and also some of the more radical national Party leaders —Krzycki, Coolidge, Lewis, Devere Allen, Maynard Krueger and Reinhold Niebuhr among them. Favoring the Old Guard were James Maurer, Mayor Jasper McLevy of Bridgeport and others, while some still tried to stay neutral and heal the breach, including Mayor Hoan of Milwaukee and Darlington Hoopes of the important Pennsylvania Party.

In line with the National Executive Committee permission to admit "unattached radicals," the entrance of some 300 Trotskyites into the Socialist Party was effected early in 1936 through the mediation of Sidney Hook, professor of philosophy at New York University, one of their number. While they were of course bitter enemies of Browder's Stalinist party and were considered Communist castoffs and free agents, and many young Militants clamored for their acceptance, Thomas was wary. He placed restrictions on their enrollment, wanting proof that they had been cleansed of the habit of ennobling treachery and that they would not bring more factionalism to the current discord. He understood Communists, but still felt optimistic about their regeneration. Unknown to Hook, the whole purpose of the Trotskyites, as later described by their leader, James P. Cannon, was to "get into the Socialist Party while it remained in a state of flux" and capture it. They were in contact with Leon Trotsky, who was then in exile in Norway and who, according to Cannon, counseled their strategy. It was Trotsky who uttered the jeer about Thomas calling himself a Socialist "as the result of a misunderstanding." Cannon's account of the parleys with the Socialists demonstrated his fanaticism. He and his henchmen met with Militant leaders including Altman, Porter, Gus Tyler and Herbert Zam —once with Thomas himself at Eighteenth Street. He wrote:

> Our problem was to make an agreement with this rabble to admit us to the Socialist Party. . . . It was a difficult and sticky job, very disagreeable. But that did not deter us. A Trotskyist will do anything for the party, even if he has to crawl on his belly in the mud. . . . [The Socialist Party men] wouldn't allow us the honor and dignity of joining as a body. . . . No, we had to join as individuals, leaving every local SP branch the option of refusing to admit us.

Cannon's honor and dignity were also affronted because his group was required to end its Trotskyite propaganda publications. His denunciation of the young Militants with whom he dealt was sweeping: "They were ignorant, untalented, petty-minded, weak, cowardly, treacherous and vain. They had other faults too." He forbore from specifying the other faults. During this same time Browder appealed to Thomas for a total organic united front which would enable them to work together in the formation of a farmer-labor party. Browder was so anxious for union that he offered to be running mate on a ticket headed by Thomas for President. But Thomas repeated publicly his suspicion of old and new Communist wiles:

> The differences between us preclude organic unity. We do not accept control from Moscow, the old Communist accent on inevitable violence and party dictatorship, or the new Communist accent on the possible good of war against Fascism and the new Communist political opportunism. We assert genuine civil liberty in opposition to Communist theory and practice in Russia.

The primary election for control of the Party in the state was the final executioner of Socialist solidarity. The Old Guard had every advantage of money and publicity. In addition to The Forward and The Leader, its allies controlled two foreign-language Socialist dailies, the German

Volkszeitung and the Finnish Raivaaja; all of these poured vituperation on Thomas as inclined toward Communism and violence, as an ambitious intriguer, and as one who had used the Party (and a handsome League for Industrial Democracy salary) as a stepping-stone to fame which drew him large lecture fees and enormous audiences for his books. WEVD was also an exclusive Old Guard outlet over which Waldman and McLevy assailed him and urged his repudiation. The Thomasites had only the young and feeble Call. Against this disadvantage, Thomas achieved a personal victory when his group won by 4,405 votes to 3,453, electing thirty delegates to the Party national convention against twelve for the Old Guard, which demanded recounts to no avail.

The split now extended to the May Day celebration, Thomas and the Militants (with what seems more spite than judgment) having agreed on a joint gathering in Union Square with the Communists. The Old Guard joined with anti-Communist unionists in having their own celebration at the Polo Grounds, The New Leader saying 70,000 attended, The Call placing attendance at 45,000 while claiming the Thomasite gathering to be the "mightiest . . . in 50 years." Thomas himself was in the Midwest. Harry Laidler, still the mediator, read a message from Thomas to his own Union Square multitude, then hurried to the Polo Grounds to read a Thomas greeting there to a reception not unmixed with boos. David Dubinsky, a member since 1911, resigned from the Party, attacking Thomas for "tying up with Communists for a joint May Day parade" and for abandoning the policies of Morris Hillquit. Thomas's suspicions of the Old Guard–American Federation of Labor brand of Socialism were soon to be realized. The Call shrewdly surmised that Dubinsky would support Roosevelt, and the shape of things to come became clearer a week later when Waldman told a reporter, "Personally I admire Roosevelt, and I have said publicly that if I could not support a Socialist candidate I would support him." The Socialist Old Guard, which had fussed about Thomas's incorrect Marxism, seemed ready to commit that final treason in the book of Marxism and go bourgeois.

At the Party convention, which began May 24, 1936, at the Cleveland auditorium (and which the Party could scarcely afford), the New York Old Guard was voted out and Thomas's faction became the official Party in New York City and the state. Browder was there, urging a joint Socialist-Communist ticket, which Thomas forcefully rejected. There is some question whether the convention could have been held had not Thomas a month earlier made a grueling speechmaking tour to the

Coast via Colorado and Arizona and back via Montana and Wisconsin, charging only his second-class hotel and restaurant bills and handing over to Senior his total profit of $782.15. Senior being ill from overwork, his wife wrote Thomas to thank him for "your sacrifice in not taking any salary and in cutting on little things throughout the whole trip."

Violet Thomas attended every convention session—"even far into the night," said The Call, "and continually plying her knitting needles." She was knitting a sweater for seven-month-old Paul Norman Senior. Thomas, who would have preferred to run for Congress where he felt he had a chance, won an ovation and was nominated for President. Leo Krzycki was regarded by some delegates as an attractive running mate, but Krzycki's boss in the Amalgamated was Waldman's friend and Thomas's enemy, Sidney Hillman. He got word from Hillman that he had better not adorn any Socialist ticket since he would be expected to support Roosevelt. Krzycki backed away and the nomination went to the unknown George Nelson of Wisconsin, a former dirt farmer, now a farm cooperative official. Thomas received congratulatory telegrams from his children, one from Becky Thomas (now at Vassar) containing a jest that turned out truer than intended: "Congratulations and sympathy on nomination. . . ." "Thomas Wins Nomination But Wrecks Party," The New Leader headlined.

With the Party split now irrevocable, the convention voted to undo the measures which had nominally caused the split. The afflictive Declaration of Principles was amended and any further united-front negotiation with the Communists was banned. The convention nevertheless represented a victory for the Militants, many of them young and cocky and from New York. Political tact dictated a judicious attitude that would mollify those middling Socialists still uncertain which way to go. Here Thomas apparently had a failure in delicacy, for he was partial enough toward the Militants to offend Hoopes of Pennsylvania and perhaps others of the same persuasion. "[You seemed] much more cordial to our self-styled Lefts than to the older Comrades who have built the movement . . . ," Hoopes later complained.

The Party, with the loss of the Old Guard, had lost its almoner and its school, its radio station and its summer conference meeting place. It had lost many American Federation of Labor union men and had added the enmity of Dubinsky to the enmity of Hillman. The paid-up Party membership in the forty-eight states had dropped from around 21,000 to 11,711, some of the loss represented by the departed Old Guard but some also by Socialists all over the country who left out of discouragement over the long schism. But Thomas was confident that the break ended dissension at last and made way for new progress. He agreed with Niebuhr, who said, "The vital forces of the Party are not with the [Old Guard]. . . . In New York there is already a remarkable burst of new energy in the Party since the hand of the Old Guard has been removed from the wheel of power."

But within two months, the national office in Chicago would be broke again, Herling would be unable to pay his rent and expenses in Washington, the Trotskyites would be sowing dissension, more members would resign and Thomas would be running for President virtually at his own expense.

## 5. Too Soft-Hearted?

There was something lacking in Thomas as a party leader, but there was disagreement about what it was. Some felt that he lacked decision —that he disagreed in important respects with the Militants and yet mostly gave them their way because they were young, enthusiastic and could be expected to grow up to better sense. A leading Centrist, Sol Levitas, thought that Thomas had the kind of courage it took to face goons or the police but that when he addressed a throng of Militants singing, "Thomas is our leader—we shall not be moved," he did not have the heart to tell them they were mistaken. Ben Gitlow said Thomas's eternal busyness was a disrupting factor: "[He] was so engrossed in his own activities, which kept him moving all over the country . . . that he had no time to watch his own house." He also seemed inherently unable to confine himself to his central purpose, to ward off the many appeals for his attention which less sympathetic men instantly declined or referred to aides. Because he became known as an easy mark, he constantly heard from friends of friends or utter strangers who begged him to solve their problems. Bad treatment of anyone by anyone distressed him, but it was worst of all if someone was mistreated by a branch of the government that was supposed to protect him. He was invariably spending valuable time looking into the case of some man said to be unjustly imprisoned, someone claimed to be falsely confined in a mental institution, someone in a snarl with the immigration authorities or even a widow in need of food or hospitalization.

There was the case of philosophy professor Arthur J. Kraus of City College who had fled Poland in 1930 because of anti-Semitic injustice, entered the United States on a temporary visa and joined the faculty. City College had dismissed him after he had gone on a hunger strike to call attention to continuing injustices in Poland. When he was unemployed, his status lapsed to that of alien and his deportation was ordered. In Poland his life might well be in danger. Thomas, who knew Kraus not at all, conferred with John Dewey, Niebuhr, John Haynes Holmes and others about this problem, which hung unsettled for months. Again, he wrote the President himself in defense of Charles Krumbein, a New York Communist official who had been anything but friendly:

> I have been acquainted with Mr. Krumbein for many years, during most of which time he has been a bitter critic of the party to which I belong and of me personally. I know him well enough to know that he is a man of character and devotion to his cause. That cause is Communism and although he is in jail for using a United States passport alleged to have been obtained by false statements, it is clear that the severity of his sentence of eighteen months plus four years' probation is solely due to his political beliefs. . . .

He was working to liberate some Kentucky miners from the prison in which he believed they had been unjustly confined, on mine company say-so, for strike activity. He was bending his own efforts and trying to enlist Attorney General Cummings to punish Klan violence against Socialists in Tampa, Florida. He debated Dr. Townsend on radio. He traveled again to Hillsboro and other mill towns in North Carolina to speak for cruelly underpaid textile workers who were striking, and met the wealthy young Socialist worker Jack Fies, a spastic cripple, whose subsequent death created an unusual situation. Thomas was not only the Party strategist but also its quartermaster, propagandist, adjutant, investigator, cavalry and tank corps, always moving into enemy territory.

There was his advance on Terre Haute, Debs's town and a holy place to Socialists, where Governor Paul McNutt placed the city and whole county under martial law because of a reasonably peaceable strike at the Columbia Enameling and Stamping Company. One hundred and fifty-eight union workers were jailed for several days, many of them without being charged or permitted to see an attorney. Assembly was forbidden. A Socialist organizer, Leo Vernon, was locked up when he sought to hold a street meeting. Powers Hapgood, a colleague of Thomas on the Socialist National Executive Committee and a native of

Indiana who had been Socialist candidate for Governor there in 1932, arrived in Terre Haute to protest against the arrests. He was promptly jailed. Thomas, appealed to by unionists who probably voted for Roosevelt, reached the city by plane August 30, 1935. He was outraged by McNutt's raw abuse of power. He never pretended to be heroic about such confrontations, admitting on another occasion that they made him nervous but that he was buoyed up by a sense of duty. On this occasion his twenty-fifth wedding anniversary was just two days off and he badly wanted to be in Cold Spring Harbor, not in jail, that day. As it turned out, his prestige was such that McNutt saw to it that Vernon and Hapgood were freed and stood beside Thomas on the courthouse steps as he delivered to a crowd of 2,000 some pungent remarks about civil liberty. The heat was on again after Thomas left, Vernon and Hapgood were again arrested and others went to jail. The Party retained a Chicago Socialist attorney, Joseph Jacobs (who luckily gave his services gratis) and McNutt ultimately ceased his ruthless and illegal use of troops for intimidation. But he gave up with such reluctance and delay that he was one of the comparatively few for whom Thomas invented an opprobrious tag—"the Hoosier Hitler."

Thomas and Violet made careful plans to head a Socialist motor caravan and sound-truck tour of Louisiana "to expose the demagoguery of Huey Long's share-the-wealth plan." Long scoffed, saying, "Mr. Thomas won't get three people to listen to him," and proved to be right, for Long was assassinated three weeks before the invasion was to begin and it was canceled. Thomas made a speaking tour with Violet as far west as Nebraska. He visited Toronto to look into the organization of the Canadian Cooperative Commonwealth Federation, a political alliance of farmers and workers that the Party might learn from. He drove his invaluable secretary, Miss Straus, so hard that typos crept even into letters to Roosevelt and Secretary Wallace. He was troubled by a series of disconnected letters from a woman in Chicago, obviously unbalanced, who rambled on about having a baby, for which at times she blamed Thomas and at other times other persons including a Chippewa Indian.

His activities would surely have kept three men of ordinary vigor hopping. He flew to Miami to address an American Federation of Labor meeting and urge that organization not to hold its convention in Tampa unless the Klan complicity with officialdom there was broken. He wrote an article for Foreign Affairs about labor under Hitler and another for The New Republic about the Socialist Party schism. He contracted to

198

write a book for Macmillan to be called *After the New Deal, What?* His daughter Frances filled in briefly as his secretary while Miss Straus went on vacation and found the work exhausting because he did everything at top speed: "He would say as he whizzed out the door, 'Call so-and-so at such-and-such a number and tell him this-and-that.' I couldn't remember all that." He censured Ray Murphy, national commander of the American Legion, for parts of his radio speech on national defense including Murphy's claims about American purity of motive and the certainty that the nation would never fight except to repel attack:

> Oh, yeah? Ask the Indians, the Mexicans, the Spaniards, the Haitians, the Nicaraguans, yes, the Germans. Did these people attack us? How and where?

And Thomas even managed to be jailed briefly himself—his first pinch in New York—as he led forty strike-sympathizing pickets in front of Mays department store in Brooklyn, a mishap that made him telephone Columbia University, where he was due to speak next, to say that he was "being delayed by a policeman."

## 6. It's a Stone Wall

Against the Thomasites the Old Guard took revenge so swift that it seemed long planned. They immediately founded the Social Democratic Federation, which was even smaller than Thomas's party but had important friends. Hillman and Dubinsky had recently merged their big unions with the new Congress of Industrial Organizations, headed by John L. Lewis. Dubinsky and Hillman, wanting to back Roosevelt but to steer clear of the Democratic Party's tainted Tammany, joined with Waldman in launching the American Labor Party in New York State,* a catch-all which was assured of a huge union following. The Social Democratic Federation went capitalist and aligned itself with the American Labor Party.

Thomas scoffed at the Social Democratic Federation as "neither Socialist, democratic or [sic] a federation but merely a halfway port to Tammany Hall," and saw it as a vehicle for bargaining for power. The new alignment brought complications. Leo Krzycki, still nominally

---

*"Labor's Nonpartisan League" was the name given the national political association through which labor would help elect Roosevelt.

chairman of the Socialist Party, embarrassed the Party by resigning and declaring (on Hillman's order) for Roosevelt. Two members of the Socialist National Executive Committee, Powers Hapgood and Franz Daniel, were also CIO officials, though not in Hillman's or Dubinsky's union. Their loyalty to Thomas and the Party was diluted by their loyalty to the CIO and their fear of union reprisals against them if they did not support Roosevelt, and they urged Thomas to "go easy" in his Presidential campaign. Thomas was elected chairman in Krzycki's place, to head a confused and divided party.

Some of the Militants who had been impatient with him for holding off the split so long were now appalled to find that they had been backed into a corner. The split hurt both sides but was more immediately disastrous to the Socialist Party. Sidney Hillman, saying rightly that the Socialists were "forever talking, talking, talking," attacked Thomas as an "outsider" who could not form a real labor party. David Dubinsky was talking about Thomas when he said, "We must bear in mind that all enemies of labor are now combining against the New Deal, against FDR, and that means against labor . . ." With them were other powerful unionists including George Meany and Joseph Ryan. Thomas's Socialist Party, instead of showing the expected unity and energy, was soon rent by new factional quarrels. In place of Waldman, Lee and Gerber to deal with in New York, Thomas now dealt with such determined men as the young union official Jack Altman, the young college professor Frank Trager and the young attorney Max Delson. Clarence Senior still ran the Chicago office, virtually unpaid, but his health was so damaged by overwork and discouragement that he decided to quit after the campaign was over—a severe blow. The Party sought to replace the lost Rand School with what it called the Debs Labor School in makeshift quarters on Twenty-first Street with a faculty including Trager, Professor Coolidge (who had to travel from Cambridge), Harry Laidler and others, but there was little money for organization and the school's subsistence was precarious.

Nineteen thirty-six was the Presidential year Thomas had pointed to in 1932 and afterward—the year when he could build on his previous campaigns, the year when the public would be educated to Socialism and the Party would be strong, the year when the New Deal's sophistries would be clear, when workers and farmers would at last drop their capitalistic illusions and not only elect Socialist Congressmen but give Thomas himself a rousing vote that might actually mean a chance for election in 1940. It was instead a catastrophe and he knew it. The Times was interested enough to send the artist-reporter S. J. Woolf to interview and sketch him at Cold Spring Harbor. Woolf saw a sign in front telling of spaniels for sale—an indication of practicality in this wealthy neighborhood where most of the surrounding houses were more magnificent than that of the Thomases. He found Thomas magnanimous in his willingness to give Roosevelt credit for initiative and effort which was, however, strictly capitalist and had increased corporation profit by 36 percent in 1935 while increasing employment only 2 1/2 percent.

"He has adopted and adapted some Socialist ideas and used them for props for a shaky, falling structure," Thomas said. "Without their support it would have already collapsed. . . . There are 12 million men and women out of work. A sixth of our population is on relief." He grew vehement as he talked of the country's needs, then checked himself and smiled. "Do you remember what Queen Victoria once said to Mr. Gladstone when he became too explosive . . . ? 'You know, Mr. Gladstone,' she said, 'you are not addressing the House of Commons.'. . . . But I cannot help getting excited when I think of the possibilities in this country, and of the way these possibilities have been neglected."

The League for Independent Political Action had largely switched to Roosevelt and the Independent Committee for Thomas and Nelson had thinned down mostly to local loyalists such as John Haynes Holmes (back in the fold), Niebuhr, Freda Kirchwey and John Dewey. The Socialist Party got on the ballot in only thirty-six states, being disqualified on technicalities in such important states as Ohio, North Carolina and Florida. On tour, Thomas discovered that when he made a speech he was usually followed very closely by Leo Krzycki, speaking against him and for Roosevelt. In Buffalo, where Thomas had both Violet and Jack Herling in tow, Herling was in the lobby of the Statler Hotel when Krzycki came in. Embarrassed, Krzycki said he was sorry he was required by Hillman to do this. "Why don't you go up and see Norman and Violet?" Herling suggested. "Will they see me?" Krzycki asked. Herling telephoned their room. "Bring him up," Thomas said. Herling did so and watched while Krzycki, an emotional man, burst into tears as he explained to the Thomases that he was forced to counter-campaign, and both Thomas and Violet were much moved by his penitence.

Violet, asked by a reporter how she liked to campaign with her husband, said it was "good sport," adding, "Besides, how would I ever get a chance to see him if I didn't go along?" Thomas, concentrating his fire on Roosevelt, still had his very real fear of a Fascist takeover and had been impressed by Sinclair Lewis's *It Can't Happen Here.* Browder, for all his talk, was running for President on the Communist ticket after all, but really campaigning slyly for Roosevelt* by treating him gently and attacking Landon as Fascist, an idea Thomas derided. Thomas had looked over Kansas personally and had had some correspondence with Landon, finding him refreshingly direct and honest, if reactionary—no McNutt or Futrell. "They want Coolidge, not Hitler," Thomas said of Landon's backers, and he remained a lifelong friend-in-disagreement of Landon's.

He also had to contend with the Union Party candidate, Congressman William Lemke, whose connections with Father Coughlin and Gerald L. K. Smith made him suspect. But worst of all were the growing defections in his own Socialist Party. Darlington Hoopes and his Pennsylvania brethren may have merely found a convenient excuse in complaining that they were annoyed by visits from Militants who took it upon themselves to instruct them in politics. Hoopes resigned from the National Executive Committee and the Pennsylvanians assured Roosevelt most of the Socialist vote simply by refraining from any mention of Thomas. Much of Massachusetts was lost to the Old Guard, half of Connecticut jumped the traces with McLevy, Oregon was virtually dead, California too, and Roy Lancaster, state Party secretary in Indiana, gave up and handed in his resignation because interest was gone, writing, "It was no accident that Norman Thomas spoke to less than 2,000 people at six meetings in the state, while during the last [1932] campaign he spoke to 10,000 in one meeting." Even Wisconsin, that homeland of successful Socialism, had been weakened by the dissension spreading from New York, to which was now added hurtful eruptions by the Trotskyites. Mayor Hoan worked hard as campaign chairman for the Thomas ticket but let it be known that this was his last big chore, writing, "I cannot much longer serve on the NEC." He stoutly denied an Arthur Krock story that Wisconsin Socialists were cool toward Thomas, but Hoan seemed fed up with the troubles of the national Party and ready to let it go. Enthusiasm had fled. When one Militant urged that Pennsylvania Socialists be disciplined for their desertion, Professor Coolidge commented, "A man sick unto death does not talk about 'discipline.'"

---

*The Kremlin wanted Roosevelt elected. In Moscow, the foxy Browder had told his superiors, no doubt correctly, that open support of Roosevelt by the American Communist Party would lose him votes.

Adding to the dolor were the confusion and ill feeling that the Trotsky-ite infiltrators were already causing in the Party. "Some of them are very useful," Thomas wrote hopefully. ". . . On some counts they will have to be watched." When Thomas commented in his "At the Front" column in The Call about the astonishing Moscow trials without show-ing proper certainty that the condemned Zinoviev and Kamenev were heroes and martyrs, he received a flood of angry letters from new Trotskyite Party members. The Trotskyites seemed to have all but taken over some of the Yipsel organizations. One officer of the Boston Yipsels sent an adulatory cable to Trotsky in Norway which caused Thomas to admonish her that the Yipsels were not making Party policy: "It is up to the Socialist Party of America to formulate its own line. . . ."

And money—if money before had been a problem, it was now a humiliation. Violet and Thomas invited the wealthy and liberal Mrs. Bayard James and her mother to dinner and managed to coax $2,500 from them, but money was going down the endless drain of Party debts and to pay for the Chicago and Washington offices. A speaking trip through five New England states netted Thomas less than $100 in donations. It seems probable that Thomas, who now had little time to give lectures for fees, was actually paying some of his own campaign expenses.

From one old Socialist, Charles E. Randall of Kansas, who had once published a Party paper in Salt Lake City, Thomas received a cultivated cry of disillusion that must have struck a responsive chord in him:

> . . . I have been forced to the conclusion that it looks like a waste of money to continue the efforts that I have made, over a period of more than 50 years, to help build up a strong Socialist Party. The recent schism in your state is sufficient evidence that there is no unanimity in believers in our principles, any more than there was in times past. . . . With our locals full of paid spies and disruptionists, just as in the case of the labor unions, and with the vast masses of the workers ignorant, stupid, indifferent and suspicious, devoid of power to reason or differentiate between potential benefactors and self-seeking demagogues of the Townsend, Huey Long and Coughlin type, it is hopeless to expect any progress along political lines. . . . I am as good a Socialist as ever, of course, and should like exceedingly to see you in the White House—but you won't get there, nor receive anything like as many votes as Debs got 30 years ago. It's a stone wall.

Thomas replied cordially and threw himself at the stone wall, succeeding in keeping his spirits up for a time despite dwindling audiences, writing Senior, "We may suffer a little from our internal troubles . . . but not much. . . . This year we may get quite a silent vote that is not so anxious to go to meetings." He managed to look confident when he and Violet burst into the Lovett home in New Haven and Thomas rushed upstairs to change his shirt, saying he had to speak at the Arena in a half hour. In Cleveland he debated with Dr. Townsend at the national convention of his followers, who believed firmly that a federal pension of $200 monthly to those over sixty would bring back prosperity, and not only to them. As Thomas himself noted, his argument that the plan was economically impossible was like questioning the belief of children in Santa Claus. The Townsendites booed. Between Thomas and Townsend, a kindly if misguided man, the crowd was finally persuaded to allow Thomas to speak a few sentences, then boo while he waited to utter his next paragraph.

His *After the New Deal, What?* was published in September and got glowing comment from Marquis Childs. It was in reality a hasty campaign book but with some of the Thomas quality, asserting that the New Deal was already over, insisting that capitalist panaceas were unavailing and making clear the great difference between Roosevelt's stratagems and Socialism. This was an explanation he had to make ad nauseam, even to Al Smith when the transmogrified Smith told the Liberty Leaguers that the New Deal had carried out one Socialist plank after another—had "caught the Socialists in swimming and had run away with their clothes." Thomas conceded that the New Deal had cribbed some Socialist ideas and had partially fulfilled some of what Socialists called their "immediate demands"—the preliminary ameliorative steps undertaken before the real business of nationalization and production for use could begin. But Roosevelt had not nationalized the banks. He had saved them and then turned them back to the bankers. His social security was a pale imitation of a Socialist program. His National Recovery Administration aimed to stabilize capitalism by regulating production and maintaining private profits. The Agricultural Adjustment Administration was a capitalist program to subsidize scarcity, and so on. "Roosevelt did not carry out the Socialist platform," Thomas said, "unless he carried it out on a stretcher."

He knew that his vote would be low, and warned at least one Socialist leader of this (in Idaho, where the Party had been kept off the ballot and bad news made no difference). On his return from a twenty-state tour late in October he predicted a "tremendous majority for Roosevelt" and added, "It is foolish for the labor unions to waste more of their good money on the Roosevelt campaign." (Thomas had spent $5,614 with the campaign almost over, and George Nelson $323.47, while the Liberty League alone disbursed almost a half million.) The fact that Communists by the thousands had flocked to the American Labor Party–Roosevelt standard, after the insistence of the Old Guard that they had left the Party to escape Communists, furnished wry amusement. But things were so bad that some of the brave young Militants were now talking of the necessity of coming to terms with the ALP—a repugnant thought that also afflicted Thomas. He had made more than 160 speeches plus several radio addresses, and he was weary. To Maynard Krueger, a University of Chicago economics professor and Party leader, for the first time he admitted something close to despair:

> I am frankly much more depressed about the outlook than I expected to be last spring. . . . I do not now know the best way out . . . I wish Clarence's health were better, in which case I would go down on my knees to try to get him to stay. . . .
>
> As for myself, if the Party decides that we are forced to play the kind of game that some New Yorkers think we must play with a very unsatisfactory labor party [ALP], I shall, of course, stay in our Party and shall go along with what has to be done. But I am through with any attempt at leadership. I shall speak and write and support the Party rather passively. . . .

The same day he wrote this letter he wound up the campaign by addressing 12,000 people at Madison Square Garden who gave him a ten-minute ovation but still left about 8,000 seats empty. On election day, Thomas polled only 187,572 votes, .4 percent of 45 million votes cast and about 22 percent of what he had polled nationally in 1932. The Socialist Party had taken heavy losses in Massachusetts, Connecticut, Pennsylvania and Wisconsin and, worst of all, had been thrashed by the ALP in New York State, 274,924 to 86,897.

"We Have Lost a Battle; We Shall Win the War," The Call headlined, taking what comfort it could in the fact that Thomas had bested Browder's vote—Browder, who had really campaigned for Roosevelt. The New Leader savored revenge: "Thomas Polls Smallest Vote . . . Socialist Party Wiped Out in Nation as Workers Repudiate Left Wing Leadership and 'Militant' Control." One story referred to the "Trotskyist party led by Norman Thomas," said with some truth that "the so-called Socialist Party has virtually ceased to exist as a political factor," and remarked that the Party which until recently had been the third largest in the country had barely received enough votes to retain its place on the New York ballot. The real story of Socialist humiliation was told at Party headquarters, where Thomas said little while Harry Laidler made cautious overtures to the ALP: "It is our fervent hope that the American Labor Party will become a party of independent political action, free of the two parties of capitalism . . . When it becomes that, the Socialist Party will be willing and anxious to cooperate."

### 7. Ruin

The Socialist Party lay in ruins. Politics was Thomas's life, and now his nineteen years of arduous building lay in rubble around him. In his "family autobiography" he covered this episode with quick and non-specific paragraphs that showed an anxiety to get on to happier subjects, and it was not until the pain had somewhat subsided that his charming candor returned and he confessed error. He had indeed failed as a political leader if political leadership meant holding factions together. Following his dream of an "inclusive" party, he had committed blunders in his dealings with the Communists, the Trotskyites and other splinter groups. He had failed to hold Hoopes and his Pennsylvanians. The farmer-labor following had refused to materialize. The "liberal anti-Roosevelt vote" he had hoped to capture proved a myth. A little more than four years earlier he had been regarded as a coming political power, and now the Old Guard with their union connections were laughing at his discomfiture.

The hurry-for-a-train Thomas could not hit the trail and run a party simultaneously. Things went on during his absence which he was not always able to overtake on his return, and the kindly Laidler was not a political leader. Besieged by factions among his own followers—there were factions even among the Militant group itself—he had frittered away precious time in hearing disputes that were never settled and had not maintained firm control. The Old Guard had settled on its right-wing course and had achieved discipline. The judicious and fair-minded Albert Sprague Coolidge believed that the largest blame for the split lay with the Old Guard, but that Thomas had allowed himself to become emotionally involved and had not been an effective leader.

The question was academic to those who believed that nothing could have prevented the split even if Thomas had been an angel of mediation. Some were convinced that the Old Guard, whose links with the Hillman-Dubinsky unions were if anything more important than those with the Party, would have bolted to ALP in any case—may have been glad for the excuse. Roosevelt had triumphed over them all.

The art of ruthless political management, of deals and horse trades, eluded Thomas. He was the inspirer, the agitator, the idea man, the reformer—not the man at a desk in a smoke-filled room giving orders. He was a moralist seeking to uphold morality in a profession dominated by the wily. If he had shown, as he would continue to show, that the mechanics of successful party leadership were not his métier, he had demonstrated qualities of idealism more important for his own astonishing future and for the country. The Old Guard, who had complained of his derelictions in Marxism, had sold Marx and Socialism down the river and gone the way of expediency with such unanimity as to bear out Thomas's doubts of their integrity. Thomas had stood by the Socialist-pragmatist principles he had spelled out in articles, books and hundreds of speeches.

# XI

## 1. Clergymen and Jailbirds

Failure or no, the suggestion that Thomas be given a fifty-second birthday party only three weeks after the electoral disaster and while Party wounds still gave torment snowballed into a showy affair. There was appreciation of his energy and gallantry in fighting the '36 campaign when he could see it was lost even in the modest Socialist terms, and admiration for his confrontation of thugs in Passaic, gun-toting planters in Arkansas and McNutt's troops in Indiana. There was an understanding that he was a personage of such stature that the Party had better capitalize on him and hang on to him or it might not get any votes at all. The celebration also had in it an element of bravado, of a Party determination to show the world it was not yet dead.

Thomas was nearly equal to Jim Farley in remembering names, and in his constant speeches, travels and attendance at meetings he met and became friendly with a similar number of people. The testimonial dinner at the Edison Hotel in Times Square was a demonstration of the rich gallery of characters included in his acquaintance.

The chairman was the philosopher John Dewey, the toastmasters were Laidler and Devere Allen, but the thousand dinner guests and the hundreds who sent congratulatory messages ranged from Thomas's very proper old friend Theodore Savage, now executive secretary of the New York Presbytery, to Tom Mooney, unable to attend because he was still #31921 at San Quentin. At the dinner were at least seventeen clergymen and eleven guests who had seen the inside of jails, not including Thomas himself, who by stretching things could fit into both categories. Two of the guests were Elizabeth Gurley Flynn and Carlo Tresca, no longer living in sin together but still good friends and friends also of Thomas. There were B.A.'s, B.D.'s, LL.D.'s and Ph.D.'s, and also quite a few who had never finished grade school. There was a message from Dr. Frank Kingdon noting that Shakespeare died on his fifty-second birthday and wishing Thomas better luck. One guest was A. Philip Randolph, the tall black president of the Sleeping Car Porters, one of the few union leaders to stay loyally with Thomas after the split. There were congratulatory cables from Socialist dignitaries in foreign places including England, Belgium, Sweden, Czechslovakia and Jerusalem.

One remarkable guest was the short, plump, beautifully complexioned Dr. Angelica Balabanoff, the sixty-year-old Russian-Jewish revolutionist and poet who had been an early colleague of Mussolini in Switzerland, but only so long as he hewed to his Socialist beliefs. Later she had been a member of the Zimmerwald peace movement before the war, and after the 1917 revolution had become first secretary of the Communist Party in Russia under Lenin, with which she broke irrevocably a few years later when she saw its developing tyranny. She had "known everyone" in the revolution business from Rosa Luxemburg to John Reed and Louise Bryant. It was said that she still carried as an object of detestation Communist Party card No. 1, signed by Lenin himself. Miss Balabanoff, who had attended several European universities and spoke five languages fluently, had a habit of writing the same poem in all five of them with a charm that drew praise from Edmund Wilson. Born to Czarist wealth near Odessa, a Doctor of Philosophy at the University of Brussels, she had a compassion for the poor and a forgetfulness of self that would make her both a lifelong friend and lifelong problem for Thomas. Now and then he would discover that she was literally starving, having given her money to the needy. Among his intermittent responsibilities for the next twenty-nine years was that of keeping in touch with Angelica, helping her get visas for foreign travel, rescuing her from Ellis Island, getting lecture dates for her, finding markets for her writings and seeing to it that she was not starving. Perhaps one could not take time for such kindnesses and still be an efficient party leader. His admiration for Angelica was another illustration of his conviction that the best human being was the one who worked at improving the condition of the world at the cost of some self-sacrifice, as she continued to do until she was eighty-nine.

From the proceeds of the dinner, Thomas and Violet were presented with a purse of $387.50. This was intended for their use on a trip to Europe, including Russia, planned for the spring. However, the Party was, as usual, destitute. Clarence Senior soon would leave with his family for Mexico for his health, still being owed several months' salary. And Thomas was the signer of one note for The Call and another for the New York Party, without entire confidence that they would be repaid. It is not unlikely that the purse helped keep the Party afloat rather than send the Thomases to Europe.

## 2. Dreadful Times Are Coming

In December, 1936, Thomas (along with President Roosevelt, Landon, Lemke and Browder) was roasted at the Washington Gridiron Club dinner, spotted Governor Happy Chandler of Kentucky there, refrained from buttonholing him on business at that pleasant function but wrote to him the very next day to ask clemency for four imprisoned miners. He also met the Spanish ambassador, Fernando de los Rios, with whom he agreed so ardently about the civil war in Spain that he shocked and affronted almost half the Socialist Party. In fact, some of Thomas's policies for the next five years shocked and affronted many people both inside and outside the Party, though they were the logical consequences of his experiences and his ideals. His revulsion for Hitler and Mussolini found expression in his crusade against General Franco. He assailed President Roosevelt for his essential support of the rebel general by refusing to permit American arms and supplies to be sent to the Spanish Republic despite all the aid lavished on Franco by the two dictators. Roosevelt held to this policy despite his own sympathy for the republic (and that of Eleanor Roosevelt, Sumner Welles, Henry Morgenthau, Harold Ickes and others), Thomas was certain, out of expedient regard for the support of Franco by well-organized, reactionary American Catholics.

There was strong but unorganized American sentiment for the Spanish Republic, and Thomas's earnest effort was to organize it. Notice of his commitment came with the startling announcement that the New York Socialist Party was recruiting and financing 500 volunteer fighters for the republic to be sent to Spain as the Eugene V. Debs Column. He had, of course, given up pacifism when he lost his faith in God. His rationale for supporting the move was his conviction that it was the lesser of two evils—that the military defeat of Franco would prevent the surrounding of France by Fascists on three sides, would inspire the laggard European democracies and would so intimidate Hitler and Mussolini as to prevent an otherwise inevitable second world war.

The protest from Socialists who were also pacifists was immediate, in part because the step had been taken, astonishingly, by the New York local without any consultation with the National Executive Committee. Jack Altman appears to have been the originator of the Debs Column idea, but if so, Thomas gave it his full blessing. This was another of those instances when he had too many irons in the fire to watch every one of them. Pained letters came from such valued colleagues as A. J. Muste (now a Party member), Elisabeth Gilman, John Nevin Sayre and—most indignant of all—the absolute pacifist John Haynes Holmes:

> . . . It is difficult for me to express the degree of amazement and outrage I feel on reading this news. I cannot believe it true. . . . Certainly the members of the Party have not been consulted. . . . By what right does any Socialist today profane the sacred name of Debs by using it to designate a regiment of soldiers enlisted for the work of human slaughter?
>
> You and I, Norman, have been through this business before. We stood fast when Belgians lifted cries as pitiful as those lifted by Spaniards today, and when Paris was beset no less terribly than Madrid. We refused to listen to the specious pleas of 1917 that the world should be made safe for democracy, civilization saved, and war forever ended by use of arms for the killing of men in battle. . . . I appeal to you as the successor of Gene Debs, and as yourself an uncompromising pacifist of consistent and heroic record, to save the Party and the nation from this madness before it is too late.

Thomas replied immediately, ". . . in many ways I would be a much happier man if I could agree with you," and explaining his position as one which in his opinion would lessen the chance of world war. "You speak of putting out the fire. The fire will never be put out in our time, I am afraid, if Franco wins." Holmes responded in disagreement but with a touching and prescient affirmation:

> I have received your letter . . . with a feeling of love for you which nothing that may happen can ever change. Please believe this, and believe it always! I emphasize this because I feel in a kind of trembling way that dreadful times are coming, and divisions of opinion and action are going to try us to the uttermost. But you and I must never misunderstand one another, whatever may happen in this tragic world. . . .

Holmes also wrote the State Department and discovered that it could be illegal to enlist in the service of a foreign state at war—something neither Thomas nor Altman had thought of. Immediate steps were taken to make Altman's Committee for the Debs Column legally independent of the Socialist Party. Thomas even called on Secretary of State Hull to make sure that men could legally be sent abroad if it was done on a "foreign legion" basis. Thomas's brother, Dr. Evan, an absolute pacifist, opposed him. Meanwhile The Call, now a poorly edited and not always reliable propaganda sheet, whooped up the Debs Column with misleading headlines such as "200 JOIN BRIGADE FOR SPAIN IN WEEK," told of the "hundreds" of "self-sacrificing men and women" joining up, and featured an Altman appeal that Socialists raise $50,000 to transport the 500 to Spain. The plea for $50,000 seemed inappropriate at a time when The Call and the New York local were in hock, the national office in Chicago was seven months behind in rent and threatened with eviction, Party workers were being paid a dollar a day to keep them going and the salary of the new national secretary, Roy Burt, was in arrears before a dent was made in the debt owed Senior in Mexico. Thomas was simultaneously embarrassed because The New York Times published a list of high-salaried people, which at that time meant anyone making over $12,000 a year, and included Norman Thomas of New York, listed at $16,600. Despite Thomas's urging, The Times did not explain that the high-salaried gentleman was a sales executive, no relation, and Thomas continued to be suspected of drawing a juicy salary from an indigent party.

Aid to Spain was another issue that rent the Party, the pacifists opposing any aid at all and some Trotskyites opposing aid except to the Trotskyite POUM organization in Catalonia, while another faction clamored for aid only to Largo Caballero and still another favored aid to anybody and everybody fighting Franco. Some outsiders were misled about Thomas's own position because he was a member of the American Committee for the Defense of Leon Trotsky (who was undermining Thomas and his party at that very moment), whereas this meant neither that he approved nor disapproved of Trotsky's politics but that he believed simply that Trotsky should be given political asylum. The Debs Column, the truculence of The Call and the constant quarrels caused the resignation of a substantial number of comrades, a Syracuse member of long standing writing bitterly as she resigned:

> When by folly after folly we succeed in reducing the Party to the irreducible minimum of the pure essence of revolutionary Socialism, I'll be glad to join a committee to build a suitable museum for the strange creature who will be left as the result of our efforts.

National Secretary Burt put it differently when he complained of Party unity being achieved "when by one means or another certain elements are forced out of the Party. This will give a unity of a very small group which will spend all of its energies in gaining unity by constantly growing smaller." This was one reason Thomas was too indulgent with the Trotskyites who were sabotaging him, since their expulsion would mean the loss of a considerable number, but his dander was rising and he wrote of them to Altman, ". . . I have believed that they could do much good within [the Party]. . . . Nevertheless it is fair to say that the things which disgust us have been enormously intensified since the admission of these comrades into the Party . . ."

The Call's irresponsibility about the Debs Column was exposed three months later by a letter from Ed Melnicoff, a Socialist member of the group, from Perpignan, saying that "the Debs Column has been a terrible flop and should be liquidated at once," that it had transported only twenty men to the Spanish border and had left them on their own, so that most of them joined an Italian anti-Fascist brigade. This was Altman's headache but was scarcely comforting to Thomas, who left on a lecture tour to raise money for his own trip to Europe. In Chicago, when he stepped into a bathtub at the La Salle Hotel, the shower fixture came off in his hands, and he fell with hot water pouring on him; his skin was burned so that he looked like a "boiled lobster," as he described it. He left a damage claim with the Socialist attorney Joe Jacobs, instructing him that if he collected as much as $50, it should go to the Party. At the going rate, Thomas's anguish would pay a Socialist worker for fifty days of labor.

### 3. A Pall of Fear

The Thomases sailed on the Aquitania March 31, 1937*—a European honeymoon delayed twenty-six years. Thomas hoped for answers to the two largest questions in his mind: Why did not England and France give substantial aid to the Spanish Republic to counteract the Savoias and Junkers and pilots Franco got from Mussolini and Hitler? And what, really, was the answer to the Russian riddle (about which he had "solemnly promised before witnesses not to write a book")? He had had

---

*The male chauvinist New York Times of April 1 told of his departure and did not mention that Violet was with him.

great trouble getting a visa for Russia—he thought it was because of his membership in the Trotsky defense committee. Finally the Russians had given in and Ambassador Troyanovsky had actually expressed a wish to talk with him—granted—at the Russian consulate in New York the day before he left.

In London, where they were the guests of the Crippses in Elm Court, Thomas argued at Transport House with the fiery unionist Ernest Bevin about Labor support for the Baldwin nonintervention policy so helpful to Franco. Bevin said with a straight face that his party's action was in support of Socialist Léon Blum of France, who had urged that policy on England, and Bevin resented Thomas's condemnation of it. "Besides," he added more amiably, "I have a lot of [Irish] Catholics in my union." Thomas's opinion of Bevin as an internationally minded union leader was not high. Thomas deplored the British truckling to Franco and rejection of Gandhi in India. The dynamic, travel-loving, perpetually inquiring tourist was on another of his track meets, hurrying from place to place, seeing people who could be expected to know something, shaking hands and smiling his genuinely kindly smile, watching closely, asking endless questions and of course delivering speeches. He visited the aging Beatrice Webb, who "talked his ears off" about Socialism and international affairs. He spoke repeatedly to Labor crowds in London and again in Cambridge and Bristol. He "vigorously led the singing of the Internationale" at a London meeting organized in his honor, he called on Kingsley Martin at The New Statesman and Nation and many others, he saw the beginning of the English arms boom but thought war unlikely for a year or more.

Both Thomases lunched in Brussels with the Socialist Camille Huysmans, and in Paris they called on Ambassador William Bullitt and then on Premier Blum, who flatly contradicted Bevin's yarn. The truth was that Blum had favored heavy shipments of planes and armaments to the Loyalists but had let himself be dissuaded by the British as well as by noninterventionists in his own country. Thomas was appalled by the British and French failure to see Franco's victory as a threat, and indeed, as in the case of Churchill, by the upper-class disposition to see the left-wing republic as the threat.

In Moscow the Thomases were steered by Loy Henderson, then chargé d'affaires in the absence of Ambassador Davies. With the American military attaché they had second-row seats at the ballet and saw Stalin enter the old imperial box after a Red Army general (identified by the attaché as General Feldman) had carefully scrutinized the audience as if for potential assassins. They saw Kiev and Leningrad and some places in between. Thomas was impressed by the national vigor; he thought Russia had solved racial problems wisely and that "village life is far ahead of what the cotton plantations have to offer in America." But housing was "wretched," consumer goods poor and scarce and "I had to pay two rubles for one lemon in a country store." He disliked the huge Soviet wage differentials and the suspicion that required him to produce his papers at every turn. He was shocked by the throngs of what he took to be the people who had heard the midnight knock on their doors—political prisoners, slave labor—working under armed guards on national projects. The people were poor but the Red Army was well clothed and housed and the military show it mounted on May Day was formidable:

> . . . I heard that only Russia could put 830 airplanes in the air at one time. . . . [I had a] strong feeling . . . that Russia is not moving toward a classless society, but on the contrary, perpetuating, and even strengthening, new class divisions. . . . Don't let anyone tell you that there is no feeling of class distinction. . . . I felt, along with my great admiration for great social achievements, a pall of fear almost as if it were a tangible thing. . . . A Russian reads precisely what news the government gives him to read. . . . I breathed the purer air of democracy . . . in Denmark. . . .

Still he remained ambivalent because Russia remained a bulwark against Fascism and was helping the Spanish Loyalists. The Thomases were most impressed by Finland, Sweden and Denmark. After stops in Poland, Germany, Czechoslovakia and Austria, they visited Spain just after the Negrin government had taken power. In Barcelona Thomas was greeted at the palace by the Catalonian president, Luis Companys, while Violet received a bouquet "tied with a ribbon in the colours of Catalonia's ancient flag." There was a tour of the damaged city and a visit to a refugee camp, and Thomas spoke encouragement by radio to the troops, after which they were escorted to Valencia. Here, while Violet rested at a hotel, Thomas was driven at breakneck speed to the front near Teruel, which was then relatively quiet, although just before he reached the front Insurgent planes bombed the nearby village of Villalba. He told Loyalist soldiers that their fight "is not only for the interests of Spain but for those of the United States and the whole world." He placed enormous importance on the outcome of the Spanish struggle. He was amused to visit a dugout and find Marxian pictures displayed—not Karl, but Groucho, Harpo et al. He was impressed by

Loyalist morale and felt sure the republic would win unless the already huge help from the Axis increased.

At the Valencia hotel that night, he and Violet were aroused by a thunderous air raid that drove them and other guests downstairs in the darkness to a place someone believed to be a shelter. The raid, carried out by Axis bombers based on the Balearics, wrecked fifty buildings and made front-page headlines in the New York papers including, "Explosion Near Hotel of Norman Thomas"—more male chauvinism. "My first clear thought," Thomas recalled, "was how angry the children would be with me for letting their mother come to Spain." The children were indeed indignant, although they also knew that their mother was not one to accept solicitous sidetracking when there was excitement on the main line. After the raid, Thomas wrote, the lights went on in their "bombproof" and "behold we had gathered for safety under a stained glass dome."

He met and talked with Juan Negrin. He believed that the Negrin government was not Communist but was influenced by Communists in and out of Spain because Russia was giving limited aid which the West in its folly denied the legitimate government. His activities were so well chaperoned that "I got the definite impression that I was deliberately being kept from seeing some things and people whom I wished to see." Negrin gave him a copy of a white paper documenting the heavy involvement of the Italians and Germans, which he promised to take to President Roosevelt. His inquiries about the Debs Column confirmed his opinion that the idea had been hasty and unwise. Most of its few men had finally been incorporated into the Communist International Brigade, which was well cared for. The republic had little need of mere soldiers. What it did need badly was war equipment and such specialists as aviators and mechanics.

Thomas the observer and questioner was himself an object of interest, according to The New York Times:

> Norman Thomas has proved an eye-opener to European Socialists. Wherever he has stopped . . . he has been eagerly questioned on the differences between the American and European brands of Socialism. Europeans have been astonished by his view that the hope of American Socialism lies in the farmers, and perhaps more astonished by his belief that in some farming areas it has already taken root. To most of his questioners, Socialism has been a growth of the industrial areas; and his admission that American factory hands usually vote for the old parties rather than the Socialist Party has aroused a good deal of respect for his frankness.

In Paris, before sailing home on the Queen Mary, the Thomases stayed with their cousin Carlotta, daughter of the late Frank and Anna Welles, on the Boulevard Suchet. There they read of the latest Russian purge, this one liquidating Marshal Tukhachevsky and seven generals, one of them being General Feldman.

### 4. Something Wrong with the Pump

When Thomas reported on his tour at the New York Hippodrome three days after his return, The Times estimated an audience of 1,500 while The Call said that "4,800 people jammed" the auditorium. Thomas, the skilled propagandist, familiar with every major newspaper in the country, was aware that The Call was a poor Party sheet not only on the score of accuracy but for more important reasons. If he made suggestions to the editors, the paper nevertheless went on looking and reading more like The Daily Worker than seemed wise. He was perhaps doubting himself because he had so misjudged the Old Guard split. There were several Party crises to face at once, and he was trying to do too much, as always. Two statements he made later suggested the candor as well as the failings of the irrepressible humanitarian as Party leader and administrator. He said:

"We wouldn't have had the factional troubles in the Party that we did have . . . had any of us on any side fully understood what was going on in Russia. . . . It took the purges, really, to awaken us fully, myself in particular." And he said:

"Well, this [problem of Spain] was terribly absorbing, so that I forgot pretty completely about Party fights . . ."

He did not forget them long. The peppery Socialist and writer Lillian Symes (the same who had invaded Passaic with him in 1926) warned him from California not only that the Trotskyites had virtually taken over the Party in that state but that there were Trotskyite spies among the many volunteer Party workers, even at the national office in Chicago. He must be careful not to confide in anyone not known to be loyal, or to dictate confidential letters to any stenographer whose allegiance was not certain. She went on:

> . . . [In] the fight ahead, the honesty and integrity of people like yourself are the very weapons with which your opponents [Cannon and his Trotskyites] hope to destroy you. . . . You are slated for decapitation—or capitulation—once they get around to it.

Thomas delayed the confrontation although the Party was torn by the question of how to deal with the Trotskyites, who contributed little to it but factionalism about Russia and Spain. There was danger that their expulsion would make them seem martyrs to Socialist innocents, who might quit the Party with them. There was also the certainty that the Old Guard would enjoy a great I-told-you-so belly laugh, and that the expulsion would delight the Communists. "The last thing I want to do," Thomas wrote ruefully, "is to escape from Trotsky by falling, or seeming to fall, into the arms of Stalin."

He called on the President, who had lampooned the Debs Column at a press conference simply by calling it "the Debutantes' Column" with his broadest grin and highest tilt of cigaret. Roosevelt gave him a courteous hearing but would not be budged either on the embargo on arms to Loyalist Spain or on the question of imposing an embargo on supplies or arms to Franco. ". . . I pleaded with the President," Thomas said later. ". . . . he told me we didn't send many arms [to Franco] anyway and rather brushed off my suggestion that the moral weight of the embargo would be important. In his own inimitable way he changed the subject. . . ." All his life, Thomas regarded Roosevelt's Spanish policy as one of his greatest errors, one that made World War II inevitable and brought decades of tragic oppression to Spain herself.

The Trotskyites had been contaminating the Party for only fourteen months when the Socialists, with Thomas's blessing, expelled them by vote in August, 1937. It had been fourteen months too long. Cannon, with the charming logic of these backstabbers, declared, "[Norman Thomas] broke his word, double-crossed us." But he was proud of his work, writing:

> Partly as a result of our [work] . . . the Socialist Party was put on the sidelines. This was a great achievement, because it was an obstacle in the path of building a revolutionary party. The problem is not merely one of building a revolutionary party, but of clearing obstacles from its path. Every other party is a rival. Every other party is an obstacle.

The Trotskyites, who had entered about 300 strong, took more than 1,000 with them when they left, including part of the Socialist youth organization, which Thomas had treasured as the Party's future. With their departure the California Party became virtually extinct, as was the one in Minnesota, and Illinois, Ohio and Massachusetts were among those badly hurt. Thomas himself was humiliated, having been taken in by sharpers and also finding his policy of the "inclusive party" exceptionable. A few more inclusions like the Trotskyites and there would be no Socialist Party left at all.

His smiling front was legendary and his Party letters were ordinarily optimistic, but during this period a note of desperation crept in. The Party, which until 1934 had been growing, had not only lost badly in membership since that time but was racked with angry discord that took the joy out of politics. The Thomas optimism, which long had been real, became a trifle forced. The great dream of a Socialist America with production for use and human misery all but eliminated, which once had seemed not impossibly beyond reach, had collapsed into very nearly a nightmare. The fighter whose courage had never broken was showing deep wounds when he went so far as to admit to Paul Porter that at times he was "near despair." The older Devere Allen, perhaps his closest ally and confidant at this time, had answered Thomas's inquiries in the kindliest way, ". . . while I might at times think you made errors of judgment, as all of us must, it would be ridiculous to think you were liquidating the Party or becoming a reformist."* Thomas replied, ". . . you and I have got to get together and talk. I confess to being in a very low state of mind about lots of things, including myself and my own capacity for the sort of leadership that apparently is required." Even his ox-like constitution broke down briefly and he was hors de combat for two days. The saddest thing was that the departure of dissidents in no way reduced Party dissidence—a phenomenon true also after the Trotskyite expulsion. As Porter (who himself had been scarcely free from factionalism) put it to Thomas:

> This sectarian factionalism feeds on itself. It tends to bring to the fore in the branch meetings or in the Party press the people who specialize in hairsplitting and intolerance. The comrades who are occupied with important mass work find themselves bewildered (or disgusted) . . . and drop more and more out of the Party.

The Call, under Gus Tyler and Herbert Zam, was the angry and officious organ of the "Clarity" faction of the Party which sought to make it an elite corps of disciplined super-revolutionists rather than an expanding body of mere voters. The Clarity group was incensed because Thomas, backed by Laidler, Altman and other leaders, bowed

---

*The term "reformist" in Marxist parlance was an insult, indicating one satisfied with mere superficial reforms instead of thoroughgoing nationalization, etc.

enough to expediency to carry on negotiations with the union-affiliated American Labor Party and to join them in backing the honest La Guardia for reelection as Mayor. He withdrew as Socialist candidate, permitting Socialists to give La Guardia their vote, although there remained Socialist candidates for lesser offices. In this he was urged by the practical Charney Vladeck, who reasoned that in politics it was wiser to take the most satisfactory alternative than to demand perfection, writing, "I do sincerely hope that you will . . . act in the interest of Labor and Socialism as a Movement,—not as a Church." Within a few weeks, Thomas "returned to the church" because of La Guardia's endorsement of the scarcely 100-percent-pure Republican George U. Harvey for Borough President of Queens as the price for Republican support. He assailed La Guardia (in whose favor he had withdrawn) for his ties with that same old "kept woman of Tammany," the GOP. This odd bifurcation was another example of Thomas's inner moral struggles which at times confused his followers and reduced his effectiveness as a political leader, but which later were sharpened and perfected into his soundest resource. The New York Clarityites, however, saw only the Party support for "union bureaucrats" and Republicanism and issued an eleven-page mimeographed manifesto attacking the "Thomas-Altman Right Wing" (the Old Guard had called them the left wing) in purplest Marxist prose and picturing themselves as the last bastion of pure revolutionary Socialism:

> . . . The Thomas-Altman attitude now is the attitude which the Old Guard advanced for years. To . . . them, making headway with the unions consists of licking the boots of the trade union bureaucrats. No Socialist principles . . . keep them from groveling in front of them. . . . We must begin, at long last, the hard and patient work of rudimentary Marxist education. . . . The hour is late for such a new beginning. But it must be made. . . . With us lies the fate of revolutionary Socialism. We cannot betray this trust.

The Clarityites were anxious to oust Thomas and seize control. Thomas survived the assault and asked the National Executive Committee to remove Tyler as editor of The Call, which was done. But by this time the Party had organizations in only twenty-four of the forty-eight states and a grand total of little more than 7,000 paid-up members. National Secretary Burt's salary was thirteen weeks in arrears, money was still owed Senior, employes under Burt were from two to twelve weeks in arrears, and the Party machinery was creaking. While Thomas was still trying to get a settlement for his bathtub accident, Dubinsky's

International Ladies' Garment Workers' Union was rich enough to give $50,000 outright to the American Labor Party. Thomas hopefully turned to the rich and generous Professor Coolidge. Coolidge, though a faithful friend and admirer, wrote a discouraged and discouraging reply about "my waning faith in the effectiveness of Party priming, and my growing tendencies to wonder if there might not be something wrong with the pump."

### 5. Meeting Adjourned

One could depend on Thomas getting national headlines at intervals by defying a governor or sheriff, by being menaced by shotguns or by being tear-gassed, arrested or bombed. Not until 1938 was he kidnaped. He had a special bone to pick with Mayor Frank Hague of Jersey City, Democratic boss of New Jersey and powerful vice chairman of the Democratic National Committee. When Hague denounced the Congress of Industrial Organizations as Communist-controlled and forbade it to hold public meetings in Jersey City, Thomas came to the defense of free speech. He crossed the Hudson with a few friends including Oswald Garrison Villard, held a meeting in a Jersey City Methodist church and spoke to 300 labor sympathizers in observance of the 150th anniversary of New Jersey's signing of the Constitution. He pointed out that Hague was much more than a local boss and that President Roosevelt deferred to him in matters of state politics and patronage.

"He is the man who chooses your governor, isn't he?" Thomas asked. "And your United States Senator?"

"And the judges too!" a listener shouted.

"I was coming to them," Thomas nodded.

Hague was displeased at news of this. "We hear about constitutional rights and the free press," he said. "Every time I hear these words, I say to myself, 'That man is a Red, that man is a Communist. You never hear a real American talk in that manner." He decreed that thenceforth an official permit would be required for public meetings. When the Socialist Party asked permission to hold an outdoor May Day meeting in Jersey City, it was denied by Hague's Director of Public Safety, Daniel Casey, "to avert trouble threatened by the Catholic War Veterans if Norman Thomas was allowed to speak."

On May Day afternoon, 1938, Thomas addressed 3,200 people in Madison Square (leaving Union Square to the Communists) and finished off by announcing that he would test Hague's edict by speaking in Journal Square in the heart of Jersey City at 7:30 that night. He invited his listeners to be there, warning that there must be no provocation or violence.

Norman and his brother, Dr. Evan Thomas, arrived with Violet by car in Journal Square that evening to find 200 policemen keeping a large crowd moving. "When Mr. Thomas stepped from his car," a reporter noted, "he was surrounded by police and hustled around a corner into a waiting car." He was whisked away so quickly that no one knew what had become of him. A sympathetic group accompanied Violet and Dr. Thomas to the nearby police headquarters. There, Police Chief Harry Walsh said he had no idea where Norman Thomas was. He invited Violet and Dr. Evan to sit down and be comfortable.

Thomas meanwhile had been driven to the ferry by other policemen and forcibly put on board. He landed in wrath at Liberty Street in Manhattan, walked two quick blocks north and boarded the Hudson tubes back to Jersey City. He walked through the milling crowd and the police in Journal Square without being recognized, and entered the office of The Jersey Observer, a newspaper. There he made a statement enumerating the illegalities perpetrated against him and said, "I have every intention of taking whatever legal action that is possible against Mayor Hague and his brand of Fascist administration." News of his presence there spread like magic. He received great applause when he emerged, to be joined by Violet and Evan and surrounded by police, who managed, perhaps by error, to strike Violet in the jaw. The coppers escorted them to the tubes, meanwhile beating with their nightsticks a few Socialists who jeered and a photographer who tried to take pictures, and forcibly deported all three Thomases.

Thomas received a deluge of telegrams and letters of support. Upton Sinclair wired Eleanor Roosevelt, "Please tell Mayor Hague it is not polite in a democracy to hit a lady on the jaw." But Public Safety Director Casey said, "I want the public to know that Thomas is nothing more than an agent for the Red-Communist group." Roger Baldwin readied the American Civil Liberties Union (Thomas was still on its board) to defend free speech in New Jersey. Thomas wrote J. Edgar Hoover to inquire whether his forcible removal did not constitute kidnaping, so that Hague's men could be prosecuted under the Lindbergh Law. (It appeared not, there having been no actual imprisonment or demand for ransom.) He also wrote President Roosevelt in part, "I ask you whether it is not time for you to state quite frankly whether or not you approve of the policies which a man of such prominence in your party [Hague] sees fit to employ so far with impunity."

A month later, Thomas secured a permit to speak at Military Park in Newark, adjoining Jersey City, where he intended to attack Hague and his regime. Among those waiting for him were crowds of American Legionnaires and other patriotic pro-Hague groups. As Thomas started to speak, a Legion brass band waiting nearby struck up a deafening tune, marched directly in front of his platform and came to a halt with every instrument at full volume so that not even the stentorian Thomas voice could be heard. Jeers came from the crowd—tomatoes and rotten eggs as well. He had encountered hostile crowds often enough so that he had a list of approaches to contain hostility depending on his appraisal of its nature. They included (1) a frank appeal for fair play, (2) "a wisecrack . . . that tickles the audience and turns the laugh against the trouble-makers," (3) beginning the speech on a note of agreement to soften belligerence, and (4) occasionally a bold attack to silence hecklers. All, however, presupposed that he could make himself heard. This was impossible with trombones and tubas all but thrust into his face. This was the third time in his life that he was prevented from speaking entirely, the first having been at Birdsong, Arkansas.

"Mr. Thomas made repeated efforts to speak," The New York Times said, "but each time the band struck up again." A hurled egg spattered off his head and was caught by a news photographer in a scene that won the year's prize for spot news pictures. A policeman backed his horse into Thomas's platform, knocking it and Thomas down. Fistfights broke out between Hague men and Thomas supporters, the latter badly outnumbered. A police official bellowed that the meeting was adjourned and warned Thomas to leave or he might get hurt—a distinct possibility in view of the number of hoodlums in the crowd and the hoodlum character of the policemen themselves. Two of his companions, David Clendenin and Morris Milgram, both officers of the Workers' Defense League, had taken painful punches from the crowd. "I expect I will be given safe conduct back to America," Thomas snapped. He was driven to the railroad station in a police car and once more deported to New York.

Inquiries disclosed that among the Hague thugs who broke up the meeting were a Democratic ward leader with a record for robbery and white slavery, and a teamster union official who had a string of sixteen arrests on charges ranging from rape to assault and battery and larceny. Thomas had always regretted that he had taken no legal action against Governor McNutt of Indiana, who had therefore continued his jackboot rule unmolested. He brought immediate suit against Hague, and would sweat for many months to pay court costs. His opinion of the President continued to decline because of his bedfellows—Senator Robinson, McNutt and now Hague. Five days after the Newark imbroglio Thomas was a commencement speaker at Kent School, where his son Evan, who had been captain of the crew, was one of the graduates.

### 6. Discrimination

Those who said Thomas could not make up his mind politically perhaps misunderstood his criteria. Some thought mistakenly that what he needed was a big, poverty-stricken church parish that he could love and help and dominate. Even Charney Vladeck, who urged him to regard politics as "a Movement, not as a Church," may have missed the point somewhat. Thomas did not of course thrust the religion he had rejected into the politics he had adopted. He did take the astonishing stand that politics should be intelligent, honest and honorable. His faith in progress, though dimmed, included the belief that the political process could be enlightened and cleansed to keep pace with the advances, for example, in sanitation. To these heresies he added others which should have closed the field of politics to him altogether. One was the strength and frankness of his convictions—something any ward heeler knew could make enemies and lose votes. Most veterans of twenty years in politics accommodated themselves to its sleaziness to a degree according to their nature. Twenty years in politics had made Thomas admit the necessity of a soupçon of expediency but had not diluted his revulsion for the sleazy. On the contrary, his moral outlook was steering him into a confrontation with his friend, admirer and fellow intellectual, Niebuhr. To these political handicaps he added still another, discrimination, a quality cherished by philosophers but rejected by most politicians.

Hence his knowledge that La Guardia was the best Mayor New York had had within long memory had made him withdraw as a candidate in La Guardia's favor. It could not make him suspend his code and refrain from criticizing the Little Flower for paying off the Republicans with an unworthy appointment. Thomas's frank concession that President Roosevelt had brought the country out of the Hoover depths and had done about as much for labor as could be done under capitalism could not stop him from attacking that system or from condemning Roosevelt's political alliance with the likes of McNutt and Hague or his view of the Spanish crisis as a matter of American votes rather than of world peril. Discrimination made him reject the easy answers which were politically useful but which really did not answer. Discrimination closed him off from the quick herd impulse. Indeed there were times when he seemed to become entangled enough in filaments of discrimination as to lose sight of the main threads.

The conservative Socialist Daniel Bell wrote that Thomas "surrounded himself almost entirely with considerably younger men who stood in an admiring and uncritical relation to him." True, he liked young people, just as he had in Harlem—saw them as the future. Still, he had invited in the Trotskyites who held him in contempt; and the Clarityites, who accused him of bootlicking, could hardly be called uncritical. His perennial association with such critical men as Roger Baldwin, John Haynes Holmes, A. J. Muste, Devere Allen, Albert Sprague Coolidge and Charney Vladeck himself did not argue incompatibility with his own generation. He could be tyrannical in his nice way. He believed he knew better than anyone else what was best for the Party, and yet his admission of despair to Porter and Allen was hardly the attitude of a party boss. A fine platform actor, he was ready to make a speech any time, delighting in his power over an audience, admitting that "in all the world there are few satisfactions greater" than to win over a crowd. But he used his wit not for cuteness but to illuminate substance, and he told the Townsendites their plan would not work and let them boo. Language, he knew too well, could be used to mislead, and yet "upon this faculty all human culture depends."

He was open to the charge that he did not realize that politics was the art of the possible. Holmes's "trembling" premonition of "dreadful times" and "divisions of opinion" was soon realized. As war drew nearer, disparagement began to replace the admiration he had known. Violet's illnesses persisted, other troubles mounted, and he seemed the victim of the kind of testing reserved for saints, though he was not of their number. He could probably have gone to the Senate—a post he coveted next to his independence—had he taken the La Guardia solution early enough. Instead, he was getting on in his fifties, his party was failing instead of gaining and his star apparently descending. Being the greatest of mavericks, a devastating critic, as confirmed in his rejection of the two-party system as the American people seemed satisfied with it, he was outside the pale, unelectable to office, his great abilities lost to the nation unless he found some new way to make them count.

# XII

## 1. Growing Deficits

Thomas's plan was to ally his little Socialist Party with the big American Labor Party in New York State to an extent that might grow as and when the ALP grew in independence from the old capitalist parties. The Socialist Party would keep its flag flying and would remain free to nominate its own candidates for those offices for which the ALP supported capitalist candidates. There were now cautious moves for reunion between the Socialist Party and the Social Democratic Federation, still identical with the Old Guard and still a part of the patchwork ALP. This was not inspired by love but by the Federation's unhappiness over its subsidiary role in ALP and the Socialist Party's own desperate need for more members, more strength, more money. Meanwhile Thomas resigned from the League for Industrial Democracy, leaving Laidler in full charge, but remained as unpaid chairman of the board, and settled down to his chairmanship (also unpaid) of the Socialist Party, using the office in his own home and hiring his own part-time secretary. In January, 1938, at a meeting of a large group of Socialists in the spacious Thomas drawing room, he founded the Keep America Out of War Congress, of which he was also chairman (also unpaid). Clarence Senior, back from Mexico, temporarily became his paid deputy in Washington.

KAOWC was the first Thomas gun against American involvement in a European war which he feared with a passion explained by his vivid recollection of the war against the Kaiser, the harm it had done Evan and many others and its shameful aftermath in America. ". . . [E]ntry into new war means Fascism at home without corresponding benefit anywhere," he wrote. He was as certain of this as if it had been graven on tablets. As it turned out, it proved a mistake to organize KAOWC

226

under Socialist auspices because it soon developed that not all Socialists opposed entry into the war and some would shout *for* it. There was of course nothing inconsistent in Thomas's continuing appeal for equal aid to Loyalist Spain—a war already begun which if won by the republic might prevent the bigger struggle—and his crusade against entrapment in a general European war he still hoped might not occur. In pushing KAOWC he burdened himself with new financial obligations on top of the grave Socialist Party deficits and the continuing charges for his protracted lawsuit against Frank Hague.

Meanwhile, Sam Romer, an idealistic young New York Socialist who had worked on The Call and of whom he was fond, had gone to Spain with the luckless Debs Column, been switched to the International Brigade and been taken prisoner by the Franco forces. Thomas corresponded anxiously with the American ambassador to Spain, Claude Bowers, whom he had known in New York and who was working for the exchange of American prisoners. The Call had sent another Socialist friend of Thomas's, the young union official Sam Baron, to Spain as a correspondent. Baron, arriving in Spain committed to the Loyalist cause, was dumfounded to find that the Communists in that government were murderous rather than democratic toward some of their non-Communist Loyalist comrades. He sent back some scorching dispatches to The Call, which Thomas believed overblown. Next thing, Baron was arrested by the Communists in Valencia as a "Trotskyite." Thomas corresponded spiritedly about this with his friend the Spanish ambassador in Washington, de los Rios, who was now less friendly and complained about Baron's "contempt for the Spanish People's endeavor to win the struggle against Fascism." Thomas knew perfectly well that Baron was as anti-Fascist as a man could be. The Baron case illuminated the growing strength of the Communists on the Loyalist side and made it plain that the choice between Franco and the Loyalists was a choice between evils, but Thomas still had no doubt that the Fascist cause was easily the more dangerous and was doing everything he could to defeat it.

In 1938 also he was prevailed on by the Party to run for Governor against the popular Herbert Lehman (Democratic *and* American Labor Party candidate) and the up-and-coming young Republican Tom Dewey. It did not take much persuading. He felt that the Party could not unprotestingly go along with the ALP's backing of a capitalist candidate—a banker at that—and thought it vital that the Party make a showing that would keep it on the ballot and improve its bargaining position vis-à-vis the ALP and the Social Democratic Federation. "I honestly feel the future of the Party is involved in making a showing in New York," he wrote Burt.

But what with KAOWC and other involvements, he was unable to mount a vigorous campaign. Violet was ill again, and his anarchist friend Carlo Tresca was one of the many who inquired solicitously about her. Thomas was truly saddened when Charney Vladeck died suddenly, some saying that part of the reason for his decline was the feeling against him of some Old Guard leaders. Thomas attended the funeral and was reminded there of the bitterness caused by his 1932 Milwaukee alliance with Vladeck in the effort to unseat Hillquit. Abe Cahan, who since then had never spoken to Vladeck, refused to attend the services. There was excitement when Thomas's youngest daughter Becky, after two shining years at Vassar, sailed for England to spend her junior year at the London School of Economics. There was a larger commotion when the still-unwell Violet went to New Haven in anticipation of the birth of the second child of her eldest daughter, Polly Miller. Violet chose this time to suffer an acute attack of appendicitis. She was rushed to the hospital where Mrs. Miller also had her child—a daughter, Patricia—thereby setting a record: It was the first time the New Haven hospital had ministered to three generations of the same family at once.

"Violet is doing as well as we can expect," Thomas wrote Senior in Washington. "I have to remodel my schedule, but I will keep on with the campaign." He was promised a substantial contribution for KAOWC in three weeks, but he added forlornly to Senior, "Can we last till then?" Burt in Chicago was worse off, writing Thomas, "May I call your attention to the very serious financial situation . . . ?" The whole national organization, including the central Chicago office, was struggling along on barely more than $500 a month, and workers were taking a week off without pay. What with one thing and another, Thomas's vote was a minuscule 24,890 in the Lehman victory. That was about half the 50,000 votes required by law for any party to stay on the ballot. The Party was at least temporarily wiped out in the state where it had once been a considerable influence. While it continued its own organization, its flag was drooping indeed when it announced that the ALP was the "electoral expression of the working class" and advised Socialists in New York State to enroll. Thomas had had to pay $100 in Party debts, had sent $25 as a loan to Mitchell in Memphis, and wrote, "I am honestly nearly swamped with financial responsibilities. . . ." He was now a trustee of New York's thriving Town Hall organization along with

such people as Wendell Willkie, Eleanor Roosevelt and Dorothy
Thompson, and a regular on their popular radio program "Town Meeting of the Air." From some of the wealthier members, including the
very rich Mrs. B. M. Milliken, he secured life-saving contributions and
also advice about other possible contributors. He wrote to Mrs. Milliken:

> Dear Alida: I am going to ask a frank question to which I know you will
> give an equally frank answer.
>
> Would it do harm or good were I to talk to Mrs. [name left blank] about
> a generous gift to the Keep America Out of War Congress? Would I be
> a good or a poor person to approach her? . . .
>
> Violet joins me in greetings.

His efforts were instrumental in getting the two Sams, Romer and
Baron, safely back home, although Baron was now saying things embarrassing to the Loyalist cause. Thomas watched Princeton beat Yale and
enjoyed a family Thanksgiving at Cold Spring Harbor. Violet was still
a little unsteady, young Evan came up from Princeton, the Gateses
were there with their first child, and "Big Evan," as the doctor was
called, discussed politics and war with his older brother, the two passing
each other repeatedly during their ambulant argument. Thomas, quite
unconsciously, was apt to eat anything in sight while pacing in thought
and speech. Once, when Frances was doing the cooking, turning out
codfish cakes which she dried on a table behind her, her father was
walk-talking with her. She discovered too late that each time he passed
he ate another fish cake and they were all but gone. It was then so late
that she had to open cans of pork and beans.

## 2. The Pact

On his return from Spain, Sam Baron flouted Socialist precepts by
going to Washington without warning and testifying *voluntarily* before
a crew loathed by Thomas and the Party, the Dies Committee. He
described the Communists in Spain as "murderers" and "monsters"
who kept hundreds of Americans rotting in jails. His statement that the
Franco people were "even worse" did not take the curse off testimony
that might very well snuff out once and for all Thomas's still-glimmering
hope that the President might lift the embargo on aid to the Loyalists.
An excitable man, Baron compounded his crime by laying it on generally and saying, for example, that the Communists supported Thomas's

fight against Hague in New Jersey because the Congress of Industrial Organizations, to whose aid Thomas had come, was heavily Communist. The Dies Committee pumped Baron about other organizations including the American Civil Liberties Union. Baron's testimony that Baldwin and the ACLU were *not* Communist (the committee said he was wrong about that) did not save him from the wrath of Thomas, who wired Washington to disavow Baron as a Party spokesman.

Baron thereupon resigned from the Party "with regret." To Devere Allen, Thomas wrote, "This madness of Baron's [is] pretty nearly the last straw." Not the least of the Dies Committee's sins was its false denunciation of Thomas's own League for Industrial Democracy as a Communist front. Thomas wrote Senator Robert M. La Follette, Jr., pointing out that the committee's appropriation was a mere $25,000 but that it continued making headlines as if it had many times that amount, suggesting that "private interests with their own axes to grind" might be subsidizing Dies. (In later years Thomas admitted that Baron was probably generally correct about the Spanish Communists, though he was unwise in taking it to Dies.) Thomas was getting occasional insulting letters, such as the following, which attacked his action in the Baron matter and went on:

> Do you ever take a good laboratory look at yourself? . . . Are you still just a muddleheaded ecclesiast with an exhibitionist hangover, capable only of the preconditioned reflexes? 'Twould seem so, Norman, 'twould seem so!

With admirable control he replied without reference to the insults that the Dies Committee was wholly discredited and that Socialists only compromised their position by voluntary appearance before it.

Violet's failure to recover her vitality, the Party doldrums, the threat of war, the loss (though expected) of his suit against Hague in the Hague-controlled Jersey courts and the cliffhanger role he was playing with all of his political and social projects on the verge of insolvency or worse made him occasionally snappish. It was flattering that both Florence Bowers of Dutton's and Edward Aswell of Harper's wrote to him that he had written plenty about Socialism and wasn't it high time for him to write his autobiography? Their agreement on this reflected their knowledge of his wide public acquaintance and the interest in him all over the nation stimulated first by his public speeches and now most of all by his frequent appearances on radio. He was not interested. He had just published *Socialism on the Defensive* and his *Keep America Out of*

*War* (with Bertram D. Wolfe) would come next, the former pretty much printed as he had dictated it into a recorder, with little time for revision. He had sat very briefly (and furnished photographs) for the elderly but vigorous Milwaukee-born Socialist sculptor, Louis Mayer, one of those wonderful but rare persons who contributed generously to the Party. Mayer had sculptured Debs, the elder La Follette, Dan Hoan and others. The head he produced showed Thomas with his mouth open. To Mayer, this was a tribute to Thomas's eloquence (he titled it "The Speaker"), whereas to Thomas, much as he liked Mayer, and especially to Violet, it suggested a man always talking which, while relatively true, did not seem flattering in stone.

Thomas's amiable debate with Mayer about the head would continue for many years. Meanwhile his letter to the President urging that he reject a man recommended by Hague for a Jersey judgeship got a very pleasant "Dear Norman" reply which made it appear certain that the Hague man, the puppet of the despoiler of the Constitution, would get the job: "I am looking around hoping to find someone who does not owe his appointment to anybody but me! But it is a difficult job. I hope to see you one of these days soon."

A couple of times when Thomas was away, his family was awakened at night by men on the street, perhaps drunk, who shouted imprecations at him. Once, while the entire family was at Cold Spring Harbor, the New York house was broken into by marauders who apparently took nothing but pawed through many of his papers. The thought entered his mind that political enemies—possibly even Hague hirelings—might be seeking to embarrass him. While he could scarcely believe that he had enemies of that kind in his own party, some of the Clarity people were working against him. He was astounded to discover that a group of them had quietly tried to swing enough influence in the National Executive Committee to secure the discharge of National Secretary Roy Burt, whom they could not control. Burt and his wife had worked loyally for the Party under the most trying financial pressures, for one small salary which was still far in arrears. This effort to unseat him was enough for Burt, who quit and took a religious education job in Minneapolis. Party efficiency did not improve while a successor was sought. For one thing, the Party and Thomas himself somehow missed noticing that Roosevelt had appointed Paul V. McNutt, of all people, as Federal Security Administrator and Thomas therefore failed to request a public hearing on the appointment. Thomas immediately complained to the President by mail, but this time got a cool reply that the appointment had been carefully considered and that "I am perfectly satisfied with the choice I made."

### 3. *Thunderclap*

Party life for Thomas became a nightmare as the unity which his wing of the Party had gained in fighting the Old Guard collapsed. For the last decade or more, an important factor in a politician's effectiveness had been his judgment of the political intentions of the Soviet Union and its Communist Party in America. Thomas for years had been in the unusual position of being comparatively well informed about Russian lies and treacheries but still taking a sympathetic historical view of the Union of Soviet Socialist Republics from its beleaguered beginnings and being well aware of the automatic hatred of all capitalists and all good Presbyterians and Catholics and Republicans and English imperialists and Hitlerites for it. Another large factor in his tolerance for Communism was the not entirely disinterested loathing of the Old Guard for it. With Fascism always looming in his mind as the great American danger, he had leaned over backwards (some said on his back) in tolerance, looking for improvement in the Communists that would permit an ultimate union of American radicals against Fascism. He had done this despite the disapproval, for one, of Angelica Balabanoff, his admirer in other respects. Angelica had once known personally many of the principals in the Moscow trials. Her disillusionment with the Soviet regime was complete and bitter.

At last, the cumulative terror of the purges brought Thomas around to the same view. To this was added his new understanding of the Communist creed of nobility-in-treachery—his experience with the Lovestonites and Trotskyites, Browder's long and Machiavellian pleas for a "united front," and Browder's cynicism in running for President as a means of backing Roosevelt. On top of this came the loss of the Socialist Party's valued Student League for Industrial Democracy when Thomas, much against his will, permitted its amalgamation with the Communist-influenced National Students' League, since this was demanded by the students themselves. Before long the League was virtually a captive of the Communists, who had also taken over the largely Socialist Workers' Alliance. It took overwhelming evidence to convince Thomas that Communists could be as bad as or worse than Democrats and Republicans who starved sharecroppers, deprived blacks of the vote, shot down textile strikers and imprisoned striking miners, but the evidence was now in hand.

His discovery that his honesty had been repaid by fraud, that his anti-Fascism and his support of the Spanish Loyalists and his dream of an "inclusive party" had all been used by the Communists to exterminate him politically and to advance a Russian regime that was itself as evil as Fascism, was a thunderclap that reverberated in his mind for years. In his "family autobiography" he glossed over some of his own errors but wrote feelingly of the Communist practice "deliberately to make a virtue of bad faith and of completely unscrupulous tactics" and of methods which made men "tend to be sheep in the hands of shepherds who treat them like mutton."

When the Communists invited the Socialists to join them in a united May Day parade in 1939, the Thomas who a few years earlier had accepted with enthusiasm now curtly declined. Instead, wonder of wonders, the Socialist Party joined the Social Democratic Federation in a somewhat uneasy celebration at the Hippodrome where, The Times said, "About 4,000 Socialists and sympathizers applauded statements by Louis Waldman, Norman Thomas and Algernon Lee . . ." It was their first public display of reconciliation, a little like the meeting of terriers which on last encounter had bitten each other. Negotiations about the exact details of reunion still continued between these two small but sensitive groups, and would never reach perfection. Thomas could not have failed to please Waldman and Lee with his ringing denunciation of the Communists, but he could scarcely go along with Waldman's call for all progressives "to unite behind President Roosevelt's foreign policy as an instrument for checkmating the dictatorships and averting war."

By June Violet was well enough so that Thomas took a month's trip west, attended six conferences on international relations (possibly induced by the "thunderclap") at various universities, gave lectures, conferred with Socialists, sounded out the country and, when opportunity offered, accepted contributions for the gasping Keep America Out of War Congress. In Hollywood he encountered Morrie Ryskind, of the memorable "Of Thee I Sing," who joined KAOWC, chipped in $100 and advised him on magazine markets for an article on nonintervention he had written. "You can hardly know how much good that hundred dollars has done," he later wrote Ryskind. "I treated it as a sort of revolving fund and was able to use part of it twice or three times getting meetings started where later there were collections. . . ." Shortly after his return, the Hitler-Stalin pact stunned the West, made the American Communists switch to their "Yanks are not coming" choreography and caused many honest Communists to quit the party in disgust. To Ryskind Thomas wrote:

> . . . Stalin's duplicity . . . ends the notion, I hope, that it is Communism which is the arch enemy of Fascism. Communism and Fascism will only be enemies to the extent they are both rivals for power in a totalitarian society.

On September 1, 1939, Hitler invaded Poland and World War II had begun.

# XIII

## 1. How About 1940?

Thomas wanted the Keep America Out of War Congress to become the unifying center for a whole covey of peace organizations already existing—among them the Fellowship of Reconciliation, the National Council for Prevention of War, World Peaceways, the Women's International League for Peace and Freedom, the War Resisters' League (of which Dr. Evan Thomas was an officer), the left-wing American Peace Mobilization and the right-wing America First Committee. Each was operating inefficiently on its own, duplicating much effort and failing entirely to cover other issues. If all these protesting voices could be schooled to sound in unison, it would make a sizable roar. There were opposing roars from people such as Dorothy Thompson, who argued in her Herald Tribune column that the neutralniks were really aiding Hitler. Thomas's reply included a masterful definition of guilt by association and a reproof for Miss Thompson for using it, though Thomas at intervals would use the tactic with telling effect himself:

> Many of us who hate Naziism . . . resent Miss Thompson's attempt to lump us with Nazi propagandists. It is a world where the disciples of Machiavelli change sides so often one cannot guide one's conduct primarily by the company in which one temporarily finds oneself but rather by principle. Miss Thompson ought to know that, because for many months she and the Communists were exceedingly vociferous members of the same group . . . the war party.

To Mary and Paul Blanshard, who were in London seeing lovely old squares desecrated by conversion into air-raid shelters, he wrote: "The greatest difficulty in every organization that I am interested in is to get any money at all." The Socialist Party revenue had shrunk drastically with its reduced membership, now below 5,000 nationally. Thomas's opportunity for large contributions had suffered in the decline of the Party and his own vote. The angels—mostly wealthy widows—who had blessed him with largess had flown.

The new Party national secretary was the tall, blunt Californian Travers Clement, a writer and the husband of Lillian Symes (the two of them had put Angelica Balabanoff's astonishing but disorganized autobiography into publishable form). Clement saved the Party money by also becoming editor of The Call, now published in Chicago. He was as strongly anti-interventionist as Thomas—the war issue was beginning to split the Party once again. A simply wonderful thing about the able and dedicated Clement was that he had a private income and for months drew no salary at all. He managed out of Party funds to pay the current rent for the Randolph Street office, though not the considerable back rent nor the $160 still owed Burt and the lesser sum owed Senior. Such debts haunted Thomas, but what haunted him more was the specter of American involvement in the war, and his tactic was to combine the Party and the Keep America Out of War Congress in the fight. This caused rising disagreement. Professor Coolidge, who was contributing $50 a month to the Party and $25 to KAOWC, at length withdrew from KAOWC when he decided that America must aid the allies against Hitler. The burden of debt and the occasional threat of lawsuits against the Party and other Thomas enterprises at times became well-nigh unbearable. The North Carolina Party member who wrote Thomas that he was down on his luck but saw sure success in a small business enterprise he could take over if the Party would kindly lend him $500, did not know what he asked.

Thomas found it necessary to dun politely several persons who owed him or Violet. "The bank is after me again about loans [to the Party]," he wrote Clement. Violet came to the rescue with a $500 loan to the Party, whose New York offices had moved from Seventeenth Street to cheaper quarters on Fourth Avenue. The Call had to retreat from weekly to fortnightly publication. KAOWC was meanwhile being pressed for $995.12 in printing costs, and there were final bills to pay in the lawsuit against Hague. It was not surprising that the distracted Thomas looked for some escape from this financial morass and ultimately found it in a direction that brought invective down on him. He was troubled by the other rich Cantabrigian, Alfred Baker Lewis, who, like Coolidge, now opposed Thomas's neutrality and called it "isolationist and in effect pro-Hitler." The majority of the Party membership in New York City was still Jewish. Not a few had relatives or friends in Germany who were Hitler's victims, and more and more of them favored whole-hearted American aid to the Allies. Thomas did not budge, writing one of his Jewish supporters:

> Personally, affectionate as I feel toward a great many of the [Jewish] comrades and warmly as I sympathize with their emotional position, I have comparatively little hope that we shall be able to hold to the Party people whose obvious interest is getting America into war. . . . it is our whole philosophy of life, our whole program for Socialism which is at stake. I do not think we have much of any message to America unless it is a message to the effect that Democracy will not be won or maintained by totalitarian war between rival imperialist powers and that it is our duty for ourselves and mankind to keep out. That this position seems to put us temporarily into the company of undesirable folks is regrettable but can no more be helped than in the first world war, when also we were called pro-German and what-not. If Debs could stand it, we can.

He sent his written resignation as chairman to Maynard Krueger of the National Executive Committee with the understanding that it must be accepted if and when Party policy on the war differed from his own. Though some members saw this as a threat, it was simply a statement of principle. He loved the Party and expended great thought and effort on it, but it would no longer be his Party if it went to war. His anti-war program included all-out support of free speech, which had been so cruelly throttled in the first war. He commended Mayor La Guardia for permitting the egregious German-American Bundist Fritz Kuhn to speak in New York City. He urged Dean Christian Gauss at Princeton to permit Earl Browder to speak there. Browder had been indicted for violation of the passport law, but Thomas felt there were mitigating circumstances:

> What prejudices I have in the matter are . . . all against Mr. Browder. I regard Stalin as at least as much the enemy of civil liberty and everything I care for in this world as Hitler. . . . In no sense is Earl Browder a true friend of civil liberty. Nevertheless I believe that tolerance proves its virtue by its success in dealing with intolerance.

Russia's attack on Finland a few days later, and the Daily Worker line that it was Finland, at the behest of Wall Street, that was invading Russia ("Red Army Hurls Back Invading Finnish Troops") made him send Browder a telegram challenging him to repudiate the Soviet acts or "stand branded as Stalin's stooge." Browder refused to comment. The Finland issue also inspired a Thomas drive to purge the thirty-five-member board of the American Civil Liberties Union of its Communist-tolerant chairman, the Reverend Harry F. Ward, and the Communist board member Elizabeth Gurley Flynn. Thomas had a steadfast affection for Miss Flynn, who had been an Industrial Workers of the World worker until she joined the Communist Party in 1937, regarding her as utterly sincere and utterly mistaken. Ward had been one of his professors at Union and in fact had joined the ACLU board in the twenties at Thomas's urging. He honored Ward for his long labors and would have defended his freedom of speech to the death but rejected the idea that one could protect civil liberties in America while winking at their denial in Russia. He wrote Ward bluntly in an open letter charging that his chairmanship of the Communist-oriented American League for Peace and Democracy disqualified him from further ACLU service. The League had flipped unerringly in principle along with Russian deviations and now seemed ready to agree that Finland threatened Russia—as Thomas put it, "that the bulldog must be ready against the dastardly attack of the rabbit." His attack on Ward and the rest was attacked in turn by another board member, Osmond K. Fraenkel, as Red-baiting. Thomas replied:

> You are neither a Communist nor a fellow traveler and I consider you one of the wisest friends of civil liberty in America. But nevertheless I think that you and many liberals like you are doing very serious harm now to true liberalism in the United States by a kind of tolerance of intolerance, which makes you give a color of support to a Communist Machiavellianism which is destroying the soul of American labor and will inevitably hasten the rise of an American Fascism, Black or Red. The support of civil liberties for Communists and Fascists is only valid and effective when we exclude Communists and Fascists from leadership in what is to them a wholly temporary, partial and pragmatic defense of civil liberty.

He succeeded after a sharp struggle in ousting Ward (John Haynes Holmes succeeded him as chairman) and Flynn. He was so busy that he was unable to attend a father-and-son affair at Princeton with Evan, and his sister Agnes, now teaching at the Quaker Westtown School near Philadelphia, wrote to him in a birthday greeting, "The time or two you've been in Phila. this fall, I've heard about it only after you've left." In the midst of these convulsions the Thomases moved from the big

Eighteenth Street place where they had lived for fifteen years to an apartment four blocks uptown at 235 East Twenty-second Street. "I'll miss the big living room for Party conferences, etc.," Thomas admitted to Clement, but the smaller domicile would be cheaper and easier on Violet's heart. There was little time that Christmas at Cold Spring Harbor for caroling, for Violet was ill, Becky (returned from England and now in her last year at Vassar) came home from college ill, and Frances Gates was taken to hospital where the Thomases' fourth grandchild was born on Christmas day.

These events did not divert Thomas from the thought that 1940 was around the corner and that it might be well to run for President on a peace platform. "How do you and some of the Buffalo Socialists feel about 1940?" he wrote one upstate member, sending similar queries to many others.

### 2. Lonesome in the Party

"Well, Mrs. Thomas," asked a friendly Toronto newspaperman at the Thomas home, conducting a novel interview based on the fiction that the Socialists could win, "what are you going to do when you get into the White House?"

"There is not much cause for immediate worry," she replied. "It will not happen but if it did, then just as I am doing now—help my husband, listen to discussions as I have today, and stay at home as much as possible."

Her reply suggested more pliancy and domestication than the forceful Violet possessed. Perhaps Thomas's endless political crusade, which impinged on her privacy and freedom, antagonized some of her family and friends, cost her money and such unexpected experiences as tussles with policemen and a punch on the jaw, repaid her in its talk, movement, suspense, personalities, surprises and excitement. She could be sure that her husband, who already belonged to at least twenty-three civic or benevolent or political organizations, and was a prime and sustaining mover in some of them, would start a new one such as the Keep America Out of War Congress whenever he felt one necessary. KAOWC had a sponsorship of some seventy-five "names," most of whom supplied only their names, a few who gave effort but very few who gave money. The sponsors ranged from Elmer Davis, A. Philip Randolph and Jay Lovestone to at least three Senators, Nye of North

Dakota, Capper of Kansas and Clark of Missouri. An active member was the hulking Carlo Tresca, a maker of exceptional salads whose wife now was the well-heeled Margaret De Silver, a firm Thomas supporter on the American Civil Liberties Union board. Another was the young but balding Jack Altman, who lived in the Bronx but spoke with the accent of his native England.

Thomas's motive for wanting a Socialist Presidential campaign joined with his motive in founding KAOWC—to fight intervention in Europe's war. The Republican candidate, whoever he was (he turned out to be Willkie, Thomas's fellow member on the Town Hall board), would in all probability be as interventionist as Roosevelt, a likely candidate for a third term. "Only Socialists will make the kind of war case that ought to be made," Thomas argued; "otherwise we leave the apparent anti-war question to the Communists who can't be trusted because they favor a war that would help Stalin. . . . [N]ot to run a national campaign this year would be to commit suicide or, at least, to betray our trust. . . ." He held to this despite considerable discouragement: The Socialist International Ladies' Garment Workers' Union official Murray Gross said it "made no sense" to run this year; the Saratoga Socialist professor Coleman Cheney said the upstate Party organization was a shambles; Paul Porter in Wisconsin was opposed; and Jack Altman said it would be unfair to the American Labor Party for Thomas to run as a Socialist.

But the ALP would support Roosevelt, which meant supporting capitalism *and* war. Nothing could stop Thomas from making the fight although he knew it would be unpleasant. Only one of the difficulties was the failure of unity negotiations between the Socialist Party and Social Democratic Federation, mostly because the Federation now favored aid to the Allies short of war. To Thomas, steps short of war were steps into war. In The New Leader, Algernon Lee attacked him in a long and savage article suggesting a Thomas entente with the American Nazi leader, Kuhn:

> It should now be clearly evident to all Social Democrats that we were right in not rushing into a merger with the people who so piously sing "Thomas is Our Leader."
>
> When Fritz Kuhn's paper . . . can reprint one of Dr. Thomas's manifestoes with a note of praise . . . no doubt remains as to where Thomas actually stands in the worldwide conflict between democratic and dictatorial tendencies. . . .

"He sounds like a raving maniac," Travers Clement wrote Thomas. "I hope you will let Lee have it right smack between the eyes." Thomas, whose prose could bite with subtleties unknown to Lee, maintained a dignified silence. The Pennsylvania Socialists under Hoopes, at any rate, had come back to him, being anti-war. He was nominated at the Socialist convention in Washington in April although a vocal minority, including Jack Altman and the persistent Alfred Baker Lewis, favored aid to the Allies. His running mate was the thirty-four-year-old pipe-smoking Professor Maynard Krueger, a native of Missouri and an excellent public speaker who had aided Thomas on economic questions in previous campaigns. The New York Times, though it favored aid for the Allies, commented approvingly, "The Socialist Party . . . isn't afraid to argue in a meeting. It did not have to wait for permission from any foreign country before naming Mr. Thomas. . . . One can disagree with his views on economics but it is impossible to dislike or distrust him."

Rebekah Thomas, graduating from Vassar and about to marry John Friebely of Philadelphia, said she planned to "campaign for dad" on her honeymoon. He would need lots of honeymooner support. Lewis resigned from the Party with his customary courtesy (Thomas wrote him how "lonesome it is going to be in the Party without you"). Professor Coolidge told Thomas he could not support him but would continue as a member, and there were other defections. Then came Hitler's blitzkrieg, Dunkirk and the fall of France. The Socialist split became a crevasse. (During this tumult, a friend discovered Angelica Balabanoff starving in her small West End Avenue apartment, not having eaten for several days. Thomas arranged a secret collection for her and a check was sent her representing "additional sales of her last book.") Altman now resigned from the Keep America Out of War Congress, having swung to the conviction that a Hitler victory would mean the "death of civilization." He put his resignation in the form of a letter to the enemy New Leader. What Thomas perhaps did not know at the time was that Altman had tried to put the letter in The Call, but the anti-war Call had refused to print it. In any case Altman had done it without consultation with Thomas, who felt all the more wounded because Altman included in his letter an attack on KAOWC and a plea for support for William Allen White's Committee to Defend America by Aiding the Allies.

"Few things have hurt me personally as much as what has seemed to me his sabotage of the Party," Thomas wrote. Thomas and the state executive committee asked him to resign, since he publicly opposed

Party policy. This angered Paul Porter, usually a staunch Thomas supporter, and others, who urged Altman *not* to resign. Altman followed the latter course and was expelled by the committee's vote in the midst of a campaign in which solidarity was the watchword. (Altman later felt that Thomas never really forgave him, though they did exchange cards on their identical birthdays.)

The shocking Hitler successes made Thomas's support dwindle as the campaign progressed. British imperialism in India and elsewhere being a constant factor in his mind, he was irked by the general American approval of a stream of British lecturers, some distinguished and some quite ordinary. "Outwardly," he observed, "most of these speakers are liberals, but their liberalism almost never goes to the extent of any basic attack upon British imperialism. With few exceptions, these ladies and gentlemen are all sure that America ought to be proud to help, once more, to save civilization, or democracy, which is amazingly synonymous with the British Empire." Henry Sloane Coffin, now head of Union Seminary, wrote him, "I cannot see how any intelligent American can fail to see that the wise course for this country is to arm at once, and meanwhile to give Britain every possible aid." The Reverend Ralph Harlow, the friend of Thomas's youth, seemed to be slipping in his anti-war determination (though in the end he held firm). Thomas felt that he was seeing a rerun of an old drama, infinitely tragic, the church of Christ preparing to wade into blood again, preachers shouldering arms just as they had done before, none of them understanding that war would not solve anything but would make things worse, just as the first one had. He remained offended by a church catering to the narrowest human caprices and prejudices and abandoning, as it had all through history, its own holy teachings. To a Methodist functionary he wrote:

> Any religion to have value in these days when men are weighed down by great tragedy, must be more than a religion of escape for individuals. It must speak with authority on values. It must set before men worthy ends to be achieved by appropriate means. . . . Such a religion is desperately needed.

Some of the old faithful were still with him for nonintervention—the Lovetts in New Haven, the Darrs in California, John Haynes Holmes, John Nevin Sayre, A. J. Muste. "In spite of all the stupidities of the statesmen during the last 25 years," Lovett wrote Thomas, "I somehow refused to believe that you and I would ever live to see another crisis

similar to that which we endured together during the years of 1914-18.
. . . Power to you now as then . . ."

### 3. Down the Fire Escape

Thomas appeared repeatedly before Congressional committees to
testify against aid, against conscription, against armaments, against the
new Smith "anti-subversion" bill which he foresaw (in one of his fairly
frequent bursts of prevision) as the first overt move against civil liberties
which he felt sure were fated to be crushed if war came to America. He
had a considerable correspondence with the President, who wrote him
kindly and at length, evidently hoping to win him over, saying in part,
"Frankly, I am greatly fearful for the safety of this country over a period
of years, because I think that the tendency of the present victorious
dictatorships is to segregate us and surround us to such an extent that
we will become vulnerable."

Thomas, on his first campaign tour, took Violet with him by car into
the Midwest. ". . . [S]he was usually my sole traveling companion,
secretary, and general assistant," he wrote later. He was amused when
an Indiana woman, hearing of Violet's spaniels, said that Socialists were
more favorably impressed by children than by dogs. "I have had six
children, five of whom are living," Violet replied. "How many more
would you suggest?" He had managed to get on the ballot in New York
and twenty-seven other states. Later, when he was traveling alone, the
Northern Hotel in Billings, Montana, caught fire and he was one of
seventy-five guests aroused in time to seize their belongings and descend fire escapes. From his Socialist friends in Wisconsin, the Walter
Uphoffs, came word of a new arrival: "Name: Norman Thomas. Birth-
mark: The Union label." The alert American Legion barred him from
speaking in the auditorium at Carbondale, Illinois, a ban he circum-
vented by addressing a crowd at the teachers' college there. Other
similar efforts to muzzle him made him especially irked at the slanted
reporting of Time magazine, which among other things declared incor-
rectly that he had been jailed during World War I, a statement not only
libelous but which he felt might have played a part in the Carbondale
difficulty and others and was not likely to help his vote.

He complained to Time. He listed outright errors in addition to the
slant, calling them "entirely inexcusable in a paper of your standing,"
noting that of recent years "you have a uniform record of rather serious

errors in connection with every story concerning which I have had specific information," and that "I am beginning to wonder how much you are to be trusted in your general reports." In reply he received courteous assurances of the care taken by Time researchers, that accuracy was Time's first concern, that the management was troubled by his comments and that corrections of errors were welcomed in the Letters column.

In publicizing his various causes, Thomas depended heavily on good relations with the press. He had punctiliously thanked the Times for Louis Stark's accurate coverage of the Washington Socialist Party convention, and he got considerable free airing of his views in the letters columns of The Times, The Herald Tribune, The World-Telegram and other publications including on occasion Time. Newspapers and magazines usually found his discussions of issues so lucid and diverting that they made excellent reading. The Nation, The Christian Century and The New Republic were favorite outlets, U.S. News often wired him questions on current issues and published his replies, and he was expanding his correspondence with out-of-town newspapers. He did not know how many millions of people he reached only through this medium but the number was sizable and he sought to enlarge it as the Socialist Party declined in every respect including publicity. Though he may have disliked to risk losing one of these outlets, he was beginning a new and less agreeable relationship with Time, to which he now wrote:

> May I say, bluntly, that I am not very hopeful of the result of any work by your research department. Nothing has ever come of my other letters in the direction of improved accuracy. . . . The damage you do with your enormous circulation is not easily repaired, when you permit someone to put a letter in your column, correcting what you have said.

The more forthright Harvard Crimson observed, "Mr. Thomas is not trimming his sails to the change of wind. He is sticking to his principles, upholding a stand that would probably get him expelled from Columbia, ostracized from the best society, and punched in the nose in Congress." Campaign tours invariably inspirited Thomas ("we are really making progress," he wrote Senior), but he was more realistic in a letter to Devere Allen:

> Remember that in 1936 about 50% of our total vote came from New York State; 25% from New York City. We shall lose almost all of these voters in New York City because they are predominantly Jewish and do not like

our stand on war and conscription. . . . Frankly, many of us think that unless we at least do as well as we did in 1936, there won't be any Socialist Party worth talking about after the election.

He was right on both counts. His vote sank to 116,796—70,000 less than in 1936, and 66,000 of those votes had been lost in New York State. It was a blow, and his public efforts reduced his 1940 income to less than $2,000. Nevertheless he and Violet relaxed with the Lovetts at the Princeton-Yale football game.

### 4. American Century

Although Thomas was delighted when Colonel Charles A. Lindbergh came out against intervention, he knew enough of his background and temperament to wonder as to his value in any public role against American involvement. But he wrote to the Lone Eagle to praise his stand. The Lindberghs had rented a house at Lloyd Neck, only a few miles from the Thomas Long Island place, and soon the two families were visiting each other on occasion. Thomas sized up the colonel—still youthful and handsome at thirty-eight—as the kind of heroic and glamorous person the anti-war movement could use if he would only take a little tutoring. Though friendly, he was as independent as his late father, blunt and tactless. He had uttered and written undemocratic sentiments and had made enemies. Thomas wrote him, with apologies for his unasked advice:

> I think your influence for keeping America out of war . . . would be far greater if you could see your way clear to do the following things: (1) Emphasize your personal opposition to the cruelty, intolerance and tyranny of Fascism. (2) Make it clear that at the very least, a desirable peace would mean the continuance of Great Britain and her self-governing dominions as absolutely independent nations with real power, not as puppets to Hitler. (3) Clarify your own position on cooperation by us with the winner of this war. I do not think you mean to imply that American business is temporarily to share with the German state the profits of exploitation, yet some of your enemies so interpret your remarks.

Immediately after the election, R. Douglas Stuart, a son of Princeton who was director of the anti-interventionist America First Committee, urged Thomas to speak under their auspices. They would pay all expenses but no fees. America First was preponderantly right-wing and

Roosevelt-hating. Thomas replied that he was a Socialist and "it might be more appropriate for me to speak under different auspices."

But the Keep America Out of War Congress, though Thomas now had the vigorous Mary Hillyer Blanshard as executive secretary, was chronically broke. America First had bagfuls of money. Its chairman was General Robert E. Wood, the Kansas-born, West Point–educated Sears, Roebuck magnate. Other men of wealth including Henry Ford contributed to it, it was nonpartisan and it had a sprinkling of Democrats and liberals among its members or supporters including Chester Bowles, Oswald Garrison Villard, Harry Emerson Fosdick, William Benton and Robert Maynard Hutchins. All were concerned with preserving American civil liberties. John T. Flynn, the liberal journalist (whose turn to the right began at this time unknown to Thomas) was Thomas's most energetic colleague in KAOWC and was as active in America First. Thomas was corresponding on a Norman-and-Burt basis with Senator Burton K. Wheeler, his colleague of 1924, about strategy. Both believed, as did America First, that passage of Lend-Lease would give Roosevelt almost dictatorial powers and make war certain. When Thomas returned from a February lecture in Detroit, he found that KAOWC had arranged a joint meeting in New York with America First. He did not object, and spoke there along with Senators Wheeler and Nye and John T. Flynn against Lend-Lease. He caught it from Dorothy Thompson, whose Herald Tribune column was syndicated all over the country:

> ... The Mr. Thomases of Germany, whose names were Herr Braun and Herr Severing, were in power in the Prussian government in 1932, with 300,000 armed police under them. They gave up that power on a mere ultimatum from Hitler ... they, too, were honest pacifists who fainted at the thought of blood. What blood has flowed since then! What migrations, exiles, concentration camps, torture barracks! What wars! ... His [Thomas's] side doesn't exist, except in his own mind. ... The reality is that this is *not* an imperialist war, except on the side of the Axis. ... The reality is that this is a world wide defense against a tidal wave of red-brown counter-revolution, falsely calling itself revolution, which aims to sweep away all the institutions of civilized man and the civilized values that you, Mr. Thomas, prize. ...

There was much more, painful to Thomas because he had criticized those same German Socialists and implored the American Socialists not to do likewise. Britain's freedom from imperialism was news to him as a champion of India—he had recently written Lord Lothian, the British ambassador in Washington, to protest against the British sentencing of Jawaharlal Nehru to four years' imprisonment at hard labor for advocating passive resistance to India's participation in the present war. Britain's use of colonial forces to fight her wars had always revolted him. (He was not forgetting the lack of sympathy on the part of such as Ernest Bevin and Winston Churchill for the Spanish Republic—saving democracy had not been so important to England then.) Thomas was dubious of Miss Thompson's libertarian logic. She had subscribed heartily to Henry Luce's recent "American Century" essay in Life, which urged American military and economic supervision of the world, with Britain as junior partner, after entering the war and winning it. Thomas, alarmed by the growing imperialist sentiment he heard from rostrum and radio, wrote:

> It is clothed, to be sure, in beautiful and glowing words It is the "American century" of Henry Luce, the "American destiny" of Dorothy Thompson; but the words merely clothe in language the nakedness of imperial ambition. The English-speaking nations are to police in God's name such places as we think necessary for our advantage, doing justice, as that British Nazi poet, Rudyard Kipling, told us was our duty, to the "lesser breeds without the law."

Thomas twitted Miss Thompson for failing to recognize Luce's imperialism, or any imperialism on her side of the fence. But the lady who could be so inconsistent could also strike telling blows, as when she replied, "Mr. Thomas, I hope that you and I never have an opportunity to discuss this matter further in the same concentration camp."

### 5. You and Hitler

This was Thomas's third exposure to heavy artillery, his first having been as a "traitor" in the early twenties and the second during his long struggle with the Old Guard. He entertained no doubt that American entry into the war meant American Fascism. The passions stirred up by the question split old friends, broke up families and ended romances. Noninterventionists were under the hottest fire in New York, with its high proportion of Jews and other interventionists. Thomas was assailed as an isolationist, a charge totally in error since it was his international view that furnished much of the rationale for his noninterventionism.

Villard, another who had gone through the mill with him in the first war, felt so outlawed that he suggested to Thomas "a dinner club to meet informally every three weeks and made up of men who have not hauled down the flag," meaning become pro-war. Lindbergh's speeches caused him to be attacked in New York as a Nazi and a man on horseback, whereas in the West he was hailed as a voice of wisdom. Polls indicated that the great majority of Americans still opposed intervention. Thomas, though distressed by Lindbergh's failures in propagandist finesse, applauded his theme that American intervention would damage the moral order both here and abroad. Thomas was so anxious not to exacerbate Jewish feelings that he urged Senator Wheeler to avoid attacking pro-war Jews, writing, "To avoid even a suspicion of racial implication, why not always put the House of Morgan in . . . and perhaps the Chase National Bank." Thomas had raised enough money to have a weekly anti-war speech broadcast by recording over an extensive network of smaller radio stations. He was being scorched in the press and by mail:

> . . . [The] world is aflame, mad dogs are loose destroying civilization as we know it, and you want us to . . . disregard what is happening. . . . You are giving aid and comfort to the enemies of democracy, freedom and Labor.

> Same old empty noise. You still talk like you know it all. You and Hitler.

> Mr. Thomas is applauded by Communists, Nazis and Christian Fronters. . . . His new allies are blind appeasers, the quitters and Quislings, and the fifth columnists of Moscow and Berlin.

But he was also getting letters of praise from plain people, some of whom sent a dollar or so to help keep him going, and from Senator Charles W. Tobey of Vermont who called him "Valiant for Truth." To bitterness he often managed to reply calmly, as to the prominent New York Socialist (his former friend) Nathaniel Minkoff, who accused him of disgracing the Party:

> You are one of the men with whom I hate to differ, but I should hesitate to try to psychoanalyze your motives or your state of mind, lest I be as badly mistaken about you as you are about me. I am fighting for what I believe with all my heart. It is the best thing we can do in a world we did not make; you are doing the same. Congratulations on your help to the refugees.

Reinhold Niebuhr was also one of those who Villard would have said had hauled down the flag. Six months earlier he had recoiled at the thought of a Hitler victory, conceded error, resigned from the Party and praised the Roosevelt foreign policy. He became a founder of the Union for Democratic Action (later called Americans for Democratic Action), linked America's cause with the Allies and attacked Thomas's position as Marxist utopianism, idealism minus realism.

Thomas declined an invitation from General Wood to become a member of America First, wanting to retain his freedom to criticize the organization, as he occasionally did. There was a scattering of Nazi and Communist camp-followers in it, to be sure, but there were also sincere pacifists and older people who regretted participation in World War I. America First came out for strong military preparation, which made the pacifist Villard resign and which Thomas still opposed. On May 23, Thomas joined with Lindbergh, Senator Wheeler, Kathleen Norris and John T. Flynn in addressing under America First auspices a mammoth gathering at Madison Square Garden (22,000 inside and 10,000 outside listening to loudspeakers). Lindbergh got a four-minute ovation, and Thomas led the crowd in "an ironical recitation of President Roosevelt's election pledge that American boys were not going to be sent into any foreign wars, the audience repeating each line after he said it." For Thomas there was a special irony in the virtual collapse in New York of the traditional Socialist rejection of war and the constant Socialist attacks on him for following that hallowed Socialist line, though his reasons for following the line were not Marxist. To one of those assailing him for the company he kept, he replied, "it would be a very great mistake for us to retire to some monastery to preserve our purity. We have got to go where people are if we are to have any hope of helping to block war."

Frank Trager had already raised the question in The Call as to whether Lindbergh was a Fascist. Thomas, who had never been satisfied with all of the colonel's thinking, had politically welcomed the influence he could exert against war even if some of his reasons might be wrong. Answering Trager in The Call, Thomas agreed that in several magazine articles Lindbergh had "advanced the unscientific and certainly anti-Socialist theory of the supremacy of the white race and its duty to preserve its imperial supremacy," ideas Thomas rejected. Also, "Colonel Lindbergh has not publicly and emphatically condemned Hitler and Hitlerism. This is true and I think very regrettable." He *had* said that the defeat of Britain would be a tragedy, but Thomas thought this scarcely adequate. He agreed that the complaint that Lindbergh had accepted a Nazi decoration was valid even though he received it while in Germany in the service of America at the American Embassy, and even though the medal "came as a surprise, and the colonel has kept it in storage with other medals from other foreign powers." Thomas did not mention that he personally had urged Lindbergh to speak out against Hitler and to clear up other ambiguities. Despite them, it would not serve the Socialist cause to exclude Lindbergh as a spokesman against intervention: "It is our job, if we can, to draw Lindbergh, and millions of less conspicuous Americans who want to keep out of war, closer to the Socialist position on war and Fascism." Thomas repeated that he was not a member of America First and did not subscribe to all its works even though it had dropped from its membership "America's richest and most reactionary industrialist [Henry Ford]."

He was on one of his track meets, speaking on the platform and over the air whenever and wherever he could. The American Legion prevented him from speaking against war in Wilkes-Barre, and he was repulsed in other places, but he took time (with Violet) to speak at the commencement at Westtown School, where his sister Agnes taught. His invaluable Mary Hillyer, an effective speaker also, went to Washington to debate with Irving Berlin, who favored intervention. She rode back with the composer through bumpy air and upchucked in his lap, thereby defeating him twice. So militant was her stand against involvement that when her husband, Paul Blanshard, came out for intervention, he had to move out for two days before she relented and invited him back.

When a Thomas speech at Haverford College included an attack on Henry Luce's "American Century" imperialism, one of his listeners was Luce's brother-in-law, Leslie Severinghaus, headmaster of Haverford School. Severinghaus wrote to him to assure him that Luce's essay was devoid of imperialism. Thomas, who had long seethed at the Luce-press's skillful derogation of noninterventionists, replied:

> . . . I'm sorry to tell you that my criticism stands. Most imperialists are sincere in believing their imperialism will serve certain gains. Mr. Luce, the son of a missionary, would be very likely to have that point of view. But imperialism is imperialism, even when it is benevolent, as it is occasionally. Slavery was a human institution by the benevolence of slave owners.
>
> Moreover the logic of imperialism if given American racial attitudes,

will not be along Mr. Luce's lines in a totalitarian age. May I add that I would have far more confidence in Mr. Luce's stuff if his own magazines . . . had not been so grossly unfair in this fight about the war.

### 6. *The Eastman Flip*

The winds of war kept blowing men in surprising directions. In June, Max Eastman published the article that overnight made him the most famous of turncoats, titled, "Socialism Does Not Gibe with Human Nature." As a professor and world traveler presumably trained in human nature, always sure of himself and visibly fast in love and wit, he was expected to have made up his mind more quickly than the average. His strictures on the unworkability of Socialism would have aroused less furor had he not spent a quarter-century advocating it and had they not appeared in that encomiast of business, church and flag, The Reader's Digest, which only in April had featured the condensed Luce "American Century." This, coming from the old editor of The Masses, was as if the Pope had denounced the Virgin Mary in The Christian Century. Actually, Eastman had moved to the right over a period of years and would have offended fewer leftists if he had been less cocky and more apologetic over his change of front. His defection was felt not to be accompanied by suitable breast-beating over decades of error and a decent admission that the brain so long deluded might not be trustworthy this time.

The Call printed a three-column funeral service, "In Memoriam, Max Eastman." The Daily Worker attacked him savagely and said he was a British agent, and his old friend Harry Elmer Barnes denounced him publicly as a renegade. Thomas urged the Reader's Digest to assign him or someone competent to write an answering article, but the Digest seemed not really interested in presenting the other side. When Eastman's extended opinion appeared in book form, *Reflections on the Failure of Socialism,* in which one of the things he said was that there was no such thing as "democratic Socialism," Thomas titled his answering Call article, "Reflections on the Failure of Eastman." The swerve of history's locomotive had shaken him too, but was modifying rather than overturning his opinions. It did seem to him that Eastman made the switch with relative painlessness; and Eastman went on to become a "roving editor" of The Digest, preaching the new gospel at that magazine's comfortable salary. Even the cool Roger Baldwin, who had a place near Eastman's on Martha's Vineyard, was unable for some years to resume the friendly talks he had had with him. Still, the Eastman turn was a landmark, another sign of growing doubt in idealism and growing faith in crude power, à la "American Century." Carlo Tresca warned Eastman that his life was in danger at the hands of vengeful Communists—a curious mistake, since it turned out that it was Tresca's life that was in danger.

Thomas was continuing his broadcasts, getting a big donation from the poet Lenore Marshall and smaller ones from others, but badly needing money both for the Keep America Out of War Congress and the Party. At this time Jack Fies, the crippled Socialist he had met in Carolina, was killed in an automobile accident and left $5,000 to be used by the Party at the discretion of five trustees, of whom Thomas was one. Much as he regretted Fies's death, that $5,000 was much needed. Thomas pursued it like a bird dog, writing the attorney handling the matter, ". . . I shall be honored to serve as one of the trustees of the fund . . . About when will this money be available?" and asking later, "For myself I should, of course, be ready to accept the legacy as soon as it may be paid. Is it necessary for you, however, to get formal acceptance from each of the five people named as trustees?"

## 7. Fallen Eagle

On learning of the sudden Nazi attack on Russia June 21, Thomas observed, "We shall watch with interest to see how fast American Communists . . . will become propagandists for American entry into the war on the side of those 'great democracies,' Stalin's dictatorship and the British Empire." The Daily Worker choked off its anti-intervention line and, after a couple of days of confusion, dutifully printed a front-page editorial clamoring for full Lend-Lease aid to Russia. The influential American Council on Soviet Relations followed with a mass meeting presided over by Corliss Lamont, asking "full and unstinting [American] support to the Soviet Union in its struggle to defend its land, its people and its freedom." The fellow-traveling American Peace Mobilization, which until then had fought all aid to Britain, pulled hard on the tiller, found peace not paramount after all and besought American help for the Soviet war machine. It proved, Mary Hillyer said scornfully, that APM was "a puppet for peace on a string from Mr. Stalin's finger," and she advised those members who resented this to rally to the Keep America Out of War Congress.

Indeed the Nazi move altered the guilt-by-association opportunities inconveniently for the interventionists. Socialists who had taxed Thomas with echoing the Communist peace line now found themselves parroting the Communist war line. Even such people as Dorothy Thompson, Henry Luce and the President himself had to come around to the Stalinist line preached by The Daily Worker. Thomas, who had all along been against both Stalin and Hitler and against British imperialism too, was still against all three, still against intervention. He would not have been human had he not permitted himself a chuckle at the embarrassment of the oddly assorted crew who had pointed fingers at him. The Russia-oriented Sir Stafford Cripps, with whom he had disagreed in friendly letters about the degree of trust one could place in the Soviets, was now British ambassador in Moscow, praising the "magnificent" Russian stand against the Nazis, a "stand" that at first seemed more like a fall.

Cold Spring Harbor was full of vacationing Thomases, children and grandchildren, in August. Thomas himself, now helped by a black hired man, had a big vegetable garden going, and he liked to swim before dinner at the Cold Spring Harbor Beach Club—a private club favored also by John Foster Dulles and permitting no Negroes, which young Evan Thomas wryly thought pretty exclusive for his Socialist father. Thomas kept rushing into the city on super-heated Long Island Rail Road trains. He took time to look for a defense-industry job for his hired man, who had asked his help in that, though it meant finding another man. Seeking to stop the abuse heaped on Lindbergh and increase the latter's anti-intervention influence, Thomas volunteered to write an article for The Saturday Evening Post, "The Case Against Colonel Lindbergh," which of course would really present the case *for* his thinking on the war. It was an idea America First applauded, and since Thomas knew Demaree Bess of The Post and had probably discussed it with him, it might well have appeared there had not Lindbergh himself scotched it.

He did this with his September 11 speech in Des Moines in which he said, "the three most important groups which have been pressing this country toward war are the British, the Jewish and the Roosevelt administration." He agreed that "No person with a sense of the dignity of mankind can condone the persecution of the Jewish race in Germany," but he urged Jews to oppose intervention in the war, adding that "Their greatest danger in this country lies in their large ownership and influence in our motion pictures, our press, our radio and our government." He was applauded by the Iowans. He saw nothing anti-Semitic in his words, noting in his journal, "It seems that almost anything can be discussed today in America except the Jewish problem." He was astonished at the outcry and the headlines he caused, especially in the East.

"Didn't our friend Lindbergh do us a lot of harm?" Thomas mourned. ". . . . I honestly don't think Lindbergh is an anti-Semite, but I think he is a great idiot. . . ." "Not all Jews are for war and Jews have a right to agitate for war if we have a right to agitate against it. The point in both cases is the way the job is done and here I think a great many Jews have been at fault. [But what] about Dorothy Thompson and Henry Luce?" "It is an enormous pity that . . . the Colonel will not take the advice on public relations which he would expect an amateur in aviation to take from an expert." When asked who wrote Lindbergh's speeches: "Most emphatically he writes his own speeches. That's why part of them have been so bad."

Thomas gave a statement to the press criticizing the speech and dissociating himself and the Socialist Party from it. He spoke no more for America First. To Lindbergh himself he wrote:

> I believe that you meant good, not harm. . . . Nevertheless, it did great harm. . . . I think you exaggerated the solidarity of the Jews in this matter . . . I don't think that if Jewish groups or British groups would drop their propaganda, we would necessarily stay out of war. . . . I honestly don't know what you can do completely to clear up the matter. . . . Nevertheless for the sake of the cause of peace and tolerance I hope you will find some way to say something in your next speech to help clear up the situation. . . .

Lindbergh did not reply. When Thomas received a telegram from Reinhold Niebuhr criticizing him for his connection with America First and Lindbergh, which was also given to the press by the Union for Democratic Action,* he let loose with both barrels, not to "Dear Reinie" but to "Dear Dr. Niebuhr," saying in part:

> I have mentioned times without number to all honest men who want to be informed that I am not a member of the America First Committee and that I have always reserved the right to criticize it, a right which I have frequently exercised publicly. It didn't take a telegram from you to suggest to me a line of action to take after Colonel Lindbergh's extraordinarily unfortunate speech. . . .

*The telegram was mistakenly sent out by the UDA secretary before reading Thomas's statement in the papers.

Moreover, I am somewhat surprised that you sent the telegram after the New York Times had carried rather prominently the gist of the careful statement which I issued in behalf of the Socialist Party, in condemnation of Lindbergh's handling of the Jewish issue in his speech. It seems to me that the timing of your telegram suggests at least a subconscious desire to play up this thing politically in behalf of war propaganda rather than a desire to find and use those tactics which would most fairly abate the dangers of anti-Semitism which unquestionably Colonel Lindbergh's speech increased. . . .

He was overworked, angry, unhappy about being smeared and losing old friends—catching it from both sides, since he was assailed now by some America Firsters who accused him of betraying Lindbergh and the organization. He wrote testily to his lecture agent, testily about his electric bill and complained to the garage that charged a dollar to drive Violet's Packard home after servicing it. Invited to go to Washington again to fight intervention, he replied that he had made so many trips there that "the business of coming to Washington at my own expense is getting more than I can stand." Particularly disturbing to him was the idea, so invariably used by warmakers, of "peace through war," as he wrote Villard:

> . . . My contacts throughout the country convince me that to a surprising and disquieting extent good people, more or less unconsciously, are being bribed off from their opposition to war by fantastic hopes of what they, operating through a war system, will do to make a good peace.

Yet he took time to seek a market for a book on labor written by a Pennsylvania Socialist unknown to him—he was always helping people with manuscripts they hoped to publish. He worked in behalf of five conscientious objectors lodged in the federal prison at Danbury—he was starting all over again his advice for and defense of CO's. He wrote President Roosevelt to ask clemency for Earl Browder, much as he loathed Browder's agile conformity with Stalin, believing the sentence given him for passport fraud out of proportion. He wrote Assistant Secretary of State A. A. Berle asking intervention with France to save the lives of Largo Caballero and other Spanish Republicans whom the prostrate French seemed about to hand over to Franco and sure death. He urged the broadest asylum in the United States for Jews and others imperiled or uprooted by European Fascism—a refrain he returned to again and again, having endless sympathy for refugees and believing that one of the noblest of America's functions was that of refuge and protection. He took Violet on one of those swift trips to the West Coast, speaking against war from Seattle to California and debating Clarence Streit in Los Angeles about Union Now. (Thomas opposed Union Now, fearing that in practice it would develop into an American-British-Lucean arrangement for global supervision.) He fought step by step Roosevelt's assumption of warmaking powers which included not only such direct action as the ordering of Atlantic patrols, the "shoot-on-sight" policy and the sending of troops to Iceland but the use of quietly undemocratic procedures—asking for an investigation of America First's finances, the wiretapping of opponents' phones and the identification of anti-interventionists with Naziism.

While the Thomases were in California, their twenty-one-year-old son Evan decided to quit Princeton, though he was a senior with an excellent record, and join the English service, not as a combatant, since he opposed war, but as an ambulance driver. On returning home, in a farewell note to Evan, the man who seemed to have spoken with fluent ease to uncounted thousands of strangers, admitted the constraint he always felt when addressing his own kin in a matter of deep sentiment:

My very dear Son: You know how hard it is for our family to say what's most on our hearts. But on this day of parting, and all the days that come, I want you to know how we love you, how much we've hoped for and from you, and how proud of you we are. In a cruel and ugly world you never made you've chosen what is for you, I'm sure, the best possible course. I'm glad that we can help you in it. In the months that lie ahead you'll find opportunities of great service to others and real education for yourself. I am very confident of the intelligence with which you'll meet what life and fate will bring.

Of course I dread the dangers that await you and also the long days of boredom that will bring their own temptations. It isn't, I think, Puritanic in any barren, life-denying sense to tell you that all your life—and after all the chances are that your days may be long in a world you'll help to make a better place—if you'll steer clear of the temporary consolations and forgetfulness of too much liquor and the far more powerful urges to sex satisfactions, of a sort always obtainable, you will rejoice. This sort of continence will deepen the priceless joys of marriage with the girl of your choice.

I suspect that you will find much that makes for cynicism about us men and our ways, but I've found it a help to consider that if God must be disappointed in us, so must be the devil in the presence of such courage and comradeship as plain people show.

More than I can tell you we shall be missing you and loving you and wishing for you the external good fortune and still more the inner courage and hope which may sustain you. Despite our follies and madness men are made for better things than constant exploitation and ever recurring wars. It will be a great happiness always to carry your watch till you return to claim it.

Love,

Dad

God and the devil were, of course, mentioned metaphorically. Thomas wrote Time about its account of Evan's decision, which implied disagreement between father and son: "As I have often found to be the case, your facts aren't quite accurate. . . . I warmly approved his act. . . . My quarrel has never been with young men who enlist in such services, but with older and more ambitious men who would send our youth, under compulsion, to war in the service of an Anglo-American imperialism." He later sent Time seven dollars for a year's subscription to be sent Evan in Cairo.

He and Violet, who had for some time been living alone in New York, moved from Twenty-second Street to an elegant if fairly compact apartment at 20 Gramercy Park, on the south side of the square. He received less than the usual flood of greetings on his fifty-seventh birthday, November 20. On December 7 he drove with Violet to Princeton to pick up some of Evan's belongings. As they talked with one of Evan's professors, the news came through of the Japanese attack on Pearl Harbor.

# XIV

## 1. I Am for Us

Thomas's anguish over America's entry into the war was best told in his letter to Krueger: "I feel as if my world has pretty much come to an end, that what I have stood for has been defeated, and my own usefulness made small." Although he had written urgently against Roosevelt's policy in the Far East and about the possibility of war with Japan, the reality stunned him. It also confronted him with the obligation to determine his own policy and (he more assumed than hoped) that of the Party toward America-at-war. In addition to being chairman of the Party, he had long been regarded as its senior foreign minister, which was not to say that he deferred entirely to others in domestic policy. World War I and Debs were no longer appropriate parallels. The Kaiser was an angel compared with Hitler. The provocations then had been minor compared with the shattering strike in Hawaii. The American people then had been sharply divided about entering the war. Now they were virtually unanimous, as was the vote of their representatives in Congress for war. It was still an imperialist war, to be sure, but the nation had been attacked and had little choice but to respond. The savagery of the attack and the frightful American loss were emotional factors that even the hard-headed Thomas could scarcely suppress. Before the world went off the track years earlier, Socialist repudiation of all war had been automatic. The majority of the Party rank and file, anti-war until now, would of course be pro-war, with only the die-hard Marxists and Tolstoyans holding out. If these latter had their way, as a practical matter the Socialist Party would be dead.

Or was it not dead already, with less than 3,000 members nationally? In New York City, which had once had dozens of branches from the Bronx to Queens to Staten Island, there remained only three, and where there had been thousands of active members in the metropolis, one had to scratch to find a few hundred—and those few hundred usually quarreling. Thomas had often shaken his head over those endless, debilitating, bootless, nerve-racking quarrels. Each one of them drove a few more members out of the Party, leaving the survivors to turn on each other in new quarrels. Thomas had his own life to live, his own family to love, his own organizations to promote, his own lectures to give and his own books to write. He could easily have concluded that the Party was no longer of political value, no longer worth his while. But he knew perfectly well that he had started some of those quarrels and and that some concerned valid and difficult issues. Contention was his own meat and drink, even if the Party comrades served it to surfeit. He never would have been satisfied with stodgy Republicans or Democrats too unaware of the issues to quarrel about them. The Socialist Party was a rebellious and wayward child but it was in large part his own. If the Party sometimes drove him mad, he still had affection for it and for many individuals in it as well as a sense of moral obligation to encourage its political responsibility. It was mostly his personality and prestige that held the remnants together. And, if he was sometimes tempted to drop the Party, he could scarcely have failed to consider the triumph his exit as a Socialist leader would have furnished Algernon Lee and his fellow mandarins of the equally feeble Social Democratic Federation.

Although the policy of the Socialist Party was hardly awaited breathlessly by the nation, Thomas thought for two days after Pearl Harbor before giving his opinion in a memo to the National Executive Committee, treating it with the seriousness of a man leading a party of millions:

> Events and popular reactions since American involvement in war convince me that our little Socialist Party has a great role to play in difficult days in complete loyalty to its past, on the basis of an active program of working for civil liberties, democratic Socialism, and an anti-imperialist peace. It should be alert for the day when a peace offensive may offer far more hope to the people than an indefinite continuance of war. Any Party statement to be effective, wants to command the widest possible support and that task involves some compromise, especially in phraseology, but no compromise that need impair our usefulness.
>
> What I am convinced both as a matter of principle and tactics, we cannot use, or seem to use, is a commitment to oppose this war now. . . .

He was a propagandist addressing a different audience when he wrote to The New York Times to ask them not to publish an anti-intervention letter he had written them before December 7:

There is now no point in any letter. The war is upon us. I believe it could have been honorably avoided and America and the world made better off. . . . But now it is rather literally "we or they" which Americans face. I am for us!

It was not really that simple. As usual when confronted by a deep moral dilemma, Thomas helped clear up his own thoughts by putting them in writing, this time in a detailed 700-word letter to a Chicago Party member. Its central argument read:

. . . I see no escape from the choice: military success for the Axis or its enemies. . . . The ship of our hopes has been wrecked, not only by the stormy sea . . . but by the bad work of our captain. What is left us is a poor sort of lifeboat but I doubt if we can stop rowing now or make our main concern an attack upon the captain . . . we are in a literal hell but the deepest pit of all would be an Axis victory.

So his policy was to give the administration "critical support" in the war effort. The Party, which had previously lost so many members who were impatient for American intervention, now lost a batch who considered Thomas pro-war. (His own pacifist brother Evan still opposed anything more than home defense.) A bitter Party struggle arose over the issue. Pillars of the Party who had supported his anti-interventionism, including Travers Clement, Lillian Symes and Walter Uphoff, now opposed him on the ground that the policy should be one of "political nonsupport." A few of the practical-minded, including young Harry Fleischman of New York, urged that the difference between critical support and political nonsupport when translated into Party action was negligible and not worth a fight. But a fight there was. The Party finally waffled in its phraseology so that the remaining members of both factions could stay in.

## 2. The Kernel of the New Order

The outbreak of war which he feared meant a long night of horror and the end of liberty in America sent Thomas into an agony of spirit that he revealed in a handwritten diary which he kept sporadically for four months. The diary was another evidence (as he conceded in it) of his great need in times of special stress to write and to speak his thoughts as a mental and emotional catharsis. To his upset over the war was added his own ambivalence toward it—his realization that despite his repugnance to American participation, his repugnance to German and Japanese militarism was such that he probably would not have been a conscientious objector if he had been of draft age. While he thought young Evan's choice was "right and wise," Evan would be gone for a long time, and meanwhile "Big Evan," who was required as a physician to register with the army, had his pacifist temper up, refused to register and might well land in jail. Thomas wrote:

> What a world for Mom and me! . . . Thank God we have each other and the love of our family. [Later:] What has made these . . . eight days since expected war actually broke—so poignant is that to Violet & me life has been so good, our growing tribe of grandchildren so delightful, the charms of both our real home in Cold Spring Harbor and our little apartment so great. . . . Even the weather . . . by its loveliness has contributed to my mood & this poignant contrast. And it needn't have been! . . . Roosevelt—who is by no means an utter villain, much of whose domestic policies I have admired—will, I think, come to a place in history & the feelings of our countrymen which I don't envy. . . .

Ten days later:

> Christmas in the country & with the family was better than I had thought. Children and the dear & peaceful fields & trees and weather and work (I planted tulip bulbs Xmas day and chopped a lot of wood) all helped out. It helps rather absurdly to have some outlet on the radio—WQXR in person today; other places—four or five by transcription. . . . It's terrible to hate a war & the process by which we got into it as I hate this and yet have no alternative to offer at least until conditions internally and externally are more favorable to a peace offensive. But there are differences between the first and the lowest pit of hell and the German-Japanese brand of military imperialism represents the lowest.

> [On January 3, 1942:] New Years Day like Christmas was happy for us —this time because of the letters. Outside, the skating pond, Tommy, Patricia, little Frances [his grandchildren] in their several & different ways are delightful. Herb & Polly [the Millers of New Haven] have useful work, fine children, good & cooperative friends. . . .

His comments on the Socialist Party reflected his impatience with the large minority which took a stand he described as "verbal escapism," urging "no political support to an imperialist war," and he ranged back over the stormy years:

I don't know the Party's future. Not only old loyalty but present conviction that with all its weakness & faults it carries as will nothing else political, the kernel of the new order . . . hold me to it. Hence I'm compelled to fight for my point of view which constantly isn't orthodox Marxism (whatever that is) or revolutionary in the accepted (and erroneous) sense. Maybe the chain of events beginning with my unsought nomination as Governor of N.Y. in 1924 which made me so much the spokesman & the leader of the Party—a diminishing party since '32, was unfortunate for me and the Party. I'm not sure the political work (i.e. within the Party) & fraternal fighting forced on me was my best role. But recognizing specific mistakes I still think my major choices in Party matters were forced by conviction. In the Old Guard–Militant fight which now seems remote I wasn't fighting for militant Marxism but for sincere & active Socialism as I saw it in the belief that time & continued work would soften extremism & test the boundaries of useful cooperation. If that fight hadn't occurred it would have come in somewhat different form on the war issue. And that too, is now changed by fate. Events & party reactions may make me soon resign the Party chairmanship (as I've often wanted to do) probably in favor of Krueger who is well fitted for that kind of thing if only he'd be more responsible; e.g. about correspondence. . . .

A cable from Evan from Bombay, Jan. 1 rec'd here Jan. 2 said "Safe; happy New Year."

His entries grew more irregular, and on April 10, 1942, he gave the reason and soon thereafter dropped the diary entirely:

I am as bad a diarist as I feared. The continuance of my radio speeches has given me an outlet—out of all proportion in their subjective value to me as compared with their objective value which also I hope is considerable. The months have made family happiness even greater by contrast with the world. Yet it's a kind of agony to wake up each morning to wonder how Bill and Evan fare [his older son Bill had followed Evan into the ambulance service] & to worry about Big Evan. The boys at least have adventure & a sense of service that shows. . . .

The ability of the Russians to draw eastward Nazi divisions which might otherwise be ravaging Kent or Sussex was appreciated even by conservatives. American Communists had been made respectable by Marshal Timoshenko, and Thomas was simultaneously criticized in his own party for being too warlike and assailed as a quisling by The Daily

Worker. After Dieppe, for example, he reduced the Communists to rage by his judicious opinion that Stalin was precipitate in his demand for a second front:

> . . . [O]utspoken criticism coming from him is something less than gallant. Certainly he did not open a Second Front against the Japanese when they attacked us at Pearl Harbor. Doubtless he had good and sufficient reason and exactly the same sort of reason which may operate against a great sacrifice of men in an unsuccessful assault just now in Western Europe. Nor is that all. At the outbreak of this war Stalin not only failed to open a second front; he made a quasi alliance with Hitler. . . . If, as his eulogists now insist, he did this from necessity to gain time, he ought to be charitable to others who must gain time. Moreover, if he, Stalin, is so aware of the importance of a second front, why was he not aware of it in 1939 before the collapse of France?

Israel Amter, New York State Communist Party secretary, charged that Thomas was Fascist. Thomas was attacked regularly in the pro-Soviet newspaper PM, which ran a cartoon showing him handing ammunition to the Russia-hating William Randolph Hearst, Clare Boothe Luce and Elizabeth Dilling for a war against the Soviets. The now thoroughly Rooseveltian Jewish Daily Forward hinted that he favored Hitler. Rex Stout, head of the Communist-dominated Writers' War Board, heaped insult as high as misinformation when he said over CBS:

> During [Thomas's] America First career before Pearl Harbor, doubtless his fellow worker Laura Ingalls spoke to him, but she can't now because she is in jail as a Nazi agent. Probably George Sylvester Viereck spoke to him too, but Viereck is also in jail. Senator Wheeler and Charles Lindbergh apparently aren't speaking to anybody. . . .

Thomas wrote William S. Paley, head of CBS, to say mildly that this was a "rather reckless use of names," that he had not been a member of America First, had never known either Laura Ingalls or Viereck, and that he applauded CBS for not censoring speeches, "but I did think you had certain standards. . . . If Mr. Stout's speech meets those standards, I want to know it to guide my possible future course." His own standards were high and he never descended to such smearing even when he hit hard. And he kept nursing along the Party: "I look at the Socialist Party as carrying the kernel of the seed of the new forces which may yet bring a better world, and I want to keep that kernel, yes, and help it grow."

### 3. Like a Lost Love

For years Thomas had flouted the traditional Socialist undiscriminating veneration of labor by praising its legitimate achievements but criticizing its corruptions and expediencies and exhorting it to honesty and democracy. In this he was moral and correct, and would be vindicated by time, but not politic in the short run. He had been repaid (as the Socialist Party doubtless would have been repaid in any event by power-seeking union leaders even if led by Louis Waldman) by labor's virtually complete desertion of Socialism and its collaboration with Roosevelt. This was one of the things which, with his bias, he found hard to forgive either in labor or in Roosevelt. But his impartiality in his attitude toward labor—his defense of its rights and his attacks on its excesses—was another example of the moralist defeating the politician. Sidney Hillman was only one of the many union leaders he felt not aggressive enough in driving out racketeers.

In an article he wrote for Harper's, "How Democratic Are Labor Unions?" he defined himself as pro-labor and praised the accomplishments of unions, but his answer to his own question could be summed up as, "Not very." He criticized union featherbedding, union racism, union demands for excessively high wages while soldiers fought for a pittance, union opposition to labor-saving devices, exorbitant initiation fees and high union dues, and the union habit of favoring friends and punishing enemies in the awarding of jobs. He singled out Hillman as wielding "an almost dictatorial power" and pointed out that he was now labor adviser to the War Production Board. It was not coincidence that when Thomas was later to speak at the University of Minnesota, the local Congress of Industrial Organizations asked the regents to bar him. The regents, widely believed to be reactionary, rejected "free labor's" demand and Thomas was permitted to speak.

Meanwhile the Keep America Out of War Congress, liquidated by Pearl Harbor, was instantly rechristened the Post War World Council with the same chairman, Norman Thomas, the same executive director, Mary Hillyer, and the same office at 112 East Nineteenth Street but with the lettering and purpose changed. Into its board Thomas had brought time-tried activists such as John Haynes Holmes and A. J. Muste along with newcomers who combined in varying degrees ideals and cash, among them Lenore Marshall (already a dear friend and ardent collaborator), Mrs. J. P. Marquand and Morrie Ryskind. His membership on the board of Town Hall and his prominence in their discussions and radio programs caused him to fraternize with other directors including Marshall Field, David Sarnoff, Mrs. Theodore Roosevelt, Jr., Floyd Odlum, Russell Maguire and John W. Hanes, all individuals whose power and influence he would solicit if the need arose (he later hit Sarnoff for a job for a grandson, also urging on him explicit standards in the fair reporting of news). Added to these were the trustees and members of the many other organizations to which he not only belonged but usually contributed time and thought (a few of them, in addition to the League for Industrial Democracy and the American Civil Liberties Union, were the Friends of German Freedom, the Workers' Defense League, the Metropolitan Opera Association, the National Committee on Conscientious Objectors and Legal Service to Conscientious Objectors). Other acquaintances in New York City included people encountered at meetings, lectures and radio studios. Outside the city were his cherished circle at Princeton, the enlarging group of friends at colleges all over the country and his now considerable acquaintance in cities he visited regularly—Boston, Washington, Philadelphia, Chicago, Saint Louis, San Francisco, Los Angeles and even the small Owensboros and Marked Trees and Pocatellos. The grand total was enormous, though Thomas's warm smile and amiable exterior still enclosed a core of privacy and reserve and he was by taste and inclination the inquirer and teacher rather than the deliberate handshaker and friend-seeker. Some Socialists understood that he had so many causes afloat that he could easily have dropped the Party and its endless headaches but for the fact that he believed in it. As one of them wrote privately to Harry Fleischman, the new national secretary who had succeeded Travers Clement:

> ... [No] matter what anybody tries to do about it, Norman is our foremost spokesman, and will always be thought of that way. Therefore, the Party must continue to seek ways of keeping him on the radio, and under the auspices of the Party or its press. Before anything is done that would endanger that, you must call upon all of us to use every bit of strength at our disposal to maintain it.

The spell he cast over some followers was as visible as the wounded feelings he caused in others who lost faith in him, such as one who replied to his form letter asking moral and financial support for the Party:

. . . I came to believe in you as the finest interpreter of the Socialist ideal in America. Then something happened. With the advent of the New Deal and Roosevelt liberalism, I—we—began to lose faith in your leadership. . . . In 1933, I believe you could have inspired the organization of a mass base political party on Socialist-liberal principles. The Party of course would have had to support Roosevelt. . . . You chose to stick to a biblical rigidity in your application of Socialist theory to political action. You could have had millions of followers. . . .

Then came the war in 1939. And whatever faith we still had . . . vanished entirely. You could not see through the mist of hatred for British past sins the horrors that were facing all of us in the event of British defeat. . . . And now when I read your appeal, the memory of my faith in you in the past, gave me a twinge of pain. . . . It's like the memory of a lost love. It never completely dies.

No one had put so poignantly the attitude of the thousands of Socialists who had been willing to compromise about Roosevelt and were unaware that, as Thomas saw it, it was they who had not kept the faith —toward the sharecroppers, the textile workers, the blacks and the subjects of Paul McNutt and Frank Hague among others, not to mention the ideal of Socialism itself. Thomas replied courteously to put his correspondent right on two misstatements and thanked him for his letter.

### 4. Worrying About the Natives

"I should like to offer my services . . ." Thomas wrote, and was accepted as an air-raid warden at Cold Spring Harbor on an occasional basis because of other duties including efforts to save Japanese-Americans from internment. This federal action outraged him and gave him some reason to believe that the Fascism he had predicted that war would bring was on its way. "We are practicing a kind of race discrimination for which we blame the Germans," he protested. The Issei and Nisei were said to own 82 percent of Los Angeles County farmland and 40 percent of California truck farms, and 3,000 of them were coastal fishermen. The state buzzed with rumors that they were traitors in touch with their compatriots across the Pacific, that they were sabotaging industry, that they had flashed signal lights for the submarine that shelled the coast near Santa Barbara. There was contrary talk, much in the minority, that the rumors were spread by those who wanted to take over the Japanese farmlands and fishing grounds. But the army was fearful and by Presidential order the Japanese-Americans were uprooted, shipped to concentration camps and paid convict wages for their labor—"like burning down Chicago to get rid of gangsters," Thomas remarked.

"There is far more concrete evidence of active espionage by Germans and Italians, including German and Italian Americans . . ." he wrote Villard. "No one proposes, thank God, to put all of them into concentration camps." He tried in an article in The Christian Century to stir up opposition to this tyranny. He conceived a misplaced respect for J. Edgar Hoover because it appeared that the Federal Bureau of Investigation opposed the internment. He was furious at his long-beloved American Civil Liberties Union because by a two-to-one vote of its thirty-five directors—many of them Jewish—it decided against fighting the internment. Americans refused to believe that there were concentration camps in this country, or that the imprisoned Japanese would lose about 60 percent of all their holdings. Thomas appealed directly to Attorney General Biddle, Assistant Secretary of War McCloy and to the President himself. That failing, he marshaled the forces of his new Post War World Council against the ACLU which he had helped found in 1917 and had served faithfully ever since.

The Post War World Council was and would remain the most "perfect" of all his organizations because its goals were so broad that it enabled him to poke his nose into any humanitarian issue almost anywhere. It would carry Thomas for twenty-seven years on a magic carpet of global do-gooderism imbued with a fervor of internationalism scarcely seen until then. The Socialist Party, although he would continue to love and support it, was a shaky reed. In PWWC he could forget Party wrangles and exert his genius in propaganda (in which he was little hampered by his board of directors)—the use of the telephone, the letter, the pamphlet, the newsletter, the committee, the picket line, the press, the radio, the Congressional hearing, the speech or debate or any medium for wielding influence toward desirable ends anywhere in the world. Since he could not be elected to public office, PWWC became his seat in the Senate, his Secretaryship of State and occasionally his Presidency and his secretary generalship of the United Nations.

It sent him spiritually to India while he still worked for the Japanese-Americans. He wrote "My dear Stafford" Cripps, who had been added to the War Cabinet and given the job of trying to satisfy India, urging

Cripps to use his influence for justice. Cripps offered India an interim government in which England would control only defense and foreign policy; the Indian Congress rejected it, wanting full independence, and initiated civil disobedience. When Britain responded by outlawing the organization and jailing its leaders, Thomas wrote President Roosevelt:

> [For the Socialist Party, Post War World Council and millions of Americans] I express a deep concern that our country shall in no way . . . be involved in the British war against the Indian national Congress. . . . I urge you to make it plain to our people and the whole world that American arms and American men under no circumstances will be employed against the Indian people. Anything else would be a betrayal of every profession of devotion to the Four Freedoms.

He became friendly with forty-year-old Jagjit Singh, a handsome, six-foot Sikh who was a prosperous importer of luxurious Indian silks and other goods on East Fifty-sixth Street and president of the India League of America, working for Indian independence. The bachelor Singh, born in Rawalpindi, had attended college in Lahore and had been in the United States for eighteen years. He was a friend and admirer of Nehru. He and Thomas found each other such valuable collaborators that Thomas became a member of the executive committee of the India League while Singh joined the board of Thomas's PWWC. The British occasionally sent over Indians favoring British rule who would challenge Thomas to radio debate on the issue. This Thomas and the League refused to do, recognizing it as a ploy to make it appear that the Indians were divided on the subject of independence. Singh discovered in Thomas an invaluable ally, outspoken for Indian independence, and the importer was an occasional guest of Norman and Violet Thomas.

Thomas called on Secretary Hull about India, finding that "the old man was nice, pleasant and well meaning, but vague and indecisive. I don't think he knows too much." Roosevelt also answered indecisively, scratching out the "My dear Mr. Thomas" and writing "Norman" in with his own flowing hand as he did when he wanted to exert his warmest influence, but saying only, "As the Secretary indicated, the responsible officials of this Government are following developments in India very closely. . . ." He did not, however, heed Thomas's April letter asking that Japanese aliens and citizens not be treated as a herd but as individuals, and at least given hearings before a civilian board to attest their loyalty. The President let them be treated as a herd. Thomas's indignation at the American Civil Liberties Union boiled over in a letter to Baldwin who, along with Holmes and other directors, agreed with his stand:

> . . . I do think there is a decent honesty which ought to compel people who say they are for civil liberty to stand for it. . . . The worst service that could be rendered to a cause is for its friends to betray it. I am not charging conscious betrayal; I am simply saying that what the Civil Liberties Union is now doing amounts objectively to betrayal of a cause. . . .
>
> It becomes more and more a question in my mind whether some of us do not owe it to . . . a real advocacy of civil liberty to resign from the Union, with a serious statement of the reasons, to which we would give the widest publicity. . . .

He was speaking weekly now by recording over more than fifty radio stations, and his listeners heard plenty about the strange kind of democracy and freedom which those upholders of the Four Freedoms, the United States and England, were giving to the Japanese-Americans and the Indians. During odd intervals of time, he and his brother Evan took up a collection for the burial of an old Socialist he had known, Fred Horowitz, who had died broke. He wrote "Dear Freda" Kirchwey, editor of The Nation, opposing her editorial "Curb the Fascist Press":

> I am as sure as I am that I am dictating this letter, that in the inevitable post war reaction the principles you seem to advocate . . . will be turned with a vengeance against the Nation and every other liberal paper or person. It is a rather terrible thing that liberals should now be the spokesmen for a jittery program which, if it means anything, can only be interpreted to mean no criticism of the Administration except from us. . . .

He made a strenuous protest, unsuccessfully, against the appointment of still another Hague-approved federal judge in New Jersey. On the earnest entreaty of Louis Mayer, who deserved attention both because of his Socialist fidelity and his generous donations for Thomas's radio talks, Thomas had pictures taken of him which Mayer could use in his second effort to correct the oral prominence in "The Speaker." He wrote the Selective Service director, General Lewis B. Hershey, in behalf of Socialist and other conscientious objectors, making plain his belief in their rights even though he and the Socialist Party did not oppose the war on conscientious grounds. It continued to be outrageous to him that members of certain sects were spared combat duty because of fine print in their books of revelation, whereas sincere objectors to war on ethical grounds became cannon fodder.

Most Socialists were accepting the draft—a thing never thought possible a few years earlier. Sam Romer, once imprisoned in Spain, had actually enlisted, whereas the forty-two-year-old Professor Coleman B. Cheney of Skidmore College, who had fought in World War I and thought that enough, had no sooner been nominated as Socialist candidate for Governor of New York than he was drafted—a punishment, Thomas suspected, for having the nerve to oppose the Democrats. He wrote regularly to Romer and Cheney and others at their training camps, asking what other trainees thought of the war and what its aims should be. He was distressed to hear that most of them did not bother to think of such things, taking the war for granted and only wanting to get it over with. He agreed, since Cheney was at Lowry Field near Denver and was denied (Thomas suspected in chastisement) any furlough to push his candidacy, to campaign for him: "I am arranging personal broadcasts . . . over this good new station in New York City, WLIB. . . . I also hope to go upstate." In June he wrote Aswell at Harper's that he was keen to write a 200-page book on planning for peace—could have it ready by September 1, which gave him seventy-five days. But Aswell urged him instead to write his autobiography, which he still resisted: "I doubt if there would be much interest in it. I think it would be pretty tame stuff in these times. . . ."

A pamphlet he wrote opposing the Japanese internment was credited in any case with improving the treatment of the 116,000 internees spread in barren camps across the West. He got letters of praise from some, including the displaced San Francisco newspaperman Sam Hohri and the Reverend Hideo Hashimoto of Fresno. For the rest of his life he would receive surprise shipments of choice lettuce, celery or avocados from these grateful people, just as he got cheese from the Uphoffs in Wisconsin, citrus fruits from the Socialist Halvorsens in Florida, occasional boxes of apples or candy and, in one instance, initialed handkerchiefs. When he saw the movie "Little Tokyo" by mistake, having entered a double feature at the wrong time, he was upset enough to write Elmer Davis, head of the Office of War Information (and one of the non-Socialists who had supported him for President in 1932): "It is . . . Grade B or C melodrama, obviously designed to explain and support the mass evacuation of Americans of Japanese ancestry. . . . Did any government agency inspire this production?" Davis's negative reply was so reassuring that Thomas wrote him again: "It gave me some new hope for the country." He had a continuing cooperative correspondence with Davis, but not with Rex Stout, who was so critical of a Thomas-sponsored pamphlet and so tart in refusing to answer courteous Thomas questions about the functions of the Writers' War Board that Thomas took a swipe at him:

> I want to insist that I asked you some questions which you cannot evade by going off on this tangent. Being Chairman of the Writers' War Board, whatever that is, does not make you a kind of dictator of opinion immune to questioning. Please look over my letter and answer the questions.

He campaigned for Cheney and his ticket—a cause so quixotic that The Times commented:

> Ten years ago the Socialist Party wound up one of its most successful campaigns with a meeting that overflowed Madison Square Garden at which Norman Thomas was the hero of 20,000 wildly enthusiastic voters.
>
> Yesterday afternoon, in a ballroom of the Hotel Diplomat, the party closed a campaign in which its candidate for Governor was a private in an army camp and unable to campaign personally. Fewer than 300 persons attended the rally. The voice of Private Coleman B. Cheney . . . was heard in a recording made "somewhere in Colorado" and sent here by air mail.

Worse, Thomas was heckled by a gaunt woman who disputed his statement that democratic rights should not be sacrificed in wartime. Still worse was the fact that at that very moment, the Communists had rallied 17,000 at the Garden for their candidates, Israel Amter for Governor and Elizabeth Gurley Flynn for Congress. Among the speakers was the elastic Earl Browder, who heaped praise on Wendell Willkie for urging a second front. A few weeks later, when Vice President Henry Wallace made a Roosevelt-approved speech defining the goal of the United Nations as a new worldwide democracy for liberty and equality, Thomas could not stifle a Bronx cheer, saying that such "democrats" as Churchill, Stalin and Chiang were "just panting for the sort of world" urged by Wallace. Churchill, Stalin and Chiang were often pictured together with Roosevelt as the Big Four of freedom's cause, and Thomas's skepticism was unpopular. One of his speech topics was "Averting World War 3," which he said candidly could not be averted unless this second one could be ended with a modicum of justice toward all races and nations. Nor was it likely to be averted if America sought to "police the world"—a phrase brought to mind by the persistent "American Century" theory of stern (though high-minded) military governance, a phrase he used as early as 1942. Surprisingly, he managed to stomach Roosevelt's deal with Admiral Darlan better than others such as Walter Lippmann and Dorothy Thompson, thinking of the lives it would save but hoping that this kind of huggermugger would be the exception rather than the rule and adding, "To me, the most dubious feature of our North African policy is that no one worries about the natives, neither De Gaulle, Giraud, Roosevelt nor Churchill, and they outnumber the French about seven to one."

As he had observed earlier, "In all the furore of discussion of Indochina everybody has been mentioned except the Indochinese." Giving consideration to the natives was a concept given lip service after World War I. It was a basic Thomas principle of justice and common decency. Worrying about the natives had started with him in the early years of the century at Spring Street, continued in Harlem and spread to Arkansas, Indiana, New Jersey, India, Algeria, and indeed anywhere where the indigenous and powerless were imposed upon. He was one of the first few to whom worrying about the natives on an international scale became an article of faith not only for reasons of justice, though that consideration was enough in itself, but because it was a practical necessity for world peace.

### 5. Murder on Fifth Avenue

At 9:40 P.M. on January 11, 1943, sixty-eight-year-old Carlo Tresca left the office on lower Fifth Avenue where he edited his Italian anti-Fascist fortnightly paper Il Martello, and had hardly gained the blacked-out street when an automobile stopped nearby and someone fired three bullets into his head and back. He fell dead only a half-block from the Rand School on Fifteenth Street and a block from the park in Union Square where he had made revolutionary addresses in his native tongue. Thomas, in addition to being his close personal friend and his colleague in the Post War World Council and other organizations, was also the friend of his one-time inamorata, Elizabeth Gurley Flynn (though she had turned Communist) and of his present wife, now his widow, Margaret De Silver Tresca, a valued contributor to liberal causes and a colleague on the American Civil Liberties Union board. Thomas led the nonreligious service for the enormously popular Tresca, which drew 5,000 to Manhattan Center. He denounced the crime as a political assassination, as did another of the speakers, Angelica Balabanoff, who had known Tresca since they were both in Italy forty years earlier. To Thomas, a political murder was infinitely worse than a mere killing done in personal rage, implying as it did the deliberate disfranchisement of the victim and the disorganization of his followers by assassination and the extinguishing of his influence.

But the suspected political motivations were not easily apparent; Tresca had swung his Hammer with equal abandon against the Fascists and the Communists. Thomas knew a right-wing Italian publisher and a left-wing (but anti-Communist) Italian publisher, each of whom had been attacked by Tresca, the latter of the two having written Thomas recently to complain of Tresca, saying, "He is against the whole world." Thomas truly missed his late comrade, who for a time had joined the Socialist Party but had grown dissatisfied with it and indeed was so unclassifiable that even his anarchism was unorthodox. Hundreds had admired his immense gusto, friendliness and courage. Thomas became the detective sorting out clues, and the gadfly nipping the police for their sluggishness while he juggled his more customary causes.

Discovering at the same time that Angelica was impoverished again, he wrote an acquaintance at the American Friends Service Committee to learn if she could be used as teacher, lecturer or linguist: "She is a person of high social ideals. She is at the moment almost starving. Her status as an alien in this country cuts her out from much work and from much public speaking. She will not be deported during the war and that's about all." He urged New York radio program directors, with whom he was now familiar, to use her as a lecturer over the air. He encouraged her to submit the outline of a book to Harper's, promising to go over her work before she submitted it and make whatever suggestions he thought useful. Angelica, who never pushed her own interests as she pushed the interests of others, adored him as the greatest of humanitarians, even if she sometimes disagreed with him politically. Other duties Thomas assumed at this time, in addition to his function as Party spokesman and planner of the postwar world, included a different kind of detective job in collaboration with an artisan named Anthony Kinch; a temporary alliance with Herbert Hoover, of all people; a sharp skirmish with The Reader's Digest; and an effort toward promoting racial integration.

Kinch had been a machinist for the Falk Corporation of Milwaukee, which manufactured gears for the navy. He thought he discovered that Falk was defrauding the government by charging work on private contracts to government time. His investigation into this so displeased his employers, he told Thomas, that he not only lost his job but found that word had got around and he was not wanted by other concerns—this at a time when skilled mechanics were at a premium. Kinch, a man of determination, went to Washington and took the case to several government departments, wearing out several pairs of shoes in inter-office locomotion. After more than a year inquiries were made by the Bureau of Internal Revenue, which settled with Falk on a basis of delin-quent taxes. Falk made restitution in the amount of some $500,000. Kinch had been told by agents of the bureau that he would be en-titled to a reward of up to 10 percent if error was proved. No reward materialized, though he made formal application for it. This was where Thomas came in, urged by a young and idealistic Milwaukee Socialist named Frank Zeidler, who had introduced him to Kinch and was inter-ested in the case. The Socialist Party had fallen on evil days even in Wisconsin. Paul Porter had gone over to the Democrats on the theory that Socialists had to work through more viable parties, and Daniel Hoan, that sterling Party showpiece, had failed of reelection in 1940 after twenty-four admirable years as Mayor of Milwaukee and had be-come a New Dealer: All the more reason why Thomas admired young Zeidler, who later became Mayor of Milwaukee himself. Kinch had described the case to several union leaders, whose "So what?" reaction fueled Thomas's fears that unions, so vital to labor's cause, were sinking deeper into the rapacity and corruption once linked habitually with capital.* Thomas's weekly broadcasts commented on such current events. He admired Kinch's dogged courage and thought the case might be shaped into a half-hour radio talk that would shock taxpayers and help mend the ways of government contractors as well as unions.

His interest quickened when he wrote the navy, the Department of Justice and the Treasury Department and got from them what seemed either evasion or more than usually obscure Potomac jargon. He im-plored the active attention of young Senator Robert La Follette. He sent out a release to the press suggesting that the government and the company had plenty to explain. But, he discovered, "although I as-sumed full responsibility for the release which I read word for word at a public meeting in Milwaukee, not a single newspaper or radio station in Wisconsin would carry it. Such, I think, is the power of the Falk [firm]." Now more determined than ever, he sought to bring the case

---

*It developed that one official of the steelworkers, however, was looking into the Falk case.

out into the open by giving its details to Arthur Krock, Demaree Bess, Drew Pearson, Walter Reuther, Bruce Bliven, Marquis W. Childs, William Green, John L. Lewis and others. Their replies suggested that the material might be libelous unless more facts were known (an odd response from newsmen whose job was to find facts), and to Pearson and a few others the sum involved seemed too small to get excited about.

When Kinch was paid $12,715.30 by the government for his work, without being told in plain language what the reward was for, Thomas's suspicions increased. As a propagandist whose method was always to throw light on enterprises that might be dishonest, he seemed helpless in his efforts to publicize this one. In desperation he wrote Upton Sinclair in California, whose reformist passion went back to his *The Jungle* of 1906, which had wrought such purification in the meat-packing industry, hoping that Sinclair might write the Kinch story: "I know how busy you are with your remarkable and successful serial novel but here is a chance for you to do a lot of good. . . . The Wisconsin press is intimidated into silence. . . ." But Sinclair failed him, his zeal now diverted to the adventures of Lanny Budd: ". . . I can't take up the very interesting story. The reason is that I plan to write two and possibly three more volumes of my "World's End" series. . . ."

Zeidler, with Thomas right behind him, now undertook to publish Kinch's story in pamphlet form. While they awaited possible lawsuits, Thomas joined forces in a project with a man with whom he was usually in total disagreement, Herbert Hoover of the Waldorf Towers. This odd alliance was based on their common interest in trying to arrange for legislation that would permit the dispatch of food to hungry nationals of European countries occupied by the Nazis. There was strong opposition to this on the ground that to do so would help feed the Nazis. To Thomas, who could easily conjure pictures of starving French, Dutch or Norwegian children, this was as much as to subscribe to the starvation of the French, Dutch and Norwegians in order to discommode the Nazis. He debated the issue with Dr. Frank Kingdon, who was still nominally a clergyman and who quoted the Bible in support of his argument against feeding the children of victims of the enemy. Thomas saw this as the same kind of betrayal of Christian ethics as he had deplored in the first war and which appeared now, for example, in the deliriously popular song, "Praise the Lord and Pass the Ammunition," a song he loathed, and he was pretty hard on Kingdon. On one Saturday, when Thomas was at a Friends' conference at Hershey, Pennsylvania, he took a train to New York in order to speak in the afternoon with Hoover at Carnegie Hall, then by fast cab caught another train that got him back to Hershey for an evening appearance. He constantly tolerated, in causes he believed in, inconvenience and nervous strain which others would automatically reject. So earnest was he in advocating such causes that people who had no cash occasionally contributed other items of value. At one meeting in New York, a woman from the audience handed him a folded piece of paper which he later opened to discover that it contained a pretty bracelet which Pickslay, the Fifth Avenue jeweler, appraised at $100—a sum he turned over to the Friends. Although Thomas and Hoover found that their plan would have to await the war's end, they had a friendly collaboration for many months and Hoover even sent Thomas praise along with banter: "Your fight is so honest and steadfast . . . that I can forget your (mistaken) economic views!"

While some Nisei were now distinguishing themselves in the American army and some others were gradually permitted to leave their concentration camps and return to civilian life at heavy cost to dignity as well as purse, Thomas continued to battle racism at several levels. He took up with Roger Baldwin the case of Winfred Lynn, a black who was willing to serve in a mixed unit but declined to become part of a Jim Crow army. He complained to the War Department about "mistreatment of negroes at the Army Air Base, Lincoln, Nebraska." He asked the Governor of Virginia for clemency for a black convict sentenced to death, writing, "It is doubtful whether [he] would have been convicted on the evidence and sentenced to death had he been a white man." (He was executed nevertheless.) He objected firmly to Dean Christian Gauss about Princeton's continuing refusal to admit Negroes, saying he was "torn between love of [my] alma mater and a decent regard for elementary requirements of justice. . . ." To a plea for a contribution for his Class of 1905 fund, he replied, "Frankly, I'd be more enthusiastic about giving it if I were not rather distressed by the failure of the authorities to meet the clear demands of the times for the end of race exclusion. . . ." He carried on the argument with his old classmate of 1905, Alfred Carton, now a wealthy attorney and capitalist and a Princeton trustee, as conservative as ever. Carton replied in friendly fashion but totally opposed to Thomas's view that loyalty to truth and learning were sacrificed when admittance was racially exclusive. Soon Thomas was working with A. Philip Randolph in preparing for a joint radio discussion of racism. In one instance he scored a modest success. As chairman of the nominating committee for trustees of Town Hall, he strongly backed the nomination of the black attorney Elmer Carter—the first black ever to be nominated to that body—and saw him elected.

At Cold Spring Harbor he patriotically enlarged his garden, bought laying hens and rented a cow for the summer, taking some pride in milking the animal with his old skill. While on a lecture trip to Wisconsin, he made a fast side trip to Taliesin, Frank Lloyd Wright's establishment at Spring Green, talked with Wright and admired his Broadacres City plan as one that would work out ideally under democratic Socialism. He also consulted with Zeidler and looked deeper into the Falk case. For a year and a half he had sought to publicize the mystifying transactions between the Falk Corporation and the government. Now, in the November, 1943, Reader's Digest, the publication with the world's largest circulation, almost four and a half million monthly, he found that Falk was indeed publicized—praised to the skies. The article, by Jack Stenbuck, was an admiring account of the excellence of Falk's labor relations. Not a vestige of criticism—just praise. Aroused, he sent a copy of the Zeidler-Kinch pamphlet to the emperor of Reader's Digest, DeWitt Wallace, along with a letter of protest. Getting no reply, he wrote Wallace again a fortnight later:

> . . . [W]ill the Reader's Digest make any amends for publishing so glowing a eulogy of a company [whose activities are described in the pamphlet I sent you]? . . . I should like a prompt answer because considerable time has passed, and the Call wants the facts for an article. . . . I don't suppose the Digest knew all the pertinent facts. But now that it knows them some statement seems to me in order for its own great fame—yes, its own honor.

But The Digest seemed to differ entirely with his view. Its belated reply came not from Wallace, who perhaps preferred to delegate the less pleasant tasks, but from an editor, Marc Rose. Rose wrote in effect that all The Digest's article had said was that the company's labor relations were good. No one had contradicted this, so why should The Digest make any statement?

With a few exceptions, such as the Lucepress, Thomas's experience had been with publications having some serious concern for truth. The philosophical and moral implications of his difference with The Digest seemed to him like those of his quarrel with the church during and after World War I which had caused him to leave it—that is, that its most solemn canons were a sham. The Digest adopted the high moral tone of its Presbyterian founder. It specialized in articles about people or corporations (like Falk) of inspiring courage, patriotism and integrity. Now and then it ran crusading pieces against Americans lacking in this kind of courage, patriotism and integrity, such as a recent one condemning gouges practiced by some garage keepers. Thomas the agnostic moralist was as disturbed about the pettifoggery of powerful people who made commercial use of the sanctions of the church as he was about union leaders who laughed off the corrupt practices of employers so long as union employes got fat wartime checks and double time for overtime. Dependent though he was on the goodwill of American propaganda outlets (The Digest would later condense and publish a homily of his from Harper's), he did not pull his punches in two letters to the magazine totaling about 800 words and including some stingers:

> . . . . I think the low standards of what constitutes honest policy in dealing with the Government illustrated, may I say, by your own apparent indifference to this case, are very bad signs of the times. . . . [D]o you think your entire obligation has been fulfilled in what is certainly an issue of public importance . . . ? . . . I am not trying to threaten you. That would be rather ridiculous. Anything that I might say, any approach that I might have to the public as against your enormous worldwide circulation, would be very small. What I am trying to do is to appeal to your own sense of responsibility for the correct use of the extraordinary power you have. But emphatically I do not intend to drop [this] case in all its angles. It is important because of the sinister light it sheds on the uncommonness of common honesty. . . .

That phrase was one of Thomas's good ones. The uncommonness of common honesty would grow so increasingly common in the postwar years as to envelop White House as well as capital and labor in a unanimity of national decay in which the churches became onlookers. The moralist discovering such decay, being human and imperfect, would scarcely be popular or free from criticism himself. Now, on his next trip to Milwaukee, he made inquiries at the local newspapers, at one of which Stenbuck had been employed. The Falk case and the restitution made to the government was well known to newspapermen there. It seemed strange that Stenbuck as a Milwaukee insider and still more in his investigations for the article had not encountered the facts which had been made known by their own strenuous efforts along with those of Kinch. But for all their continuing endeavors, and despite the pamphlet, the Washington bureaucracy did not alter its view that it was all a simple tax matter, nor did The Digest see any error in its course.

That was the end of a detective investigation and crusade to which Thomas had devoted many hours spread over many months. Not quite the end. He did at last in a kind of despair write Senator James E. Murray of Montana, "I am glad that your subcommittee is going to look into cost plus war contracts." And to Senator La Follette of Wisconsin he wrote, "I am genuinely impressed with Kinch . . . I hope you can help further in Kinch's effort . . . ." The Falk case, however, antedated the war. There was never any proof, of course, that the corporation had engaged in the activities alleged by Kinch, Zeidler and Thomas.

### 6. The Married State

"I would like to be rejoicing over Mussolini's plight," Margaret De Silver Tresca wrote Thomas, "but it is so sad that Carlo's not here to do so. . . ." Thomas had several times prodded District Attorney Frank Hogan about the police failure to solve the case. "Would that Carlo were with us!" he wrote Mrs. Tresca. ". . . . I'm not too optimistic about any sort of future but I do think we've got to keep working on it and that work does count. Carlo did."

Again it was his admiration for the activist, the individual who sought to improve society or correct injustice—which amounted to the same thing—and who kept working at it. The phrase "We've got to keep working at it" appeared in scores of his letters to Party members or people who wrote to comment on his radio talks and the difficulty of achieving needed reforms. And that work did count was to him an infallible law of human nature. To a chairman who introduced him as "the defender of lost causes" he said firmly so that the audience got the point, "*Not* lost causes—causes not yet won." On January 11, 1944, the anniversary of Tresca's murder, he led a memorial meeting and criticized the district attorney. He had to keep trying.

He was proud of the war service rendered by his sons. William was invalided back from Egypt with a serious infection that made him 4-F, and on recovery joined the Red Cross. Evan returned with a touch of malaria and a book manuscript about the desert war, but immediately joined the United States Navy and married Anne Robins before leaving again for the European theater of war. En route in the morning to the Cold Spring Harbor station, Thomas could see the harbor: "Rarely did I pass it without seeing again Evan and his companions as they were when they were about 11 or 12 years old and sailed little dinghies. . . . So vivid was memory that for an instant of time I would look for them again. And then would come the realization in what dangerous places all over the earth I should have to seek them." All of the children were now married, leaving their parents alone at 20 Gramercy Park with Dr. Evan, Unk—a warm companion always and priceless when Violet had one of her occasional attacks. She was amused to learn that Minowa, one of the servants, called her "the First Lady" on the sly because Thomas should have been in the White House. Young Evan's bride was touched at the unconcealable affection between Violet and Norman Thomas after thirty-four years of marriage, and at how Violet powdered her nose and looked her best before meeting him at the door when he returned from wherever he happened to be returning from. A young woman employe at 112 remarked unnecessarily that he "never made passes" in a world where office passes were expected. Violet's gayety was irresistible. She wrote her new daughter-in-law:

> I got pretty well tired out with all our excitements here and the doctor sent me to bed for a few days but it didn't seem to be enough because so much was going on and I couldn't stay still. So when the Old Man [Thomas] went west last week I took a room at the Lowell! . . . . Stayed in bed for breakfast and till noon every day and just luxuriated and went out and bought a new hat and shoes and went to some movies and came back Friday a new woman.

This smelled more of the Social Register than of Marx. It would have shocked some of Thomas's more serious Socialist friends who knew her only in her demure Party role. The double life of Violet and Norman Thomas had long since been accepted by them both. Thomas in effect had achieved a redistribution of wealth in his own family which, when viewed from the comfortable estate of Violet's relatives, seemed a great sacrifice, whereas to the earnest Socialist egalitarians it appeared sybaritic. Thomas could easily have been a prosperous church official like Ted Savage, or a rich attorney like his classmates Fosdick and Carton —or simply a wealthy lecturer who gave the public what it wanted and charged the going rate—and added substantially to Violet's wealth. He had rejected these things for a career which instead subtracted from it. In his Party and Post War World Council role he nursed nickels, wore gravy-spotted neckties, had a humble office in a run-down building, rode second class and typically wrote to Milwaukee, "Please get me the cheapest room with bath at the Pfister." At Cold Spring Harbor he lived simply, ate whatever was put in front of him, but swam at the fancy beach club and argued politics on the sundeck with Dulles. Violet, for her part, believed in, subsidized and gave time and effort to his Party career without renouncing the capitalism he could not defeat and some of the luxuries which would have been greater but for her considerable social contributions. Between her illnesses her vigor seemed unabated. She made more use of the Princeton Club than her husband, took his sister Agnes to see *Othello*, tried without much success to keep Thomas looking spruce, supervised the care of about 100 dogs, wrote to both sons copiously when they were in service and in fact maintained a bubbly correspondence usually banged out on her typewriter because her handwriting, though distinctive, was almost illegible.

Thomas, in sending congratulations to bridegrooms, usually wrote, "All I need wish is that you will be as lucky as I have been," sometimes varied with, "I am a firm believer in the married state." He saluted the birth of a Socialist baby by addressing his letter to the baby and praising its choice of parents. He was now dashing off autobiographical recollections which eventually ran to some 75,000 words, hastily done as always but true to the man and his beliefs. He never carried it beyond 1946 and, being dissatisfied with it and also stayed by his innate reserve, refused to publish it despite the pleas of Aswell and others. As a speaker, he so delighted the girls at the reformatory for women in New Jersey (he spoke without fee) that the superintendent wrote to him, "Let us make it an annual event!" Never a prude, he defended Lillian Smith's "shocking" *Strange Fruit:* ". . . I believe [it] to be one of the most powerful and useful novels published in America in years. . . . The banning of the book . . . is the only thing that might give it any evil significance in anybody's mind." The sculptor Louis Mayer arrived to lunch with the Thomases and later wrote of his pleasure in "that glimpse of perfectly simple and serene home life . . . It did my heart good . . . and I want to thank you both again . . ." Mayer went home to his studio near Fishkill to finish his third try at the Thomas head and to send photographs when he had finished it. Thomas had to write to him with all the tact he could muster that it still did not seem right. That open mouth! Mayer's patience was endless. He complimented Thomas on the kindliness of his criticism:

> You couldn't have said anything more striking than that the head is a stranger to you, not looking as you do on the outside nor as you feel yourself to be inside. . . . [John Haynes] Holmes, too, wrote me he is not satisfied with the mouth though he thinks I've caught your features otherwise. . . . With unchanged devotion & my kindest regards to Mrs. Thomas.

Violet, who did not like the head either, wrote Anne on another matter: "Dad is on jury duty for a fortnight and we miss him and his garden doesn't do well without him. . . . I have an old dress turned into a scare crow to keep the corn safe and wasn't I glad to get rid of that dress. . . . It was just meant to frighten crows."

## 7. At the Stork Club

The vigorous, independent-minded Professor Albert Sprague Coolidge, an authority on the chemistry of metals and an enthusiastic model-railroad hobbyist, had let his Socialist Party membership become quiescent after he joined Niebuhr's Union for Democratic Action. He regretted this because he appreciated Thomas's veritable arsenal of talents and especially his fluency and eloquence in upholding the ideals which in practical politics invariably became squeezed and pressed and pummeled to death. The idealist in America was not merely valuable. He was indispensable. But to Coolidge's friendly disagreement with Thomas over nonintervention had been added his doubt of Thomas's skill as a party leader and his conviction that the Union might *get* somewhere, whereas the Socialist Party seemed headed for extinction. Coolidge, whose wealthy mother maintained an apartment in Washington, ran into Thomas in the capital in 1944 and later wrote to him, "I came away with the impression that you were more bitter against Stalin than it is good for any man to be," and added, "Of one thing I am sure —there is no future in Russophobia as a main drive in life, whether on the emotional or the intellectual level."

Thomas replied truly that he was not anti-Russian—the Russian people had his sympathy—but "passionately anti-totalitarian." He was, however, becoming more and more hostile to Stalin and a little bitter against Roosevelt. Added to the other Soviet horrors had come the murder of the two leaders of the Polish Jewish Socialists, Viktor Alter and Henryk Ehrlich. Thomas had met Ehrlich when he visited the United States and had liked him. Thomas had interceded for the pair both with the State Department and with Harry Hopkins on one of the latter's trips to Moscow. Their execution, on the trumped-up charge of collaborating with the Nazis, put the seal on Thomas's conception of Stalin as the barbarian of all barbarians. Thomas's attitude toward the Katyn massacre was less suspicion of the Russians than certainty that they were guilty. Despite his scorn for Max Eastman, Thomas said in his autobiography that events in Russia and elsewhere "have constrained me to change some of my judgments of Socialist theory and practice," but still had "strengthened my basic belief in it." Thomas's revulsion toward political fraud had been heightened, he had seen that "men covet power as much as profit," and he had been reinforced in his awareness that Socialism must "encourage diversity of organization against a monster all-inclusive state." The regimentation of war, he thought, had increased a "trend toward a modified American version of a Fascist economy rather than toward democratic Socialism."

He did not trust Roosevelt, against whom his list of grievances was long, though Thomas never forgot the President's "rescue" of the sinking country in his first term. The transfer of Socialists and unionists either into the Democratic Party or some "independent" but pro-Roosevelt group like Niebuhr's Union for Democratic Action had sounded in his ears like the thunder of an army marching to join forces with the enemy. The departure of Paul Blanshard, David Dubinsky, Alfred Baker Lewis, Paul Douglas, Paul Porter, the Reuther boys, Dan Hoan, Reinhold Niebuhr and all the rest in their hundreds and thousands had hurt him deeply and impressed him as a terrible mistake. From all directions came reminders of the decay of the Party. He heard from Ed Johnson, the former Socialist organizer, who with his wife Martha had started him on the sharecropper campaign. Martha had died and Ed was now a New Deal bureaucrat in the Department of Labor. Thomas wrote Johnson kindly but with a gentle dig: ". . . I wish you were free to work more actively with us." Thomas's fear of Fascism was increased by Roosevelt's push for universal conscription. Thomas's resentment over Spain still burned. And had not Roosevelt shrugged off the sharecroppers, interned the Japanese-Americans, failed to furnish an American haven for Jewish and other refugees? Were not the armed forces still basically Jim Crow, and was not the President now failing to give genuine support to the Fair Employment Practices Commission?

Thomas was now more than half convinced that Roosevelt had deliberately goaded Japan into the attack on Pearl Harbor. The millions of American unemployed up to the very beginning of the war proved to him the failure of the administration and provoked some cynicism about Roosevelt's war motives. He attacked the Anglo-American "obliteration bombing" of Germany as unnecessary militarily and counterproductive psychologically, saying it also might lead Balkan peoples to choose Stalin's leadership—an opinion that flooded his office with angry and sometimes abusive letters saying in effect, What those Germans need is obliteration bombing until they're obliterated. Roxana Wells was not having her usual easy time booking lectures for him. The San Francisco Town Hall returned his contract because it was felt that "such a person with a repute of destructive ideas on winning the war for democracy should not be allowed to further his disruptive cause . . ." Hatred was as popular as unconditional surrender. Sober men in clubs discussed the forcible return of Germany to a peasant economy or the sterilization of the Japanese. Thomas wryly enjoyed quoting Irwin Edman's lines, "To Some Bloodthirsty Writers," in The New Yorker:

> *At the Stork Club very late,*
> *Let us drink and drum up hate.*
> *Another round, and while we swill,*
> *Arrange to kill, kill, kill, kill, kill!*
> *Let's make sure when victory's won*
> *We'll be more savage than the Hun. . . .*
> *Soldiers have little time for loathing,*
> *That's for us chaps in tailored clothing.*
> *Waiter, some caviar, some wine,*
> *We're planning bloodbaths on the Rhine. . . .*

Thomas was not one of those zealots who demanded instant negotiation for peace the moment America entered the war. In 1943 he had opposed the Peace Now movement formed by his Socialist friend, the psychology professor George Hartmann (who had been fired from the Columbia faculty for his beliefs, then hired and fired by Harvard). Peace could not be courted while Hitler had the upper hand. Nevertheless, the administration should have a master plan for peace ready for use at that precise moment when the Axis was beginning to lose and its more reasonable adherents, worrying about their own skins, would listen. Such a plan might shorten the war appreciably and, unlike vengeful Versailles, nurture reconciliation that would make peace stick. Thomas had worked on plans for peace and for peacekeeping from the beginning with his customary intensity of study. He had reexamined the old League of Nations. He had given sympathetic attention to the ideas of that unusual New Yorker Ely Culbertson, who was widely known as an expert on contract bridge. Culbertson was the Rumanian-born son of an American engineer who had married a Russian woman. The son had traveled extensively with his parents and had become so deeply absorbed in the problems of peace that he had composed an ambitious and complex design for a peacekeeping world community of nations. Thomas worked with him in correcting some of its presumed flaws. He sent copies of the plan to many knowledgeable friends for comment and criticism. He conferred about it with others including Edwin Borchard, professor of law at Yale. Thomas so steeped himself in the subject that he was well aware of the enormous difficulties that must be solved—and were worth solving—in order to realize the bright promise of a union of nations for peace. Over the radio and through his Post War World Council propaganda and The Call, he had steadily advocated a peace plan to be held in readiness for the favorable opportunity and had suggested some of its provisions.

America, however, seemed to lean toward obliteration. Gradually it became clear that Roosevelt, despite opposition among his own Chiefs of Staff, meant what he said about unconditional surrender. To Thomas it meant that the Axis would fight virtually to the last man and the hatred engendered would make lasting peace unlikely. His opinion of Roosevelt was not enhanced by the latter's chumminess with that old Thomas bête noire, Sidney Hillman, nor by his reluctance to return Japanese-Americans to their homes. To Senator La Follette, Thomas wrote:

> A lot of us are counting a great deal on you for the fight against the President's lust for power and his desire to remake the world with Stalin and Churchill without consulting the Congress and the people. . . . I know that you will fight the [universal] draft but I am particularly eager that you'll press for more information on our commitments to Stalin and Churchill. The President's irritated assurances that he had made no new commitments [at Teheran and Cairo] mean nothing. . . . As you yourself —and as your father's son, you have a great opportunity and a lot of us here, regardless of party, will be eager for your leadership.

He criticized the Moscow agreement as a plan to Balkanize all of Europe and to perpetuate imperialism, saying, "The United States and Great Britain underwrote Russia's desired boundaries, while Russia and the United States underwrote Britain's colonial empire." What little correspondence he had now with the President was stiffly formal and there were no more "Dear Norman" letters. He sent a long letter to Secretary Hull, part of it protesting that

> the Cairo declaration by its silence on the restoration of Hong Kong to China and more especially by its failure to say one word of hope of

freedom to the peoples of the French, Dutch, and British Empires in the Far East, clearly implied that the United States, however firm in its opposition to Japanese militarism, was ready to underwrite with the lives of our sons the reestablishment and maintenance of white empire over peoples to whom even the Japanese have given a semblance of self-government. That way lies new and more dreadful wars.

And again, in a letter to Sam Romer, he used that phrase that would become a cliché of the Vietnam doves: "I mistrust . . . the whole business of our policing the world or any part of it indefinitely." As the Presidential year of 1944 approached, the Socialist Party was at a low ebb despite its hopeful song, sung to the tune of "The Battle Hymn of the Republic":

> *There's another camping coming up in 1944*
> *When we'll take the same position as we have in days of yore—*
> *We'll still be for the underdog, and still be anti-war,*
> *With a Socialist President.*
> > *We'll campaign for Norman Thomas,*
> > *We'll campaign for Norman Thomas,*
> > *We'll campaign for Norman Thomas,*
> > *In Nineteen forty-four!*

### 8. Norman and Reinie

For at least the tenth time, Thomas fruitlessly explored the possibility of forming a Socialist coalition with dissatisfied mass groups. He had firmly decided not to run in 1944, having groomed Maynard Krueger for the race. Early in the year, though it could not have been easy, he appealed to "Dear Reinie" Niebuhr and the Union for Democratic Action to abandon the alliance with Roosevelt, which Thomas felt could scarcely be satisfactory, and to come back to the fold with all the Socialists they had kidnapped and all the liberals too. Niebuhr replied courteously but made it plain that he had abandoned Socialism (and Thomas) as utopian and that he and his group were dealing with the best political possibilities as they existed.

When Thomas arrived in June at the Socialist Party national convention in Reading, declaring that he was not a candidate this year, newsmen laughed, saying he sounded like Roosevelt. He was in earnest, but so was Krueger in declining the nomination, saying he wanted to run for Congress in Illinois. Krueger agreed to remain national chairman, and Thomas accepted the nomination (by acclamation) for the fifth time without visible dismay, the firehorse heeding the bell. Darlington Hoopes trotted along as his running mate. Hoopes, a forty-seven-year-old Reading attorney, had served three terms in the Pennsylvania Assembly. The Party adopted a Thomas platform, asking as usual for the socialization of basic resources and containing a plank condemning the unconditional surrender policy of the administration as "prolonging this war and inviting the next," and another demanding "an immediate political peace offensive based on the offer of an armistice to the peoples of the Axis nations." Interestingly, after Niebuhr had criticized Thomas for unwillingness to make concessions essential in practical politics, another observer, the partly sympathetic Dwight Macdonald, faulted him mistakenly from the opposite point of view—that he was too "opportunistic," too ready to compromise with capitalism, insufficiently aware of the Big Four's imperialism, too subservient to such intriguers as Roosevelt and Churchill, and that he veered too much in policy.* It was true that some of Thomas's beliefs were common among liberals and that he was moving slightly to the right, although his faith in public ownership remained. He was "liberal" enough to have lunch a couple of times with Arthur Hays Sulzberger, but he received attacks as well as commendation in Sulzberger's New York Times, which supported Roosevelt.

The divergence between Niebuhr and Macdonald was if nothing else another indication of the fragmentation of Socialist philosophy which had all but eliminated the Socialist Party. Thomas nevertheless campaigned across the country as if he had a chance, his only companion again being Violet. On a crowded train in Kansas, they had as seat companion a young air force man going home to Texas on leave.

". . . I've been in Europe," he said, "and I don't know much about this political campaign. May I ask who you're going to vote for?"

"Myself," Thomas replied with a twinkle.

---

*Macdonald also censured Thomas for his collaboration with America First and his participation in an "idiotic" radio program in which a panel of "experts" essayed to solve personal problems for unhappy wives and moony adolescents. Thomas indeed had a passion for radio (and later television) programs, appearing on them constantly. Most were intellectual but a few were light and even corny. He once hammed it up as leader of a pickup orchestra on the Cal Tinney show. He made every available use of the printed and electronic media to spread his views. Later he was to cause some disapproval even in his own family by permitting a long Thomas interview to appear in the most luxurious of cheesecake magazines.

The airman looked disconcerted. "Well, of course . . . I know any man can be President, but . . ."

Thomas explained that he was the Socialist candidate. The young man pondered for a moment, then said, "Well, if you weren't running yourself, who would you vote for?"

The Thomases had to laugh at that, but it was not really funny for it epitomized the automatic exclusion of the Socialist candidate in the public mind. Some of their troubles came to vivid life in Violet's letter to "Dearest Frankie," her daughter, Frances Gates:

> Everywhere we have been late—out of 4 nights have gotten to bed 3 of them at 3 AM. The meetings have been terrible. At Albuquerque there were only 2 Socialists to plan our meeting, one was 70 & deaf & the other was dead—died just before we arrived—after having scheduled us for *Oct* 24th instead of *Sept.* Poor Dad was wonderful & we spoke to about 100 in a huge gymnasium at the Univ. of New Mexico. Our hotel (which we reached at 3+ AM was disreputable dirty & with no food) but we fared well by barging in on a lovely Spanish one. . . . Newspapers are hard to get & I just live for 48 hours in San Francisco. Due there tonight. . . .

Her companionship obviously lightened the rigors of barnstorming. Once more, in a long open letter to Niebuhr in The Call, Thomas asked the Union for Democratic Action, which had declared for Roosevelt, to switch and support the Socialist ticket. He denounced Roosevelt as the candidate of corrupt bosses, the seeker of fourth-term "absolute power," the President who had pushed "no major progressive legislation since 1937" and who lacked any plan for avoiding World War III. "You left us because of honest differences over an interventionist policy before Pearl Harbor," Thomas wrote. "We got war. . . . Now, how about winning the peace? How about insisting that the demand for unconditional surrender be replaced by terms which may hasten a constructive people's revolution in Germany?" He urged the Union for Democratic Action that "you and thousands of men and women of like opinion will be very unhappy if you throw away your vote by voting for what you don't want, and getting it—as you will if either Roosevelt or Dewey wins," and he welcomed them back "with open arms" to the Socialist standard.

It was unfortunate that these two men, so admirable in intellect and in good will toward mankind, should have fallen out at all, much less that their differences should have been founded to some degree in misunderstanding. Niebuhr, eight years younger, believed as did the agnostic Thomas that political action was a Christian duty. Both had been early believers in the Social Gospel. Niebuhr had supported American intervention in World War I and had later regretted his support. He had not come to New York from Detroit until 1928 and had little knowledge of what that war had done to Norman and Violet Thomas and Evan Thomas, and to Norman Thomas's political thinking. Niebuhr had been a loyal Socialist, a member of the staff of The World Tomorrow, a supporter of the League for Industrial Democracy and Thomas's ardent backer in 1932 and 1936. He had also supported Thomas against the Old Guard and had believed that their exit meant a vigorous and reborn Party—a judgment in which both were in error. The crumbling of the Party, the looming European war and Niebuhr's revulsion at Hitler had brought Niebuhr around to an admiration for the "realism" of Roosevelt's policies. In 1940, when Niebuhr had voted for Roosevelt, he and Thomas had argued over United States foreign policy and, according to Niebuhr, Thomas had said:

"Reinie, if you can prove to me that America is absolutely disinterested in espousing the anti-Nazi cause, I'll be with you."

To which Niebuhr said he replied: "My dear Norman, I don't have to prove this to you—that it is disinterested—because I approach politics with the axiomatic principle that all nations have mixed motives, at least as mixed as individuals have, and that the matter of national self-interest is bound to play a part in this." He concluded that "that was the basic difference between us. He had a rather pure moral idealism. I had an impure one." Niebuhr said elsewhere that Thomas was a symbol of the harm Marxist dogmatism could do to the most independent of minds.

But their differences were not so easily defined. Thomas had risen above narrow moral considerations in his support of the Spanish Loyalists, not as unadulterated libertarians but as the best European weapons available at the time against that same Hitler. His pragmatic willingness to tinker with Marxism, which had disturbed Hillquit, and the fact that he was still tinkering, seemed to clear him of Marxist dogmatism. Certainly a large part of the difference between Thomas and Niebuhr lay in matters other than principle—Thomas's growing distrust of Roosevelt at the very time that Niebuhr became his admirer, Niebuhr's rejection of Thomas's belief in a third party against those two similar Democratic and Republican bottles of "useless medicine," and in Niebuhr's hurtful success in leading so many prominent Socialists out of the Party when it needed them most.

Now, Niebuhr's reply to Thomas's appeal for reunion was a classic repudiation of utopianism, expressed so sharply and effectively that it took courage to print it in The Call:

> ... One of the more interesting ironies of this time lies in the spectacle of American Socialists talking of the necessity of "winning the peace"; if America and the democratic world had listened to those Socialists who before Pearl Harbor were telling us that our capitalistic society was not pure enough to take up arms against Fascist aggression, Hitler would be making the peace today. ... Indeed, although you profess many progressive ideals ... there is an exasperating quality of irresponsibility about the whole Socialist position. . . . This irresponsibility . . . stems from your inability to conceive of politics as the act of choosing among possible alternatives. . . . Americans will not . . . be called on to make a choice between Socialism and reaction. A sizable Socialist vote in November will prove nothing and influence no one. . . .
>
> ... We are not defenders of the Northern machine bosses and Southern poll-taxers who still dominate the Democratic Party. . . . I remind you once again that the battles ahead will not be contests between unmitigated evil and absolute good. . . . Americans cannot afford the luxury of a gesture toward a perfect program, while real issues are being decided on a much more modest level. . . . I reiterate that the course we have chosen represents a fighting chance for a sick society. . . .

Niebuhr could not forgive Thomas's pre-war opposition to intervention,* while Macdonald on the contrary approved that opposition and only lamented its cessation when war came. *Chacun à son goût!* The American left was in disarray. That Thomas was utopian was true to an extent. He admitted having had an excessive belief in "progress," some of his hopes in Socialism seemed far-fetched, and he had sniped more than was necessary at the admirable La Guardia. The fact remained that Roosevelt had borrowed and put into practice many of the social reforms Thomas had urged in 1932, and that the utopian Thomas was in a sense their godfather.

During the campaign he could hardly be accused of cadging votes by evading issues or buttering up individuals or groups he may have offended. Earlier he had attacked James C. Petrillo, czar of the musicians' union. Now in an open letter he assailed Sidney Hillman,

---

*Thomas himself, years later, had doubts of the wisdom of his opposing intervention against Hitlerism.

his "undemocratic" Political Action Committee and its support of Roosevelt and his Hagues, Bilbos and Pendergasts. And his letter to an official of the United States Council of Church Women was anything but apple-polishing: ". . . [The] average white Protestant church is, in respect to its own membership, one of the most thoroughly Jim-Crow organizations in America. No wonder its influence for justice . . . is not greater."

For all his long efforts to establish asylum in America for Jewish and other refugees, Thomas was attacked by several Jewish papers of the unconditional-surrender-is-too-good-for-the-Nazis school. His old friend The Jewish Daily Forward (Abe Cahan was now eighty-four) charged that the Socialist platform offered peace to Hitler on a silver platter, while a Jewish Morning Journal cartoon portrayed Thomas as a quisling. Worst of all was an attack in The International Teamster, organ of the Brotherhood of Teamsters, whose president, Daniel Tobin, was chairman of the Democratic Party's national labor committee. It said in part:

> Norman Thomas has a postwar plan. It is the kind of plan you would expect from a man who has spent so much of his time fawning on the Germans and Japs while they were killing Thomas's fellow countrymen. His "plan" fits in perfectly with Hitler's plan for future conquest, which is not surprising when you remember that Thomas is the head of the Socialist Party in the United States while Hitler is the leader of the Socialist Party in Germany.
>
> Just a couple of Socialist boys looking at the world through blood-smeared glasses.

For the first time in his life, Thomas took to the law for this libel, bringing suit for $500,000 against Tobin and the author of the article.* He won the lawsuit but was snowed under in the November balloting, receiving only 80,518 votes, his worst Presidential shellacking. He sent dutiful, if not flowery, congratulations to Roosevelt, who had got some 312 times as many votes as Thomas and who was dead five months later and succeeded by Harry Truman. During the campaign Thomas had disparaged Truman's political background. After V-E Day he pressed on the new President evidence that Japan was prostrate, that the unconditional surrender policy would play into the hands of Stalin, that

---

*Thomas was represented by his friend, the Socialist lawyer Joseph G. Glass (whose office was on Wall Street!). In 1946 the Teamsters settled out of court, printed a full retraction, and the generous Glass donated his fee to the indigent Party.

the "earliest possible peace" should be sought, and that "I speak with some intimate knowledge of Communist tactics at home and abroad." The atom bomb dropped on Hiroshima shocked him. The second one on Nagasaki outraged him. His protests by radio and in the Post War World Council newsletter drew opposition, one Florida physician writing:

> . . . [When] I read of the way our men were treated, I only regret that atomic bombs were not used to blast the four Jap islands into oblivion. There may be innocent women and children, but they only in my opinion breed more of the same kind of soldiers to make us trouble in the future.

# XV

## 1. War Is Obsolete

Three months before the Japanese surrender, Thomas and Violet visited Haverford College, where they stayed with the Felix Morleys, Morley then being president, and Thomas gave the commencement address. As he looked back on that speech, he commented:

> Had I been speaking after the bombs were dropped, first on Hiroshima, then on Nagasaki, without waiting for the political effect of the first horror, I should have voiced, as I did elsewhere, my condemnation of their use over unfortified cities, but also my hope which millions shared that somehow the terrible power now in men's hands would mean the end of war; science had made it obsolete.

His overriding purpose for the rest of his life was to steer the nation (despite his awkward position so far from the tiller) away from World War III, in which Russia would be the enemy. He held firmly to this course even though his loathing for Stalin made Thomas appear ambivalent and caused him to be attacked as a warmonger by PM and The Daily Worker. He could not resist an occasional I-told-you-so remark about the war that was to solve the Hitler problem raising the Stalin problem instead. But that the public had to be made to understand that war now must be obsolete, and that machinery had to be devised to prevent its recurrence, were central with him. He met occasionally with Jagjit Singh (known as "J.J.") and the India League at the Ceylon India restaurant on West Forty-ninth Street, where turbans were common, Tagore was often read, and British imperialism was passionately denounced. Just before the war ended, Thomas was so annoyed at the

293

British Labor Party for its apparent blind approval of Churchill and Stalin that he wrote Aneurin Bevan:

> Scarcely anybody in America thinks that the British Labor Party is in earnest against imperialism. . . . It seems to me that opposition to imperialism includes also opposition to Stalin's brand of imperialism in Eastern Europe, as well as to British imperialism in Burma, Malaya, or India. . . . Where does the British Labor Party stand?

He was pleased but still wary when, a month later, the British shelved Churchill for Attlee and the Labor Party—Socialist if not Marxist—was in power. "Its success will be an immense blessing to all mankind," he wrote, adding, "I confess that I should have more confidence in it . . . if its leaders were showing more powerful and imaginative leadership in substituting a new pattern of world cooperation for the old imperialism." He read Richard Wright's *Black Boy* and found in the serfdom experienced by Wright and millions like him in the world's richest country more proof that a Socialist-oriented third party was essential and could be successful—perhaps a utopian belief in the face of his 1944 rout. The party should not be patterned after Britain's Labor Party, he reasoned, which suffered from too much union control, but should have labor support—a dilemma that he never really resolved. "Congress today with all its faults," he observed privately, "is a better expression of democracy and has a better regard for individual rights than an AFL or CIO convention to say nothing of John L. Lewis's hand picked outfit." But he had been almost as blunt in public statements about the unions, which did not relish his candor. Two minor details demonstrated that the support he got from labor now was hardly stronger than the support he himself gave the Almighty. One was a $100 contribution he received from an official of the Brotherhood of Locomotive Firemen and Enginemen (which barred blacks), along with the request, "Please keep this confidential," the donor well aware that having it known that he had contributed to Thomas would do his union career no good. The other was a concluding sentence in his unpublished autobiography in which he mentioned "the younger men [of the Party] who, pray God, may succeed where I have failed." He struck out "pray God" and substituted "I earnestly hope." Whatever embarrassment attended his Party failure did not stop him from advising the country on all matters concerning all politics, all issues and all nations. He had almost concurrent articles on national and international affairs in The Christian Century, Commonweal, The Progressive, Common Sense

and Human Events, the latter a conservative publication co-edited by
Felix Morley. He was in some demand for radio appearances, one
woman listener writing:

> . . . I tuned in to the American Forum of the Air . . . and heard a very
> stimulating voice which proved to be Norman Thomas debating with
> someone. (His voice, like Roosevelt's, is unmistakable.). . . . It did my heart
> good to hear so courageous and logical a contestant in these days of
> confused thinking. Too bad there are so few men like him. And he's
> growing older!

He neither felt, looked nor acted old, though he was over sixty and
had eleven grandchildren. He was tireless and not forever serious,
writing one Socialist who had sent in a dollar, "I am passing [it] on to
the thoughtful consideration of our National Secretary . . ." He had so
far betrayed Violet's faith in cockers that he bought a black standard
poodle, Jester, of which he was very fond. The sale of the Gramercy
Park building in which they lived forced the Thomases to move a block
south to the building at 71 Irving Place which Violet owned and in
which she had had her tea room.

Thomas had been suspicious of Dumbarton Oaks and its secrecy,
fearing it might turn into a "dangerous attempt to underwrite a temporary and unstable cartel of empires." He applauded the San Francisco
United Nations conference but testified before the Senate Foreign Relations Committee against provisions which he thought would make the
United Nations an imperialist alliance of the strong instead of a truly
democratic body. He had racked his own brains and those of many
others over the problems that had to be solved in forming a workable
and democratic congregation of nations and he probably knew more
about it than any Senator in the room. Elsewhere, he urged that America continue rationing in order to feed Europe. He appeared before the
Senate Committee on Military Affairs to ask for a "positive peace policy" and an end to the draft. "There must be an international disarmament," he reasoned, "without which talk of international police power
is a stupid fraud." He asked and got the advice of Bernard Baruch on
disarmament. He had a long talk at Princeton with Albert Einstein on
the control of atomic energy and general disarmament. If there
was anyone as early, insistent and informed as Norman Thomas in
propagandizing the need for universal controlled disarmament, he
does not come to mind. Thomas fairly purred with delight when England offered India her freedom and sent congratulations to Prime

Minister Attlee, who then and there became for Thomas a Socialist hero.

## 2. Chip on His Shoulder

Thomas's most anxious preoccupation, as he worked for disarmament, was what he felt to be the mistaken love affair between American liberals and the Russians. "You always have a chip on your shoulder against Russia," complained his Boston friend George L. Paine. The wealthy and liberal Mrs. Thomas Manley Dillingham of Santa Barbara, who had contributed to the Socialist Party though she was not a member, wrote that she thought the way he was "denouncing" Russia and Communism "was not the way to attain unity." He met with the conservative manufacturer Russell Maguire and Father Robert Gannon to discuss methods of fighting Communism in the United States. He sought a talk with Freda Utley in Washington to learn what she knew of the situation in China, writing, "I confess I am more and more skeptical about Chiang's government and more and more worried about the Communists." He wrote an old adversary, Secretary of Commerce Henry A. Wallace, to complain that in his anxiety to encourage friendship with Russia, Wallace seemed to ignore "the ruthlessness of Soviet imperialism, both in its treatment of the common man at home and in occupied territories." Having heard from Socialists in the MacArthur military government in Japan, Thomas warned Colonel Bonner F. Fellers, MacArthur's military secretary, of the "large and growing number of Communists or Communist fellow travelers who somehow manage to worm their way into important posts." Congresswoman Clare Boothe Luce, whom he had met at a Town Hall affair (he met everybody), sent him information about the evil nature of Chinese Communists as given "confidentially" to her, which he acknowledged with thanks.

He scarcely missed a book on politics, national or international, requesting and getting free copies in his capacity as radio commentator. He read David Dallin on Soviet Russia, was fascinated by Arthur Koestler's explanation of Communism in *The Yogi and the Commissar* and was simply carried away by Victor Kravchenko's *I Chose Freedom.* Kravchenko, a Soviet metallurgist and Red Army captain who had been sent to Washington with a purchasing commission, had become aware of the "unspeakable oppressions and cruelties" of his homeland and had defected, to the rage of The Daily Worker and the delight of American anti-Communists. His book was at once an exposé of Soviet ruthlessness and an attack on American naiveté as shown in such books as Joseph E. Davies's *Mission to Moscow* and by the attitudes of Americans themselves: "The extravagance of the adulation sometimes made me wince." "Americans seemed intent on explaining everything *in Stalin's favor,* to the discredit of the democracies." "Stalin's grip on the American mind, I realized with a shock, was almost as firm as his grip on the Russian mind." Kravchenko and his book of course were being exploited by hard-lining American Century promoters like Henry Luce and DeWitt Wallace, and Kravchenko wrote an article for Luce's Fortune magazine.

Thomas became friendly with Kravchenko and questioned him in detail about life and politics in Russia. The enmity between American Socialists and Communists had been traditional (and Thomas's own enmity was something other than merely traditional), but he now seemed to be supporting an alignment of the Party on the Soviet issue with American conservatives and opposing most liberal sentiments. The Thomases gave a large reception at Irving Place for Kravchenko, inviting forty Socialists and intellectuals, including Angelica Balabanoff, Bertram Wolfe, Louis Fischer and Harry Fleischman, still national secretary of the Party and a close friend. Kravchenko, whose personality proved abrasive, was criticized by some of the guests—a few of them ex-Communists themselves—for taking so long to break with the Soviets. "This bothered Mrs. Thomas," Fleischman recalled, "who whispered to me that apparently these ex-Communists could only believe that supporting Communism was understandable until the date they rejected it, but impossible for any sane person to support thereafter." Angelica, however, whose detestation of the Soviets was complete, thought Kravchenko ignorant and arrogant and departed from her usual tone of Thomas-worship in her note of thanks to her hosts:

> I must say that if I had met him elsewhere and if you would not have spoken of his book as you did, I would have thought that he is (A) not quite normal or (B) a charlatan, or (C) both. And if he had not written that book (which I have not yet read) I would be inclined to think that he is a Bolshevik agent. . . . As you may have noticed I told him what I thought of his way of treating you & your guests & I would have told him much more if he were not at your house.

Louis Fischer was as frank in his note to Thomas: "I thought Kravchenko gave a miserable performance. . . . Thanks for inviting me. He confirms my conviction that the worst effect of the Soviet dictatorship, as of all dictatorships, is to cripple the capacity of its victims to think."

Indeed the guests gave Kravchenko a hard time. Thomas reassured him in a note, "No one who reads your book with a warm heart and open mind could fail to be in your debt," and to Fischer he wrote, "I think if you talk longer to Kravchenko and without the confusion of so many people you would get a better point of view and like him." As a propagandist himself, he was showered with the propaganda of other propagandists who wanted him to become *their* propagandist. But he became only slightly entangled in the web spread by the China Lobby, which sent some of its first persuasion from the office of Alfred Kohlberg at Fifth Avenue and Thirty-seventh Street.

Kohlberg was a rich dealer in gloves and handkerchiefs (called "Kohlkerchiefs") mostly made in China. He had offices in Shanghai, Swatow and Chefoo. He always insisted that his affection for Chiang Kai-shek had no commercial motivation but was inspired solely by Chiang's democratic government as opposed to the tyranny of the Chinese Communists. Kohlberg, who was supported by the Luces and others including Walter Judd and Max Eastman, went so far as to declare in a letter to Thomas that Ho Ying-chin and others surrounding Chiang were really a group of Socialists, though their Socialism might not be quite identical with Thomas's, necessarily containing Asiatic mutations. In an excess of haste, Thomas signed the first "Manchurian Manifesto" which appeared in the newspapers; but that was the end. "I am exceedingly dubious about America supplying and training any military forces in China," he wrote Kohlberg. "I am worried about the nature of Chiang's government."

Professor Coolidge, however, agreeing with the Niebuhr philosophy of enlightened pragmatism and the need for giving some ground to Russia, was alarmed by the vehemence of Thomas's anti-Communism and wrote him so. He agreed that Stalin was being impossibly ruthless and expansionist. Still, Stalin could not live forever, and Coolidge foresaw pitfalls in aligning with conservative politicians on this issue:

> What scares me is the danger that any serious conflict of wills with Russia will almost inevitably grow into an all-out struggle, in which all anti-Communists are drawn together[,] with the reactionaries emerging on top. . . . I am afraid that the little people [in Eastern Europe] are going to be out of luck for a while, and about all we can do is to be honest in saying we don't like it.

"I find it rather ironic," Thomas replied in part, "that so many of those who denounced me because although I abhorred Fascism I wanted to keep America out of war against Germany and Japan now denounce me as a warmaker against Russia simply for wanting the truth known. Who are the appeasers now?" But he added that he wanted "the liquidation of all forms of imperialism," American and European as well as Russian, and that one of his arguments against peacetime conscription was that it was directed against Russia. His opinion of Russia and its Communism could hardly change until *they* changed, but he was merely being practical, wanting Americans to know the nature of the Russia with which it had to stay at peace. He invited Coolidge to join the Post War World Council, whose policy was "in no sense" anti-Russian. His later letter to Foreign Commissar V. M. Molotov at the Russian delegation to the United Nations at Lake Success showed that he could bend when Molotov did: "Dear Sir: The Post War World Council has read with delight your statements on limitations of arms and in particular your statements of yesterday on supervision for the control of the use of atomic energy. . . ."

Thomas was simultaneously immersed in involvements which most busy men rule out of their lives. He coaxed his doctor brother Evan to travel to Bethel, Connecticut, to minister to Lillian Symes Clement, seriously ill with a heart ailment. It was in vain, and Thomas himself went to Bethel to attend her funeral, remembering that she was one of those who accompanied him in 1926 to the Botany mills in New Jersey. Although he did not like *Bernard Clare,* the latest novel of his "sort of Socialist" friend James Farrell, he defended it, writing Prime Minister Mackenzie King in Ottawa, "I do not think the book is pornographic and I fear censorship." As a member of the International Association of Poets, Playwrights, Editors, Essayists and Novelists, he addressed that group and rubbed elbows with such writers as Van Wyck Brooks, Carl Carmer, Pearl Buck, Norman Cousins and Manuel Komroff. Out of sympathy for the wife of George Johann Dasch, one of the wartime German saboteurs who had been landed on Long Island by submarine, he was working for clemency for Dasch. It was a case on which Thomas would work intermittently for many years. While addressing a National Association for the Advancement of Colored People group in Illinois, as he put it, "it occurred to me that it was about time I joined myself," and he remitted the five-dollar membership fee. Paul Porter, for whom Thomas had once envisioned a high post in the Party, was now going to England for the administration's Mission for Economic Affairs, and

Thomas sent him a letter of introduction to Stafford Cripps. (It was in London that Porter encountered Dorothy Thompson by chance and took her to dinner to repay that debt of long ago.) In the last year of the war, Thomas had resumed his sleuthing role and tipped off Office of Price Administration Director Chester Bowles about black marketing in New York; they became good friends and occasionally dined together in Washington. Thomas worked to get conscientious objectors out of prison. He ran into a childhood friend from Marion, now living in Queens, learned that he had an invalid wife and looked for a nurse for her. To the editor of *Robotnik Polski,* a Polish Socialist paper in New York, he wrote, "Yes, I will be glad to write an article for your anniversary issue. About how many words and when do you want it?" He visited a school for Negro children in Elkhart, of which that city was proud, and wrote the superintendent, "we shall not build a common citizenship in a democratic country by practicing segregation, and I hate to see a city in Northern Indiana conform in this point to the prejudices of the South." To one correspondent, however, he admitted that he had not had time to look into the exploitation of the Hopi Indians, and to another he explained that he had been so involved in European and Asian affairs that he had not been able to follow developments in Armenia.

Though he failed the Hopis and Armenians, he took a continuing kindly interest in people with mental troubles. He corresponded with a young and confused Puerto Rican–American in the Bronx, complimented him on his intelligence but found him unstable and advised him to see a competent psychiatrist. He wrote the director of the Rockland State Mental Hospital in behalf of a man who claimed he had been sent there illegally, adding, "I feel a certain human sympathy for cases like this and would like to know the facts." He invariably had at least one and sometimes several persons of uncertain stability on his list of correspondents. He was charmed by one Socialist comrade in Illinois who wrote to him that he was leaving for a mental hospital, saying, "It isn't bothering me as much as it might. The way the world has gotten today it will be just simply a miniature world." "Won't you let me know your address and where I can write you?" Thomas replied, and began a correspondence of several years' duration with the man, who was in and out of the hospital. To Thomas, the man was exactly right. The world was just a large insane asylum, and the term "crazy world," only half in jest, became common with him.

### 3. A Sense of Failure

Dr. Evan Welling Thomas, who had abandoned the church in maturity and became a physician in mid-life, now married a nurse-administrator, Ruth Bills, at fifty-six and took an apartment uptown with his bride. Later they moved to Albany when he joined the state Department of Health. The removal of the cherished Unk from the family circle was a blow to Thomas's peace of mind. There was no longer a doctor in the house, and Thomas virtually took Violet's temperature and pulse now before leaving on a trip of any duration. Both Thomas and Violet decided reluctantly that the big house at Cold Spring Harbor was too much for her to cope with, even with servants. They put the place on the market and built a small house in nearby Lloyd Harbor for themselves. "Lookers" paraded through the big house but it did not sell, and since the indecision seemed as hard on Violet as anything else, they sold the small place instead. It went to George P. Hunt, an editor of Fortune, who was delighted to get it at cost in that time of housing shortage and wrote Thomas that he was overwhelmed at such an "unselfish, open-handed transaction." With the Gateses living nearby, the "big house" had become a family rallying place in the summer. At Christmas, a half-dozen or more of the grandchildren, all of whom called Thomas Big Dad, would join him and the others as he led in his resonant bass the singing of Christmas songs. The Thomases had the customary postwar difficulty in keeping servants, and now and then applied to a New York agency for a replacement. One Chinese cook who arrived at the Cold Spring Harbor station and was met by Thomas asked him immediately if there was a movie theater in town, and when Thomas said there was not, would not budge from the station and took the next train back to the city. One Japanese servant named Fujita, however, remained for years and became virtually a member of the family. Violet had recently taken up bridge, so Thomas did too. He proved to be as maladroit at cards as he was at driving a car, playing the wrong cards but, his son-in-law John Gates observed, always having a good reason for it.

As for the Party, although Thomas lent his name and efforts to fundraising, it was "bust," as he wrote inelegantly to Walter Uphoff. There were periodic crises in paying the rent for the cheap Fourth Avenue office and in keeping The Call afloat. The Chicago office had long since

301

been abandoned. Thomas was now well enough launched with the Post War World Council, which gave him a platform for most of his causes (and for which he had to solicit money), that he might have been forgiven for dropping the Party as a lost hope and as a competitor for both his time and money. He remained loyal out of sheer belief and new optimism. See what Socialism was doing in England and the Scandinavian countries! One of his great efforts, now that the United Nations was in town, was to bring Socialists of many countries together in a unity symbolic of the international dialog essential for world peace. It exasperated him that they resisted such gatherings and when brought together were anything but free from the nationalist feelings Socialism condemned. In December, 1946, the Irving Place house was the scene of a reception for seventy-five internationally prominent Socialists. Among the dozen-odd who made brief speeches were Léon Jouhaux of France, Percy Welys of England, Hartvig Frisch of Denmark, Jose A. Encinas of Peru, David Wilson of New Zealand and, of course, Angelica Balabanoff, soon to leave for Italy to help the struggling Socialists there. (Angelica had recently written Thomas, "once more I have to admire you, your courage, and to regret—and how!—that the masses do not listen to you.")

At such gatherings Fujita, known as Fuji, was on hand to serve sherry. Thomas himself, though he had originally favored Prohibition and hoped it would succeed, had enjoyed wine after repeal and occasional spirituous liquors. He was a one-drink man. Liquor had not been served with any regularity in the Thomas home, however, until Evan came of age. Thomas and Violet, now alone with the servants, occupied only two floors of the Irving Place building, the ground floor (Violet's former tea room) being taken by the Sleepy Hollow Bookstore operated by the French sisters, who became good friends of the family. Irving Place, dead-ending into Gramercy Park, with little traffic, had a quiet turn-of-century gentility. In the morning Thomas was out the door, around the corner on Nineteenth Street and in his office in three minutes. Some thought his temper, which could bite, was sharper than of yore, whereas others marveled at the patience that had survived so many disappointments. When Kurt Schuschnigg lectured at Town Hall, scores of Austrian refugees and ex-GIs picketed the building while a capacity crowd listened to this former ally of Dollfuss. Thomas popped up during the question period to say that he had no connection with the pickets, "But I want to protest this whitewashing of Dollfuss and the long course of events leading to the armed assault on the Karl Marx houses in Vienna. . . ." There were such shouts, both of approval and disagreement, that the moderator had trouble restoring order and Schuschnigg conceded that mistakes had been made.

Elsewhere, Thomas applied his own logic to the Nuremberg trials: "In Germany Allied courts were punishing Germans for not being conscientious objectors to military orders to kill; in the United States . . . we were punishing Americans for being conscientious objectors to participation in the wholesale killing of war." It merely proved that it was not safe to lose. It was one thing to have "short sharp trials for atrocities and the deliberate attempt to exterminate civilian populations," and another to try all the leaders, especially when some judges "represent a Britain for whom the statute of limitations has not yet wiped out the guilt of aggressive imperialist wars while others represented the dictatorship [Russia] responsible for aggressive wars against Finland, Poland and the Baltic states in violation of some 29 treaties. . . ." Nor did Thomas think that the United States, especially after that dreadful second Bomb, could mete out justice to the Japanese with assurance of moral impeccability.

These thoughts were attacked by many as un-American, though Thomas was at some pains to show that the nation had much to recommend it. His article in Harper's, "What's Right with America," stressed such facts as that despite victory in two world wars, the United States had seized little booty, and after each of them had made generous loans to Europe. And he had to admit that in the second war, with the exception of the crime against the Japanese-Americans, civil liberties had survived much better than in and after World War I. The Reader's Digest had given a wide berth to his dozens of critical articles. They seized on this one, condensed it and made it the lead-off of their May, 1947, issue, blurbing it as the work of a man "accustomed to lambasting us for our faults." Thomas had to admit himself wrong in his certainty that war would bring Fascism here. Two years after the war was over (for all that dangerous Smith Act), Truman was in his White House and if all was not well, at any rate Thomas was not under the scrutiny of detectives, and he and others were saying things for which they would have been jailed twenty-seven years earlier. He felt sure that part of the reason was the Pearl Harbor attack which had unified Americans as they had never been unified in the other war, and also the euphoria of coming out on top as the world's greatest power, prosperous instead of suffering the want and unemployment he had foreseen.

No one yet knew that the attack on civil liberties was brewing and would come to a head later, when the American Century idea came under challenge. In 1946 his friend Congressman Jerry Voorhis had been unseated by the young Richard Nixon, whose tactics Thomas would not have praised in Harper's, and the new Senator Joseph McCarthy from Wisconsin was still feeling his way around Washington.

At the moment he was more fearful of the new Henry Wallace Progressive Party and the naiveté shown by some of its backers. To a Brooklyn friend of the cloth who had signed a Wallace manifesto, he sent a warning: "You will remember there was a time when I went in more or less for the support of these [Communist] fronts. I learned from very hard experience that it was a mistake." But he weighed each issue on its merits and was critical of the Truman Doctrine, fearing that "American intervention in Turkey [will] become more and more imperialistic, more and more tied to the politics of petroleum."

In the spring of 1947 he felt safe enough about Violet to take another of his cross-country tours of investigation combined with the usual grueling schedule of speeches. It had been fourteen months since he had been in California and he noticed a change:

> Then the tendency was too much complacency about Russia and too much appeasement. Now there is a high degree of rather hysterical anti-Communism, which is being exploited by reactionaries. While the Communists have lost their easy contacts, in some ways they may be able to profit among decent Americans from the anti-Communist hysteria and such wild proposals as the outlawing of the party and, in California, the prohibition in public schools of the discussion of "controversial issues."

This kind of thing was bad enough in California. He was incensed by Princetonians who said that the faculty should avoid partisan mention of politics:

> . . . [It] is the right, and even the duty, of officers and professors in a university to play their part as citizens in politics according to the dictates of their conscience. What kind of citizenship can be taught in universities by men who themselves are compelled to become second-rate citizens deprived of the right to express their mind in proper political channels because they are paid by people who may not like some of their opinions?

The latter was a view that William F. Buckley, Jr., would later attack at Yale. Thomas wrote Winston Churchill to applaud his efforts toward a united Europe—a step away from the nationalism that made a world view impossible. A nation that had caused him worry for several years was Israel, which with more than his usual prescience he saw as an endless threat to peace. This complex problem had to be discussed carefully, especially in New York, and he had sought light on it from his old friend of first-war days, Rabbi Judah Magnes, now president of the Hebrew University in Jerusalem. Thomas thought Zionism a mistake in its linking of state and religion and believed that peace would never come unless the displaced Arabs could return to a minimal federation somewhat "like Switzerland with its German and French speaking cantons."

Things were threatening enough so that, in his belief that the world was his personal problem, he felt that he was failing it. ". . . I have had an unusually happy and fortunate life," he reflected. "What haunts me is a kind of foreboding about the future of the world and a sense of failure." Only the United States, Canada and a few small countries could be called reasonably well fed, yet two years after the great war ended there were nineteen million men under arms in the world, with the United States and Russia spending the most to get ready for the next war. The combination of his worries about Violet and his need for a medium for his views caused him to write Edward R. Murrow of CBS, whom he knew and liked:

> This is an unconventional letter, in which I inquire about the possibility of my getting a job on some regular program, bi-weekly or weekly, as a radio interpreter or commentator on the news. As you know, I have done a good deal of radio work . . . What brings my interest to a head is the fact that my wife's health makes it desirable . . . that I should greatly reduce the traveling that I have been doing. . . . I have no expectation of competing with Winchell or even Fulton Lewis for a Hooper or Crossley rating, but I think I could contribute something to that balance which I understand networks seek. . . . I could of course not conceal the fact that I was a Socialist. My comments on foreign affairs would follow the line of the Post War World Council, but I should not propagandize. . . .

Murrow replied kindly that the offer raised both "possibilities and problems" and invited him to lunch. Obviously the problems were larger, and random comments Thomas made later indicated that large radio advertisers could be expected to object to a Socialist commentator. The commercial power which could give Winchell and Lewis sway over millions could deprive the public of the truly intelligent and stimulating Thomas, who of course still appeared frequently on various programs by invitation. In June, 1947, Thomas had to cancel a July 4 speaking date in Columbus, writing, "My wife is unwell—we have had to take two of our grandchildren . . . because their mother is sick—and another family of our children and grandchildren is coming from Kansas City on July 3." The latter were the Millers (Dr. Miller taught pediatrics at the University of Kansas Medical School), who knew nothing of Violet's illness. The two young Miller girls, Patricia and Frances, found both Violet and Thomas delightful. Thomas, who loved children in a demonstrative way he could not achieve with adults, would come in after the girls were tucked in bed and sing, "Goodnight, Ladies," and sometimes "The Bullfrog on the Bank," hamming it up so that they went to sleep laughing.

On August 1, after the Millers had returned to Kansas City and while Thomas was at a Party National Executive Committee meeting at Reading, Evan's wife Anne was talking by telephone with Violet when Anne discovered that there was no voice at the other end of the line. Violet had had her last heart attack. She had lived to be sixty-six—a life anything but sedentary despite that constant threat. Harry Fleischman, who was with Thomas when word reached him in Reading, saw his anguish, perhaps the anguish of a man who had waited so long for the blow to strike that he had gained hope that it never would. By the time he reached Cold Spring Harbor he had himself in firm control and was, his daughter Frances Gates thought, "magnificent."

The funeral, in keeping with the Thomas feeling for the privacy of grief, was limited to the family and a few of the closest friends. ("Personally," Thomas later wrote, "I suppose I am peculiar, I want to be cremated and have my ashes scattered. I do not like our main charity to be to the dead.") No church was connected with the ceremony except in the person of the Reverend Sidney Lovett. Lovett conducted the service in the big living room of the house Violet had designed—just as Thomas, in his days of religious belief, had officiated at the funeral of Lovett's young first wife thirty-one years earlier. For Lovett, to whom Violet had always been Mom, it was the saddest of rituals, lightened only by the belief in God which Thomas did not share and from which he could take no comfort. The service was indeed so personal that Mrs. Gates, for one, found it hard to bear. To Socialist comrades, some of them hurt because they had not been invited, Thomas apologized in The Call: "We kept the funeral very strictly private . . . because Violet and I shared among so many other things a very strong dislike of public funerals." After the cremation, Thomas sailed out on the Sound with Evan and John Gates and consigned Violet's ashes to the sea. Thomas again found himself unable to express his feelings orally to his own kin. Ultimately he did so in a letter to "My very dear Children," in which he paid tribute to them all, but especially to Violet:

> I'm not fool or ingrate enough to say "no sorrow is like unto my sorrow." Parting is the common lot of men and I've had 37 wonderful years. . . . Just living with her and doing things together was fun. . . . She'd let me talk about problems and worries and often helped me by her shrewd common sense; she was loyal to the same ends but she never, thank God! turned home into another church meeting or Socialist debating society. . . .
>
> . . . . I have friends and causes and some strength still to serve them. But if I seem to live as in a dream it will be no lack of affection or interest in the strange and wonderful stream of life in which we are caught but because something rare and for me entirely irreplaceable is gone.
>
> And yet I would rather have it so than that she should have known a kind of lingering invalidism that she often feared. To be spared that, to meet death in the midst of life's happiness with your main job well done, is a thing greatly to be desired. And that she had.

Well said, but he was broken for a time. He wrote Raymond Fosdick twice about his inability to shake off his sorrow. To Gilkey he wrote, "The family have been very kind. So have my friends. But I'm very lonely."

### 4. Toynbee and Jester

The Gateses, with the aid of a legacy from Violet (each of the children got one, and Thomas was left the Irving Place building and other small property) bought the big house at Cold Spring Harbor. Of the children, Frances Gates remained the most active in sympathy with her father's politics and would come closest to filling the great vacancy in his life. William Thomas and his family lived in Rumson, New Jersey; the Freibelys (Rebekah Thomas) nearby in Plainfield; the Millers (Polly Thomas) were in Kansas, and Evan and his family lived in New York City. "Violet's house" remained Thomas's country retreat, where an apartment was arranged for him by the Gateses. Occasionally he got Violet's Packard out of the garage—at great danger to life and limb—for lectures nearby. He described his dog Jester as a fine companion "when I give him a chance," meaning that Jester saw him only when he was at home. One could say that Thomas threw himself into work as an anodyne for his loss except that he could scarcely work any harder than he always had. He was busy lecturing, busy at Town Hall, busy at PWWC, ACLU, ILA, WDL, LID and other alphabetical responsibilities, busy meeting with American Socialists and with foreign Socialists from the United Nations, busy digesting Toynbee, busy also with the scores of thoughtful gestures and enterprises that were marks of his endless concern for building justice stronger, brick by brick, as when he addressed Mr. Jackie Robinson:

> Now that the Dodgers have won the pennant, it is very appropriate, I think, to thank you, not only for what you did in the pennant race but for what you have done for the colored race and for the fraternity which ought to characterize our mutual relations. You have performed a real service to your country and in general to a world which must learn to honor men for what they are and do regardless of race.

But he did not evade the difficulties involved in integration. While racial intermarriage was a justifiable goal, it required reasonable care. He advised one young white man that he would be making a mistake if he married a black girl simply out of antipathy to racism, and would be wronging the girl in so doing. Intermarriage could be successful if done with full understanding of the prevailing handicaps, but scarcely if done as a duty. And to the Chicago Negro publication The Circuit, he was perhaps annoyingly frank in his statement of some of the obstacles blacks had to surmount in their fight against discrimination:

> I am wholly opposed to all forms of race discrimination. This includes restrictive covenants for the exclusion of negroes from certain districts in Chicago and elsewhere. I agree with you that our fight against this injustice will be made much easier if negroes will make their own communities conspicuous examples, both in physical appearance and internal harmony, of the kind of homes we desire for all our people. I know this is not easy, particularly because negroes are usually relatively underpaid and overcharged for rent. It does not seem fair that negro communities should be judged as white communities are not—on a racial basis. Nevertheless it is an obvious truth that every outstanding negro athlete, musician, scientist, etc., peculiarly serves his race. By the same token, every outstanding negro community peculiarly serves the race and helps to break down prejudice. It is worthwhile to remove every faint cause for the allegation that negroes are undesirable neighbors.

43. The Thomas couple, with Dr. Evan Thomas, are rudely escorted out of New Jersey by the police of Mayor Frank Hague (*left*). Hague's status as a Democratic chieftain despite his dictatorial tyranny was only one of Norman Thomas's quarrels with President Roosevelt, who deferred to Hague.

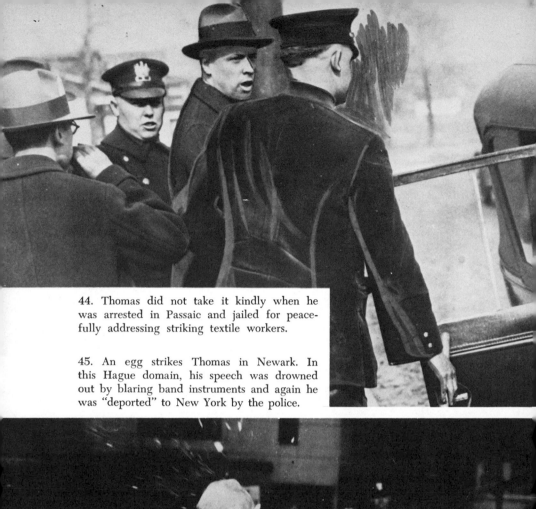

44. Thomas did not take it kindly when he was arrested in Passaic and jailed for peacefully addressing striking textile workers.

45. An egg strikes Thomas in Newark. In this Hague domain, his speech was drowned out by blaring band instruments and again he was "deported" to New York by the police.

46. Fiorello La Guardia and Dorothy Thompson were two whose lives occasionally collided with Thomas's. La Guardia, though "best of all mayors," suffered occasional Thomas criticism.

47. Thomas confers at convention with Maynard C. Krueger (*left*), his 1940 running mate, and Travers Clement, the Socialist national secretary. The Party was deeply in debt.

48. Peppery Lillian Symes warned Thomas that the Trotskyites planned to "decapitate" him.

49. Darlington Hoopes of Pennsylvania was Thomas's running mate—his fifth—in the 1944 race.

50. Thomas appears at Garden anti-intervention rally with (*from left*) Senator Burton K. Wheeler, Lindbergh and Kathleen Norris. His acceptance of America First cooperation outraged some Socialists.

51. William Gausmann and Harry Fleischman (*right*) with Thomas at 1948 Reading convention. Fleischman had risen to become a leader and close Thomas ally. Despite sign, no woman won nomination for Vice President.

52. Dr. Albert Sprague Coolidge—Thomas treasured his friendship and judgment.

53. Bridge expert Ely Culbertson joined Thomas in plans for world peace assembly.

54. Henry Wallace incensed Thomas first in 1934, then as innocent pawn of the Communists in 1948.

55. Reinhold Niebuhr was a close Thomas ally, later broke with him and labeled him as utopian.

56. J. J. Singh aided Thomas's postwar planning, while Thomas helped Singh's drive for free India.

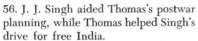

57. Roger Baldwin—he and Thomas joined in portentous affairs but always had time for a joke.

58. Thomas waits to speak at memorial meeting for his friend Carlo Tresca (*seen in painting*), shot dead on Fifth Avenue during the wartime blackout.

59. Victor Kravchenko—he charmed Thomas but stirred only contempt in Angelica Balabanoff.

60. Corliss Lamont deplored Thomas's campaign to drive Communists out of the ACLU board.

61. Allen and John Foster Dulles, Princetonians both, did not please Thomas. He lost all faith in the elder brother.

62. Tucker Smith, running mate in Thomas's last Presidential campaign in 1948, several years later received an astonishing letter from Thomas.

63. Thomas at seventy-fifth birthday is surrounded by four of his children (*from left*): Mrs. John W. Gates (Frances), William S. Thomas, Evan W. Thomas and Mrs. John D. Friebely (Becky). The only one not present, Mrs. Herbert C. Miller (Polly, *at right*), made her home in Kansas a rest stop for her fast-traveling father.

64. Though he had not revered her husband, Thomas thought Eleanor Roosevelt America's greatest lady.

65. Touring Japan and Southeast Asia, Thomas meets in Rangoon with Burmese officials and newsmen. This was one of his trips sponsored by the American Committee for Cultural Freedom.

66. Thomas is flanked by Clarence Senior (*left*) and Paul Porter, once called the "Kansas goyim."

67. He leads pickets at the Russian consulate, an assignment he performed smartly scores of times.

68. *Left:* At beach club with daughter Frances. Here he often picked political bones with John Foster Dulles.

69. *Opposite page:* At his fiftieth Princeton reunion—feather, smile, camaraderie, but not much alcohol.

70. *Below:* Shown here with the children of son Evan, he was "Big Dad" to all fifteen grandchildren.

71. C. D. Jackson—his idea of "bending the truth" in propaganda became U.S. policy abroad and at home as well.

72. Don Peretz was half Thomas's age, but the old warhorse ran him ragged on their Middle East tour.

73. Henry Luce's imperialist bias drew Thomas's fire. James A. Farley (*shown with Luce*) entered Thomas's life in three incarnations: Irish patriot, New Deal cabinet member and finally Coca-Cola capitalist.

74. Juan Bosch stands with Vice President Lyndon Johnson at Bosch's inauguration in Santo Domingo. Bosch was one of the few whose abilities Thomas (as well as President Kennedy) seems to have misjudged.

75. The fascinating lady Thomas met at Time's birthday party (*below*) he remembered only as Lola Somebody.

76. Lenore Marshall wrote Thomas, "The whole country should be grateful to you. I am, and constantly."

77. James Farmer, jailed as freedom rider, got a letter and a check from Thomas, a fellow CORE member.

78. A. Philip Randolph watches guest of honor perform the ritual at his eightieth birthday celebration. Nineteen hundred admirers attended, seeing in him qualities unique and civilized, but going out of style.

79. He managed a magnificent eightieth birthday smile which made the Times front page and concealed the arthritic agonies that failed to stop him.

80. But locomotion was painful. Below, he leans on Timothy Sullivan as he chats with faculty members at the University of Colorado.

BELOW OLYMPUS    By Inter

WE COULD USE SOMEONE LIKE NORMAN THOMAS TODAY!

WASN'T HE A SOCIALIST IN THE 30'S!

—WE'VE ADOPTED MOST OF HIS PROGRAMS

SEE! THE SYSTEM WORKS!!

INTERLANDI © 1977, LOS ANGELES TIMES

His own record against discrimination was good if not perfect. In New York City he had lived and worked among blacks and members of all races. He had always rejected any color line at his lectures and speeches except in some cases in the South during political campaigns where it would have meant that he would have gone unheard. He had steadily fought the racial discrimination practiced by some "democratic" unions and some colleges. Blacks had been among the Socialists who met at his New York home, he was now friendly with African blacks at the United Nations, and A. Philip Randolph (one of his favorite friends) was high on his list of those under consideration for the Socialist Party nomination for President or Vice President. Neither he nor Violet, however, had felt it incumbent on them alone to defeat racial discrimination. No blacks had visited them at fashionable Cold Spring Harbor—a place so firmly out of bounds for Party affairs that such old white Party colleagues as Harry Laidler had never been there. No blacks owned property at Cold Spring Harbor, the few blacks there being servants or gardeners who were effectively excluded from the private beach club simply by its cost, a matter which Thomas seems never to have made a subject of one of his crusades.

He was still handsome at sixty-three, straight, patrician of feature, his bald head encircled by a white fringe, the lines around his eyes and mouth quickly widening when he smiled and capable of a wide range of expressions. These he used so effectively on the platform and on the new medium of television that professional actors saw in him a fellow artist. The loneliness of 71 Irving Place was lessened by the arrival of his youngest sister Emma from Baltimore to stay with him while she took a master's degree in social work at Columbia at the age of forty-eight. Emma, who had both the Thomas intelligence and the Thomas sense of humor, was at first a trifle intimidated by her famous brother, mostly because of the reserve that seemed inexplicable in so articulate a man. She thought that his voice had lost some of its musical quality and been given a quaver by too much public speaking. He made no mention of Violet, obviously still avoiding the pain the subject brought him. (The loss of young Norman in the twenties had haunted him for years.) He would be away for days at a time, and Emma was busy studying and attending classes, but she became fond of Jester, who was left in her charge. "I didn't know I came here to take your dog around the block three times a day," she once remarked, to her brother's great amusement. She did much of the cooking, finding him as hearty and absent-minded an eater as in her childhood days at Lewisburg. Always hungry, he ate voraciously and indiscriminately, and his table manners, to which he never gave a thought, were terrible. The dog was trained to sit under the table at mealtime. Thomas sometimes broke his own rule that Jester must not be fed at table, slipping him tidbits. At cocktail parties, Thomas was the terror of hostesses, abstractedly denuding huge trays of canapes while others drank.

Fuji, who had been in the house when Violet died, remained part-time with Thomas until he could find other temporary work he liked. A concertgoer, he automatically had time off for musical events at Carnegie Hall or elsewhere, and his affection for Thomas—like Thomas's for him—was evident. When in town, Thomas enjoyed striding around Gramercy Park with the dog on the hydrant-and-tree circuit, the two of them becoming neighborhood fixtures. Thomas often had Socialist meetings at the house, from which Emma removed herself. Her theory was that in his peculiar shyness he made use of Jester as a conversational icebreaker with strangers, the playful and handsome dog always getting him over that first hump of constraint.

As for Toynbee, Thomas thought him "pretty good on the rise of civilization but not, I think, so sound on its fall." He especially criticized Toynbee's reliance on religion as a regenerative force. Thomas's whole quarrel with religion was that it had failed and was still failing as a regenerative force. He thought Toynbee's reasoning in this respect a "counsel of despair." He *wished* that religion would measure up to its duty to mankind but had little hope for it. Occasionally on a Sunday at Cold Spring Harbor he would go to church with the Gateses. They were convinced he did so out of curiosity and because he loved the hymns. He embarrassed them because he invariably criticized the sermon in his platform voice (he seemed unaware of its volume) even before they were out the door, causing people to stare.

Travers Clement had rather dropped out of Party activities since the death of his wife because the lives of both had been so intertwined in Socialism that it was almost unbearable for him to resume it alone. To Thomas he wrote, "You must be subject to the same stresses and strains and I certainly admire the way you have stood up under them." One of Thomas's most enthusiastic admirers was Angelica—also a problem because of her statelessness, changes of mind and carelessness of self. Returning from Italy after only a few months, she decided to go back there with a systematic program for aiding the Italian Socialists. Thomas again made her honored guest at a Socialist party at Irving Place, celebrating also her seventieth birthday, for which she thanked him with an effusiveness all her own:

And if I write to thank you personally, dear comrade Norman Thomas, I do it *not* because I want to *thank* you—I know how hurt you would be if I would try to do it. I only want to apologize for having mentioned you personally in my speech that evening—I know how you dislike it—but desiring deeply to convey to your guests my feelings I could not help mentioning what the mere existence of a person & Socialist like you means to me—to my restless soul longing for consistency. I have had the rare privilege of knowing many great individuals—what I most looked for in approaching them & what I most appreciated—was harmony—harmony between words & deeds—public and private life.

## 5. On Handling the Communists

Thomas, who was damned by some as anti-Communist and by others as pro-Communist, had in his discriminating way reached a conception of the problem for which he agreed there was no easy solution: the development of an American foreign policy toward Russia and a domestic policy toward American Communists and sympathizers consistent both with freedom and national safety. His activities and statements in which few anti-Communists would join and which caused him to be called pro-Communist were many:

His great fondness for several former Socialists who had gone over to the Communist Party was of a piece with his opposition to the military buildup and his fear that the Truman Doctrine might promote imperialism. He testified against the Mundt-Nixon bill before the Senate Judiciary Committee, admitting the problem of "deliberate use by Communists of bad faith as a tactic" but declaring that the bill would "suppress the Communist Party and drive it underground where it would be more dangerous." He insisted on the constitutional right of the Communist Party to exist, meet and politick, and reminded Americans that democratic perfection did not exist here. He attacked the House Un-American Activities Committee: ". . . the net result of the Committee's inquiry has been to do any genuine liberal position far more harm than good. The Committee has given the Communists and near-Communists valuable ammunition." He attacked movie magnates who fired Communist or fellow-traveling actors or writers out of hand:

[Their action] in firing them . . . and that in advance of any trial on contempt charges, marks the beginning of indirect and capricious government censorship far more dangerous than anything the accused men have done. . . . They are not being discharged because of any proved subversive act, but only because they refuse to answer the question "Are you a Communist?" . . . It will be a sad day for the American Bill of Rights if men like the succession of Dies, Rankin and [J. Parnell] Thomas, who have set no standards of what constitutes unAmerican activities . . . should directly or indirectly be allowed to say who can write in our press, speak on our radio or be employed in the movie industry.

On the other hand, he was called anti-Communist because he thought Communism as it existed in Russia brutal—the slave camps particularly sickened him—and its proponents in America either misguided or treacherous. (He had long since given up trying to reason with Elizabeth Gurley Flynn, who insisted that he would love Communism if he would make a long stay in Russia.) The Moscow-ordered cashiering of Browder had been typically ruthless and in fact had inspired Thomas with some sympathy for Browder despite the harm Browder had done him and the Socialist Party. Thomas had gone before the Senate Foreign Relations Committee to praise the Marshall Plan, which American Stalinists dutifully assailed. He drew the line sharply when it came to the matter of Communists (any more than Nazis or Kluxers) holding any important position from police chief to President, and that included membership on the board of the American Civil Liberties Union, for Communists holding such power could "simply invalidate our defense of civil liberties." He thought it foolish to permit dedicated Communists to teach American children. He was so concerned about African freedom that he persuaded Alan Paton to address a group Thomas gathered at the Dorset Hotel apartment of James and Lenore Marshall, among them Roy Wilkins, Lillian Smith, Jagjit Singh and Channing Tobias. After Paton spoke, Thomas stressed the point that non-Communists must put the case before the American people before the Communists seized it and exploited it as their own.

In foreign policy he advocated a line aimed at wearing down Russian intransigence and building toward peace. He vehemently opposed the preventive war urged by zealots anxious to obliterate Russia before our nuclear monopoly ended. He disagreed with George Kennan's famous policy of "firm containment" of Russia and agreed that Walter Lippmann made an impressive case against it. But he was almost as opposed to Lippmann's argument for the old balance-of-power idea, with the democratic countries allied against the Russian sphere. That had never worked before. He was realistic about history even if, as many believed, he was utopian in his hopes. What he wanted now, especially while the nuclear advantage existed, was a mighty, concerted drive under American leadership for the gradual relinquishment of national sovereignty and for world disarmament under strong international controls:

> I am pleading that the one hope of peace lies in bringing home to the nations the fact that disarmament under genuinely effective international control is its essential condition. Here, the United Nations might serve an interim usefulness, with comparatively minor changes in machinery. On no other terms will it be much more than a debating society whose acrimonious discussions may contribute more to the coming of war than to the preservation of peace.

But this could be no tentative or half-hearted proposal. It must represent the total dedication of the administration. It must be announced and pushed and kept alive by the President himself. It must be given the same national urgency usually given to war. It must never stop. It must accept rebuffs and continue the effort, forever propagandizing for peace. Thomas did not rule out the possibility that the Soviets might ultimately come to agreement, but the policy was valid in any case:

> Whether . . . the Soviet dictatorship would accept . . . is, I grant, very doubtful. But much depends upon the persuasive power with which reasonable proposals of universal benefit are presented. No iron curtain could keep them altogether from the knowledge of the people of the Soviet Empire, and popular feeling has some weight even in a totalitarian state.
>
> Assuming the worst—that is, the complete rejection of any sound plan of control for universal disarmament [a security league should be established] under Article 51 of the U.N. Charter within the framework of the United Nations. If that security league should, as it must, continually reiterate to all peoples and governments its invitation to come in, the peace of the world would be saved. Meanwhile, the division within the United Nations between nations which are in earnest about establishing enough world government to control armament and the international anarchist states would be in every way less hurtful than the present poorly defined cold war between the leading Powers within the United Nations.

Although he never said it in so many words, he proceeded on the assumption that if only utopianism could save the world from self-destruction, then the world had better get busy and make utopianism work.

## 6. A Work of Art

As chairman of the Tresca Memorial Committee, Thomas marked the fifth anniversary of his friend's murder with a firm letter to District Attorney Hogan pointing out that the crime was obviously political, that if Communists or Fascists were involved there might be national and even international ramifications, and urging Hogan to call in the Federal Bureau of Investigation on that ground. It irked him, too, that the district attorney's office had never questioned an intimate of Tresca, a union official whose check for $640 was found in the slain man's pocket and who was one of the last persons to talk with him. The detective in Thomas would not down. Through his friend Roger Riis of The Reader's Digest he tried vainly to get that publication to run a story on the case. In a speech at the Rand School—yes, the Rand School—Thomas asked Governor Dewey to appoint a special prosecutor, and Roger Baldwin announced a $5,000 reward in behalf of the committee for information leading to the arrest and conviction of the killer.

The Rand School of course was sacred to the Old Guard, the moribund Social Democratic Federation, and Thomas had been persona non grata there since the great schism a dozen years earlier. His admittance marked another effort of the two splinters to unite. Tresca's murder remained unsolved (as it does to this day), but the warmup between the Socialist Party and the Federation was one of those illusory signs that encouraged Socialists to look for a great upsurge in the Party vote in 1948. Other signs were the death of Roosevelt, the seeming insignificance of Truman as his successor and the severe Congressional setback the Democrats had suffered in 1946. The most powerful spur was the candidacy of Henry Wallace who, heartily backed by the Communists, threatened to steal the third-party movement.

But perhaps Socialists did not need any excuse to nominate a Presidential candidate.

Thomas sincerely preferred not to run. In the last pages of his unpublished autobiography, finished in 1946, he announced his retirement from candidacy and his intention to remain only as a member of the Party National Executive Committee. His candidate was again Maynard Krueger. But now it became clear that Krueger had lost hope in the Party—so much so that he later decided to run for Congress from Illinois on an independent rather than a Socialist ticket. Thomas knew even before the Party convention assembled in Reading in May that he was "it" for the sixth time. There was no one else who could get a vote big enough to influence labor and liberals. Thomas assumed that Dewey would be the Republican candidate and would win, and that one Republican administration might be enough to cause labor and progressive forces to reflect that the Democrats had done nothing for them since 1937 and that they must form a new coalition of their own. "The best thing our confused Democratic President has done," he said, "his support of recommendations of his Civil Rights Committee, is precisely the thing that damns him the worst in his own party—a fact which exposes the terrible inadequacy of that party as the servant of the people." The Socialist platform, largely reflecting his own thinking, stressed the urgency rather than the mere advisability of careful planning and a great national effort for peace. It advocated the permanent liquidation of all colonialism, renewed efforts to reinstate the Baruch Plan, an international police force, access to raw materials by all peoples,* internationalization and demilitarization of strategic waterways, and admittance of at least 40,000 displaced persons under unused immigration quotas from the war years. Thomas's running mate this time was Tucker P. Smith, a forty-eight-year-old Missourian who had served as a union official and was now professor of economics at Olivet College in Michigan. A few weeks later Thomas wrote Krueger to urge that if he ran for Congress, he do so as a Socialist: "If you run as an independent after refusing to run for President, it will be an obvious slap in the face of the Party."

Thomas's nomination was front-page news in The Times and caused a flurry of friendly editorials in newspapers in all parts of the country except the South. Even many editors opposed to Socialism were beginning to recognize his unique role as a highly informed and intelligent political critic and educator, useful beyond party lines. Since newspapers invariably stressed his striking analogies or flashes of wit, he wrote the more important dailies to urge that they give him serious coverage rather than featuring his wisecracks. Sulzberger of The Times candidly admitted the difficulty of allotting space to a candidate "who obviously has no chance of winning," but said The Times would try to do him justice and would print two of his most important speeches in full. Thomas appealed for donations, not forgetting to remind Upton Sinclair

---

*"Access to raw materials by all peoples" was an issue of little interest to raw-material-rich America until the 1973 embargo on Arab oil.

that Lanny Budd should do something for the Party. Professor Coolidge backed him and Thomas hoped to win many others from the Union for Democratic Action (now called Americans for Democratic Action) and from the Democrats. To Alfred Baker Lewis, still clinging to the Democrats, he pointed out "the pernicious effects of Southern racism and reaction in the Democratic Party" and "Truman's complete inadequacy," and added, "I should like to remind you that the well-nigh complete desertion of the Socialist Party in favor of action within the Democratic Party has got mighty poor results." He made no appeal to Niebuhr, though they were not unfriendly, but replied to a question from Daniel Bell about Niebuhr's criticism of utopianism and his definition of politics as a dilemma only solvable by realistic compromise: "The dilemma which you state exists and I have never been able to find a perfect verbal or logical solution of it. Political action always requires compromise and it is difficult to say in advance . . . at just what point compromise becomes betrayal."

Through the enterprising National Secretary Fleischman, Thomas made an arrangement with E. Palmer Hoyt, publisher of The Denver Post, to attend all three major political conventions (Republican, Democratic and Progressive in that order) and write a daily column about them. By now, Thomas was so favorably known, except in the South, that Hoyt was able to syndicate the columns to fourteen important dailies ranging from the Los Angeles Times, Portland Oregonian and San Francisco Chronicle to the St. Louis Post-Dispatch, Indianapolis Star, Trenton Times and Worcester Telegram.

"I want to use whatever I make on the syndicate," Thomas wrote Hoyt, "over and above actual expenses, to advance the [Socialist] campaign . . ." This added some $3,000 to the Party kitty, which totaled only $60,000. Nothing had pleased Thomas so much for years. The born publicist and propagandist had suddenly added a total of three millions in newspaper circulation to his daily audience, a factor that would surely help his vote. It meant that a book on which he had been working for an unparalleled two years would be further delayed, but he joined the Newspaper Guild and fell to, Fleischman working as his legman. All three conventions were at Philadelphia's Convention Hall. Thomas mingled with veterans of the press including Westbrook Pegler, Elmer Davis, Inez Robb and Arthur Krock, and with politicians ranging from the young Hubert H. Humphrey and William O. Douglas to that oddball from out of his past, Henry Wallace, who became officially the nominee of the Progressives. For the friendly, liberal Mayor Humphrey, Thomas conceived an admiration that would become a long friendship because of the Minnesotan's introduction of what Thomas called "the bravest and best resolution on civil rights which any of the major parties had ever offered up to that date." As for Wallace, though Thomas was not one to hold grudges over trifles, he had never forgiven the Iowan for his neglect of the sharecroppers and his slaughter of pigs. He wrote a friend that Wallace's refusal to face situations forthrightly was "fairly illustrated by his conduct when Secretary of Agriculture in refusing even to talk with committees of sharecroppers and their friends, myself included, about the terrible effects of AAA upon their interests."

Thomas agreed with Wallace on a few issues such as his anti-militarism, his concern for the poor of the world ("a quart of milk a day for every Hottentot"), and above all the deep desire for peace with the Soviet Union that caused his break with the Democrats. It was just that Wallace was an innocent who reminded Thomas with embarrassment of his own earlier innocence about the Communists. The first essential in dealing with the Communists was a hard-headed understanding of them. To The Daily Worker, Wallace was now a hero while Thomas, a target for years, was a warmonger. Thomas was amused by the Progressive conventioneers' sensitivity to colors on the red side of the spectrum and their quick shift to the Green Room at the Bellevue-Stratford when a committee had been assigned by some bungler to the Pink Room.

As the campaign wore on, Thomas discovered that the votes of many liberals and even some Socialists would go to Wallace in the hope that this earnest man could bring America and Russia together in peace. Thomas's final run for the Presidency was, as always, simply an effort for a good showing. "A large Socialist vote," he said, "will mean constructive pressure on the likely winners, the pro-capitalist Republicans." He traveled alone, without a press representative, without a secretary, without Violet for the first time in many years. In Baltimore, where he spoke to about 150 people in an International Ladies' Garment Workers' Union hall above a Chinese restaurant, he inspired that scoffer at all politics, H. L. Mencken, to write that it was a pity the crowd was not bigger:

> . . . [They] would have at least enjoyed a rare and exhilarating pleasure, to wit, that of listening to a political speech by a really intelligent and civilized man. . . . [Thomas] poked gentle but devastating fun at all the clowns in the political circus, by no means forgetting himself. There was not a trace of rancor in his speech and not a trace of messianic bombast.

. . . He never starts a sentence that doesn't stop and he never accents the wrong syllable in a word or the wrong word in a sentence. . . . It is not often in this great Republic that one hears a political hullaballoo that is also a work of art.

"I blushed when I read that article . . . ," Thomas wrote Mencken. "Honestly, I regard it as a sort of compensation for campaigning. You are my favorite anarchist. . . ." Thomas also charmed a less famous reporter for The Christian Science Monitor who called on him at Irving Place and found him romping with Jester, tossing a wooden dumbbell which Jester would retrieve and attempt to hold in unilateral imperialist possession. (Jester was now a grandfather, one of his daughters, a gift to the Blanshards, having produced a litter of pups punctually on Mother's Day.) The Monitor man observed of Thomas, "His thinking processes resemble Grand Central Station at rush hour; ideas arrive and depart rapidly and on schedule." Thomas still treasured human foibles —the woman who, after he had spoken in favor of public ownership of natural resources, came up in indignation and said, "Why, that's *Socialistic* talk."

He was forever being reminded that he was growing old, going through political rituals that he had performed since the twenties, recognizing some of the same old dust-laden halls and aging chairmen, meeting politicians such as Wallace, Herbert Hoover and Harold Ickes in their second or third incarnations—discovering even that Dorothy Thompson, once so hostile, had endorsed him and that The Jewish Daily Forward, long vindictive, was this time his supporter. Now he was feted at the Waldorf by the fun-loving Circus Saints and Sinners, among them Jim Farley, whom he had known as an Irish patriot three decades earlier, then less pleasantly as a New Deal wheel, now as an amiable Coca-Cola capitalist. Thomas began his speech, "Friends, if there are any here," described Truman as a candidate who asked his speech writers, "What's it going to be tonight?" and Governor Dewey as a man "clad each day in a pair of platitudes." He rushed away for another meeting, saying he had to "win over some honest voters," emphasizing the adjective and leaving the Sinners in laughter. An old lady of Gramercy Park wrote to him:

> . . . I was walking up Irving Place when I passed an elderly gentleman with a beautiful black dog. I was attracted by both and involuntarily stood and watched them go up the steps of No. 71 . . . The gentleman (I am sure) was Norman Thomas. It is . . . highly probable that when I cast my vote

next Tuesday it will be for the last time. So it seems a serious and important occasion to me. . . . I'm going to vote for . . . a gallant gentleman, the Socialist Norman Thomas.

Although this one was hardly in that category, Thomas occasionally received flirtatious letters from admiring widows. He replied with his usual careful propriety, "This is just a brief note, during very rushed days, to tell you how much I appreciate your letter . . ." Some Socialists thought he might get a half million votes. Thomas knew better, but as always when campaigning he had moments of euphoria, writing to a friend, "We are having the best response since 1936, in many ways since 1932." Alas—when all the votes were counted that the counters bothered to count in the thirty states where Thomas was permitted on the ballot, Thomas got 140,260. It was better than 1944 but not enough better to encourage the Socialists.*

"On election night," Fleischman wrote, "I accompanied Thomas to the studios of the TV networks, where we watched the returns come in. As it became obvious that Truman, despite all expectations, was winning, we realized that the Socialist Party's last hope of creating a new political alignment through a new mass party had gone down the drain. Of far greater importance than the meager Socialist vote was the fact that all the labor and liberal forces which had expressed interest during the campaign in a possible new party immediately jumped back on the Truman bandwagon."

From Salt Lake City, the Japanese-American Citizens' League sent Thomas some prize Utah celery.

From Rome, a radiogram from Angelica: "ADMIRING GRATEFULLY YOUR INDEFATIGABLE WORK FOR PEACE AND SOCIALISM. SEND WARM GREETINGS."

From South Yarmouth on Cape Cod, a hand-written note from Gilkey, now retired: "I have just written in your name on our Massachusetts ballot [that was one of the states ruling the Socialist Party off the printed ballot]—and have reason to believe that Geraldine and Mary Jane [his wife and daughter] have done likewise. . . . I know well enough that you have run only from a sense of party and even more of public duty—but you have had your reward in what has been said about you . . . all the way from the N.Y. Times and the Sat. Eve. Post to E. R.

*Wallace, with a half million to spend, got 1,156,103. Truman was the surprise winner with roughly 24 millions, Dewey getting 21 millions and the Dixiecrat J. Strom Thurmond 1,169,021.

Murrow. I hope you have copies of it all for your grandchildren. They will some day be as proud of you as your old friends are right now!"

And from the elderly sculptor of "The Speaker," riding the Chicago-bound North Shore Limited on election day:

> The returns are not yet coming in & I will not be too greatly interested in the result. . . . Our morons & hypocrites would prefer excitement to education, rather be fooled than reformed. . . . I merely registered my protest when I voted for you before making this train. However, I do want to go on record as having stood by you with more than words & vote & knowing that there must be a deficit connected with the "defeat." But more than anything else the check is a personal tribute to you & a token of my loyalty. . . .
>
> With love and appreciation, Louis

# XVI

## 1. A Continual Pain

When the Stafford Crippses visited New York and lunched with Thomas and a mutual friend, the talk turned to the suicide of John Winant, former United States ambassador to Britain. Lady Cripps remarked that in these tense times one could see why any sensitive man might seek such an escape. Sir Stafford disagreed: "Not Norman or I; we have too much faith in Socialism."

It was all very well for Cripps to say that. He was now Chancellor of the Exchequer in a British government formed by a powerful Socialist party of which the labor unions had become part and parcel. While Thomas was not contemplating anything rash, he could scarcely be cheery about Socialism's influence in America. Here, labor had never warmed up to the Party in good times, and in the dreadful thirties had marched off to the tune of the Pied Piper in the White House, with Hillman leading the betrayal. Thomas, blaming himself in part since he had been unquestioned Party leader for a dozen years, was gloomy enough to write Darlington Hoopes, who was now Party chairman, "It is a continual pain, almost physical with me, to reflect on our failure. . . ." By dint of earnest effort he had restored friendly relations with many Old Guardsmen, James Oneal and William Feigenbaum among them, but had never found real forgiveness in Algernon Lee, Julius Gerber and Louis Waldman. He had pondered the Party's failure. He could not agree with Ibsen's argument against the proposition that since the stupid are in the majority, democracy means the rule of the stupid. Ibsen's answer was that many of the stupid would in their folly vote on the right side.

Thomas had not attracted either the wise or the stupid. He had long

321

since decided that the overwhelming mass of voters did not vote on a basis of reason or principle but in response to one or another of four trivial considerations. There was what he called the Grandpappy Voter who merely aped the loyalty of his ancestors. The Good Man Voter was moved by some real or fancied virtue in the candidate without even knowing his program. The Horse-racing Voter just wanted to vote for the winner. And the "Throw the Rascals Out" Voter had a grudge, often mistaken, against some official believed to have erred. Yes, American voters needed education, and Thomas was convinced that the Socialist Party had better stop running for any but carefully selected offices and devote its main effort to instructing the public.

Thomas unwound after the election by watching Princeton beat Yale at Palmer Stadium, an event that always made him crow at his next sight of Sidney Lovett. While he still thought Truman inadequate, he admired his plucky fight, which he felt had two good results: It discredited the arrogant pollsters and at least showed that the public, for all its folly, had gone against the heavy newspaper sentiment for Dewey. Nineteen forty-eight was a watershed year for Thomas. He would never be a candidate again. (Later, when there was talk of nominating him for Governor, he put it down firmly: "My decision not to run is really definite and reasonable. . . . I should like to nip in the bud any talk of nominating me." He was still a member of the National Executive Committee, whose meetings he attended faithfully and to which he gave his best thought. He remained a loyal lifelong Socialist and continued to address Party meetings free. But he was moving into the wider and freer sphere of the Post War World Council and its various spin-offs, seeking to accomplish there what the Party had failed to accomplish, taking the role of international ombudsman with an influence remarkable for a man never elected to office. His central theme —how to keep the world from self-destruction—was obviously the overriding, all-encompassing issue of the postwar decades. No one worked at it as he did. He started right in with a memo sent to Truman's secretary during the President's absence:

> My . . . deep desire is that the President, perhaps in his Inaugural Address or his Message to Congress, should take in behalf of America a great lead in demanding universal (not unilateral) disarmament under effective international control. Even the demand for it would have immense values for our leadership in democracy. . . .

## 2. *The Chautauqua Voice*

Thomas's secretary, in transcribing his Dictaphone reply to a letter from the Duke of Bedford about disarmament, consulted her style book and decided that the salutation should be "My Lord Duke," and that it should be concluded, "Your Grace's most obedient servant." That was one letter she had to redo, for Thomas, seeing this as he signed the letter, caused it to be changed to "Dear sir" and "Sincerely yours." He flew into a telephone tantrum at his brother Ralph, who asked him to speak free to the prosperous men's club at Ralph's church in Baltimore, the Brown Memorial. He apologized by mail but let Ralph (who had not voted for him since 1936) know the score:

> . . . [If] I were to accept that sort of thing as a custom, I would practically destroy any earning capacity I now have. My [lecture] agent worries about it. It is one thing to speak for the Socialist Party on various causes in which I am interested, for nothing. It is another thing to make a special case of the type of club which has never done anything for any cause in which I am interested. Repeatedly . . . I have found that clubs—not only church clubs—have imposed on me while they pay other people who, if I may say it myself, are by no means as competent. . . .

Though he doubtless derived some satisfaction out of letting Ralph know what he thought of his club, he nevertheless spoke to the men's club at Brown Memorial Church—free. His regular fee now ranged from as little as $50 when he felt sorry for a worthy group, to $350 plus all expenses. The agent of course took 30 percent. If he had few personal financial worries, his enterprises were seldom secure. The Socialist Party was always broke. The Post War World Council, his dearest brainchild, was repeatedly snatched from insolvency by a check from some generous person like Lenore Marshall, or tided over by an infusion of his own cash. In 1949 he kept the Council alive on a budget of a mere $7,600, out of which he paid his office rent, the salary of his valued executive director Madeline Trimmer, that of his part-time secretary and the considerable cost of newsletters. He stayed afloat only because he donated his own energies—hence when PWWC lay gasping and the men's club wanted him to speak free, his annoyance was understandable. He was still deeply interested in the League for Industrial Democracy, which always needed money. The League published occasional pamphlets, which were the special province of the handsome and well-heeled Mrs. Katrina McCormick Barnes. Mrs. Barnes, whose husband was a Republican, had been a Democrat and now described herself as a Socialist fellow traveler, for she had never joined the Party but often befriended it. Since she was also on the American Civil Liberties Union board, Thomas knew her well and was doubly pleased because she not only worked for good causes but contributed to them generously. At that time the ACLU board met at the Hotel Diplomat, where the food was terrible, and Thomas would sometimes meet her on the way out and would say in what she called his Chautauqua voice, "Let's have tea together, that is, provided you have some gossip." His love of gossip—extra-marital affairs, marriages foundering, political shenanigans—was as keen as ever. Unaware as always of the power of his vocal foghorn, he would let diners twenty paces distant know all about items supposedly *entre nous*. She admired his mastery over committees, his ability to define issues and get people down to business on good causes, enjoyed his conversation and thought him "the most charmingly simple and at the same time utterly sophisticated person on earth." Added now to his schedule were monthly lectures on politics at the New School for Social Research, limiting his time for tea. (He had recently written his Socialist friend Gunnar Myrdal, "I have the honor of being one of the sponsors of the dinner given in your honor tonight, but unfortunately I shall not be able to be present," to which Myrdal replied in part, "I wonder very much if we are never going to meet again?") He now had to refuse to read long manuscripts sent him, or to serve as unpaid literary agent. When Margaret De Silver Tresca wrote to ask if she could see him about a personal problem, he replied immediately:

> I find myself in the most curious situation. I literally haven't time for any long talk because of various dates, conferences and so forth before I leave on a trip that will keep me out of town until about the end of March. Is that too late? I could perhaps speak to you very briefly first, but it would be very unsatisfactory. I'm awfully sorry to seem so ungracious. . . .

The fact that Thomas had labored long on the memorial committee for her late husband, and that six months earlier she had refused to donate to the desperate Call, may have been a factor. He opened his house to relatives, the Socialist Party or friends, saying, "I want it used." The Blanshards, who had a place at Thetford Center, Vermont, where Thomas had paid a flying lecture-tour visit to see them and Jester's grandchildren, were his New York guests for a time during which Mary Blanshard worked for him at the Post War World Council. When Thomas's sister Emma got her degree and returned to Baltimore, her place as escort to Jester was taken by Harrison Moyer, a Columbia student planning to do Lutheran church work in India. "I shall be glad to give you room at 71 Irving Place free, with linen, bedding, etc.," Thomas wrote him. "You will be able to make considerable use of the apartment both when I am in New York and when I am away. I get my own breakfast and shall probably be out usually for other meals. . . . In my absence I should ask you to look after mail. . . . Jester and I look forward to your coming." He gave Moyer a dressing-down on one occasion for putting an ad in the paper that kept Thomas's phone ringing, but they occasionally had breakfast together and got along so famously, having long conversations about India, that Moyer later wrote that he would "always cherish the memory."

Thomas's newspaper column during the conventions was successful enough so that The Denver Post continued syndicating it thereafter on a twice-weekly rather than a daily basis and to a smaller group of papers. When Jester died in 1949, the saddened Thomas wrote a touching column about it, "The Death of a Friend," which brought in an avalanche of mail from dog owners such as his political comment did not draw. "I am still getting notes of sympathy," he wrote a fortnight later. ". . . Well, I do like dogs, and I might get more votes as a dog lover than a Socialist." His status as a syndicated columnist increased his leverage with government and United Nations officials over what he had had as plain Norman Thomas. His mail to and from Washington had quadrupled since the 1948 election. Letters by the score poured out of his backstreet office to Dear Hubert, Arthur, Wayne and Foster, as he addressed Senators Humphrey, Vandenberg, Morse and Dulles with arguments for Post War World Council policies. "I confess to getting quite a kick out of writing these columns . . . ," Thomas wrote Palmer Hoyt in Denver. "I appreciate the fact that you are the only man in America who would have thought it worth while to try [me]."

His column bore chiefly on politics, with occasional forays into philosophy or social mores. He did not always conceal his opinion that the Catholic was the most benighted of the various Christian churches, none of which was sufficiently enlightened. If he was resentful of the Babbittry of the Brown Memorial Men's Club and disapproving of Zionism as a collaboration of church and state, he was as perpetually indignant at Franco as he was at Stalin. He was also indignant at the Catholic Church for supporting the brutal Catholic Franco while it assailed the brutal anti-Catholic Stalin. He received a flood of Catholic letters accusing him of bigotry when, on a radio forum, he suggested that the church ought to oppose brutality among its own. He kept it up in letters to the major American newspapers, pointing out the great fuss the Pope made about Cardinal Mindszenty and recommending that he "add weight to his righteous campaign for justice in Hungary by urging standards of justice upon Franco, son of the church." "I cannot accept the theory," he wrote Angelica, "that in order to fight Communism we must shut our eyes to every other evil." Though he liked Father Gannon, Cardinal Spellman was often an affliction to him. The separation of church and state was an absolute article of faith with Thomas. The cardinal's famous attack on Eleanor Roosevelt for her opposition to federal support of parochial schools inspired Thomas to write the soon-to-be Senator Lehman to praise him for his politically courageous public defense of her and to praise Mrs. Roosevelt herself for her measured reply:

> I don't usually bother people with fan letters, but I should like to break my rule and tell you how much I value your reply to Cardinal Spellman and its dignity, sincerity, and the soundness of its argument. You have done us another great service.

He kept a solicitous eye on the English Labor government, which was creaking audibly, and he fenced with The Chicago Tribune and others who joyously exaggerated its failings:

> . . . I think it is outrageous misrepresentation to blame the English difficulties on Socialism. Actually it is Socialism of a democratic sort that is saving the country if it can be saved. The trouble is the English people called the doctor too late. Not a single nation went totalitarian which had first went [*sic*] Socialist. Consider New Zealand and the Scandinavian countries in this connection.

His prescience about Israel was matched by his opposition to American intervention in China, Indonesia and Indochina. Before the Senate Foreign Relations Committee he testified largely in favor of the North Atlantic Pact (which the Socialist Party opposed), insisting that Franco's Spain be excluded. He argued that steps should be taken, through the United Nations if possible, "to make it clear that the pact will not furnish moral or economic aid . . . [for] the wretched colonial wars which have been waged by the Netherlands and France in Indonesia and Indochina. These wars create a situation made to order for racist and Communist exploitation. From Asia may yet come a greater peril to us than from Europe." Though he occasionally missed the mark,

Thomas (as in this instance) seemed to be reading the book of the future, which few but he possessed. By now he was far and away more seasoned and expert at commenting on legislation than most Senators and his influence, while not measurable, cannot have been negligible. Richard Lee Strout, who conducted the "T.R.B." column in The New Republic, listened and was impressed, writing in his telegraphic style:

> Last week we watched Norman Thomas testify for Atlantic Pact before Senate Committee. Democrats, Republicans, treated him respectfully, deferentially. We felt at all times he was master of situation & ablest man in room. What a President he would have made. . . . The bulk of the Norman Thomas–Socialist platform has been adopted over years by New Dealers, gets lip service now even from G.O.P. Victory is so complete even Bob Taft has been called "Socialist" in world where epithet has all but lost its meaning. . . . We brood over Norman Thomas sometimes. Why haven't American Socialists ever got farther as a party? Was it pacifist-isolationist slant of some elements in World War I & II—? Even last week Thomas explained "division of opinion" within his organization forced him to speak for Treaty as an individual. We'd like to offer Norman Thomas access to this cramped but sympathetic column sometime to give his version of why leader so able as he hasn't ever mobilized bigger party.

Well, that was a long story, too long for T.R.B.'s "cramped column." The death of Oswald Garrison Villard at seventy-seven removed an old pacifist colleague, and John Haynes Holmes, another colleague, read the eulogy. Holmes himself was now in semi-retirement at seventy, aided at his new non-sectarian Community Church on Thirty-fifth Street by the young and strapping Reverend Donald S. Harrington, a Socialist admirer of Thomas, who helped make that church a forum for free discussion where Thomas often spoke. Roger Baldwin, only a few months older than Thomas, retired to a less demanding post with the American Civil Liberties Union (and was shocked that it was necessary to pay his successor, Patrick Malin, $13,500 for the job for which Baldwin had refused to accept more than $3,600 a year). Thomas himself felt fine except for a touch of arthritis in one knee and was entering into an expanded career involving considerable foreign travel. He sold 71 Irving Place for $16,000 and got advice from his banker son-in-law John Gates (whose profession he had denigrated) on the investment of that money and the proceeds from other small properties Violet had left him. While he did not feel precisely pinched, he was scarcely easy either because his extravagant need for independence made him resist any sort of help and sometimes filled him with forebodings of extended illness that might ruin him and bring hardship to his children. He built a modest portfolio of capitalist stocks, including Quaker Oats, Consolidated Edison, American Tobacco and Johnson & Johnson, the latter company being as it happened the employer of his son-in-law John Friebely as an executive. These investments brought in about $3,000 a year in interest and dividends, an amount which of course gradually increased. He could easily have earned $40,000 a year as a lecturer if he had set a stiff fee and held to it. This he was temperamentally unable to do because he was chiefly interested in spreading his message and there were too many worthy groups that could not afford more than a nominal fee. What with his high expenses and his give-away talks, his income was modest and there is no telling how much of it went to pay the pressing debts of the Post War World Council and other causes.

He moved to a small one-bedroom apartment at 39-A Gramercy Park, at the northeast corner of the square, from which (though he seldom had time) he could look down on its greenery and see children playing in the fenced enclosure. Now it took him five minutes instead of three to get to his office. For The New York Times Sunday Magazine he wrote an article in praise of dissenters and again sounded The Theme:

> The particular dissent which haunts me day and night is against the notion that peace for my children and grandchildren can be guaranteed by the present race in arms. . . . Already so tied are we Americans to an arms economy that our fantastic military expenditures are even now hailed as a bulwark against depression. A proclamation of universal peace would mean economic panic. [There were, he agreed, no easy answers in Stalin's world.] And yet so afraid are we of dissent from habitual reliance upon arms and yet more arms, so unable are we to match our boldness in physics with boldness in politics, that neither our Government nor people seems willing even to try the effect upon Governments and masses of men of a well-thought-out appeal for the universal end of the armament race, under supervision of the United Nations, with international arrangements for security. . . . We live in a time when certain dissents against mass folly have become an essential condition of the progress if not the very life of mankind.

On his sixty-fifth birthday, November 20, 1949, The Times paid him an editorial tribute:

There are not many men in American public life who command greater esteem or fewer votes than Norman Thomas. . . . The influence which Mr. Thomas has exercised as a Socialist leader is difficult to assess [but much Socialism has found its way into American law]. Today, on his 65th birthday, we extend our congratulations to this great dissenter, who has six times been his party's nominee for the Presidency, and whose sincerity, eloquence, perseverance and faith have earned him an honored place in America's political annals.

"Upon my word," wrote John Haynes Holmes, remembering the twenties and thirties when The Times was ready to suspect that Thomas was subversive, "I never expected to live to see you thus worthily praised in this place."

### 3. A Sophomore Again

As the McCarthy era began, Thomas was too discriminating—and too stricken with ghastly memories of Communist deceit—to fall into the camp of either the pros or the antis. He was critical enough of Roosevelt, convinced enough of the guilt of Alger Hiss and seriously enough opposed to permitting fervent Communists to teach school, to pass these McCarthyite shibboleths. He placed more credence in Louis Budenz than later appeared prudent. But he battled the House Un-American Activities Committee, Mundt-Nixon, the McCarran bill and the China Lobby with the zeal of an anti. His admiration for Eleanor Roosevelt would have outraged any McCarthyite. He had only contempt for McCarthy himself as the crude and ruthless exploiter of an issue that was indeed real and deserved serious consideration. There were not Communists under every bed, but some under some beds. He drew a sharp distinction between those who (like himself) had once had faith in the Soviet experiment and hence had been friendly with American Communists, and those who still humored the Kremlin in 1950. He was alarmed, for example, by what he regarded as Corliss Lamont's tendency to put the kindliest construction on what Thomas saw as Soviet horrors. Yet he worked so fairly with Lamont, who was also one of the members of the American Civil Liberties Union board, on a resolution concerning Communism, that Lamont wrote him that it was a "pleasure" to collaborate with him. On other occasions he and Lamont would come near to quarreling.

Some who had been fire-breathing young members of the Socialist Party in the hungry thirties were now middle-aged and portly Democratic government bureaucrats being investigated and questioned about former associates and about rash things they had once said. Thomas received numerous letters from the Federal Bureau of Investigation or other investigative bodies inquiring about their true-blueness. He was impatient about these suspicions of good men who once may have grown a trifle excited and he devised virtually a form-letter reply not only giving a ringing defense but attacking the nature of the investigation: "Finally, I desire . . . emphatically to protest against the kind of loyalty proceedings which led to charges against Mr. ———."

He was surely alone in combining such a painful knowledge of Communist falsehood with such a determined campaign for universal disarmament under international control which he admitted Russia would not immediately permit. He had put exhaustive thought into a true world federation and knew its problems were so gigantic that it would take years to perfect—years during which there was hope of Stalin's passing and new wisdom in the Kremlin. During this interim period it was essential to slow the arms race lest world government come second to world destruction. Thomas, working as if he were a minister without portfolio, meanwhile pulled what strings he could to save distant countries from falling into the Soviet orbit. Yet he had given up on Chiang Kai-shek almost from the beginning and commended General Marshall as "emphatically right in his judgment of Chiang." He had opposed American interference in China and, he wrote the persistent Alfred Kohlberg, "I do not want to repeat the performance in Indochina." He actually supported for a time the Vietnam-American Friendship Association, an arm of the Ho Chi Minh government, against the renewed French colonialization evidenced by the installation of the puppet Bao Dai, who was heralded by the Lucepress, Cardinal Spellman and the China Lobby. Some members of the India League felt that Thomas, with his friendship with Cripps and other British Socialists, had had some magic influence in the freeing of India. He had in any case worked hard for it. On January 26, 1950, when the last English apron-string was broken and India's independence as a republic became official, Thomas was the principal speaker at a celebration held at Community Church and attended by J. J. Singh and other Indians, some ready to represent the new nation in the United Nations. This was a celebration of deep significance for Thomas. He assumed rather than hoped that India, with its American-style constitution and the sizeable sprinkling of Socialists

330

among its leaders, would be a bulwark of freedom—more specifically, a stronghold against Communism. He did not believe that American imperialists could impose Chiang Kai-shek on China or that French imperialists could impose Bao Dai on Vietnam. Those two countries must be permitted to settle their own problems of nationhood. India *had* settled hers, with the enlightened aid of a Socialist British government—a combination to his mind nothing short of glorious. A little homily he penned in a letter to Everett R. Clinchy breathed his loathing for Stalin's Communism:

> Without some notion of brotherhood, civilization, indeed the very life of the race, would have been impossible. But, through the ages, the idea of brotherhood has generally been restricted to members of the same family, tribe, nation or race, or to believers in the same religious or political creed. There always will be a particular sense of fellowship resting upon common loyalties. But today the peace, and certainly the happiness, of the world requires a larger and more inclusive sense of brotherhood for all the sons and daughters of earth. . . . This brotherhood must take account of the existence of important differences of opinion. Its emphasis must not lie on imposed unity of thought, but on a common abhorrence of cruelty, oppression, and everything that would reduce human life to the status of a commodity and man himself to the level of a thing.

Thomas was well launched on his career of indignation against and enlightenment of those so ignorant as to confuse Socialism and Communism, when in fact Socialists were the most seasoned and knowledgeable of all opponents of Stalin's perversion of Communism. Such wisecracks as "A Communist is a Socialist in a hurry" set him by the ears. He was aroused by a speech by Congressman Franklin D. Roosevelt, Jr., whom he had considered the late President's most promising son, in which Roosevelt said, "As a Democrat, I hate Socialism just as much as I hate Communism or Fascism or any other ism." Thomas reminded him that many Socialists had voted for him on the Liberal Party ticket* and he had not mentioned this when he needed their votes: "It would logically follow that you hate Attlee and the Labor government as much as you hate Stalin and the Communist government. That's outdoing Winston Churchill himself." Thomas agreed to give the baccalaureate

---

*The Liberal Party had been organized in New York in 1944 by dissident members of the American Labor Party who opposed totalitarianism and favored a strong United Nations. It often backed "reform" Democrats.

at Bloomsburg State College, near the well-remembered Lewisburg, Pennsylvania, but Ivan Boxell, publisher of the nearby Danville News, editorialized against this invitation to a man "who would dislodge the American way of life." Bloomsburg, in immediate fear, canceled Thomas's appearance, though paying his $250 fee, and he speculated about the timidity of teachers' colleges in general and the unlikelihood of independent thought coming from graduates of such places: "They train second-class citizens, an order of scared rabbits." When Dr. Elmer Henderson, president of the American Medical Association, fearful of socialized medicine, declared Socialism and Communism to be the same except that Socialism was only a little slower in making "human liberty and dignity die," Thomas wondered if Henderson "wants to make the ridiculous claim that Britain's program of seeing that every one of her children gets adequate medical care is a blow at human liberty and dignity." For almost a year Thomas battled with Commissioner Watson D. Miller of the Immigration and Naturalization Service because the service used as its official citizenship "instruction book" a thick manual published by the Daughters of the American Revolution. The manual, as reactionary as its sponsor, warned candidates for citizenship that Socialism and Communism should be equally shunned. Miller backed down when Thomas got the American Civil Liberties Union on his trail and thereafter the service used its own more objective manual.

At the Socialist Party convention held in Detroit in June, 1950, Thomas delivered the keynote address to 150 delegates representing a national membership of fewer than 3,000. For the world he urged controlled disarmament. To the Party he declared that running candidates for the Presidency was "breaking our backs" and recommended a new policy emphasizing a Party role as an educator in Socialism and the nomination of candidates only where they had a fighting chance. The quiet Quaker Hoopes was one of those who opposed the idea. There may have been a feeling that Thomas, after losing six times running, ought to give someone else a chance to lose, but there were also those who rebelled at the consequent necessity to vote for capitalist candidates. The convention made the New York Times front page because of an astonishing headline: "SOCIALISTS REJECT THOMAS PROGRAM." His power was further clipped the following day in the election of a National Executive Committee in which for the first time in almost two decades he was part of a minority. Among the tributes paid him was a resolution affirming faith in him as "the spokesman of

American Socialism," but the defeat vexed him and he thought the decision to run candidates hopelessly was a grave error. He was the Party's spokesman, to be sure, but he was much more than that—its only personage of national prominence, without whom the Party would likely dry up and blow away. His close ally, Fleischman, resigned as national secretary after eight years in the post. He was succeeded by a dark-eyed and determined young lady, Robin Meyers, who was taking a master's degree in history at Columbia.

Thomas returned in time for the forty-fifth reunion of his Princeton class of 1905. He was one of the few strictly sober persons in the crowd. Some of his classmates, much as they liked him, rather wished he would skip *this* celebration because he tended to put a check on their essential commemorative bibulousness, for they could not bear to look silly before his smiling austerity. He took this philosophically, musing, "I may regret that, on the whole, reunions are too greatly inspired by the prayer: 'Make me a sophomore again just for tonight,' which prayer, with the aid of a sometimes excessive consumption of the spirituous . . . often seems to be granted. Nevertheless, I have known other times at reunions and have enjoyed a very valuable renewal of old friendships."

### 4. The Speaker Speechless

A few days later, Katrina Barnes walked into Thomas's office at 112 to see him raise his head from his hands. "Tears were streaming down his face," she recalled. It had just been discovered that his son Evan had multiple sclerosis. If it followed its usual course Evan, who was only thirty and had two small children, might be incapacitated within a year or two.* He had become an editor at Harper's on returning from the navy and his swift rise there had been a matter of pride to his father. Thomas immediately canceled a speaking trip he had planned to Seattle-Portland on the ground of expense, believing that it might be necessary for him to help out financially. "As long as he can work," he wrote a Seattle friend about Evan, "things will be all right. But I don't want to put myself in a position where the most I could do for the family is to keep from being a burden on them."

Since he now had a New York apartment too small for any entertain-

---

*It developed that Evan had a long and unusual remission.

ing, he had recently joined the bookish Coffee House Club on West Forty-fifth Street where friends, including Professor Irwin Edman and August Heckscher, were members, and he occasionally invited members of his family there. Strangely, though his arms were wide open to his grandchildren, he had been less successful in establishing easy intimacy with his own children in their adulthood. Those he saw most often were Frances Gates, with whom he lived when in Cold Spring Harbor, and Evan. Both were persons of unusual intelligence, ability and independence of mind. Frances, however, had of all the children been most sympathetic with Thomas's Socialism and continued to be. Evan had grown doubtful of Socialism's feasibility and become at least a nominal Democrat. He resented having been sent away to school at eight, several years earlier than the other children. The argument that the parade of family infections was responsible had not impressed him. He blamed his father's insistence on running for President and saving the world. For a brief time after the war, when housing was scarce, Evan and his wife had lived with his parents, and father and son had sometimes clashed on political or intellectual matters. Here, Evan was up against one of the most gifted of all debaters, who had given thought to all the issues, had handled hundreds of hecklers in his day and could pick apart any argument that was not firmly based—possibly even one that was. Thomas tended to win these discussions with the immemorial certitude of parents. The only argument Evan could remember that he ever won concerned his criticism of his father's approving review of a book highly critical of Roosevelt. After a long talk, his father had astonished him by saying, "You're right and I'm wrong." Obviously, it would have been endearing if he could have said that more often. Evan as a talented editor also disapproved of his father's habit of dashing off books, dictating them into a recorder with little or no revision. He recognized his father's literary gift, told him that he should spend serious effort on revision, but went largely unheeded.

Thomas's failure to give due weight to his son's arguments was all the more remarkable because in public debates he was known for his fairness toward opponents, and in his own Socialist circles he would listen to arguments pro and con. He was a good listener in his own line of work —that is to say, in a committee, a National Executive Committee meeting, an alumni group, a Congressional or a United Nations inquiry. At times he was less so with his own family. When his sister Emma lived with him—always admiring, voting for him every time he ran for President (as did Agnes), but feeling his constraint, seeing him use his dog as a conversational icebreaker—she felt that his flow of language, once started, was hard to stop. Fenner Brockway had noted that Thomas in private conversation often seemed to be making a speech. One is reminded also of Louis Mayer's declamatory sculpture and Thomas's sensitivity about it. Harry Fleischman, on the contrary, found Thomas attentive, never breaking in except when he anticipated one's thoughts, which, with his quick mind, he sometimes did. Anticipated thoughts can be wearing on the one whose thoughts are anticipated, but Fleischman was a lifelong admirer. J. J. Singh found Thomas in conversation admirable, to the point, wasting no time on small talk, though he would lighten heavy discussions with flashes of wit.

Thomas mentioned that as a boy he often talked too much to hide his shyness. Possibly the trait persisted, and the tendency toward monologue included at times a tendency toward positiveness. Yet, despite his years of public speaking and his enjoyment of it, he still admitted nervousness about the next speech. His strong sense of family privacy caused him to tell his secretary to destroy all his family letters, while all the rest concerning the Socialist Party and his other affairs were deposited in the New York Public Library at the library's request. (He continued to throw away the original manuscripts of his books and articles, thinking them worthless, until 1957 when the Princeton librarian asked for them.) If his children occasionally had to humor his foibles, familial love was strong on both sides. At the Thomas family gatherings, his deep laughter was frequent and he was part of a stimulating conversation which everyone joined and enjoyed.

John Gates, who had had to live down his profession as banker, was a political liberal and on good terms with his father-in-law, though at times he too suffered from Thomas's certitude. The other three Thomas children, all living at some distance, saw him less often. Thomas stopped in with the Millers in Kansas when touring, and the Millers and their three children visited the Gateses and their three children during this summer of 1950, to Thomas's great delight. In the fall, Thomas spent a day with his son William and family at Rumson—an occasion when the fourth of William's children was baptized by that admired link with the family past, Sidney Lovett, in a ceremony filled with memories of Violet.

## 5. *The Acheson Axe*

"I suggest, at least for discussion," Thomas wrote shortly after the beginning of the Korean War, "a proposal by the U.S. to recognize the Communist Government of China which undoubtedly controls the mainland, on condition that this government will loyally cooperate in the United Nations and prove it by appropriate action in regard to Korea. We might also consider the advisability of urging a popular plebiscite in Formosa under the United Nations to determine its ultimate fate."

These proposals, so abhorrent to the China Lobby, indicated his readiness to give Mao a chance to show he was better than Stalin. They were withdrawn when the Communist forces drove south and Korea exploded into full-scale war. Though describing himself as "crushed" by this new struggle, Thomas wrote, "On the whole, I think it is better to back the U.N. against this aggression than to have permitted it to go unchallenged. That would have certainly invited ultimate world war."

Unhappy though he was that Communists ruled China, their control was obvious and had to be granted, just as did the corruption and failure of Chiang. "This organization [the Post War World Council] and I personally," Thomas declared, "have consistently opposed the Time-Life policy of building up Chiang Kai-shek." His opposition to the similar buildup of Bao Dai in Vietnam continued, but as it now appeared that Ho Chi Minh was a dedicated Communist and that native sentiment was not unanimous in his favor, he dropped Ho and awaited further light. But still, like the theme in Beethoven's Fifth, came his repeated efforts for universal controlled disarmament. The Cold War had reached a level of endless debaters' points and ploys. To his Cold Spring Harbor friend John Foster Dulles, now Ambassador at Large, he wrote:

> You have heard me more than once expound my belief that the immediate position of America in the minds of the people of the world would be enormously improved by a bold and imaginative type of peace propaganda which has heretofore been absent from our diplomacy.

Dulles's reply indicated that he missed the point entirely and was thinking in terms of the very offensive and defensive ploys Thomas hoped to escape. The same day, Thomas tried Secretary Acheson for at least the second time, using the identical phrase "bold and imaginative type of peace propaganda" and continuing:

> Any hope of peace requires transfer of conflict from the realm of war. And that means universal and enforceable disarmament under a strengthened United Nations, with provision for its own police force. Only with disarmament would it be possible for us Americans to do the other thing absolutely necessary, which is to present a practicable plan for a cooperative war, under United Nations direction, against the world's desperate poverty. It could be easily financed out of what the world would save on arms. Hence, we of this organization [the Post War World Council] believe that an official American spokesman, preferably the President himself, should go before the Assembly of the United Nations to offer this way of escape from war and to assure the peoples of the world of American eagerness to participate in a conference to implement this program.

Acheson thought this utopian. "My constant appeal to American liberals," he later observed, "was to face the long, hard years and not to distract us with the offer of short cuts and easy solutions begotten by good will out of the angels of man's better nature." Later, after Thomas's friend Senator Brian McMahon made a disarmament speech in the Senate, he and his wife went to a diplomatic reception. When they reached Acheson, the Secretary said to his own wife, "My dear, I want you to meet the most beautiful woman in Washington, but as for her husband, I could hit him over the head with an axe." On August 25, Thomas called on President Truman to praise him for opposing a bill for a $62-million loan to Spain. He had come around to a greater appreciation of the President for whom at first he had felt something close to scorn, and Truman's cordiality did no harm. While there, Thomas urged the peace drive on him as he had to Dulles and Acheson. Three days later, in a note of thanks to Truman, he repeated The Theme in more detail:

> Since I knew you had another appointment, I did not take time to urge that if you appeal for disarmament you make the appeal very specific. We [the Post War World Council] don't mean reduction in arms; we mean prohibition of weapons of mass destruction under effective and continued inspection; the universal end of peacetime military conscription; the reduction of all armies to a police level to preserve internal order; and the

creation of an international police force under a strengthened United Nations.

Two months later he was at it again, writing the President: "Your able speech in San Francisco emboldens me once more to raise the question of your pleading for universal and enforceable disarmament under a strengthened United Nations when you address the Assembly of the United Nations on October 24. Your letter of September 28 heartened me by saying that you are still considering this matter."

Lo and behold, Truman at the United Nations did speak, if not with quite the force, eloquence and detail Thomas might have wished, for effective disarmament. Thomas wired his appreciation. Tucker Smith wrote Thomas, "It looks as though your visit with the President must have done some good." Hugh Sheehan wrote him, "Congratulations on the President's speech at Lake Success!" But it was a one-day "PRESIDENT URGES WORLD PEACE" splash. At that very time, General MacArthur's disastrous dash to the Yalu took over the headlines, and peace was not the subject of the general's confusing dispatches. The President and the world were immediately enveloped by problems of greater war instead of an effort for peace which must be as energetic and concerted as that for war. The dove—if it had ever taken wing— was shot down in Korea.

### 6. This Mad World

When Angelica Balabanoff arrived again from Italy on the Vulcania, she was held incommunicado for three days at Ellis Island. This was due to the McCarran Act, which required official suspicion of anyone once a Communist, though Angelica decades earlier had renounced Communism and become one of its most ardent enemies. She was exhausted when Thomas finally managed to free her and send her to the home of a friend. She found a cheap apartment on West Seventy-seventh Street —she had a remnant of a fund raised in New York for her work in Italy —and Thomas set about to help her reestablish herself.

"Dearest Comrade Thomas," she wrote, "I have no words to thank you for your trying to have my article published. It goes without saying that I have no objection to its being revised, corrected and if necessary, abbreviated." At Harper's, The Atlantic and The Reporter, Thomas tried to land articles she wrote, in at least one instance doing considerable revision himself. To Edward Weeks at The Atlantic he wrote, "I have before me now a piece in which [Angelica] discusses Malik against the background of really Bolshevik practice. Would you like to see it . . . ? I repeat, one of your editors would have to give it a little more attention than some articles." To a group to whom Angelica was to lecture, he urged that they pay her more than expenses because "her sources of revenue are few." Through his efforts and those of others it seemed as if she made ends meet, although one could never be sure about her, and she was the Socialist Party's honored guest at the Debs Day dinner at the Henry Hudson Hotel—one occasion at least on which she ate well.

Thomas protested to Attorney General McGrath and to President Truman himself about the "absurd and dangerous McCarran Act," which the American Civil Liberties Union was fighting. He also made a discreet but vain effort to achieve the removal of the jowly Vermonter, Warren Austin, as ambassador to the United Nations. He had often seen Austin in action and thought him terrible, though in a letter to Truman he stressed that the "intolerable strain" Austin had been working under might have induced a manner that "tends to alienate some of our potential friends." That was a job Thomas would have dearly loved himself and could in all probability have held with distinction, but of course he had no chance. He wanted it held by the most qualified person available, and in any case (whether he knew it or not) was serving the nation more importantly in his own unique role. He also kept a benevolent if critical eye on the Voice of America, a propaganda arm which he hoped would project an honest and attractive (he did not think the adjectives irreconcilable) image of the nation to the world. As a skilled propagandist himself, he gave the benefit of his advice to Foy Kohler, who headed the operation, spoke over the Voice repeatedly, urged J. J. Singh to speak to India and Upton Sinclair to address Britain, and helped Harry Fleischman land a job at the Voice of America.

When Earl Browder was indicted along with other Communists, Thomas was incensed to see the Communist Party put up bail for the others while leaving the cast-off leader in jail. He offered through an intermediary to provide bond for Browder. A few months earlier, Browder had written his opinion of Thomas to Professor Robert J. Alexander as a nabob who enjoyed going slumming among the poor. Now he wrote Thomas gratefully to say that another friend had supplied bond. Thomas replied in his coldest of letters:

You are entitled to know what I did and why. I thought it grossly unfair that all those indicted with you for contempt arising out of your refusal to answer certain questions should have been bailed out, some of them by the Communist Party or Communist front organizations or members, while you remained in. I thought that those of us who really believe in civil liberty had a chance to show up this kind of hypocrisy and, in so doing, we would perform a public service.

I am, as you know, vehemently opposed to the Communism you support, in spite of the treatment you have had from the American party. . . . But I thought you were entitled to a day in court and to an opportunity to prepare your defense.

In using the phrase "those of us who really believe in civil liberty," he meant that Browder did not. He was at the same time concerned over the strange case of the elderly Aaron Cohn, whom he had known for years as a kindly and reputable merchant having ever more difficulty in supporting his ailing wife and family. Enraged by what he considered the unfair competition of a large chain, he had begun writing legally libelous letters to its executives. Thomas, though understanding the resentment of a neighborhood storekeeper against a powerful corporation, had several times, as he put it, "tried to moderate Mr. Cohn's increasingly excited methods of speech and writing." Cohn had spent a session in a mental institution and now again he was in the hospital under observation while attorneys were considering charges against him. Thomas went to the hospital and talked with Cohn and also with the psychiatrist who had examined him. He wrote one of the plaintiff's attorneys:

As I understand the psychiatrist's findings, Mr. [Cohn] is in no way dangerous. It occurs to me that it would be possible for us, with the addition perhaps of some of his relatives, to persuade him to stop writing and mailing defamatory letters. . . . He gave me a sort of promise to stop writing this type of letter . . . I cannot guarantee either the time or the money to act as his guardian, but I could guarantee to give some time and attention to helping him keep [his promise].

This he later did, and gave Cohn $10 to tide him over when his social security payment was held up. Meanwhile he acknowledged Angelica's holiday card, not having sent any himself because it was Violet who had always attended to that:

I am one of the many to whom your life and your courage are treasures for every year. Will you forgive me if I ask a question about money? Has

that fund which you have earned a thousand times over been exhausted?
How do your plans stand on a return to Italy? With all good wishes for the
best possible year in this mad world, believe me, fraternally yours. . . .

### 7. What's More Than Truth?

Thomas had missed the June meeting in West Berlin of a flock of
anti-Communist intellectuals from twenty-one countries—a gathering
that would have profound consequences for him and others. It seemed
quite innocent and well-intentioned, being sponsored by Americans
including Mrs. Roosevelt, Walter Reuther and Upton Sinclair, and by
Europeans including G. A. Borgese, Suzanne Labin and Dr. Hans Thir-
ring. Arthur Koestler was one of the prominent ex-Communist delegates who insisted that neutrality between Communism and the "free
world" actually meant siding with the Communists. The five-day meeting resulted in the founding of an international anti-Communist organization called the Congress of Cultural Freedom, cultural freedom being
what anti-Communists had and Communists had not. The Congress
opened an office in Paris headed by Nicolas Nabokov. Its Cold-War
purpose was to spread cultural freedom in opposition to the Communist
spread of false propaganda. Among its honorary chairmen were such
noted people as John Dewey, Salvador de Madariaga, Benedetto Croce,
Bertrand Russell and Karl Jaspers.

The chances are that Thomas read about the meeting, which was
covered by The New York Times. He may also have heard directly
about it from two of his friends active in it, James Farrell and Sidney
Hook. In any case, an American affiliate was soon formed, the American
Committee for Cultural Freedom, with an office on East Forty-fourth
Street. Professor Hook was the American chairman, and vice chairmen
included Reinhold Niebuhr, Roger Baldwin, Arthur Schlesinger, Jr.,
Daniel Bell and James Burnham. Schlesinger wrote Thomas, giving
information about the organization and inviting him to join. "I shall be
delighted to become a member of the American Committee," Thomas
replied. "What are your dues going to be?"

Before long, Thomas was listed on the Committee's stationery as a
vice chairman. He was aware of his weakness for joining too many
organizations, and at times he performed a ritual of self-reproach for
being unable to give some of them sustained attention. But the committee was his element, his native heath, the place where, as one who could
not be elected to office, he could exert influence, work together with

341

other people of similar beliefs and get things done. He joined no committees frivolously. He was so active and skilful a parliamentarian and so eloquent in presenting arguments that he could often swing more weight in a committee by appearing only during its infrequent crises in policy than could others who attended every meeting. The committees and organizations to which he belonged at this time, in addition to the Socialist Party itself and its National Executive Committee, its Public Affairs Committee and its Call Association, included the Post War World Council, the League for Industrial Democracy, the American Civil Liberties Union, the India League of America, Town Hall and its board of trustees, the Citizens' Committee for United Nations Reform, the Inter-American Association for Democracy and Freedom, the National Sharecroppers' Fund, the National Association for the Advancement of Colored People, the International League for the Rights of Man, the American Committee on Africa, the Coordinating Council of the Fifteenth Precinct, the American Association for a Democratic Germany, the Newspaper Guild, the International Rescue Committee and the Workers' Defense League. There were undoubtedly more.

Especially in his capacity as propagandist for disarmament in the face of Soviet refusal to permit inspection, Thomas saw the international promotion of cultural freedom as one honest and effective way to bring world pressure against Russia. But he deplored the cultural implications of the opinions of C. D. Jackson, publisher of Luce's Fortune magazine, given at a subsequent Princeton panel discussion of propaganda. Jackson, a Princetonian of a vintage almost a generation later than Thomas, had been Eisenhower's psychological warfare chief in the war and was regarded as an expert in the field. Jackson said bluntly that truth was not enough in propaganda and that the skilled purveyor must not shrink from manipulating or "bending" the truth.* Thomas of course had criticized the Lucepress manipulation of news. He did not believe the answer was to emulate Russian tactics. He wrote The Princeton Alumni Weekly in reply:

> I protest most vigorously C. D. Jackson's remarks that we "need more
> than truth," that "truth must be bent," and that there should be no

---

*Henry R. Luce, the boss of Jackson and of Time, Life and Fortune, a superpatriot with little humor, believed it the duty of his publications to manipulate the news in what he conceived to be the national interest. He was so upset at the "loss of China" that in an impassioned speech to his staff he denounced objectivity in newswriting as "phony" and as having been in part responsible for the loss. He defended the past use of "value judgments" in his publications and demanded more in the future.

Marquis of Queensberry rules in propaganda. What's more than the truth? A lie? What sort of university is it that would be devoted to more than the truth? And what sort of propaganda for democracy is it which seeks to rival Nazism or Communism in the use of the lie, big or little?

Mr. Jackson is head of a committee which I thought might have more faith in propaganda as the voice of the people rather than of government. Imagine the effect if, after that committee has told the truth about slave labor behind the Iron Curtain, a Communist or fellow traveler can instantly comment: "You have just listened to a report by a committee headed by a man who says that the truth must be bent in order to win and that there are no Marquis of Queensberry rules in propaganda." . . . I would like to see the University make it clear that the bending of truth is no part of its philosophy. The proper presentation of the truth is another matter.

Thomas enclosed a copy of that letter in one to his friend Allen Dulles (Princeton 1914), Foster's younger brother, both of them sons of the Presbyterian divine who had once offered Thomas an assistantship. Allen had been an Office of Strategic Services executive during the war and was now about to enter upon his career in the Central Intelligence Agency, which he was to head within two years. In his reply he was more frank than his older brother, who had earlier written Thomas that the United States must never descend to the Soviet practice of justifying any means to gain an end. Allen Dulles said that of course propaganda attributable to the United States government must be truthful. But he had no qualms about bending and breaking the truth in the inner struggle against Russia, where he said effective lying which could not be traced to the administration was essential.

This was one solution to the terrible problem posed by the Russian and international Communist use of institutionalized falsehood—a problem that had to be countered in the most effective way by United States policy. Indeed the Central Intelligence Agency had already been in existence for three years and was well embarked, though secretly, on a policy of falsehood not only against enemies but against loyal Americans, among them Thomas himself.

Spymasters such as Allen Dulles would doubtless have considered Thomas naive in his belief in truth, his confidence that truth crushed to earth would indeed rise again and that even in Russia, once Stalin was gone, truth would begin fighting its way back. But the supposition that the nation's representatives could, as Dulles suggested, lie only when they would not get caught, and *not* get caught, was perhaps as naive.

Human nature being what it was, the "successful" lie would be likely to be used closer and closer to the edge of discovery until it slipped over and was exposed to the world. American policy in propaganda would come to assume extra importance because the ethics of the secret propagandists would influence the ethics of the administration, and lying abroad would facilitate lying at home. A factor that perhaps was not given due weight was the great advantage afforded the Soviet use of falsehood in a Russian society with no history of freedom and no illusions to lose. In America, popular government conducted in honesty was a tradition, an article of faith. The damage to public confidence and hence to the fabric of democracy if this tradition was exposed as a sham could be grave. Thomas was familiar with Justice Brandeis's warning against official dishonesty: ". . . [Our] government is the potent, the omnipresent teacher. For good or for ill, it teaches the whole people by its example."

It seems unlikely that Thomas would have permitted Dulles's letter to go unchallenged had he not been terribly pressed, having another date to see the President and then being scheduled to leave for India in March. Truman seemed impressed by Thomas's engaging personality. His relations with the President were so cordial that he sought to expand his influence with him and use it for peace. His talk with the President on February 28, 1951, was again on the subject of foolproof disarmament, Thomas's hope that the campaign for it could be made more insistent and dramatic and could be put on the agenda of any Big Four meetings that might occur. "Truman very sincerely desires peace and disarmament," he observed, but he knew that the administration's effort for it lacked imagination and the vital spark of urgency. The very day after seeing Truman, he pressed that point diplomatically in his note of thanks. The day after that he begged the President's pardon for addressing him again, this time urging that the administration spell out its faith in peace and international fair play in a carefully written national credo which could be spread by the Voice of America and other outlets (including Thomas himself). Truman replied from Key West with the warmth of a man who did not mind at all getting good ideas from a politician who had never held office, and actually invited more.

## 8. Visiting Nehru

"When the Korean War emphasized America's second failure to win peace by military victory in total war," Thomas reflected, "I found myself repeatedly recalling Dante's famous lines: 'There is no greater sorrow than to remember a happy time in misery.' For me, the happy time was the years of my faith in certain progress, the misery my present doubt whether right can ever achieve its own appropriate might so that man and his civilization may endure."

Although no one knew it—Thomas would later pour it out in a confessional private letter to Tucker Smith—he was also troubled because his faith in all-out Socialism was slipping. This was partly because of what had happened in Russia and his fear (a fear felt by many others even including Max Eastman) that massive collectivism and its inevitable bureaucracy might kill individual freedom despite all good intentions. His changed beliefs were evident in his first book in four years, *A Socialist's Faith,* in which his already curtailed formula for Socialism in power had been revised still further. Private ownership was permitted a larger sphere, nationalization being limited mostly to the "commanding heights" of the economy. He thought capitalism to be dying but far from dead, he cited the Soviet Union as a warning against complete collectivization, and with his usual candor he admitted that "there are men with a deep-seated desire to work for themselves," and that "the working class is not the Messiah which some of us thought." He had mellowed in his view of the Roosevelt administration, but his assessment of recent times was bleak: "In general, with the single and important exception of the growth of a better conscience on race relations, the years through which I have lived have been years of moral retrogression."

Thomas had been selected as one of the delegates of the American Committee to help install the new Indian chapter of the Congress for Cultural Freedom in Bombay and New Delhi. Before leaving, he wrote to his children, saying that he did not expect to die while away (he was sixty-six) but wanted to make prudent provision for the off chance:

In the event of my death abroad, I want no nonsense and expense about bringing my body back to America . . . Preferably I should like to be cremated where I die. . . . If I should die where it would be practical I

345

should like a hospital to be permitted use of my body or any part of it which might be helpful to medical science or to some individual. I wish my remains to be cremated, not buried, and the ashes scattered much as we did for your mother. If at all possible, keep the funeral private and have a memorial service. You know my feeling about funerals. If Sid Lovett is alive and available, ask him to do as he did for us when Mom died. . . . When I get back I will try to find time to get as many of you as possible together at the Coffee House Club to make up for what will probably be my lax correspondence as I will be traveling rather fast and furiously.

He took off by Trans World Airlines March 17, 1951, for Bombay, leaving his Post War World Council office in the charge of a new secretary, Stephen Siteman, a former officer of the Socialist Party in Newark. His book was receiving generally friendly reviews. He felt the need of whatever prestige he could gather. Though India's Socialist Party was a poor second to Nehru's huge Congress Party, it was almost twice as big as the Communist Party—so big, in fact, numbering some twelve million voters, that Thomas felt humiliated as the leader of a party whose membership was measured in still fewer thousands. Among his fellow American delegates were Louis Fischer, James Burnham and Dr. Max Yergan, a black educator; among the Europeans were Salvador de Madariaga, Ignazio Silone, Stephen Spender and Denis de Rougemont. Arriving in India, Thomas was struck by Madariaga's excoriation of Franco and his opinion that Stalin was if anything worse.

The Lord Mayor of Bombay gave them a reception at which he boasted that his city contained ten language groups, each numbering more than 100,000. Thomas was billeted at the home of a kindly Socialist, Purshottam Trikamdas, where he made friends with the family including the little daughter. He became friendly with Asoka Mehta, secretary of the Bombay Socialist Party, and the Socialist Minoo Masani, an English-educated lawyer who had been Mayor of Bombay and was now a member of the Indian Parliament. But Thomas was discouraged by the pervasive Indian pessimism as well as by the policy of strict neutrality toward Soviet Russia and the "free world" which India was expected to embrace. At a Rotary Club he addressed, an elderly gentleman told him, "At any rate you didn't tell us that India was the hope of the world. We can't even feed ourselves, and where is there hope in that?" Similar remarks he heard were "We Indians lack character; the English at least had character," and "Gandhi is dead and he has no

346

successor." There were even some who said that only ruthless Communism could discipline the country into improvement. There was also a suspicion of America as the nation of militarism which had bombed Hiroshima and Nagasaki, General MacArthur seeming a personification of Mars—a man who loved to bomb Asians and who seemed more powerful than his own government. When Thomas spoke at Lahore (which he had visited forty-three years earlier with the Reverend Bates and Ted Savage) he was heckled by listeners who insisted that the American bombing in Korea was indiscriminate. He had never thought so before, but now he began to wonder.

It had been planned that some of the meetings would be held in New Delhi, but these were scratched because, the neutralist government said, a pro-Communist congress had been turned away and it would be wrong to admit an anti-Communist gathering. Some Indians boycotted the congress as a United States propaganda device. Jaya Prakash Narayan, the Wisconsin-educated Socialist leader, said talk of cultural freedom seemed frivolous among the hungry. When Denis de Rougemont likened Indian neutrality to "that of the lamb that is neutral between the wolf and the shepherd," an Indian delegate thought the choice unhappy either way, since the shepherd "shears the lamb and possibly eats it"—a remark some of the earnest Westerners thought in execrable taste. In New Delhi, Thomas picked up titillating rumors about Nehru's alleged affair with a high-born English lady which he later related to Clarence Senior and Mrs. Barnes. He had a private talk with Nehru, during which the Prime Minister's neutralism receded enough for him to condemn Stalinist expansionism, while Thomas assured him that the American people strongly disapproved of his proposal that Mao's China be admitted to the United Nations "with his guns still smoking."

He was disappointed in the great nation he had championed for decades, and in the leaders who seemed unable or unwilling to give sufficient direction or inspiration to the freedom recently won after being so long sought. But he agreed that India was not without reason for her suspicions of the West. "French foreign policy jeopardizes the whole West," he wrote. "France hangs on to her bit of India and illustrates, the Asians think, colonialism at its worst in Indochina and North Africa. . . . Criticism of America in the matter [of the Korean War] is fairly general. . . . We should have no support in Asia on any use of Chiang on the Chinese mainland. As for General MacArthur, he has become pretty much a red flag to the Asian bull. . . ." He also noted the

347

great fondness felt for Eleanor Roosevelt, a recent visitor, and the positive good she had achieved simply by her personality in cementing relations with the United States. Thomas followed what was now a firm policy in calling on the American ambassador, who happened to be Loy Henderson, whom he had last seen as a lesser functionary in Moscow in 1937. Proceeding on to Karachi, he paid his respects to Ambassador Avra Warren and spoke with Pakistan's Prime Minister Liaquat Ali Khan. He flew to Rome, where he composed his newspaper column and was entertained by the New York Socialist Amicus Most, now with the Economic Cooperation Administration at the American Embassy on Via Veneto. Here he read of Truman's sacking of MacArthur. He promptly wrote the President, supporting him, and noted in his column, "I am amazed by Republicans so blinded by party feeling that they cannot see how disastrously this talk of impeaching the President for exercising his constitutional right is affecting our prestige over here." Next came sixty hours in Belgrade, where he thought Tito's dictatorship might be susceptible to American overtures; then he went on to West Berlin, where he talked with and was deeply impressed by the Socialist Mayor Ernst Reuter.

Home after six weeks abroad, he encouraged his twelve-year-old granddaughter, Nancy Gates, to advance international concord by corresponding with the daughter of his hosts in Bombay, and he sent several fatherly letters to his hostess, Leela Trikamdas, mistakenly addressing her as Lulu. He had scarcely caught his breath when he had to give his views to State Department officers specializing in India and report to President Truman, following this with a letter of appreciation in which he urged (1) that more wheat be sent to India, (2) that our bombing in Korea be rigidly restricted to essential military targets, and (3) that, since the year marked the 175th anniversary of the Declaration of Independence, the President might find it possible "to make a kind of anniversary statement or proclamation in which you could state positively America's intention to promote freedom throughout the world . . ."

Truman replied in general agreement. A month later Thomas addressed him again on the subject of publicizing our aid for peaceful pursuits in connection with the airplane death of an American crop-sprayer in Iran: "Would it not be a good idea to honor the heroism of men who do this type of Point Four work? . . . . Might this not be valuable in terms of American relations with Iran as well as in terms of dramatizing what is involved in the Point Four program?" The President replied appreciatively, "I think your suggestion is a good one," and promised to look into it. Another month passed and Thomas reverted to his

> . . . earnest hope that, in your answer to the Russian note asking a Five-Power conference to end the cold war, you will find a way to present an alternative approach to peace which will command the respect of all nations as obviously more honest, more logical, and fairer to the rights of the smaller nations. . . . I found that the plain people of the world—some of them even in our own country—are not convinced that it is we Americans who love peace simply by the excellence of our negative case against the Kremlin. . . . My father used to tell me it was a mistake to let the Devil have all the good tunes. Why let Stalin have, in the minds of the multitudes, the tune of peace which is their hearts' desire?

The President acknowledged this with a cheerful note saying he hoped that a program of that kind could be developed. Next, Thomas (for the Post War World Council) wrote Truman to urge strong support for his appointment of that target of McCarthy, Dr. Philip C. Jessup, to the United Nations, and was promptly assured by Presidential Secretary Hassett that this was being given. Ten days later, Thomas, once more at his most diplomatic, wrote of his fear that Stalin had succeeded in posing as the friend of peace and that part of the reason was "our failure dramatically to present ourselves in the role which you stated so well in your speech of October 24th, 1950, when you declared that we wanted universal fool-proof disarmament. Cannot that theme be magnified and developed by the American delegation at the United Nations and in any conference with Stalin which you and Mr. Churchill may decide to hold [?]"

Again Truman replied in the most amiable agreement. But what with the Acheson point of view and the pervasive McCarthyism, the kind of insistent, dramatic, ingenious, enterprising, well-planned drive that Thomas was talking about was never mounted. He would have to try the next President. Meanwhile, he wrote A. A. Berle, he found the country more and more pervaded by "the kind of fear which is seriously undermining American freedom," the kind of thing which "makes Acheson act as if McCarthy were always looking over his shoulder."

### 9. I Could Break My Heart

Babette Deutsch had called on Angelica, found her starving again—
only a pot of jam in her tiny refrigerator—and Thomas was collecting
a new fund for her. Another problem was the death of Mother Bloor,
and a telegram from Elizabeth Gurley Flynn inviting him to speak at
the services. Flynn, the Irish charmer who had helped him at Passaic
and elsewhere, was now sixty-one, a contributor to The Daily Worker
and Mother Bloor's successor as the foremost woman Communist. His
previous friendly attentions to these two had been misinterpreted. He
wrote carefully to "Dear Elizabeth":

> . . . I have another previous engagement at that hour and cannot come
> to the funeral services. I doubt if I should come anyhow and certainly I
> should not speak at them and I want to tell you why so that you will not
> think I am evading the issue.
>
> I once had a great admiration, almost an affection for Mother Bloor. I
> have never lost it altogether but I am convinced that she, like you your-
> self, took a very dangerous wrong path. I literally should prefer death to
> life under the system that Communism has established in the USSR and
> seeks to establish wherever it gets power. . . . Holding these beliefs, there
> is nothing I can say at Mother Bloor's funeral that would not be misunder-
> stood by most non-Communists and resented by Communists.

"Don't let PWWC be only anti-Communist," Mary Blanshard wrote
him. But Thomas's anti-Communism was still discriminating. "Special
interests and reactionaries have cashed in pretty successfully on the
anti-Communist fever," he wrote William Gausmann, a Socialist friend
who was with the Economic Cooperation Administration in Paris.
"They manage to involve somehow even Socialism and Trumanism
with Communism." It pained him to see the administration flinch before the McCarthyite assault: ". . . all of us should take more effective
steps to stop the excessively apologetic tone of the administration's
defense of its own past. It was its business to consider the recognition
of Red China even if it should decide against it." He wrote to every
member of the Senate Foreign Relations Committee, from Brewster of
Maine to Smith of New Jersey, in defense of Dr. Jessup:

> Messrs. McCarthy, Stassen and their supporters hardly have a right in any
> event to demand from public officials a record of infallibility in the diffi-

cult years through which they have lived. Dr. Jessup never paralleled Harold Stassen's extraordinary suggestion . . . that the U.N. should keep peace by a force of 25 bombers, recruited from five different nations, presumably the Big Five, each to be presented with one of our atom bombs. The builder of that glass house is in no position to throw stones.

William F. Buckley's book *God and Man at Yale* made Thomas raise his eyebrows at Buckley's "virtual identification of religion with capitalism" coupled with the hope that the Yale alumni, so largely composed of stockbrokers and corporation officials incompetent in education, would take over the university, which would mean the ruin of its educative function and the end of its freedom. "To me the fear that Yale or any other American university is turning out radicals is grimly humorous," Thomas wrote. "The contrary is conspicuously the case." He deplored the anti-Communist tendency to be soft on dictators, telegraphing Secretary Acheson: "NEW YORK TIMES WHICH ANNOUNCED BEGINNING CONVERSATIONS ON SPANISH BASES REPORTS EXECUTION TOMORROW OF FIVE CONDEMNED LABOR LEADERS. CAN YOU NOT PROTEST? WHAT SHALL IT PROFIT AMERICAN DEMOCRACY TO GAIN SPANISH BASES AND LOSE ITS OWN SOUL?" His argument that we should "disrecognize Chiang" offended at least two of his old Socialist friends, Bertram Wolfe and Arthur McDowell, both of whom had turned visibly to the right, their anti-Communism including support for Chiang. In his column Thomas remarked that "the Luce magazines continuously harp" on the theme that in Indochina France was not fighting a colonial war but was fighting for the United States and the United Nations: "Actually France is fighting a colonial war made necessary by her stupid imperialism. French government in Indochina was a disgrace before World War II."

Although Katrina Barnes thought him philosophic about the decline of the Socialist Party, his letters showed deep concern underneath. "Frankly," he wrote Gausmann, "what is left of the S.P. is a pitiably weak party and I could break my heart about it if it would do any good." After attending a National Executive Committee meeting, he wrote, "my feeling as I sat there in Philadelphia was that few men had more conspicuously failed than I in the things I have tried hardest to do in the last 35 years."

This was in a memo about Party matters shown also to Martin Diamond of Chicago, a young college professor and member of the National Executive Committee, who replied at great length and with the astonishing affection which Thomas could evoke, saying that "There is a sense in which [your] judgment is true," but that, "This is a different and better country precisely because of what you and we did. . . . There is so much richness in what you have done that for me all sting is taken out of the judgment even in the sense that it may be valid."

"We shout the old slogans," Thomas lamented, upset especially because the National Executive Committee had decided to run national candidates in 1952—a move he was sure would be disastrous and perhaps even finish off the Party. To Fleischman he wrote that he wanted to help the Party (or replace it if it died) with a new Fabian type of society, purely educational, which he called the Union of Democratic Socialists.

This was a movement he started virtually undercover. Fearing that he might be suspected of undercutting the Party, he first asked the advice of people totally in his confidence such as Fleischman and Upton Sinclair. Sinclair thought it an excellent idea and said Thomas could put down both him and his wife, the effervescent May Craig Sinclair, as members, but warned that the name would never do, that the American people would take Socialism but not the label. Hadn't the League for Industrial Democracy proved that, and Sinclair's own experience of getting 60,000 votes on the Socialist ticket and 879,000 on EPIC? Thomas kept the name nevertheless. Socialism was Socialism and it seemed to him dishonest to conceal it. He queried to learn if there was interest among radical intellectuals including Dwight Macdonald and C. Wright Mills. (Macdonald had recently written a New Yorker profile of Roger Baldwin, for which Thomas had been one of many sources. Baldwin had been incensed by some details and had thought of suing, which Thomas had advised him not to do.) The Union was proof of Thomas's eternal faith in Socialism, however attenuated. Not until later did it get under way, at which time Thomas invited the whole Socialist Party into it—an invitation some declined. Thomas was delighted to sign up A. Philip Randolph as vice chairman (Thomas himself of course being chairman) and collect such members as Albert Sprague Coolidge and Van Wyck Brooks, but although he worked and fussed over the Union for three years, it never really got up steam. It died leaving the gaunt Socialist Party still barely alive.

The 1952 Presidential election was one Thomas was going to sit out. He decided even to skip the Socialist Party convention, knowing that if there he could not help opposing any nomination of candidates and that "a big fight would be practically fatal to the Party." Meanwhile he and A. Philip Randolph were selected by the American Committee for

Cultural Freedom to visit its counterpart in Japan in the spring. From there, Thomas alone was to go on to Hong Kong and five Southeast Asian countries. He made his usual careful preparations, writing in advance to politicians, newspapermen, and businessmen, keen in anticipation over a journey that should teach him more about world politics and enable him to pass the knowledge on in his newspaper columns. He also changed his will and named his son Evan and son-in-law John Gates as executors.

### 10. God Save the President

He left April 23 ("As usual when you leave we feel like orphans," Angelica wrote him), with one of his greatest admirers beside him in the plane. Thomas in the twenties had helped Randolph start his Union of Sleeping Car Porters by getting him a grant from the Garland Fund, and the two had cooperated ever since, Randolph also being on the Post War World Council board. A firm Socialist, Randolph had in 1948 been proposed as a candidate for Vice President (he declined, being too busy with his union), and Thomas had spoken frequently to Socialist groups at the Hotel Theresa and elsewhere in Harlem. Just as Randolph was one of the leading blacks in the fight for civil rights, so was Thomas high among the whites. "He had the stature of a father to me," Randolph said later, although Thomas was only five years older. "We never had differences."* This was not literally true, but their only recorded disagreement came in 1940 when Randolph could not follow Thomas's anti-war stand and briefly left the Party. Rather than complain about Thomas's utopianism, Randolph saw something "spiritual" in Thomas's greatness because he moved beyond national and racial boundaries and sought to help "all mankind," giving meaning to the one-world idea so much voiced and so little embraced. The two had discussed their approach to the Japanese before leaving, and on the long plane trip continued conversations which Randolph recalled as wonderfully pleasant.

In Tokyo (where the newspaper Nomiuri carried Thomas's column), they were guests of the Japanese Congress for Cultural Freedom. The Tokyo committee was poorly organized, but Thomas and Randolph

---

*When I interviewed Randolph in September, 1973, he spoke of Thomas with such fervent admiration that I suggested that Thomas, being human, must have had faults. "If he had any, I was not aware of them," Randolph replied. —Author.

took part in round-table discussions, talked with college students, were interviewed by press and radio and traveled to the southern island of Kyushu to speak to coal-mining union members. "The miners looked with admiration on Norman," Randolph recalled. But America's racism and militarism were scarcely unobserved; the Bombs were still a vivid memory. Thomas remarked, "It is a good thing to send over a Negro, if he is the caliber of Philip Randolph. I noted . . . that his statements about America were more readily accepted than mine." The neutralism Thomas deplored was strong. On May Day, when it was arranged that Thomas and Randolph should speak to a huge Tokyo outdoor rally, Communists arrived in strength enough to disrupt the meeting and furnish Life with a picture of the scene, showing Thomas and Randolph watching the skirmish with interest. In a note of thanks to Masaburo Suzuki, chairman of the Japanese Social Democratic Party, Thomas defended the American role in Korea, adding:

> I am very fearful of our arms economy. It gives workers as well as industrialists a vested interest in the horrible "prosperity" it brings. But [the war] was not begun for imperialist reasons. And the hope of its end is universal, controlled disarmament for which we should unceasingly work.

The two Americans separated, Randolph going directly to Burma, his last stop, while Thomas made inquiries about Red China in Hong Kong and then visited Thailand. In Bangkok, wearing rumpled white ducks, he was greeted both as grandson of the missionary collaborator of King Mongkut and as what the newspaper Kiattisak described as "the aged and reverence-inviting politician." One cynic informed Thomas that "Siam's two parties are the army and the navy," and that it would be necessary to have a police license to organize anything like a Committee for Cultural Freedom. A friendly Siamese "urged me tactfully . . . not to make it appear as if I were organizing a committee. I followed his instructions." He did, however, take continuous political and economic notes for his column, sip quarts of tea at gatherings and work far into the night. He was given a reception at the American Embassy; he gave a press conference of his own at the Oriental Hotel and was given a "tea party" at the Suriyanon Hotel by the Serirat Weekly, always towering a foot above his short Thai hosts. The local translation of the Ratanakosin Weekly's long story was shaky but colorful:

> Mr. Thomas . . . is leader of American Socialist Party and was nominated to the election for several offices including those for American President.

Besides, he is a writer and lecturer . . . he has always been contributing to more than ten newspapers. . . . As a pro-Socialism, he said, he had been once quite interested in Russian affair; but he was utterly disappointed only after having seen actual practices in Russia which had a slavery taste in every stage. The high paid. The oppressed labor is at a low one. The state acted as sole capitalist. Himself . . . does not approve in the least. . . .

Himself proceeded to Rangoon, where he stayed with his former Party colleague Professor Frank Trager and his sociologist wife (Trager being stationed there with an educational mission), was feted at the Union of Burma Club and talked with the Socialist Prime Minister U Nu and other officials. In Singapore he was embarrassed because the papers headlined "panty riots"* at American colleges, a phenomenon causing Asians to think more than ever that Americans were excessively rich, trivial and frivolous. He went on to Jakarta, noting, "The Dutch were even worse than the British in their failure to provide popular education for the people. . . ." In Manila he talked with President Quirino and many others, observed "certain police state tendencies" and remarked on "the well-nigh universal dislike, mistrust or hatred for Chiang Kai-shek and Syngman Rhee, and the general Asian resentment at French colonialism in Indochina." He reported his discoveries in his twice-a-week syndicated column and also in The Call, sometimes pecking away on a portable typewriter in a sweltering hotel room into the wee hours. He turned homeward, troubled by American mistakes in foreign policy which played into the hands of the Communists—our chumminess with Franco which made Asians skeptical about the Land of the Free and nourished their neutralism, and "our too complacent support of French colonialism in Tunisia and Indochina."

He returned June 10, a week after the Socialist Party convention in Cleveland had nominated Hoopes for President with Samuel Fried-man, a New York publicity man and former editor of The Call, as his running mate. Much as Thomas liked Hoopes, whom he had known for a quarter century as a high-principled Quaker lawyer, he felt his grasp of foreign affairs inadequate and his speaking voice too muffled for this ambitious effort, and he feared the worst. Yet he immediately supported the Socialist ticket, asking radio and television stations for time for Hoopes to rebut a charge by General Eisenhower that Socialism

*The "panty riot," or raid, was a military operation, since fallen into disuse, in which male collegians invaded girls' dormitories and captured panties.

implied "pure dictatorship."* He had dinner with John Foster Dulles and observed to Gausmann, "in a queer sort of way, [Dulles] is something of a split personality." Thomas praised Chester Bowles's former partner, William Benton, now a Senator, for his fight against McCarthy. He made war on the Bohn Aluminum and Brass Company ("Accent on the brass," Thomas said), whose radio announcer always lumped Socialism and Communism and likened them to noxious weeds in the democratic rose garden. He actually persuaded NBC to give him free time to educate Bohn. Less than a month after his return from the Orient he was in Chicago to cover the Republican and Democratic conventions, his column for these events again being purchased on a daily basis by an expanded group of papers.† As a Socialist he had always stayed at eight-dollar hotels. Now as a columnist he stayed in splendor at the Drake, while the Republicans nominated Eisenhower and Nixon and the Democrats Stevenson and Sparkman.

He regretted that neither party had any plank on civil liberties nor had mounted any real attack on McCarthy, but he did conceive an unsocialistic admiration for Adlai Stevenson. Stevenson's Princeton background was an advantage, but what attracted Thomas even more was his lucidity and the courage he showed later in addressing the American Legion convention at Madison Square Garden—the Legion had been witch-hunting in his own state of Illinois—denouncing McCarthyism (without precisely using the name) and making an eloquent plea for the kind of patriotism that defended civil liberties. Thomas admired a good speaker with courage. "You did the whole country a great service," he wrote Stevenson.

But the sensation of the campaign was the discovery of the Nixon "secret fund" and the Checkers speech. Thomas abhorred the electioneering ruthlessness of the young California Senator and had already made a shrewd appraisal of his character. He wrote in his column:

---

*Thomas continued to surprise people who opposed all Socialism on principle by reminding them that such things as schools, water supply and highways were Socialistic—a fact often forgotten. As for the often-execrated Socialistic mail service, he blamed its annual deficit on big-business interests which required it to handle a vast tonnage of fourth-class and other mail at rates low enough to bankrupt any privately owned operation.

†The Portland Oregonian, Trenton Times, Indianapolis Star, Cincinnati Enquirer, Milwaukee Sentinel, Worcester Telegram, Denver Post, St. Louis Post-Dispatch, Minneapolis Star and Tribune, Seattle Times, San Francisco Chronicle, Los Angeles Times, Houston Post, Des Moines Register and Tribune, New York Post and Washington Daily News took this temporary daily column whereas only seven of them used his regular twice-weekly column.

The Republican candidate for Vice President has made the crusade of the Republican candidate for President a piece of political hypocrisy. . . . secretly he accepted some $18,000 from a group of rich men. When this important and highly pertinent fact is made known by a responsible newspaper, Nixon, admitting the facts, yells "Smear" intended by "friends of Communists and crooks" to call off his campaign against them. And that is low demagoguery outrageously unbecoming to a possible Vice President of the United States . . . his sense of honor and propriety in accepting this money without public accounting is shockingly low. . . . The Nixon episode should lead to a law compelling full publicity on the source and use of all gifts to all legislators or high officials.

The election which swept in Eisenhower and Nixon was indeed a disaster for the Socialists. Hoopes and Friedman, for whom Thomas had campaigned, polled 20,203 votes. Thomas had been critical of Eisenhower—particularly when in Wisconsin at McCarthy's request he omitted from his prepared speech his defense of his old friend General Marshall—but he was more fearful of Ike's running mate, Nixon, writing:

"As [Stevenson] said, 'We vote as many but pray as one'—for our country. My prayer—especially when I contemplate the next Vice President—is 'God save the President.'"

# XVII

## 1. Man About Town

"Dear Norman," Mary Blanshard wrote with the freedom of an old friend, "It is always such great fun having dinner with you at your nice club—but always you have to dash before I have caught up on half the news. I & all your friends wish you would consider retiring—& then you could be more active than ever by circulating among your friends & family. When will you?"

Age had scarcely slowed him. Some said that the most characteristic picture of Thomas would show only his coattails flying out the door or his hand waving as he disappeared into a cab. His friends told amused stories of talks or meals with him terminated in mid-sentence or mid-coffee. "Dear August," he wrote August Heckscher, "I think I explained why I had to get out in such a hurry Saturday night." To Mrs. Jonathan Bingham, who had questioned him in connection with a biography she planned of Niebuhr, he wrote, "I was sorry to leave you so abruptly to find your own way out of the Club yesterday but I had to be on time for a radio appointment." Samuel Friedman wrote to him in some reproach that Thomas had never had time to talk things over, though the two had known each other for many years. "Dear Hugh Gaitskell," Thomas wrote to the Right Honorable Member of Parliament who had visited New York and whom Thomas had been anxious to see, "I was awfully sorry I had to leave so abruptly the other night. . . ." "Norman," wrote his old friend Ralph Harlow, "I would treasure an opportunity to sit down and talk with you again." Niebuhr wrote, "I wish we could talk." To A. A. Berle, Thomas wrote, "I thank you for adjourning things for me since I had to catch a certain train."

It does not seem right to call him a driven man, since he seemed to

358

enjoy a full schedule and seldom appeared harried. He knew that the things he wanted to get done got done by virtue of the Thomas Track Meet, but he still answered every letter. "The best general rule for a speaker," he wrote an inquirer, "is to believe in what he is saying, to want to make other people believe in it, and then to work hard to find the best language to convey his ideas." He believed in his Long Island Rail Road conductor, bitterly though he assailed that capitalist road for its service, and when the conductor was laid off for some infraction, Thomas wrote the railroad to say he knew the man well, that he was "cheerful, friendly [and] reliable," and hoped he would be returned to his job, which he was.

When in New York Thomas was in his singular way a man about town, a radio-television-political personality, still appearing weekly on WEVD, frequently on "Author Meets Critics," "American Forum of the Air," "Tex and Jinx," "Meet the Press," "Town Hall Forum," "Keeping Posted" and the George Hamilton Combs "Spotlight," besides his serious political broadcasts. He even filled in for a time for Barry Gray on his midnight-to-two talk show. Martha Deane found him easily approachable and had him several times on her WOR morning show; once he appeared with Arthur Schlesinger, Jr., and the executive secretary of the state Communist Party, the latter being utterly snowed under by Thomas's volley of arguments. Even the articulate Schlesinger acted chiefly as onlooker or referee. Thomas had appeared on the first "Town Meeting of the Air" in 1935 and ever since had received more audience requests for his appearance than anyone else. Town Hall's rule was that no one should appear more than twice a year, so Thomas was on the show twice a year like clockwork. George V. Denny, Jr., president of Town Hall, regarded him with some awe as one of the greatest educational forces in America, respected even by those who disagreed with him. The New York Times radio critic complained when Thomas came on after midnight: "Mr. Thomas went after everybody, Republicans and Democrats alike. . . . If radio is going to present its liveliest and most stimulating material after most people have gone to bed, it should stop whining about television's competition." Thomas enjoyed these challenges to his wit and learning and was on a first-name basis with scores of radio-television people and with the large circle of broadcasting "guests," the wise or the amusing.

His growing interest in Latin America meant closer ties with board members of the Inter-American Association for Democracy and Freedom, one of them the rather dashing, Basque-born Dr. Jesus de Galíndez, a Spanish Republican exiled since the Franco dictatorship, who had lived in the Dominican Republic until he could no longer stand Trujillo's dictatorship there and was now lecturing at Columbia University. Galíndez's life was in danger and he knew it, and this friendship was soon to involve Thomas in one of the metropolis's most disturbing mysteries. Other friends, such as Sidney Hook, Richard Rovere and the novelist James Farrell, centered around the American Committee for Cultural Freedom. Another group was connected with the United Nations, where he knew people of all skin hues. Still another numbered dozens of magazine and book editors and authors, all these besides the Princeton crowd, the Senators and Congressmen, the do-gooders, the Socialist Party and the dear old friends of dear old causes—Baldwin, Lovett, John Haynes Holmes, Muste, Clarence Senior, Harry Laidler and the rest.

But most of these he saw only at meetings, radio or television studios, or at cocktail parties. His social life was jam-packed with fleeting hellos and goodbyes. He had, and evidently wanted, only a few friends with whom he met and dined occasionally. These were the kindred spirits, such as the Blanshards and the Marshalls. Thomas had known James Marshall, a wealthy attorney and civic leader, since the thirties when both were members of the City Charter Commission. He had recently got Marshall into the Coffee House Club and through Indian friends was able to aid both Marshalls in making a journey to Sikkim. One of his favorite of all friends was the small, intense Lenore Marshall, poet and novelist, an idealist, a tireless worker for peace, an heiress and a major supporter of the Post War World Council. It took three kinds of people to launch a cause: Intelligent ones to plan the program, enthusiastic ones to push it and wealthy ones to pay expenses. It was a miracle when the three coincided in one person, as they did in Lenore Marshall, whose muse was also concordant. Thomas did not need his own experience with death to appreciate her four-line "Mortality":

> *No isle can shelter you from final grief,*
> *No tide can bear you from the coming season;*
> *The hieroglyphics on a winter leaf*
> *Must reconcile you to the great unreason.*

"The one great success of my life was my marriage," Thomas often wrote young couples about to be married. Years after Violet's death he was still writing regretful corrections to people who invited him and Violet to social events. Tears came to his eyes when he spoke of her. He now had fifteen grandchildren—the final score. Being an active promoter of world birth control, he was a trifle embarrassed at the number and often pointed out that they were the offspring of five children so that the average was only three apiece. He now had another poodle named Jester, but usually left him with the Gateses at Cold Spring Harbor where Jester was his weekend companion. He sent the Millers in Kansas careful advice about colleges for his oldest grandchild, Norman Thomas Miller. He liked to listen to music as he read, in his rare hours of leisure. In the spring of 1953 he wrote to all five of "My dear Children":

> I just ordered through Miss French a copy for each family of a book that did me a lot of good. It is enormously interesting and sooner or later even the youngest child will be in a position to appreciate it. The book I mean is "O Rugged Land of Gold" by Martha Martin.
>
> Yesterday afternoon, a beautiful Sunday afternoon, after a very busy week, I sat outdoors in front of my little apartment with a radio bringing me the Philharmonic Orchestra playing Siegfried's "Rhine Journey from Gotterdaemmerung" [sic]. I was reading one of the most moving parts of my book and the combination was terrific. Fortunately, the end of Martha's adventure was no Gotterdaemmerung.
>
> Maybe I was particularly impressed because I find it very hard to be optimistic about us human beings. . . . The natural heroism of this woman, her unaffected comments on nature and life, her extraordinary achievement: these were things that moved me profoundly. . . . Well, anyway, the book will speak for itself to you.
>
> Lots of love.
>
> Dad

The book was the personal account of a woman living in remote Alaska, whose husband's expected return from a trip was delayed interminably by accidents. She was herself injured in a landslide and had to spend the terrible winter alone, fighting for her own life and that of her unborn child. Her courage, self-reliance and intelligence had so impressed Thomas that he wanted all his descendants to read the book and profit by her standards, which he, a man of standards, admired. For the same reason he admired Laura Ingalls Wilder's books for children and enjoyed reading them to his younger grandchildren.

Few children were being named after him nowadays, but he still received admiring letters, one of them from a woman, a former neighbor he did not know:

When I lived near Gramercy Park and used to see you occasionally, walking your dog, shopping at the Co-op, or riding in the bus, I used to think: "Well, at last this man of seemingly unending energy is beginning to show his years." But when I heard you last night on Town Meeting, I would have thought you were about 35—except that no youth of 35 could have your wisdom. Your dynamic energy, your enthusiasm combined with consummate courtesy, and consideration for the other fellow's idea, your ability to stir the audience, your quick grasp of the point at issue and alertness, were a great joy to witness.

Thomas replied, "I was much pleased by your letter" and enclosed the latest Post War World Council newsletter.

## 2. Pillar of Jelly

"Let me add as a closing word a question to which I do not expect an answer," Thomas wrote the new Secretary of State Dulles. "How long can the Administration stand McCarthy?" He got what he expected. He also pressed Dulles to keep Mrs. Roosevelt on the American delegation to the United Nations, saying, "Her place in the affection of people throughout the world is unique." She was of course dropped. He had urged the Senate to reject Charles E. Wilson as Secretary of Defense while he had large holdings in General Motors. He feared a "government of the generals, Eisenhower and Motors," writing, "In a transcendental sense, Wilson may be right that the interests of General Motors are the interests of the country," but added, "millions of his countrymen would be made suspicious of certain decisions and more millions of Europeans and Asians would believe our military defense undertaken to aid private profits." Wilson was approved. The death of Stalin and succession of Malenkov moved Thomas to write President Eisenhower:

> This letter is an urgent request to you to consider replying to Malenkov's recent statement on peace by restating the American desire for universal foolproof disarmament under what would have to be a strengthened United Nations. We [the Post War World Council] grant that news tends to discredit [Malenkov's] sincerity. . . . Nevertheless, is it not profoundly significant that, on taking a position in which he cannot be as secure as his predecessor, he obviously feels it so necessary to appear to the people inside and outside the Iron Curtain as the friend of peace?

Eisenhower made a speech for peace which Thomas called "magnificent," but he still lamented that as always it did not go far enough in spelling out a campaign for "the total liquidation of all weapons of mass destruction." He tended to like Ike but still, as he put it, "didn't know yet what Ike liked" and reserved judgment. The fact that Mildred McAfee Horton, whom Thomas had often met as president of Wellesley College, was passed over for important office disclosed, he wrote, that "the State Department was so bound by its own ridiculous rules of investigation or so terrified of Joe McCarthy [that it] argues a degree of bureaucratic rigidity or cowardice which makes one fearful for the future of the Eisenhower administration." Pretty soon Eisenhower was giving so much ground to McCarthy, what with the European book-burning journey of the Senator's young aides Cohn and Schine, that Thomas felt the President had become a "pillar of jelly," and the Secretary of State as well. He cheered Ike's success in stopping the fighting in Korea but declared, "for a viable peace, we shall have to recognize Mao's government simply because it exists. Recognition would not imply moral approval any more than the recognition of Russia implies it." He let McCarthy have it in an open letter in his column:

> You first established yourself in the Senate, not as the enemy of Communism, but the friend of Joe McCarthy's bank account. I refer, for instance, to your $10,000 fee from the Lustron Corporation. But suddenly you discovered gold in them thar hills of anti-Communism. . . . You imitate Communist ethics by asserting your alleged end justifies any means however discreditable. . . . If I were Malenkov I would privately award you the Order of Lenin for arousing the resentment of Americans against both their indispensable allies and their own government . . . and for implying to us citizens that if only we would hate Attlee, Churchill, Acheson, Truman (and Dulles should he stop yessing you) hard enough, we could defeat Communism at a cheap price. What a service to Moscow!

His passion for foreign travel, which he had been forced to suppress during his middle years, got a new fillip from the offer by the American Federation of Labor and Congress of Industrial Organizations Free Trade Union Committee to cover his expenses in Europe and North Africa, where he would make a survey of labor's political and cultural groupings. This would also enable him to attend the tag-end of the International Confederation of Free Trade Unions convention in Stockholm and the whole of the International Socialist Congress immediately following it in the same city. It came about through his acquaintance with Jay Lovestone, the one-time Communist leader who made the mistake of backing Bukharin instead of Stalin, was expelled from the party, for a time ran an opposition Communist splinter, but now had "reformed" with a vengeance and become in effect "foreign minister" of the American Federation of Labor in its little-known fight against Communism in the international labor movement. Lovestone sat at the right hand of George Meany, the cold warrior who extended the war to unionism. Lovestone spent at least $300,000 annually in his encouragement of "free" trade unions abroad as opposed to Communist-controlled ones. Thomas, delighted but overworked, had one of his realizations that he belonged to too many organizations and offered to resign from the Town Hall board, the offer being indignantly rejected. Not being fluent in any foreign language, he wrote the multilingual Angelica, who was again in Rome, to see if she could join him. "You hardly can imagine how glad and happy I am to be able to meet you!" she replied immediately. Thomas, always a trifle embarrassed by her devotion to him, wrote, "I shall lean heavily on your experience and your marvelous linguistic knowledge." (Her latest book of poems, *Tears,* was again a collection in which each poem was rendered in five languages despite all the difficulties in meter and rhyme. Like most poetry it was not profitable.) Meanwhile, upset because a number of Socialists, including William Gausmann and Philip Heller, had lost or were threatened with losing their State Department or Mutual Security Agency jobs, he wrote Scott McLeod, the McCarthyist young security officer at the State Department. In this minor post McLeod had caused astonishment by uttering policy pronouncements usually regarded as more in the Secretary's province, without complaint from Dulles.

Still guaranteed to raise Thomas's temper was any governmental suspicion of Socialist patriotism or tendency to lump Socialists with Communists. He resented a housecleaning of Socialists who were serving well—resented also having to deal with a cocky young subaltern in the matter. In his letter to McLeod he defended the loyalty of Socialists and asked what the policy was toward them. McLeod took five weeks to answer with a hard-nosed three-page letter which he released to the press, saying in essence that while there was no suspicion of their loyalty, Socialists opposed America's "free enterprise" system and hence "I would never knowingly employ a Socialist to fill [a policy-making position] within the Department." By then Thomas was in Europe. The Socialists being fired were not in policy-making positions. He replied in indignation, accusing McLeod of "contributing to McCarthyism" and ending:

I submit that Socialists in MSA or State Department employment are far nearer the President's policy . . . than are the disciples and servants of our Inquisitor General and Thought Controller, Senator McCarthy. The men who tried to sabotage the Bohlen appointment, kept Mildred McAfee Horton from a post of useful service to which the President had appointed her, and burned the books, were not Socialists. Neither were those rash young book censors, the team of Cohn and Schine at which all Europe still laughs, Socialists.

In Stockholm he met Angelica, and for days bent low in order to converse with her. Now seventy-six, and having already spent fifty-two years in work for Socialism in many countries, with little success to look back on, she nevertheless maintained a kind of enthusiasm expressed in formal Old World phrases. Thomas was delighted by Sweden, a shining example of Socialist success—something he could point to now that England had regressed to Toryism. "Already I've heard enough to know how general is the feeling that liberty is dead in America," he wrote; "that all of us, and not the least President Eisenhower, live in mortal terror of Grand Inquisitor McCarthy."

After stops at Bonn and Berlin, Thomas visited Cairo, where the monarchy had fallen and Nasser was in charge with Naguib as front man. The British still clung with 80,000 men to the Canal Zone. Thomas talked with Foreign Minister Mahmoud Fawzi and with Sir Brian Robertson, the British negotiator for Suez. The Palestinian question which preoccupied Thomas could wait, as Fawzi put it, not being the immediate concern that Suez was. Thomas, so opposed in principle to British imperialism, seemed to accept calmly the English hold on Suez even with the imperialist Churchill again Prime Minister; the canal after all was not a people, and perhaps Thomas saw English-held Suez as a bulwark against Soviet imperialism. He wrote in his column:

> I am leaving Cairo rather more hopeful . . . that a reasonable and amicable solution might be reached of [the problem of] the protection of that vital seaway, the Suez Canal, and the upkeep and control of the great military base which now protects it.

His impatience with the French swelled when he visited Tunis, where Habib Bourguiba, a man he admired, was imprisoned for his nationalism. "French colonial policy," he remarked, "continues to be imperialist to a degree that makes any hope of a decent peace in Indochina very dim . . ." He noted and would remember the huge American air bases surrounding Rabat in Morocco. He touched down in Paris and

London, then took off from Prestwick after acquiring Scottish heather to give his grandchildren, and was home August 17. The state-owned Scandinavian Airlines was efficient but he was put in the wrong seat, as he let the airline president know:

> I had seat #16 which practically blocks approach to the toilets behind a green curtain. Through nobody's fault, every person, during the night, who had occasion to go behind that curtain, hit me, stepped on my feet or waved the curtain in my face. . . . Only a midget could doze in relative comfort in a seat in that position. I am not a midget.

### 3. Thomas vs. Eisenhower

In the same mail Thomas wrote President Eisenhower to protest the discharge of Socialists in foreign posts and a policy resulting in the visible decline of morale in the Foreign Service. He protested also the high-and-mighty manner of Scott McLeod and asked for a talk. Eisenhower passed the letter to Dulles, who replied this time not to "Dear Norman" but to "Dear Mr. Thomas." He did not question Socialist loyalty, Dulles wrote, and he had the highest respect for many prominent Socialists, "including, of course, yourself." But it was proper to employ people reflecting the administration's political beliefs; hence, "I believe that Mr. McLeod's position is a sound one." Thomas replied firmly to "Dear Mr. Dulles":

> I still think it necessary that I should seek to see the President himself because events show that the present policy is not confined to your Department. . . . I hear of an increasing number of little "S" socialists who are discharged. . . . One can, of course, interpret policy making positions to include almost any position in which the judgment and discretion of its occupant are important. I do not think you would tend thus to define the phrase. If you do, you will wreck the civil service. . . . It is certainly true that many of those discharged by Mr. Stassen [the Mutual Security Administrator] are far more loyal to your program than some of your Party brethren in the Senate, or than Messrs. Cohn and Schine. Finally, I do object very seriously to a situation in which announcements of Administration policy in a matter so important as this should come from a security officer in your Department or any other. It is along these lines

that I want to make the case, and to make it to the President, before trying to make it a public issue.

This was pretty sharp talk to his beach-club fellow. He won his point and saw Eisenhower October 27. Surprised to find that Sherman Adams stayed in the Presidential office during the interview, Thomas commented subsequently, "But I later learned that when Hoover visited Eisenhower, Adams was in the room too. I was relieved. It means I wasn't a peculiar character." The President, whom he found "an extremely decent man," listened carefully and "showed a much better understanding of what Socialism really was than I expected." Eisenhower accepted the Tennessee Valley Authority but believed that "once the process of socialization of certain industries and services was started, it could not be stopped"—an assertion Thomas could not accept but did not debate. "The President assured me he has no doubts of Socialists' loyalty," Thomas said later. ". . . . He was categorical that the Civil Service should not exclude Socialists." Feeling better, Thomas then visited Attorney General Brownell to protest the stand of the Justice Department in a case involving the Louisiana sugar-cane cutters and also its habit of listing persons and organizations as subversive on mere McCarthyist whims.

He headed north immediately to give several lectures, including one at the Dartmouth "Great Issues" course, and to visit the Blanshards amid the autumn wonders at nearby Thetford Center. The handsome, bearded, cultivated Blanshard, the clergyman turned humanist, had made a large part of his later career out of his opposition to the social and political policies of the Catholic Church. He had written two books on the theme, both best-sellers, although many newspapers declined to advertise them. Thomas had tried unsuccessfully to get Sulzberger of The Times to accept ads for one of them. Thomas could not, however, match Blanshard's easy dismissal of religion as an absurdity any logical man was well rid of. "I am no atheist," Thomas observed. "Indeed I am almost haunted by religion and often wish that I could regain the comfortable Christian theology of earlier years." Whenever he lectured at Dartmouth, as he did every year, the Blanshards dined with him at the Hanover Inn or thereabouts and, when they could, enticed him away to their place a dozen miles north on Sawnee Bean Hill.

## 4. Thomas vs. Einstein

The central miracle of Thomas's life was his continuing vision of apocalypse, which he worked interminably to communicate. The visions had come to him when, as a young man, he discovered the Social Gospel as the road to equality and abundance; in his opposition to World War I; in his drive for an "inclusive" Socialist Party in the thirties; in his support of the Spanish Loyalists and his opposition to American intervention in World War II. His fertility in hatching or accumulating ideas was equaled by the intense energy and ingenuity with which he broadcast and sought to put them into action. Now, in the years since the war, his crusade of crusades was to maneuver the more important peoples and governments of the world so as to solve the Soviet-Communist menace without a war. His "cultural freedom" journeys had been at least as much for the purpose of spreading goodwill for democracy and wariness of Communism as for self-education. He was a firm believer in Sidney Hook's motto, "Heresy, Yes—Conspiracy, No," and his anti-Communism was at times believed excessive by some who had never had dealings with people like Browder and Cannon and who were perhaps unaware of the breadth of his outlook and the lengths to which he went to secure justice for American Communists. Corliss Lamont was often ambivalent toward Thomas, cheering him for such things as his fight against the Dulles-McLeod position but disapproving otherwise:

> . . . Mr. Thomas for many years has been one of the most vociferous of those politicians who try to excite the public to white heat over the alleged Communist menace. In spite of his genuine services to civil liberties, he bears much responsibility for the general witchhunt both within and without the Federal Government; and so has helped to create the atmosphere in which the purge engulfs Socialists and liberals as well as Communists. I repeat that civil liberties are indivisible.

Although this surely was excessive, Thomas did appear more like a nervous dowager than his old leathery self when Lamont, I. F. Stone, Albert Einstein and others founded the Emergency Civil Liberties Committee in the belief that the American Civil Liberties Union had gone reactionary. The reason was ACLU's decision not to aid the accused Soviet spies, Ethel and Julius Rosenberg, on the ground that civil liberties were not involved.

The Rosenberg case naturally stirred passions on both sides. Thomas believed the pair guilty but wrote to President Eisenhower asking for a commutation of their death sentence lest they become Communist martyrs. He had helped drive Communists out of the ACLU board in the belief that since they (like Fascists or Kluxers) denied or supported the denial of civil liberties in certain circumstances, they were ineligible to defend civil liberties as they had to be defended for everybody including those same Communists, Fascists and Kluxers. He wrote to Lamont of "my long standing belief that Communists don't belong on the board of directors of the ACLU any more than, let's say, a Jesuit priest would belong on the board of elders of a Presbyterian church. That doesn't mean that I want to put either Communists or Jesuit priests in jail. Quite far from it." Lamont, on the contrary, took the stand that the organization defending liberty had to be open to all, even those imperfect in their own dedication to liberty: "As soon as we start making exceptions, we are lost."

Thomas's loyalty to his own ACLU was stirred when the Emergency Civil Liberties Committee held a conference at Princeton in celebration of Einstein's seventy-fifth birthday and Thomas was invited to attend. He declined "with deep regret" in an open letter to Einstein declaring that "prominent and dominant personalities in the Emergency Civil Liberties Committee . . . have shown through the years anything but a consistent love of liberty, in and out of the academic field. . . . I am thoroughly persuaded, as I think you are, that the test of freedom in America and indeed among thoughtful men everywhere is a capacity to oppose both Communism and the thing that in America we call McCarthyism." He disagreed, he said, with one of Einstein's five points in the definition of academic freedom: "I cannot agree with you that it is an infringement on liberty for proper authorities in the state, in the University, or the schools, to raise a question concerning the *allegiance* of men who seek posts in which it is of the utmost importance that their allegiance should be solely to their conscience in search of truth. It is allegiance to Communism as a dictatorial conspiracy, not as a heresy [,] which warrants proper inquiries under proper circumstances." Einstein replied to "Dear Norman Thomas":

I was very pleased to receive a letter from you, for I felt instinctively that you are one of the few whose every word carries true conviction, untarnished by hidden intentions. One feels, as well, your good will towards all. . . .

On *one* point we are of the same opinion. Russia is, in a very clear sense, a "politically underdeveloped country," about like Europe at the time of the Renaissance and a bit later. Murder, with and without legal accouterments, has become a commonplace means of daily politics. The citizen enjoys no rights and no security against arbitrary interference from the power of the state. Science and art have become wards of those who govern. All this is certainly abominable to the taste of modern civilization. But I believe that it is the problem of the Russian people to make changes there. We cannot advance a progressive development by threatening Russia from the outside. Similarly, our well intentioned criticism cannot help because it will not come to the ears of the Russians.

It seems to me, therefore, more useful to confine ourselves to the following question: How about the danger which America faces from its own Communists? Here is the principal difference of opinion between you and me. In short, I believe: America is incomparably less endangered by its own Communists than by the hysterical hunt for the few Communists there are here (including those fellow citizens whose red tinge is weaker, *à la* Jefferson). Why should America be so much more endangered than England by the English Communists? Or is one to believe that the English are politically more naive than the Americans so that they do not realize the danger they are in? No one there works with inquisitions, suspicions, oaths, etc., and still "subversives" do not go unchecked. There, no teachers and no university professors have been thrown out of their jobs, and the Communists there appear to have even less influence than formerly.

In my eyes, the "Communist conspiracy" is principally a slogan used in order to put those who have no judgment and who are cowards into a condition which makes them entirely defenseless. Again, I must think back to the Germany of 1932, whose democratic social body had already been weakened by similar means, so that shortly thereafter Hitler was able to deal it the death-blow with ease. I am similarly convinced that these here will go the same way unless men with vision and willingness to sacrifice come to the defense.

Now you clearly see the difference of opinion. Who is right cannot be decided through a logical process of proof. The future will tell. . . .*

So the argument was between one man who had seen the horror of Hitler's rise and another who had been betrayed by Communists, each giving more weight to his own horror. Thomas had the advantage in

*Einstein's letter was translated from his original German.

political acumen and knowledge of America. The two combatants withdrew after this single courteous round. (The future still has not told all, but events of subsequent years would suggest that the fears of Einstein have come closer to realization in America than the fears of Thomas.) Thomas remained the charred victim dreading the fire but thinking also of a thousand other things. Eugene Debs, in his speech before being sentenced, had said, "while there is a lower class, I am in it; while there is a criminal element, I am of it; while there is a soul in prison, I am not free." Thomas could have said, without a trace of magniloquence, that wherever he found a victim of injustice, he would defend him. Roger Baldwin, the best of judges, observed that "Norman Thomas has always been a champion of civil liberties for peoples everywhere, without exception." He meant this literally. At roughly the same time, Thomas was concerned about causes and injustices in a half-dozen countries including his own:

He asked United States intercession for Victor Raul Haya de la Torre, the Peruvian radical who had been forced by that country's dictator, Manuel Odria, to take refuge in the Colombian Embassy in Lima. There he had stayed for five years while Odria's soldiers watched the embassy night and day, mounted machine guns on adjoining buildings and denied admittance to doctors and dentists. The State Department followed the policy of "nonintervention" it found convenient when radicals were being victimized. "An elastic definition of 'nonintervention,' however," Thomas observed, "did not restrain us from giving moral reinforcement to Odria by awarding him recently our highest military honor, the Legion of Merit. . . ."

He called with a committee on Eric Boheman, ambassador from Sweden, to make suggestions for the examination of prisoners of war in Korea, Sweden being a neutral representative at Panmunjom.

He wrote J. Edgar Hoover to protest the harassment by FBI men "investigating" a man—a day laborer—who had years earlier been a member of the United States Communist Party. He also verified the loyalty of a woman who had come under FBI suspicion because she had once been a member of the Yipsels.

He greeted the black Dr. Akiki Nyabonga on his arrival from Uganda and urged Columbia and Princeton, among others, to employ him as lecturer or professor "to explain African culture to Americans."

He was fed up with the State Department's passport division and with Dulles himself because of their constant interference with suspected "radicals" who wanted to travel. When John Swomley was refused a passport simply because he was a pacifist and secretary of the Fellowship of Reconciliation, Thomas wrote the department, "it will be a sorry day for our country if it should appear to other peoples that we only allow Americans to travel who agree with the foreign policy of an incumbent Secretary of State . . . Don't we commend the very strength of our democracy by proving its tolerance of divergent views?"

He became a sponsor of yet another committee, Spanish Refugee Aid, whose honorary chairmen included Pablo Casals and which succored victims of the Franco regime. (To Dorothy Thompson, who invited him to join the American Friends of the Middle East, he wrote, "I have to confess I am scared by the number of organizations I belong to already.")

He wrote Juan Perón to protest the arrest of Socialists in Argentina.

As a minor stockholder in the American Tobacco Company, he was disturbed by the discovery that cigarets might cause cancer and urged its executives to conduct their own investigation: "But I think very great care must be taken to guarantee independence of the research."

He gave encouragement and help to a group of American Kalmuck Buddhists in their efforts to determine the fate of their Kalmuck brethren who had once been subjects of the U.S.S.R. Many had been liquidated by Stalin because they fought for Germany in World War II.

"Above all," he wrote Senator Alexander Wiley, chairman of the Foreign Relations Committee, "I think it is the business of the Senate to see to it that we don't suddenly find ourselves in an undeclared war in Indochina. . . . In general, we have to remember that the United States is not omnipotent and that sometimes we have to choose the lesser evil in foreign policy. . . ."

He came to the defense of Corporal Barry Miller, who was doing well as a radar instructor at Fort Monmouth, New Jersey, until it was discovered that he had once been a member of a Trotskyite group at the University of Chicago. Miller abruptly was reduced to private, then given an "undesirable discharge" without so much as a hearing. Thomas compared the treatment of this enlisted man with the protection the army had given General Ralph Zwicker when that officer was attacked by McCarthy. Thomas protested to Army Secretary Robert Stevens, was shunted off to Assistant Secretary Hugh Milton, then wrote Senator Alexander Smith of New Jersey (and of Princeton) and to President Eisenhower himself, following this with letters to at least twenty of the nation's leading newspapers, from coast to coast, and got Attorney Rowland Watts of the Workers' Defense League to represent Miller.

Thomas et al. made so much noise that the War Department reviewed the case, withdrew the undesirable discharge, replaced it with a general discharge and promised fair procedure in future. Even so, as Thomas pointed out, the "undesirable" discharge stuck in memories and "Mr. Miller is still looking for a job. The employment which he had regarded as certain after his Army service has been denied him. . . ."

When Milovan Djilas was discharged by Tito from his high government post and put on trial for urging greater democracy, Thomas wrote Comrade Wijono of the Secretariat of the Asian Socialist Conference in Rangoon: "Marshal Tito, who is I think about to visit Burma, evidently has a high regard for Asian opinion and I am wondering if Asian Socialists would think it appropriate to make some representation to him. . . ."

In a more specialized branch of statecraft, he wrote President Victor Butterfield of Wesleyan University that its graduate Harry W. Laidler would soon celebrate the fiftieth anniversary of his graduation and that Wesleyan would honor itself by conferring on him a degree. And to President Dodds of Princeton he urged the same for his old classmate (and best man at his wedding) Dumont Clarke, director for years of the religious department of the Farmers' Federation at Asheville, North Carolina.

In pondering mortality, which he had to do at seventy, the bargainer and negotiator in him regretted the impossibility of negotiation that would prevent long decrepitude before death. As some of his old friends died, he remarked on how fortunate they were to pass on while still functioning efficiently. Among them were Henry Sloane Coffin, who had joined him and Violet in wedlock back when God was a reality; Jessie Wallace Hughan, one of his first comrades in the Fellowship of Reconciliation and in the Party; Algernon Lee of the Social Democratic Federation, never the warmest of friends; and August Claessens, his campaign aide of 1928. John Haynes Holmes, that glorious ally and critic through the decades, was slowly failing. Angelica had suffered a breakdown in Italy and had been forced to rest for a time at a *Kuranstalt* at Bolzano, from where she wrote, "Though I do not feel 'old,' I realize that there is not much time left for me."

A thousand friends ranging from left to right gave Thomas a seventieth birthday party at the Town Hall Club, where he shook a thousand hands, then sat with a granddaughter on each knee and listened with protest more feigned than real as he was extolled. He had a grievance, he said, against Robert Browning, who had preached the virtues of age and urged, "Grow old along with me, the best is yet to be." "False advertising," Thomas complained. Truly astonished when he was presented with a check for $10,000, he scrutinized it closely, then said, "As an old-time Socialist campaigner, I always thought people forged signatures on $10,000 checks." This kind of banter, uttered with precisely the right intonation, gesture of hands and gleam of eye, was irresistible even to people long aware of his mastery of it. A Times editorial said, "His brand of Socialism consists mainly of jumping in wherever he thinks human beings are being abused or human rights ignored, and doing something about it." From Angelica in Rome came a long panegyric, one sentence reading:

> During my very long life . . . I had the privilege of meeting outstanding men and women serving the cause of Socialism with self denial and great devotion, but very, very few of them possessed such a rare combination of intellectual and ethical qualities as your guest of honor.

But Thomas's hearing was slipping, arthritis in one knee had kept him on crutches for a time, and the crusader feared the disablement that would end his crusades. To S. K. Ratcliffe, the eighty-six-year-old English Socialist whom he had met both in Europe and America, and who wrote that he was crippled by age and failing eyesight, Thomas replied with praise for his courage, adding:

> I cannot help telling you that a letter like yours increases my feeling that Providence or nature would have done us a service by providing a more dignified exit from this mundane scene, while we are still in reasonable possession of our faculties.

This was an unsentimental view he expressed repeatedly as his own disabilities grew. Still he remained tender in his family feeling. On several occasions over the years he made room in his tight schedule to join with his brothers, sisters and other relatives in summer reunions at the old Bradford County manse of his Welsh Grandfather Thomas, which was still owned by a descendant. Dr. Evan was among the several dozen who gathered there. His marriage had not been successful and had ended in divorce. It was characteristic of him that he regretted this not only for himself but also from his point of view as a pacifist, regarding himself with chagrin as one who advocated peace for the whole world but was unable to maintain concord with his own wife. He had taken a position with the Chicago health department and directed a drive against venereal disease in that city. Now and then when Thomas stopped over in Chicago, he would stay at Evan's bachelor apartment on North Lake Shore Drive, where Evan had both a bed and a couch the necessary seven feet long.

## 5. *Thomas vs. Thomas*

Thomas's "intermezzo" period of bitterness toward Communists, during which he supported the requirement for teachers' loyalty oaths and declared war on the Emergency Civil Liberties Committee, was one of those rare times when political stresses brought his principles and prejudices into a shade of confusion. When the Central Intelligence Agency, growing rapidly under Allen Dulles, engineered the coup that overturned the leftist Arbenz regime in Guatemala and replaced it with the United States-oriented Castillo Armas government, the Eisenhower administration lied about American involvement. But that America had been involved was known, though not the extent of the involvement nor that it was Central Intelligence Agency work. Thomas, who thought it was State Department work, took in his column a curiously mild view of it. "Since a Communist beachhead in Guatemala would have been a serious matter," he wrote, "one must rejoice that that particular danger seems to be over." He observed, however, that it was the more liberal elements in Latin America who complained of this "Yankee imperialism," that "there can be no doubt that revolt in Guatemala had active support morally and probably materially from Washington," and that "our American responsibility will be very great" for good government in Guatemala.

Thomas had intended to sink his $10,000 birthday gift not in the Socialist Party or its offshoots but mostly, for a change, in his "own" organization, the Post War World Council, over whose policies he had more control. But he could not resist worthy appeals even when they competed with his dearest projects. Before he knew it he had advanced $500 to the Workers' Defense League, sent $1,000 for use in a Mississippi civil rights case, given an unnamed amount to the National Committee for Rural Schools, and donated other sums that would force him to scout around for donors for the Post War World Council. He cut expenses in 1954 by quitting his Gramercy Park apartment, leaving the city where he had been a resident for forty-nine years and making Cold Spring Harbor his year-round home. His son Evan, who had a summer place down the road from Violet's (now the Gateses') house, had a comfortable apartment above his double garage which Thomas took over. Thomas had his usual garden. (A new cook at Evan's place, thinking Thomas the gardener, shouted at him to bring some corn but to leave it on the porch and not dirty the kitchen.) Thomas flew to Bermuda in March 1955 to visit his son William and family, William Thomas now being field director of the Red Cross there. He promptly encountered an exercise of religion that persuaded him that he had not satisfactorily defined his own position. The cause was his attendance on Palm Sunday with the younger Thomases at the service in the chapel at the United States Naval Station.

"The service was genuinely impressive," he remarked. "The chaplain . . . spoke with a sincerity and friendliness and a sense of message which had value for us all. As I listened to him, I hoped that my grandsons in any time of military duty might be fortunate enough to benefit by the ministry of such a chaplain. And this made more poignant my own inability honestly to join in the recital of the Apostles' Creed or to see in the events of Holy Week the guarantee of immortal life of which the preacher so confidently spoke."

The chaplain was so inspiring that he made Thomas doubt his own doubts, or at least *want* to doubt them. The hymns and prayers of his childhood, the unseen power of several generations of churchly forbears—perhaps even his yearning to see Violet in the next world that he had shut out from his beliefs—tugged at him. He could not stand apathy or ambiguity, least of all in his own conversations with himself. It set him to composing, entirely for his own peace of mind, a 6,000-word restatement of his own beliefs even though, as he read it over, he saw that the old skepticism was still there, if in different phraseology. He conceded at its end:

> As I read over what I have written, I am aware that to true believers of every sort, it will seem hardly better than an uncertain if reverent agnosticism. In writing it, I have not found nor expressed that assured peace of mind which in these days so many of us crave . . . as the highest good. . . . Yet I think that I have, for myself at least, set forth a kind of faith which however less triumphant than my eager heart might desire, justifies thankful acceptance of life, deep satisfaction at belonging to the race of men, and adequate reason for seeking to make some contributions to the marvelous pageant of human existence.

One of his contributions to the pageant was to urge President Eisenhower to "recognize the inescapable fact that the Communists do rule China," that we got along better with Russia in the United Nations than out of it, so why not China? Another was to wire the President and Senators Humphrey, Morse and Lehman, among others, against the new tendency to threaten war over Quemoy and Matsu. Another was to raise more money for Angelica, getting $200 in one lump from Margaret De Silver. Angelica was being sent $50 monthly by the Italo-American Labor Council in New York and preferred (on the chance that she might at times make a salary in Italy) that Thomas not send her money until she asked. But she never asked and he was troubled with visions of her going hungry. "Will you write me how you stand financially," he wrote her. ". . . . I need to forecast the future a little, properly to serve our Ambassador to the Italian people." In her reply she made no mention of money, so he sent her $200 which she later acknowledged with gratitude.

He had regained his old stride in producing books, having added in 1954 *The Test of Freedom*\* and in 1955 *Mr. Chairman, Ladies and Gentlemen,* a charming jumble of reminiscences of his years of public speaking and advice to speakers he derived therefrom, which he had threatened to call *Chairmen I Have Met and Dinners I Have Et.* Whenever it was permissible, he plugged his books on radio or television programs, as he also did at "book luncheons," one of them at the Cosmos Club, Washington's equivalent of the Coffee House, of which he had recently become a member. The Cosmos gave him a base of operations and overnight accommodations in the capital for an ambitious Thomas project—a great Post War World Council effort to devise a viable introductory plan looking toward world disarmament, aided by the prestige of two United States Senators. He was so busy that he resigned a committee chairmanship in the American Committee for Cultural Freedom, which was tentatively planning a "Free World Academy," an idea backed by Henry Luce and others, to train people for active service as anti-Communist, pro-democratic propagandists. While Thomas thought the idea good on paper, he was wary about association with publicists whose motives might clash with his own, writing, "I understand that Henry Luce has become the chief factor in it and my confidence is less than perfect in what he would do with it." Later, with William Benton, he attended a Plaza Hotel luncheon where Luce spoke and repeated an irritating old canard to the effect that Thomas had said the Democratic and Republican parties had carried out all that he advocated. Thomas, having corrected this a hundred

---

\**The Test of Freedom* was an analysis of what he considered the proper American line between McCarthyism on the one hand and Communism on the other.

times, was annoyed enough to speak sharply to Luce about it after the luncheon, and then to apologize by letter for his "bruskness." Luce had scarcely acknowledged this with a pleasant note when Time again suffered Thomas's displeasure for what he felt was erroneous coverage of the Galíndez case.

Thomas sent his views on a proper British policy for the Far East, with apologies, to the MPs Herbert Morrison (who had recently visited New York and dined with him at Cold Spring Harbor) and Clement Attlee. Nor was he too busy, when Prime Minister U Nu of Burma arrived, to call on him at his suite at the Pierre, attend the luncheon given him by the Mayor, and go to two other conferences with him. U Nu's Socialist government had installed the forty-hour work week and made other modest gains on which Thomas looked with considerable hope, although that country was still neutralist. At the request of the Rangoon paper Nutimes, Thomas cabled a semi-approving report ending: ". . . THE PRIME MINISTER OF BURMA TOOK VERY MUCH THE POSITION OF NEHRU ON THE DESIRABILITY OF ASIAN NEUTRALITY BUT HIS PERSONALITY, HIS HUMOR, HIS FRIENDLINESS ENABLED HIM TO AVOID THE UNFORTUNATE IRRITATION WHICH THE ABLE INDIAN LEADERS, NEHRU AND KRISHNA MENON, SOMETIMES PROVOKE."

As a lecturer, he was propagandizing (and sounding public opinion) with characteristic vigor. "I am writing this column between Butte and Billings, Mont.," he wrote for his American newspapers, "aboard a Vista-Dome car on the luxurious North Coast Limited. . . . Since October 2nd I've traveled by airplane, train and bus twice across the continent and from Hibbing, Minn. in the North to Montgomery, Ala. in the South, with much zigzagging and many difficult connections in order to make one-night stands." To Knife and Fork clubs and other organizations he spoke against American involvement in Indochina and explained that the United Nations was not really limited to those states practicing perfect unselfishness in foreign relations, so that Red China should be admitted. He stopped in Kansas with the Millers, whose oldest child—his oldest grandchild, Norman Thomas Miller—would soon graduate from college. Finally getting home, he managed to make the Yale game at Princeton with the Friebelys. Despite all good intentions he could not resist joining another committee, the American Friends of Vietnam, which supported the new Catholic Premier Ngo Dinh Diem; Thomas would discover it to be a group with which he had little sympathy.

In mid-December he took ten days off for hernia surgery. This gave him time for a backward glance over his own career and to remark on how he had come through odd bypaths into an awkward political position. It became necessary for him (as in his Bermuda disquisition on religion) to analyze his own position in writing, this time for some Socialist friend who might advise him. It was important to find the right friend—preferably one of his own generation, wise and able to keep a confidence. Earlier, Thomas had exchanged confidences with Devere Allen, but Allen was now in declining health and had dropped entirely out of Party activities. He selected Tucker Smith, his 1948 running mate, the economics professor who had inherited his father's farm near Perry, Missouri, and had stayed there:

Dear Tucker: Various circumstances, among them the fact that this is the Woodrow Wilson centenary, set me to thinking about the past and my part in it and to looking over The World Tomorrow, which I edited at the time of the first World War. All of this gave me a great urge to talk to someone who like myself had lived through that first World War and who had pretty much shared some of the religious ideas I had as well as my Socialist convictions. . . . I cannot think of anyone around here who fills the bill with whom I might talk.

As I looked over The World Tomorrow, I rather envied myself as I was: rather unsophisticated, easily filled with righteous indignation but pretty hopeful of a much more successful recovery from World War I and its hysteria than ever took place. I was starry eyed about the League of Nations until I read the covenant and considered its tie-in with the Treaty of Versailles. If I judge that treaty and the covenant less harshly now, it is because I have less hope of what can be done in human affairs, at least with any rapidity.

I suppose the difference with me between now and then could mostly be summed up by saying that then I expected more of both God and man than today. I think I like people rather better now than then partly because I expect less of them. And that goes for myself. Tolerance is easier, but hope for the future less.

Another thing that life seems to have taught me is . . . that fine moral and political generalizations have to be judged very often in terms of attainable goals. For instance, I hate war as much as I ever did but do not find an uncompromising belief in non-violence . . . as effective an alternative as once I did. I believe in the correctness of the moral, and mostly the economic, criticisms I made of capitalism both from the standpoint of Christian ethics and Socialist theory. I think that it is true that our present day capitalism in America, partly as a result of this sort of criticism is somewhat reformed although much less reformed than certain writers are claiming. But various grim experiences, including the record of the Russian revolution, make me far more doubtful of easy collectivist or Socialist alternatives. Politically I think we Socialists are in duty bound to suggest a workable alternative in the light of what we all are learning about bureaucracy and the difficulty of preserving individual freedom and initiative even under a collectivism short of totalitarianism. In our complex world, there are not many questions that can be solved simply in terms of condemnation of what is. Conceivably such condemnation can pave the way for something worse. I still believe there ought to be a great increase of collective ownership but I am far more painfully aware of the difficulties of operating collective ownership than formerly and I have become more skeptical than once I was of the ethical beauty of voluntary collective communities, noble as may be their inspiration. The tyranny of true believers living together over one another can be a pretty terrific affair.

. . . . I cannot become sophisticated enough philosophically to be sat-isfied with [a] purely philosophic concept of God. . . . I cannot escape my rational doubts by resort to mysticism. . . . I am not even a great admirer of the mystic except when his mysticism is accompanied by the kind of love St. Francis of Assisi had for men and all created things. Francis's love for Lady Poverty is, however, no solution for our problems. I think that Gandhi's devotion to spinning, and his preaching of its value, makes sense temporarily under conditions as they were . . . in India. It was no long run answer to the problem of abundance, and abundance men surely have a right to seek. . . .

All this means that I lack some of the convictions which have made men powerful in reaching the hearts of their fellows. I am, for example, not doing a good job in persuading people to the kind of Socialist inquiry and Socialist attitude which I think facts and our times require. I might do better if I were a "true believer" in a more definite creed. Yet "true believers" have done a lot of harm as well as some good. It is, I think, one of the misfortunes of men that to arouse them to do what can and should be done now, one has to promise so often an undeliverable utopia. That necessity ought not to exist if mankind is to make the progress it ought. There are, for example, abundant reasons for taking steps . . . for con-trolled disarmament to avert World War III or to do the economic things that could be done steadily to diminish poverty and to increase abundance, but how do we make these reasons have the force of the simpler Socialist faith of earlier days? How in short can we combine discrimination and enthusiasm?

Although I hope less than I once did, I am by no means crushed by my own beliefs and lack of dogmatic certainty. For myself, I see plenty to live for. The question is how more effectively to share my beliefs. This question is the more important because I am persuaded that my present less than apocalyptic convictions do point the way if not to utopia at least to the delivery of mankind from the kind of catastrophe which continuation of the present policies seems to me to [make] rather more probable than any forward march of man. This is not because man per se is becoming worse, but because the consequences of his folly and sins can be so much more catastrophic now that he has become to a large extent master of the incredible power of the atom.

I shall be grateful if you have any light to shed on this. You were a soldier in the World War who I think later became a pacifist. You were also a YMCA worker. I was an outspoken Christian pacifist who later felt obliged to modify that belief. We both were, and are, Socialists, but Socialists of a rather different type than in earlier days. That is why I am writing to you.

This remarkable letter was the appeal of a leader of men and born optimist who had been backed into a corner by his profound dissatisfaction with the existing American political system, his growing doubts about the Socialist system he had to offer as a substitute, and his inner questioning as to how and how far the Socialist substitute must be modified. The utopian in him about which Niebuhr had complained had been so far subdued that he feared he lacked the kind of buoyant conviction essential for persuading the masses. Lacking the belief in God that had once sustained him, he had to accommodate his thinking to the two most shocking political events of his lifetime—the awful perversion of Socialism in Russia and the equally awful urgency of coming to satisfactory terms with a ruthless and unfathomable Union of Soviet Socialist Republics which held the power to destroy civilization. ("Vishinsky was the one man on earth with whom I should most have hated to shake hands," Thomas wrote elsewhere. "He was evil, indefatigable, and sometimes brilliant.")

The letter was the more astonishing because of the enormous responsibility he assumed for the good of the nation and the world, despite his status as self-appointed propagandist holding no public office and technically not responsible to the electorate which had repeatedly rejected him and his party of a few thousand. He did, like St. Francis, have a singular devotion to mankind, for all the occasional crustiness age and disappointment had given him. Tucker Smith, though he had his hands full at the farm, answered with a long and warm letter which could not solve Thomas's dilemmas but did supply encouragement, saying in part, "If there is an eternity in which men personally sit and stew in their own private past, the temperature in yours will be bearable."

### 6. Again, Murder

In his statement for the 1955 Princeton Yearbook—a sobering half century after he had graduated—Thomas had told his classmates:

> I've failed—doubtless to your general satisfaction!—in the chief purpose of my career. That was to bring about, or help bring about, in our country a more realistic political alignment which might give us two major responsible parties, one of them democratic Socialist in principle whatever its name. . . . Love for Princeton—as for our country—does not blind us to imperfections. . . . Yet, looking back, I can truthfully say that my Princeton years opened the doors, or led to the connections, which largely shaped my life. Even my marriage, far and away the happiest and smartest of my achievements, I owe, at least indirectly, to Princeton. . . . I could have wished to persuade you to share more of my views, but I should be an ingrate not to acknowledge thankfully your friendship, and its more than tolerance to this heretic. . . .

". . . [When] Mr. Nixon faces a situation which he can exploit for partisan advantage," Thomas told the readers of his column, "he throws truth and good sense to the winds and causes true patriots to pray that he may never become President of the United States." (Thomas *did* have a gift for appraising character.) He had become almost as disenchanted with John Foster Dulles, although in summer the two still occasionally met at the Cold Spring Harbor beach club and argued politics, sometimes in the buff in the locker room. Right out in his column Thomas pronounced Dulles to be "indefatigable in energy if not perfect in wisdom," and he called it "egregious folly" when Dulles and Life Magazine collaborated on that shocker, "How Dulles Averted War." Blurbed on the cover: "THREE TIMES AT BRINK OF WAR: HOW DULLES GAMBLED AND WON," it seemed to place the grave business of civilization-saving statecraft on the level of a truculent boy putting a chip on his shoulder and shaking his fist. The other side of the Presbyterian elder's split personality was showing. The article declared that Dulles had prevented war by a toughness that included the threatened use of nuclear bombs in connection with problems in Korea, Indochina and Taiwan. "The ability to get to the verge without getting into war is the necessary art," Dulles was quoted as saying. "If you try to run away from it, if you are scared to go to the brink, you are lost." This fustian, coming from the threatener of "massive retaliation," brought a storm of protest from a broad American spectrum and from normally friendly Europeans. Thomas observed in his column:

> Mr. Dulles and Henry Luce launched into the world, just prior to an official conference with Sir Anthony Eden, and during an election year, an article which infuriates the British, bringing charges of untruthfulness from such friendly papers as the London Times and the Manchester Guardian, and at the same time greatly provokes Democrats in our own country. All this at the moment when the administration wants bipartisanship in foreign policy and cooperation with Britain. . . . I pass over the dubious accuracy of the article. . . . *The* necessary art is not to dance on the edge of the abyss of war but to discover an alternative to war in the struggle for freedom.

Thomas himself was working hard at this necessary art. Meanwhile, on the initiative of A. J. Muste, Thomas had joined Mrs. Roosevelt, Albert Sprague Coolidge, John Nevin Sayre and forty others in a letter to Eisenhower appealing for clemency for Communists (among them Elizabeth Gurley Flynn) convicted under the lamentable Smith Act, which Thomas had fought from the start in 1940. None had committed an overt act but had been convicted simply as Communists "conspiring to overthrow," etc., as Thomas pointed out in a later letter to the President. The anti-Communist Thomas continued in his alter ego as defender of individuals when he came to the aid of the portly Alexander Trachtenberg and his Communist colleague George Charney, both convicted under the Smith Act but granted new trials. Thomas sent out 511 letters appealing for donations for their legal expenses. He still had affection for Trachtenberg, the one-time Socialist who had brought him into the Party back in the days when Socialism seemed the answer to everything. Now seventy-two, Trachtenberg had long been head of the Communist Party's book-publishing operation. But when he gratefully invited Thomas to William Z. Foster's seventy-fifth birthday celebration, Thomas wrote "Dear Alex" as bluntly as he had Miss Flynn:

> As for William Z. Foster, I certainly don't want him in jail but neither do I want to sponsor any dinner in his honor. You surely know my position which is that I am supporting your case because of my general views on civil liberties and not because of my sympathy with Communism. I will be honest with you and tell you that I would be a Christian of a rather unusual type if I should be on [Foster's] committee considering his systematic misrepresentation of my position . . .

Trachtenberg was convicted anyway, and all Thomas could do was appeal for leniency. Earl Browder, now living in Yonkers and no longer a Communist, stopped in at Thomas's office for the first chat the two had had for years. He had not been invited by Thomas, who participated "as a matter of courtesy." The death of Charles Gilkey's wife in Massachusetts, and Thomas's sympathetic letter, brought about his first meeting with his friend of his youth in several years. "Bless you for your letter," Gilkey wrote, mentioning that Thomas had invited him to Cold Spring Harbor the previous year, that he would now like to visit him and would be preaching at Union College March 11, an easy train ride from New York. It caused the busy Thomas to make special arrangements:

> Dear Charlie: Your letter . . . brought much joy until I looked at the calendar and found I am leaving early on the evening of Monday, March 12th. My engagements are at Lafayette [College] and I think I can leave Easton around 1 or 2 and get back for the night of Tuesday, March 13th, if you can stay over. If you get down to New York by noon on the 12th, we can have lunch at the Coffee House Club and spend most of the afternoon. . . .

This was one of those occasions when Thomas regretted that he no longer had an apartment in town. Gilkey did indeed meet him at the club and spend most of the afternoon with him. Gilkey was now seventy-three to Thomas's seventy-one, a time of life when split-second planning is not usually necessary between friends of such vintage, but Thomas had a "call" beyond the usual churchly summons. A new cause was thrust upon him when his friend Dr. Jesus María de Galíndez vanished from sight—obviously kidnaped, possibly murdered. His doctoral dissertation at Columbia had been a study of the Trujillo tyranny in the Dominican "Republic" which he had expanded and was arranging for general publication. He had received threats intermittently for four years. Trujillo had sedulous agents in America (his attorney in New York was none other than the firm of Franklin D. Roosevelt, Jr.) and in Galíndez's bachelor apartment at 30 Fifth Avenue, police found a note instructing them to seek his Dominican enemies if he should be killed. His apartment was only a few blocks south of where Tresca had been shot dead—a crime which Thomas still held to have been incompetently investigated—and in his public outrage over the new case he seemed quite willing to attract the attentions of Dominican thugs himself. As days passed it appeared more certain that Galíndez must have been murdered. A Dominican friend of Galíndez, Andres Requena, had been shot dead in New York in 1952 after publishing a pamphlet critical of Trujillo—another unsolved case—and several anti-Trujillo Dominicans who had fled to Cuba had also received threats and were believed in danger.

Again Thomas was convinced that it was political murder, the suppression of decent government by terror. At the Inter-American Association, of which he was a board member, he read to the audience the notes of an address Galíndez was to have delivered there—an attack on the Trujillo regime. He wrote the President (whom he was also urging to suspend nuclear tests), asking for an FBI investigation. He wrote the State Department, the Attorney General, several union leaders and leading newspapers, not forgetting Drew Pearson, all in the effort to get more official and unofficial attention focused on the case. The Trujillo people fought back with protestations of innocence and the routine charge that Galíndez was a Communist, which he never was. Thomas was irate that young Roosevelt should continue to draw a reported $5,000 a month retainer from the Dominican butcher. When Roosevelt chaired a Democratic committee meeting at the Commodore Hotel, Thomas wired the county leader, Carmine de Sapio: "AS FRIEND OF DR. JESUS DE GALINDEZ AND ENEMY OF TRUJILLO AND OTHER DICTATORS I RESPECTFULLY PROTEST IMPLIED DEMOCRATIC PARTY SUPPORT OF TRUJILLO BY YOUR DINNER CHAIRMAN'S POSITION AS LAWYER-LOBBYIST FOR GENERALISSIMO TRUJILLO. . . ."

He wrote Roosevelt (with whose mother he was carrying on a correspondence about several public matters) to ask, "do you not think you owe it to your name and your associates and your professions of interest in democracy to resign your position which inevitably and increasingly compromises you in the public mind?" Roosevelt waited a month, then replied courteously but with no mention of resigning, though he did resign considerably later. Thomas appeared on CBS to tell of the case and his favorite Spanish-language magazine Iberica* was featuring it, but it was an election year and he could not spend all his time on Galíndez. He noticed, as he frankly wrote Jacob Javits, that both Javits and Mayor Robert Wagner in their race for a Senate seat were so eager for the Jewish vote that "I was . . . worried for a while that both of you thought you were running for Mayor of Tel Aviv." Nationally he was dissatisfied with both Eisenhower and Stevenson, for despite the latter's intelligent speechcraft and responsible attitude toward the Bomb, he weaseled on civil rights to save his southern vote. (Thomas was beginning a correspondence with a previously little-known Alabama preacher, Martin Luther King, whom he praised for his leadership of the bus boycott and above all for his adherence to nonviolence.) He went to the Socialist convention in Chicago and found it largely taken over by youngish and middle-aged people he did not know as well as he wished.

"The convention showed some life and adopted a pretty good platform," he commented, adding, "I was pretty lonesome . . . thinking of the people who used to go to those affairs." The convention nominated Hoopes and Friedman again, which Thomas thought foolish, this time mostly for write-in votes since the Party had been forced off most state ballots. Always a job-hunter for deserving people, he was looking for a teaching position for Robin Meyers, the resigned Socialist Party national secretary, knowing that some would look askance at her Socialism and writing to many prospects, "I would be glad to have any of my grandchildren sit at her feet in a history class. . . ." But his major effort of 1956 was the conception, organization and financing of a disarmament conference of respectable scope—an enterprise which got him into something that seemed impossible, a quarrel with Mary Blanshard.

*Iberica, dedicated to a Spain free of Franco, with Victoria Kent as editor and Louise Crane as publisher, was edited at Thomas's own 112 address. Thomas and Salvador de Madariaga were honorary chairmen.

## 7. High Life in Mexico

Thomas had earlier been impressed by what he called a "very carefully worded and prepared resolution on universal disarmament" presented by thirty-four Senators headed by Flanders of Vermont and Sparkman of Alabama. He did not want the idea to die, and since no one else seemed ready to breathe life into it, he accepted the duty. He took the two Senators to lunch at the Cosmos Club and got their cooperation in extending the idea into the realm of practical plans. He had prepared the way with a meeting with other believers in disarmament, including Thomas K. Finletter, James P. Warburg, Ernest Gross, Charles Bolté and Christopher Emmet, and he secured the cooperation of the distinguished lawyer Grenville Clark. During the war, Clark had been told in advance about the atom bomb by Secretary of War Stimson, who was a law associate of his—a weapon so horrible, Stimson said, that he urged Clark to devote himself to thinking of methods by which it might be controlled. Clark, a Harvard Phi Beta Kappa two years older than Thomas, had been thinking about it ever since and was soon to produce a book on the subject. The proposed disarmament conference was scheduled for the fall of 1956; meanwhile Thomas had to raise money for its expenses, and it happened that two world-shaking political events which no one could foresee—the British-French-Israeli attack on Egypt and the Soviet invasion of Hungary—intervened.

Almost as explosive had been the arrival in the United States in 1955 of the slight, intense and somewhat mysterious Sacha Volman, thirty-five, an anti-Communist propagandist. Born in Bessarabia, Volman was said to have been imprisoned by the Nazis when they invaded Rumania, then imprisoned again by the Russians when they arrived, and to have "finally fled Rumania hidden in a wooden box." Now an American citizen, he had plans for the printing and disseminating in Tunisia, Japan, Hong Kong, India and selected countries in South America of carefully prepared anti-Communist pamphlets. Volman had discussed these ideas with the Free Europe Committee, which had promised to finance some of them if their own propagandist stipulations were met. Volman needed the money and prestige of a substantial American group backing him, which Thomas began to organize. He took a great liking to Volman, and the newcomer obviously reciprocated his affection. Volman seemed to have that combination of idealism, brains and energy that he admired, plus a kind of soldier-of-fortune derring-do that enabled him to deal effectively with people of all races in all countries and to escape trouble, if need be, in a wooden box. Soon Thomas was deep in plans with Volman to spread pamphlets and also to open a "school for democracy" somewhere in Latin America.

Thomas was thinking in large, almost grandiose terms, planning a disarmament conference, seeking to persuade America that the idea of negotiating disarmament with the Soviets was feasible, and meanwhile contemplating a program for strengthening through propaganda weak points in the world against Soviet expansionism. What with the American elections and the Galíndez case, Thomas—always in danger of spreading himself thin—seemed to be approaching the gossamer.

He was angered by the steady effort of Trujillo agents to blacken Galíndez's reputation. They spread rumors in New York, Washington and elsewhere that he not only was a Communist but a crook, having appropriated monies he collected from Spanish Republicans. Also, Thomas noted, "I got an amazing telegram from Ciudad Trujillo asking me to go down and visit them in the name of the so-called Popular Socialist Party about which I know nothing. . . . Whether I am invited . . . to be eliminated or bribed I do not know." The Federal Bureau of Investigation said it was New York's case, the same District Attorney Hogan was in charge who had failed in the Tresca murder, and the Galíndez case was fated also to remain officially a mystery, the body presumably well hidden—a circumstance which if anything increased Thomas's outrage against the Dominican dictator.

Thomas's secretary, the sober-faced Stephen Siteman, was able and industrious enough to take part of the load. As if to fill in interstices of time, Thomas, whose acquaintance with foundations was wide and friendly (he had actually asked the Roebuck-Marshall Fund for money to defend Trachtenberg, without success), was knocking at the doors of several for several purposes. The Twentieth Century Fund had just rejected his plea that it finance a thorough study leading to the proper regulation of political campaign contributions, a field in which his worries were well substantiated but ahead of their time. The Ford Foundation rejected his request for a grant for an objective study of the kind of teaching given at parochial schools—Protestant and Jewish as well as Catholic. He had better luck at the Christopher Reynolds Foundation, which gave him $5,000 to finance his coming disarmament conference.

Meanwhile a Congress for Cultural Freedom conference was held in Mexico City in September, which Thomas attended with Roger Baldwin, Ralph Ellison, John Dos Passos and others, to meet many delegates from Latin America. Its chief purpose was to strengthen its representation in nations south of the border and to encourage democracy in states too often subject to the Communism of despair or to banana- or copper-corporation Fascism. Salvador de Madariaga presided, and Thomas made one of the principal speeches. Here again Thomas met that astonishing man, Jose de Figueres, known as "Don Pepe," the then democratically inclined President of Costa Rica, and his wife Karen. He had met them earlier at an Inter-American Association meeting in Havana. Both spoke English and would aid Thomas's propagandist efforts in Latin America. In Mexico City, Thomas felt hampered by his limited knowledge of Spanish and was disappointed in the conference's lack of preparation and intellectual content. The activist in him sought not only talk but results, which he would soon seek through Sacha Volman. Baldwin, who for decades had watched every dollar for the American Civil Liberties Union, was struck by something else—the open-handedness with which he and other visiting delegates were treated. "I was surprised," he recalled, "at the automatic way the Congress paid our hotel bills and other expenses—laundry, telephone calls, whatever was on the hotel bill." This might indeed have aroused curiosity, since the American branch of the Congress for Cultural Freedom was having trouble keeping financially afloat, and in fact Thomas had solicited money for it himself. But Thomas was preoccupied with many things including the Suez crisis, over which tension was mounting. Another was the fairly general and sometimes uninformed criticism of the United States by Latin delegates, and still another was the matter of the unexpected vaccination.

Thomas was surely the first person to become so exercised over a vaccination that he complained about it to a Secretary of State. The victim was Dr. de Madariaga's secretary, Mrs. Emilia Rauman of Oxford, England. Although she had been told at the American Embassy in London that it was not required, when she landed at Idlewild (later John F. Kennedy) Airport in New York for only a two-hour layover before catching a plane for Mexico City, she was told otherwise and vaccinated then and there. The vaccination took severely and reduced her usefulness in Mexico. Thomas, unhappy about the anti-Yankee feeling he had found, thought the kind of State Department bungling shown in the case of Mrs. Rauman was one of the reasons. He wrote Secretary Dulles, apologizing but asking him to hand the problem along to the right assistant: "It seems to me that our authorities should be coached to be very meticulous in explaining exactly what would be required."

Dulles might rightly have complained that Thomas opposed virtually everything he or his department did—his policy on China, on Indochina, his open backing of Adenauer, his rocket-rattling, his treatment of the Foreign Service officer John Paton Davies, the abruptness of his turning on Nasser in the matter of the Aswan Dam loan—and Mrs. Rauman's vaccination. But now Thomas gave enthusiastic support to the Dulles-Eisenhower refusal to back the Anglo-French-Israeli assault on Egypt and their insistence on a United Nations solution. He cheered this American reliance on the international assembly which had exercised so little influence and even saw it as a turning point that might give the United Nations more of the prestige and power he wanted it to have. He wrote scornfully of "the blundering Eden" and "that sorry Socialist [Guy] Mollet" of France. He was more cautiously critical of Israel, as a New Yorker had to be. When on November 5 England, France and Israel accepted a United Nations cease-fire order, he was jubilant. The Arab-Israeli problem which had haunted him for years was not solved, but at any rate the international body had shown strength. He wrote Eisenhower "how deeply we respect your action in standing by the United Nations even when it is jeopardized by our friends."

In the Eisenhower-Nixon sweep over Stevenson and Kefauver, which occurred during the Middle Eastern drama, the Socialist Hoopes-Friedman ticket (which got on the ballot in only four states) was credited by possibly indifferent tabulators with a grand total, all over the nation, of 2,126 votes. No more evidence was needed that they should not have run. But Thomas's most immediate concern was the shaky health of the President-elect and the shaky character of his running mate. His early appraisal of that enigmatic personage was again emphasized by the line with which he ended his newspaper column after the election:

"With what fervor I pray, 'God save the President.'"

### 8. Hungary and Suez

The brutal trampling of the Hungarian revolution by Soviet soldiers and tanks during this same eventful interval brought the predictable Thomas reaction. Russia's vote with the United Nations moralists condemning the Suez invaders while forbidding any United Nations interference in Hungary was to be expected. But India's vote *with* the Soviet bloc on the issue truly aroused him. If India's "neutralism" had pained him, this implied approval of Soviet terror put him in a turbulent temper that rippled through his note to J. J. Singh:

> Dear J. J.: This is a letter to decline an invitation for tomorrow night which I so happily accepted over the telephone. I could give you various conventional excuses for not coming but I have decided that I owe to such good friends as you and your charming wife an honest explanation.
>
> The truth is that I cannot trust myself to act as a guest in your home should act toward those more or less official Indians who, I gathered from your phone message, will be present and with whom I should have broken bread. There are lots of things I like to debate and discuss but I find it impossible to discuss calmly Krishna Menon's vote with the Soviet bloc on the Hungarian issue at the United Nations. This seemed to me a repudiation of India's attempt to stand for moral principle as opposed to power politics in international relations. . . .

He sent copies of this to Indian friends including Asoka Mehta in Delhi, Minoo Masani in Bombay and the Indian ambassador in Washington, who had once been his dinner guest. He also cabled Moshe Pigade, president of the Parliament in Belgrade, to protest Yugoslavia's vote on the Russian side, but without the shock apparent in his messages to the Indians. It turned out that Singh agreed with him substantially, as Thomas explained in a letter to Mrs. Roosevelt:

> Singh now says he feels much the same and he begs me to urge you to take an initiative in sending a cable to Nehru pointing out to him how India's moral leadership has been compromised. Presumably other friends of India would sign such a cable if you thought best: Roger Baldwin, probably, Walter Reuther, I myself, and you might think of others.

Mrs. Roosevelt replied that she thought the timing wrong and that it was best not to cable Nehru at this moment, to which Thomas, on reflection, agreed. Meanwhile he was aiding Hungarian relief measures, referring some inquiries to his old Hungarian friend, the Reverend Ladislas Harsanyi, still in East Harlem. From Angelica in Rome came a letter pouring out her outrage at the invasion of Hungary (but not mentioning Suez). "Moscow's crimes in Hungary ought, if anything could," he replied in part, "to bring sight to the blind but I suppose some wilfully blind outside of Russia will persist in faith in the monster." Worried because she mentioned for the second time that she was living on "borrowed time" and added, almost as if in farewell, "I am very happy & grateful to have met and known you personally, dear Comrade," he sent another check for "our Ambassador." She had at any rate recently made twenty-two speeches in twenty-two different places in twenty-two days, causing him to comment, "Mrs. Roosevelt could hardly beat that."

Thomas was at the New York airport to meet the Hungarian Socialist and patriot, Anna Kethly, one of those who managed to escape the Russians and cross the border, and who soon after vainly tried to present Hungary's case at the United Nations. The New York Socialists arranged a reception for the sixty-seven-year-old Miss Kethly at the West Side apartment of Ernst Papanek, who headed the Party's international affairs committee. Leading Socialists from the United Nations attended, Asians (including an especially large group of Burmese) and Europeans including Paul-Henri Spaak of Belgium, as well as Golda Meir, Israel's foreign minister who had been deep in the planning of the attack on Egypt. Thomas helped to maintain calm in this potentially explosive gathering, for New York Jewish Socialists unanimously condemned the Soviet invasion of Hungary but were apt to condone the Israeli invasion of the Sinai. The discussion was kept strictly on Hungary. "[Mrs. Meir] used good judgment and did not intrude the question of Israel," he observed, writing later, "This Israeli business troubles me greatly. I would so like to go along with the great majority of my Jewish friends. Alas, as it seems to me, most of them have a blind spot on this subject. There are notable and honorable exceptions."

He was receiving protesting letters because at a Cooper Union forum he declared that Israel did not come to the United Nations with clean hands. Shortly thereafter, his long-awaited disarmament conference— thirty-eight conferees including politicians, scientists, economists and peace planners—met at Arden House, the former Harriman mansion in the Catskills which had been given to Columbia University. Needing more organizational and financial backing, he had succeeded in bringing in the Committee on World Development and Disarmament (of which it might almost be said "of course" he was a board member) as co-sponsor with his own Post War World Council. The formidable scope of the problem was well understood. These four days of meetings were devoted to discussions that would result in three resolutions to be presented in Congress, one for a permanent United Nations police force, a second for a monitored moratorium on nuclear tests, and the third a "comprehensive resolution favoring universal controlled disarmament." It was Thomas's conviction (later borne out) that arms "control" was a delusion. Only the truly inspiring idea of disarmament, he argued, could capture the world's imagination and could eventually work. When the conference ended, three of the conferees, Senators Flanders and Sparkman and Congressman Brooks Hays, agreed to present to President Eisenhower its suggestions for what Thomas called "immediate progress in the difficult—but not impossible—road to our goal." The three resolutions failed in Congress, but Thomas's efforts continued.

Almost a year earlier, when Thomas had first advanced the idea, Mary Blanshard had understood that she would be employed in organizing the conference and carrying it through while her husband was on a lecture tour. But what with the money pinch and the many intervening crises, the job had vanished, Thomas apparently had been remiss in keeping her informed, and she let him know that she was incensed. "I recognize that you have some right to be annoyed," he conceded in a letter in which he tried to explain. But she resigned from the Post War World Council in protest and Thomas was disconsolate at this rift in one of his oldest friendships. From Angelica at any rate, in a Christmas letter reporting her activities, came proof of continuing affection: "I can only repeat to you the question I am asking myself: Why am I to have the privilege of having met [such] a human being and Socialist as you are?"

As months passed and the estrangement with Mary continued, he was so troubled that he mentioned it to Harry Fleischman, who happened to meet her in Washington and tell her about it. Her response was to write Thomas about her unhappiness at the "strange schism" but recounting her grievances. Thomas replied instantly and humbly: "In retrospect I think that I was stupid not to find some way to work all this out and still keep you but most of the things to which I belong these days have money trouble. . . . I do not in the least exaggerate when I say that I would rather have worked with you in this whole business than anyone else. . . . Perhaps I have too much Scotch blood in me. Anyway some thrift seemed to be imposed and I didn't handle it very well. I am sorry." He ended it, as he never ended any but family letters, "My love to you both." Her heart melted, to his immense relief.

From a third lady in his life, Lenore Marshall, came an offer to help pay expenses for a vessel that peace workers proposed to send into a Pacific area which the British planned to close off, unilaterally, in order to make nuclear tests—a ship whose voyage would be highly publicized and whose venture into the forbidden area to stop the tests might awaken world realization of the deepening danger.

Still another woman, Karen Figueres, wife of the president of Costa Rica, wrote him from San Jose, " 'It was a treat rather than a treatment'* to hear you the other evening on the TV program Night-Beat!"

His correspondence with a fifth lady touched on different problems:

> Dear Elizabeth: I am delighted to hear that you are out of the jail to which you never should have been sent. This, as you well know, means no conversion to your point of view on Communism but rather a statement of my opposition to the Smith Act and my belief that you, even as a Communist, weren't jeopardizing the security of the U.S.A. Now that you are out I hope that your health is reasonably good and that, among other things, you can urge along your party in what seems to me to be the right direction toward a more democratic position.

Elizabeth Gurley Flynn, now sixty-seven, replied with a long, affectionate letter which she ended: "Do give my warmest regards to your wife [Violet had been dead for ten years], to Roger [Baldwin] and to all others of my good friends of long ago, whom I never cease to regard as such."

*This was a wordplay on a ubiquitous cigaret ad of the time.

# XVIII

## 1. More Infallible Than Moses

Thomas's global interests were reflected in the gift of table linen from Ngo Dinh Diem, President of South Vietnam; his correspondence with Aneurin Bevan about the necessity for international Socialist cooperation; correspondence with Mohammed Hatta in Indonesia protesting the political imprisonment of two distinguished Indonesians in Jakarta; correspondence with Chester Bowles about organized opposition to nuclear tests; Thomas's effort to persuade Secretary Dulles to exert pressure on Tito for the liberation of Djilas; his protest against the sale of American tanks to Saudi Arabia in return for an air base; his acquaintance with Julius K. Nyerere, the Tanganyikan leader, and Foreign Minister Salah el-Bitar of Syria at the United Nations; his protest against the American appeasement of Trujillo (as of Franco) for anti-Communist purposes; and his increasing apprehension over the Vietnam and Arab-Israeli problems.

On the strength of a grant from the well-heeled Free Europe Committee, Thomas had founded a new organization misnamed the Institute for International Labor Research and had sent Sacha Volman to Costa Rica, where Volman got under way with the beginning of his school, aided by President Figueres. Called the Institute of Political Education, the school was planned as an outgrowth of a domestic institution founded by Figueres for Costa Ricans. Its aim was simply to instruct young Latin Americans in the democratic processes which were little known there. The busy Volman was soon visiting South American countries to gain moral support from liberal leaders and to recruit students.

Thomas meanwhile had sent copies of his carefully written report on the Arden House conference to the newspapers and to all influential Senators and Congressmen, and sought to propagandize it in other ways, writing Loy Henderson in the State Department: "Would it lie within your province to convey to the President the suggestion that he might proclaim a disarmament Sunday as a time for prayer?" He urged on Eisenhower a moratorium on nuclear tests. As for Indochina, he had accepted Diem's table linen, similar gifts undoubtedly having gone to all of the American Friends of Vietnam, but he grew progressively more skeptical both of Diem and the American Friends. Diem was jailing political opponents. Reports from Asia including a long article in Life suggested a withdrawal of civil liberties in South Vietnam and, as Thomas observed, "hardly justified the seemingly unconditional praise that Henry Luce bestowed on Ngo Dinh Diem." In one of Thomas's quotable lines, he wrote that "we Americans cannot be true to our own convictions about democracy and freedom if we pass over in silence acts done by our friends which we would strongly condemn if done by our enemies." When General John W. O'Daniel, chairman of the Friends of Vietnam, announced that "American private enterprise" and American "capital and know-how" would solve Vietnam's problems, Thomas let the general know by return mail that he was finished with O'Daniel and the Friends too, which contained an assortment of members from left to right including Van Wyck Brooks, Senator John F. Kennedy and Conrad Hilton.

Thomas was planning his usual trip to the West Coast and also one to the Middle East. He had written an editorial in The World Tomorrow in 1919 about Zionism and Palestine and had been caught up in the problem ever since. He had supported his friend Rabbi Magnes's proposal for a bi-national state governed jointly by Jews and Arabs, and since 1948, when Israel proclaimed itself an independent state and defeated its Arab attackers, he had clearly seen the seriousness of the threat to world peace so long as the Arab-Israeli enmity continued. Some Jews still fumed over his pre-war anti-interventionism. His present opposition to Zionism, which arose from his intense belief in the separation of church and state, and the blame he laid on the Israelis for the recent attack on Egypt, did not improve his standing with Jews. The Jewish Daily Forward was sniping at him again and opposing a new plan for the unification of the Socialist Party and the Social Democratic Federation (each now a mere shadow) because Thomas was not "right" on the Israeli question. "Unfortunately," Thomas wrote Gausmann, "I think the majority of the New York Jewish community seems to believe that Ben Gurion is more nearly infallible than Moses ever was, and that any criticism of Israeli action is a kind of blasphemy. . . ." He agreed that "the few Arabs I have listened to are equally intransigent." Now at least three persons whose opinions he respected—Mrs. Roosevelt, the Reverend Donald Harrington and Reinhold Niebuhr—saw more justice on the Israeli side than Thomas did, the pragmatic Niebuhr being impatient enough with Eisenhower for his opposition to the tripartite attack on Egypt to call him "the Chamberlain of our day." As Thomas wrote Erich Fromm, whom he had known as a psychoanalyst and teacher in New York and New England and who now lived in Mexico, "I am tremendously concerned for some solution to the present stalemate of bitterness in Arab-Israeli relations. It helps to poison [the] peace and happiness of the world. I find it hard to know how to act." As always, it was mental anguish for him to encounter a problem for which he could not propose a logical solution. His instant impulse was to make an investigation at the scene. He did not feel he could afford such a trip, but the Free Europe Committee solved the difficulty, agreeing to pay his expenses in return for his effort to arrange for the publication by reputable Arab groups of such anti-Communist works as Djilas's *New Class* and the five-nation report on Hungary, condensed in pamphlets. His companion on the journey would be the thirty-five-year-old Don Peretz, a non-Zionist Jew who had taken his doctorate at Columbia in political science and was a specialist on the Middle East.

Now, in September, 1957, Thomas called on Foreign Minister Salah el-Bitar of Syria, still in New York on United Nations business. The Syrian, who as a student in Paris had flirted with Communism, was co-founder of the Socialist Baath Party in Syria. That country's quarrel with Israel and its arms deal and friendship with Russia had so alarmed the State Department that in 1956 the Central Intelligence Agency had joined with English and Iraqui conspirators in a vain effort to overthrow the purportedly pro-Communist government in Damascus. One result was that Bitar was treated in America as an enemy. No State Department representative had met him when he arrived and he had been studiously avoided ever since. His alleged ties with Russia and alleged enmity toward Israel made politicians shun him. They felt that any commerce with Bitar would mean a sure loss of Jewish votes.

Loy Henderson, though approving of Thomas's contemplated trip to the Middle East (the area of Henderson's specialty), strongly urged him to avoid Syria because of its "consistently anti-American policy." Bitar, a lonely man in New York, speaking through a secretary-interpreter, welcomed the attentions of Thomas and Peretz. "He talked calmly and logically," Thomas wrote Chester Bowles. ". . . . I personally was impressed by his statements that Syria wasn't Communist; that he was a Socialist and therefore not a Communist; and that Syria took aid from Russia only because she must under the situation which confronted her." Bitar was anxious to talk with American liberal politicians, especially Senator Kennedy. The Senator agreed to meet Bitar but in strict secrecy, which was arranged, with his wife Jacqueline the only other person present, translating Bitar's French. Kennedy evidently wanted to run no risk of losing Jewish support.

"All profile and no courage," Thomas remarked tartly to Peretz of the Senator whose book of similar title had celebrated politicians whose backbone forbade this kind of concealment.

Thomas also arranged meetings (not furtive) between Bitar and Senators Flanders and Humphrey and with Bowles. "I am not happy," Thomas admitted to Flanders, "over the fact that it is probably true that we have a lot more men in uniform in Turkey than Russia has in Syria. If the Russians had an equivalent number in Mexico, there would have been a war a good while ago." Thomas also borrowed the Fifth Avenue apartment of Mrs. W. Murray Crane, mother of his friend Louise Crane, for an informal reception at which Bitar met a group of Socialists and others. ". . . I have been urging various editors . . . to try and get in touch with you before you return to Syria," Thomas wrote Bitar. "I spoke to the editors of the New York Times, and of the magazines Life, Look and Harper's."

All in all, Bitar could thank Thomas for bringing him out of quarantine during his brief stay. Thomas also prepared the way for his own trip with a visit to the Israeli Embassy in Washington, and a flood of letters to friends and officials in the Middle East and to such people as the Israeli ambassador to the United Nations, Abba Eban. To President Eisenhower he sent a characteristic letter, again sounding The Theme:

> Before I go, there is what the Quakers would call a concern on my heart involving the lack of progress in disarmament negotiations. . . . I had the good fortune to be at the United Nations Assembly when you made your impressive and ultimately successful speech on Atoms for Peace. I witnessed the extraordinary change in the atmosphere of the Assembly after that speech. I am wondering, therefore, whether there might not be a chance to do something of the same sort on disarmament by appearance before the Assembly at a suitable moment. Could you not yourself in a

speech challenge all nations to accept that very important feature of the American proposal in London: namely, the diversion of all new nuclear materials solely to works of peace? . . . I think some dramatic act like this might make it impossible for the Russians to refuse and win for us a solid leadership for effective progress in disarmament. . . .

### 2. The Mideast Quickstep

At seventy-three, Thomas, instead of resting up for his journey, returned from lectures in Philadelphia and the University of North Carolina (cramming on the Middle East on planes and in hotels), to join Peretz and take off on November 2. He made such a fetish of independence that he could be crusty when his companion offered to carry his luggage. On the long flight, Peretz noted that Thomas's original reserve soon melted. For the younger man, to observe his partner was as interesting in its way as to achieve the formal objectives of the tour. Thomas had with him Herbert Muller's *The Uses of the Past,* which he felt gave him perspective on present world crises with its sketches of earlier civilizations. At Cairo they were surprised to be met by the chauffeur-driven car of a kindly American businessman there, Francis Kettaneh. The car was at their disposal during their ten days in the city—an unexpected result of one of Thomas's advance letters.

They checked in at the American Embassy, saw the Pyramids and had a long talk with Nasser at home. Peretz felt that an important Thomas quality was the immediate impression of integrity and absence of guile which had first struck Peretz himself and now, he was sure, had the same magnetic effect on Nasser and others. It invited friendship and confidence.* Nasser told them of his plans for Egyptian reform (which he called democratic Socialism although he was vague about details) and seemed taken aback by Thomas's question as to whether Jews and Copts were to share in the reforms. He replied that the mass exodus of Jews from Egypt after the recent war had been caused by groundless fear and that he had tried to halt it, though he admitted that some sympathizers with Israel had been arrested. He "agreed with Mr. Thomas on the need for separation of church and state in a democratic

---

*Years later, when Henry Kissinger was conducting Middle East shuttle diplomacy, Peretz thought that this quality of Thomas's might have made him even more successful than Kissinger at this assignment.

society," Peretz noted in his report, "but said that conditions in Egypt preclude such an approach . . ." He spoke with some resentment about recent American "unfriendliness" and United States support of the Baghdad Pact whose organization broadcast anti-Nasser propaganda from Cyprus. (Nasser was to send them both handsome Christmas cards for several years, causing Thomas to comment to Peretz on the religious paradox of a Moslem sending Christmas greetings to a Jew.) In a later interview the Minister of the Interior told them with a straight face that there was no press censorship but admitted that mail was examined, which Thomas found true: "We later discovered that all of Mr. Thomas's mail from Egypt had been censored and some did not arrive in the United States at all."

Except for the most basic sightseeing, Thomas could not endure an idle moment. The number of interviews with government officials, Jewish and Coptic leaders and embassy people, varied by such things as an unscheduled Thomas speech at the American University in Cairo, ran into scores. The two visitors found the Jewish community troubled by uncertainty about the future, though admitting that there was no repression at the moment. Thomas soaked up information, ate everything placed in front of him, and kept up a pace that had Peretz, half his age, breathing hard. When they left Cairo they discovered that their entire bill at the new Shepheard's Hotel had been paid by the Arab League—an embarrassment to Thomas but one he could do nothing about. In Baghdad the two Americans dined with the anti-Communist and also anti-Israeli Dr. Fadil Jamali, former Prime Minister and United Nations delegate, and several of his cabinet-minister friends. In Beirut, Thomas was surprised and not displeased when United States Ambassador Donald Heath (who was later to occupy an even hotter spot in Saigon) said, "I feel like addressing you as Mr. President." They had talks with President Camille Chamoun of Lebanon, the well-known Foreign Minister Charles Malik, religious leaders, Quaker relief directors and members of the Socialist Party, some of whom poured out such strong anti-Israeli sentiments that it struck Thomas that their motto must be "liberty, equality and revenge." At the Syrian border, the pair cooled their heels for an hour while the guards got clearance from Damascus. In that city they were at last greeted by Bitar, who exerted himself to return the hospitality Thomas had shown him in New York. The Foreign Minister was a leading proponent of Syrian union with Egypt and a moderate on the Israeli question. The country, however, was faction-ridden, his power had its limits and Thomas and Peretz found that one of their primary aims—to arrange better treatment of some 5,000 Jews in Syria—was beyond him. The Anglo-American-Iraqi interference in Syria a year earlier was not in the visitors' favor. Their talk with the rich, pro-Soviet Minister of Defense, Khaled el-Azm, who had on one wall a mural-sized photograph of his recent meeting with Khrushchev, demonstrated the opposing hues events could assume when seen through different propagandist lenses. Thomas warned him of Soviet untrustworthiness, saying, "If you sup with the devil you must use a long spoon," and reminded him of what had happened to Jan Masaryk in Prague—pushed out of a window to his death. Azm nodded and remarked that Secretary Forrestal in Washington had also fallen from a window to his death.

"But he was not pushed," Thomas said.

"But our information is that he *was* pushed," Azm replied.

At the invitation of Bitar, who seemed determined to counter the drift toward the Soviet Union and to improve relations with the United States, Thomas addressed 200 Baath Party leaders, including government officials and university professors. Bitar advised the group to listen and learn, although "Mr. Thomas [will] say things with which the group could disagree . . ." Thomas did indeed court disagreement in his sharp criticism of the Soviet Union and his emphasis on Socialist ideals not well observed in the Middle East—the suppression of narrow nationalism and the cultivation of an internationalist concern for justice for Jewish minorities in Arab countries as well as for Arab minorities in Israel. He was politely received but he had no ready answer for the Arab who said, "You Christians and Westerners, not we, persecuted the Jews; yet you make *us* pay the price." And he became uncomfortably aware that in his litany of Soviet crimes in Hungary he was using a double standard, for all his effort to judge both sides fairly. ". . . I was met," he noted, "by reference not only to the Franco-British attack on Egypt, but the allegation that France in Algeria had killed and tortured more Algerians than Russia had Hungarians, crimes, they alleged, made possible, at least indirectly, by aid of American arms."

The Americans returned for more interviews in Lebanon before going on to Jordan, with Thomas often attending evening meetings and then working into the night on reports, letters and his newspaper columns. Peretz watched for signs of the older man's collapse. Instead, Thomas rose each morning with new zest. His trousers were always baggy and he sometimes seemed to have slept in his clothes. In Amman, Hussein was king of a divided and rickety nation with military checkpoints everywhere. "Bombs go off very frequently around homes of officials," Thomas reported in his column; "—there was one incident the night after we arrived." He found Jordan flooded with "outrageous Egyptian radio propaganda" against Hussein, adding, "I wish I had known about this propaganda . . . when I saw President Nasser and he complained of the propaganda against him by the 'Baghdad Pact' radio network." But the young king seemed confident when the Americans interviewed him, telling of plans for the resettlement of refugees and of a possible federation of Jordan, Saudi Arabia and Iraq as a counterbalance to the union with Egypt being proposed by Syria.

In Israel—necessarily the last stop because entrance to contiguous Arab countries from Israel was forbidden by the Arabs—Thomas groaned at the commercialization of religious shrines in Jerusalem and Bethlehem. The two successful Soviet sputniks of October and November—triumphs in the field which had been believed America's own—had given Russia a new prestige in the five countries previously visited. Now, during the Thomas-Peretz nine-day stay in Israel, occurred the humiliating American failure to put its first and much smaller satellite into orbit—an event causing jeers all over the world about the "Flopnik" or "Kaputnik." The two conferred with government officials, newspapermen, and leaders of many Jewish groups and of the Arab minority, whom they found relatively well off. Prime Minister Ben-Gurion was "too busy" to see them—doubtless a reflection of his pique at Thomas's well-known criticism of the war against Egypt. Golda Meir, who received them at her Jerusalem home, was cordial at first but less so, Peretz recorded, when Thomas "raised the question of our concern about Israeli expansionism." Although they had more freedom to travel, discuss and disagree in Israel than in any of the Arab states, Thomas was troubled by what he saw as an Israeli inflexibility when he felt conciliation was called for, and a failure to solve the moral problem raised by Israel's appropriation of the property of the refugees. He wrote in part:

> A beginning of progress might be made if the Israeli government would say convincingly that the Arab war which enlarged her territory has not changed her willingness to work out economic cooperation or union with Jordan. . . . Further, Israel should convincingly renounce any thought or plan for territorial expansion by force of arms, but agree to negotiate rectifications of the present fantastic boundary . . . Then she should agree to the maximum possible repatriation of refugees on Palestinian soil, with indemnification for those who do not desire repatriation. . . . As evidence

of her good faith Israel might urge joint patrols of borders by a mixed force of her troops and her Arab neighbors. She should hasten the process already begun of turning the Arabs who did not leave Israel into first rather than second-class citizens. . . . The hate and the arms race in the Middle East which it inspires can only lead to an Armageddon.

A necessary underlying ingredient for peace was, he said, an end to United States–Russian Cold War contention over the region. He and Peretz finished their tour in great pessimism, feeling that "the brinkmanship policies of . . . Dulles only worsen the situation and add oil to the smouldering fires in the area."

The two Americans had spent six hard weeks together without disagreement or tension. Thomas's eagerness to detect and follow the bewildering currents and eddies in this roiling sea of discord had been unflagging. The two of them, Gentile and Jew, were in basic agreement on the main issues, and Peretz was left with an enduring admiration for his "student." As they flew home, Thomas spun yarns about his political career and occasionally talked of Violet. "He talked of her," Peretz recalled, "as if she had died only the previous year instead of ten years earlier."

### 3. Funeral Directions (Revised)

Thomas had scarcely touched his native soil when he asked to see President Eisenhower, his purpose being to tell him politely that his Secretary of State was wrong in almost everything he did and to propose a better course. The President as usual replied through a subordinate who urged him instead to talk with Loy Henderson and Robert Murphy, the two pre-eminent State Department specialists in the Middle East. Thomas responded:

I am a little embarrassed about talking to either Mr. Henderson or Mr. Murphy, highly as I esteem them, because I should hardly feel I could say to them what I would have said to the President; namely, that I think Mr. Dulles has so lost confidence all around in the Middle East that I doubt whether he can successfully deal with the situation. I do not say this, I assure you, out of love of criticism for criticism's sake, or for any lack of personal friendship for Mr. Dulles. It just seems to me to be a fact.

I should be glad if you could call the attention of this letter [sic] to the President.

Thomas's camaraderie with Bitar and the Syrian Baathists seemed to inspire in the Central Intelligence Agency the idea that friendliness might be as good an avenue for winning American favor in Syria as conspiracy. From Allen Dulles came a proposition: Would Thomas invite the leading members of the Baath Party to America—all expenses paid by the CIA—with the assurance of an official welcome here instead of the freeze given Bitar? Thomas thought it over, discussed it with Peretz and decided against it because of the CIA backing. Although he had written to congratulate the younger Dulles on his appointment to head the agency, he was not enamored of undercover work and institutional deceit and was critical of some of the agency's rumored operations. His enterprises after his return showed his feeling that time was running short both for himself and for the continued existence of a civilized human race on the planet unless the luxury of Cold War animosities was sacrificed for determined negotiation. In March, 1958, he was the moving spirit in a second disarmament conference at Arden House, with much the same group attending plus two more Senators, Hubert Humphrey and John Sherman Cooper. One of the primary obstacles to success was the familiar argument, "You can't trust Russia," which the conference felt no longer prevailed under the political conditions now faced by Premier Khrushchev. ". . . [T]here was general agreement," Thomas reported, ". . . that Khrushchev generally wants approaches to disarmament at least as much as Dulles and that both bargain for relative advantage. But both want to live. Common interest in the defeat of Germany made even Stalin tolerably cooperative during the war."

At his Nineteenth Street office Thomas was mounting an assault of which the heaviest shelling was aimed squarely at his Long Island neighbor and fellow Princetonian, John Foster Dulles. He felt more than ever that Dulles's policies were aggressive, undemocratic, basically untruthful and terribly dangerous, placing the country "at a low pitch," he remarked, ". . . in the quality of its world leadership." One might have thought the Post War World Council office a large one, heavily staffed, from the work done and the propaganda issuing from it. Siteman was now Thomas's only full-time helper, typing his letters, keeping abreast of his affairs, holding the fort when he was gone. From 112 came a steady stream of pronouncements, advocacies and incitations:

The United States stand that the Soviets had no rightful interest in the Mideast was absurd, Thomas wrote the White House. We should put the recent "surprisingly decent" Russian proposals for a settlement there to the test "by proposing, for example, that Russia join the United States, France and Britain in underwriting a United Nations guarantee that no boundaries will be changed by force in the Middle East."

He endorsed Senator Humphrey's proposal to negotiate an agreement with the Soviets to suspend nuclear testing, independent of all other issues.

He mentioned the ferocities of three dictators, Trujillo of the Dominican Republic, Fulgencia Batista of Cuba and Alfredo Stroessner of Paraguay and commented: "Now these dictators have been indiscriminately included by John Foster Dulles as among the leaders of 'free nations'; that is, nations friendly to our [capitalist] interests and which usually vote with us at the United Nations."

As Cuba weeks later seemed ripe for rebellion under Castro, Thomas joined Louise Crane of Iberica and others in urging Dulles to stop sending arms to Batista.

With a group of peace advocates he visited Arkady Sobolev, Kremlin ambassador to the United Nations, and reflected that Sobolev "gave me a feeling that on this subject a common interest in living made the Soviet Union in earnest in desiring not only an end of tests but considerable disarmament."

He attacked Dulles's underwriting of the Baghdad Pact "to defend nations right up against the southern border of the Soviet Union."

In Washington, with Linus Pauling, Bertrand Russell and others, he had the nerve to bring suit in Federal District Court to enjoin the Secretary of Defense and the Atomic Energy Commission from conducting any more nuclear tests—although the current House Un-American Activities Committee chairman, Congressman Francis E. Walter, saw Thomas as "simply serving as a screen of respectability while the black hand of the Communist conspiracy remains clearly visible." The suit, which was of course a propaganda effort to awaken the people to their peril, was dismissed four months later, whereupon the plaintiffs appealed the ruling.

Thomas addressed the United Nations Trusteeship Council (without success), asking for an immediate halt in United States nuclear tests in the Marshall Islands area on the ground that the tests were scarcely beneficial to the Micronesians living there.

He characterized our landing of 10,000 Marines in Lebanon as "the new American imperialism," saying, "our support has been given, not to the awakening peoples of the Middle East, but to corrupt, reactionary governing cliques so long as they were anti-Communist."

He was hardest of all on Dulles's threat to fight for the Quemoys, "within a slingshot distance from the Chinese mainland," which could cause the "stupidest, wickedest, possibly the most catastrophic war in American history." He employed his knack for making distant and confusing events understandable by comparison: "The Chinese would no more leave [the islands] in enemy's [*sic*] hands than our forefathers would have left Block Island in British hands after the revolution if they had held it necessary for the defense of Newfoundland." He worried as he had worried for forty years over the failure of the majority of the people to rise to an understanding that it was their own welfare that demanded their political participation, except that now in the nuclear age the word "welfare" had to be replaced by "survival":

> The apathy of the people or their fatalistic resignation in the face of this danger indicates a collapse of democracy in the face of issues most vital to us all. The Quemoys mean nothing to us. . . . They mean much to the mainland Chinese, whose harbor and shipping are within gunshot of them. . . . So great has been [Chiang's] proved incompetence, the corruption of his officials and his wife's family, so great his unpopularity among the Taiwanese . . . that it is far from certain whether he would carry a fairly conducted plebiscite on Taiwan.

The American people had rejected Socialism, which he believed a cure for apathy. Socialists in the United States were many times outvoted, say, by the Loyal Order of Moose. The English Socialists had gloriously abjured imperialism but had failed at home and been replaced by the Tories. The French Socialists, when it came to North Africa, Egypt and Indochina, were as imperialist as Napoleon. The Indian Socialists had failed to achieve an international outlook. The Burmese Socialists were neutralist and ineffective. The Socialists in the Arab countries were as bitterly nationalist as Ben-Gurion. "The truth is," Thomas wrote Angelica, "no Socialists at present are making the kind of records that arouse people." He asked her opinion of the portrayal of Russian society in *Dr. Zhivago,* and he worried about her solvency: "Remember that I am really a custodian of the funds which keep our Ambassador to the Italian people."

Meanwhile he found time to attend the graduation of his granddaughter Nancy Gates from Wells College, and her marriage in an Episcopal ceremony in June, 1958. And one night in the fall he suffered excruciating pains which inspired a handwritten note to his children:

Sitting up awake & not in expectation of death, I decided to modify a bit my directions as to my funeral.

In general it will be your trouble & I don't want to dictate—but I have certain strong feelings—

1. I prefer cremation to burial.

2. I want nothing resembling a non-religious Socialist funeral with lots of speakers.

3. If convenient keep the funeral small & private and if so desired have a memorial service later.

4. Since I know no ritual substitute which in dignity ranks with a Christian burial, I'd like Sid Lovett or some understanding friend (perhaps Donald Harrington of the Community Church) to conduct the service. He should understand that I am not an orthodox Christian, that I do not believe in the resurrection of the dead or most of the formal dogmas of the Church. But the Christian tradition is so much a part of our life, or my life, and Christ is to me so commanding a figure who so released all that I care most for that I feel justified in asserting a Christian service which should *not* play up personal immortality.

Where to have the service is your problem.

All my love,

Dad

He shunned the "non-religious Socialist funeral" because it offended his sense of dignity. For all his decades of dissent, he wanted his leave-taking to be appropriate. But the removal of his gall bladder saved him. Word of his illness upset Angelica, who had written him in one of her more enthusiastic flights: "If we would have had Norman Thomas in more than one country!" and who now wrote solicitously of his overwork and need for a rest: "Please *do* let me know how you feel presently." ". . . I convalesced very satisfactorily," Thomas assured her, "and got back to the office earlier than was expected . . ."

## 4. Welcome, Khrushchev

Thomas's twice-weekly newspaper column, which he prized above jewels, was gradually dying. It now appeared in only three outlets, the Denver Post, Los Angeles Mirror and Trenton Times, and they occasionally skipped him if space was needed. His writing was urbane (if always too hasty), and his experience and political wisdom were rich, but the Thomas smile and charm which could reconcile listeners to advice they did not like could not always be translated into type. His criticism of Republican and Democratic heroes tended to alienate members of those parties, and since these partisans represented most of the population, the wonder was that he still had three willing newspapers. His honest animadversions against revered institutions—even motherhood in excess—doubtless lost him readers.

"Next to the prevention of war," he wrote undiplomatically, "birth control is probably the most important single issue before mankind. It is immoral to oppose it." Such opinions increased the number of Catholics who saw him as an enemy of the Church of Rome. A few undiscriminating Jews thought him anti-Semitic. To his often disparaging comment about Protestant services he occasionally attended was added his latest published censure of Protestantism as interested in "a way of escape from the world rather than salvation of the world." So he kicked about Catholics, Jews, Protestants, Republicans, Democrats (and Socialists too, though less publicly), and what was there left to praise?

He *had* given praise where he thought it due. He had praised every peaceable move of Presidents Truman and Eisenhower, of Senators McMahon, Morse, Humphrey, Flanders, Sparkman and many others down to the redoubtable William H. Meyer, the first Democrat to be elected to Congress from Vermont in generations, who campaigned for an end to nuclear tests, for banning the H-bomb and for recognition of Red China. (Thomas gave Meyer more than praise—a campaign contribution—but an ungrateful constituency was to turn Meyer out of office.) Thomas's priorities were consistent. He had always regarded religion and politics as related at least in being ideally aimed at the betterment of man. Foreign relations was the overwhelming issue in the nuclear world and the churches that ignored this, treated it lightly or exacerbated the curse of nationalism, were failing the people, especially since in America there was no longer any party of substantial political dissent. Unlike those in England, America's two great parties were fundamentally similar with respect to the vital issues—capitalism, anti-Communism and reliance on weapons of destruction. There was far more contrast among individual Democrats, or individual Republicans, than between the two collective parties. "The voter will still have to inquire," Thomas observed, "is this candidate . . . a Barry Goldwater or Nelson Rockefeller Republican, a James Eastland or Hubert Humphrey Democrat?" He would later write seriously to Elmo Roper, "How about a question [in your poll] concerning a new and meaningful alignment of parties so that you wouldn't have to examine each Democrat and Republican separately to tell them apart?"

The old warrior, now a little stooped and bulging at the belt, his face furrowed by expressive lines, his bald head encircled by a white fringe, was for all that a superb athlete in his mission of attempting to push the public and the Congress toward disarmament. Now second to Dulles in his list of the enemies of reason was Dr. Henry Kissinger of Harvard. Dulles had built up the nuclear terror, which seemed to rule out war except as a last, and indeed final, resort. This had been seen by critics as having a numbing effect on foreign policy, since any aggressive foreign policy must depend ultimately on the credible threat of war. Now Kissinger, in a book revolting to Thomas, *Nuclear Weapons and Foreign Policy*, had evolved a way in which, he said, limited wars could be fought with comparative safety to noncombatants and the country could therefore avoid profitless peace. Thomas, always trying to place obstacles in the way of war, was stunned at the spectacle of a brilliant professor removing those obstacles for the good of the country. Dulles died in 1959, but his alliances, bases and policies would live on, and Kissinger was to be heard from later. Angelica disagreed that the Russians could be trusted, writing Thomas, "The Bolsheviks will never keep their word . . . and with them there can be no 'new beginning.' " Thomas's belief that the fight against the nuclear terror was a simple necessity for civilization was one of the considerations that thawed his own long cold war. He actually invited Earl Browder to tea at the Coffee House Club, setting an afternoon hour "when practically no one is there." He was kind to him, suggesting that he might give a series of talks at the New School, and Browder thereafter referred to him as "my dear friend." Events in Russia had encouraged Thomas, whereas American moves and attitudes caused him to write:

On May 10, 1955, Russian representatives on the United Nations Subcommittee on Disarmament accepted previous Western proposals for reduction of the size of conventional armies. . . . On September 15th, the Western Powers withdrew the proposals which the Soviet had accepted. . . . [In] 1957, the Russians offered a suspension of [nuclear] tests under inspection. This was flatly rejected by the United States largely on the grounds of the impossibility of adequate inspection. But the Americans offered a package proposal including the suspension of tests and other matters far more difficult of inspection. . . .

. . . . The false moralism that sees in Communism only a criminal conspiracy to which the West can say nothing but *no*, and that primarily by military might, is a dangerous thing. . . . We Communists and non-Communists will have to live together or die together . . .

Thomas welcomed Premier Khrushchev's 1959 visit to America. He attended the official luncheon given the Premier in New York and was "impressed by the way Mr. Khrushchev handled himself and his case." He cheered the Camp David talks and wrote, "We who believe in controlled disarmament have reason for satisfaction that Khrushchev supported it as earnestly as he did before the U.N."

### 5. A Considerable Moocher

". . . [It] is wonderful to have Mr. Thomas around," The New York Times editorialized. "We hope he will be here for long years to come." The occasion was his seventy-fifth birthday, celebrated by a dinner party at the Waldorf-Astoria Starlight Roof. Eleanor Roosevelt and Norman Cousins were co-chairmen and more than 700 guests turned out. ("I'm not old," Thomas said, "but I'm horrified at the age of my children.") Typically, the busy Mrs. Roosevelt was "on the road" at the time of the dinner she helped organize and sent her sentiments on a recording, in which she said that Thomas could always be counted on for "causes that our democracy needs." It was a significant phrase. In a fat nation where so many comfortably believed that democracy alone was enough, self-sustaining and self-perpetuating, the reminder that there were causes badly needed was important. While there was of course no head-count, it was believed that a minority of the guests were Socialists. The majority were Democrats or Republicans, opposed (as was Mrs. Roosevelt) to some of Thomas's beliefs but believing in him as a stimulator of thought, catalyst and civic watchdog. The praise of The Times did not mean that the old Socialist had simmered down to mere liberalism. He valued The Times as the world's greatest newspaper, read it avidly, missed it when he was out of town but assailed it, for example, when it editorially supported the Marine landings in Lebanon. And The Times would never, never agree to the nationalization of even the "commanding heights" of industry.

Thomas still lived alone in his son's Cold Spring Harbor apartment, sometimes did his own cooking (though he was a terrible cook; and since the Evan Thomases and the Gateses were nearby, "I am a considerable moocher," he said) and caught the 8:15 to the New York office he had occupied for almost three decades. In his Waldorf talk, always the artist, he kept the diners attentive and often chuckling but he did not fail to sound The Theme. "You've got to have co-existence or you'll have co-nothingness," he said, suggesting that Khrushchev "in his own interest and his country's may be more serious about disarmament than our Pentagon."

For a nonofficeholder without visible political clout to draw 700 to the Waldorf was an anomaly. Listeners who for years had tried to analyze the Thomas fascination knew that it was something more than eloquence, more than wit or personality or integrity and had to settle for that inclusive word *style*. Three days after his birthday he telegraphed President Eisenhower that his forthcoming visit to Spain was widely interpreted as approval of Franco, urged him to "emphasize America's continued belief in the principles of freedom and true democracy," then hurried to address a Senate subcommittee on the wretched conditions in migrant labor camps right on his own Long Island.

### 6. What Devil of Ineptitude?

The growing threat to all mankind of nuclear weapons ticked like a time bomb, with scant time left to stop it. Thomas had had to wait for a relatively receptive climate both in Russia and the United States—until well after the death of Stalin and until McCarthyism waned—before he could get qualified conferees together at Arden House with any hope of impressing Congress. But by then time was already running out on at least two essentials for success, one of them technical, the other political.

Technically, once nuclear weapons had proliferated and were known to many scientists, not even the best intentions could get the cork back in the deadly bottle. Late in 1958, seventy-one leading nuclear scientists from many countries including the Soviet Union had met at Kitzbühel, Austria. Linus Pauling and H. J. Muller, both Nobel prize winners, were among the American delegates. The seventy-one agreed that setting up a reliable system of controls for international nuclear disarmament had become "extremely difficult, perhaps impossible," and that even though negotiation might eliminate such weapons, the knowledge of how to make them would be, "for all time, a potential threat to mankind."

Politically the world had had the misfortune of containing a Russia racing to defend itself against a nuclear might it had to match or excel, and a United States determined to keep ahead. The Dulles policy of massive retaliation and of spreading nuclear weapons among allies had increased both the terror and the skills which could create even greater terrors. Congress, lacking any compelling leader working resolutely for disarmament, had capitulated to Dulles. Of the private crusaders such as Thomas, Grenville Clark and Pauling, Thomas had spent the most prolonged and dedicated effort and had succeeded through his remarkable propagandist skills in getting a peripheral hearing for disarmament. But his only hope as a private crusader was to reach the public and the Congress with his message.

This hope was dwindling because the arms race based on nuclear weapons had produced an American affluence which—though short-run and later to be paid for bitterly—was domestically so popular that it was political suicide to oppose it. Americans had grown so bored with the balance of terror that, with the exception of a thoughtful minority, it no longer terrified. Thousands of great arms factories, with more going up all the time, made their owners wealthy and gave well-paying jobs to millions. The home swimming pool, once reserved for movie stars and rich executives, now was enjoyed by plumbers and truck drivers, and the second or third car was mandatory. Both capital and labor had a vested interest in manufacturing more and more weapons of death. Socialism had always believed that capital gloated over arms profits, but labor was supposed to be made of better stuff. It was not. Bitterly anti-Soviet leaders such as Meany and Lovestone urged higher and higher wages with plenty of overtime for the producers of bombers and missiles. Already, so large a part of industry was devoted to weapons that the certainty of peace would mean temporary economic disaster. Naturally, politicians like Congressman Meyer, who opposed rising military expenditures, were virtually asking for retirement to private life. Public officials, union leaders and even gentlemen of the cloth joined in the fierce competition among the different states for factories to make planes, tanks, submarines, tactical and strategic hydrogen bombs and all the thousands of parts that went into them.

Thomas observed that The New Yorker—the only popular publication that had given responsible editorial treatment to the Bomb ever since Hiroshima—sent Daniel Lang to Alamogordo after a four-year lapse. He found that the scientists working there on these weapons, many of whom had earlier been uneasy or even haunted at the potential destruction over which they presided, were now of good conscience. They were serving their country. It was true that the time did not seem propitious to reverse this public psychology except in the sense that it was now or never, but startling political events would emerge to make the effort appear worthwhile.

As always, when Thomas had an idea he thought important for the people, he made speeches about it, wrote articles about it and summed it all up in a book. This time the book was *Prerequisites for Peace*, his most important of all in the sense that it concerned issues and programs he deemed essential to saving man from self-destruction. *Prerequisites* —not much noticed at the time—gave a striking portrayal of a national state of mind at once materialist and suicidal. Thomas insisted that disarmament, sneered at by "realists," was still politically possible and with skillful management would usher in a world of great prosperity and serenity. To do so it was necessary to persuade the people that the armaments gravy train was en route to catastrophe.

The horror of all-out nuclear war had already been described by Kissinger in his *Nuclear Weapons and Foreign Policy:* In terms of the comparatively undeveloped hydrogen weapons of 1957, a successful attack on the fifty most important American cities would kill from fifteen to twenty million people and leave twenty to twenty-five million injured. There would be vast areas of devastation. The contamination of ground, air and water would kill millions of others or doom them to lingering death. With government personnel and facilities largely destroyed, caring for survivors would be impossible, it would be every man for himself and social life would return to the brutish. The result would be such panic and horror that, as Thomas put it in a favorite phrase, "the living would envy the dead."

To be sure, he agreed, Russia could not be trusted, but neither could the United States, as one had only to scan scores of American Indian treaties continuing into the twentieth century to verify. "The basis of any international agreement," he argued, "is not brotherly love but mutuality of interest. . . ." He thought the signs were clear that the longing of the Russian people for peace and a higher standard of living was pressuring their leaders: ". . . [No] dictator can forever ignore this popular feeling . . . Khrushchev isn't ignoring it. He is concerned about the Russian desire for more consumer goods. . . . It can't be satisfied without cutting military expenditures." Khrushchev was believed to have eliminated most of the ghastly Russian slave camps. Some of the dreadful fear behind the Iron Curtain had abated. "Khrushchev's denunciation of Stalin's crimes let loose forces which he has not the power . . . entirely to force back . . ." Russia's growing industrialization would increase its desire for conciliation with the world of trade, the world itself. Of late, evidence of a Soviet wish for arms reduction had been growing and it was the United States which had pulled back—notably in the 1955 offer which some had called "the moment of hope." "The withdrawal," Thomas wrote, "convicted the West of the same sort of insincerity or uncertainty in disarmament negotiations of which its representatives commonly accuse its opponents."

The United States had some 275 military bases or installations surrounding the Soviet Union, a situation hateful to the Soviets. Some were located in Turkey, a nation contiguous with Russia and a traditional enemy. "If the Russians had tried to establish one base in the Caribbean," Thomas argued with more prescience than he knew, "it would have meant war." Our circle of bases, which he agreed was an advantage so long as our security depended on retaliatory power, would not last. "An unfriendly government or a hostile people could make these bases untenable, or, if tenable at all, on terms of ill will and struggle against sabotage which would completely offset their military value."*

Many were later to agree with his criticism of the Dulles system of alliances which, especially in the Far East and Middle East, overextended the United States in commitments not clearly spelled out. He urged our withdrawal from the Southeast Asia Treaty Organization and the Central Treaty Organization, the latter earlier known as the Baghdad Pact: "Today, the United States appears to have some 47 allies to whom we are bound in varying respects and to varying degrees not clearly known to our people, or to most Congressmen, or, one suspects, the State Department itself."

The unhappy fact was, he said, that on either side there could be no responsible governmental control of armaments that could destroy civilization. Tactical nuclear weapons were, for example, taken into Lebanon by our Marines. Nuclear weapons of various kinds were at some of our 275 bases surrounding Russia. With our allies already or soon to be furnished with nuclear weapons, the final disaster could be triggered by a local incident unknown to Washington or to Moscow, just as the Civil

---

*Thomas has been borne out only in part in this prediction. Some American bases have been eliminated entirely by unfriendly governments, as in Libya. Some countries, such as Turkey and Greece, seem to be reducing the number of American bases, and Spain denied us the use of our bases there for the emergency airlift during the 1973 Middle Eastern war.

War shooting began over a disagreement at Fort Sumter. "In our era of peace under threat of massive retaliation," Thomas observed, "our fate is literally in the hands not merely of heads of governments but of hundreds of anonymous colonels—our own, our allies', and our enemies'."

So new hope emerged when Eisenhower treated Khrushchev with consideration in this country, talked seriously with him at Camp David and agreed to meet him, de Gaulle and Macmillan at a Paris summit in May, 1960. It did not seem impossible that the Cold War might thaw a little and that the political climate might attain a salubrity wherein disarmament might seriously be discussed. It was another time of promise during which the leading participants of all four nations—but particularly those of the Big Two—could be expected to take every precaution against error or misunderstanding.

Hence the downing of an American U-2 spy plane in Russia just eleven days before the four heads of state were to meet not only stunned Thomas but bore out his point that the power to foil grand designs lay in the hands of underlings. (The spy plane of course had been developed by the Central Intelligence Agency and its pilot was a CIA agent, that agency still being headed by Allen Dulles. Was it Dulles, or one of *his* subordinates, who "forgot" that these planes had been spying over Russia for four years and that it might be well to suspend the flights at least until after the summit?) Thomas wrote at the time the first reports came out of Russia:

> How would we feel if in Mexico or Cuba the Russians had half as many bases and planes and flyers as we have in Turkey? . . . How much worse would we feel if one of those flyers got almost to Washington, taking pictures from on high, before our defenders brought him down with all the story book paraphernalia of spies, including a pistol and a poison needle for suicide?
>
> This time there seems small doubt that Khrushchev is telling substantially the truth about an episode that puts the West at a grave disadvantage in the summit conference (if that is to be held) and discredits us thoroughly in the opinion of the world. . . . what devil of ineptitude manages our policy? Or has the State Department surrendered wholly to the Atomic Energy Commission and Dr. Teller?

There followed the gruesome procession of American errors: The denial of the spy plane, the proof that the denial was a lie, Khrushchev's effort to present Eisenhower with a chance to evade responsibility for the flights, the President's admission and justification of them, the statement that the flights were vital to United States security and would be continued, followed by Eisenhower's announcement that they were ended permanently. "Now, more than ever," Thomas mourned, "if nothing comes out of the summit conference but a continuance on both sides of 'defense' by increasing power to overkill and perpetuate a competition in diplomatic lies, espionage and deceit, the end of the road will be annihilation. . . . The whole episode fairly shrieks to the world how extraordinary are the risks that the cold war will become hot by accident or blunder. The one hope is to end the cold war." The Premier overplayed his tantrums in Paris and that ended the summit, Thomas later conceded, but "There is no question that President Eisenhower and Dictator Khrushchev both wanted progress toward disarmament." The opportunity was gone. Thomas voiced a lament felt by many countrymen:

> We now know what most Americans hadn't believed: that in the widely played game of peacetime espionage we lie and cheat like the rest of them—only better, we now boast, because of our technical skill. In the anarchy of the relations of sovereign nations there are no morals, there is no crime, except to be caught.

# XIX

## 1. The Seventh Circle of Hell

Although Thomas was early aware of kinks in Nixon's character, he was not satisfied with Nixon's Democratic Presidential opponent, Senator John F. Kennedy, either. The country-club nabob, he remarked, had replaced the log cabin hero in the voters' esteem and the engaging Kennedy, with money to burn, flying in his own plane, beat Thomas's friend Humphrey in the primaries. Thomas, who never ducked issues, met head-on the question of the effect Kennedy's religion might have on his politics:

> . . . [W]e citizens would have not only a right but a duty to find out whether a Christian Science candidate would oppose all federal appropriations for medical investigation and service, or how a Quaker candidate would do his job as commander in chief of our armed forces. . . . The Roman Catholic church claims greater ecclesiastical control over the beliefs and actions of its members than most Protestant churches or Jewish synagogues. Hence the legitimacy of inquiring how far a Catholic candidate would feel himself bound by the hierarchy's stand on the exceedingly important issue of birth control, or negotiations with Khrushchev which the church seems bitterly to oppose.

Before Kennedy was even nominated, the foxy Thomas had written the birth-control advocate Margaret Sanger—a logical one to pop this sort of question:

> I was delighted to read your letter in the Times. . . . Can't you prompt someone to ask Senator Kennedy a question which no one has yet asked him? It might run something like this:

"Senator Kennedy, you and your family are prominent and influential Democrats in the important state of Massachusetts. This state, apparently under pressure of the Roman Catholic hierarchy, tries absolutely to forbid any artificial means of birth control. That is to say, a church is using its power over a political legislature to make a crime out of that which is no crime at all but rather a social virtue in the eyes of a great many American citizens. Have you ever protested this or in any way disapproved of it? Does your sanction of this sort of legislation in Massachusetts imply submission to hierarchical demands for similar action elsewhere?"

Mrs. Sanger (who in 1917 had joined Thomas in supporting Morris Hillquit for Mayor) took the hint and sent such a query, writing Thomas later: "You will be interested to know that I did not receive a reply to my letter to Senator Kennedy, written at your suggestion."

Thomas: "I think it is worthwhile calling attention to Kennedy's failure to reply to you, don't you?"

But in the campaign, Thomas found Kennedy's statements about his religion "forthright, honest and satisfactory," adding, "I personally am rather more afraid of Senator Kennedy's earthly father than of any spiritual father of his church." While in general he thought the Democratic Party less pernicious than the Republican, reactionary southern Democrats were worst of all: "Your civil rights planks are hardly worth 50¢ on the dollar with Senator Eastland chairman of the Senate Judiciary Committee and . . . Howard Smith chairman of the House Rules Committee." For years Eastland had outraged him. He had once wired Lyndon Johnson when Johnson was Senate majority leader:

SENIORITY HAS FOISTED ON SENATE AND COUNTRY MANY INAPPROPRIATE CHAIRMEN IMPORTANT COMMITTEES BUT TO HAVE EASTLAND, LEADER OF WHITE CITIZENS COUNCILS, PREACHER OF MODERN NULLIFICATION, AS CHAIRMAN IMPORTANT JUDICIARY COMMITTEE CRIPPLES AND SHAMES DEMOCRATIC PARTY AND AMERICAN SYSTEM IN EYES OF WORLD.

Eastland was still crippling and shaming the system and Thomas was still outraged.

One evening at his son Evan's he chatted with his grandchildren, Wendy, Louisa and Evan III, who asked him questions about politics. With them, he made up for his sometimes stern insistence on exemplary behavior by his attentiveness and charm. He would greet them elaborately with, "How do you do, and how do you do, and how do you do again," and his extensive repertoire of camp songs included "The Poor Old Slave" in all its variations down to "The piggety-poor old sliggety-slave," etc. Now he followed his habit of talking to them almost as adults, discussing the issues of the election point by point, and their interest was total. He saw all of his children and grandchildren when he had the opportunity. After his usual speaking tour to the West Coast, he planned another almost as extensive, writing in his customary hurry to Polly Miller, his daughter in Kansas:

> I am dictating a letter that I won't be around to sign. It is simply to let you know that, as it now appears, I should like to come to you from San Antonio on March 26th, and leaving to go to Boulder, Colorado, on March 29th. From Boulder, I shall go to Des Moines and from Des Moines, come to you on Sunday, April 3rd. Thence to Fayette, Mo., April 5th and then back to you and on April 7th, go to Seattle. Is this going to be convenient?

His enjoyment in visiting the Millers was enhanced by Dr. Miller's belief in socialized medicine and by occasional Miller gatherings at which he met such remarkable people as Thomas Hart Benton. He was now working closely with Lenore Marshall, one of the founders and chief financial supporters of the Committee for a Sane Nuclear Policy. Now that he had no New York apartment, the Marshalls occasionally put him up for the night in their apartment when he arrived back in the city late. He would retire exhausted and rise brimming with energy. He listened to as many of the Kennedy-Nixon debates as he could, unhappy because the two young men were too much alike in tactics, dodging the China issue, going along with a welfare state that had been called Socialist a couple of decades earlier, but both committed to the garrison state—more and more arms when the world already had stockpiled the equivalent of ten tons of TNT for each luckless human being. Thomas was shocked when Kennedy, asked what he would do for the economy, "merely replied that he had already recommended two or three billions more for arms." He was further jolted when the Kennedy office urged that Castro be crushed by our direct economic intervention and our aid to anti-Batista rebels against the dictator (advice it later withdrew, saying it was not the candidate's), which Thomas pointed out would flout our treaty with the Latin American nations in the Organization of American States. He added, as if he were peering beyond the veil: "It will give Castro every reason to draw still closer to the USSR and will excuse Khrushchev for giving him outright military aid." It was all very well for Nixon to condemn Kennedy's proposal, but in the next breath Nixon spoke with satisfaction of the Central Intelligence Agency intervention in Guatemala under Eisenhower, which Thomas with full information now condemned. "I find it frightening," he admitted, "to contemplate the sort of leadership in the White House indicated in the last debate."

He saw that Nixon was following his habit of speaking not quite truthfully, manipulating the facts. But Thomas succeeded in avoiding the posture of the viewer-with-alarm, for although he saw clearly that truth was going out of style and that American society was deteriorating instead of improving, his innate optimism somehow insisted that the trend was not irreversible. When the Sales Promotion Executives Association had the courage to invite him to address them, he performed his feat of letting them have it and making them like it. While the public was admittedly lazy, he told them, "It has an intermittent desire for the facts and that desire can be built up." On the contrary, advertising was tearing it down in the fever to sell goods and was ruining the language in the bargain. He cited the cigaret that "tasted good like a cigaret should," asked if Shakespeare ever wrote a play titled "Like You Like It," and said that that kind of ad made him wish he smoked so that he could quit in protest.

To Newsweek he said, "As a man who has lived many years and seen the world become steadily more dangerous, I regard the current political scene with the highly qualified equanimity of Dante when he arrived at the seventh circle of hell, convinced that there must be an eighth." He had written both major party organizations to grill them about their platforms, bearing down on civil rights and asking, "Will your platform evidence a passionate concern for universal disarmament down to the police level . . . ?" To a friend in Americans for Democratic Action (which he had finally joined himself) he wrote that that organization was foolish simply to endorse Kennedy unconditionally, for it "should be putting pressure on the Senator in a good many fields, including, certainly, foreign policy." To Nehru, on whom he had also kept an eye, he wrote, "May I add my personal assurance of profound hope that you will be able to work out an honorable agreement with Chou En-lai during his visit?"

Twenty-one-year-old Patricia Miller, one of his granddaughters from Kansas, worked in Thomas's office that summer of 1960, doing research for his projected book on great dissenters. Thomas could scarcely be expected to remember the circumstances of the births of all fifteen of his grandchildren, but he could never forget that Patricia had been born in the New Haven hospital at the time Violet was there losing her appendix and setting that record of three generations under simultaneous care. She remembered him fondly not only from her childhood visits to Cold Spring Harbor with the family and his own visits to Kansas, but from his calls on her when he happened to be in Madison while she was a student at the University of Wisconsin.

This summer, Thomas refrained from travel. Each morning, Patricia drove him to the Cold Spring Harbor station, where they each got The New York Times, which he would absorb with incredible speed as they rode in, even to the baseball statistics, which he liked to have if only because his grandson Danny Friebely loved baseball and it aided his conversations with Danny. He walked fast, with long strides. "It was all I could do to keep up with him from train to subway," Patricia recalled, "and from subway to 112." She was astonished at the way he dictated his newspaper column in a half-hour. When they rode home together, he would listen to her report on Tom Paine, one of "his" dissenters, then engage in lively talk on any subject that came to mind. Before dinner with the Gateses, he drove to the beach club for a ten-minute dip, coming back refreshed while Patricia—like Don Peretz in the Middle East—was ready for bed after a hard day.

Her affection for him was awakened by several attributes, not least among them, she said, that "He gave you the feeling that he was delighted to be with you." When *Great Dissenters* was published the next year, it contained Thomas's punctilious acknowledgment of the valuable help of Patricia Miller and Stephen Siteman.

## 2. What Are We Doing in Laos?

One of Thomas's letters to Lenore Marshall began typically, "Bayard Rustin is telephoning me just as I am running to catch a train to say that he is organizing a march of young people on election day for peace and equality." Thomas was pushing two good ideas: that the duration of the election campaign should be halved, and that television and radio time should be given free equally to candidates—even of small parties. "No rich party should be allowed to buy unlimited time beyond this," he wrote.

Marshal Tito was ready to see Thomas at the Yugoslav mission to the United Nations, but unfortunately Thomas, who had sought the meeting, was out of town. He also missed Nyerere and Tage Erlander but got back in time to see his old Indian friend and host of 1951, Purshottam Trikamdas, also at the United Nations. Thomas had decided that Kennedy was the lesser of two evils, having more candor than his opponent as well as good advisers like Chester Bowles. He voted—for the first time since Wilson in 1916—for the winning candidate, but was less enthusiastic about the victory than he was downcast over the defeat of Meyer in Vermont. In Meyer, peace had lost one more of its few soldiers. Thomas wrote in his "syndicated" column of the growing secrecy of United States foreign policy, the difficulty of learning our intentions in Cuba and the Congo:

> But [that] is simplicity itself as compared to Laos. . . . What are we doing in Laos? How deeply involved are we? How much money have we spent on arms and military supplies including what may have been given by CIA?. . . . Why is Laos important enough to us to risk millions of dollars and quite possibly the lives of our sons in a war to determine who will govern its poor people? The usual answer to the last question, of course, is that our security depends upon our keeping this backward little country, strategically placed, out of the hands of the Communists. . . . [Have] we not far more to fear from a war in Southeast Asia which would soon get out of hand . . . than from any attack or aggression against our basic security directed from that distant part of the world?

He was prophetic indeed. "Frankly," he wrote the friendly Congressman Henry S. Reuss of Wisconsin, "I am not too sanguine about Congress since you liberals have been unable to keep us from being insulted by keeping outspoken enemies of [the Democratic] platform in key chairmanships." Eastland and his fellows were still there. "We'll get a little better aid to the aged," Thomas predicted in the new Socialist paper New America,* "but not socialized medicine. And the Pentagon will be asked to help shape disarmament policy which means that we'll have as much disarmament as we should have abolition of cigaret smoking for cancer control if the American Tobacco Company were chief planner." But he was so grateful for Eisenhower's farewell warning to the nation about the swollen "military-industrial complex" that he sent Ike his thanks and plugged the warning repeatedly in his column, newsletter and speeches. He was delighted with Kennedy's inaugural

---

*Succeeding The Call, it was the organ of the Socialist Party and the Social Democratic Federation, which had united, one might almost say, in death.

eloquence and his use of Robert Frost, not even complaining about Kennedy's rather extravagant claims of United States authority; but he worried about the young man's willingness to match his words with deeds and about such things as his appointment of Kissinger as a special adviser.

Thomas traveled to Harvard to debate with Kissinger in February, 1961, telling him among other things that arms control was a delusion in the nuclear age, that disarmament was the only workable solution. According to Gabriel Kolko, one of the listeners, Thomas was "magnificent" and the audience at least agreed that he demolished Kissinger. Chester Bowles was now Undersecretary of State, and Thomas not only advised him freely on foreign policy but also recommended Don Peretz for a job with State. He was irked enough by a note from Bruce Barton praising his speech at the Dutch Treat Club without a word about its call to action that he thanked Barton but added pointedly, "I am very much in earnest about what I said about finding an alternative to war." An enemy comparable to Dr. Kissinger appeared in Dr. Herman Kahn, whose *On Thermonuclear War* impressed Henry Luce as strong and hopeful and made Thomas sick. Kahn said such a war would not be so bad after all if we met it intelligently and were reconciled to some losses. Thomas assailed Kahn in The Saturday Review and in his column: "[He] has prepared tables to show us how happily we could survive wars costing up to 100 million people. We could recover in varying lengths of time and be ready for a fourth world war. Dr. Kahn talks no nonsense about wars to end war but only a national security which may quite likely involve these holocausts." Life Magazine, seeming to get its figures confused, blurbed on its cover a story, "How You Can Survive Fallout," predicted that only five million Americans need be killed with fallout suits and other prudent preparation and said, "The best first aid for radiation sickness is to take hot tea or a solution of baking soda." The Lucepress, in the Dulles tradition, was simultaneously warning Khrushchev and steeling the United States to face nuclear war over Berlin. Thomas sent identical letters to a score of the nation's biggest newspapers urging the recognition of East Germany as a fact of life and deploring the "present horrible game of 'chicken' as played crassly by Moscow and only a little less so by Washington":

Are we Americans ready to die by millions rather than admit that the question of some recognition of East Germany in the process of guaranteeing freedom for West Berlin is very definitely and honorably negotiable?

The optimistic Herman Kahn tells us that we can survive if a first attack costs us only 20 to 100 million, provided that our retaliation attack can destroy more Russians. Are a majority of Americans willing to pay those lives and agony of the survivors in the name of the goddess of liberty who will not be found in any country walking serenely among the corpses of the dead and the ruins of great cities?

The mass use of fallout shelters costing billions might make war inevitable, he argued, by encouraging public acceptance of the idea of nuclear conflict and also gulling people into the belief that sheet metal or brick could save either them or their freedom: "Liberty cannot be preserved in a fallout shelter. Even if we survive a nuclear war, we will have to live under the worst form of dictatorship afterward."

### 3. More Than the Truth

Thomas had hardly returned from California (where he impressed a Stanford teacher almost to tears) and attended a three-day conference on disarmament in Washington sponsored by the Americans for Democratic Action, the Friends and other organizations, when the Central Intelligence Agency–planned invasion of Cuba was disavowed by the administration and by Ambassador Stevenson at the United Nations; then it collapsed in ruin and the truth came out. Only a week earlier Thomas had praised the President for his explicit renunciation of any United States military intervention in Cuba but had observed with his usual keenness, "He was rather more ambiguous on possible American aid to Cuban rebels than one could have wished." The indignation of Americans of integrity was universal. Thomas joined a dozen others in an immediate telegram of protest to Kennedy. He wrote Bowles, who had opposed the invasion:

> Because of our long friendship, I pick out you to pour out my pained regret over the Cuban incident. . . . Assuming that . . . Stevenson honestly believed [his United Nations denials], I think he might perform a service to mankind by resigning in protest at having been made the mouthpiece of falsehood. This, on top of the U-2 episode, leaves the U.S. government with no reputation for telling the truth in the opinion of mankind. . . .

He drafted an open letter to the President protesting not only the intervention but its knavery and got scores of signers from Edmund Wilson to I. F. Stone to A. J. Muste to Donald Harrington and Lenore

Marshall ("Bravo!" she wrote Thomas). Again, as in the U-2 affair, Thomas could have heard echoes of C. D. Jackson's insistence that "more than truth" was needed to fight Communism and the suave assurance of Allen Dulles (the same Dulles who "commanded" the Cuban invasion) that falsehood was useful when not traceable to the administration. Stevenson did not resign. The administration made no apology for its fraudulence and another standard of decency had fallen, with the inevitable corrosion of general political morality and the redoubling of the cynicism of a public which until very recently had clung to old-fashioned American ideals. Thomas kept encountering alarming extremes of opinion. At a California lunch counter his neighbor had been a kindly-looking man full of John Birch Society sentiments who said he had liked Earl Warren as Governor, but as Chief Justice "the Communists must have got him." Thomas could only shake his head at the many "well-meaning but terribly confused human beings" who "denounce lovers of peace all the way from Quakers to General Eisenhower as secret Communists or dupes of Communism." Back home, at a suburban forum discussing Cuba, Thomas met William F. Buckley, Jr., whose views he described as:

> the coldest advocacy of an American imperialism that I have yet heard or read. . . . Our young advocate of the gospel of human liberty as revealed to William Buckley, erstwhile champion of Senator McCarthy . . . wants no more nonsense and delay in "raking the island clean of Communists." Why? Simply because our national security requires it. . . . This was his whole point. No consideration of good as well as evil in the Cuban social revolution. No treaty agreement, no United Nations, no Organization of American States, no respect for world opinion, no fear of Khrushchev's threats, should deter us from protecting our own interests in Cuba or anywhere else. We should not allow a Communist government to exist 90 miles from our shores. Wasn't this argument analogous to the Russian argument on Hungary, or to a possible Russian intervention in Turkey where we have many bases close to the Soviet border? The Russians might think so [Buckley replied] but it was a question of our power and our interest against theirs. . . . This power doctrine points a sure road to ultimate world war. It is the enemy not only of our leadership for democracy and peace in the world but also of the security it seeks to serve.

Karen Figueres, staying at the time with her husband in New York, sent Thomas "Don Pepe's" statement of cautious criticism which urged the United States to take the long-run view and said, "You cannot 'stop'

Communism. You have to run faster." Thomas had one of his exchanges with an ex-Socialist friend, the Vienna-born philosopher Max Nomad, now living in the Bronx, who had discovered that even the working-class revolt was in the end like all political movements, a ruthless struggle for power. This idealist-turned-cynic sent Thomas, whom he admired extravagantly but felt was wasting his time on a humanity too corrupt and rotten to salvage, a copy of his *Aspects of Revolt* in which he quoted two Thomas statements in The Call, sixteen years apart:

> [1936:] ". . . the Soviet regime . . . is a workers' state, to be defended by the international working class whenever it clashes with the powers of capitalism."
>
> [1952:] ". . . the Messianic hope which consciously or unconsciously inspired most of us to become Socialists is scarcely tenable in America or elsewhere in the world. . . . History and our better knowledge of our human psychology has destroyed or profoundly altered that particular scheme of earthly salvation. We have learned much about the temptations of power and we know that there is no Messianic working class nor any sort of elite that we can trust automatically to save 'mankind.'. . . . [T]here will never be an absolute final victory."

Thomas conceded to Nomad that his hopes had dwindled but rejected total cynicism: "For many years, life for me has been a struggle to find compensatory incentives and encouragements for the more nearly absolute faiths that I have lost. . . . I was never a very orthodox Socialist, but I had Socialist hopes that I have lost. . . . [But] I don't think we're incapable of realizing that to live we must find alternatives to war. . . . I do think you might give a little more explicit recognition that men, who are not saints, Socialists or otherwise, are capable of some sense of fair play and human affection and are often motivated by desire for justice independent of their own power." From Sandra Levinson of Stanford's political science department, who had escorted him to speaking appointments around the campus, came the opposite of cynicism:

> You were absolutely magnificent. . . . I am surrounded by would-be political scientists to whom disarmament, capital punishment, civil rights and civil liberties are mere labels for things about which they read and attempt to teach, but about which they do not *act*. They have not participated, they have not partaken of the "bread of affliction," they have remained "above" the subjective interpretation of social events. They are "scientists" by golly, and everyone *knows* that *scientists* must remain

disinterested, unconvinced and, most importantly, uncommitted. . . .

. . . [The] label "reformer" appears a little out of date for people in this atomic age, but that label is precisely the one I claim for my own; it is through my students that I hope to carry on some of this reforming. . . . These past two days have revived me, simply observing you in action, with a passion and an intellectual honesty all too rare in American politics today. I have heard the Stanford students ask you . . . if you don't feel very satisfied that so many of your once "radical" proposals are now taken for granted . . . and your answer that you're too much concerned about the future to dwell on the past. Don't these students realize that they have the chance of an age to redirect the course of mankind's future, to, in fact, assure that mankind *has* a future? Have they become so scientific that they no longer see anything in terms of morality and immorality, of good and bad (except when it comes to those assuredly evil Communists . . .)? These are the questions to which I attempt to direct my students—these are the reasons for listening to you and taking heart with you. That is why I write to you: because you have assured me beyond all expectations (and they were very high) that your commitment is a very beautiful and worthwhile thing. . . .

It was enough to warm an old man's heart—to convince him that the pebbles he was dropping were causing widening ripples in the pond. It was the answer to the surrendering cynicism of Nomad. The only hope of the old propagandist was to inspire young propagandists. Otherwise there was no reply to the Central Intelligence Agency, the Bay of Pigs, Kissinger and Kahn, Buckley and the Birchers and the salesmen who spent millions to put across that jingle, "like a cigaret should." He knew that the question was whether there were enough Sandra Levinsons to prevail over such power and such counter-propaganda. Thomas occasionally admitted that the odds were formidable but never did he concede defeat. It is a safe assumption that admiring letters helped him keep going, as they always had. There were other encouragements that kept his arthritic frame on the run. The Post War World Council was holding its own, the Committee for a Sane Nuclear Policy was gaining in influence and he was ready (aged seventy-six) to launch Turn Toward Peace, an organization aiming to coordinate existing but scattershot peace groups and to stress the typically Thomasite slogan: "Peace is the personal responsibility of every American." There were the surprising windfalls that came his way. A New York widow of modest means gave him $200 every year. A woman in Brookline, Massachusetts, sent him several shares of Texaco stock to aid his work. And Mrs. Julia C. Phillips of New York, whom he had never heard of but who had seen him on television, left him $10,000 in her will "to promote peace and love . . . among all people and a belief in the one universal God." Ten thousand dollars! But God stood in the way. Thomas wrote the attorney for the estate:

> I am deeply concerned in the promotion of peace and a feeling of unity and brotherhood among all people. I think I believe in something which I would call a universal God but I should be hard put to it to carry out Mrs. Phillips' instructions in her belief that "promotion of world peace and world brotherhood is dependent upon acceptance of the one God." . . . Does this morally disqualify me from accepting the legacy?

It did not. Indeed, Thomas was receiving as well as dispensing encouragement and inspiration. He absorbed it from people like James Farmer of The Congress of Racial Equality (of which Thomas was inevitably an officer), who as a Freedom Rider was jailed in Jackson, Mississippi, where Thomas wrote him to "send greetings and to hope that your vacation is not too uncomfortable." He promptly sent Farmer $25 out of his own pocket and $100 from the Julia Phillips fund (which melted like June snow) for the Freedom Riders. There was his good Socialist friend Walter Uphoff, now a professor of labor relations at the University of Minnesota, whose sons (one named after Thomas, another after Debs) were chips off the old block; Eugene was a Freedom Rider temporarily occupying the same jail as Farmer, while Norman worked for the Sane Nuclear committee and the Student Peace Union at Minnesota. There was young Michael Harrington, writing *The Other America* and working for decency as if his life depended on it. Lenore Marshall, no longer young, was yet an inspiration with her enthusiasm, her poetry and her money. There was Mary Farquharson, a loyal Socialist for many years in Seattle, who wrote Thomas, "You have helped to save some of us from giving up in despair"—a reminder that along with the young who needed inspiration were the mature who, without leadership, would logically quit the fight against Democratic-Republican rule. Thomas's constituency was often unknown and unnamed and always uncounted, and if some of it disagreed with him except on disarmament and peace, that portion of agreement was precious and had not only to be encouraged but enlarged. Thomas, perfectly aware of his gift for inspiration and how badly it was needed, could scarcely desert his constituency simply because his bones ached and some people asked, Why doesn't the old man retire?—especially when this was the life he loved and would miss as sorely as the Bernhardts and Barrymores would have missed theirs and who kept giving farewell performances until their mortal curtains fell. He was by no means decrepit, although John Haynes Holmes probably laid it on a trifle when he saw Thomas on a television panel and wrote him, "You looked and acted exactly as I remember you in years gone by. . . . How do you do it? Where is your fountain of youth?" Still, the San Francisco woman who saw him on David Susskind's "Open End" with John Crosby and others exercised an imaginative talent in the other direction when she wrote the station:

> That Mr. Thomas you had on your show last night—did he separate the man from the boys! He must be 100 years old, his voice is quavery and his hands shook—but I loved him. His mind is so clear & sharp & he could see so straight—the man must be from outer space.
> Why don't we try to keep him here & make him our Governor—at least. Are men like him NEEDED!
> So bring him back soon if you can find him again. —Sadie

## 4. South of the Border

Meanwhile Thomas had gathered an organization to supervise the work of his Institute for International Labor Research. For once he wore one of his hats away from 112 East Nineteenth Street, for the Institute had its own modest office at 113 East Thirty-seventh Street. As chairman he had selected a board of eight directors including the former Socialist Professor Robert J. Alexander of Rutgers, Katrina Barnes, Leon Dennen and Thomas's old Socialist comrade Professor Frank Trager of New York University, who had clipped his left wing and turned politically to the right. A Thomas adviser was Clarence Senior, his Socialist collaborator of the thirties and a warm friend ever since. Senior had become a professor of sociology at Brooklyn College, a specialist in the Caribbean and a consultant to the government of Puerto Rico. Sacha Volman was secretary-treasurer of the Institute and director of its school at the scene in Costa Rica.

Evidently the project, after its first encouragement by the Free Europe Committee, had received only minor contributions. It operated frugally until 1960, when Thomas interested the wealthy Jacob M. Kaplan in it. Kaplan, himself a story-book character, had made a molasses fortune decades earlier in Central America and had added to it later through his ownership of a New York department store chain and dominant holdings in the Welch grape-juice firm and other enterprises. A self-made man, now sixty-seven, he lived handsomely on East Eightieth Street and Long Island. He was a trustee of the New School and a liberal, though he seemed to retain some of the attitudes characteristic of men who made early fortunes in the banana climes: He felt that Kennedy, instead of covertly backing rebels in Cuba, should have waded in openly and deposed Castro by military force. He had retired into philanthropy, heading the small but well-established Kaplan Fund on lower Fifth Avenue. Thomas, who had dealt with foundations of all descriptions for many years, got $35,000 from the Kaplan Fund. This temporarily eased Volman's worries in Costa Rica. By 1961 his school near San Jose had forty-seven students from eleven Latin American states, a batch of them being Dominicans opposed to the Trujillos, and a faculty of six including Figueres. Another faculty member was Juan Bosch, the Dominican professor and novelist whom Trujillo had forced into twenty-five years of exile. Bosch, a man of enormous charm and considerable idealism, unfortunately had weaknesses of which Thomas never became aware and which in the end would thwart Thomas's designs. Bosch was highly emotional and filled with more resentments than a politician should harbor. For the furiously energetic Volman, the older Bosch developed an affection like that of a father.

Thomas won the support of President Romulo Betancourt of Venezuela, Haya de la Torre of Peru and former President Eduardo Santos of Colombia as sponsors of the school and of the Institute's bimonthly Spanish-language magazine Combate, devoted to social advancement and inter-American cooperation. There was mutual affection between Thomas and Volman, who flitted between Costa Rica, Washington and New York and was an ardent promoter, not at all backward about calling on Senators. Correspondence was steady between Thomas and Volman, the latter sending careful reports. Thomas hoped Washington would take notice of the school and perhaps learn a lesson about the cultivation of democracy after its blunders in Latin America, most recently in Guatemala, Cuba and the Dominican Republic. Volman seemed to be doing an excellent job. The New York Times sent a reporter to look over the school, and published a long and approving dispatch. In May, 1961, the Brookings Institution sent a mission of three professorial experts to live at the school for ten days, attend classes and scrutinize it in general. They came away with high praise. Young

Latinos—not all of them admirers of the Yankees—were learning the politics of a kind of government as far away from the Communism of Castro as from the dictatorial terror of the lately assassinated Trujillo.

The Brookings report, Kaplan wrote Thomas, had attracted several donors to the Kaplan Fund, which would pass the money along. It did so with a generosity that, so long as it continued, kept the Latin American operation free from financial need and indeed encouraged Thomas to solicit money from Kaplan for other good causes.

The omnipresence of the Central Intelligence Agency was a subject of gossip after the U-2 and Bay of Pigs fiascoes and eventually there were rumors that the agency had its fingers in many pies. Despite its secrecy, it could hardly spread money around as it did without leakage and suspicion. Dwight Macdonald, who in 1956 had written to Thomas gaily from London about how wonderful it was to write for the London-based magazine Encounter, which was subsidized by a rich American foundation and lavish toward its writers, suspected its integrity in 1958 when it refused to publish an article of his which did not absolve America of imperialist designs. His suspicions, however, were of Encounter's fear of antagonizing its American angel—not that behind the angel might lurk the CIA. John Kenneth Galbraith later suggested that he had heard rumors as early as 1960 that the CIA was subsidizing the Congress for Cultural Freedom, of which he was a member. The Congress was the sponsor of Encounter, which had two American editors, Melvin Lasky and Irving Kristol, and many American contributors. Thomas of course had not forgotten the CIA's effort to use him in extending hospitality to the Syrian Socialists as an anti-Communist ploy. He was, however, a little deaf and terribly preoccupied with his peace crusades. Now, Irwin Suall, the Socialist Party–Social Democratic Federation national secretary, informed him of the columnist Robert J. Allan's statement that the new CIA director was investigating subsidies that the agency was paying to "nearly every international Socialist conference in recent years," and was going to end payments to such "questionable conferences." The Socialist International was the responsibility of its secretary, Albert Carthy, in London, who said that no such subsidy had ever been received and asked questions about it. At Suall's request, Thomas wrote John McCone, successor of Allen Dulles, whose CIA career had been finished by the Cuban debacle:

.... Mr. Carthy requests . . . that you tell us which conferences were promoted, which financed and which persons and organizations were associated with the Agency. I can understand that the CIA quite legitimately, directly or indirectly, might help some international conferences of a definitely non-Communist sort but I never heard of any aid to any Socialist Party conferences in any country.

Although he was asking a favor and being courteous, his "I can understand that the CIA *quite legitimately, directly or indirectly*" might help causes which furthered its own designs, could permit the inference not only that he might have heard something of such CIA help but that indirect or secret help would not surprise or outrage him. But this interpretation is so far from what would be expected of the forthright Thomas, and clashes so sharply with all the other evidence, that such an inference from a hurriedly dictated letter may be ruled out.

McCone replied stiffly that the CIA did not comment on public statements concerning it, but that Thomas could be assured that Allan's report was based on no interview with McCone or any responsible CIA official. That was that.

### 5. Angelica Starving

Thomas had joined the American Association of Retired Persons, provoking jokes about how such a workhorse had the nerve to call himself retired. Although his major crusades kept him hopping, he was still unable to say No to smaller ones, of which he always had a dozen or more bubbling on back burners and troubling his conscience because he could not give them full attention. At intervals he would explode to the State Department about its refusal to issue passports to such places as Cuba or China, an unwarranted denial of freedom. After two decades he was still trying to get Mrs. Dasch's saboteur husband back from Germany to join her. For several years he asked for clemency for Morton Sobell, convicted of spying for the Russians in a trial Thomas thought dubious, and he worked steadily both on President Kennedy and Attorney General Robert Kennedy for the release from prison of Junius Scales, a young ex-Communist especially victimized by the Smith Act.

Scales, son of a banker who had lost heavily in the depression, left the University of North Carolina in 1940 to become a textile organizer for the Communist Party. He enlisted after Pearl Harbor and was moved from post to post for the duration of the war, the army being uncertain of how it should treat such individuals while Russia was our ally. He resumed his life as a Communist functionary in North Carolina, stuck with the party despite the Czech coup of 1948, and in 1954 was arrested on that same, simple Smith Act charge of membership in the Communist Party. Given a six-year term, he fought the sentence for six years during which he joined the John Gates group of dissidents in the party in their effort to declare independence from Moscow. He finally quit the party in disgust over the Russian invasion of Hungary and Khrushchev's denunciation of Stalin. His disillusionment was authentic. The Justice Department pressed the case hard, because Scales refused to implicate others he had known in the party. His six-year sentence— twice what others such as Elizabeth Gurley Flynn got—was obviously punitive and unfair, even if the Smith Act itself had been just. He began serving his term long after quitting the party and becoming the object of Communist vituperation. Thomas persuaded Reinhold Niebuhr, President Goheen of Princeton and Grenville Clark to join him in sending out a petition for Scales while Thomas himself began a year and a half of efforts by mail and in person in Washington.

Meanwhile his estimate of the Soviets jumped a notch when he saw the charming and totally nonpropagandist Russian motion picture "A Summer to Remember," encouraging him to think that reason was gaining behind the Curtain. He was further encouraged because Palmiro Togliatti in a Moscow speech was permitted to dwell on the horrors of nuclear war and describe it as something civilization must at all odds avoid. Thomas accepted new civic duties, such as the chairmanship of the United Fund for his home town on Long Island, gave interviews to representatives of the local high school paper, and solicited Mrs. Agnes Meyer of The Washington Post for money to ease "the plight of the Seneca Indians, whose holy land is to be inundated by a flood control dam." Seeing Yugoslavia as a hopeful object lesson in the possibility of Communism moving toward democracy, he congratulated Tito on releasing Djilas from prison—an approval he had to withdraw sixteen months later when Djilas was again imprisoned, this time for his *Conversations with Stalin.* Thomas had to reprove the Marshal for a sentence that was "unjust" and which "certainly will not help Yugoslavia's standing among men of good will." He took time to praise Elizabeth Gurley Flynn for her letter to The Times, getting an affectionate reply including, "I wish you could visit the Soviet Union." He was appalled to hear from the Bertram Wolfes, visiting Angelica in Rome, that she apparently had run out of money, was a trifle vague and

433

was suffering from malnutrition after buying a newspaper daily, reading it and returning it for a crust of bread, which constituted her food for the day. The Wolfes of course befriended her and Thomas immediately sent money which, typically, she had not requested.

"Looking back on my life," he wrote an East Indian friend, "one of my regrets is that I think my family life, happy as it was, suffered a little and my education in and appreciation of music, theater, etc., suffered more because I had so little time and energy left for what I should have liked to do. . . ."

By now seventy-seven years old, his natural alacrity dwindled at times, he suffered pain in his arthritic legs, his hearing and eyesight were failing and he showed what was becoming an obsessive fear of invalidism and lingering death. Certainly one cause besides age was the ebbing of the enormous confidence in the forward march of mankind that had once sustained him. First, God had been the force he saw as propelling man toward inevitable progress. God had been replaced by the inspiring belief that man's own Socialist rationality would usher in equality, peace and abundance. Hiroshima and the Cold War arms race had weakened that assurance. Now the question of survival was as important as that of progress. That he was neither bitter nor cynical testified to his resiliency. But he had been driven slowly backward to the last fortress—a belief in man's capacity for good as well as evil, and the hope that human affection, honesty, fair play and justice would prevail against the evil. *It was up to man himself.* It involved patience. Hence Thomas's upset when he debated Goldwater or Buckley, and his dismay at such scandals as the Bay of Pigs, the repudiation of party platforms, the secret war in Southeast Asia, and the growth of groups such as Birchers or Minute Men, who breathed hate rather than intelligent effort to solve a problem that was everyone's. It seemed that as the disreputable Soviet Union moved ever so slightly toward accommodation, the once-reputable United States moved away from it. ". . . I wish I could see clearly," he said, "a sure and hopeful way of deliverance—to which I might better contribute—for the generations of my children and grandchildren from the deep night of our civilization's end."

### 6. Freedom of the Press

For years, Thomas had kept colliding with the propaganda of the Luce magazines, as he did with their campaign to instil the idea that American courage and principle required the nation to stand firm on the Berlin issue even if it should mean nuclear war. In California Thomas had observed the quick success of Dr. Frederick Schwarz's "Christian Crusade," with its whipping up of hate against Communists in public meetings and in "classes in anti-Communism" for which it charged substantial fees, turning a handsome profit. Even Life Magazine had derided the Crusade in a two-paragraph news squib, offending several large Life advertisers. C. D. Jackson, now publisher of Life, had thereupon flown west and apologized to a vast Christian Crusade rally in the Hollywood Bowl attended by such dependable anti-Communists as John Wayne, Senator Dodd, George Murphy and Congressman Walter Judd. Thomas wrote Jackson:

> I was, of course, sorry to find you making common cause with Dr. Schwarz, the John Birchers, et al, at that great Hollywood rally. That is not the way to fight against the worst features of Communism or advance either liberty or peace. . . . I have heard from a source not to be dismissed as either uninformed or malicious that your appearance in Hollywood and your speech virtually retracting things said in Life and Time on the general subject was directly the consequence of advertising pressure. My informant was rather specific. The advertisers in the meanwhile had been stirred up by the Crusaders to use economic coercion. . . . I need not tell you how contradictory I think this situation is to pious talk about freedom of the press in America.
>
> I shall be traveling and speaking in a great many places, including Los Angeles, and in some of my speeches I shall want to elaborate the theme I have set forth. I don't want to do it before putting the matter before you and hearing your side of the story. This, both for friendship's sake and in common fairness.

Jackson, in a careful, 400-word reply, agreed that advertisers had complained but said this was common and had nothing to do with his apology, which was tendered out of admiration for Dr. Schwarz and his movement and realization that Life had been wrong. Thomas, unlike most others with publishing connections, did Jackson the honor of accepting his assurance, though with some reservations:

> You say that Dr. Schwarz is a "non-rabble-rouser teacher." If [his] leaflets are not rabble-rousing, I don't know what is. . . . He is not an open advocate of war but the effect of his books as well as his leaflets, like the effect of the Birch Society and a number of others, is to create a popular hysteria on Communism which tremendously complicates any sort of

peaceful settlement of any issue and makes it far easier to blunder into war.

You and I are both anti-Communists who would probably differ at some points in our statements about Communism and the way to fight it but I simply cannot imagine you in the same company with the Christian Anti-Communism Crusade. I can see how Senator Dodd and Walter Judd and probably Henry Luce could be but not you.

The growth of the right-wing lunatic fringe had no parallel on the left, which had dwindled in size if not in lunacy. When Thomas debated in Tucson with Barry Goldwater, then a second-term Senator, Goldwater took the line that if the Birchers were extreme they were balanced by the Americans for Democratic Action on the left, whereas Thomas could not agree that the likes of Robert Welch deserved space in the same category as Humphrey, Niebuhr and Schlesinger. Goldwater, said Thomas, "denounced the rash spending of the federal government and the centralization implicit in it." But the military budget of about $50 billion did not trouble the Senator, who said he "expected to support the military budget and didn't think it made for centralization." The Thomas who ten years earlier had seen the chief threat to America in the Communist left now saw it in a war-happy right wing seemingly oblivious of nuclear realities. When he attended a huge Garden rally sponsored by the right-wing Young Americans for Freedom, Thomas's blood ran cold (and the great auditorium rocked with cheers) when a speaker demanded that the President win Cold War victory by issuing the following orders:

To the Joint Chiefs of Staff: Make the necessary preparations for a landing in Havana. To our commander in Berlin: Tear down the Wall. To our chief of mission in the Congo: Change sides. To the chief of CIA: You are under instructions to encourage liberation movements in every nation of the world under Communist domination—including the Soviet Union itself.

To Thomas, peace was now far more indivisible than when Litvinoff had coined the phrase. Any backslide into violence anywhere in the world was a blow to the United Nations and international safety. He was wounded when India—*his* India—swallowed up Portuguese Goa in a quick military operation after only perfunctory United Nations representations, the Indian Socialists supporting Nehru in this. To Asoka Mehta he sent one of his sugar-coated letters, thanking him and Krishna

Menon for New Year's cards ("You know how I prize the friendship of both of you"), then lowered the boom: "It is because of the strength of this feeling that I find myself under a kind of compulsion to write you about the Goan episode and to tell you how deep is the injury that your government's course has done to the influence of India and Prime Minister Nehru in support of the United Nations and that search for alternatives to war upon which the life of mankind now depends. . . . Many of India's warmest friends are saying, 'So Gandhi's country is like all the rest. It is against other people's wars but never against its own.' " Mehta did not reply immediately, and J. Edgar Hoover did not reply at all when Thomas taxed him for his acceptance of a $5,000 award from the Freedoms Foundation at Valley Forge, a right-wing propagandist group.

In February, 1962, Thomas's Turn Toward Peace group sponsored a two-day demonstration of 4,000 collegians from forty states—strictly non-Communist, guitars banned, neckties obligatory—carrying such signs as "Peace—The Cause That Refreshes" and "We Condemn Both U.S. and Soviet Testing." They flooded Lafayette Square and encircled the White House in orderly ranks, while eighty Young Americans for Freedom counter-picketed with such signs as "A Test a Day Keeps the Communists Away." Thomas later addressed the throng from the Sylvan Theater near the Washington Monument, deprecating a descent to man-made caves and warning, "You will not live to my age . . . unless you stop the arms race." But the President heard a different drummer, as Thomas noted in his column:

> In Vietnam, the Kennedy administration has already taken a long chance
> on full scale war by the degree to which it is involving American military
> forces in aid to a numerous South Vietnamese army which is apparently
> reluctant to do its own effective fighting. . . . Our military power is not
> going to stop Communism in the long run simply by shoring up govern-
> ments like Diem's. . . . This sort of thing . . . may indeed grow into a new
> sort of imperialism to manage governments which mismanage their own
> affairs. Still worse, it could grow into a cruel guerilla war. . . .

## 7. *Missiles in Cuba*

In a post-inauguration courtesy visit to the White House and a considerable correspondence with Kennedy, Thomas invariably was treated with respect. The President sometimes took the trouble to explain his reasons for decisions Thomas deplored, signing with his indecipherable scrawl, so different from Roosevelt's pellucid, patrician signature, Truman's plain-Jane and Eisenhower's handsome legibility. Thomas was uncertain about Kennedy, giving him high marks for his separation of church and state, his speeches and his official "style" but faulting him because "his genuine but moderate liberalism doesn't stand up well against the pressures of the military-industrial complex" and regretting his lack of any instinct for crusade, his nervous responsiveness to public opinion and his use of the kind of Machiavellianism perfected by Roosevelt. About Laos and Vietnam, Thomas peered into the future with clear vision. He soon found fault with Kennedy's Secretary of State, Dean Rusk, who had come in with so mild a reputation and had become a confirmed cold-warrior, praising Franco and Chiang and sending the disagreeing Chester Bowles into bureaucratic mazes so remote, Thomas wrote, "that a search party for him has been suggested." To the President's brother Bobby, Thomas mentioned another complaint: "I still have some hopes that the Democratic Party and the Administration will find some way to end the everlasting disgrace of having James Eastland of Mississippi as chairman of the Judiciary Committee in the U. S. Senate." The hopes proved unwarranted.

Thomas had become so much an institution that the days of being attacked with tear gas, stink bombs or vegetables, or being refused permission to speak, seemed over. True, the watchful American Legion and Veterans of Foreign Wars protested against his speaking in New Orleans, but they were overruled and he spoke. Senator Thurmond, whom Thomas had tagged as a "bigoted mediocrity," got even as chairman of an Armed Services subcommittee by rejecting Thomas's complaint that Governor Rockefeller's military chief of staff invited radical rightists to indoctrinate state militia groups. Thurmond said Thomas's attitude was identical with that of the Communists, but added cautiously, "my recognition of this fact should not be distorted by any implication that I am trying to label Mr. Thomas as a Communist."

As if reflecting that his time was limited, Thomas indulged what was for him a riot of sociality. He had moved from his apartment at Evan's place up the road to the big, memory-filled house where the Gateses lived year-round and a septuagenarian could have company. He had tea with his brother Ralph and sisters Agnes and Emma at the Coffee House Club. He dined with Upton Sinclair, in New York to see his publisher —Sinclair, whose second wife Mary Craig had informed him before she died that he needed a helpmate and must marry again. He had done so promptly after a brief search, writing Thomas, "The lady is 79, so don't worry." Thomas, a one-woman man, had now been alone for fifteen years. He arranged a meeting with Gilkey, now retired in Boston, met Ralph Harlow in New York (both comrades at Spring Street when the century and they were young) and topped it off by meeting Walter Uphoff, in New York from Minneapolis, and taking him to see *My Fair Lady*.

When he was besought by Long Island admirers to run for Congress as an independent, he took them seriously and consulted his physician —proof of how strongly he still yearned for the kind of power that came not from his own appeals and organs of propaganda but from the people's votes. "If I had been, say ten years younger," he admitted, "I think I would have agreed . . ." True, he was working harder than most Congressmen half his age and would soon appear before the Senate Commerce Committee to argue for equal radio-television time for minority candidates. He joined Pauling and 200 others in a petition to Ambassador Dobrynin asking an end to Soviet executions for "economic crimes," joined a smaller group in a protest to the Argentine government at the imprisonment of the deposed President Arturo Frondisi, and limped at the head of fifty pickets at the New York Yugoslav consulate, protesting Djilas's imprisonment.

He traveled to the Kansas side of Kansas City for the wedding of his granddaughter Patricia, joyfully joining Sidney Lovett there, Lovett having been the Millers' New Haven neighbor and baptizer of the children, and now assisting the minister performing the ceremony. The Thomas who had been restricted to an anteroom when Violet's sister was married forty years earlier was now the center of attention at the reception, Mrs. Miller observed, "holding court for a crowd of people surrounding him." He suffered anguish from arthritis in his legs but was too courteous (and perhaps was enjoying the homage too much) to break up the crowd and find a chair. The Cuban missile crisis in October, 1962, was a warning to such young married couples and indeed every person of awareness everywhere that the life expectancy of the race was uncertain. Thomas, knowing that many Americans outraged at the thought of Russian missiles in Cuba were unaware of our scores of bases surrounding the Soviet Union, cautioned:

> The President . . . knows, as the American people must not forget, that we have very many bases around the Soviet Union. Whether or not any of them are missile bases or have nuclear warheads, many of them harbor airplanes, carrying the most dangerous weapons. The Kremlin has not challenged our right to service those bases. It may now, e.g. in Turkey.

He breathed relief when Khrushchev agreed to withdraw the missiles. A few weeks later, Thomas's many months of work, along with others, for Junius Scales, were rewarded when the President commuted Scales's sentence on Christmas Eve. ". . . [H]e got home late the night before Christmas," Thomas wrote Grenville Clark, "to the immense happiness of everybody, especially his wife, who had been rather seriously ill. . . ."

## 8. The Thomas Track Meet

Sacha Volman, that prodigy of publicity, had written Thomas that he was coming to the States with the new Foreign Minister of Costa Rica and asked Thomas's help in making appointments for them with Senators Humphrey, McCarthy, Morse and Mansfield. He had earlier arranged other Washington appointments with the aid of the Presidential assistant Arthur Schlesinger, Jr. Volman planned that the Foreign Minister should lunch at New York's Overseas Press Club and appear on a nationwide television program. The need for money, which so hounded Thomas in other pursuits, had been no problem in the Costa Rica school, thanks to the generosity of the Kaplan Fund. Turn Toward Peace was so pinched that Thomas gave it $100 outright plus $400 to be repaid if possible, "but I shall not be a difficult creditor," which meant that the whole $500 was a gift. Lenore Marshall and a few others could not carry the whole financial load.

But at the end of 1962 Volman's school seemed about to founder when the Kaplan Fund ended its support. The reason, it was said, was that the school was sufficiently interfered with by Costa Rican politicians to threaten the Fund's tax-exempt status. Prospects to reestablish the school elsewhere brightened with the election of Juan Bosch as President of the Dominican Republic, succeeding the late Trujillo. Thomas, not forgetting the Galíndez case, was delighted at this first free election for decades in that luckless island, and so was Kaplan. When Bosch spent a fortnight in New York in January, 1963, soon after his election, he had lunch and long talks with Thomas and Volman. An intellectual of great charm with a stand-up brush of stiff white hair, in politics a moderate Socialist, he had impressive credentials. At Thomas's urging, the Bosches were dinner guests of Kaplan, whose years in Central America furnished a common bond. The ardent Bosch, Kaplan later wrote, embraced him and said he would be Bosch's real ambassador in the United States. Bosch invited Thomas to his inauguration (Thomas had to decline), then went on to Washington to be received warmly by President Kennedy. The President-elect of a small sugar republic was getting unusual official attention. Bosch was described as the "chosen instrument for the Alliance of Progress in the Caribbean," expected to build a shining republic that would expose the nearby Communist evil of Castro as well as make amends for the thirty years of Trujillo. "I need not repeat my hope," Thomas wrote him, "that you will make of the Dominican Republic a showcase to the world of what can be done for the people under democracy."

Arthritis or no, Thomas was still in the track meet, speaking at Brown, Cornell, Choate, Princeton, Michigan State, Colorado—an average of a speech a day for almost a month. He took a breather when Time Magazine gave its fortieth birthday party at the Waldorf, honoring many who had appeared on its cover. Grudges laid aside, he accepted Luce's invitation to attend. Time and Life had made so many errors about him, and had presented and still presented "value judgments" so obnoxious to him that he truly deserved a dinner and extravaganza in recompense. Here, for a change, he *listened* to speeches. One woman guest said to him, "I remember you running for President when I was a little girl." "Madam," he replied, "I've been running for President since I was a little boy." Returning home, he told the Gateses he had enjoyed the event and he named people he had met, one of them an actress with a foreign accent with whom he had been photographed. Her name, he thought, was Lola. Lola what? He did not know. Lollobrigida? Ah yes, that was it. He was at Princeton again in June to celebrate the simultaneous graduation of two of his grandsons, John, oldest son of the Gateses, and Norman, son of the William Thomases. He was the guest of a good friend, Dr. Julian P. Boyd, the Princeton historian who was engaged in his enormous task of editing the papers of Thomas Jefferson in preparation for a complete edition. Like Jefferson, Boyd felt, Thomas had consummate poise and equanimity and great ethical concern, but unlike Jefferson, who avoided center stage and preferred to work by indirection, Thomas was as direct as a man could be. Thomas posed for the Princeton professor and sculptor, Joe Brown, sitting on a slowly revolving turntable and spinning yarns while Brown worked. By now, Thomas had an inexhaustible fund of stories out of his own experience which he told with zest and perfection of intonation and gesture, and when Brown picked up the conversation at one point and spoke of a clergyman he knew, Thomas chuckled and said, "I was in that racket once myself"—raillery, of course, since the religion dear to his heart though not to his mind was not a racket except in the way some exploited it. Thomas said not a word about Louis Mayer's earlier open-mouthed bust "The Speaker," and Brown happily finished the head with the mouth closed and a faint smile. Thomas worried about his alma mater, writing in the Alumni Weekly:

> The more I have thought about McGeorge Bundy's defense of federal aid to universities and the fact that Princeton gets a little more than half its total budget from federal grants, the less I am satisfied with the situation. I by no means object to the principle of federal aid. You would hardly expect a Socialist to protest on this point. . . . Are these grants all for special projects?. . . . To what extent are grants made by or in behalf of the Pentagon? To what extent are they related to the kind of research or other work which underlies the steady expansion of the general capacity to overkill?

### 9. *A Low State of Mind*

Meanwhile Bosch was inaugurated in Santo Domingo with Vice President Lyndon B. Johnson's approving presence as proof of Washington's hope in him. From the start, in this volatile, faction-ridden island republic, Bosch seemed embittered by his long exile and cursed by imprudence and tactlessness. Instead of delivering the expected conciliatory inaugural, he came out fighting with a three-hour speech attacking Dominican groups he should have soothed. He excluded from the ceremony most of the members of the Council of State, gaining powerful enemies. Those leaders of the Inter-American Association for Democracy and Freedom who were present, were appalled. The newcomer who had been counted on to kiss hands was instead slapping faces. Thomas's friend Frances Grant, secretary-general of the Association (of which Thomas was a member) later observed that Bosch "began to alienate almost every sector of Dominican life, including his erstwhile comrades in the fight against the tyranny." It was a customary precaution for a new Latin American president to send away influential military officers known to oppose him, either into exile or to safe diplomatic posts. Bosch did not do so, permitting known enemies to remain in high military stations. Having done this, he would have been expected to conciliate them. On the contrary, Bosch assailed them repeatedly.

American Ambassador John Bartlow Martin, trying to help the new regime make the showing Washington expected, was frustrated by the President's moods and eccentricities as well as by right-wing plots against him. Washington, very much in the picture, arranged for Bosch to set up an agency for Dominican improvement called CIDES, which was headed by Sacha Volman. CIDES was the acronym for *Centro InterAmericano de Estudios Economicos y Sociales* (Inter-American Center for Economic and Social Studies). Volman began organizing a great public education program to be broadcast on television. Money was now pouring in for the project from the Kaplan Fund and the Ford Foundation too. Among other CIDES plans were to promote public health with tent clinics, aid agrarian reform, build farm-to-market roads, encourage decent housing and train schoolteachers. The aim of CIDES was to make the Dominican Republic so wonderful that other Latin nations would copy her democratic methods and scorn Castro. Ambassador Martin took a quick dislike for Volman:

> Volman was probably the only confidant Bosch had. . . . [His] briefcase [was] full of plans and his head full of plots. His mind was quick and devious; he could be charming and ingratiating or murderously tough; his basic instinct was conspiratorial . . .

He did not explain this appraisal. Thomas, who was not accustomed to associating with conspirators or murderous toughs, would have been astonished at this characterization of his valued ally. Volman, who resided in the luxurious villa of Trujillo's departed daughter, was rumored by some to be a Central Intelligence Agency operative—perhaps with no more accuracy than the constant talk among Dominican right-wingers that Bosch was a Communist. But the unhappy fact seemed to be that Thomas (like President Kennedy and the Washington bureaucracy) had seen Bosch at his most charming and idealistic and was totally unaware of his political failings. Bosch, who had sympathy for the masses and scrupulous dollar-honesty, was even more richly endowed at making enemies. Ambassador Martin worked furiously to save the President who was to have ushered in democracy, prosperity and love, but failed. In September, 1963, after Bosch had been in office only seven months, a general strike was arranged by Dominican business leaders, the military took over and Bosch was driven from office in a typical Caribbean coup. Volman went into hiding and later fled to Florida; this time his project was finished for keeps.

Thomas, who had not yet visited the Dominican Republic and was unaware of much that had gone on there, was disconsolate. "I write in a low state of mind," he wrote to Lenore Marshall, "because [of] the news on the radio of the overthrow of the Bosch government . . . by a rightist coup."

### 10. Splendidly Opinionated

When a minor heart ailment forced Thomas to give up his now infrequent driving, it was a relief to the Gateses, who had long expected him to kill himself and others. He gave his ten-year-old Ford to a granddaughter. While his routine slowed, it could hardly be called sedentary. He spoke at thirty-one colleges in the first six months of 1963 and continued his usual medley of other events—appeared on a CBS political discussion with Tallulah Bankhead, was a featured speaker at the great March on Washington headed by A. Philip Randolph and sponsored by a consortium of black organizations, attended a White House luncheon for President Victor Paz Estenssoro of Bolivia, later accepted in New York a decoration which President Paz Estenssoro pinned on him, and inaugurated for the Post War World Council a campaign for the repeal of the "anti-subversive" laws—the Smith Act, the McCarran Internal Security Act and the Communist Control Act. His fears about the Smith Act when it became law under Roosevelt had been prescient indeed. His foresight on many issues had been borne out by events, though he looked back on Roosevelt with a selective approval not felt at the time. He used the Nelson Rockefeller divorce, in which the Governor's wealth permitted him to bypass New York law as poor people could not, as a text for his belief that "a mistaken marriage should not be irremediable" and stated his lack of enthusiasm for the Governor:

I believe that the New York law, permitting divorce only for adultery, is in error and I have been one of those who for many years have sought its amendment. So far as I know, Nelson Rockefeller has never been one of our company. Like scores of hypocritical legislators throughout the years, he has managed to evade the weight of a law which he has lacked the courage and sense of fair play to seek to change. The politicians fear the power of the Roman Catholic Church which supports the New York law.

He managed to be splendidly opinionated and, with occasional exceptions, urbane with those who disagreed with him. At one meeting where a member of the audience under forty monopolized the floor interminably, Thomas finally snapped, "Sit down, young man," in the manner of one brushing off a fly, and the man sat down. Thomas's onetime Socialist colleague Art McDowell, a rabid anti-Communist, tried to convert him to belief in the holiness of the Vietnam war, to which Thomas replied, "It almost makes me physically ill to contemplate the death of Americans in support of that [Diem] government." The Thomas who *never* lost his temper in debate did lose it once or twice while opposing Buckley, who impressed him as a throwback to the McKinley era, the embodiment of the religious-capitalist self-righteousness whose ideological victory would come at the expense of a world turned to cinders. To Bertram Wolfe, with whom he had once been in close political agreement but who now hewed to the anti-Communist hard line and thought Thomas utopian in believing that any agreement with Russia could have meaning, Thomas wrote, "it is no longer possible to talk in terms of thermonuclear war about peace or freedom," adding:

> . . . I am inclined to go back to the conflict of churches for certain rough analogies. Catholics and Protestants did not love each other after 1648 much, if any, more than they did before but they managed to coexist without war. Something of the sort must happen between us and Russia especially with China in the offing where the evolutionary process has hardly begun.

Perhaps he forgot that the fatigue of 100 years of war had aided peace in 1648.

The young professor of international law Allard Lowenstein, a New Yorker who taught at North Carolina State College, was one of those idealist-activists of whom Thomas felt the world contained too few, and whom he had met while speaking at the Raleigh campus. Thomas was so attracted by Lowenstein's support of the Freedom Ballot in Mississippi—in which disfranchised blacks dramatized their eagerness to vote by doing so in an unofficial election in which their votes did not count —that he flew to the state of Senator Eastland, spoke at Greenwood and at Tougaloo College in Jackson, and was chased in a car by local white nightriders. Aaron Henry, a Clarksdale druggist and president of the state National Association for the Advancement of Colored People, was the "candidate" for whom Thomas and some fifty collegians campaigned for votes. Only the two white candidates, Democratic and Republican, were eligible for election and, said Thomas, differed chiefly on "who hates the Kennedys the most." One collegian worker was jailed in Natchez for "loitering" and Lowenstein was also behind bars for a short time. "You almost have to have a passport to get into Mississippi," Thomas commented. ". . . . It's a pity that [the state] is absorbed so much in race that it doesn't discuss any other issues."

He complained whimsically to the Socialist magazine Dissent, edited by Irving Howe, for dedicating its tenth anniversary issue to him: "It makes me feel as if I had died which I have not done yet." In November he turned up at Stanford University as Guest in Residence for four days at $125 a day plus air fare. This arrangement, showing an appreciation of him as an adviser, leader of bull sessions and general cultural influence as well as formal lecturer, had also prevailed when Haverford College in June paid him $1,000 to stay on campus a week and then deliver the commencement address. As always, the fee interested him only because he expected as a matter of principle to be paid as much as anyone else of equal eminence, and the more he was paid the more he could plow back into his needy causes. He invariably sandwiched in free speeches to Socialists or other indigent groups while on tour. Bruce Bliven, the veteran New Republic editor who had crossed swords with Thomas when that publication had backed Roosevelt's war preparations, was now in semi-retirement, teaching at Stanford, his alma mater. Five years younger than Thomas, a mere seventy-four, he had agreed with him on some liberal issues, though never on Socialism. He now appraised the visitor objectively, noting his foresight in predicting such events as the Hitler-Stalin pact, the Cold War and the nuclear stalemate long in advance, and going on:

> He stayed in one of the men's dormitories, talking nonstop with groups large and small, all day and half the night. Now and then he barnstormed off 20 or 30 miles to speak at other institutions, and when his time was

up, he departed for a distant part of the state, where he repeated the performance. . . .

. . . He has spent his life trying with fabulous energy to persuade the world to be good by talking to it. He is not a very skillful orator: his voice is loud and a little harsh;* he speaks rapidly and extemporaneously; his thoughts are sometimes too complicated to be fully grasped at such speed. Yet he is enormously popular with audiences, partly because he has a good sense of humor and does not take himself too seriously, partly because of his obvious, passionate sincerity, but chiefly, I think, because you get the sense that he is holding nothing back for political reasons, that he is doing his best to tell the truth as he sees it.

Thomas had hoped to meet his grandson Norman Thomas Miller, now working in Los Angeles, but was too pressed for time. Earlier he had written feelingly of the death of Eleanor Roosevelt, with whom he had worked in many causes and whom he called "First Lady of the world." Now, when President Kennedy was killed, he wrote in his column, "If sorrow can save the nation, our country is on the road to salvation," and to Michael Harringon, then in Paris, he wrote "under the shadow of our great tragedy but with considerable hope in President Johnson." He even retained hope in the Party itself, small as it was, in arrears in its New York rent and its bills for New America, its national drive for a mere $15,000 getting scarcely more than half that sum. He was thinking of the Party's future, telling Harrington, "I cannot think of anyone to whom I look with more confidence [than you] to carry on the struggle for an enlightened Democratic Socialism in our country."

". . . I did manage to get home . . . for a family Thanksgiving dinner," he wrote another friend, and again at Christmas he joined "quite a big proportion of the family, including "[two] of my great-grandchildren, aged two and four. . . ."

---

*Bliven's reaction to Thomas's voice was unusual, though Thomas's sister Emma thought he had damaged a fine singing voice by so much speaking. It had a quality which some called a quaver but which Donald Harrington called an "inspiring crackle," and Mary Blanshard thought his voice "beautiful." Recordings of it show (in the author's opinion) great range and appealing timbre. It was indeed loud even in his old age.

# XX

## 1. Creeping Socialism

". . . I will not stand for election as delegate to the Convention in Chicago," Thomas wrote the Party. "I make this decision because various of my handicaps are increasing. . . ." To his brother Evan in Chicago he wrote, "Everything has to end some time," and to Walter Uphoff, "My main hope for myself is that I can keep going and avoid a long old age of invalidism in which my family have to say, 'Oh, the poor old man.'" He preferred to die as Elizabeth Gurley Flynn had, though not *where* she had. She died quickly at seventy-four while visiting Moscow, having become head of the American Communist Party. Izvestia devoted half its front page to her obituary, while Mrs. Nikita Khrushchev headed her full-scale state funeral. (". . . [S]he put life into a meeting as practically no other speaker could," Thomas wrote Dr. Harrington, thanking him for the memorial service she was given at Community Church.) He did not want to die as John Haynes Holmes now did, after long helplessness due to Parkinson's disease. The lucky Roger Baldwin, on the other hand, ten months older than Thomas, was eighty in January, 1964. Thomas attended the anniversary celebration at Baldwin's Greenwich Village home and found him, though slight and somewhat fragile-looking, untroubled by arthritis, jaunty and nimble.

Thomas at times made histrionic use of his aches, as at one Long Island hall when he seated himself at the far end of the platform so that when he was introduced he limped very slowly to the podium, cane in one hand, other hand on back, then turned to the audience and rasped, "Creeping Socialism!" But at times he was in such arthritic pain that he wrote both "family doctors"—his brother Evan and his son-in-law Dr. Miller—to ask about a new treatment with bee venom reported to be

448

helpful. They did not recommend it. He wrote the North Shore Medical Group in his home town:

> I address you collectively because it is likely that one or more of you will take care of me in any serious sickness. I am in earnest when I say that I beg you, if the sickness is actually or virtually incurable, to do the minimum that the law and your conscience allows to keep me alive. Recently I have seen a friend who would have hated it, kept alive for almost two years, when it is doubtful if he was even fully conscious. . . . I do not want to be kept alive when life means only capacity to breathe. It would be a terrible burden to my family and friends.
>
> I am giving a copy of this letter to my children.

He was delighted at a biography of him by Harry Fleischman, written with Thomas's cooperation in recollection and also with the affection and wisdom of Fleischman's three decades of friendship with him. He was glad to be collaborating occasionally on peace and civil rights issues with the young Reverend William Sloane Coffin, who succeeded the retired Sidney Lovett as chaplain at Yale and was as dynamic as his late father, whom Thomas had known and loved more than a half-century earlier. It was a moral victory when Albert Sprague Coolidge rejoined the Party on Thomas's urging, on condition (granted) that he would not be addressed as "Comrade Coolidge." When Upton Sinclair came to town on a lecture tour, they did not merely shake hands, they embraced. ("We argued every time we met," Sinclair wrote later, "but we loved each other just the same.") Thomas accepted with pleasure an honorary LL.D. from Johnson C. Smith University—the institution where his grandfather Mattoon had served as president from 1870 to 1886 and where the audacious Mattoon couple were buried. With equal alacrity he accepted in New York the Order of Solidarity from the Italian government, which he suspected that Angelica had urged on the Socialist Giuseppe Saragat (now Foreign Minister), writing to her, "for some reason and at somebody's suggestion, Saragat saw that I got the Order. . . ." Carrying a sign, "Stop Nuclear Arms for Germany," he led 300 housewives to Pier 90, where the guided missile destroyer Biddle was docked.

"The garrison state mentality" was one of his favorite lecture subjects. The Republican nomination of Goldwater, whose "tough and dangerous and superficial" discussions of foreign relations appalled Thomas, made him go not "All the Way with LBJ" as the campaign slogan had it but, in Thomas's revision, "part of the way with LBJ." "His own policy in Vietnam means war," Thomas declared with customary prevision, "the kind of war in which an American plane can stray over a line and destroy a Cambodian village. It is a war which cannot be won and which, if continued, will increase, not decrease, China's influence and power in Southeast Asia." To Senator Morse, with whom his correspondence was heavy, he wrote, "Every day's news from South Vietnam scares me." Hearing from Juan Bosch in Puerto Rico where he had taken refuge, Thomas replied, "The coup, which deposed you, was a tragedy and I still yearn for a return of your constitutional government." Returning to the subject of Vietnam, Thomas urged Senators Morse and Gruening to push for a plank against the war in the Democratic platform. Morse replied that it was impossible because they would be repudiated by the party and their influence would then be nil.

With both major parties now pro-war, Thomas tried vainly to persuade Walter Reuther to take a stand against the Meany-Lovestone policy, also pro-war. He traveled to Washington to ask the Democratic platform committee for an anti-war plank, and of course did not get it. He had to take comfort in a Chicago debate with Robert Welch, shaman of the Birchers, about which a local columnist wrote that "if this debate was a boxing match, they would have had to call it off in the second round because Robert Welch was completely outmatched by the young Mr. Thomas."

In September, a Congressional subcommittee investigating tax-exempt foundations conducted hearings at which it was learned that the Central Intelligence Agency had made large payments to the Kaplan Fund. It was believed that the fund had been used as a conduit through which the CIA had helped support the Institute for International Labor Research enterprises, now ended for a year. The first payment of $35,000 to Thomas had come from the Kaplan Fund itself. However, the fund's biggest grant in 1963 had been $395,000 to the Thomas-Volman project and most or all of this was believed to have come from the CIA. Other grants had been received from the Ford and Parvin foundations and from individual donors. Newsmen seeking to check the CIA report, said The New York Times, met a "wall of silence" at the Kaplan Fifth Avenue offices. Whether Thomas also met a wall of silence is not known; he wrote an immediate reply to The Times in which he made no mention of anything Kaplan had said, as he surely would have if he had been able to reach Kaplan. Volman, questioned in Washington by The Times, denied any knowledge of CIA involvement, said there had been no strings tied to the Kaplan payments and that "We believe our activities have been good activities."

Thomas, in his letter to The Times, said the story surprised him since it was the belief of some Dominican insiders that the CIA had aided the military coup that exiled Bosch because he was thought to have Communist sympathies. Volman had been forced to flee and the coup put an end to CIDES and the school and publications which it was now claimed the CIA had subsidized. Thomas had the "highest confidence" in Volman, and said the Kaplan Fund "never interfered in any way" and that "I have never ceased to believe that the Kaplan Fund was enabling us to do a work which deserved the gratitude of all lovers of intelligent, progressive democracy." While Thomas was troubled at the possibility that the project had been a CIA beneficiary, it had been supported by other donors, its work had been constructive and the matter rested there for the time.

## 2. The Portcullis Falls

"Today in Art my teacher wanted to know if you had big ears, since he's convinced they are signs of greatness," Thomas's granddaughter Louisa Thomas wrote him from Concord Academy, where he had lectured. "Have you? I can't remember, but if you haven't, don't despair; they aren't required." He replied promptly, answering other questions she had asked and advising her on how to choose a college but forgetting about his ears, which were average in size. To his enlisted grandson, Private John W. Gates at Fort Riley, Kansas (the same place where big-eared Evan Thomas had suffered in 1918), he wrote, "I think you can learn something useful about people and life this hard way and I respect you for not suddenly trying to be a conscientious objector when you have not really been convinced of that position."

At the request of the Associated Students of the University of Hawaii, he took off for Honolulu on a Tuesday, made three speeches and was back in New York Thursday. Jet-lag did not affect him and he slept well aboard planes. A few days later he left to speak to Party gatherings and Turn Toward Peace groups in Cleveland and Indianapolis; at Indiana University; in Chicago and Boulder, Colorado; and in Houston, Tucson, Los Angeles, San Francisco and several other cities, speaking against Goldwater at every opportunity. "The only principle he represents," Thomas said, "is the one of always standing firm, even if you are on quicksand." Thomas's eightieth birthday would be November 20, 1964.

451

He was given an early birthday party in Chicago, another in Los Angeles, and he still had to face one in New York. His disparagement of Goldwater brought him some vicious telephone calls, and he was astonished at the moonshine some of the right-wing extremists believed—that President Johnson had a private "Siberia" in Alaska to which he sent his enemies, and that somewhere on the new Kennedy half-dollar, if you looked at it right, was a hammer and sickle. "In this sort of society we have a big work to do," Thomas wrote his fellow Socialists in New America.

The new intolerance bothered him: "There is now much more organized persecution of dissenters than there was when I was the not-too-popular candidate for President. A man dissents, and the super-patriots on the nut fringe plague him with anonymous phone calls. They send hearses and funeral wreaths to his home. They send his wife advance copies of his obituary." To his brother Evan he wrote, "I had . . . a pretty satisfactory trip and was modestly elated to have stood it as well as I did." After the election, he commented on the ineptitude of the Goldwater speeches: "If he'd kept on long enough, he would have got an even lower vote." His fame was such, and his remarks so dependably salty, that on his birthday (he was at the University of Nevada at the moment, saying, "My future is mostly in the past") wire-service dispatches about him flowered in newspapers all over the country. ". . . [I]t lies in my worsening memory," Gilkey wrote him, "that for some weeks you are going all over the country to attend birthday dinners in your honor. . . . Of all my contemporaries, you are one of the few whom our troubled world cannot do without."

His official eastern zone birthday party, the biggest of all, was at the Astor, with A. Philip Randolph in the chair. Ralph and his family came up from Baltimore and rented a suite at the hotel, which all the Thomases—brothers, sisters and the three succeeding generations—used as a base. More than nineteen hundred persons paid $2.50 each to honor him. One of them was that political enigma, Juan Bosch, still a democratic hero to him. Saving his legs, Thomas sat "somewhat apologetically" in a red plush chair to receive hundreds who lined up to talk a bit, to reminisce over incidents years or decades ago, most of which he remembered with an instant smile, being a veteran of this sort of thing who really loved it for all the harrumphing he had done about it behind the scenes. "The world is going your way, sir," said one congratulator, to which Thomas replied in all honesty, "I'm not so sure." His disillusionments, which were many in the age of the Bomb and the Lie, were thinly cushioned by what some might call local and minor successes. But the successes were no more measurable than was his influence on the college generation, to which he was devoting most of his remaining energies. One of the nonmeasurable inspirations was his refusal to accept defeat. The world was not going his way at all and he knew it, but after each repulse he marshaled his nonmeasurable forces and charged again. There were hundreds of congratulatory telegrams from prime ministers, justices and Senators—from Vice President–elect Humphrey, whom he had long admired, who had supported Thomas's second Arden House peace conference and who was now following Johnson into war, not peace. From Meany and Dubinsky—leaders of the labor movement which he had tried and failed to make a force for peace, both war men. The huge, frilly birthday cake, fashioned by Cake Bakers' Local 151, was the work of artisans who accepted the war their leaders backed.

The series of birthday parties and honors given this perpetual loser, this greatest of also-rans, was remarkable in a nation addicted to success and it requires explanation. It was surely not a mere show of sympathy for his failures. Perhaps there was still some belated recognition of the political successes he had achieved by indirection, the demands he had made decades earlier and which the New Deal had incorporated. But there was much more than that. Probably some in the Astor crowd would have been hard put to it to analyze the reasons for their admiration. To be sure, there was no one like him in his care for all humanity. He was the nonchauvinist personified. Who else was there with such a capacity for caring—who would lavish his time and effort on Milovan Djilas, Junius Scales, the Long Island conductor and Alexander Trachtenberg as well as on the Seneca Indians, the Kalmucks, the blacks of America and Africa, the oppressed of Spain or the Dominican Republic or any part of the world?

The tribute was given to a kind of success no one else—literally no one else—in the country had achieved. Although its central magic ingredient was biblically simple, people on the long road he had traveled had not always seen it. Angelica had defined it as integrity and had said, "Could every country only have a Norman Thomas!" Sandra Levinson had called him "magnificent" because of his commitment. The bubbly Sadie had said he could "see so straight" that he "must be from outer space." Old Bruce Bliven, a lecturer himself, had looked for the secret and thought it was that "he is doing his best to tell the truth as he sees it." Max Nomad had paid him the highest compliment possible from such a thoroughgoing believer in man's depravity and hopelessness, simply by admiring him. Thomas in his answer to Nomad had said it all, that man was both good and evil, that he did have a choice, that one must appeal to his better nature, always his better nature. True, Thomas's integrity *was* impressive, his commitment powerful, his vision extra-terrestrial, his honesty especially remarkable in the new American age of institutionalized falsehood. But the true wonder of Thomas, with all his faults, was that he appealed to the good in mankind. His hearers knew he appealed to the good in them. It elevated them. The world seemed better when one's intelligence and nobler impulses were importuned. It made some even believe that a still better world was possible if men everywhere would only banish hate and cultivate goodwill. In the world of McCarthy, Dulles, Nixon, Kissinger and Frederick Schwarz, to have one's angels petitioned instead of the devils was a unique event.

It was so rare that the magic of it spread across the country, though too thinly to measure. Some of the wonder affected Senators and Congressmen—alas, not enough to make a difference, because the tide was against Thomas. The United States, in its twin drives of fighting Communism and winning affluence, had opted for the morals of the Communists and the sharpers. There seemed no drawing back from the turns made at the Bay of Pigs and Tonkin Gulf, any more than there was repentance in the advertising boardrooms or the labor unions. In a sense—and some of them must have realized it—the nineteen hundred people at the Astor were honoring the last great American idealist. There would always be more Dulleses and Nixons, but Thomas, in his red plush chair, was on the way to becoming a lost national asset.

"When I was campaigning," he said with a straight face to a birthday interviewer, explaining his failure to win, "my advisers were always telling me to smile. I did as I was bade. But I happen to have a rather fatuous grin—some would say even foolish. Anyway, I'd smile, the camera recorded it, and the next day the newspapers would use a picture of me with that horrible grin, along with a headline that said, 'Thomas Predicts End of the World.' "

Some of his friends objected. "You are the great moral leader of our political life," Lenore Marshall had written him. "The whole country should be grateful to you. I am, and constantly." The eighty-five-year-old Ethel Clyde sent $500 and insisted that his picture in The Times was anything but horrible: "It is an inspiration to know that anyone can live that long, still be handsome, and express in his face such kindliness, humor and joy in living. More power to you, Norman!" Angelica Balaba-noff wrote from Rome to "Dearest Comrade and Friend!" to celebrate "your genuine authentic altruism . . . your incomparable devotion to a cause the triumph of which is still so far and the road which leads to it so thorny!"*

He gave the Astor celebrants a rousing fifteen-minute speech, the old sorcery still in his voice, eschewing mere peevishness, managing to maintain relative calm even while condemning unnecessary poverty, the arms race and the napalming of villages—"often the wrong villages"—in Vietnam. He did not neglect to propitiate up-from-slum Socialists: He was pretty lucky himself, he said, never having had to pay the price of poverty. He was presented with a check for $17,500 to spend as he saw fit, but which of course would go to the causes. "It won't last long," he said cheerfully, "because every organization I'm connected with is going bankrupt," which The Times printed as its quotation of the day. He had also been given smaller parties by his own family and by his colleagues at 112—the League for Industrial Democracy, the Sharecroppers' Fund, the Post War World Council, Iberica and the rest. "I'm so sick of being 80," he said before the Astor affair. "I was 80 at a party in California on the 31st, and I was 80 in Chicago on the 28th, and now I'm going to be 80 in New York . . . But after [that] the portcullis falls, and I will absolutely not be 80 any more."

### 3. Not Too Respectable

When the Chase Manhattan Bank lent money to the apartheid-rid-den South African Republic, Thomas wrote to the bank's president, David Rockefeller, courteously explaining that he must withdraw his account after being a customer for a half-century and hoping that this would not reflect on his son-in-law, John W. Gates, a rising executive with the bank. He still sent regular notes of encouragement to old Socialists such as Joel Schmedekamp in Illinois, who was a mere sixty-five and troubled by arthritis perhaps no more than Thomas himself. Thomas had mentioned jocularly that "the line forms at the right" for applicants for shares of his $17,500 birthday money, but it was hardly

---

*Some determined Socialists had continued to write in votes for Thomas for President at every election. The baseball impresario William Veeck was among the uncounted who voted for Norman Thomas after Thomas's death.

a joke. New America asked him for $2,000 plus "an additional offer to match funds beyond that." Other deserving organizations extended their hands in sharp competition. Thomas exercised diplomacy to avoid hurting feelings, writing to the National Sharecroppers' Fund:

> You rank very high . . . but my principle of distribution has had to take account of my various special responsibilities for certain organizations and, to a lesser degree, the ability of organizations to raise money. . . . In no way does [my contribution] imply any appraisal of the relative merit of the organizations to which I give.

He gave $4,762 to his own indigent Post War World Council, $3,000 to the Workers' Defense League, $2,500 to Turn Toward Peace and smaller amounts to other organizations including the National Association for the Advancement of Colored People, the League for Industrial Democracy and Students for a Democratic Society, though the latter group's growing rashness worried him. Michael Harrington of LID, returning from a speaking tour, telegraphed Thomas that he was shocked at his small contribution to that body, though Thomas had earlier paid a $500 debt troubling LID and had written, "I am not so poor but what I will continue giving you some of my own money."

Thomas had greater vexations to worry about, among them the continuation of Senator Eastland on the Judiciary Committee and the deeper drift of President Johnson into war. He had recently learned from Paul that Mary Hillyer Blanshard, that dear apostle of fair play, was dying of cancer, and when he spoke at Dartmouth the snows were so heavy that he could not get to the Blanshard place. He gave Mary what comfort he could by telephone—his last conversation with her.

Arthritis kept him out of Martin Luther King's march from Selma, but he felt now that civil rights (one area in which he had praise for Johnson) was making better progress than work for peace, which accordingly had higher priority. He was now infirm enough so that he carefully selected meetings and speaking dates on a basis of importance. He sugar-coated an appeal to the President, praising his petition for racial understanding and adding: "May I respectfully submit that a similar appeal, properly timed, initiated by you in the hearing of the whole world, might do for the Vietnamese situation what you are doing in Alabama?"

Johnson's replies always complained of his own unappreciated efforts and prayers for peace. A Thomas letter to Secretary McNamara protesting against the cruelties practiced by Americans on the Vietnamese brought the reply that it was quite the other way around, that Americans practiced no cruelties but were often victims of Vietcong cruelties. In writing to "Dear Averell" Harriman, Undersecretary of State for Political Affairs, Thomas condemned the idea "that we ought to be God's policeman, especially when the devil is Communism. . . . I would honestly like your point of view." He was spurring Turn Toward Peace to greater efforts and was suggesting to John P. Roche of Americans for Democratic Action a plan to hit the poll-conscious President hard, perhaps with "an avalanche of letters." To The Christian Century he wrote in part:

> Once more in the Vietnam crisis we seem to be observing the Christian churches in their familiar role of opposing all wars except the one they are in. . . . By what right has the church of Christ so long accepted cruel guerilla war in Vietnam, fought by American conscripts alongside unwilling Vietnamese as a war nominally for liberty?. . . . Has the Christian church no answer to Communist progress but the bombs of which we have enough to destroy the world?

He had not seen his birthplace in Marion since 1948, and he had accepted an invitation to speak to the Rotary Club there, one of whose members was the present pastor of his father's Presbyterian church. Thomas was picked up at the Columbus airport, given a standing ovation when he spoke, had a long visit with the retired shoe dealer Homer Waddell—one of only three high school classmates still living—then flew on to speaking appointments in Flint and Kalamazoo. Waddell sent him a clipping from The Marion Star containing a letter critical of his speech because he had opposed the war. Thomas thanked him, writing, "I feel better not to be too respectable." President Johnson's dispatch of 23,000 Marines to the Dominican Republic to make certain of a right-wing government there—in defiance of the United Nations charter and the Organization of American States agreements—aroused something more than a routine Thomas protest. The action reduced what was left of his hope that the President might have peaceful intentions in Vietnam, and the widespread public acceptance of the intervention was even more distressing. To Meany and Dubinsky, Thomas sent sorrowful protest against their support of the President's belligerence. Adlai Stevenson, so heroic in 1952 at the Garden when he talked turkey to the American Legion, now repeated in the United Nations the administration's tired fictions about the Dominican Republic as he had those about the Bay of Pigs and Vietnam, and became a melancholy symbol of the nation's fraudulence. Thomas's newspaper column contained an open letter to Stevenson, saying that his latest United Nations performance "raises serious questions concerning the quality and strength of your liberalism" and asking, "Are you not forced to admit that our action [in the Dominican Republic] exactly parallels the Russian action at the time of the Hungarian revolt?" He sent it to Stevenson in advance, writing, "I beg you to believe I do it not to score a point against you but really to appeal to you at least to try to tell us how you can do some of the things you have to do at the United Nations." Stevenson, always the gentleman (he had only two months to live and was obviously unhappy about what he "had to do") replied that he would not think of regarding Thomas's letter or his column in a personal way but did not go into the motivation of a dissembling United Nations ambassador. From the hard-nosed McGeorge Bundy, Thomas got a reply on the Dominican affair so dubitable that Thomas shot him a letter beginning, "Let me say quite frankly that I find your reply to my letter unsatisfactory."

### 4. Class of 1905

When Life Magazine proposed to do a picture feature on him, Thomas was busy but willing, even though the Lucepress was hailing the Dominican militarism: "I have my calendar before me and I simply cannot see any good time in New York . . . before the end of May." It would be good to have Life, with its huge circulation, spreading *his* message for a change. Life arranged to send a writer, Sylvia Wright, and a photographer, Leonard McCombe, with Thomas during a tour. Miss Wright, interviewing him at home, found him amiably talkative about his background and generously crediting Violet's help as well as her money with making his life and career easier. Wright and McCombe then accompanied him by air to California, surprised that so much energy could persist within the bent, baggy-suited frame, that his voice could be so strong, that he could maintain good humor despite pain. "I have only one request to make of the world," he said half jokingly, ". . . and that is to let me go out with a bang, not a whimper." They watched him bang away at Berkeley and other campuses, a man nearing eighty-one commanding the attention of student crowds usually scornful of anyone over thirty. (Tom Hayden said there were only three people over thirty whom his generation would trust: Thomas, C. Wright

Mills and Michael Harrington.) Thomas shrewdly analyzed the New Left which now made up a vocal part of his audience:

> J. Edgar Hoover is greatly mistaken if he thinks they have been mainly inspired and guided by the American Communist Party. There are Communists in the New Left[,] which contains many individuals and groups with various ideas. But the most prominent Communists are definitely sympathetic with the Chinese, not the Russian version of Communism in action, and they are not members of the American Communist Party. In the Thirties the old Left and, today, the New Left among the students represent a significant revolt against what is now called the establishment and its mores, but there are significant differences. The old Left was primarily concerned with economic conditions. Its members were Socialists or Communists or sympathizers . . . and they placed great emphasis on the working class as the bringers of social salvation. A much higher percentage of their members came from the working class than is the case with the New Left, most of whose members seem to come from a prosperous middle class.
>
> Theirs is most definitely a revolt against what they regard as bourgeois values and they are more conscious of the infallibility of youth as against middle age. They are more inclined to find "the poor" as bearers of salvation rather than the working class, certainly as it expresses itself in the unions. In the Thirties we had no beatniks but they are numerous in the New Left. The New Lefters are . . . more concerned about foreign policy than the old Left and they are . . . anti-Washington's version of Americanism.
>
> But to my mind the chief difference is that the members of the old Left had pretty definite programs, chiefly economic, Socialist or Communist. The New Left is very amorphous in program, inclined to be nihilistic, anarchistic rather than Socialist. Freedom from dogmatism is a good thing but lack of program is not . . . I deeply regret the tendency of some rather conspicuous members of the New Left to appear more interested in a Communist victory in Vietnam than in a constructive peace. . . .

That last sentence was especially applicable to Berkeley. The central theme of one student speaker he heard there was an incitation to more bitter war—he urged student volunteers for the Vietcong. The man who for years had placed a large share of his hope in guiding the student generation toward intelligent political action for peace was shaken by the trend toward violence and political alienation. But he had to keep his lines of communication open. He was able to quell his inclination to illuminate their folly with a biting remark and he insisted on the need for well-considered political action to get results: "You march off demanding the impeachment of Lyndon Johnson and what will you get? I'll tell you what. You'll get a lot of people who are fed up with him suddenly coming to his defense. Instead, go out and be missionaries. If you can convince enough American people that you have the right idea in wanting us out of this war, then you'll convince Johnson." He added with a wink, "He's a great believer in consensus, you know!" and joined them in laughter. One of his listeners was his New Jersey granddaughter, Joan Friebely, now a student at Stanford. To see him so crippled that he almost had to be carried to the rostrum shook her, but the strength of his voice was reassuring.

Thomas discovered that his eyesight, now poor at best, was even dimmer and saw an ophthalmologist, who could do little for him.

His preferred breakfast was an enormous stack of hotcakes. En route with the Life couple to Havre, Montana, where he spoke at the Northern Montana State College, he made use of one plane stop to destroy a huge steak with French fries, half a loaf of garlic bread and several brownies with coffee. Next stop, the Twin Cities, his eyesight seemed worse than ever. He was indeed going blind from retinal arteriosclerosis, and little could be done about it. "I'm falling apart piece by piece," he grumbled.

He dined with another granddaughter, Patricia Miller Libbey, now living with her husband in Saint Paul. He seemed to her less upset over his impaired vision than over the Berkeley nihilism. A Minneapolis eye specialist treated him before he was driven to the University of Minnesota to participate in a teach-in on the Vietnam war. Here, in his disgust at the war, he behaved scandalously. Seated next to the rostrum, he let the dovish Hans Morgenthau speak undisturbed. But when Frank Sieverts of the State Department spoke in defense of the American role in Vietnam, Thomas interrupted him, heckled him, contradicted him so that Sieverts was in difficulty and the audience shushed Thomas. He won back the crowd when his own turn came to speak and, among other things, he gave them his favorite parable about the peculiar logic in the administration's continual additions to arsenals which could already wipe out the human race and calling such additions a deterrent:

"Such nonsense. It is like saying that if Harry and David are fighting a lot at kindergarten, the thing to do is give them each a gun and say, 'There now, boys, go deter each other.' "

Returning to New York, he got stronger glasses but could not read without much greater magnification. For all that, he flew back to California a week later to appear on a television panel with an old friend sometimes politically to his left, I. F. Stone. Flying home again, he spoke at two consecutive Madison Square Garden rallies. His children were not free from the suspicion that he might be driving himself purposely in search of death in harness so that he might die while still active and escape the invalidism he dreaded.

But next he turned to an event dear to his heart, the sixtieth reunion of his Princeton class of 1905. He joined his brother Ralph there— Ralph, whose wife had recently died and who had been grateful to Thomas for his support at the time—but apparently Evan and Arthur did not attend. Thomas joined the parade and watched the baseball game, which appeared to him as a blur. He wore an orange-striped 1905 cap and flashed a smile which was caught by one photographer as proof that age and aches and failing eyes could not quench his gayety, even though his classmates of 1905 had been dying year by year and the parade was small, bent and slow. He was the guest of the Boyds, who were unaware of how bad his eyesight was until they took him to the home of a friend who had a Brancusi sculpture which Thomas squinted at and took to be a Franklin stove; then he laughed at his own blunder.

These frivolities over, he resumed his effort to round up a group of labor leaders who would speak and write against Johnson's war policy as a counter to Meany and Dubinsky. "President Johnson and perhaps the Chamber of Commerce must be glad to know," he wrote Walter Reuther a trifle bitterly, "that they can always trust labor when it comes to policing the world with bombs." Thomas letters in like vein went out to A. Philip Randolph, Emil Mazey and a dozen others. (Reuther and the United Auto Workers came out for Johnson and the war, citing the enemy's "refusal to negotiate.") Thomas's letters directly to the President were now answered by aides with protestations of the administration's passion for peace which was always foiled by Hanoi or Peking. One of Thomas's letters presented a point of view not favored in Washington:

All the elements seem to show that this is essentially a civil war, not primarily caused by aggression from without. . . . To give a somewhat extreme illustration, it seems to me that when the President talks to North Vietnam about negotiations, ignoring the Vietcong or National Liberation Front, it is pretty much as if King George III had proclaimed to the world his willingness to discuss the American revolution with Louis XVI but not with George Washington. French aid was an important item in our revolution but it wasn't the revolution.

He yearned for an end to face-saving: ". . . I want the President to take a dramatic initiative and proclaim his desire for an immediate cease-fire." He called on the new ambassador to the United Nations, Arthur Goldberg (to whom he had sent congratulations containing an uncharacteristically loaded sentence: "I judge you must have identified yourself pretty much with the general Johnson policies in the Dominican Republic and Vietnam . . . and that is why my admiration of your patriotism and sacrifice is considerably limited.") He came away without real hope in Goldberg. Thomas's crusade for world disarmament had to take second place to his campaign against the war in Indochina. He was working for peace with men as old as himself—Roger Baldwin, A. J. Muste and Grenville Clark; with the "middle-aged" including Allard Lowenstein, Dr. Coffin and Michael Harrington; and of course directly with the college generation. Clark, like Thomas, was affected by the moral issue—"the sheer cruelty and horror of our protracted bombing of helpless and very poor people"—and urged civil disobedience, which had an honorable tradition in public opposition to the Fugitive Slave Law and Thoreau's refusing to pay taxes and going to jail during the Mexican War. Muste, the absolute pacifist, had paid no taxes since 1948, notifying the Internal Revenue Service that he was withholding payment entirely rather than support nuclear and bacteriological armament. He had finally been brought into court for nonpayment in 1960, Thomas and Nevin Sayre appearing as character witnesses for him. Thomas nonetheless disapproved of Muste's stand, saying, "I don't think you do any good by disrupting organized society." He paid his own taxes in full but with a letter saying that that part going into warfare was paid under strenuous protest. Nor did he favor Clark's idea of civil disobedience, feeling the pulse of collegians all over the country as he did and being among the first to realize that the problem was not to start but to control civil disobedience, to keep it from defeating the cause it professed to support. The anti-war movement was already being hurt by young people who outraged middle-class respectables by strewing garbage, burning draft cards, cheering the Vietcong and indeed merely by letting their hair grow long and overtly insulting Americans over thirty. Thomas was irate at the excesses of the "ardent young Americans who have been led to hate America more than to love peace" and was trying to alter his technique to counter them.

## 5. Pieties, Pieties

The death of Thomas's brother Ralph at seventy-eight, with the lucky quickness of a heart attack, caused Thomas to gather with the clan in Baltimore for the funeral. Five days later he cabled the Social Democratic Party in Rome: "WE MOURN WITH YOU THE DEATH OF THAT MAGNIFICENT COMRADE AND FRIEND OF HUMANITY, ANGELICA BALABANOFF." The multilingual poet of Socialism had been a peculiar treasure to him. He was on that last plateau of age where friends and contemporaries and those younger still were dying—Ed Murrow, Leo Krzycki, Sam Romer, Art McDowell and blessed old Charlie Gilkey. He could not allow inevitabilities to stop him. The day after the cable he was in Washington addressing (with Dr. Spock and others) 25,000 young and middle-aged marchers for peace. "I cannot help but think," a friend wrote him, "that Angelica Balabanoff would have been pleased to know that you led the march on Washington yesterday." Actually, he was too lame to lead the march but he was there. While there, he was not too lame to call on Secretary of State Rusk and have a "quite heated" discussion of Vietnam, emerging from it to say, "I went. We talked. . . . But we made no converts." Cheering every sign of aid given the lonely Senators Morse and Gruening, he congratulated Senator Fulbright on his speech against the war. To Victor Reuther he argued that the United Auto Workers' support of the war made no sense when "even the State Department admits [peace] feelers from North Vietnam which it never reported to the public, even at the time when Johnson was running as the friend of peace in contrast to Senator Goldwater. I cannot tell you what a disappointment it is to all my hopes and beliefs about labor's role that in these matters labor continues to be to the right of the Wall Street Journal."

He put most pressure of all on Vice President Humphrey—a decent man with a record of political courage not lately evident. The two had been personally friendly for years. He sent repeated adjurations to Humphrey, realizing his difficult role under the powerhouse Johnson, without conceding that this absolved him from effort. Humphrey replied with customary courtesy and all too customary repetition of the President's asserted great but thwarted efforts for peace. Thomas tried him with a three-page letter of careful political analysis, suggesting that

463

Johnson was now getting support from those supporting "Richard Nixon or worse," but losing many to the left of Nixon, and that public opinion against the war was growing: "Is there any way of honorably suggesting to President Johnson that we, who sympathize with his desire for greatness in history, a desire partly satisfied by his performance in the field of civil rights, believe that he will lose what he wants unless he can promptly get out of the Vietnamese war by negotiation[?]" Humphrey's reply was a rewording of previous pieties. But by now Johnson had started his short-lived "peace drive" and suspension of bombing in North Vietnam. Thomas urged Humphrey that the suspension be made permanent:

> I know the pressures must be great from the Pentagon and elsewhere but I think the country, properly informed, would stand behind the President in refusing to renew this horror of destruction from the air. . . . My special plea is not to renew the bombing at the request of Nixon or Dirksen or anyone else.

The words "properly informed" should have been writ large. The public was not merely being poorly informed about Vietnam. It was being actively deceived. Thomas's Christmas newspaper column began, "We awoke at the beginning of Christmas week to a sickening mixture of Christmas carols and the score of the slain in Vietnam."

### 6. We All Need You

"I like human beings," Thomas told an interviewer. "I'm very glad I'm one of them. But I think we're crazy. We're irrational. Look at our race prejudice, look at our inability to get out of the war, look at the crazy things we do in our personal lives." He admitted to the peace worker Mildred Scott Olmsted his diminishing optimism about humanity, adding nevertheless what always had been and still was his law of life: "But it's worthwhile to keep on in our struggle." If the fight was abandoned, then the world was indeed lost; the Goldwaters or Welches and Eastlands would have their way by default. He was attacked ungrammatically in The Long Island Press by a parcel of Birchers who hailed the three great Americans, J. Edgar Hoover, MacArthur, and Goldwater. He caused a skirmish in his home-town government in Huntington when a Republican councilman introduced a resolution to condemn him for appearing at peace rallies and saying, "There's no fool like an old fool." Two other councilmen defended him warmly although not agreeing with all of his opinions. A local doctor, totally mistaken about Thomas's aims, wrote him to stop sending him "peace literature" because "calling for unilateral disarmament in Vietnam is too actively participating in the killing of American troops in Vietnam. I do not wish to join your murdering clan." Thomas, who had dealt all his life with people who misunderstood him or were ignorant of issues or both, wrote back patiently that he had never advocated unilateral disarmament but asked for negotiation and a cease-fire which "probably would save the lives of our boys in Vietnam," and sent along his latest newsletter giving his position.

The Life article on Thomas did not appear until January 1966; it bathed him in the respectability and fame many Americans associated with that magazine. His indomitability and wit had touched Sylvia Wright, whose account was so warm and admiring as to startle many readers accustomed to the Lucepress line. He received hundreds of letters, mostly laudatory, from readers in various parts of the world. "This is a love letter that needs no answer," one American woman who had met him in 1915 wrote from Taxco. "(Do not be alarmed—I am too old for nonsense—going on 90.). . . . I am thankful that I have lived long enough to see those 'dangerous creeping Socialist ideas' quietly incorporated into the political thinking of most intelligent people. Even, thank God, to see the tide rising, however slowly, against terror as an instrument of national policy." Irving Laucks wrote to him from the Center for the Study of Democratic Institutions, "Times are sure changing! Yesterday afternoon I talked with a Catholic priest who is organizing a union of priests. . . . But my greatest shock came when somebody gave me a copy of Life in which [you were presented] of all things, in quite a commendatory style." Margaret M. Gage, who had been so generous to the Socialist Party over the years, wrote, ". . . that is one magazine in which I never expected to see you featured." A. J. Muste wrote, "it is, to my mind, a great contribution to the desperately needed education of the American people to have your views so clearly and attractively presented in a magazine like Life which will reach millions of people who ordinarily would not hear these views and, very likely, wouldn't listen to them if they appeared in another medium."

So there were knocks and there were boosts. He won the benediction of an interview with Walter Cronkite, but when he became the central figure in a New York Channel 13 "round table" in which Frank Graham, James Farmer, Harry Fleischman and Allard Lowenstein took turns heaping praise on him, he claimed to be embarrassed, describing the program as a "discussion of what, if I were an applicant for sainthood, the church would call my life work and miracles. The last named have been conspicuously absent." He was legally blind, which was far from total blindness but a great handicap. When he was at Cold Spring Harbor, Frances Gates or her younger son, Norman Thomas Gates, a high school senior, read him The Times, and he listened to radio news and recordings for the blind. ("He did not like rock music," young Norman noted.) Thomas had taken a small kitchenette apartment in town at the Gramercy Park Hotel on the north side of the park, so that he did not have to fight train and subway to get to 112. He had been a denizen of the neighborhood for thirty-five years—almost as much a fixture as the Friends' Meeting House—and an elderly neighbor lady who saw him groping his way along—so different from his long stride before his blindness and arthritis—wrote to him in a birthday greeting, "I just saw you passing my window . . . My thoughts are often with you, in admiration and affection. Take care of yourself—we all need you, and more than ever."

He made his usual late-winter speaking trip to California, though this time Siteman accompanied him. Shortly after his return, he got out of a cab in front of 112, slammed the door on his own raincoat and was dragged cruelly when the cabbie drove away. At Beth Israel Hospital he was found bruised but unbroken, and when Mrs. Gates arrived to read him Helen Howe's *The Gentle Americans,* she recalled, "His nose was scratched and swollen, he had two black eyes and he looked terrible." One of his get-well cards came from Humphrey, though he had written to the Vice President sternly after his fox-in-chicken-coop remark about Vietnam. Siteman sat with him, taking letters. Thomas had been upset by a Times story containing new driblets of information about the activities of the Central Intelligence Agency in Latin America. It said in part:

> Congressional investigation of tax-exempt foundations in 1964 showed that the J. M. Kaplan Fund, Inc., among others, had disbursed at least $400,000 for the CIA in a single year to a research institute [meaning Thomas's Institute for International Labor Research]. This institute, in turn, financed research centers in Latin America that drew other support from the Agency for International Development . . . the Ford Foundation and such universities as Harvard and Brandeis.
>
> Thus, the ramifications of CIA activities, at home and abroad, seem almost endless.

A comment by James Reston on this news impelled Thomas to write again to President Goheen—the fifth Princeton president he had known, including his late father-in-law:

> I have just had read to me James Reston's column in the New York Times today that stirs again my curiosity and concern about a matter which I think I once took up with you; namely, the amount and purpose of Federal grants to Princeton which I know come to a very large part of our budget. Are any of them from the CIA and, if so, for what?

Assured by Goheen that Princeton received no CIA grants, Thomas replied that one couldn't be too careful: "I, myself, have been engaged in enterprises which I now think received CIA money, through foundations. The enterprises were good and were worth government support through open agreements such as you say Princeton negotiates for research projects. There is quite a distinction between such contracts and the roundabout aid from the CIA, by no means all of which is for good causes."

Again he tried sweet-talking the President, praising him for his program televised in Texas "which so admirably related your attachment to the country of your fathers in the days of your youth," and ending with the snapper: "It gave me some hope that the man I saw there would find a better way than he has yet found out of the Vietnamese mess." He wrote to Helen Howe to tell her how much he had enjoyed her book, whereupon she visited Beth Israel to read to him and discovered him gone to a SANE-sponsored peace rally in Washington. "I am amused at my picture of your father," she wrote Mrs. Gates, "in a darkened hospital room, with me tiptoeing in to read to him—while all the time he is marching on Washington . . ." The Gateses, worried about him, flew to Washington. "I hardly recognized my father when he came tottering onto the platform," Mrs. Gates recalled. "His eyes were still black and it seemed impossible that he could deliver a speech. But his voice came out powerfully and he spoke splendidly."

## 7. The Dominican Repulse

"I have a terrible time keeping up with necessary correspondence," Thomas lamented. "I can only do what I do because of Stephen Siteman's help, which goes far beyond his professional duties." He was so grateful to his devoted aide that he mentioned this repeatedly in letters which Siteman took by shorthand and typed himself, so that the latter well knew he was appreciated. The taxicab accident made Thomas's children unanimous in their insistence that he always have a companion while traveling. Since Siteman was needed in the office, Thomas advertised in The Saturday Review ("Peace leader needs young assistant . . .") and hired Timothy Sullivan of Philadelphia, a twenty-six-year-old graduate of Villanova, who had taken graduate work at the University of Chicago. Sullivan had seen Thomas speak a couple of years earlier in Philadelphia and was surprised at how handicapped he was now by blindness and arthritis. The young man happened to be broke when he was hired, and until he got his first paycheck his night's rest, unknown to the boss, was enjoyed in Thomas's big leather chair at 112.

Thomas assailed the stepped-up bombing near Hanoi and Haiphong, accusing the President of making "the terrible light of burning villages and oil tanks" the new American symbol replacing the traditional light from "liberty's torch." But when it was rumored that the North Vietnamese would execute captured American flyers, Thomas cabled President Ho Chi Minh:

> As worker for peace and strong critic of American bombing I respectfully report that execution of captured American flyers would have disastrous effects upon American public in our efforts to win it for peace and justice in Vietnam. It would make almost certain great intensification and prolongation of war.

Although Ambassador-at-Large Harriman and others had sent appeals to Hanoi on this subject through the United Nations, the International Red Cross and several Communist countries including Russia, it appeared that Thomas was the only one who got a direct answer from Ho:

> Thank you for your message. No doubt you know that the policy of the Government of the Democratic Republic of Vietnam with regard to the enemies captured in war is a humanitarian policy. Wish you good health.

His health could have been better but he was so concerned about the presidential election to be held under Organization of American States auspices in the Dominican Republic on June 1, 1966, that he arranged to watch over it in person. The leading candidates were his friend Bosch and Dr. Joaquin Balaguer, a one-time Trujillo collaborator in whom Thomas understandably had little faith and who was widely regarded as being secretly promoted by the United States. There had been terror for a time preceding the election. "There lies before me," Thomas wrote, "a long list of Dominicans murdered, 'vanished,' wounded, imprisoned, beaten, etc. . . . Most of these victims . . . were neither Communists nor ultra-right militarists, but members of the PRD [Bosch's party]." Indeed Bosch's son was wounded by a mysterious assailant and Bosch had threatened to withdraw. He stayed in the race in large part because Thomas urged that otherwise the election would have no meaning. Thomas had been thwarted first in Costa Rica and then in the Dominican Republic in his fond plans for implanting a seedling of democracy that would sprout and flower in Latin America. Clarence Senior, now a member of the New York City Board of Education, in addition to his professorial and Latin American duties, was astonished by Thomas's determination, despite the evidences of it he had seen during their long friendship. Thomas had been foiled by political forces and machinations beyond his control in a country foreign to him, and the plausible course for a bent and blinded eighty-two-year-old would have been to quit the field with regret and relinquish the salvation of Latin America to younger hands, while focusing his own remaining energies on curing Washington's madness in Vietnam. His return to the Dominican fray was the ultimate demonstration of an old man who simply would not give up.

But inscrutable influences were working against him, not least of them Bosch himself. Ellsworth Bunker, later to serve as a militant ambassador in Saigon, was in Santo Domingo as the United States member of the special small peace committee set up by the Organization of American states, which had no adequate force to guard against fraud at the country's 3,400 polling places. There were 7,000 United States troops on the scene to "keep the peace" and, some said, to promote the interests of the Washington-supported candidate, Balaguer. Dominican officials agreed to Thomas's astonishing suggestion that he furnish a body of qualified and impartial election observers. Thomas arrived late in May, his nose still scarred, but otherwise recovered. He had had time to round up only seventy observers from the United States and Latin countries, among the Americans being Bayard Rustin, Allard Lowenstein and Victor Reuther. Thomas and his crew were given the cold shoulder by Bunker and the American Embassy personnel, who looked on them as interlopers. "If the [United States] government will be embarrassed," Thomas said, "it will be the fault of the government." The seventy observers were sent out on election day in teams of two, at least one member of each pair being Spanish-speaking. Their function was merely to make themselves visible at polling places as a discouragement to the open intimidation of voters, and to hear complaints.

The word spread about the blind, aged Yanqui with the wonderful smile, and "people left their places in the long voting lines to shake his hand." Bosch was of course again labeled as a Communist or fellow traveler, less being said about his grave temperamental flaws. Though a strapping man, he seemed fearful and left his heavily guarded home only three times, not once appearing on television, a medium on which he had scored heavily in 1963. The lawyer Balaguer, a manikin whose feet dangled when he sat in a big chair, conducted a vigorous campaign, ridiculed Bosch as timid, and won by a margin of 235,000 votes. Thomas, surprised and discomfited by the result, gave some credence to the claims that many Bosch ballots had been found in graveyards and in the sea. Bosch himself, though claiming irregularities, later conceded Balaguer's election. It appears that Balaguer's large plurality was due less to fraud than to his undeniably effective campaign against a poorly qualified opponent who virtually let the race go by default.*

Thomas sent congratulations to Balaguer which were correct if not truly enthusiastic and which expressed confidence that Balaguer would investigate the charges of fraud—charges which Balaguer, addressing Thomas as "Distinguished and prominent friend" in his courteous reply, said were unworthy of serious consideration. Thomas said publicly that in any case Dominican democracy had been advanced. His own pocket had not, for contributions covered only part of his committee's bills and he paid out $7,000 of his own for some of his seventy observers. He had made a good try, but the Dominican situation was more than he could handle.

*Frances R. Grant, secretary-general of the Inter-American Committee for Democracy and Freedom—a friend and admirer of Thomas—felt him mistaken in his stubborn loyalty to Bosch. Ms. Grant, along with others of the committee, had lost faith in Bosch because of his earlier failure as President. She believed Balaguer honestly elected.

# XXI

## 1. Thomas in Playboy

"Dear Norman," wrote Louis Mayer, still active at ninety-seven, almost if not quite old enough to be Thomas's father, "We often think of you & are always glad to think of you as on the job, trying to put wrong things right." He had "two good tinted plaster casts" of "The Speaker," wondered if Thomas's sons might want them, and could Thomas visit him at Fishkill? Thomas replied with delight, less over the sculpture than his admiration for this remarkable old man, but evidently he did not get to Fishkill. He did get to Terre Haute, where he had preached Debs's funeral sermon forty years earlier, when Socialist ideals had seemed gloriously attainable. Thomas was honored by the Debs Foundation and a head of Thomas by the sculptor Pietro Lazzari joined the sculpture of Debs (by Louis Mayer) at the old Debs home on North Eighth Street, now a Socialist museum. The student council at Muhlenberg College meanwhile tried to arrange a debate for Thomas with Richard Nixon, but acknowledged (in a comment which would later evoke irony) that "[Nixon] is a man who is difficult to reach." Thomas permitted himself to be interviewed at great length by Playboy. Some of his children—and one grandchild—opposed this but he went right ahead and got some fifteen thousand words of his philosophy off his chest in a question-and-answer session. The following gives the flavor:

Well, if I were President—which my fellow citizens have taken the greatest pains to prevent—I would announce my willingness, indeed my anxiousness, to get China into the family of nations. . . .

. . . . I was shocked at a recent CBS television survey of a group of 16-year-olds. . . . The majority of them expected there would be a nuclear

471

war in their lifetime. You see, they have accepted the unthinkable. . . .

. . . . I've found today's young much more militant in criticism than in proposing practical alternatives. . . .

. . . . [I want] more Peace Corps varieties of aid. But all of these . . . I would like to see handled as much as possible by the UN. The unilateral relationship between a rich uncle and a poor nephew is not necessarily the best kind of relationship. . . .

. . . . We've got to stop interfering in other peoples' civil wars—in Santo Domingo and Vietnam and God knows where else. That doesn't mean I think there's a sacred right for everybody to have a civil war, but when outside control is essential, it has to be exercised through a much more developed UN, rather than by one self-appointed policeman like the United States. . . .

. . . . The working class in America is middle class in practically every respect. . . . [The] dilution of labor's down-the-line militancy has been one of the greatest disappointments in my life . . . we have not found a substitute for the working class as the agent for change. . . .

. . . . [Capitalism] twists people's values. You know, like: "My son, whatever you do, make money—honestly, if possible.". . .

. . . . I think the joy of life is the acceptance of challenge, and in that respect, I've known joy. Nor have I lost faith in Socialism. It needs new applications, but Socialism—with its emphasis on planning and with its deep desire to make that planning democratic—still points the way to the future. . . .

. . . . I do *not* believe that man is perfectible, to be honest with you. The best I can say is that we are not damned by our gods or by our genes to stay the way we are or the way we have been.

Some lingering doubt or fear that Socialism might conceivably get out of hand was suggested in his mention of its *deep desire* to make its planning democratic.

So it came about that Thomas, whose books rarely sold more than 10,000 copies, reached his two greatest audiences in the space of a year in the millions who read Life and Playboy. This enormous impact could hardly fail to aid the slow turning of the public mind against the war. The spate of publicity was augmented by his appearance on Esquire's cover in full color, with a group including Marianne Moore, Helen Hayes, Joe Louis and Jimmy Durante, all described as "unknockables" whom "nobody hates"—an appraisal truer then of Thomas than it once had been, but still contradicted by some of the angry or scurrilous letters he received. Playboy was so pleased with his blend of wit, wisdom and morality that he was invited to write an article on the peace movement for the magazine. His first grandchild, the Reverend Norman Thomas Miller, now thirty-one and the pastor of a sectarian church in Colorado Springs, wrote to him tactfully to importune him not to appear again in a publication which tended to glorify sex and belittle marriage.

Thomas wrote "Dear Bill" Coffin at Yale: "For obvious reasons I strongly disapprove of the way the Playboy magazine exploits sex, and would not want to seem to commend it. . . . I think it is an article worth writing and publishing but this time they will pay for it, and they didn't for an interview and I would be seeming to give a different degree of approval to the magazine; at least that is the way some of my friends think, particularly one young man dear to me who writes in great distress about building up so reprehensible a magazine." Coffin replied waggishly that had they asked Thomas to write about sex, Coffin might consider him a trifle old. But they wanted him to write about the peace movement, which he was "the man most qualified" to write about. The readers of Playboy would not read him on that subject elsewhere, and Coffin felt the subject of peace so urgent that Thomas could safely risk appearing in a spicy publication. Thomas sent a copy of Coffin's letter to his grandson, saying that he agreed generally, "So I am going ahead with it, with the hope that it will give a lot of young people a straighter idea than they now have of the peace movement. . . . It was good to hear from you."

### 2. How Many Times?

With Siteman as companion, Thomas spent a weekend at the luxurious camp at Blue Mountain Lake in the Adirondacks of Harold K. Hochschild, a mining magnate strongly opposed to the Vietnam war and who had contributed generously to Thomas's campaign against it. Possibly it brought Thomas recollections of his Adirondack sojourn in 1909—fifty-seven years earlier—with another mining tycoon, Cleveland Dodge, when Thomas had eaten thirteen pancakes and sung hymns while Violet was sailing to India. Professor Jerome Blum of Princeton, one of the guests this time, found Thomas a pleasant companion, full of yarns, enjoying a brief swim and a visit to the Adirondack Museum of which Hochschild was a benefactor, though Thomas could dimly descry only the larger exhibits. Thomas took time out to have Siteman read him The New York Times. "[Thomas] was one of the best raconteurs I have ever heard," Hochschild recalled. If he was not always that sunny of disposition, he seldom succumbed to real bitterness over the increasingly apparent erosion of governmental integrity—the lying by the administration that was designed to foster a belief that the war was being won and to conceal the escalating horror of the American onslaught.

In December Thomas was the final speaker in a SANE-sponsored protest against the war with 18,000 in the audience at the Garden. This was the new Garden, the third in which he had appeared repeatedly —the first being the one that was really on Madison Square, the second uptown off Broadway and the third at Penn Station. There were too many events and speakers as usual—I. F. Stone, Floyd McKissick, Tony Randall, Jules Feiffer, Pete Seeger, a thousand blue balloons released bearing doves, and finally Gunnar Myrdal and Thomas. Myrdal said, "There's not a single government in Europe which would dare to send a squad of soldiers to Vietnam as a gesture of support for the United States, not even Britain." Dwight Macdonald, covering the affair as a journalist, admitted admiration and even awe at Thomas's long record of civility and courage in protest and saw him as heroic:

> So now he is 82 and he has to be helped to the speaker's stand, but once there, in the old, familiar stance, facing the crowd—they are on their feet applauding, calling out to him—he takes a firm grip on the rostrum, throws his head back, and begins to talk in a voice that is quavering (as it has been for many years) but also strong and resonant, easily reaching the highest galleries. For ten minutes he baits the President, modulating from irony to polemic to indignation to humor to fact to reasoning, speaking in a rapid businesslike way without rhetorical effects. At his first pause there is the usual automatic clapping, which he waves away impatiently with both hands, he's too old for such nonsense: "It's late. You probably want to get home and I certainly do, so if you must applaud, please do it after I'm finished." As the high-pitched, virile voice throws out unanswerable questions with a kind of contemptuous sympathy for the President, it occurs to me he is an old hand at talking to Presidents, though I'd be surprised if he'd been invited around recently.
>
> He winds up briskly, professional brio, as how many times, how many times? We get to our feet again to clap, to cheer timidly, to smile at one another as members of the same family do when one of them acquits

himself well in public. The old man endures the applause politely for a reasonable time, then begins to make his way back to his seat, slowly, uncertainly, inclining his patrician gray head and smiling his bony smile, more of a grin, as his peers on the speaker's platform pay their respects. He looks tired, and a little bored. Eighty-two years is a long time.

Late in 1966 Harrison Salisbury of The Times got to Hanoi and sent back dispatches telling Americans of the civilian toll taken by American bombers which they had been led to believe hit only military targets. Thomas had watched the Presidential lie expand from a patchwork device to cover an unexpected error (Eisenhower and the U-2) to a network of deception designed to conceal from the public what was going on in Vietnam. The artful expedient of administration team play had increasingly curbed the free flow of honest news as American officials both in Vietnam and Washington sought to hide ghastly failure. Secretary Rusk was irate over the Salisbury revelations, managing to suggest that they were unfair and unpatriotic. The cultivation of the lie had so far progressed that there were important segments of the Congress, the press, the church and the public agreeing that it was unpatriotic to publicize American lies even to America itself. To Johnson, two days after Christmas, Thomas sent the toughest letter of the hundreds he had written to the nine Presidents in the White House since 1912:

... Harrison Salisbury's dispatches in the New York Times of December 27th have just been read to me. I have heard all this with an emotion which I devoutly hope you may come to share. Can you not see how it discredits America? Is your own heart not touched by the sufferings of civilians in a war which we have not even declared? The horror of the means applied is in no way atoned for by any conspicuous success in achieving the end of interdicting supplies to South Vietnam.

It is no secret to you that on the subject of Vietnam and some others that [sic] your administration here and abroad is under almost continual attack for lack of credibility. Did you ever think of how you would regard Russian statements about bombing in situations parallel to our bombing in the Hanoi area? The Pentagon even dares to complain in an injured tone because the North Vietnamese have the effrontery to try to deal with our bombers by emplacing "their air defense sites, their P.O.W. sites, and radar and other military facilities in populated areas. . . ." How unsportsmanlike.

I want especially at this season to be proud of my country. This sort of thing makes it practically impossible. . . .

### 3. Gnarled and Bulgy

To Timothy Sullivan, working for Thomas was a new experience under the sun. Sullivan was not in the favored position that Patricia Miller had been as a member of the family, or that Siteman was after fifteen years of service. There was a sensitivity and reserve in Thomas that Sullivan found had better not be pressed. He could bristle at a thoughtless intrusion. Sullivan knew also that Thomas suffered frequent arthritic pain which was endured without groan or complaint but which at times twisted his face or shortened his temper. "He eschewed self-pity," the young man noted. The man who never wanted to be taken by the arm and helped, now had to submit. He sometimes said wryly, "I'm ancient, used-up and probably crazy." His body was now bent and ungainly, but he had "the head of a great man," as Sullivan saw it, and an electric presence.

To Thomas, after his long collaboration with the now middle-aged Siteman, the collegiate Sullivan was a new experience and he told his daughter, Mrs. Gates, that he liked him. Sullivan was well-educated and well-read, intelligent and helpful, quick at taking letters although without shorthand, a good companion on speaking trips whose academic background put him at ease with the college people he had to deal with. Sullivan found Thomas to be completely without condescension. He would ask Sullivan's opinion on important matters and treat it seriously. He was innocent about money in the profit-motive sense, thinking of money as something apart from his personal needs but vital for his causes. He would ask for a first-class plane seat apologetically, regretting the need to pay the extra fare and not ride with the masses as he had in day coaches a half-century earlier, the regular seats being too cramped for his arthritic legs. His body was now so gnarled and bulgy that a custom tailored suit was essential. He had one made at Brooks Brothers and was appalled at the price—something like $300. He remembered that in 1955 his good friend, the Socialist tailor Meyer Schneider in Detroit, had taken his measurements and insisted on sending him a suit as a gift, a wonderful suit. That was the way the Socialist Party was, or had been. He doubted that such a thing could happen in the Republican or Democratic parties.

## 4. The Secret Police

The banner-headline sensation of 1967 was the disclosure that for fifteen years the Central Intelligence Agency had infiltrated and subsidized—of all groups which old-fashioned American tradition directed should be led in paths of openness and honesty—the National Students' Association. Secret grants of money and secret coaching had shaped the students' organization into something like the well-drilled anti-Communist propaganda machine the agency wanted. With that, the dam of secrecy broke in other places, adding to Thomas's discomfiture over the Kaplan Fund. In its global offensive against Communism, the CIA had made the same clandestine use of dozens of other organizations, most of which learned only now how they had been conned. "Before very long," one observer remarked as the headlines named still other groups, "every political society, philanthropic trust, college fraternity and baseball team in America will be identified as a front for the Central Intelligence Agency." If no subsidized baseball team materialized, the list grew to include college professors, labor leaders, women's clubs and, yes, the National Council of Churches, as well as seamen's unions and goon squads in various parts of the world. The CIA's usual method was to give money to these individuals and organizations through a dummy charitable foundation or an agent planted in such a foundation, or both. As Andrew Kopkind saw it in The New Statesman: ". . . [The] CIA supported Socialist cold warriors, Fascist cold warriors, black and white cold warriors. . . . [B]ut it was a sham pluralism and it was utterly corrupting."

On the contrary, it was not corrupting in the least, however disillusioning and humiliating it was, to Norman Thomas and other honest men who had unknowingly used CIA money for purposes they knew to be good. The corruption lay in the government secret-police agency which had abandoned the Marquis of Queensberry rules. The CIA had resorted to a Communist code which we were presumably fighting.* No

---

*Nothing came out at this time about the subversion of the Federal Bureau of Investigation under Hoover, or about the CIA's even more blood-chilling roles and its designs for assassinating foreign leaders regarded as opposing the "American Way." The agency had some vigorous defenders, among them Thomas's old adversary, Time Magazine, which made CIA director Richard Helms its cover hero and his agency the subject of a long encomium.

one could estimate how seriously this studied practice of a government agency victimizing its own patriotic citizens through fraudulence shook the underpinnings of a nation whose democratic strength depended on public faith. Thomas defended the National Students' Association, with which he had had dealings as a lecturer and whose rank-and-file members had known nothing of the "arrangements" between their top officers and the CIA. He wrote early in his column, before other victimized groups were listed:

> What was wrong, and very wrong, was that the CIA, a spy organization, secretly dispensed these funds, a fact which, if known, would have immensely damaged a great deal of [the students'] work. . . . [As a Socialist favoring open government support of good causes and no government support of bad ones, he urged that such aid should be dispensed by the Department of Health, Education and Welfare. He had a refreshing frankness found in few others similarly embarrassed:] I speak feelingly because I was chairman of the Institute for International Labor Research, which received very considerable funds from the CIA through the conduit of the J. M. Kaplan Fund—which, in general, has done very good work with its money. . . . I can testify that neither the Fund, nor the CIA ever made any kind of demands upon us. [But this practice] reflects upon the foundations which covered for the CIA [and] upon the government itself. . . . My only regret is that I was not more particular in informing myself.

But he could scarcely have been expected to "inform himself" when the CIA's whole purpose had been to deceive him and the other recipients. The newspaper disclosures were followed by a Saturday Evening Post article by a former CIA agent, Thomas W. Braden, "I'm Glad the CIA is 'Immoral.' " A stout defender of the agency, he said the CIA's kind of immorality was essential and intrinsically moral because of its anti-Communist achievements. Braden told of huge agency sums paid to Jay Lovestone of the American Federation of Labor–Congress of Industrial Organizations (which Lovestone denied and George Meany called "a damn lie," adding carefully, "to the best of my knowledge") and to Walter Reuther of the Automobile Workers (Reuther confirmed this). Braden also told of the CIA subsidization of the Congress for Cultural Freedom and one of the many magazines it sponsored, Encounter, in London. It came out elsewhere that the Free Europe Committee was a CIA front, though it had been so anxious to appear "private" that it had vigorously advertised for public contributions. Among its directors were C. D. Jackson and Allen Dulles, the latter having been head of the CIA when it first began its secret excursions into private foundations and other organizations and the enterprise's enthusiastic backer. As the revelations continued, the Thomas score in unknown subsidizations was seen to be impressive:

The Free Europe Committee had sent him to the Middle East in 1957 and had helped to subsidize his Institute for International Labor Research.

The Congress for Cultural Freedom had sent him on three journeys —to India, to Japan and Southeast Asia, and to Mexico.

The American Federation of Labor and the International Confederation of Free Trade Unions had sponsored his visit to Stockholm and thence to several North African countries (though the AFL did use its own money for foreign work and there was no proof that the CIA had defrayed these Thomas expenses).

The Kaplan Fund of course had passed on to him the largest total of all in CIA cash—a million dollars in round figures—for his work in Latin America.

Since Thomas for decades had directed causes requiring financial backing and he had become expert at coaxing money from foundations, it was not surprising that he had become entangled with the CIA. That agency had not only infiltrated many legitimate foundations but had founded some fake ones which were simply CIA transmission belts. Thomas's Institute, at the time it closed in 1966, had had a little money left which it used to publish a pamphlet attacking the 1965 United States military intervention in the Dominican Republic. "The CIA didn't get much for that money," Thomas remarked. Nevertheless, old Mr. Integrity was embarrassed and hurt. The Richmond News Leader published a contemptible editorial headed, "Norman Thomas, CIA Agent," and a few other antagonistic newspapers seized the opportunity to ridicule him. Several confused Socialists wrote to him to criticize his "CIA connections" and one non-Socialist wrote him, "Long after the Communist menace here was dead, the CIA still thought you a dependable tool for their inflated anti-Communism." Christopher Lasch's criticism of him was misleading except for one point:

Norman Thomas . . . admits that he should have known where the money . . . was coming from, but . . . what he chiefly regrets is that a worthwhile work has had to come prematurely to an end. The Kaplan Fund, Thomas insists, "never interfered in any way"—which merely means that he was never aware of its interference. He does not see that he was being used [for different purposes] from the ones he thought he was advancing. *He thought he was working for democratic reform in Latin America, whereas the CIA valued him as a showpiece, an anti-Communist who happened to be a Socialist.*

But he was indeed working for democratic reform in Latin America (as Lasch suggested he was not) because by coincidence that was what the CIA wanted at the time. What he did seem to overlook was that the agency undoubtedly valued him also as a showpiece. At eighty-two, forced to have everything read to him—so unhandy and time-consuming a business that it would be surprising if he had not missed some of the comment entirely—Thomas was not at his best in this fusillade of controversy. He was unhappy about the Kaplan Fund, saying that when he first heard rumors of CIA backing, "they were always denied when I asked Mr. Kaplan about them." Ten years earlier he could have been expected to launch a new crusade against Central Intelligence Agency abuses. Now he was steadily winding up his affairs. He planned to close down his Post War World Council at the end of the year, and meanwhile he resigned from the board of the International League for the Rights of Man, the American Emergency Committee for Tibetan Refugees and other organizations. He ultimately made his peace with Kaplan and by the fall of 1967 was asking the Kaplan Fund for money to aid a civil rights program.

This time of scandal had offered the nation its opportunity to bring its undercover work under responsible control. But the tumult ended with the appointment of a presidential commission of investigation with the perhaps intended result that nothing was done. The CIA continued untrammeled into new and greater license.

From Max Nomad, Thomas received checks for $40 and $28 which Nomad offered to the Post War World Council because they were paid him by the magazines East London and London Survey which he had since learned were CIA-connected and he therefore rejected their money. So did Thomas, who wrote to him, "In the light of what the Institute for International Labor Research took unknowingly from the CIA, I, as chairman of that organization, simply cannot take your checks."

# XXII

### 1. Anti-Antis Are Ahead

Thomas fretted because he could scarcely see his food and could transfer it to his mouth only with exasperating slowness. At home, he seized a round object and gnawed at it before his daughter could tell him it was not a cookie but a cork coaster. "My God!" he said with relief. "I had begun to doubt your cookery." He now accepted speaking dates tentatively, explaining that his rickety condition forbade certainty and also required him to charge extra for the expenses of his companion. "... I have now sunk so low in decrepitude that I need to have someone to guide and support me," he wrote. Yet when he declined an invitation to a Princeton class dinner it was not because of decrepitude but: "Unfortunately I have to speak at Alfred University on the 7th." Letters from some of his older friends now contained an elegiac note, covering matters of affection or remembrance indicating an uncertainty as to how many more letters could be written. Jack Darr, now retired with his wife in Seattle, sent him holiday greetings: "After Herb Bates, no one has had greater influence on my life and thinking than you. . . . And it is good to have been in the same world, crazy and heartbreaking as it is, with you."

Thomas kept retrenching, dropping out as a sponsor of Spanish Refugee Aid, resigning even from Sigma Delta Chi, but that was not to say he had given up looking ahead. To Erich Fromm in Mexico he wrote, "What do you think about planning to try to get Martin Luther King to run as a kind of coalition candidate for President in 1968?" In 1965 King—unaware that the FBI was bugging his hotel room—had stopped in at 112 for a talk with him and Thomas had been impressed. Another who dropped in was H. L. Mitchell, co-founder almost thirty-five years

481

earlier of the Southern Tenant Farmers' Union, bringing memories of masked nightriders, beatings and killings. Thomas took Mitchell to lunch, after which Mitchell helped him into a cab for an appointment with U Thant.

Thomas's February, 1967, trip to California was shorter than usual and Siteman was his companion. Thomas spoke against the war at Stanford, Berkeley, Irvine and other places and had luncheons with Lura Oak, an old family friend, and two of his grandchildren, also enjoying a new experience, a helicopter ride from Irvine to Los Angeles. In the spring he took off again, this time with Sullivan, for the University of Connecticut, Windham and Williams colleges and points west, one of them being the University of Colorado, where he spoke and stayed overnight with the Uphoffs, who had moved there from Minnesota. The Uphoffs, who had known him since 1932, were in the special category of friends who had named children after Thomas and had been faithful to the Socialist ideal despite the Party's eclipse. Professor Uphoff, while in Wisconsin, had run for Governor and Senator on the Socialist ticket, and both in Wisconsin and Minnesota had campaigned for Thomas and other Party candidates. He liked to repeat Thomas's axiom, "I'd rather work for something I want and not get it, than work for something I don't want and get it." All previous Thomas visits had been part of the track meet, but this one was leisurely, as if it might be the last. Before Uphoff drove him and Sullivan to Denver to catch their plane, Thomas sat on a screened porch with the professor and his wife—it was a sunny April day—and reminisced with his hosts about the time when Socialism was more hopeful. He could not see the inspiring view of the Flatiron Range, but he sniffed the bracing air with gusto.

Paul Blanshard had married again, this time to another graduate of 112, Estelle Mayer, who had worked for the City Affairs Committee in the Walker years; Thomas had heard from them from Capetown. Could Thomas help get them into Tanzania? Entrance was not normally permitted by the black Tanzanians from South Africa. Thomas wrote his friend President Nyerere at Dar-es-Salaam—something shading on political wirepulling—and it was arranged. When Thomas spoke at Boston University, Albert Sprague Coolidge was there with his wife to greet him, writing afterwards, "It was certainly good to see you . . . and to witness such a triumph over physical handicaps." Strongly though he resented being seen publicly in this tottering condition, Thomas could really not stop himself from speaking against the war as long as he could lean against a rostrum.

# NORMAN THOMAS

He attended his sixty-second reunion at Princeton, conceding to a classmate who was ill, "I wasn't in good shape for the reunion but managed with help to get around to quite an extent." Part of his spare time went into a continuing effort to get Morton Sobell out of prison. A. J. Muste, one of the octogenarian duo who had fought with Thomas for civil liberties and other causes since before the first war, passed on to his reward not long after Thomas had written to him, "You, Roger [Baldwin], and I were all born close together, and I am honored to be of your company." "He leaves no successor," Thomas wrote in tribute although his affection for the obdurate Muste had never been as warm as for the roguish Baldwin. And where was Baldwin? In Russia, visiting the Kropotkin house, Baldwin in 1927 having edited Kropotkin's revolutionary pamphlets. Baldwin could still snorkel and waltz; his eyesight and hearing were good. In the endurance contest among these three, all born within the same twelve months, he was the winner, but he had taken things fairly easily in the last two decades compared with the other two.

Thomas attended to family amenities—a birthday present for his daughter Frances, another for his grandson Evan Thomas III, another for his sister Emma,* who arrived with Agnes and also Dr. Evan that summer for a visit. It was another of those possibly final gatherings which Thomas, with his great family pride and affection, enjoyed despite the gloom which his infirmities occasioned in himself. To Baldwin he wrote, "Couldn't you get your account of your visit to Kropotkin's house and your reflections published in the New Yorker or the Saturday Review?" With politics in mind, he wrote to Lowenstein, Bayard Rustin and Michael Harrington, trying to arrange a day on which these three busy men could visit Cold Spring Harbor and talk with him. He was astonished to be named beneficiary of the insurance policy of a woman in her twenties whom he did not know, who wrote to him that she did not expect early death, but "I guess they will notify you if my expectations prove invalid," adding:

> From the day of my first political memory, you and Eleanor Roosevelt were held up to me as great people. I have never been disappointed by any political position you have taken. You remain the only consistently honorable person I am aware of.

---

*Being too busy to shop, Thomas always gave his family gifts of money and apologized for doing so.

Thomas was touched and delighted. He allowed a new anti-war group, Negotiation Now, to persuade him to ask Lenore Marshall for a $1,000 donation although she had given them $1,000 three months earlier. "I always hate to ask for money . . ." he wrote Lenore, "since you give so generously without being asked." He added in a later note to her: "I am now so horrified by the war . . . that I am joining the Writers and Editors War Tax Protest . . . We are saying that we will not pay the new surcharge on taxes made necessary by the war, nor the 23% of our income tax which is estimated to go to support the war. I'm not advising other people . . ." "No isle can shelter you from final grief," she had written appropriately, and something else appropriate for them both:

> *I was happy, I could whistle*
> *Till he got his anti-missile,*
> *I felt better when I read*
> *Anti-antis were ahead,*
> *Now I'm safe again but can't he*
> *Make an anti anti-anti?*

### 2. Wash the Flag

By request, since he could not attend, Thomas wrote a statement to be read at the interracial New Politics Convention slated for Chicago. He had been deeply troubled by the outbreak of black rebellion and burnings in Los Angeles, Cleveland, Newark and other cities, regarding these methods as certain to lose rather than gain objectives. His overriding concern, he wrote, was peace in Vietnam and, he added, "It is obvious that practically and spiritually peace in Vietnam is tied in with peace in the streets of American cities. In your discussions you will be thinking and working for an America whose slogans will not be 'BOMB BABY, BOMB!' or 'BURN BABY, BURN!' but 'BUILD BABY, BUILD!' for peace, justice and fraternity." He seemed overoptimistic, for the black temper was strained by such atrocities as the Birmingham bombing. Thomas wrote protestingly to William Sloane Coffin, who had attended the convention, for the black caucus had taken charge and (according to the New Yorker account read to Thomas) had presented a list of thirteen proposals along with an ultimatum that all should be endorsed without modification as a sign of interracial unity, and the whites had supinely agreed:

I haven't been so low in my mind about the Left, or some big chunks of it, at any time. What troubles me is not the naivete and immaturity, but what seems to me to be a kind of dishonesty. . . . What I can't understand is the belief that either white guilt consciousness or any practical solution of our very serious race problem call for the amazing abnegation of whites in Chicago. This is not the way to bring about genuine fraternity or true integration.

What with his physical miseries and spiritual concern, he enjoyed the one alcoholic drink he permitted himself before dinner. He was looking for a job for Timothy Sullivan, who would be out of work at the end of the year. The sudden death of Thomas's youngest brother Arthur, who had recently sent him McIntosh apples and had seemed in good health, proved again that one never knew the day or the hour. Thomas joined the family at the funeral, later writing inevitably to Arthur's widow Christine that "he was fortunate in dying promptly," and "I was extraordinarily fortunate to belong to a group of brothers and sisters who didn't agree on a lot of things, but who found it very easy to feel a continuing respect and affection for each other."

Next came a surprise—Thomas's "last" of his thousands of speeches. At least it was so announced by some unknown functionary before Thomas addressed 109 students from thirty countries at the Sheraton-Atlantic Hotel (the McAlpin to Thomas and other old-timers)—an affair sponsored by the same National Students' Association that had not long since lost its Central Intelligence Agency benevolences. It had become a public sensation to see Thomas guided and helped to the rostrum, pale and bent, to expect a squeak and hear instead a quavering roar. The word that it was the end of the road for the old spellbinder made it more than ever a significant event. Alistair Cooke, one of the reporters present, began his story for The Guardian, "A gaunt old giant, gray with fatigue, contorted with arthritis and blind as Tiresias was helped up to a podium in an hotel room here yesterday . . ." Cooke told his Englishmen of Thomas's many local and national political campaigns, wrote, "He always lost the election and always grew in influence and dignity with every defeat," and added, "He has sharper opinions than most of the Presidential hopefuls . . ." That was something which, in the current idiom, Cooke could say again. The United States, Thomas told the students, should stop the bombing, declare a cease-fire on its own initiative, reconvene the Geneva Conference, withdraw from Southeast Asia and stop its arrogant pretense of writing the orchestration for the world and rewriting the Ten Commandments, a new version being, "Thou

485

shalt not kill—retail; thou shalt kill wholesale at my command." But he reminded them that the United States "has a pretty good record of letting people say what they think," and said, "I don't like the sight of young people burning the flag of my country, the country I love. . . . If they want an appropriate symbol they should be washing the flag, not burning it."

It turned out that this was *not* his last speech, that the student group had been in error. "Tiresias" was irked at the error. Yes, he had several infirmities but "doubted that the public wanted a catalog of them." He would close the Post War World Council and retire from his other activities at the end of the year, but that was two months away. While he did not precisely say that he would keep on speaking until then even if he had to be carried to the platform, there was something of that tone.

But The Times even ran an editorial marking his "last" appearance, saying that Thomas "may not be as indestructible as he once was, but he is still as indispensable," and hoping that he would be able to "log more 'farewell appearances' than Mme. Schumann-Heinck." The letters came pouring in. "Well," Darlington Hoopes wrote, "I see you made the front page of the New York Times again without dying, which is more than the rest of us could do if we did." Thomas was busy explaining that the announcement was made "without my knowledge or consent" and was mistaken. He had speaking dates at Yale and Harvard and places as far west as Pocatello and Seattle, and he intended to visit the Darrs in the latter city. The story of his "retirement" had gone out over the wires and he would have to write to all these places to assure them that he would be there as scheduled—that is, of course, unless Providence, or whatever controlled these things, should decree otherwise, which was always possible at his age. On November 7 he packed the Yale Law School auditorium in a debate with Robert Welch —incidentally greeting Sidney Lovett, William Sloane Coffin and Allard Lowenstein, the latter visiting Yale to start organizing his "Dump Johnson" movement. The Yale Daily News noted the "thunderous applause" Thomas received as he entered, whereas Welch arrived unnoticed. It seemed impossible to some observers that he could last out the debate, but his voice held strong to the end. "Of course it was a mismatch," The News said, "rather as if Teilhard de Chardin had consented to discuss the phenomenon of man with Oral Roberts."

Four days later, he was at the University of Chicago with Siteman to join Senator Eugene McCarthy, Martin Luther King, John Kenneth Galbraith and others in addressing 500 members of the National Labor

Leadership for Peace. The name of the group was itself enough to gladden Thomas. It was an insurgent group, including old friends of Thomas such as Patrick Gorman of the Meat Cutters and Emil Mazey of the Automobile Workers, opposing the war in Vietnam. Light and reason were returning where there had been little but the blustering bomb-belief of Meany. Again in Chicago, Thomas was impressed by King's powerful religious faith, which a blind man could hear in his voice. Unfortunately, Thomas, the last speaker before lunch, was placed on the platform in a hard chair and had to sit there through several speeches. He was in agony by the time he was called. It took strenuous help to get him to the rostrum. Nevertheless, he was so delighted at this decision of a significant portion of organized labor to do what he had urged on them two years earlier that he spoke for twenty minutes, praising them and satirizing the Johnson fluctuations. One of his listeners was Professor Uphoff, whom he had invited to join him and Siteman at the University Club for lunch. Thomas was exhausted. He had great difficulty negotiating, with help, a short flight of stairs to the restaurant. Uphoff had never seen his face so ashen and his whole frame so shaky. Thomas listened to Siteman read him the menu and recovered only slightly when luncheon was served, apologizing for his failure to enliven the conversation.

Then came the long ride to O'Hare Airport and the flight to New York. Siteman helped him to his hotel room—he was too tired to eat—and read to him from Edmund Wilson's *Patriotic Gore* before leaving. Around dawn, Thomas telephoned Frances Gates in a feeble voice that he felt very ill. He was taken to the hospital at Huntington, near his Long Island home, so weak from a stroke that the room-filling voice was down to a whisper. Still, he was so happy to hear next day that Princeton's football team had beaten Harvard that he had his son Evan read him all about it and took special pleasure in Princeton's superiority in the passing department. But he regretted missing a speaking engagement in Vermont, where he was due at that very moment.

For the second time he made the front pages without dying, though the newspapers were readying their obituaries and not only Vermont but Harvard, Pocatello and Seattle would have to do without him. Letters, cards, telegrams and cables flooded in. There were bushels of flowers. The Thomas missives, normally so personal, now amounted to a form letter of thanks for such attentions. A Pennsylvania Socialist unknown to Thomas sent him home-made doggerel:

*May God bless you with his gracious love, His heavenly gifts increase,*
*And in his tender loving care may you find strength and peace.*
*May God's dear presence guide you and keep you ever strong*
*And grant the gift that will comfort and bless you all life long. . . .*

For almost a half-century it had astonished Thomas that people could place such faith in a God who managed things so poorly. But Sidney Lovett and Ralph Harlow, both dear old friends, were able to reconcile this implausibility. They wrote to him, as did Albert Sprague Coolidge, who had missed the news report and was looking forward to seeing him when he spoke at Harvard November 29 and had a guest suite of two rooms and bath "vacant and ready" for him. Thomas spent his eighty-third birthday flat on his back, terribly weak but determined that he would get up and learn to walk again. From Vincent Sheean in Helsinki, who had heard the report of his retirement but not his denial: "HAPPY BIRTHDAY YOU WILL NEVER RETIRE NOT FOR ME." From Lenore Marshall to "Norman my dear":

> I've been thinking that, when some of your strength returns, perhaps you will do something that for a long while I have been waiting for: Your autobiography, or at least pieces and fragments of it that stand out especially in your mind. In a way it would be a history of sorts of the Socialist movement of our time, but it would also be a great personal record— dramatic scenes that you could describe in your own special way, whether they are of large or small events. Have you considered it? I hope you will.

Siteman had written the Darrs that the visit to Seattle would have to be scrubbed, probably forever. From Darr came a moving letter in which he quoted the last stanza of Felix Adler's hymn "Hail the Glorious Golden City" as a symbolic if perhaps inadequate tribute to the efforts and services of Norman Mattoon Thomas over the sixty-two years and five months since his graduation from Princeton:

*And the work that we have builded,*
*Oft with bleeding hands and tears,*
*Oft in error, oft in anguish,*
*Will not perish with our years.*
*It will live and stand transfigured*
*In the final reign of Right;*
*It will pass into the splendors*
*Of the City of the Light.*

Although Thomas did have twinges of sentiment over the hymns of his fathers, had suffered anguish aplenty and had come close to tears over the injustices of the world, he would admit to only a modicum of error. Darr added something for the accomplishment of which Thomas surely wished that there was a benevolent God who could and would answer prayers and create a miracle:

"It may take a long time, but I am confident that the youth whom you have influenced through the years will yet win in the causes which you have served with such dedication."

### 3. To the Mountaintop

Thomas, who had repeatedly criticized Providence, or whatever one might call it, for protracting one's terminal uselessness, and had celebrated the blessing of prompt death, was denied prompt death. It was as if the God he had reproved and disestablished for his folly in making man so stupid had resumed his throne to even the score. Thomas dictated the final Post War World Council newsletter, saying at the end, "I had hoped to work until I died, but fate, which has been very good to me in most things, declared otherwise . . . And so goodbye, although I hope I may occasionally be granted another chance to communicate with you." So thin and pale as to be almost translucent, he declined just to lie and wait for death. He wrote Palmer Hoyt of The Denver Post —the first paper to take his column and now the last and only one to keep it—of his illness:

Obviously I cannot do two columns a week for you. Would it be possible, however, for me to send from time to time a column on some subject in which I was interested? The last regular column will probably be the one for release on the Christmas weekend.

I want to express my personal gratitude to you for taking the columns these past years. I never thought I was Walter Lippmann but I am glad to have had a chance to write many of the things on my mind. . . .

The office at 112 was vacant. To other seventh-floor occupants the place seemed strangely quiet without The Voice spilling out into the narrow hall. Siteman was taking a vacation and Sullivan still had a job after all. Thomas had letters to send, reading to listen to, politicians to harass and, if one could believe it, one more book to write. He was moved to a Huntington nursing home only a few miles from the house Violet had built, where he had round-the-clock care. He was also required to submit to their routine of serving five small meals a day instead of three big ones, a plan aimed at keeping elderly patients busy and happy, but which Thomas loathed. In fact he loathed being there at all, though this nursing home was the very best. The private man in a public place, subject to restrictions and regulations, was impatient but unfailingly courteous. Occasionally he was well enough to get home to the Gateses for a Sunday dinner, an event he treasured although the ordeal of transporting his brittle frame was considerable both for him and the transporters. One Sunday, when the dinner guests were to be Sylvia Wright and her husband, a freezing rain coated pavements and walks with ice. Frances telephoned him that it was too dangerous to drive.

"If Jack is afraid to pick me up," Thomas snapped, "I'll call a cab." Jack Gates picked him up.

He could sit in a wheelchair when he was at his best. When Sullivan read him the news that Dr. Spock, William Sloane Coffin and three others had been indicted for urging resistance to the draft, Thomas breathed fire and held a news conference in his room. He praised the Spock-Coffin group for "doing the equivalent of what many of us still reproach the Germans for not doing; that is, speaking out against fighting in a war which is indefensible morally and politically." As for those who argued that dissenters really prolonged the war they sought to end, Thomas replied in the first place that he doubted it, and in the second place that to those believing the war immoral the view was comparable to that of a thief who grabs your purse, saying, "Give me that pocketbook. Let go or you'll only be prolonging the strife." He recalled with relish the story about Thoreau, imprisoned at Concord for refusing to pay the war tax, and his friend Ralph Waldo Emerson, arriving to pay the tax and to free him. "I am surprised to find you in there," Emerson said. "I am surprised to see you out there," Thoreau replied.

Assassination—first of Martin Luther King, then of Robert Kennedy—was part of the measure of news Sullivan had to read to him. Thomas had been one of that huge assemblage in Washington in 1963 when King had said, "I have a dream that one day this nation will rise up, live out the true meaning of its creed . . . that all men are created equal." He had been thrilled by the roll of King's voice and the grandeur and solemnity of the event, calling it "one of the happiest days of my political life" because it seemed a great leap toward brotherhood; but it was only to be succeeded by "Burn, Baby, Burn." To young Sullivan, Thomas said he had envied King because King had been to the mountaintop. "I've never been there," he said. "I've never been to the mountaintop." Sullivan, who revered him, wanted to shout that he had indeed been to the mountaintop, that he was a regular visitor there. But probably it was a cryptic suggestion of regret at his inability to reach accord with God—something which King, though a victim of greater injustices than Thomas had ever endured, had been able to do.

Thomas enjoyed the telephone beside his bed. When Roger Baldwin called to ask how he was, he replied, "I could be worse." "How?" demanded the prankish Baldwin. "I might lose my mind," Thomas replied. He was dictating his book little by little to Sullivan, reflecting in it: "It's my own guess that Abraham Lincoln would not have been elected if, in 1860, he had been compelled to present himself over television, or possibly, due to his very thin voice, even the radio. His angular awkwardness, which Americans have come to cherish in their love for this great man would have counted against him . . ."

In June, Clarence and Ruth Senior visited him before leaving on a sabbatical journey around the world. They were one of many couples who had named a son after Thomas. "Norman was asleep," Senior recalled. "His white skin was stretched over his skull like a death mask, his hands were bony and cadaverous. But when the nurse woke him, there was a wonderful transformation. His face lighted up and the old charm was instantly there." The curved lines around eyes and mouth, deepened during a half-century before audiences all over the land— from the frame auditorium in Trinidad, Colorado, to the International Ladies' Garment Workers' Union hall over the Chinese restaurant in Baltimore, to three different Madison Square Gardens—became translated into the irresistible Thomas smile. He could see the Seniors only dimly, but recognized their voices. The memories of the two men— Senior was twenty years younger—could have ranged in sentimental recall over the time in 1929 when Senior had come to New York and been made national secretary of the Socialist Party, of their collaboration in two Presidential campaigns, and of that bloody struggle with the Old Guard. Senior had not always agreed with Thomas, and had thought his friend's collaboration with America First before the war a great mistake, but the affection between the two was enduring—nor did Mrs. Senior forget Violet's $35 that got her out of the hospital. But Thomas had little time for reminiscence. He was still exclaiming over the withdrawal of Lyndon Johnson from the 1968 race—part of that, he said, was Lowenstein's work—and the prospect it held out for a peace candidate in the fall election.

"We'll be back in seven months," the Seniors said as they were leaving, although from his appearance neither of them thought him likely to last seven days. "We'll see you then."

Thomas's smile turned rueful. His expression and his eyerolling glance around him conveyed as eloquently as words his repugnance at the thought of seven months more of invalidism added to the seven months he had already had. "I hope not," he said, and wished them a pleasant journey.

There were visitors whenever he was able to receive them, ranging from Sidney Lovett and Lenore Marshall to local high school students. When not working on his book, he worked to end the war, writing to Humphrey after his nomination:

> I have been your friend since the first time I met you, at the Democratic Party convention in 1948, when you introduced the bravest and best resolution on civil rights which any of the major parties had ever offered up to that date. . . . I rejoiced when President Johnson selected you as his running mate in 1964. . . . Are the many statements in which you, if anything, "out-Johnson" Johnson in support of his Vietnam policies to be taken as your present position?. . . . After these terrible weeks, it is less than ever appropriate for a man of your standing to campaign on the issue of a "happy America," an America presumably rejoicing every day in the box scores of the slain in an atrocious war. . . .

Humphrey's position soon became clear, and Thomas gave him up: "No memory of personal friendship should make us endorse a politician who has been so opportunistic about the terrible war in Vietnam." He urged the forces of Senators McCarthy and McGovern to unite against Humphrey. From his nursing-home bed he saw his world ripped apart with sit-ins and strife on the campuses and fires and riots in the cities. The younger generation was aroused, to be sure, but no one seemed content to wash the flag. "The effect of the war has been totally bad," Thomas told an interviewer, "spiritually, morally and economically. Think what we could have done to improve the quality of life at home with the money that's been spent in Vietnam!" The McGovern-McCarthy coalition failed to materialize and the voters were left with a choice between Humphrey and Nixon. A few days before the election Thomas declared for Humphrey only because of the alternative, saying with less spark than was his wont, "I don't think [Nixon] has much principle."

He had had an "Elect Lowenstein" banner on his wall for weeks. After the returns were in on election day, he called the Nixon victory "a calamity" but was delighted over the election of Lowenstein to Congress. And for all his gloom about the country, which he admitted was "quite capable of going to hell," he was in an exuberant mood as he celebrated his eighty-fourth birthday at the nursing home. Inundated by messages and telegrams from all over the world, he enjoyed a champagne-and-cake party at which the guests had been restricted, because of his condition, to his children living nearby, Frances Gates and Evan Thomas, and a select group of the faithful—Baldwin, Fleischman and his wife, Siteman, Sullivan, Fay Bennett, Rowland Watts, Louise Crane, Michael Harrington and a few others. The room was crowded. Thomas in pajamas sat up in bed and raised his glass cheerfully when toasted by his daughter, then by Baldwin, who was clearly the victor in the tripartite battle against superannuation. Birthday parties had been splashy events in Thomas's otherwise businesslike life, but no one mentioned those milestone extravaganzas which accentuated his present limitations—the first one at the Edison when he was a mere fifty-two, the celebration of his seventy-fifth at the Waldorf and that of his eightieth at the Astor.

One who arrived to join the guests was Alden Whitman, who Thomas knew perfectly well was the obituary chief of The Times, a man who arranged his important obits in advance and (although now writing about his birthday) was looking him over with the final reckoning in mind. During his Harvard days in the thirties, Whitman had heard Thomas at the Ford Hall Forum in Boston. He had interviewed him twice for The Times. Now he saw Thomas looking as if the merest breeze might blow him into the beyond and yet filled with optimism for America and the world. "He was on his deathbed," Whitman remarked, "but he had a simply unquenchable spirit. Change was coming for the better, he said, and far gone as he was, he spoke in rounded sentences that you could parse." His humor was unquenchable too. When one of the guests brought out a camera, Thomas observed, "You can't take a moving picture; there isn't much that moves."

A few days earlier, he had finished dictating to Sullivan his twenty-first book, a slim one called *The Choices*. Now he had four more weeks to look back over the long road he had traveled. His life had been incredibly rich in concern, involvement, thought, action and friendship. He had not been one of those eased gently and accidentally into events, as had been his fellow-townsman Harding. Thomas had thrown himself into history by opposing the majority, fighting the easy drift, dissenting and instructing, torn between confidence and gloom. In his last big book he had written, "At this moment if I looked from some distant planet on our struggles as one looks at a horse race, I should be inclined to bet on disaster, the triumph of ignorance, hate and greed. But . . . [somehow,] through the ages, we men have won for brotherhood victories which have kept our race alive and moving forward, even when the odds against it were great. Our obliteration, or our social damnation, is not inexorably decreed by fate . . ." In *The Choices* he had stressed that man *could* choose reason and decency, that the question "is not, *can we,* but, *will we* save ourselves?"

But it was his birthday cheer that reflected the inner philosopher. The man who had at times known despair could not now rule out hope. Nixon had been elected, Eastland still desecrated the Senate, and yet the Thomas faith in America, in the slow but irresistible wisdom of its commonalty, would not down. Men were not saints but they had goodness in them. The same belief in people that had made him harangue and instruct them all his life forbade the thought that all his haranguing and instructing had been useless. There were good portents. The people had taken forever to do it but had finally dumped Johnson and let it be known that the war must end. Labor had been as slow, but had at last begun to turn against the warmakers. Some of the Vietnam lies were coming home to roost.

A world that had produced such people as Violet, as Baldwin, Randolph, Holmes, Angelica and Lenore, was not a hopeless world. Thomas, the grandfather of fifteen and great-grandfather of ten-and-more-coming, could scarcely deny hope in his own genes.

Lucid to the last, he died on December 19, 1968. Whitman's obituary was one of the long ones, starting on Page One and jumping to a full eight columns farther back, and adorned with five pictures. Thomas was right again in predicting the fact that would seem outstanding about him: Included in the headline was the clause, "He Ran Six Times for Presidency." The news traveled quickly around the world. In a Honolulu hotel, the Clarence Seniors were on the last leg of their journey. Senior finished his shower bath and entered the room to find his wife weeping by the radio. "Norman is dead," she said.

# NOTES

There have been four previous biographies of Norman Thomas: *Norman Thomas, Respectable Rebel,* by Murray B. Seidler (Syracuse University Press, 1961); *Norman Thomas: A Biography,* by Harry Fleischman (W. W. Norton, 1964, 1969); *Leader at Large,* by Charles Gorham (Farrar, Straus & Giroux, 1970); and *Pacifist's Progress,* by Bernard K. Johnpoll (Quadrangle, 1970). A fifth, *Mr. Socialism,* by Dwight Steward (Lyle Stuart, 1974), written apparently from the extreme left point of view, is slight, splenetic and unworthy of serious attention. Johnpoll's work confines itself strictly to Thomas's political activities. It is well researched and insightful, though it blames Thomas excessively for the decline of a Socialist Party which was self-destructive in its sectarianism and hopelessly divided in its responses, first to the New Deal, then to World War II.

Letters and papers cited below without mention of source are from the Norman Thomas Papers at the New York Public Library. In some letters quoted, unnecessary paragraphing has been elided. The chief sources consulted, and abbreviations for them where abbreviations are used, are:

NTP: The collection of Norman Thomas Papers at the New York Public Library
NYPL: New York Public Library
NT Autobiog: Thomas's unpublished autobiography in NTP above
The Frances Gates collection of Thomas family letters
The Evan Thomas II collection of family letters
A NT letter in possession of William S. Thomas
Fleischman: The Fleischman biography mentioned above
Johnpoll: The Johnpoll biography mentioned above
Seidler: The Seidler biography mentioned above
Fleischman tape: Transcriptions of Fleischman's taped interviews with NT
Call: The Call, a Socialist newspaper
NL: The New Leader, a Socialist newspaper
New America: A later Socialist newspaper
DW: The Daily Worker (Communist)
NT Col.: NT's column of comment in the Denver Post and other capitalist newspapers; passages are quoted from NT's own typescripts, many of which were sent out as suitable for papers for either of two days—hence the frequent double dates
NYDN: New York Daily News
NYHT: New York Herald Tribune
NYP: New York Post
NY Trib: New York Tribune
NYT: New York Times
NYWT: New York World Telegram
NR: New Republic
SR: Saturday Review
SP: Socialist Party
CP: Communist Party

# Notes

2 *"A frock coat"*: NT Autobiog, 5.

3 *"Both were the kind"*: NT Autobiog, 20. *Hymns mother sang:* Prof. Alexander interview with NT. *Left-handed:* NT Autobiog, 10.

5 *"Invited by King Mongkut"*: Mrs. K. E. Wells to Harry Fleischman, after Jan., 1963. *Elephants:* Carl Sandburg, *The War Years* (Harcourt, Brace, 1939), Vol. II, 301–302.

7 *Harding's marriage:* Francis Russell, *The Shadow of Blooming Grove* (McGraw-Hill, 1968), 85. *Thomas on the Hardings:* NT to Samuel Hopkins Adams, after Jan. 15, 1939. *Kissing games:* Henry A. True to Prof. Alexander, Alexander notes.

8 *Speakings and debates:* NT to Prof. A. Craig Baird, May 7, 1940. *"My father spoke"*: NT, *As I See It* (Macmillan, 1932), 155 and 160. *"What a setup"*: NT Autobiog, 5.

9 *"We children"*: NT Autobiog, 6.

10 *"With the years"*: NT Autobiog, 16. *"Emma under one arm"*: Emma Thomas told author.

11 *Cheating at Bucknell:* NT Autobiog, 25; Fleischman tape, 25. *"Stand up straight"*: NT to Ben Sweeney, Dec. 29, 1954.

12 *Rang the bell:* Fosdick told Prof. Alexander.

13 *Dark trousers:* Fleischman tape, 35.

14 *"What class were you?"* NT Autobiog, 33.

17 *"Papa's killing Mama"*: NT Autobiog, 46.

18 *"Mother thought"*: Carter to NT, Oct. 12, 1906.

19 NT letter from Pyongyang, dated Sept. 1, 1907, property of William S. Thomas.

20–22 NT letter to mother, dated Nov. 17, 1907, Frances Gates collection.

23 *"Can a man of your"*: Dumont Clarke to NT, June 24 [1908].

25–26 *John Aikman Stewart:* Information from his obituary, NYT, Dec. 18, 1926.

26 *Violet's father's disappearance:* NYT, Sept. 26 and Nov. 24, 1888. *Pink undergarments:* The niece, Mrs. Richard N. Pierson, told author.

27 *"Most of the people"*: Savage to NT, June 16, 1908. *"For ten weeks"*: Gilkey to NT, Nov. 13, 1908. *"I am waiting"*: Dumont Clarke to NT, undated, 1909.

29 *"We the undersigned"*: Mr. and Mrs. Dodge to NT, Sept. 15, 1909.

29–30 Violet's letters to NT, dated Sept. 28 and 30, Oct. 2 and 15 and Nov. 4, 1909, Frances Gates collection.

30 Woodrow Wilson letter to NT, Nov. 5, 1909. *"We'll not make a fuss"*: Violet to NT, undated, Frances Gates collection. *"I was very much in love"*: NT Autobiog, 55.

31 *Palm Sunday sermon:* Some librarian has marked NT's notes "Easter 1911?" But they fulfill his own description of the Palm Sunday sermon. See NT Autobiog, 56–57.

32–33 *Lovett meets NT:* Lovett told author.

33 *Holding hands:* Emma Thomas told author. Ralph's letter to NT, July 10, 1910, Frances Gates collection. Gilkey letter, July 1, 1910, Frances Gates collection.

34 *Thomas wedding:* NYT and NY Trib, Sept. 2, 1910.

35–36 *"I had been well schooled"*: NT Autobiog, 59–60.

36 *"Mr. Thomas was charged"*: NYT, Jan. 17, 1911. *"These sensational rumors"*: Fleischman, 49. A. R. Ledoux letter, dated Aug. 31, 1911, Frances Gates collection.

38 *Jews "united with the Irish"*: Oct. 8, 1951, NT to Paul Blanshard. *Dinner for Hungarians:* From Prof. Alexander's notes.

39 *"I was of a generation"*: NT to Max Nomad, Apr. 26, 1961.

40 *"With all my love for Princeton"*: Fleischman, 52–53.

42 *Pirazzini's pistol:* In tape recording by Rev. Darr.

43 *"I enclose check"*: NT to Emil Schlegel, Dec. 13, 1916. *"Egg coal"*: NT to Herman Harjes, June 18, 1917.

# NORMAN THOMAS

# Notes

69 *"While in confinement"*: To Mrs. Welling Thomas, Nov. 22, 1918, Frances Gates collection. *"The news about Evan"*: Ralph Thomas to NT, Nov. 6, 1918.

69–70 *NT's application for membership:* To Alexander Trachtenberg, Oct. 18, 1918.

70 *"Four cases of influenza"*: NT to Mrs. George B. Case, Nov. 6, 1918. *"In all this sudden break"*: NT Autobiog, 72.

71 *"I cannot close"*: Rev. Chaffee to NT, Aug. 4, 1918. *"Several of her family"*: NT to Dr. Miller, Aug. 7, 1919. NT to Gilkey, Jan. 16, 1919.

71–72 NT to Dr. Mott, Dec. 18, 1918.

72 NT to brother Ralph, Jan. 10, 1919.

73 *The radical list* appeared in NYT and NY Trib, Jan. 25, 1919.

74–75 *"My own feeling is"*: NT to "Dear Gilbert," otherwise unidentified, after Mar. 17, 1918.

77 *NYT article on Socialism:* In Jan. 11, 1920, issue.

78 *"Bolshevist theories and morals"*: NYT, Jan. 3, 1920. *Attack on New York Socialists:* NYT, May 2, 1919.

78–79 *"Sentinel" activity:* Frederick Lewis Allen, *Only Yesterday* (Bantam, 1959), Chapter III; Max Eastman, *op. cit.*, 136, 181; Symes and Clement, *op. cit.*, 329–330; Weinstein, *op. cit.*, 169–170.

79 *Mt. Vernon confrontation:* John Haynes Holmes, *I Speak for Myself* (Harper's, 1959), 192.

79–80 *Speaker Sweet's proscription:* NYT and NY Trib, Jan. 14, 1920.

80 *"To prove that Socialism"*: Morris Hillquit, *Loose Leaves from a Busy Life* (Macmillan, 1934), 261. *Claessens's promise:* August Claessens, *Didn't We Have Fun!* (Rand School Press, 1953), 109. See also Zecharia Chafee, *Freedom of Speech* (Harcourt, Brace, 1920), 332–364.

81 *"All the religion"*: NYT, Mar. 8, 1920. *Thomas at wedding:* Mrs. Richard N. Pierson told author.

83 *Giraffe Club story:* Mrs. Herbert C. Miller told author. *"If you disagreed with him"*: Stewart quoted in NYT, Dec. 18, 1926.

84 *"I cannot discover a God"*: NT to Dr. Stuart Cole, Dec. 1, 1954.

86 *Cahan and Socialism:* Moses Rischin, *The Promised City* (Corinth, 1962), 157. *B. Charney Vladeck:* See Devere Allen, *Adventurous Americans* (Farrar & Rinehart, 1932), chapter on Vladeck.

87 *"I have heard Republicans"*: NYT, Feb. 11, 1923.

88–89 *NT and The New Leader:* NT Autobiog, 85; Fleischman, 95; NYT, Aug. 12, 1923.

89 *NT's nomination:* NYT, July 26 and 28, 1924; NT Autobiog, 89.

90 *NT article in NYT:* In issue of Mar. 2, 1924.

91 *NT on young Roosevelt:* NYT, Sept. 26, 1924.

91–92 *Times story on NT candidacy:* Issue of Oct. 9, 1924.

92–93 *Calles guest of Thomases:* Mrs. Herbert C. Miller told author.

93 *The hate lists* are given in Allen F. Davis, *American Heroine: The Life and Legend of Jane Addams* (Oxford, 1973), 263–265. *Horses swerving:* Claessens, *op. cit.*, 93–94.

94 *NT visit to Princeton:* Author's conversation with William S. Thomas.

95 *"Everybody like me"*: Max Eastman, *Heroes I Have Known* (Simon & Schuster, 1942), 19.

96 *Thomases escape to hotel:* Mrs. Miller told author. *"He said he was reluctant"*: NYT, June 21, 1925.

97 *"I have another question"*: Granville Hicks, *Part of the Truth* (Harcourt, Brace & World, 1965), 71. *La Guardia on NT:* NYT, Oct. 19, 1925.

98 *Debs at Carnegie Hall:* NYT, Oct. 12, 1925.

PAGE

99   *NT greets churchmen:* NYT, June 4, 1926.

100   *Gitlow on NT:* Benjamin Gitlow, *I Confess* (Dutton, 1940), 364–365.

100–101   *NT visits miners:* Mrs. Eleanor Shatzkin told author.

101–103   *NT and textile strike:* NT Autobiog, 104; NYT, Apr. 15, 16, 20, 21, 29, May 1 and Oct. 19, 1926; Irving Howe and Lewis Coser, *The American Communist Party* (Beacon, 1957), 241–242.

104   *NT on Kerensky:* NL, Dec. 5, 1925.

108   *NT on Al Smith:* NYT, Oct. 13, 1926.

109   *Death of Stewart:* NYT, Dec. 18, 1926. *NT nominated for President:* NYT, Apr. 14 and 17, 1928.

110   *"Take the woodchuck":* Claessens, *op. cit.,* 179–180.

111   *NT meets Porter:* Porter told author.

115   *Senior, Blanshard and Herling:* Author's conversations with the three.

116   *Brockway on NT:* A. Fenner Brockway, *Inside the Left* (London: Allen & Unwin, 1942), 233.

117   *"We Socialists":* NYT, Sept. 29, 1929.

118   *NT vs. La Guardia:* M. R. Werner, "Fiorello's Finest Hour," American Heritage, Oct., 1961.

119   *North American Review article:* Feb., 1929, issue.

120   *Holmes, Hillquit and NT:* NYT, Nov. 18, 1929.

121   *The LIPA:* R. Alan Lawson, *The Failure of Independent Liberalism* (Putnam, 1971), 40–41. *Blanshard on NT:* Blanshard told author.

123   *The Dartmouth grad:* Bruce Bliven, *Five Million Words Later* (John Day, 1970), 213.

124   *Depression joke:* NT to B. H. Feldman, Apr. 5, 1949.

125   NT letter to Hoover, Apr. 23, 1932, Hoover Library, West Branch, Iowa. *Vladeck review:* In NL, Mar. 28, 1931.

127–128   *"Of Thee I Sing" anecdote:* Mrs. Paul Blanshard told author.

129   *"Its leaders hated Communism":* NT, *The Choice Before Us* (Macmillan, 1934), 130.

130   *"Awful heresies":* NT, *As I See It.*

132–133   *Milwaukee convention:* Senior, Blanshard and Waldman told author. Also, NYT, May 24, 1932; NL, May 28; and Shannon, *op. cit.,* 217.

134–135   *"Men and women search":* NYT, July 31, 1932; Time, Aug. 8.

137   *NT speech to collegians:* NYT, Oct. 26, 1932.

138   *"Not a candidate for anything":* NYHT, Oct. 9, 1933. *"I do hope":* Gilkey to NT, Dec. 17, 1932.

140   *Thomas on FDR program:* Johnpoll, 102.

140–141:   *May Day:* NYT, May 2, 1933.

141   NT letter to the five publications, Feb. 8, 1933.

142   NT to brother Arthur, Nov. 8, 1933. *Blanshard resignation:* Paul Blanshard, *Personal and Controversial* (Beacon, 1973), 80, 134. NT to Blanshard, Sept. 14, 1933.

143   *"It is emphatically":* NT to Most, Oct. 5, 1933. *Communist attack on Violet:* DW, Nov. 1 and 2, 1933. *"Given the necessity":* NT to H. J. Ashe, Oct. 6, 1933.

145   NT letter to Whitehead, Dec. 28, 1933. NT to Senior, Nov. 20, 1933.

147–148   *NT at dog commencement:* James Marshall told author.

148   NT to Senior about Krzycki statement, Nov. 24, 1933.

151   *Garden brawl:* NYT, Feb. 17, 1934. *"New York learned":* NL, Feb. 24.

152   *"What hope there is":* NT, *The Choice Before Us,* 155. Alexander letter, Apr. 2, 1934.

154   *NT on violence:* NT, *The Choice Before Us,* 148. *"America with its lynchings":* From NT's "A Socialist Program," undated but before Mar. 1, 1934.

# Notes

155 NT to FDR, Nov. 14, 1933. *Inez Robb story:* Memphis Commercial Appeal, Jan. 2, 1969 [*sic*]. NT to Streator, Nov. 3, 1933.

156–157 *NT urges FDR:* Dec. 18, 1933.

157 NT to Olson, Apr. 10, 1934. Olson reply, Apr. 28. NT to Senior, Jan. 16, 1934.

158 Martha Johnson to NT, Nov. 7, 1933. NT to Gen. Johnson, Dec. 20, 1933.

159 *"The sharecroppers":* NT to Henry Wallace, May 9, 1934. *"Now, under the operation":* NT to Wallace, Feb. 22, 1934. Wallace reply, Mar. 8. *"I'd rather sit":* Arthur M. Schlesinger, Jr., *The Coming of the New Deal* (Houghton Mifflin, 1958), 77.

160 Mitchell to NT, Mar. 20, 1934. Amberson to NT, Apr. 2. *"These things are":* Mitchell to NT, Apr. 12.

161 NT to Leach, Mar. 15, 1934. Voorhis to NT, Apr. 2. NT to FDR, May 4. NT to Rautenstrauch, Aug. 31.

162 Mrs. Jessen to NT, Apr. 10, 1934. NT to Otto Jessen, June 22. NT to the three magazines, Aug. 9.

163 Schilpp to NT, Aug. 16, 1934. Mitchell to NT, Sept. 5.

164 *"To put it brutally":* NYT, Mar. 2, 1934. *Debate with Long:* T. Harry Williams, *Huey Long* (Knopf, 1969), 694; NYT, Mar. 3, 1934.

165 *Taylorville incident:* NL, May 26, 1934; NYT, May 22; also Oct. 6, 1934, clipping from Decatur, Ill., Herald in NTP. *Rockford incident:* NYT, May 29, 1934.

166 *"Those whom we must win":* NT, "A Socialist Program," before Mar. 1, 1934.

167–169 *Declaration of Principles:* Included in Devere Allen to NT, June 16, 1934. Senior and Waldman told author of details of convention. Also, American Socialist Quarterly, July, 1934; Waldman, *Labor Lawyer* (Dutton, 1944), 267; NYT, June 4; NL, June 9.

169 *Shaplen story:* NYT, June 4, 1934. *Waldman statement:* NYT, June 5. *Hendin statement:* NL, June 16.

170 *Holmes statement:* Socialist Voice, undated. NT to Waldman, June 6. NT to Porter, June 7. Vladeck to NT, June 14.

171 NT to Vladeck, June 13, written before Vladeck's warning. Senior to NT, Aug. 15. NT to Hoan, July 12.

172 NT to Senior: July 2, 1934. Also, NYT, July 2; NL, July 7.

173 *"Even the memory":* NT, *The Test of Freedom* (Norton, 1954), 21.

174 *Oregon SP resignation:* State chairman to Senior, Sept. 8, 1934.

175 NT to Father Sill, Kent School, Sept. 17, 1934. Browder to NT, Aug. 17. NT reply, Aug. 21. *"Anyone can see":* New York member to NT, Sept. 17.

176 NT to Sinclair, May 1, 1934. *"It is a joy":* NT in NL, Oct. 13.

177 *"I am working":* NT to Maynard Krueger, Oct. 13. *"I go to towns":* Ibid. Feigenbaum to NT, Oct. 19.

178 NT to state committee, Nov. 7. NT secretary to Frank E. Baker, Nov. 23.

180 *Rodgers statement:* Howard Kester, *Revolt Among the Sharecroppers* (Covici Friede, 1936), 68–69.

181 Naomi Mitchison to NT, undated. Frankfurter to NT, Mar. 21, 1935.

182 *Birdsong incident:* STFU bulletin; Kester, *op. cit.,* 80–81.

183 Kester-Mitchell telegram, Mar. 27, 1935. NT reply, Apr. 2; NYT, Apr. 18.

184 *Wallace speech:* Kester, *op. cit.,* 53. NT to FDR, Apr. 9. *NT-FDR meeting:* Schlesinger, *op. cit.,* 378–379. Mitchell to NT, Oct. 4.

185 *Chicago crisis:* Seniors told author; Gitlow, *op. cit.,* 578–579. NT to NEC, Nov., 1934.

186 NT to NYT, Dec. 5. Hoan to NYT, Dec. 5. NT to Hoopes, July 8.

187 *"Imagine the picture":* Unidentified clipping, NYPL. *"Boxing gloves":* Hoan to NT, Mar. 7, 1935.

PAGE

188 *Porter to Indiana:* Porter told author. Gerber to NT, Mar. 2, 1935.

189 *Yipsels at picnic:* George Goebel to NT, Aug. 24, 1935. *NT cannot raise money:* NT undated memo to Hoopes, Allen et al. *"Spilt milk":* NT to Anderson, Mar. 7. De Witt to NT, Mar. 31. Porter to NT, Oct. 6.

190 *NT-Browder debate:* NYT, Nov. 28, 1935; Call, Dec. 7. Also, M. S. Venkataramani, "United Front Tactics of the CP (USA) and Their Impact on the Socialist Party of America, 1932–36," in International Studies, Quarterly Journal of the Indian School of International Studies, Vol. I, No. 2, Oct., 1959.

191 NT to Lewis, Nov. 18, 1935. Vladeck to NT, Dec. 13. Hughan to NT, Dec. 22.

192 *Waldman on left wing:* NYT, Dec. 2, 1935. *NT reply:* NYT, Dec. 15.

193 *Cannon account:* James P. Cannon, *History of American Trotskyism* (Pioneer Press, 1944), 222 and 224–227. *NT on CP wiles:* NYT, Apr. 16, 1936.

194 *Handsome salary:* Actually, NT had voluntarily ended his LID salary so that his only income came from lecturing. *SP primary:* NYT, Apr. 2, 3 and 7, 1936. *May Day:* Call and NL, both May 9. Also, Max Danish, *The World of David Dubinsky* (World, 1957), 95. *Waldman on FDR:* Call, May 16.

195 *"Your sacrifice":* Ruth Senior to NT, June 8; NL, May 30. *NT gave offense:* Hoopes to NT, Aug. 26.

196 *Niebuhr optimism:* Daniel Bell, *Marxian Socialism in the United States* (Princeton, 1967), 169–170. *Thomas too busy:* Gitlow, op. cit., 581.

197 *NT on Krumbein:* NT to FDR, Sept. 14.

198 *NT in Terre Haute:* Call, Sept. 7 and 21; NT, "Hoosier Hitlerism," The Nation, Sept. 18.

199 *Frances fills in:* Mrs. Gates told author. *On American purity:* NT to Murphy, Nov. 11, 1935. *NT arrested:* NYT, Feb. 13, 1936. *NT on the SDF:* NYT, June 4, 1936.

200 *"Forever talking":* Matthew Josephson, *Sidney Hillman* (Doubleday, 1952), 398. *Dubinsky view:* Danish, op. cit., 94.

201 *Woolf interview:* NYT, June 7, 1936. *Krzycki incident:* Herling told author. *Violet remark:* Akron Beacon Journal, Sept. 15.

202 *"Coolidge, not Hitler":* NYT, Sept. 9, 1936. *"Sick unto death":* Contained in Oct. 20 Senior letter to NEC.

203 *NT on Trotskyites:* To Hoopes, Aug. 19. Randall letter, Aug., undated.

204 *"We may suffer":* NT to Senior, Aug. 18. *Booed in Cleveland:* NT, "I'm Glad I'm Not Running This Year," American Magazine, Oct., 1952. *"On a stretcher":* Fleischman, 171.

205 *"Depressed about the outlook":* NT to Krueger, Nov. 1, 1936; Call and NL, Nov. 7.

206 *Laidler statement:* NYT, Nov. 4. *Coolidge opinion:* Related by Coolidge to Prof. Alexander.

208–209 NTP has large folder on NT birthday party. *About Angelica:* Balabanoff, *My Life As a Rebel* (Harper's, 1938), Chapters I and II.

211 *"Amazement and outrage":* Holmes to NT, Dec. 23, 1936. NT replied Dec. 24, and Holmes responded Dec. 28.

212 The Call, Jan. 2 and 9, 1937.

213 Burt to NT, Jan. 23, 1937. NT to Altman, Dec. 5, 1936. *Melnicoff statement:* Contained in David Felix to NT, Mar. 17, 1937.

214 *NT on tour:* NT Autobiog, 183, 190; NYT, Apr. 15; Call, May 1. Also, NT interview with Prof. Alexander.

215 Call, June 5; NYT, June 20 [*sic*]; NYT, May 28.

216 NT Autobiog, 185, 186; NYT, May 29. *"Eye-opener":* NYT, May 2.

217 *Hippodrome estimate:* NYT, June 11; Call, June 12. *"We wouldn't have":* Fleischman tape, 186. *"Well, this problem":* Fleischman tape, 207. Symes to NT, Feb. 16.

# Notes

PAGE

218 *"The last thing"*: NT June report, "The Party Situation." *"I pleaded"*: NT recollection, Nov. 24, 1965, over WBAI. *"Partly as a result"*: Cannon, *op. cit*, 352–353.

219 *"While I might"*: Devere Allen to NT, July 7, 1937. NT reply, July 8. Porter to NT, Jan. 27.

220 *"I do hope"*: Vladeck to NT, July 19. *Clarity manifesto: circa* Oct.

221 Coolidge reply, Aug. 20. *NT speaks in Jersey City:* NYT, Dec. 22, 1937.

222 *Thomases deported:* NYT, May 1, 1938. NT to FDR, May 3.

223 *NT methods of handling hostility:* NT to Prof. A. L. Capuder, Mar. 5, 1939. *Newark repulse:* NYT, June 5, 1938.

225 *Bell's criticism:* Bell, *op. cit.,* 189. *"Few satisfactions greater"*: NT, *Mr. Chairman, Ladies and Gentlemen* (Hermitage, 1955), 87.

226 *"Entry into new war"*: NT warning in his Jan. 21, 1938, invitations to his home to form KAOWC.

227 *Baron dispatches:* Call, Sept. 11 and Oct. 30, 1937. De los Rios to NT, Nov. 16.

228 NT to Senior, Oct. 19, 1937. Burt to NEC, Sept. 3, 1938. *"Electoral expression"*: Dec. 25, 1938, SP news release. *"I am swamped"*: NT to Peter Grimm, Dec. 7, 1939.

229 NT to Mrs. Milliken, Oct. 11, 1938.

230 *"This madness of Baron's"*: NT to Allen, Nov. 20, 1938. To La Follette, Nov. 23. *Insulting letter:* Nov. 20. NT, *Socialism on the Defensive* (Harper's, 1938); *Keep America Out of War* (Stokes, 1939).

231 FDR to NT, Nov. 28, 1938. *Move against Burt:* Johnpoll, 190–191; NT to Laidler, Feb. 17, 1939. FDR to NT, July 26, 1939.

233 *Hippodrome meeting:* NYT, May 1, 1939. NT to Ryskind, Oct. 25, 1939.

234 *"Stalin's duplicity"*: NT to Ryskind, Aug. 25, 1939.

235 *"Many of us"*: NT to NYHT, Sept. 12, 1939. NT to Blanshards, July 18.

236 *"The bank is after me"*: NT to Clement, May 18, 1939. Alfred Baker Lewis to NT, Sept. 30.

237 *"Personally"*: NT to Aaron Levenstein, Oct. 23, 1939. *"What prejudices"*: NT to Gauss, Nov. 20. DW, Dec. 1.

238 *NT vs. Browder:* NYT, Dec. 2, 1939. NT to Ward, Nov. 29. NT to Fraenkel, Dec. 19. See also Corliss Lamont, *Freedom Is As Freedom Does* (Horizon, 1956), 266–277; and Lucille B. Milner, *Education of an American Liberal* (Horizon, 1954), 262–270. Agnes to NT, Nov. 20.

239 *"How do you"*: NT to Herman Hahn, Jan. 15, 1940. *"Well, Mrs. Thomas"*: Included in Dec. 10, 1938, R. J. Deachman to NT.

240 *"Only Socialists"*: NT to Walter O'Hagen, Feb. 13, 1940, and to "Comrade Horn," Feb. 29. *Lee attack:* NL, Sept. 16, 1939.

241 *"Raving maniac"*: Clement to NT, Sept. 16, 1939. *NYT approval:* Apr. 9, 1940, issue. *Rebekah campaign:* NYT, June 8. NT to Lewis, June 3. *"Few things"*: NT to Lena Tulchen, Aug. 5.

242 *NT on British lecturers:* NT to NYT, Aug. 10, 1939. Coffin to NT, Aug. 3, 1940. *"Any religion"*: NT to T. Otto Nall, Aug. 9, 1940. Lovett to NT, Sept. 25, 1939.

243 *FDR's fears:* To NT, July 31, 1940. *Violet on tour:* NT, "I'm Glad I'm Not Running This Year." *Hotel fire:* NYT, Sept. 12, 1940. Uphoffs to NT, undated, 1940.

244 *NT complaints to Time:* Oct. 1, 8 and 15, 1940. Harvard Crimson, Oct. 9. NT to Senior, Aug. 3. NT to Allen, Aug. 14.

245 *Advice to Lindbergh:* NT to him, Aug. 9.

246 NT to Stuart, Nov. 19. *Thompson column:* NYHT, Feb. 24, 1941.

247 *"It is clothed"*: NT, "How to Fight for Democracy," Annals of American Academy, July, 1941. NT to Thompson, Feb. 24. Her reply, undated.

PAGE

248 *"A dinner club":* Villard to NT, Dec. 3, 1940. NT to Wheeler, Mar. 4, 1941. Tobey to NT, Mar. 27. NT to Minkoff, Jan. 27.

249 *NT at Garden:* NYT, May 24, 1941. *"It would be":* NT to Joe Friedman, May 26. Call, May 17 and 31.

250 *Mary Hillyer militance:* Paul Blanshard, *op. cit.,* 153. NT to Severinghaus, July 16, 1941.

251 *Eastman article:* RD, June, 1941. Eastman, *Love and Revolution,* 638. Eastman, *Reflections on the Failure of Socialism* (Devin-Adair, 1955).

252 *Jack Fies bequest:* NT to Edward T. Rice, July 7 and 18, 1941. *"We shall watch":* NT to NYT, June 23. DW, June 24. *"Full and unstinting":* NYT, July 3. *Mary Hillyer charge:* NYT, July 4.

254 *Wartime Journals of Charles A. Lindbergh* (Harcourt, 1970), 539. NT comments to Bertram Wolfe and Emanuel Muravchik, Sept. 16, and to Brendan Sexton, Oct. 8. Wayne S. Cole, *America First* (U. of Wisconsin, 1953), 147–148. NT to Lindbergh, Sept. 24. NT to Niebuhr, Sept. 15.

255 NT to Villard, after Oct., 1941.

256 NT to son Evan, undated, from Evan Thomas II.

257 NT to Time, Nov. 6, 1941.

258 *"I feel":* NT to Krueger, Dec. 11.

259 *"Events and reactions":* NT to NEC, Dec. 9.

260 *"I see no escape":* NT to Ken Cuthbertson, Jan. 2, 1942.

261–262 *NT diary:* Among NT Papers.

263 *On Stalin:* NT to NYT, Oct. 6, 1942. *Rex Stout attack:* Included in NT to Paley, May 14. *"That kernel":* NT to Mr./Mrs. Philip Gray, Jan. 7.

264 *NT on unions:* Harper's, May, 1942.

265 *"No matter what":* Judah Drob to Fleischman, July 31, 1942.

266 *"Lost love" letter:* ———to NT, July 23, 1942. *"We are practicing":* NT to Hugh Macbeth, Mar. 9, 1942.

267 Call, Mar. 7, 1942. NT to Villard, Aug. 20. Christian Century, July 29. NT to Cripps, Feb. 20.

268 NT to FDR, Aug. 11. *NT on Hull:* To Villard, Aug. 18. FDR reply, Aug. 25.

269 NT to Baldwin, Sept. 1. NT to Kirchwey, Apr. 3.

270 NT to Cheney, Sept. 21. NT to Aswell, June 12. NT to Davis, Sept. 18 and 25.

271 NT to Stout, June 30, 1943. NYT, Nov. 2, 1942. *"Just panting":* NYT, Dec. 30.

272 *On Darlan:* NT to NYT, July 28, 1943. *Tresca murder:* NYT, Jan. 12 and 17, 1943.

273 *"She is a person":* NT to Clarence Pickett, Jan. 12, 1943.

274 *Falk matter:* Explained in NT to Assistant Secretary of the Treasury Herbert E. Gaston, Apr. 21, 1942. *"Although I assumed":* NT to Paul Ward, Oct. 29, 1942.

275 NT to Sinclair, Mar. 22, 1943. Sinclair reply, Mar. 29.

276 Hoover to NT, Nov. 2, 1942. NT to War Department, Aug. 19, 1943. NT to Darden, June 8, 1942. NT to Gauss, Nov. 17, 1942. NT to Philip L. Gill, Dec. 10, 1942.

277 NT to Wallace, Nov. 21, 1943. Marc Rose to NT, Nov. 23.

278 *"I think the low standards":* NT to Reader's Digest, Nov. 21 and 24, linked.

279 NT to Sen. Murray, Mar. 6, 1944. Mrs. Tresca to NT, July 30, 1943. NT reply, Aug. 5. *"Rarely did I pass":* NT Autobiog, 209.

280 *Violet's letter:* Postmarked Apr. 20, 1944, to Mrs. Evan Thomas, Evan Thomas collection.

281 *NT on "Strange Fruit":* NT to Alfred A. Albert, June 19, 1944. *Mayer's thank-you:* Apr. 16. *Mayer on the sculpture:* Dec. 10, 1945.

282 Violet's letter, undated, Evan Thomas collection. Coolidge to NT, May 11, 1946. NT to Coolidge, May 7, 1944 (this was an ongoing debate of long duration).

# Notes

283 *NT comments on Socialism:* NT Autobiog, 227, 232, 237. NT to Johnson, Sept. 13, 1943.

285 *"A lot of us":* NT to La Follette, Jan. 12, 1944. *On Moscow agreement:* NYT, Nov. 20, 1943. NT to Hull, June 26, 1944.

286 *"Policing the world":* NT to Romer, Sept. 14, 1943. *Song:* In NTP. Niebuhr to NT, Jan. 5, 1944. *Reading convention:* NYT, June 2, 4 and 5. Call, June 2 and 16. Rev. Donald S. Harrington, a delegate, told author.

287 *Macdonald criticism:* In "Politics," Oct., 1944. *Airman's questions:* NT, "I'm Glad I'm Not Running This Year."

288 Violet to Frances, Sept. 25 [1944], Frances Gates collection. Call, Aug. 4, 1944, had NT letter.

289 *Niebuhr-NT argument:* In "Norman Thomas and Reinhold Niebuhr," by Paul Merkley, doctoral thesis at Fresno State College (in NTP); see also *Reinhold Niebuhr*, by Ronald H. Stone (Abingdon, 1972), 68–69.

290 *Niebuhr answer:* Call, Sept. 8, 1944. See also Christopher Lasch, *The New Radicalism in America* (Knopf, 1965), 300. NT open letter to Hillman, Sept. 26, 1944.

291 NT to Mrs. E. M. Bowman, Sept. 19, 1944. International Teamster, Nov., 1944.

292 *"Earliest possible peace":* NT to Charles Ross, May 22, 1945.

293 *NT's comment* on the 1945 address was given to the Haverford class of 1963.

294 NT to Bevan, June 6, 1945. *NT on Laborites:* NT Autobiog, 236. *On John L. Lewis:* NT Autobiog, 231.

295 *On Dumbarton Oaks:* To George Wells, Dec. 23, 1944. *On UN:* To Raymond Leslie Buell, May 9, 1945. *"There must be":* NT Autobiog, 221.

296 Paine to NT, Sept. 26, 1946. Mrs. Dillingham to NT, June 1. NT to Freda Utley, Aug. 7. NT to Wallace, Sept. 18. NT to Col. Fellers, May 7. Mrs. Luce to NT, June 20.

297 Kravchenko, *I Chose Freedom* (Scribners, 1946), 466–467. *NT reception for Kravchenko:* Fleischman told author; also, Fleischman, 220. Angelica to Thomases, May 11. Fischer to NT, May 11.

298 NT to Kravchenko, May 14. NT to Fischer, May 13. Kohlberg to NT, July 17. NT to Kohlberg, July 16. Coolidge to NT, May 11.

299 *"I find it ironic":* NT to Coolidge, May 7. NT to Molotov, Dec. 5. NT to Mackenzie King, Aug. 19. NT to NAACP, June 18.

300 *NT on segregation:* To R. N. Douglas, Nov. 2, 1945. NT to Rockland director, May 6, 1946.

302 Angelica to NT, Oct. 21, 1946. *NT and Schuschnigg:* NYT, Feb. 11, 1947.

303 *"In Germany":* NT Autobiog, 207. NT to NYT, Oct. 7, 1946.

304 *"American intervention":* NT to George V. Denny, Apr. 21, 1947. *On California:* NT report on trip, Apr. 22, 1947. NT to Princeton Alumni Weekly, June 12, 1944. NT to Churchill, Jan. 21, 1947. *"Like Switzerland":* NT to Sam Romer, May 27, 1947. *Foreboding:* NT to Irving Stone, Feb. 20, 1947. NT to Murrow, May 26, 1947.

306 *"I suppose I am peculiar":* NT to Frank Cutting, undated [1948]. Call, Aug. 6, 1947.

307 NT to children, Frances Gates collection.

308 NT to Robinson, Sept. 23, 1947. NT to Circuit, June 12, 1945.

309 Emma Thomas told author of her sojourn with NT.

310 *NT on Toynbee:* To S. K. Ratcliff, Sept. 15, 1947. Clement to NT, May 10, 1948.

311 Angelica's letter, June 10, 1948. *NT on Mundt-Nixon:* May 28, 1948. *On HUAC:* NT to Edna Lonigan, Nov. 7, 1947. *On firing actors:* NT to George Sokolsky, Dec. 5, 1947.

313 *"I am pleading":* Sept. 26, 1947, PWWC statement. *"Whether":* NT to NYT, May 6, 1948.

504

PAGE

314 NT to Hogan, Jan. 6, 1948. NYT, Jan. 11.

315 *"The best thing":* NYT, May 10, 1948. NT to Krueger, May 28. Sulzberger to NT, May 26.

316 NT to Lewis, Oct. 15, 1947. NT to Bell, Nov. 4. NT to Hoyt, May 28, 1948.

317 *"Bravest and best":* NT to Humphrey, June 3, 1968 [*sic*]. NT to Prof. E. S. Allen, June 28, 1948. *"A large Socialist vote":* NYT, Aug. 22, 1948. *Mencken praise:* Reprinted in Baltimore Sun, Dec. 20, 1968.

318 NT to Mencken, Oct. 29, 1948. Christian Science Monitor, May 15, 1948. *"Socialistic talk":* NYHT, Nov. 22, 1964 [*sic*]. *Sinners:* NYT, Oct. 27, 1948. Old lady to NT, Oct. 30.

319 Fleischman, 237. Balabanoff to NT, Nov. 3, 1948. Gilkey to NT, Nov. 2.

320 Louis Mayer to NT, Nov. 2, 1948.

321 *Cripps scene:* NT to Mrs. Morris Rubin, Oct. 11, 1949. NT to Hoopes, Sept. 16.

322 *NT voter analysis:* Found in his 1948 papers. NT to Truman's secretary, M. J. Connelly, Nov. 26, 1948.

323 *"My Lord Duke":* NT to Bedford, Sept. 14, 1948. NT to Ralph, Apr. 28.

324 Mrs. Barnes told author. NT to Myrdal, June 2, 1948. Myrdal reply, June 19. NT to Mrs. Tresca, Feb. 10, 1950.

325 *"I shall be glad":* NT to Moyer, Feb. 1, 1949. *Death of Jester:* NT to Fred Colvig, Apr. 15, 1949. NT to Hoyt, Aug. 29.

326 *Advises Pope:* NT to Baltimore Sun and other papers, Mar. 2, 1949. NT to Angelica, July 28. NT to Mrs. Roosevelt, same day. *On Labor government:* NT to W. D. Jamieson, Nov. 22, 1948. NT testimony, May 11, 1949.

327 Strout sent NT the column, May 13, 1949.

328 *NT article:* in NYT, Nov. 20, 1949. Same issue paid him editorial tribute.

329 Holmes to NT, Nov. 21, 1949.

330 *On Chiang:* NT to Robin Meyers, Sept. 18, 1950. NT to Kohlberg, May 26.

331 NT to Clinchy, May 16, 1950. NT to FDR Jr., Jan. 30.

332 *"Scared rabbits":* NT to NR, June 26, 1950. NT to AMA Journal, July 31. *SP convention:* NYT, June 4 and 5, 1950.

333 *"I may regret":* NT to Scott W. Reed, Apr. 21, 1949. Mrs. Barnes told author. NT to Hugh Sheehan, June 13, 1950.

334 Evan Thomas II and Emma Thomas told author.

335 Fleischman told author. *Singh opinion:* Prof. Alexander's notes. John Gates and William Thomas told author.

336 *"I suggest":* NT to John L. Lewine, July 5, 1950. *"On the whole":* NT to Bruce Barton, July 12. *On Chiang:* NT to M. D. Schneider, Oct. 24. NT to Dulles, Aug. 7.

337 *"Any hope":* NT to Acheson, Aug. 7. *"My constant appeal":* Acheson, *Present at the Creation* (Norton, 1969), 379. *Axe story:* NT, *Prerequisites for Peace* (Norton, 1959), 50. NT to Truman, Aug. 26, 1950.

338 *"Your able speech":* NT to Truman, Oct. 18, 1950. Tucker Smith to NT, Oct. 25. Sheehan to NT, Oct. 25. *Angelica:* NYT, July 8 and 11. Angelica to NT, Sept. 14.

339 NT to Weeks, Oct. 19. NT to Truman, Nov. 29. Browder to Alexander, Mar. 19, Alexander notes.

340 NT to Browder, Dec. 12, 1950. The name "Aaron Cohn" is necessarily fictitious. NT to Angelica, Dec. 29.

341 *Founding CCF:* NYT, June 26, 27, 28, 1950. Christopher Lasch, *The Agony of the American Left* (Vintage, 1969), 63–69. NT to Schlesinger, Nov. 10.

342 *"I protest":* NT to Alumni Weekly, Feb. 23, 1951. See also W. A. Swanberg, *Luce and His Empire* (Dell, 1972), 467–468.

343 Allen Dulles to NT, after Feb. 23, 1951.

PAGE

344 NT to Truman, Mar. 1 and 2.

345 *"When the Korean War"*: NT, *A Socialist's Faith* (Norton, 1951), 9–10. *"Commanding heights"*: *Ibid.*, 186. *"There are men"*: NT, "Democratic Socialism" (pamphlet, LID, 1953), 38. *"In general"*: NT, *A Socialist's Faith*, 13. *"In the event of my death"*: NT "to my children," Mar. 13, 1951.

346–347 *NT in India:* NT Col., Feb. 2, 1956; NT, "India on the Verge," The Progressive, Oct., 1951; NYT, Mar. 29, 1951. *"Guns smoking"*: NT to Truman, May 14. *"French policy"*: NT Col., Apr. 10.

348 NT Col., Apr. 12. NT to Truman, May 14 and June 29.

349 *"Earnest hope"*: NT to Truman, Aug. 7, Oct. 24 and Nov. 2. NT to A. A. Berle, Aug. 23.

350 *"Dear Elizabeth"*: Aug. 13. NT to Gausmann, Aug. 3. *"All of us"*: NT to Reginald Zalles, Oct. 18. NT to the Senators, Oct. 23.

351 *"To me the fear"*: NT Col., Mar. 23, 1952. NT to Acheson, Mar. 13. NT Col., Jan. 24. NT to Gausmann, Aug. 14, 1950. *"My feeling"*: NT to Aaron Levenstein and Hy Fish, Sept. 16, 1951. Diamond to NT, Oct. 11.

352 Sinclair to NT, Sept. 25, 1951.

353 *"As usual"*: Angelica, Apr. 15, 1952. Randolph told author of tour.

354 *"It is a good thing"*: NT report to ACCF, June 18, 1952. NT to Suzuki, Apr. 30. Kiattisak, May 16, Frances Gates collection. Ratanakosin Weekly, May 19, Frances Gates collection.

355 *"Panty riots"*: NT Col., June 6. *In Manila:* Call, June 13.

356 NT to Gausmann, Apr. 24, 1953. NT to Benton, Sept. 18, 1952. NT to Stevenson, Aug. 28.

357 NT Col., Sept. 25. *On Nixon:* NT Col., Nov. 9–10.

358 Mary Blanshard to NT, Feb. 13, 1952. NT to Heckscher, Feb. 1, 1954. NT to Mrs. Bingham, Mar. 5. Friedman to NT, July 2, 1956. NT to Gaitskell, June 14, 1956. Harlow to NT, Apr. 24, 1956. Niebuhr to NT, Dec. 5, 1956. NT to Berle, Feb. 2, 1956.

359 *"The best"*: NT to David Braveman, Sept. 8, 1953. NT to LIRR, Sept. 18, 1951.

361 *"My dear children"*: Mar. 23, 1953.

362 *"Let me add"*: NT to Dulles, May 15, 1953. *"Her place"*: NT to Dulles, Dec. 23, 1952. On *"the generals"*: Call, Apr. 10, 1953. NT to Eisenhower, Mar. 19, 1953.

363 NT Cols., Apr. 23, May 28, May 17–18 and May 21, 1953.

364 *AFL anti-Communist war:* Ronald Radosh, *American Labor and United States Foreign Policy* (Random House, 1969), 308. Angelica to NT, June 7. NT reply, June 15. McLeod to NT, July 14. NT reply, July 21. Call, July 24.

365 *"Already I've heard"*: NT Col., July 16. NT Cols., Aug. 20 and Aug. 23–24. NT report to Lovestone, Sept. 9.

366 NT to SAS, Aug. 18. NT to Eisenhower, same date. Dulles to NT, Sept. 8. NT reply, Sept. 10.

367 *Eisenhower interview:* Call, Nov., 1953; NYT, Oct. 28. *"I am no atheist"*: NT to James Farrell, May 25, 1952 [*sic*].

368 *Lamont on NT:* Lamont, *op. cit.*, 127–128.

369 NT to Lamont, Mar. 24, 1961. *Lamont view:* Cedric Belfrage, *The American Inquisition* (Bobbs-Merrill, 1973), 186n. *NT to Einstein*, Mar. 9, 1954. Einstein reply, Mar. 10.

371 *Baldwin on NT:* "Norman Thomas, a Combative Life," NR, Jan. 13, 1968. *Odria case:* NYT, Dec. 15, 1953.

372 *On passports:* NT to Mrs. Ruth Shipley, Oct. 11, 1954. NT to Dorothy Thompson,

PAGE

Jan. 3, 1954. NT to John W. Hanlon, American Tobacco Co., Mar. 2. NT to Sen. Wiley, Feb. 15.

373 *Barry Miller case:* NYT, June 17, 18, 19, 1954. NT to Wijono, Dec. 31. Angelica to NT, July 10.

374 *NT at 70:* NYT, Nov. 20 and 22, 1954. Angelica letter, Nov. 12. NT to Ratcliffe, Oct. 27.

375 *On Guatemala:* NT Col., July 18–19, 1954.

376 *NT religious reappraisal:* "Good Friday, 1955," Frances Gates collection. NT to Eisenhower, Mar. 22.

377 NT to Angelica, May 2. *On Luce:* NT to Chester Bowles, May 10.

378 *Cable to Nutimes:* July 6. *"I am writing":* NT Col., 1955, date missing.

379 *"Dear Tucker":* NT to Smith, Jan. 5, 1956. *On Vishinsky:* NT Col., Nov. 28–29, 1954.

382 *On Nixon:* NT Col., Feb. 23, 1956. Life, Jan. 16.

383 *"Mr. Dulles and Henry Luce":* NT Col., Jan. 19.

384 *"Dear Alex":* Feb. 28. Gilkey to NT, Feb. 21. NT reply, Feb. 27.

385 *Galindez case:* NYT, Mar. 19, Apr. 5 and 8. NT to de Sapio, Apr. 12. NT to FDR Jr., Apr. 20.

386 NT to Javits, Nov. 7. *"The convention":* NT to Martin Diamond, June 19.

387 *"Resolution on disarmament":* NT to Jay Lovestone, June 19, 1953.

388 *"I got an amazing telegram":* NT to Drew Pearson, Apr. 13, 1956.

389 *In Mexico City:* Baldwin told author. NT to Dulles, Oct. 4, 1956.

390 *"Blundering Eden":* NT to Chicago Sun-Times, Nov. 14. NT to Eisenhower, Nov. 12. *"God save":* NT Col., Nov. 11–12.

391 NT to Singh, Nov. 12, 1956. NT to Mrs. Roosevelt, Nov. 13. Her reply, Nov. 16. Angelica to NT, Nov. 10. His reply, Nov. 15.

392 *"Mrs. Meir used good judgment":* NT to Bjarne Braatoy, Nov. 19, 1956. *"This Israeli business":* NT to Anne Fremantle, Jan. 3, 1957. *"Comprehensive resolution":* NT Col., May 16, 1957.

393 *"Immediate progress":* NT Col., Dec. 23–24, 1956. NT to Mary Blanshard, Sept. 10, 1956. *"In retrospect":* NT to her, Apr. 17, 1957.

394 *"It was a treat":* Karen Figueres to NT, Jan. 27, 1957. NT to Mrs. Flynn, June 12, 1957. Her reply, June 13.

396 *"Would it lie":* NT to Henderson, Apr. 25, 1957. *"We Americans":* NT to Gen. John W. O'Daniel, June 27, 1957. NT to Gausmann, Jan. 25, 1957.

397 NT to Fromm, July 3, 1957. Henderson to NT, Sept. 20. Peretz told author.

398 NT to Bowles, Sept. 26, 1957. NT to Flanders, Oct. 23. NT to Bitar, Oct. 3. NT to Eisenhower, Oct. 31.

399 Dr. Peretz told author many details of the tour. *"He agreed with Thomas":* From Peretz's written report, 7.

401 *"I was met":* NT, "Are We As Right As We Think?" SR, Apr. 18, 1959.

402 *"Bombs go off":* NT Col., Dec. 19, 1957. *"A beginning":* NT in Peretz report, 26–27.

403 *"Brinkmanship policies":* Peretz report, 27. *"I am embarrassed":* NT to Presidential Assistant Robert Gray, Dec. 30, 1957.

404 *CIA offer:* Peretz told author. *"General agreement":* NT Col., Mar. 26, 1958. *NT on Dulles:* NT Col., Jan. 5–6, 1958.

405 NYT, Dec. 30, 1957. *Humphrey proposal:* NYT, Feb. 19, 1958. *On Sobolev:* Call, May, 1958. *HUAC charge:* NYT, Apr. 9. *NT before UN:* NYT, June 20 ff. *On Lebanon:* Call, July–Aug., 1958.

406 *On Quemoys:* NYT, Sept. 7, 1958; NT Col., Sept. 20–21; and Call, Oct. *"The apathy":* NYT, Sept. 7, 1958. NT to Angelica, Apr. 2, Sept. 23 and July 29, 1958.

# Notes

PAGE

407   *Funeral directions:* Sept. 14, 1958, Frances Gates collection. Angelica to NT, Sept. 28. NT reply, Dec. 27.

408   *On birth control:* New America, undated, 1960. *On Democratic-Republican sameness: Ibid.* NT to Roper, June 23, 1960.

409   Kissinger, *Nuclear Weapons and Foreign Policy* (Harper, 1957). Angelica to NT, undated, July, 1957. NT to Browder, Mar. 22, 1957. *"On May 10":* NT, "Are We As Right As We Think?" SR, Apr. 18, 1959.

410   *"We who believe":* Call, Winter, 1959. *NT 75th birthday:* NYT, Nov. 19 and 20, 1959.

411   *Warns President, condemns labor camps:* NYT, Nov. 23 and Dec. 8, 1959. *Kitzbühel meeting:* I. F. Stone, *The Haunted Fifties* (Vintage, 1963), 257.

412   *Alamogordo scientists:* NT, *Prerequisites for Peace,* 27.

413   *"The basis": Ibid.,* 33; also 34, 38–39.

414   *"The withdrawal": Ibid.,* 44; also 49, 93, 89.

415   *"In our era": Ibid.,* 25. *NT on U-2:* NT Col., May 11, 1960.

416   NT Col., May 14–15, May 18 and May 21–22, 1960.

417   *"We citizens":* NT Col., May 6. NT to Mrs. Sanger, Jan. 5.

418   Her reply, July 5. His rejoinder, July 8. *On Kennedy:* New America, undated, 1960. *On Eastland:* NT Col., Oct. 12. NT to LBJ, Feb. 29, 1956.

419   *"I am dictating":* NT to Mrs. Miller, Mar. 15, 1960. *"It will give Castro":* NYT, Oct. 31, 1960.

420   *NT to salesmen:* NYT, Oct. 19, 1960. Newsweek, Aug. 22. NT to Sen. Charles Percy, July 18. NT to Prof. Samuel Beer, Sept. 19. NT to Nehru, Mar. 18.

421   Patricia Miller Libbey told author. NT to Lenore Marshall, Oct. 31, 1960. NT Col., Oct. 29–30.

422   *On Laos:* NT Col., Dec. 21, 1960. NT to Reuss, Jan. 23, 1961. New America, undated, 1960. NT to Eisenhower, Jan. 19, 1961.

423   *Reproves Barton:* Jan. 5, 1961. *On Kahn:* NT Col., Apr. 1–2, 1961. Life, quoted in I. F. Stone, *op. cit.,* 315. *"Are we Americans":* NT to Dallas News and other papers, Sept. 19, 1961. *On shelters:* NYT, Nov. 12.

424   *NT on JFK:* NT Col., Apr. 15–16, 1961. NT to Bowles, Apr. 26.

425   *On Birchite:* NT Col., Apr. 8–9, 1961. *On Buckley:* NT Col., May 27–28.

426   Max Nomad, *Aspects of Revolt* (Bookman, 1959), 68. NT to Nomad, Apr. 26, 1961. Sandra to NT, Apr. 5.

428   *"I am deeply concerned":* NT to W. A. Campbell, Jan. 20, 1960.

429   Holmes to NT, Oct. 13, 1961. Sadie to Channel 9, San Francisco, Feb. 17.

430   Juan Bosch, *The Unfinished Experiment: Democracy in the Dominican Republic* (Praeger, 1965), 170. Author's conversations with Senior and Mrs. Barnes. NYT, Oct. 7, 1961.

431   *The Brookings report:* Kaplan to NT, June 6, 1961. Macdonald to NT, Oct. 24, 1956. Lasch, *Agony,* 74–75. NT to McCone, Dec. 22, 1961.

433   *Seneca Indians:* NT to Mrs. Meyer, Oct. 13, 1961. NT to Tito, Jan. 24, 1961, and May 15, 1962. NT to Flynn, Nov. 21, 1961.

434   *"Looking back":* NT to A. S. Venkataramani, Apr. 20, 1961. *"I wish I could see":* Fleischman, 296.

435   NT to Jackson, Nov. 3, 1961. Jackson reply, Nov. 8. NT rejoinder, Nov. 15.

436   *On Goldwater:* NT Col., Jan. 24, 1962. *Garden harangue:* Same NT Col. NT to Mehta, Jan. 2, 1962.

437   *Peace demonstration:* Washington Post, Feb. 18, 1962. NT Col., Feb. 21 and Mar. 28.

438   *On JFK:* NT Col., July 14–15, 1962. NT to Robert Kennedy, Dec. 1. Thurmond statement to AP, May 31.

PAGE

439 *"The lady is 79"*: Sinclair to NT, Oct. 8, 1961. *"If I had been"*: NT to Sanford Gottlieb, July 11, 1962. Mrs. Miller told author.

440 *"The President knows"*: NT Col., Oct. 27–28, 1962. NT to Clark, Dec. 16.

441 *"Chosen instrument"*: Peter Nehemkis, *Latin America: Myth and Reality* (Knopf, 1964), 130. NT to Bosch, Feb. 13, 1963. Time, May 17.

442 *Jefferson and Thomas:* Dr. Boyd told author. Prof. Brown told author. NT to Alumni Weekly, Feb. 12.

443 Ms. Grant in Hemispherica, July-Aug., 1966. *Martin on Volman:* John Bartlow Martin, *Overtaken by Events* (Doubleday, 1966), 310. Author's conversations with Ms. Grant, Prof. Alexander and Clarence Senior.

444 *"I write"*: NT to Lenore Marshall, Sept. 25, 1963.

445 *NT on Rockefeller:* NT Col., June 1–2, 1963. NT to McDowell, Sept. 4. NT to Wolfe, Nov. 2, 1962.

446 *NT in Mississippi:* NYT, Nov. 1, 1963. NT to Dissent editor Stanley Plastrik, Oct. 21. *"He stayed"*: Bliven in review of Fleischman, NYT, Feb. 16, 1964.

447 *"Under the shadow"*: NT to Harrington, Dec. 3, 1963.

448 *"I will not"*: NT to Betty Elkin, Jan. 20, 1964. NT to Evan, May 5. NT to Uphoff, Nov. 15, 1962. NT to Dr. Harrington, Sept. 9, 1964.

449 *"I address you"*: NT to Medical Group, June 24, 1964. *"We argued"*: Sinclair to NT, Dec. 17. NT to Angelica, May 15. NYT, July 16. *"His own policy"*: NT to NYP, Mar. 26.

450 To Morse, July 28, 1964. NT to Bosch, Mar. 4. *"If this debate"*: Quoted in Max Weinrib to NT, Oct. 25, 1964. *Probe of CIA:* NYT, Sept. 3.

451 NT to NYT, Sept. 4, 1964. Louisa to NT, Sept. 22. NT reply, Sept. 28. NT to Pvt. Gates, Nov. 29. *On Goldwater:* Newsday, Sept. 12.

452 NT to New America, Nov. 12, 1964. *On persecution:* NYHT, Nov. 22. NT to Evan, Nov. 4. *Goldwater speeches:* Washington Post, Nov. 26. *"My future"*: NYT, Nov. 21. Gilkey to NT, Nov. 20.

454 Lenore Marshall to NT, Sept. 23, 1963. Ethel Clyde to NT, Nov. 19, 1964.

455 Angelica to NT, Dec. 14, 1964. *On party:* NYHT, Nov. 22, 1964; Washington Post, Nov. 26; NYT, Dec. 7; Park East, Nov. 19; official recording of Astor party.

456 *"You rank"*: NT to Sharecroppers, Mar. 1, 1965. NT to LBJ, Mar. 16.

457 NT to Harriman, Jan. 20, 1965. *"I feel better"*: NT to Waddell, Apr. 15.

458 NT to Stevenson, May 6, 1965. NT to Bundy, July 6. NT to David Maness of Life, May 5. *"One request"*: Life, Jan. 4, 1966.

459 *"J. Edgar Hoover"*: NT Col., Oct. 30–31, 1965.

460 *"You march off"*: Life, Jan. 4, 1966. Sylvia Wright memo to Hugh Moffett, June, 1965. Patricia Miller Libbey told author.

461 *Guest of Boyds:* Author's conversation with the Boyds. NT to Reuther, May 14, 1965. *"All the elements"*: NT to Assistant Secretary of State J. L. Greenfield.

462 *"I want the President"*: NT to James P. Warburg, July 26, 1965. NT to Goldberg, July 21. *NT on Muste:* Nat Hentoff, *Peace Agitator* (Macmillan, 1963), 126. *"Ardent young Americans"*: NT to Arthur I. Waskow, May 26, 1965.

463 *"WE MOURN"*: Nov. 26, 1965. *Call on Rusk:* NYT, Nov. 30. NT to Victor Reuther, Nov. 18.

464 *"Is there any way"*: NT to Humphrey, Dec. 16, 1965. Again to Humphrey, Jan. 21, 1966. *"I like human beings"*: NYT, Nov. 21, 1965. NT to Ms. Olmsted, Sept. 7, 1965. The Long Islander, Dec. 19, 1965.

465 *Life article:* "The Dean of Protest," Jan. 4, 1966. Laucks to NT, Jan. 18. Ms. Gage to NT, Jan. 26. Muste to NT, Jan. 14.

466 *"Applicant for sainthood"*: NT to Lowenstein, Feb. 24. NYT, Apr. 27.

467 NT to Goheen, May 4 and June 15. NT to LBJ, May 12.

# Notes

PAGE

468 Sullivan conversation with author. *NT and Ho:* NYT, July 20. *"There lies before me":* NT to NYT, May 15.

469 *"If the U.S. government":* Clipping, Chicago Daily News, undated. Eugenio Chang Rodriguez, ed., *The Lingering Crisis: A Case Study of the Dominican Republic* (New York, 1969), 85 and *passim.*

470 *NT in Caribbean:* Rodriguez, *op. cit.,* 90–91, 67–70; NYT, June 1, 3 and 14, 1966.

471 Mayer to NT, July 9, 1966. *"Nixon is a man":* William Hoffman to NT, Oct. 17. Playboy, Nov., 1966.

473 NT to Coffin, Feb. 6, 1967. Coffin reply, Feb. 10. NT to grandson, Feb. 13. *In Adirondacks:* Recollections of Hochschild and Dr. Blum.

474 *At Garden:* Myrdal told author; NYT, Dec. 9, 1966; Dwight Macdonald in Esquire, Mar., 1967.

475 NT to LBJ, Dec. 27, 1966.

476 Sullivan conversation with author.

477 *CIA scandal:* Ramparts, Mar., 1967; New Statesman, Feb. 24, 1967; NYT, Feb. 20.

478 *"What was wrong":* NT Cols. for Feb. 18 and 25–26. Saturday Evening Post, May 20; Time, May 19; NYT, Feb. 20, 21, 22, May 8 and 9.

479 NT Col., Mar. 15. *Lasch criticism:* Lasch, *Agony,* 109.

480 *"In the light":* NT to Nomad, Mar. 7, 1967.

481 *"Sunk so low":* NT to Morris R. Abram, Jan. 18, 1967. Darr to NT, Jan. 9. NT to Fromm, May 3.

482 *In Colorado:* Uphoffs and Sullivan told author. Coolidge to NT, Apr. 28.

483 *Princeton reunion:* NT to Philip Gill, June 22. NT to Baldwin, Sept. 27.

484 NT to Lenore Marshall, Sept. 8 and 20. New Yorker, Sept. 23.

485 *"I haven't been":* NT to Coffin, Sept. 27. Guardian, Oct. 31.

486 NYT, NYDN, Oct. 30. Hoopes to NT, Nov. 1. Yale Daily News, Jan. 9, 1969.

487 *Chicago meeting:* Uphoff told author; NYT, Nov. 12; NYP, Nov. 14.

488 Sheean to NT, Nov. 20. Lenore Marshall to NT, Nov. 21. Darr to NT, Nov. 15.

489 *"I had hoped":* In The Long Islander, Jan. 25, 1968. NT to Hoyt, Dec. 6, 1967.

490 *Icy Sunday:* Mrs. Gates told author. *Thoreau story:* The Long Islander.

491 *Baldwin banter:* Baldwin told author. NT, *The Choices* (Ives Washburn, 1969), 66. The Seniors told author.

492 NT to Humphrey, The Long Islander, June 20, 1968. *"No memory":* NT to NYT, Aug. 19, 1968. *"The effect of the war":* NYT, Nov. 21, 1968.

493 Newsday, Nov. 21, 1968. *84th birthday:* Described to author by five participants and by Whitman. NYT, Nov. 21.

494 *"At this moment":* NT, *Socialism Reexamined* (Norton, 1963), 211. NT, *The Choices,* 83. *Obituary:* NYT, Dec. 20, 1968.

Thomas left an estate estimated at something over $100,000 and bequeathed substantial sums to the Socialist Party and other causes he espoused. His son Evan sailed out on the Sound and let his father's ashes mingle with what might have remained of his mother's, placed there twenty-one years earlier. Thomas had his nonsectarian memorial service at Community Church, conducted by the Reverend Sidney Lovett and the Reverend Donald S. Harrington. Lovett's eulogy made plain his belief that however unbelieving Thomas had been, he was still a child of God, not to be denied God's love. The not notably sentimental Murray Kempton recalled how constantly Thomas had appeared in "lonely, unfashionable places" to face stern issues and asked, "And who will go for me to all those places where I ought to go myself now that my Norman Thomas is gone?" There were messages from all over the world. Included were those from President Johnson, Vice President Humphrey and Governor Rockefeller, who were among those who had felt the sting of what he said in the unfashionable places.

# AUTHOR'S NOTE
# AND ACKNOWLEDGMENTS

This book is written from the point of view of one whose once extensive Socialist beliefs have undergone considerable modification, but not to the point of total rejection.

Lack of time and the gasoline shortage prevented a search of all sources in its preparation. It is based largely on a study of the Norman Thomas Papers at the New York Public Library—the most voluminous and valuable single source, containing nearly 100,000 letters and papers, but not the only one. I talked with old Socialists and non-Socialists who had known Thomas, some of whom had been close to him for decades, but there are many whom I missed. Scores of the less important (but by no means trivial) Thomas crusades are passed over here for brevity's sake. The outline of the Socialist Party which I give, even during Thomas's leadership, is condensed and incomplete.

While the book is not definitive, I think it does reflect Thomas's thoughts and deeds as disclosed in his own letters, writings and speeches and as observed and interpreted by others allied with him, opposed to him or related to him. He was that bird many people now believe all but extinct, an honest politician. His integrity, linked as it was with great energy, intellect and compassion, made a combination now unseen. Whatever his shortcomings in the artful shifts of politics—and he was shrewd indeed in his later years—he embodied a degree of civilization and decency few even then expected to find in public life. To study his career and perceive his standards from this post-Watergate juncture has been as exhilarating as to view Eden from Tophet.

All five of Thomas's children—Mrs. John W. Gates, Mrs. Herbert C. Miller, Mrs. John Friebely, Evan W. Thomas II, and William Stewart Thomas—gave me their help. It was given by mail, by telephone or—in the case of Frances Thomas Gates and Evan Thomas —by relating to me their recollections of their father, mother and family background in repeated personal interviews. Mrs. Gates, who lived near or with her father until his final illness and was politically and personally most sympathetic with him, freely gave many hours of her time and answered endless lists of questions with true Thomas patience and fortitude. As did her brothers William and Evan, she also lent me family pictures, letters and papers, including some prizes heretofore held private, among them the sparkling letters written by her mother to her father before their marriage while the future Mrs. Norman Thomas was on a journey to India.

Her husband, John W. Gates, talked of Norman and Violet Thomas from the special vantage point of a son-in-law, while the wife of Evan Thomas II, Anne Robins Thomas, gave me her recollections as a daughter-in-law and proved again that women invariably notice details that men miss. Norman Thomas Gates, a grandson, told me his impressions of Big Dad, as all the grandchildren called Thomas. And a granddaughter, Mrs. Patricia Miller Libbey, related her experiences during a summer in New York when she worked as his researcher. Norman Thomas's younger brother, the equally independent-minded Dr. Evan Thomas, looked back into his memory for my benefit, as did the two sisters, Agnes and Emma Thomas, and Mrs. Arthur Thomas, widow of Norman Thomas's youngest brother. Mrs. Richard N. Pierson, a niece of Norman Thomas, had wonderful anecdotes to tell about "Uncle Norman." I thank every one of them.

I am deeply indebted to Harry Fleischman, for many years a Socialist Party official, a dear friend of Norman Thomas and himself author of a fine Thomas biography, written while the subject was still living. Far from preempting Thomas, Fleischman was eager for more to be written about him. Fleischman supplied a friend's and insider's knowledge of Norman Thomas and of the Socialist Party, and among many other favors he lent me the transcriptions of his long interviews with Thomas.

# Author's Note and Acknowledgments

I was fortunate in gaining the cooperation of four national secretaries of the Party, each of whom worked closely with Thomas for years: Clarence Senior, Travers Clement, Fleischman and Robin Meyers. Other current or former members or officials of the Party who helped by recounting their own observations were Fay Bennett, Alice Dodge, Judah Drob, John Herling, the Reverend Donald Szantho Harrington, Paul R. Porter, Professor Walter Uphoff, Mary Jo Uphoff, Louis Waldman, Rowland Watts and Frank P. Zeidler.

Luck was with me in finding men whose acquaintance with Thomas goes back over many decades: the Reverend Sidney Lovett, a friend from the time he met Thomas in 1910 until he presided over Thomas's memorial service fifty-eight years later; Roger N. Baldwin, a friend and co-worker in the American Civil Liberties Union and other causes for fifty-two years; Thomas's own brother, Dr. Evan Thomas, mentioned previously; A. Philip Randolph, a friend as both a union leader and Party member; and Paul Blanshard, a lifelong friend though he quit the Party.

The staff of the New York Public Library Manuscript Division, where my wife and I studied the Thomas Papers for two years, were characteristically kind and efficient: Paul R. Rugen, the Keeper of Manuscripts, and Jean McNiece and John D. Stinson. So, too, was Michael Nash at the new manuscript reading room in the Library Annex on West Forty-third Street.

Professor Robert J. Alexander of Rutgers University, who left the Socialist Party but remained a friend of Thomas's and later served on the board of his Institute for International Labor Research, was generous far beyond courtesy. Having spent part of his time for years on a definitive biography of Thomas not to be immediately finished, he gave me access to some of his research. In return, I gave Professor Alexander some of my own which he had not discovered but which, I fear, was less valuable than his.

Thomas's good friend, Professor Julian P. Boyd of Princeton University, thoughtfully arranged for me a gathering of faculty members who knew Thomas in various connections and threw light on his association with the university he loved. I also had an opportunity to talk with Mrs. Boyd and with their son, Kenneth Boyd, both of whom knew Thomas from his visits there. Another Princetonian, Earle E. Coleman, University Archivist, produced information about Thomas from the archives and also led me to still other helpful Princetonians.

Dr. Henry Wexler, the New Haven psychoanalyst whose help has been invaluable to me in discussing personalities in a half-dozen books, has again applied his wisdom as well as his professional expertise in aiding my comprehension of the remarkable character of Norman Thomas.

Joseph L. Graham explored for me the Presbyterian Historical Society in Philadelphia and produced information about Thomas as clergyman. My thanks also to Harry Harrison of the Yale University Library, where I made use of the fine newspaper and periodical collections, the stacks and the Linonia and Brothers collection.

Ben Waknin, of Columbia University, consulted me on another matter and, it turned out, led me to interesting material about the post–World War I official spying on Thomas which I would otherwise have missed. And Tom Mahoney, long a denizen of Gramercy Park who now and then encountered Thomas there, lent me his aid as he has done in the past.

Again I have had the matchless professional help of that lone Doctor of Philosophy among literary representatives, Patricia S. Myrer of McIntosh & Otis, Inc. This is the ninth book concerning which I have profited from the advice and experience of my friend, Burroughs Mitchell, of Scribners. Charles Scribner, Jr., a Princetonian of a later generation than Thomas, took the time to read the manuscript and make discriminating suggestions. And the script has had a rare advantage: a critical reading by that perfectionist in tone, syntax and sense, Professor Jacques Barzun.

512

# NORMAN THOMAS

Grateful acknowledgment is also made to the following for kindness and help:

Mrs. Katrina McCormick Barnes
Jamie Bischoff
Mrs. Paul Blanshard
Professor Rufus Blanshard
Professor Jerome Blum
James McClure Clarke
Dr. William Sloane Coffin, Jr.
Crispin Cook, M.D.
Hal Cooley
Mrs. A. Sprague Coolidge
Professor Virginia Corwin
Page Cross
John W. Darr, Jr.
Carolyn A. Davis
Professor Thomas L. Derr
Mrs. Samuel De Witt
Professor Martin Diamond
Cleveland E. Dodge
Judah Drob
Mrs. Max Eastman
Edward Eliscu
Arlee R. Ellis
William R. Emerson
Professor George Fischer
Margaret M. Gage
Professor Langdon B. Gilkey
Mary Jane Gilkey
Laurie Graham
Frances R. Grant
Dorothea V. Hammond
Nat Hentoff
Harold K. Hochschild
Roger W. Holmes
Darlington Hoopes
Maggie Houston
Professor Wilbur S. Howell
Richmond C. Hubbard, M.D.
Francis Keil, M.D.
Victoria Kent
Professor Joseph M. Kitagawa
Sharon E. Knapp
Irving Laucks
Mrs. Ruth W. Lester
Sandra Levinson

Alfred Baker Lewis
Mrs. Sidney Lovett
Dr. Hyman Lumer
James Marshall
Virginia Lowell Mauck
Sandro Mayer
Carey McWilliams
Howard N. Meyer
H. L. Mitchell
Gunnar Myrdal
Mrs. Reinhold Niebuhr
Professor Roy V. Peel
Professor Don Peretz
Albert Engdahl Peterson
West F. Peterson
Harry P. Phillips, Jr.
Mrs. Paul R. Porter
Susan Richman
Professor Moses Rischin
Florett Robinson
William H. Savage
John G. H. Scoon
George Scullin
Mrs. Clarence Senior
Mrs. Eleanor Shatzkin
Leonard Shatzkin
David Sinclair
Professor Louis Starr
Daniel D. Steininger
Irwin Suall
Timothy Sullivan
Thomas T. Thalken
Estate of Dorothy Thompson
Louis Untermeyer
Henry H. Villard
Oswald Garrison Villard, Jr.
Stephen C. Vladeck
Louis Waldman
Mrs. Kenneth Walser
Alden Whitman
Edith R. Willcox
Mark Huntington Wiseman
Frank P. Zeidler
Hibben Ziesing

My wife, Dorothy Green Swanberg, the most gifted of researchers and a discerning critic, applied her shorthand and her insight—both equally swift—during our long sessions with the Norman Thomas Papers. Our conversations gradually sifted the raw material down to whatever understanding of Norman Thomas appears here.

W. A. S.

# INDEX

# INDEX

*Bernard Clare* (James Farrell), 299
Bess, Demaree, 253, 275
Betancourt, Romulo, 430
Betterton, Joseph, 165, 166
Bevan, Aneurin, 294
Bevin, Ernest, 214, 247
Biddle, Francis, 267
Bitar, Salah el-, 395, 397, 400–401
*Black Boy* (Richard Wright), 294
Blankenhorn, Heber, 88
Blanshard, Mary (*see also* Hillyer, Mary),
235, 246, 250, 252, 264, 318, 324, 350,
358, 360, 367, 386; quarrel with NT, 393;
447n.; death of, 456
Blanshard, Paul, 115, 121, 124, 128, 131;
quits Party, 142; 145, 173, 235, 250, 283,
318, 324, 360, 367, 456, 482
Bliven, Bruce, 275, 446–447n., 453
Bloor, Ella Reeve, 76, 350
Blum, Prof. Jerome, 473
Blum, Leon, 214
Borchard, Edwin, 285
Bosch, Juan, 430, 441; fails in office, 442–
444; 450, 468–470
Botany mill strike, 101–103
Bourdon, Eli, 177
Bourguiba, Habib, 365
Bowers, Claude, 227
Bowers, Florence, 230
Bowles, Chester, 246, 300, 356, 395, 398,
422, 423, 438
Boyd, Prof. Julian P., 441–442, 461
Boyd, Mrs. Julian P., 461
Braden, Thomas W., 478
Brandeis, Justice Louis, 344
Brick Church, 24, 30–32, 34, 35, 95
Brockway, A. Fenner, 116, 335
Brookings Institution, 430–431
Brooks, Van Wyck, 299, 352, 396
Brooks Brothers, 74, 134, 476
Broun, Heywood, 132
Browder, Earl, 105, 175, 190, 192, 193,
194, 202, 205, 210, 232, 237, 238, 255,
271; cashiered by CP, 312; 339–340, 384,
409
Brown, Prof. Joe, 442
Brown, Rev. William Adams, 27, 43–44, 51,
59, 63, 80
Brownell, Herbert, 367
Brubaker, Howard, 88
Bryan, William Jennings, 6, 9
Bryant, Louise, 209

Buchanan, James, 5
Buckley, William F., Jr., 304, 350, 425, 427,
434, 445
Bucknell College, 11, 12
Bullitt, William, 214
Bundy, McGeorge, 442, 458
Bunker, Ellsworth, 469
Burleson, Albert C., 63, 64
Burt, Roy, 212, 213, 220, 228, 231, 236

Caballero, Largo, 212, 255
Cahan, Abraham, 86, 114, 128, 133, 185,
228, 291
Call, The, 61, 78, 88; new Call begun, 188;
190, 194, 195, 203, 205, 210, 212, 217,
220, 227, 236, 249, 251, 285, 288; pub-
lishes Niebuhr's letter, 290; 301, 306,
355, 422n., 426
Calles, Plutarco Elias, 92–93
Canadian Cooperative Commonwealth
Federation, 198
Cannon, James D., 91–92
Cannon, James P., 193, 218
Cardozo, Justice Benjamin N., 126
Carmer, Carl, 299
Carnegie, Andrew, 13–14
Carpenter, C. T., 180, 181, 183, 184
Carter, Elmer, 277
Carter, Thomas, 12, 16, 18, 19, 23, 28, 61
Carton, Alfred T., 12, 16, 34, 54, 55, 276,
280
Casey, Daniel, 221
Castro, Fidel, 405, 419, 430, 441
Cattell, Prof. J. M., 65
Central Intelligence Agency, 343, 375,
397, 404, 420, 422; its Cuban invasion
exposed, 424–445; 427, 431–432, 436,
443, 450–451, 466, 467; deceptions dis-
covered, 477–480
Chafee, Zecharia, 78
Chaffee, Rev. E. B., 71, 100, 101
Chaliapin, Fyodor, 78
Chamoun, Camille, 400
Chandler, Albert, 210
Chase National Bank, 248, 455
Cheney, Prof. Coleman B., 171, 240, 270,
271
Chiang Kai-shek, 271, 298, 330–331, 336,
351, 355, 406, 438
Childs, Marquis, 204, 275
Chou En-lai, 420
Christ Church, 23, 28, 43

515

# INDEX

Hiss, Alger, 11, 329

Hitler, Adolf, 129, 142, 149, 151, 171, 198, 202, 210, 213; pact with Stalin, 234; 237, 241, 242, 245, 249, 250, 263, 289, 293

Hoan, Daniel W., 109, 132–133, 148, 168, 171, 182, 186, 187, 192, 202, 231, 274, 283

Ho Chi Minh, 330, 336, 468

Hochschild, Harold K., 473–474

Hogan, Frank, 279, 314, 388

Holmes, Rev. John Haynes, 17, 62, 63, 71, 73, 79, 92, 99, 100, 103; lauds NT, 120–121; 131, 142, 145, 170, 197, 201; assails Debs Column concept, 211; 225, 238, 242, 264, 269, 281, 327, 329, 360, 373, 429, 448, 494

Hook, Sidney, 192, 193, 341, 360, 368

Hoopes, Darlington, 186, 192, 195, 202, 206, 241, 287, 321, 332, 355, 357, 386, 390, 486

Hoover, J. Edgar, 222, 267, 371, 437, 459, 464, 477n.

Hoover, Herbert, 110, 112, 124–125, 128, 137, 224, 273, 275–276, 318

Hopkins, Harry, 282

House Un-American Activities Committee, 311–312, 329

Howe, Helen, 466, 467

Howe, Irving, 446

Hoyt, E. Palmer, 316, 325, 489

Hughan, Jessie Wallace, 73, 191, 373

Hughes, Charles Evans, 80

Hull, Cordell, 153, 212, 268, 285–286

Human Events, 295

Humphrey, Hubert, 316–317, 325, 377, 398, 404, 405, 408, 417, 436, 440, 453, 463–464, 466, 492

Hunt, Frazier, 183, 184

Hunt, George P., 301

Hussein, King, 401–402

Hutchins, Robert M., 246

Huysmans, Camille, 214

Hylan, John F., 57, 97

Iberica (publication), 386, 386n., 405, 455

I Chose Freedom (Victor Kravchenko), 296–298

Ickes, Harold, 210, 318

India League of America, 268, 330, 342

Indochina, 351, 355

Ingalls, Laura, 263

Inter-American Association for Democracy and Freedom, 342, 359, 385, 442–443, 470n.

International Confederation of Free Trade Unions, 363, 479

International Ladies Garment Workers' Union, 88, 89, 149, 221, 316

International Teamster (publication), 291

International Workers of the World (IWW), 65, 238

Institute for International Labor Research, 395, 429, 450–451, 466, 479, 480

Institute of Political Education, 395

Israeli controversy, 305, 326, 390, 392, 396, 397, 399–403

It Can't Happen Here (Sinclair Lewis), 202

Jackson, C. D., 342–343, 425, 435–436, 479

Jacobs, Joseph, 198, 213

James, Mrs. Bayard, 203

James, William, 13

Javits, Jacob, 386

Jefferson, Thomas, 102, 442

Jessen, Louise, 162

Jessen, Otto, 162

Jessup, Philip C., 349, 350–351

Jewish Daily Forward: Socialist Party patron, 86; 92, 128, 133, 149, 150, 151, 169–170, 173; ceases support, 185; 193, 263, 291, 318, 396

John Birch Society, 425, 427, 435, 436, 464

Johnson, Edward, 158, 283

Johnson, Hugh, 158, 175

Johnson, James Weldon, 64

Johnson, Lyndon B., 418, 442, 447, 449–450, 452, 453, 456, 457, 460, 461; NT assails his war policy, 462; 463–464, 467, 475, 487, 492, 494

Johnson, Martha, 158, 283

Johnson C. Smith University, 5, 449

Jones, Rufus M., 73

Jordan, David Starr, 48–49, 73

Kahn, Alexander, 170

Kahn, Herman: On Thermonuclear War, 423; 424, 427

Kamenev, Lev, 203

Kaplan, Jacob M., 429–430, 441, 480

Kaplan Fund, 430, 431, 440, 450–451, 466, 477–480

Karsner, David, 97

Kaufman, George, 127

519

# Index

520

# INDEX

521

# INDEX

# INDEX